THE ECONOMICS OF MONEY AND BANKING

SIXTH EDITION

Lester V. Chandler
PRINCETON UNIVERSITY

HARPER & ROW, PUBLISHERS
New York   Evanston   San Francisco   London

PREFACE

Though extensively revised and rewritten, this edition is quite similar in purpose, approach, and treatment to the five editions that preceded it. It is addressed primarily to college and university undergraduates who are just beginning their formal study of money and banking. In the selection and presentation of materials, I have kept the needs of the student constantly in mind and have not tried to write to my professional colleagues.

This is not an exhaustive treatment of money and banking. Not even a book many times the size of this one could claim to deal exhaustively with the vast amounts of theoretical, legal, institutional, empirical, and historical materials that have been accumulated in the field of money and banking. Furthermore, I do not believe it appropriate that the newcomer should be forced to wade through an encyclopedic treatment of this broad and complex subject. I have therefore selected what I believe to be the most important principles, processes, and problems and have attempted to deal with them fully enough to clarify their significance and interrelationships.

The ultimate interest of this book is in policy. However, policy cannot be understood without a theory of the interrelationships of money and banking and the functioning of the economy as a whole, a clear understanding of the institutions and processes involved, and an appreciation of the social and historical context within which policy makers operate and by which their policies are shaped. This book therefore employs theoretical, institutional, and historical approaches. It emphasizes an evolutionary view, attempting not only to explain how present-day structures, attitudes, and policies evolved but also to suggest some possible directions of future change.

While concentrating on the functioning of the monetary and banking system as a whole and on its interrelationships with the rest of the economy, this book devotes relatively little attention to the technical problems of operating and administering an individual bank. I am convinced that this is the most fruitful first approach for the student whose interest in the field is largely cultural. I believe the same is no less true for those who aspire to be leaders in banking or finance. Through formal study or experience they must, of course, master the tools of their trade. However, they will be better citizens, and in the end better bankers or financiers, if from the beginning they see their profession in its broad economic and social context and understand both the effects of their own actions on the functioning of the economy and the effects of government monetary and fiscal policies on the various sectors of the economy, including banks and other financial institutions.

A major purpose of this new edition is to bring materials up to date, including events preceding, accompanying, and following the dramatic dollar crisis of 1971. However, a number of other changes have also been made, most of them to improve exposition but some to expand coverage.

Professors Harold R. Williams and Henry W. Woudenberg have prepared a study guide, *Money, Banking, and Monetary Theory: Problems and Concepts,* Second Edition, to accompany this edition. I feel that both professors and students will benefit from its use. I wish to thank Professors Williams and Woudenberg for preparing this guide, for their assistance in preparing the *Instructor's Manual* which accompanies the text, and also for their helpful suggestions.

It is not possible to mention here all the persons who have helped in preparing this and the previous editions. However, I do thank teachers and students who have supplied comments both favorable and unfavorable, on preceding editions. I also wish to record here my deep gratitude to Phyllis Durepos for her invaluable assistance in preparing copy for the printer.

LESTER V. CHANDLER

CONTENTS

Preface

THE NATURE AND FUNCTIONS OF MONEY AND FINANCE

1 THE ROLES OF MONEY   3
2 KINDS OF MONEY   20
3 DEBT, CREDIT, AND FINANCIAL INSTRUMENTS   44
4 FINANCIAL INTERMEDIARIES   69

PART TWO COMMERCIAL BANKING

5 BANKING HISTORY OF THE UNITED STATES   87
6 THE COMMERCIAL-BANKING SYSTEM   114
7 BANK EXPANSION AND CONTRACTION   136
8 COMMERCIAL-BANK POLICIES   159

PART THREE CENTRAL BANKING

9 THE FEDERAL RESERVE SYSTEM 183
10 THE FEDERAL RESERVE CREDIT AND BANK
RESERVES 207
11 INSTRUMENTS OF MONETARY MANAGEMENT 237
12 THE MONETARY SYSTEM: AN OVERALL VIEW 270

PART FOUR MONETARY THEORY

13 THE NATIONAL-INCOME ACCOUNTS 281
14 AN INTRODUCTION TO MONETARY THEORY 302
15 QUANTITY THEORIES 325
16 CONSUMPTION, SAVING, AND INVESTMENT 347
17 A SYNTHESIS OF MONETARY AND INCOME THEORY 368
18 GOVERNMENT FISCAL OPERATIONS AND POLICIES 386

PART FIVE INTERNATIONAL MONETARY RELATIONS

19 THE INTERNATIONAL MONETARY SYSTEM 407
20 INTERNATIONAL PAYMENTS AND EXCHANGE RATES 428
21 INTERNATIONAL MONETARY POLICIES 449

PART SIX AMERICAN MONETARY POLICY

22 UNITED STATES MONETARY POLICIES, 1914–1929 471
23 MONETARY POLICY IN THE DEPRESSION, 1930–1941 497
24 MONETARY POLICY, 1941–1951 519
25 MONETARY POLICY, 1951–1959 533
26 MONETARY POLICY, 1960–1971 550
27 THE DOLLAR CRISIS OF 1971 584
28 THE FUTURE 599

Index 609

PART ONE

THE NATURE AND FUNCTIONS OF MONEY AND FINANCE

CHAPTER 1

THE ROLES OF MONEY

One need not be an economist to be acutely aware that money plays an important role in modern life; he need think only of his own experience and recall the headlines that have thrust themselves at him in recent years. From his personal experience he knows that the process of getting a living is a process of getting and spending money, and that how well he can live depends on how many dollars he can get and how many goods and services each dollar will buy. He also knows that dollars are harder to get at some times than at others, and that the buying power of each dollar has varied widely, sometimes to his benefit and sometimes to his injury.

When we recall the events of recent decades, we are reminded that the behavior of money is also vitally important to the operation of the national and international economy. During the 1930s newspapers headlined stories of "deflation and depression": the drastic decline of output, job opportunities, and prices accompanying the shrinkage of effective money demand for output; of widespread want and suffering while millions of unemployed workers and other productive facilities that were both willing and able to work were standing idle because of insufficient "demand"; and of wholesale failures of debtors to meet their obligations because of the decline of their money incomes and of the prices of their assets. Headlines in the 1940s told different sorts of stories—not stories of deflation and shrunken employment, but stories of "inflation," of rising living costs, and of discontent and distress among those whose income and wealth were relatively fixed in terms of money. The 1950s were less unstable, but they included years of inflation, years of mild deflation with unemployment considerably above minimum levels, and widespread debate over the relation of monetary policies to the rate of economic growth. The first half of the 1960s was characterized by excessive unemployment and inadequate economic growth, the second half by price inflation. Also, a new set of monetary problems appeared; we began to worry, for the first time in several decades, about the international position of the dollar—about the continuing deficit in our balance of international payments, the deterioration of our net international-reserve position, speculation against the dollar, and conflicts among the domestic and international objectives of our monetary policies. The early 1970s brought no abatement of international monetary problems, and the nation faced baffling domestic problems of coping simultaneously with price inflation and excessive unemployment.

In short, personal experience as well as some knowledge of history and economics makes it clear to everyone that money plays an important role in the economic system and that the behavior of money is somehow causally related to the behavior of employment, the rate of real output, the level of prices, the distribution of wealth and income, and so forth. What are not so clear, however, are the answers to questions such as these: Just what are the functions of money in the economy, and just how does money perform these functions? To what extent do economic disturbances "arise on the side of money and monetary policy?" To what extent do money and monetary policy amplify and spread through the economy disturbances originating in nonmonetary factors? What are the effects of the various types of money and monetary policies? Which ones promote economic objectives generally considered desirable, and which ones militate against the attainment of those objectives? With how much success can we use monetary policy to prevent unemployment, promote a steadily advancing level of output, and maintain a stable purchasing power of the dollar while preserving a basically free enterprise economy?

Such questions are the central concern of this book. The primary interest throughout is in the functioning of the monetary, credit, and banking systems and in their relationships to the functioning of the economy as a whole. Though much space will be devoted to historical, structural, and legal aspects of the various institutions that create, transfer, and destroy money, these aspects will not be studied primarily for their own sakes, but rather for their contribution to our understanding of the functioning of the economic system.

THE BASIC FUNCTION OF MONEY

Money has one fundamental purpose in an economic system: to facilitate the exchange of goods and services—to lessen the time and effort required to carry on trade. A man living and working in complete isolation from others has no use for money. He cannot eat it, or wear it, or use it to promote his productive processes; having no occasion to exchange either goods or services with others, he has no need for money. Even if a dozen persons lived together in isolation from all others, the use of money would be of only limited benefit to them; they could barter their goods and services among themselves with but little loss of time and effort. As groups become larger, however, and wish to increase their degree of specialization and the size of their trade area, they find the direct barter of goods and services increasingly inconvenient and increasingly wasteful of time and effort. They therefore search for something that will enable them to escape the wasteful processes of barter; they invent money.

We may say, then, that the sole purpose of money in the economic system is to enable trade to be carried on as cheaply as possible in order to make feasible the optimum degree of specialization, with its attendant increase of productivity. We are all familiar with the high degree of specialization that characterizes modern economies—specialization of persons, of business firms, of regions, and of types of capital. We know that without this high degree of specialization, which enables us to utilize the various regions to maximum advantage, to make the most advantageous use of native abilities, to develop skills, to amass huge amounts of specialized and useful knowledge, to employ large aggregations of specialized capital, and to achieve economies of scale, our productive powers and living standards would be far below their present levels. But this specialization would be impossible without an equally highly developed system of exchange or trade. Money is productive, therefore, in the sense that it is an essential part of the modern exchange mechanism and thereby facilitates specialization and production.

BARTER EXCHANGE

We have carefully avoided saying that exchange is impossible without money. People can, of course, carry on trade by a direct bartering of goods and services. Primitive trade was often carried on in this way, and bartering is not unknown even now. Yet pure barter is so wasteful of time and effort that little trade would be feasible if this were the only available method of exchange.

The first serious shortcoming of pure barter is the lack of any common unit in terms of which to measure and state the values of goods and services. (By the *value* of a good or service is meant its *worth*, the quantity of other goods and services that it can command in the market.) In this situation, the value of each article in the market could not be stated simply as one quantity, but would have to be stated in as many quantities as there were kinds and qualities of other goods and services in the market. For example, if there were 500,000 kinds and qualities of goods and services in the market, the value of each would have to be stated in terms of 499,999 others. Moreover, no meaningful accounting system would be possible. A balance sheet would consist of a long physical inventory of the kinds and qualities of the various goods owned and another inventory of those owed; consequently, the net worth of the person or firm could be ascertained, if at all, only by a prolonged and tedious study of the numerous barter rates of exchange prevailing in the market. Profit and loss statements would be equally difficult to draw up and interpret. A firm could only list the various kinds and qualities of goods and services acquired during the period as income and those paid out as expenses, so that again the net results could be discovered, if at all, only by a laborious study of barter rates of exchange. It is almost inconceivable that even a small department store, not to mention General Motors Corporation, could keep meaningful accounts in the absence of a monetary unit.

The second serious disadvantage of barter is often called "the lack of a double coincidence of wants." Stated more simply, it would happen only rarely that the owner of a good or service that he wished to barter could easily find someone who both wanted his commodity more than anything else and possessed the commodity that our trader wanted more than anything else. For example, suppose that he owned a three-year-old draft horse that he wished to trade for a certain kind of two-wheeled cart. To find someone who already owned or could build with maximum economy exactly the kind of cart he wanted and who would be willing to trade it, and who also wanted more than anything else the kind of horse that was being offered, would likely be a laborious and time-consuming process, if such a person existed at all. The horse owner would probably have to accept something that he wanted less than the cart, or else he would have to carry through a number of intermediate barter transactions; he might have to trade the horse for a cow, the cow for a boat, the boat for some sheep, and the sheep for the desired cart. Barter presents even more serious difficulties when the articles to be exchanged are not of the same value and cannot be divided without loss of value. Imagine, for example, the plight of the owner if he wanted to trade his horse for a pair of overalls, a hat for his wife, three dishes, an aluminum skillet, 50 cartridges, schoolbooks for his children, and numerous other inexpensive articles.

A third disadvantage of pure barter is the lack of any satisfactory unit in terms of which to write contracts requiring future payments. Contracts involving future payments are an essential part of an exchange economy; individuals must enter into agreements as to wages, salaries, interests, rents, and other prices extending over a period of time. But in a pure barter economy these future payments would have to be stated in terms of specific goods or services. Though this would be possible, it would lead to three grave difficulties: (1) It would often invite controversy as to the quality of the goods or services to be repaid; (2) the parties would often be unable to agree on the specific commodity to be used for repayment; (3) both parties would run the risk that the commodity to be repaid would increase or decrease seriously in value over the duration of the contract (e.g., wheat might rise markedly in value in terms of other commodities, to the debtor's regret, or decrease markedly in value, to the creditor's regret) .

A fourth disadvantage of pure barter, which results from its first two short-comings, is the lack of any method of storing generalized purchasing power. People could store purchasing power for future use only by holding specific commodities or claims against specific commodities. This method of storing purchasing power has often been used, and as we shall later see, is used extensively even today. Yet it has serious disadvantages when it is the only method available. The stored commodity may deteriorate (or appreciate) in value, its storage may be costly, and it may be difficult to dispose of quickly without loss if its holder wishes to buy something else.

Because of the four disadvantages outlined above, pure barter is a highly inefficient means of trade. It was to overcome these difficulties that virtually every society invented some kind of money early in its development.

THE SPECIFIC FUNCTIONS OF MONEY

Money serves its basic purpose as "the great wheel of circulation, the great instrument of commerce" by performing four specific functions, each of which obviates one of the difficulties of pure barter described above. These functions are to serve as: (1) a unit of value, (2) a medium of exchange, (3) a standard of deferred payments, and (4) a store of value. The first two are usually called the *primary* functions of money. The last two are called *derivative* functions because they are derived from the primary functions.

Money as a unit of value

The first function of money has been given many names, of which the most common are "unit of value," "standard of value," "unit of account," "common measure of value," and "common denominator of value." Through all these names runs one common idea: The monetary unit serves as the unit in terms of which the value of all goods and services is measured and expressed. As soon as a group develops a monetary unit such as a dollar, a peso, a franc, a pound sterling, or a pengo, the value of each good or service can be expressed as a *price,* by which we mean the number of monetary units for which it will exchange. For example, we say that the value of a certain hat is $10, that beef of a certain grade has a value of $1 a pound, and so on. Ours is certainly a "pecuniary" society in the sense that values typically are measured and expressed in monetary units.

The practice of measuring the values of goods and services in monetary units greatly simplifies the problem of measuring the exchange values of commodities in the market. One has merely to compare their relative prices in terms of monetary units. For example, if carbon steel is $8 per hundredweight and corn is $2 per bushel, a hundredweight of steel is worth 4 bushels of corn. This practice also simplifies accounting. Assets of all kinds, liabilities of all kinds, income of all kinds, and expenses of all kinds can be stated in terms of common monetary units to be added or subtracted.

Money is not the only common unit of measurement employed in the economic system. Units such as feet, inches, and meters are used to measure linear distance; ounces, grams, pounds, and short tons, to measure weight; gallons, liters, and barrels, to measure liquid volume; and so on. These units of physical measurement are, themselves, constant quantities. Confusion would surely result if these units of physical measurement were to shrink 25 percent one year and expand 10 percent the next. Yet the unit of value (money), perhaps the most important unit of measurement in the economic system, has too often undergone wide fluctuations in its value or *purchasing power*. The latter is the inverse of the average or general level of prices of a large number of goods and services, as measured by the consumer price index, the wholesale price index, or by an index of the prices of all goods and services included in the gross national product. For example, if the general or average level of prices doubles—if twice as many dollars are required to buy a given assortment of goods and services—the value or purchasing power of a dollar decreases by 50 percent. But if the general or average level of prices falls by 50 percent—if only half as many dollars are required to purchase a given assortment of goods and services—then the value or purchasing power of a dollar is doubled. Some of the consequences of fluctuating price levels will be discussed later.[1]

Money as a medium of exchange

Various names have been given to the second function of money: "medium of exchange," "medium of payments," "circulating medium," and "means of payment." This function of money is served by anything that is generally (not necessarily universally, but very commonly) accepted by people in exchange for goods and services. The "thing" may be porpoise teeth, bits of gold, copper coins, pieces of paper, or credits on the books of a bank; the only essential requirement of an object to be used as money is that people in general be willing to accept it in exchange for goods and services. When a group has developed such a mechanism, its members need no longer waste their time and energy in barter trade. Our horse owner can simply sell his horse to the person who will give him the most money for it and then buy the supplies that he most desires from those who will

---

[1] The succeeding sections implicitly assume that each "thing" that actually circulates as money—that is used as a means of payment—is stated in terms of the unit of account and maintains a fixed market value in terms of the unit of account. For example, a certain piece of paper money is stated as $5 and actually passes in the market as five dollar units of account. In such cases a depreciation or appreciation of the purchasing power of the unit of account is accompanied by a proportional depreciation or appreciation of each of the things used as a means of payment. However, in some abnormal cases the things used as means of payment may fluctuate in value in relation to the unit of account. For example, a certain silver coin may be equal to one unit of account (say, $1) at one time and to two units of account (say, $2) at another time. In such cases the purchasing power of the unit of account and of each of the things used as a means of payment will not vary proportionally.

give him what he considers to be the best bargain. The Ford worker need not barter his bolt-tightening services directly for the various things that he needs; he can sell his services for money in the most favorable market and spend the money as he sees fit. In the final analysis, all trade is, of course, barter; one good or service is traded indirectly for others, with money acting as the intermediary. But by serving this purpose, money greatly increases the ease of trade.

The fact that money is often referred to as "generalized purchasing power" or as "a bearer of options" emphasizes the freedom of choice that the use of money affords. The owner of a good or service need not secure his supplies from the people to whom he trades his good or service; he can use his money to buy the things he wants most, from the people who offer the best bargain, and at the time he considers the most advantageous.

Here, again, money can function properly only if it maintains a relatively stable purchasing power. If a dollar is a bearer of fluctuating amounts of generalized purchasing power, it is likely to cause confusion and injustice in trade.

Money as a standard of deferred payments

As soon as money comes into general use as a unit of value and a medium of payments, it almost inevitably becomes the unit in terms of which deferred or future payments are stated. Modern economic systems require the existence of a large volume of contracts of this type. Most of these are contracts for the payment of principal and interest on debts in which future payments are stated in monetary units. Some of these contracts run for only a few days or a few months, many run for more than 10 years, and some run for 100 years or more. By the early 1970s, the volume of outstanding debts of American governmental units, nonfinancial business firms, and households were over $1,800 billion, and debts of financial institutions were at least a trillion dollars. There are also many contracts other than debts that are fixed or semifixed in terms of monetary units; among these are dividends on preferred stock, long-term leases on real estate and other property, and pensions.

The disadvantages of writing contracts for future payments in terms of specific commodities have already been noted. But money is a satisfactory standard of deferred payments only to the extent that it maintains a constant purchasing power through time. If money increases in value through time, it injures the groups who have promised to pay fixed amounts of money and gives windfall gains to those who receive these fixed amounts. If, on the other hand, money loses value through time, it injures those who have agreed to receive the fixed amounts and lightens the burden of payers.

Money as a store of value

We have already noted the disadvantages of holding specific commodities as a store of value. As soon as money comes to be used as a unit of value and as a generally acceptable means of payment, it is almost certain to be widely used as a store of value. The holder of money is, in effect, a holder of generalized purchasing power that he can spend through time as he sees fit for the things he wants most to buy. He knows that it will be accepted at any time for any good or service and that it will remain constant in terms of itself. Money is thus a good store of value with which to meet unpredictable emergencies and especially to pay debts that are fixed in terms of money. This does not mean that money has been a stable and wholly satisfactory store of value; it can meet this test only if its purchasing power remains constant. In actual practice, it has performed this function most capriciously.

Money is not, of course, the only store of value. This function can be served by any valuable asset. One can store value for the future by holding short-term promissory notes, bonds, mortgages, preferred stocks, household furniture, houses, land, or any other kind of valuable goods. The principal advantages of these other assets as a store of value are that they, unlike money, ordinarily yield an income in the form of interest, profits, rent, or usefulness (as in the case of an auto or a suit of clothes); and they sometimes rise in value in terms of money. On the other hand, these assets have certain disadvantages as a store of value, among which are the following: (1) They sometimes involve storage costs; (2) they may depreciate in terms of money; and (3) they are "illiquid" in varying degrees, because they are not generally acceptable as money and because sometimes the only way to convert them into money quickly is to exchange them at a loss of value.

All persons and business firms are free to choose for themselves the form in which they will store their value, to determine the proportions they will hold in the form of money and in various nonmonetary forms, and to alter these from time to time to achieve what seem to them the most advantageous proportions on the basis of income, safety, and liquidity. The decisions are much influenced by a person's expectations as to the future behavior of prices. If he comes to believe that the prices of other things are less likely to decline and more likely to rise, he will be inclined to hold less of his wealth in the form of money and more in the form of other things. But if he comes to believe that prices of other things are less likely to rise and more likely to fall, he will be inclined to hold an increased part of his wealth in the form of money and a smaller part in other forms.

We shall see later that this freedom of people and business firms to determine for themselves the distribution of their holdings as between money and other assets and to shift from one form of assets to another may initiate or aggravate fluctuations in the flow of money expenditures and in prices and business activity. Sometimes people as a group show a tendency that is variously described as a desire to hold more of their wealth in the form of money and less in other forms, to use more money as a store value and less as a means of payment, to transfer money from active use to idle balances, to hoard money, to hold money longer before spending it, or to decrease the velocity or rapidity of circulation of money. But regardless of the name applied to it, such a development tends to decrease the flow of money expenditures for securities, goods, and services, thereby exerting a downward pressure on the national money income, employment, and price levels. On the other hand, a widespread tendency that has been variously described as a general movement to hold less wealth in the form of money and more in other forms, to use less money as a store of value and more as a means of payment, to transfer money from idle balances to active use, to dishoard money, to hold money only a short time before spending it, or to speed up the velocity or rapidity of circulation of money, serves to raise the rate of money expenditures and to raise money incomes, price levels, and under some conditions, employment and real output. Such fluctuations in the velocity of money, or the demand for money to hold, will occupy a very important position in our later discussions of the relationships between money and the behavior of the economy.

DEFINITION OF MONEY

Having considered the various functions performed by money, we must now ask, "What 'things' are included in money and what 'things' excluded?" Money should be defined precisely, for we shall deal at length with the supply (stock) of money and its behavior. Unfortunately, it is impossible to find a completely clear-cut answer to this basic question.

Examples of money

Anyone who begins his study of money with a belief that there is some one thing that is "by nature money" and that has been used as money at all times and in all places will find monetary history very disconcerting, for a most heterogeneous array of things has served as circulating media. An incomplete list is given in Table 1–1.

Table 1–1 An incomplete list of things that have served as money

clay	goats	hoes	iron
cowry shells	slaves	pots	bronze
wampum	rice	boats	nickel
tortoise shells	tea	porcelain	paper
porpoise teeth	tobacco	stone	leather
whale teeth	pitch	iron	pasteboard
boar tusks	wool	copper	playing cards
woodpecker scalps	salt	brass	debts of individuals
cattle	corn	silver	debts of banks
pigs	wine	gold	debts of governments
horses	beer	electrum	
sheep	knives	lead	

Some of these things are animal, some vegetable, some mineral; some, such as debts, defy classification. Some are as valuable for nonmonetary purposes as they are in their use as money; some at the other extreme have almost no value in nonmonetary uses. Some are quite durable; others could be classified as perishable.

About the only characteristic that all these things had in common was their ability, at some time and place, to achieve general acceptability in payment. And the reasons for their general acceptability certainly varied from place to place and from time to time.

Legal definitions of money

Some have tried to define money in purely legal terms, contending that "money is what the law says it is." Legal provisions are certainly relevant. A "thing" is likely to have difficulty in achieving general acceptability in payments if the law prohibits its use for this purpose, although violations of such laws are far from unknown. Laws can also help a thing to achieve general acceptability by proclaiming it to be money. They may go further and endow it with *legal-tender* powers, decreeing that it has the legal power to discharge debts and that a creditor who refuses it may not demand anything else in payment of an existing debt.

However, legal definitions of money are not satisfactory for purposes of economic analysis. For one thing, people may refuse to accept things that are legally defined as money and may even refuse to sell goods and services to those who offer legal tender in payment. Moreover, things that are not legally defined as money may come to be generally acceptable in payment and even to become a major part of the circulating medium. Commercial-bank notes and deposits are an outstanding example. We must conclude, therefore, that legal provisions are an important, but certainly not the only, determinant of the things that do and the things that do not serve as money.

Functional definitions of money

To be useful for purposes of economic analysis, the definition of money must be in functional terms. Money includes all those things that perform the functions of money and excludes all others. But this definition raises still other questions, the principal of which is, "performs what functions?" Two of the functions—those of serving as a unit of value and as a standard of deferred payment—do not help determine which "things" to include in the money supply and which to exclude, for they are abstract units that can relate to many different things. For example, we could measure values in dollars whether or not our money, denominated in dollars, was composed of gold, paper money, or porpoise teeth. And we could state contracts extending over time in dollars without reference to the nature of the things to be used in payment.

Virtually all economists agree that the money supply should include all those things that are in fact generally acceptable in payment of debt and as payment for goods and services. If a thing is in fact acceptable in payment and generally used as a medium of payments, it is money, whatever may be its legal status.

Applying this criterion to United States money, our supply includes at least coins, paper money, and demand deposits (or checking deposits) at banks. All our coins and paper money are not only generally acceptable in fact, they are also endowed with full legal-tender powers to discharge debts. Checking-deposit claims against banks do not have legal-tender powers, but they are in fact generally acceptable as payment. Perhaps as much as 90 percent of all payments in this country are made by transferring deposit claims against banks from payors to payees, the transfers being effected by checks or other orders on banks. The checks or other orders are only the means of effecting transfers; the things transferred as money are deposit claims against banks.

Throughout the remainder of this book, we shall define the money supply in this restricted sense. The public's money supply includes only its holdings of coin, paper money, and checking deposits. As indicated in Table 1–2, coins are indeed the "small change" of the monetary system, comprising less than 3 percent of the total money supply. Paper money makes up another 23.5 percent, but checking deposits are by far the largest component, representing nearly 74 percent of the total. All these things are generally acceptable and generally used in making payments and are also used as a store of value.

Table 1–2 The public's money supply, September 30, 1971

TYPE OF MONEY	AMOUNT OUTSTANDING (MILLIONS OF DOLLARS)	PERCENT OF TOTAL
Coins	$ 6,074	2.7
Paper money	51,946	23.5
Demand (checking) deposits	163,400	73.8
Total	$221,420	100.0

SOURCE: *Federal Reserve Bulletin,* November, 1971, pp. A16–19. This table actually overstates the amount of coin and paper money in the hands of the public. About $5,400 million of the amount shown above was in the vaults of commercial banks where it served as a part of their legal reserves.

Later we shall have occasion to refer to "moneyness." This relates to the characteristics of money itself, defined in our restrictive sense. Money remains constant in terms of monetary units and can be used for making payments without delay or other costs. Moneyness is therefore a protection against loss in terms of money and against the delay, inconvenience, and other costs that may be involved in exchanging some other asset for money.

Near-moneys or moneys?

Many economists consider our definition of money too restrictive. They admit that only coins, paper money, and checking deposits are generally accepted in payments, but they prefer to expand the money category to include some other things that have a high degree of moneyness and are widely used as a store of value. None would include everything used as a store of value; the concept of money would become meaningless if expanded to include land, structures, livestock, business inventories, and other such risky and illiquid assets. But some economists would include time and savings deposits at commercial and mutual-savings banks, claims against credit unions, and shares of savings and loan associations in their definition of money. Some would go further and include U.S. Treasury bills and other short-term debts of the federal government and even short-term debts of safe private debtors.

These things are not generally acceptable in payment; they yield an income to their holders, but they are not legally payable on demand, and, in most cases, there is at least a short delay or other cost in exchanging them for money in the sense in which we have defined it. Yet they do indeed have a high degree of moneyness or "liquidity." Their value ordinarily fluctuates only very narrowly in terms of money, and they can be exchanged for coin, paper money, or checking deposits quickly and at little cost other than the sacrifice of the income that they yield.

Those who favor a broader definition of the money supply believe these assets should be included because a dollar held in these forms may have almost the same effect on the willingness and ability of the public to spend as would a dollar of money in our restricted sense. These assets are almost perfect substitutes for money as a store of value, and are superior in the sense that they yield an income. Their availability reduces the quantity of money proper used by the public as a store of value and releases more of it to be used as a medium of exchange or payments. In other words, less money proper is immobilized in serving the store-of-value function, so that more money can be used to make payments. A given money supply can support a higher level of spending.

We do not deny that the availability of these "near-moneys" can affect the behavior of the rate of money spending. Nevertheless, we shall stand by our earlier definition of money for several reasons:

1. Since all assets possess the quality of moneyness in varying degrees, any other definition would leave equally troublesome borderline cases.

2. We doubt that a dollar's worth of these assets affects the public's willingness to spend as much as does a dollar's worth of money proper.

3. At times it is the purpose of monetary policy to make it more expensive or less expensive to exchange these assets for money proper. For example, it may at times be desirable to force people to take losses or to sacrifice more interest income if they try to exchange government securities for money proper.

4. The rate of spending depends not only on the supply of money and other liquid assets, but also on many other things, such as the people's total wealth, both liquid and illiquid; their expectations as to future wealth, income, and price levels; the availability and cost of credit; and so on. To include these other liquid assets in the money supply simply because they affect the rate of spending would raise questions as to why all determinants of the spending rate were not also included.

Although we exclude these near-moneys from our definition of the money supply, we shall not ignore their effects on the behavior of the rate of spending. We include these in our analysis by taking into account the public's demand for money balances. We shall argue that the behavior of spending depends not only on the supply (stock) of money, but also on the demand function of the community for money balances. The characteristics and quantities of near-moneys will thus enter the equation as one, but only one, of the determinants of the community's demand function for money balances.

THE UNPRECEDENTED IMPORTANCE OF MONEY

Money is by no means a recent invention—it is certainly as old as recorded history, and some form of it seems to evolve as soon as a group finds a significant amount of specialization and exchange advantageous, which is usually early in group life— nor are monetary problems less ancient. Historians have yet to find a society with a perfectly functioning money, and many of the ancient monetary disorders were serious. Yet money is of unprecedented importance in modern capitalistic economies. This is due to two interrelated factors: (1) the unprecedented extent of specialization and exchange, and (2) the nature of economic motivations under capitalism.

The rapid rise of specialization and trade in the United States has been outlined by Walton Hamilton:

> In the United States in fewer decades than the fingers on the hands has occurred a social revolution. An economy of small farms and petty trade, with a bit of commerce on the fringe, has been converted into "the great industry." At the end of the Civil War there was a coastal plain with a few cities, a back country with a dotting of small towns, and a West which invited settlement. The small, all but isolated, farm was dominant. The family, committed to a subsistence agriculture, undertook to produce their own livings with their own hands and formed an all-but-priceless economy. The household group was well or poorly off as they were hard working, prudent, thrifty, and had the break of the seasons. The weather could bountifully give or stingily withhold; for, because of an undeveloped technique in agriculture, it was still nature and not the market which made years fat or lean. The face of the land was covered with these almost self-contained entities. Almost—for the town was near at hand, to which the farmer took his surplus of produce; discovered the strange phenomena of the market, money, and price; engaged in verbal combat in haggling over a bargain; established an indirect contact with places far removed; and brought away tobacco, tools, and the subscription to the county weekly.[2]

Even in the period before the Civil War, money was not unimportant in this country. The farmer's enjoyment of life, if not his possession of necessities, depended to a considerable extent on the prices of farm products, the prices of the things he bought, and the real burden of his money debts. Moreover, there were already many people in the towns and cities whose dependence on money and markets was greater than that of the farmer. Yet, as Hamilton indicates, the farmers were to a considerable extent self-sufficient, and even the city dwellers were less dependent on money and markets than they are today. A social revolution has

---

[2] Walton Hamilton, *Price and Price Policies*, New York, McGraw-Hill, 1938, p. 7.

indeed occurred since that time. In 1840 about 70 percent of our people lived on farms; this figure has now dwindled to less than 5 percent and may fall still farther. And farming itself has experienced a revolution. The self-sufficient farm family is now the rare exception; to a constantly increasing extent, the farmer is a specialized businessman, producing for sale in the market and relying on the market for a large part of the equipment and supplies with which to carry on production, as well as for most of the things with which to satisfy his family's wants. He, too, provides for his farm and family by obtaining money for his production and spending the money for tractors, implements, building materials, gasoline, automobiles, clothing, food, and other supplies and services. Any lingering illusion that the American farmer was independent of the market vanished during the Great Depression following 1929. The great numbers of our people who are engaged in mining, manufacturing, transportation, communication, marketing, and service are almost completely dependent on markets and money. For them, self-support is a process of securing money in return for their specialized goods or services and then spending it for the things they want. Anything that disrupts the flow of their money income is likely to cause serious suffering and frustration.

A second reason for the unprecedented importance of money in the United States and other countries with similar types of economic systems is to be found in the nature of economic motivations in a capitalistic system. Money and monetary policy cannot safely be neglected even in a collectivistic society such as Soviet Russia, which relies primarily on centralized physical planning and direction of employment, output, and distribution. Time after time, central planners have been embarrassed by excessive or deficient money flows that create dissatisfaction and militate against the success of their master plan. But money and monetary policy are inescapably more powerful forces in a capitalistic, free-market economy. The leaders in this system are the enterprisers—those who determine the policies of business firms, whether these are individual proprietorships, partnerships, corporations, or cooperatives. They are the ones who determine whether or not to establish plants, the size and location of plants, the types of goods to be produced, the rate of output, the amount of employment to be offered, and the demand for capital equipment. Their motivation is to "make money," as much money as possible; and they supply goods and services only to the extent that this process will contribute to their primary objective of making money profits. If the flow of money spendings for their output is so great relative to their costs as to enable enterprisers to maximize their money profits by using all the available productive factors, then almost the entire work force will be employed. If, however, money spendings for their output are so small relative to their costs that they will maximize their profits or minimize their losses by stopping far short of full output, they are likely to leave large numbers in the ranks of the unemployed. If the flow of expenditures for their products rises when almost all available factors of production are already fully employed, they are almost certain to raise their prices. Such fluctuations of money expenditures are likely to be accompanied by fluctuations not only in employment and real output but also in price levels. This brings us to the difficult subject of the causative role of money.

Money as a causative factor in the economy

We must neither underestimate nor overestimate the influence of money and monetary policy on the functioning of an economic system. Many of the writings of the so-called "classical" economists who dominated British and American economic thinking in the nineteenth and early twentieth centuries tended to accord money only an unimportant causative role. Such a view of the significance, or rather the insignificance, of money was clearly stated by John Stuart Mill:

> It must be evident, however, that the mere introduction of a particular mode of exchanging things for one another by first exchanging a thing for money, and then exchanging the money for something else, makes no difference in the essential character of transactions. . . .
>
> There cannot, in short, be intrinsically a more insignificant thing, in the economy of society, than money; except in the character of a contrivance of sparing time and labor. It is a machine for doing quickly and commodiously, what would be done, though less quickly and commodiously, without it; and like many other types of machinery, it only exerts a distinct and independent influence of its own when it gets out of order.
>
> The introduction of money does not interfere with the operation of any of the Laws of Value laid down in the preceding chapters. The reasons which make the temporary or market value of things depend on the demand and supply, and their average and permanent values upon their cost of production, are as applicable to a money system as to a system of barter. Things which by barter would exchange for one another, will, if sold for money, sell for an equal amount of it, and so will exchange for one another still, though the process of exchanging them will consist of two operations instead of only one. The relations of commodities to one another remain unaltered by money; the only new relation introduced is their relation to money itself; how much or how little money they will exchange for; in other words how the Exchange Value of money itself is determined.[3]

Three aspects of Mill's statement should be noted before jumping to the conclusion that money deserves no more attention than each of the thousands of other labor-saving devices in the economy. First, Mill conceded that money "exerts a distinct and independent influence of its own when it gets out of order." This suggests the importance of keeping money "in order" to avoid disturbances. Second, he was speaking primarily of "equilibrium conditions"—those conditions that would rule after sufficient time had elapsed for all factors of production, output, costs, and prices to become so adjusted that there would be no incentive for further changes. Third, he was assuming that, at least in the long run, there was no "money illusion" and that both money wage rates and prices were perfectly flexible. That is, he assumed that decision makers responded not to the absolute level of a price but to relative prices—the prices of what they sold relative to the prices of things they bought, which are the barter terms of trade. He also

---

[3] John Stuart Mill, *Principles of Political Economy*, Book III, Chap. 7, p. 3.

assumed that money wage rates adjusted flexibly to demand and supply conditions in labor markets and that prices adjusted flexibly to changes in costs.

Modern economists tend to accord money and monetary policy a more prominent role in their analysis. In the first place, they believe money is frequently, if not virtually always, "out of order," in the sense in which Mill used the term. They have not even succeeded in defining satisfactorily the requirements of a "neutral" monetary policy, one that would not itself influence the behavior of an economy, but would enable an economy to function exactly as would a highly efficient barter economy without money. And actual monetary policies are rarely, if ever, neutral; instead, they tend continuously to push the economy one way or another.

In the second place, economists now devote much more attention to conditions and periods of disequilibrium: to business cycles, periods of unemployment or inflation, and periods of transition from one equilibrium position to another. The late Lord Keynes once quipped, "In the long-run we are all dead." This does not suggest that long-run consequences are unimportant, but it does emphasize that we cannot afford to neglect "short runs" or disequilibrium conditions which may persist for long periods and have serious social consequences. This fact is especially true if money wage rates are inflexible downward, even in the face of unemployment, and if prices of output do not decline flexibly with cost levels. Under such conditions, a decline in aggregate spending for output may be reflected not only in a decline of the price level, but also, and perhaps to a greater extent, in lower real output and in unemployment of labor and other productive factors. And a rise of expenditures for output, if it occurs when the economy is operating at a level far below its capacity, can elicit increases in both output and employment, although the rise of demand is likely to be reflected increasingly in prices as output approaches capacity. Thus, money, monetary policy, and anything else that influences the rate of aggregate expenditures can affect not only the price level or the "exchange value of money itself," but also such real variables as employment and output.

To overemphasize the role of money and monetary policy can be as dangerous as to underemphasize it. Some reformers, noting that the ability of an individual to obtain goods and services depends on the amount of money he can command, have erroneously assumed that the same must always hold true for an entire nation. They would therefore abolish poverty and usher in the economic millennium by great expansions in the money supply. How wonderful it would be if we could all become rich in any real sense simply by creating great batches of money! Unfortunately, it is not all that easy. We have already noted that an expansion of money spending may serve to expand real production if it occurs in a period of unemployment when the labor force and other productive factors are not working at full capacity. Economic policy must not ignore this fact. But neither can it safely ignore the fact that the most that monetary policy can do to promote production—and it may not accomplish this without the aid of other wise economic policies—is to achieve and maintain full employment. It cannot compensate for a paucity of natural resources or a scarcity of capital goods or a backward state of technology or sluggish and unintelligent labor or unimaginative and unenterprising economic management or inefficiency in government economic activities. In other words, a wise monetary policy may help to raise and maintain the actually realized rate of production closer to potential productive capacity (although we should not assume that it can always achieve even this objective). However monetary policy usually is not one of the major determinants of this potential capacity. Nor is a wise monetary policy by any means the only factor determining the distribution of income and wealth among the members of the community. We shall have wiser monetary policy, and certainly wiser economic policies as a whole, if we recognize the limitations of monetary policy as well as its power.

Selected readings

Sources of recent and current information

Bank for International Settlements, Annual Reports.
Board of Governors of the Federal Reserve System:
  Annual Reports, 1914 to date.
  Federal Reserve Bulletin (monthly). This is a highly valuable source of current information concerning monetary and banking developments in both the United States and abroad.
  Banking and Monetary Statistics. (Through 1941. Current statistics in *Federal Reserve Bulletins.*)
  Miscellaneous publications, see lists of these in *Federal Reserve Bulletins.*
Chase Manhattan Bank of New York, *Monthly Bulletins.*
Comptroller of the Currency, *Annual Reports.*
Council of Economic Advisers, *Economic Indicators* (monthly).
Federal Deposit Insurance Corporation, *Annual Reports.* These reports contain excellent statistics and analyses of the structure and condition of American banks.
Federal Reserve Banks:
  Annual Reports, Monthly Bulletins, and special publications.
  The Monthly Letter of the Federal Reserve Bank of New York is a rich source of information concerning conditions abroad and in the central financial markets.
International Bank for Reconstruction and Development, *Annual Reports.*
  See also its special studies.
International Monetary Fund, *Annual Reports.*
  Also valuable are its publications of staff papers and special studies.
Secretary of the Treasury:
  Annual Reports.
  Treasury Bulletins (monthly).
U.S. Congress:
  House Banking and Currency Committee, various hearings and reports.
  Senate Banking and Currency Committee, various hearings and reports.
  Joint Economic Committee, numerous hearings, special compilations of materials, and reports.

CHAPTER 2

KINDS OF MONEY

Having surveyed the various roles played by money in economic systems, we now consider the principal types of money that have been used. This is a highly important subject, for the types of money employed can influence greatly the behavior of a nation's money supply, the value or purchasing power of its monetary unit, and the ability of monetary authorities to control the money supply.

CLASSIFICATIONS OF MONEY

Money can be classified on several different bases, such as the following: (1) the physical characteristics of the materials of which money is made; (2) the nature of the issuer, such as a government, central bank, commercial bank, or other; and (3) the relationship between the value of money as money and the value of money as a commodity. We shall use all these classifications, but it will be convenient to start with the third. Table 2–1 shows the various types of money on this basis.

Since 1933, the United States has had only credit or debt money; both full-bodied and representative full-bodied money were discontinued and withdrawn at that time. The latter two should be analyzed, however, for they have played important roles in monetary history and are still remembered nostalgically by many people.

Full-bodied money

Full-bodied money is money whose value as a commodity for nonmonetary purposes is as great as its value as money. Most of the early commodity moneys, such as cattle, rice, wool, and boats, were as valuable for nonmonetary purposes as

Table 2–1 Classifications of money

I Full-bodied money
II Representative full-bodied money
III Credit money
    A. Issued by government
        1. Token coins
        2. Representative token money
        3. Circulating promissory notes
    B. Issued by banks
        1. Circulating promissory notes issued by central banks
        2. Circulating promissory notes issued by other banks
        3. Demand deposits subject to check

they were in their monetary uses. The principal full-bodied moneys in modern monetary systems have been coins of the standard metal when a country is on a metallic standard: a gold standard, a silver standard, or a bimetallic standard using gold and silver. We shall use gold in our examples, but the same principles apply to full-bodied money made of any other commodity.

Full-bodied coins need not be issued by governments. This function could be, and in a few cases has been, entrusted to private enterprise with some regulation of the purity and weight of the coins to prevent cheating. In most cases, however, governments have retained a monopoly of the issue of full-bodied coins. Three steps are involved:

1. Define the gold value of the monetary unit. This may be done in either of two ways, but both amount to the same thing: Stipulate the gold content of the monetary unit or stipulate the money price of each unit of gold. For example, for many years before 1933, the federal government defined the dollar as 23.22 grains of fine (pure) gold. This amounted to setting a price of $20.67 per ounce of fine gold because an ounce of gold (480 grains) will yield 20.67 portions of 23.22 grains each.

2. At the stipulated price, purchase all the metal that is offered and coin it without limit and virtually without charge. This prevents the market price of gold from falling below the mint buying price. No one will sell gold at a lower price for nonmonetary uses when the monetary authority is a willing buyer at $20.67 an ounce.

3. Permit the melting of coins to get gold for nonmonetary uses. It is usually unnecessary to give permission to do this; people do it anyway if they find it the cheapest way to get gold. The effect of this is to prevent the market price of gold from rising above the mint price as long as gold can be acquired for nonmonetary uses by melting the full-bodied coins. However, when market demands for gold can no longer be satisfied by melting down gold coins, the market price of gold can rise above the official mint price; that is, the monetary unit can depreciate in terms of gold.

Figure 2–1 indicates that all this may be viewed as an arrangement whereby the price of gold is stabilized in terms of money. The curve S_TS_T represents the total supply of gold in the sense of the total stock at various possible prices. The curve D_CD_C represents the demand function for gold for nonmonetary purposes. The figure indicates that the price of gold cannot fall below the level OE as long as the government stands ready to buy (represented by curve D_MD_M) at that price all that is offered for monetary purposes. And the price cannot rise above that level as long as gold can be supplied for nonmonetary uses by melting full-bodied gold coins. The supply of gold from melting coins is represented by the curve S_MS_M.

Another important point is this: When the government has fixed the price of gold and stands ready to buy in unlimited amounts and to permit melting of gold coins, it loses control of the quantity of full-bodied coins. The amount of gold in monetary use will be a residual equal to the total gold stock minus the amounts demanded for nonmonetary uses. In the figure, the amount of gold in monetary use is equal to the total stock (OB) minus the amount absorbed in nonmonetary uses (OA). The monetary value of the full-bodied coins is equal to the number of ounces in this form multiplied by the price per ounce. This is represented by the area $ADCB$.

Some consider it a merit of this type of money that its supply is limited by the cost of enlarging the gold stock and by competing demands for nonmonetary uses. They see this as a safeguard against overissue. Others see little merit in leav-

Figure 2–1 Stabilization of the price of gold

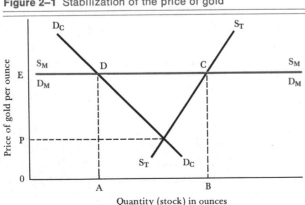

ing the quantity of money in this form to be determined by the vagaries of gold mining and of competing demands.

Two points on which there has been much misunderstanding need to be clarified:

1. To say that full-bodied coins have the same value as money as they have in nonmonetary uses of the metal is not to say that they have a constant value or purchasing power in terms of other things. If the price of a unit of gold is fixed in terms of money, its purchasing power varies reciprocally with the prices of other things. Thus, the purchasing power of gold will fall by half if the price level of other things doubles, and the purchasing power of gold will double if the price level falls by half. There is no reason to expect that the price level of other things will remain constant simply because the price of gold has been stabilized. For example, suppose that while many major countries stand ready to buy gold for monetary use at constant prices, someone discovers huge new gold deposits that can be mined and refined at very low real cost. One would suspect that the large increase in the supply of gold would in some sense lower its "value." Yet the price of gold cannot fall as long as governments will buy it at constant prices for monetary purposes. How, then, may its value fall?

2. It is not true, as some have inferred, that the value of a full-bodied coin (in the sense of its purchasing power over other things) is simply the reflected value of the metal as determined by its total supply (stock) and its demand for nonmonetary uses. Its value is determined by the total supply (stock) of the material and by its total demand for monetary and nonmonetary uses. And the monetary demand may come to be the major part of the total demand. If the monetary demand were withdrawn and the total supply made available for nonmonetary uses, the price and value of the material could fall greatly. For example, what would happen to the value or purchasing power of each ounce of gold if governments refused to buy any of the current output of gold for monetary purposes? And what would happen if in addition to not buying gold, governments threw onto the market the accumulated stock of more than 1.2 billion ounces now held in monetary reserves?

Representative full-bodied money

Representative full-bodied money, which is usually made of paper, is in effect a circulating warehouse receipt for full-bodied coins or their equivalent in bullion. The representative full-bodied money itself has no significant value as a commodity, but it "represents" in circulation an amount of metal with a commodity value equal to the value of the money. Thus, the "gold certificates" that circulated in the United States before their recall from circulation in 1933 represented fully equivalent amounts of gold coin or gold bullion held by the Treasury as "backing" for them.

In some respects, representative full-bodied money is similar to full-bodied money. The amount of it that can be issued depends upon the quantity of full-bodied money or its bullion equivalent available as "backing," and the cost of the "backing" material is as great as that of full-bodied money. This type of money has certain advantages over full-bodied money. In the first place, its use obviates the expense of coining, although against this expense must be set the cost of providing and maintaining the pieces of representative paper. In the second place, it avoids ordinary abrasion as well as the deliberate sweating, clipping, and chipping to which circulating coins are sometimes subjected. In the third place, it is easier to transport than the full-bodied money that it represents. This was certainly true of the Swedish representative money that circulated in place of massive copper coins during the seventeenth and eighteenth centuries, of the warehouse receipts for tobacco that circulated in Virginia and some of the other colonies, and of the pre-1933 gold certificates. The principal disadvantages of this type of money as compared to full-bodied money are the ease of counterfeiting it if the representative paper money is not very distinctive and its destructibility by fire.

Credit money

By credit money, or debt money, we mean any money, except representative full-bodied money, that circulates at a value greater than the commodity value of the material from which it is made. In some cases, the market value of the money material is insignificant, as in the case of most paper money. In other cases, such as copper coins, the market value of the material may be substantial, but may still be below the value of the money.

How can a money achieve and maintain a value or purchasing power as money greater than the value of the commodity of which it is made? Essentially, the method is to limit the quantity of the money by preventing the free and unlimited transformation of the commodity into money. The most common way is for the issuing authority to fix the quantity of the particular type of money to be issued and to buy only as much of the money material as is needed for the purpose. The remainder of the supply of that commodity is left for nonmonetary uses, and this residual supply may be so large relative to demands for nonmonetary uses, that the market value of the commodity will fall far below the value of the money. Note that in this case the issuing authority itself determines the quantity of debt or credit money to be issued and the amount of the money material to be purchased for the purpose.

Credit or debt money can also result as the issuing authority buys all the money material offered to it, but at a price significantly below the monetary or face value of the money into which it is transformed. Suppose, for example, that the monetary authority issues pesos, each containing $\frac{1}{2}$ ounce of silver, but stands ready to buy all silver offered to it at a price of only 1 peso an ounce. The issuing authority is clearly in a position to make large gross profits by purchasing silver at 1 peso an ounce and converting each ounce into 2 pesos of money. This gross profit to the issuer is called "seigniorage." But the main point here is that this is a way of maintaining the value of credit money above the market value of the commodity of which it is made. Each ounce of silver in the form of money is obviously 2 pesos, but the price of silver in the market could fall as low as 1 peso an ounce, the price at which the monetary authority will buy it.

Credit money can take various forms:

1. Token coins. As noted earlier, our coins (half-dollars, quarters, dimes, nickels, and pennies) are indeed the "small change" of our monetary system; they make up only a very small fraction, less than 3 percent, of our total money supply. These coins are all token money; with a value as money considerably above the market values of the metals contained in them. In general, the government creates and issues those amounts of the various denominations of coins that the public demands as "small change."

The market value of the metals contained in nickels and pennies has always been considerably below the face values of these coins. The history of silver dollars, half-dollars, and dimes has been less consistent. Until the mid-1960s, these coins consisted of 90 percent silver and 10 percent alloy. During this period, the price of silver remained low enough to keep the market values of the silver in these coins significantly below their face values. The situation changed in the 1960s as nonmonetary demands for silver—demands for silver to be used in silverware, electronics, and photographic film—rose sharply relative to silver supplies. The market price reached $1.293 an ounce, at which price it became profitable to melt down silver dollars and to exchange silver certificates for the silver bullion backing them. Silver dollars disappeared from circulation, some were converted to bullion for nonmonetary uses and some were added to rare-coin collections. As the market price of silver continued to rise, it became profitable to melt down half-dollars, quarters, and dimes. Congress modified this situation by changing the commodity content of these coins from silver to copper and nickel; once again the money value of small change is far above its market value as a commodity.

2. Representative token money. This is usually paper which is in effect a circulating warehouse receipt for token coins or for an equal weight of bullion that has been deposited with the government. This type of money is like representative full-bodied money, except that the coin or bullion held as "backing" is worth less as a commodity than it is as money. Silver certificates, which circulated in varying amounts from 1878 to 1967, are the only example of this type of money in the United States. They were backed by an equivalent number of silver dollars or by silver bullion of equivalent weight. Virtually all of them disappeared after 1967. Most of them were presented to the Treasury for redemption in silver as the market price of silver rose, but some went into numismatic collections. The silver certificates were replaced by Federal Reserve notes.

3. Circulating promissory notes issued by governments. Governments also issue credit money in a form that is usually, but sometimes inaccurately, called "circulating promissory notes." These are usually made of paper and are sometimes called "fiat" money. Some of them carry the government's promise to redeem them in other types of money on demand; this is why this type of money

is usually called "circulating promissory notes." Other forms of this money, however, lack this promise and in effect say, "This is a certain number of monetary units."

The only circulating promissory notes issued by the United States government and still in circulation are the United States notes, or "greenbacks," which were issued to assist in financing the Civil War. Over $400 million of them were originally issued, but they were reduced to $347 million by 1878 and have since remained at approximately that level.

Many people oppose the use of government paper money, fearing that it will be issued in excessive amounts. Monetary history provides a real basis for this fear, since these issues provide an attractive source of revenue to governments. By spending a small amount for paper, engraving, and printing, a government can pay its debts or cover its expenses by producing millions of dollars' worth of paper money. The temptation to sacrifice proper monetary management to budgetary needs is often strong. It should be pointed out, however, that most of the excessive issues of paper money have occurred during war periods when nations felt that their very existence was at stake and when they were in dire need of money to meet military requirements. There is no reason why a properly managed government paper money should not function well.

4. Circulating promissory notes issued by central banks. The largest part of the hand-to-hand currency that is used in most advanced countries is in the form of circulating promissory notes issued by central banks, such as our Federal Reserve banks, the Bank of England, and the Bank of France. The largest part of our paper money is made up of Federal Reserve notes, which are circulating evidences of debt issued by the 12 Federal Reserve banks. In some cases, the paper money issued by central banks is redeemable in other types of money; in other cases, it is irredeemable. Although the Federal Reserve banks will redeem their notes in token coins or other types of paper money, they are not obligated to redeem them in full-bodied money.

5. Circulating promissory notes issued by private banks. Circulating promissory notes issued by privately owned banks have played an important role in monetary systems. Promissory notes issued by state-chartered banks and by the First and Second Banks of the United States provided a large part of the circulating medium in this country before the Civil War, and the national banks chartered by the federal government issued such notes from the time of the Civil War until 1935, when their power of note issue was rescinded. Although the notes issued by privately owned banks have been retired in this country, they are still used extensively in some other nations. These notes, it must be emphasized, are only circulating evidences of bank debts—creditor claims against banks.

6. Checking deposits at banks. The major part of the money supply in this country, as well as in most other advanced countries, is in the form of demand deposits at banks. These so-called "deposits" are merely bank debts payable on demand and are claims of creditors against a bank which can be transferred from one person or firm to another by means of checks or other orders to pay. These

claims against banks are generally acceptable in payment of debts and for goods and services. They are used almost exclusively in transactions involving large payments and very widely in the making of small payments, such as payments from customers to retailers and the payment of salaries and wages to employees.

The popularity of checking deposits can be traced to their advantages:

a. They are not so liable to loss or theft as other types of money.

b. They can be transported very cheaply, regardless of the amount of the payment or the distance between payer and payee.

c. Because checks can be written for the exact amount of the payment, there is no need to make change and count bills and coins.

d. When endorsed by the payee, checks serve as a convenient receipt for payment.

The principal disadvantage of checking deposits is that checks drawn on them may not be accepted from an unknown person, but this is largely remedied by such devices as certified checks, cashier's checks, and traveler's checks which in effect guarantee payment to the payee or to anyone to whom he transfers his claim.

COMBINATIONS OF THE VARIOUS TYPES OF MONEY

The various types of money described in the preceding section have been used in actual monetary systems in many different combinations and proportions. At one extreme, the entire circulating medium is composed of full-bodied money or of full-bodied money plus representative full-bodied money. In such cases, the size of the total money supply depends on the official price of the money material and upon the quantity of that material the country can command for monetary uses. Many of the early monetary systems approached this type, but no such systems exist today.

At the other extreme, the entire circulating medium is made up of credit or debt money. Most modern monetary systems are of this type, with most of the money in the form of checking deposits and paper money. In some cases, the monetary authorities make no attempt, either directly or indirectly, to keep the various types of credit money at a constant value in terms of any commodity. These are pure credit-money systems. In such systems, the size of the money supply is not determined by the availability of any metal or other money material or limited by any obligation to redeem in a money material. It depends solely upon decisions of monetary authorities. In other systems in which the entire circulating medium is composed of debt money, the authorities do attempt directly or indirectly, to keep the various types of money at a fixed value in terms of some commodity. We shall discuss these later.

In between these extremes are monetary systems combining full-bodied money, representative full-bodied money, and debt money in various proportions. In some, credit money has been a very small fraction of the total; in others, it has been the major part. The general trend in monetary history has been for credit money to become increasingly large relative to full-bodied money. Some of the reasons for this will be discussed later. We turn now to some aspects of monetary standards.

MONETARY STANDARDS

As noted earlier, it has been common for a country to try to maintain its monetary unit and its various types of money stated in that unit at a constant value in terms of some commodity. Any commodity could be chosen—including peanuts, tobacco, cotton, or titanium—but silver and gold have been the most commonly used. A country that stabilizes its monetary unit in terms of gold is said to be "on a gold standard." A country that stabilizes its monetary unit in terms of silver is said to be "on a silver standard." Under a "bimetallic standard," a nation stabilizes its monetary unit simultaneously in terms of two metals, such as gold and silver.

Terms such as "gold standard" or "silver standard" should be used with the greatest of care. Each seems to imply that the monetary systems included under it are completely homogeneous, or at least that differences are not significant. In fact, however, each is a very broad category including monetary systems that differ greatly in form and functioning. Moreover, while the name remains constant, the systems to which it refers change, sometimes radically. We shall therefore stress differences as well as common features of a monetary standard.

To stabilize the value of a nation's monetary unit (and its various types of money stated in terms of that unit) in terms of some selected commodity, the monetary authority must meet the following requirements:

1. Define the quantitative relationship between the monetary unit and the commodity. This may be stated as the amount of the commodity for which a monetary unit will be given. Or, equivalently, it may be stated as the money price of a unit of the commodity, such as an ounce or a pound.

2. Stand ready to buy, at the stated price, all of the commodity offered to it. Payment may be made in full-bodied coins, representative full-bodied money, or new money of any sort. So long as the monetary authority can issue money to buy at a fixed price all of the commodity offered, it can keep the price of the commodity from falling; that is, it can prevent the value of the monetary unit from rising in terms of the commodity.

3. Stand ready to sell, at the fixed price, all of the commodity that is demanded.[1] This may be supplied to the market from the monetary system by withdrawal of full-bodied coins, by redemption of representative full-bodied money, or by sales out of other holdings of the commodity by the monetary authority. So long as the monetary system is able to supply all of the commodity demanded from it, the market price of the commodity cannot rise; the monetary unit cannot depreciate in terms of the commodity. However, the market price of

---

[1] We ignore here the usual small differences between official purchase and sale prices.

the commodity can rise—money can depreciate in terms of the commodity—if the monetary system is unable or unwilling to supply, at the fixed price, all of the commodity demanded from it.

These requirements suggest some of the problems of stabilizing money in terms of a commodity, especially when the monetary system contains large amounts of money in addition to full-bodied coins and representative full-bodied money. A nation can easily prevent the price of the commodity from falling—i.e., prevent its money from rising in terms of the commodity—because it can easily create the money needed to buy all of the commodity offered to it for monetary purposes. This is not to say that the monetary authority will always be happy with the inflationary pressures that may result from creating the new money to pay for the commodity. However, it can prevent the price of the commodity from rising above the official level—i.e., prevent its money from depreciating in terms of the commodity—only so long as it is both able and willing to supply at the fixed price all of the commodity demanded from it. This it can do only if it avoids "excessive issues of money"—only if it does not create or allow to be created so much money that it will be unable or unwilling to meet all demands on it to redeem its money in the money commodity.

As soon as the quantity of money becomes a multiple of a country's monetary gold, a promise to redeem all money in gold becomes a promise that cannot be kept if demands for redemption are actually made in volume. And there is often danger that such demands will be made. For example, a country may overexpand its total money supply, increase its costs and prices relative to those of other countries, and lose much of its gold to other countries to pay for an excess of imports over exports. Or some event may create fears that a country will be unable to redeem its money in gold, which will lead to large demands for redemption. For these and other reasons, countries have often been forced to suspend free redemption of their moneys in gold. In some cases in which they could have continued to redeem all money in gold, nations have been unwilling to do so because that would have required what they considered to be an undesirable restriction of the total money supply. They wanted more freedom to issue money to promote output and employment, to finance government deficits, or to use for other purposes.

Reasons such as these help to explain the historical trend for governments to limit ever more narrowly, and even to discontinue, the redeemability of money into gold or any other valuable commodity. And as governments limit their liability to redeem in gold, they achieve freedom to allow the money supply to become larger relative to the amount of monetary gold.

Let us now look briefly at some episodes in the history of American monetary standards.

Bimetallism, 1791–1861

In its first major monetary legislation, the Coinage Act of 1791, the United States established a bimetallic standard. It adopted the dollar as its monetary unit and gave it a fixed value in terms of silver and also in terms of gold. The pure silver content of a dollar was fixed at 317.25 grains. This amounted to fixing a mint price for silver at $1.293 an ounce, for one ounce (480 grains) could be minted into 1.293 dollars, each containing 371.25 grains. The pure gold content of the dollar was fixed at 24.75 grains. This was equivalent to fixing a mint price for gold at $19.395 an ounce, for an ounce of gold could be minted into this number of dollars. Thus the "mint ratio" was 15 to 1. That is, the silver content, by weight, of the dollar was 15 times that of gold. Or, to put it another way, the mint price of gold was 15 times that of silver. The government stood ready to mint, at these values, all the gold and silver offered to it. And people were free to melt down or export coins. The clear intent of the legislation was to provide the new nation with full-bodied gold and silver coins, gold coins for the larger denominations and silver for the smaller.

However, the scheme failed; silver "drove gold out of circulation" because the mint ratio in the United States valued silver more highly relative to gold than did the mint ratios of several other important countries which were also on bimetallic standards. In those countries the mint ratio was 15½ to 1. This discrepancy created an opportunity for a profitable chain of exchanges of gold and silver. For example, a person could get an ounce of gold in the United States, export it to another country in exchange for 15½ ounces of silver, use 15 ounces of the silver to buy an ounce of gold here, and have ½ ounce of silver left to cover expenses and yield a profit. However, gold would have disappeared from circulation in the United States even in the absence of such "round-robin" exchanges. This is because Americans making payments abroad found it cheaper to pay in gold, and foreigners making payments to Americans found it cheaper to pay in silver.

Responding to complaints against the de facto silver standard, Congress attempted to reestablish a bimetallic standard by altering the mint ratio in 1834. Leaving the silver content of the dollar and the mint price of silver unchanged, it lowered the gold content of the dollar from 24.75 to 23.22 grains. This was equivalent to raising the mint price of gold from $19.395 to $20.67 an ounce. The new mint ratio was 16 to 1 while that abroad remained at 15½ to 1. The situation was now reversed; the United States mint parity valued gold more highly relative to silver than did other countries. The results, although apparently unintended, should have been predictable. Gold now drove silver out of circulation. Not only silver dollars but also half-dollars, quarters, and dimes disappeared, creating inconvenience in trade. The nation came to be on a de facto gold standard. This fact is important for understanding our subsequent monetary history. Although we were legally on a bimetallic standard from 1791 to 1861, during most of the 27 years from 1834 to 1861 we were "de facto" on a gold standard.

Some viewers of this experience concluded that "it only goes to show that bimetallic standards must fail sooner or later; one of the metals will inevitably drive the other out of circulation." No such sweeping conclusion is justified.

Failure is indeed likely to result if countries adopt different mint parities. However, both metals may remain in circulation if mint parities are uniform.

Inconvertibility, 1861–1879

From soon after the outbreak of the Civil War in 1861 until 1879, the dollar was without a fixed value in terms of any metal. The Civil War was financed by highly inflationary methods, including the issue of over $400 million of greenbacks and much larger expansions of money in the form of bank notes and deposits. The American price level more than doubled while price levels abroad experienced no such increases. Under these conditions, it became impossible to redeem money in gold at a fixed price, and the price of gold rose sharply.

At the end of the war, with prices more than double their level of four years earlier, the nation faced crucial questions of monetary policy. It could not simultaneously restore the prewar value of the dollar in terms of gold or silver and maintain prices at their current high level relative to those abroad. Should it attempt to prevent a fall of prices and remain on an inconvertible paper-money standard? Should it attempt to prevent a fall of prices but reduce the gold or silver content of the dollar to defensible levels? Or should it restore the prewar gold or silver value of the dollar and allow price levels to fall as much as would be required for the purpose? The last alternative was chosen even though, as it turned out, the price level had to be allowed to decline by more than half.

The unlimited gold-coin standard, 1879–1933

Legislation enacted by Congress in 1873 preparatory to stabilization of the dollar in terms of some metal, which actually occurred only in 1879, rejected bimetallism and for the first time established a monometallic gold-coin standard. The gold content of the dollar was 23.22 grains, the same as that established by the legislation of 1834. The act provided for the free and unlimited coinage of gold at this value and also for the unlimited issue of gold certificates against full gold backing. No legal limits were placed on the redemption of other types of money in gold coin or on the acquisition of gold for export or for nonmonetary purposes. This was truly an unlimited gold-coin standard.

Under the new system established by the act of 1873, the Treasury no longer stood ready to mint or to buy at any fixed price all the silver offered to it. It did buy such limited amounts as it needed to manufacture fractional silver coins and also limited amounts against which it issued silver certificates, but its total purchases were so small that the market price of silver could and did fall far below the old mint price of $1.293 an ounce.

The American unlimited gold-coin standard lasted 54 years, from 1879 to 1933, although convertibility of at least some types of money into gold was interrupted briefly during several banking panics and for about 2 years during World War I. The functioning of this gold standard changed in several ways during the period. We shall mention here only one—the growth of deliberate monetary management. Before the establishment of the Federal Reserve System in 1914, the

American government had no agency or mechanism capable of managing the monetary system continuously and effectively. Under these conditions, increases and decreases of the nation's monetary gold tended to exert strong, if not automatic, influences on the money supply and credit conditions. Increases in the stock of monetary gold, whether from domestic production or imports, tended to increase bank reserves and induce increases in the money supply. On the other hand, decreases in monetary gold served to reduce bank reserves and bring about reductions in the money supply. These results often occurred whether or not they were wanted.

The Federal Reserve System brought first the possibility and later the actuality of a much higher degree of deliberate monetary management. Increases or decreases of monetary gold need no longer exert their old influence on the money supply and credit conditions. The Federal Reserve, with its power to create or destroy currency and bank reserves, could offset the effects of changes in the monetary gold stock, intensify these effects, or even bring about an increase or decrease in the money supply in the face of an opposite change in the amount of monetary gold. As will be emphasized later, a highly managed gold standard may function very differently from one that is not managed so much, and its performance depends heavily on the nature of monetary policies.

The American gold-coin standard came to an end in March, 1933, at the time of the great banking collapse. The government ended the redemption of money in gold; required that all gold coins, gold certificates, and gold bullion be surrendered to the Treasury in exchange for other types of money; terminated the minting of gold coins and the issuance of gold certificates; and then took deliberate steps to reduce the gold value of the dollar and raise the dollar price of gold. It would not be accurate to say that the government was forced to suspend gold payments. The government could almost certainly have kept the dollar redeemable at its old value in terms of gold if it had been willing to limit its freedom to adopt policies to promote economic recovery. But after more than 3 years of deflation and widespread unemployment it was unwilling to accept such limitations. It believed that suspension of the gold standard would be helpful in at least two ways. First, it would enable the government to lower the value of the dollar in foreign-exchange markets. As dollars became cheaper in terms of foreign currencies, American exports would be promoted and imports inhibited. Second, it would enable the government to adopt more expansionary monetary and fiscal policies without being inhibited by fears of gold losses.

The limited gold-bullion standard, 1934–

The new gold standard, which was established at the end of January, 1934, differed greatly from the unlimited gold-coin standard that had prevailed from 1879 to 1933. For one thing, the gold value of the dollar was decreased from 23.22 to 13.71 grains, a reduction of 40.94 percent. This was equivalent to raising the official price of gold from $20.67 to $35 an ounce, an increase of 69.33 percent. Also, the following policies were adopted in January, 1934 and prevailed until mid-March, 1968. The Treasury stood ready to buy, at this new price, all gold offered to it. However, no gold coins were minted and no gold certificates were issued to or held by any entity other than the Treasury and the Federal Reserve. Sellers of gold were paid with bank deposits or other types of money. To the extent that dollars were redeemable in gold, they were redeemable in gold bullion; however, the Treasury sold gold only for limited purposes. Gold might be bought, sold, held, or used only in accordance with Treasury regulations. In practice, the Treasury sold gold only to foreign central banks and official institutions and for "legitimate" domestic industrial, artistic, and professional uses. This is indeed a limited gold-bullion standard.

In adopting a gold-bullion standard, the United States followed the practice adopted by most other gold-standard countries in the 1920s. Prior to 1914, most of these countries, like the United States, were on unlimited gold-coin standards. These were suspended in the inflationary period during and immediately following World War I. When these countries returned to gold, most of them in the latter half of the 1920s, they rejected gold coinage and redemption of their moneys in gold coins and adopted gold-bullion standards. Typically, they stood ready to sell gold only in bullion form in bars worth not less than about $4,000. Some of these nations adopted unlimited gold-bullion standards; gold bars were sold without limitation on the purpose for which they were to be used. Other nations established limited gold-bullion standards; gold was sold for some purposes but not for others.

The replacement of an unlimited gold-coin standard with a gold-bullion standard, and especially with a limited gold-bullion standard, serves in at least two ways to "economize on gold"—to enable a given amount of monetary gold to support a larger total supply of money. First, it lessens the liability of the monetary authority to redeem money in gold and concentrates a larger part of the gold in the central reserves of the government or central bank. And second, a given amount of gold in the central bank can support a larger money supply than can the same amount of gold outside the central bank. For example, $1 of gold circulating in the form of gold coin or gold certificates supports only $1 of money. The same $1 in gold held as reserves by a commercial bank with a reserve requirement of 10 percent can support $10 of money in the form of checking deposits. But the $1 in gold held in a central bank which can create $5 worth of currency and commercial-bank reserves for every dollar of its gold reserves may support a total money supply of $40 or more.

In mid-March of 1968, the United States modified in two salient respects its gold policies that had prevailed for the preceding 34 years. In a statement issued jointly with several important foreign governments and central banks, the United States Treasury and the Federal Reserve announced that henceforth: (1) The cooperating institutions would continue to sell gold to each other at $35 an ounce, but they would not sell gold to anyone else. Others who wished to acquire gold for hoarding or any other purpose would have to buy it in gold markets. (2) The cooperating institutions would continue to buy gold from each other at $35 an ounce but they would not buy gold that was not already in official monetary reserves. They would refuse to buy newly mined gold, gold scrap, and gold from private hoards. Thus they created a "two-tier price system for gold"—a price of $35 an ounce for transactions among central banks and governments, and the possibility of a different price in gold markets, this price depending on supplies and demands for nonmonetary purposes. The points to be stressed here are both the further limitation on redeemability of money in gold and the limitation on monetization of gold.

A further change occurred in August, 1971, when President Nixon terminated convertibility of the dollar into gold, even for foreign central banks and governments, and indicated that for at least an interim period the United States would buy no more gold for monetary purposes.

The long-run implications of the policy actions in March, 1968 and August, 1971 are not yet clear. Monetary authorities are unlikely to return to their old policies of purchasing at a fixed price all gold that its offered to them, although they might buy limited amounts. They could even sell, for nonmonetary purposes, the gold already in their possession, although this seems unlikely in the short run. If they do this, gold will be "demonetized" and become just another commodity in the marketplace. What is most unlikely is that the monetary authorities will ever again redeem other moneys freely in terms of gold.

Summary

Our brief excursion into the history of monetary standards has produced evidence supporting two earlier statements: "Terms such as gold standard or silver standard should be used with the greatest of care." And "While the name remains constant, the systems to which it refers change, sometimes radically." Some of the most radical long-run changes in gold standards have been these:

1. Composition of the money supply. Under unlimited gold-coin standards, full-bodied gold coins and gold certificates typically made up a considerable part, although usually not all, of the actual circulating medium. Under modern limited gold-bullion standards, neither gold coins nor gold certificates circulate. The entire money supply is credit money—checking deposits, paper money, and token coins. And the total money supply is typically a large multiple of the country's monetary gold.

2. Monetary management. Most of the earlier gold standards were not highly managed. Some countries, such as the United States, did not have central banks or other agencies for the purpose of monetary management, and some of the existing foreign central banks managed only intermittently and to a limited extent. Under these circumstances, the size of a nation's monetary gold stock was usually a strong, and sometimes a dominant, determinant of the size of its total money supply. In contrast, the gold standards of today are highly and continuously managed, and the money managers typically refuse to allow changes in their monetary gold stocks to dominate their money supplies. To cite an extreme example, while the monetary gold stock of the United States fell by about 50 percent between 1950 and the early 1970s, the total money supply rose by about 100 percent.

3. International reserve and source of international liquidity. Almost from the beginning of gold standards, gold served as an international monetary reserve and as a source of international liquidity. Nations used gold as a medium for meeting deficits in their balance of international payments and for buying their surplus supplies of money in foreign-exchange markets, thus supporting their exchange rate. Gold still serves in this role; in fact, this is its major remaining monetary function. However, even in this role its relative importance has declined as supplements and substitutes have been invented and adopted. Among these are official holdings of claims against foreign moneys, such as the U.S. dollar and the British pound; borrowing arrangements with the International Monetary Fund (IMF) and among the leading central banks; and so on. One of the latest, and perhaps in the long-run the most significant, substitutes for gold is the system of paper gold that was initiated in the beginning of 1970. Known more formally as "Special Drawing Rights" or "SDRs," these units of paper gold are simply created claims against the IMF, with each unit declared to be equal to the gold value of one U.S. dollar. A total of $9.5 billion of this currency was created and issued to the monetary authorities of the participating countries during the first three years of the program—$3.5 billion at the beginning of 1970, $3 billion at the beginning of 1971, and $3 billion at the beginning of 1972—and more SDRs will be created in subsequent years. Just as individual nations have become unwilling to allow their domestic money supplies to be dominated by gold, the community of nations is no longer willing to allow gold to dominate its supplies of international reserves and liquidity.

Such marked changes in the monetary roles of gold remind us that monetary systems, far from remaining static, are subject to continuous, and sometimes abrupt, changes in both form and functioning.

THE GENERAL ACCEPTABILITY OF MONEY

Although many countries, including the United States, have long used credit money and this credit money has often not been redeemable in gold, silver, or any other money with a substantial nonmonetary value, the feeling still persists in some quarters that pieces of money cannot be "good" or even generally acceptable unless they themselves have an equivalent value for nonmonetary purposes or are kept redeemable in other types of money that have an equivalent value for nonmonetary uses. At the risk of excessive repetition, we must reiterate that this view is erroneous. That token coins, paper money, and other circulating debts can be overissued, and on too many occasions have been, is undeniable. But if their issue is properly limited, they can be given a scarcity value and can circulate at least as satisfactorily as any full-bodied money. In fact, with proper management, their quantities can be adjusted to the needs of the economy better than can the quantities of a gold or silver full-bodied money whose supply often reflects the capriciousness of gold or silver mining and of nonmonetary demands for these metals.

Money can have a value simply because it is limited in supply and is demanded for use as money. Barter, as we have seen, is inconvenient. To escape these inconveniences, people want some kind of "tokens" or "tickets" that can be used as means of payment. In determining whether or not to accept such tickets in payment of debt or for goods and services, each person is interested in only one question: "Can I pass them along to someone else in exchange and without loss of value for the things I want to buy?" He is interested in their acceptability as money, not in their usability for some other purpose.

To describe how all this came about, we shall sketch some of the major forces that have strongly influenced the development of money and monetary institutions. As monetary history our discussion will not be complete, but the purpose is rather to concentrate on major forces and motivations.

Coinage

Let us start with the use of uncoined metals, such as copper, gold, and silver, as circulating media. These metals probably came to be generally acceptable in payment because they were widely desired for religious and ornamental purposes, they did not deteriorate, their large value relative to their weight and bulk made them relatively easy to transport, and so on. At this stage, money was not differentiated from the material of which it was made; the metals flowed freely into and out of monetary uses. The use of bullion as money had serious disadvantages, however, especially if payors were not averse to short-weighing and adulteration. Precision weighing apparatus was not widely available and assaying was both laborious and inaccurate. Coinage solved both these problems. At first, coinage amounted merely to an official certification as to the weight and purity of a lump of metal. The imprint of a king's stamp meant in effect, "I hereby certify that this contains a certain weight of metal of a certain purity." The names of many monetary units (such as pounds, lire, livres, and shekels), which were originally units of weight, attest to this fact.

Coinage was an important monetary innovation. It greatly expanded the use of metallic substances as money. More important, however, it was a long step toward the differentiation of money from its component material. Not metal, but *coined metal,* became money. People gradually ceased to think in terms of the *weights* of metal; they thought in terms of the *number of coins*—not the weight of silver in a payment, but the number of shekels or lire. Debts and other contracts came to be stated in monetary units. This habit often persisted after the pure metallic content of the coins was reduced through abrasion, clipping, sweating, or deliberate action of the sovereign. When coinage was limited, the value of the coins as money often rose above the commodity value of their reduced metallic content; token coins appeared.

The evolution of banking

Despite their other advantages, full-bodied gold or silver coins had some disadvantages for those who held them or used them to make payments.

1. Danger of theft and robbery. Safekeeping may have been easy for a king with an armed entourage or a wealthy businessman with strong vaults, but it could be a serious problem for others, especially when law enforcement left much to be desired.

2. Cost and risk of transporting to make payments over distances. Transport costs alone were high; even more onerous in many cases were risks of robbery. The bad guys who held up stage coaches, now so frequently portrayed in TV westerns, were by no means the first brigands to take their toll on roadways, and bad guys in ships were problems on many seas. Nor were the cattle barons the first members of nobility to encourage their men to pick up a little money on the side.

3. Loss of weight of the coins through abrasion, clipping, chipping, and sweating. The payor lost nothing as long as the coins were acceptable at face value. But after coins had reached some stage of deterioration, payees might accept them only by weight, with losses to the payor.

4. Absence of interest or any other return on the money. People began to look for ways to overcome these disadvantages.

Largely because of the danger of theft and robbery, the practice arose of leaving gold and silver in the custody of some reputable person (a wealthy merchant, a money changer, or a goldsmith) who owned a strong box or other means of safekeeping. At this stage, the "depositor" undoubtedly expected that the custodian would indeed hold all the specie intact. The custodian performed this service as a favor for his friends or made a charge for it. It is also probable that at this initial stage, a depositor who wished to make payments would himself go to the goldsmith or other custodian, get the required amount of coins, and use the coins themselves to make payment. But this was inconvenient; how much easier it would be to transfer claims against the metal. And such claims were at hand, for the goldsmith or other custodian usually gave some sort of evidence to the depositor. One type was a receipt, which said in effect, "IOU so many florins." The next step was for payors to make payment by giving these IOUs to a payee. The latter could then claim the specie from the goldsmith, or use the IOU to make payments to others. As these IOUs came to be used in payments, the bank note was born. A bank note is simply a bank debt or promise to pay, evidenced by a piece of paper. The earliest bank notes may have been acceptable only because they were believed to be fully backed by specie. Nevertheless, this was an important step in the evolution of money, for the community was becoming accustomed to using in payment not the precious metals themselves but paper claims against those metals.

Another method of payment soon developed. The person leaving gold or silver with the "banker" would not receive a piece of paper representing the debt of the banker, but simply a "deposit credit" evidenced by an entry on the bank's books. The practice soon arose of making payments by writing an order on the banker to pay someone else. For example, Jones would write an order on the bank saying, "Pay Smith X florins and charge to my account." Smith might then claim the gold or silver. But as such orders became more widely acceptable in payment, it became increasingly common for payees to leave the specie with the goldsmith or other banker and to pay others by transferring claims to deposits. Thus, deposit claims, not specie itself, came to be used as a means of payment.

The high cost and risk of transporting precious metals over distances created an opportunity for profit that did not go unnoticed by shrewd goldsmiths and merchants. One can imagine a canny goldsmith-banker in Lübeck writing to his counterpart in Genoa:

> As we both know, trade between our areas has grown rapidly in recent years. Large amounts of specie flow every month from my area to yours, at great cost to the merchants and great risk to property and life. At the same time, almost equally large amounts of specie flow from the Genoa area to the Lübeck area, at comparable cost and risk. We can easily abolish these unnecessary costs, spur the development of trade, and add to our own pitifully low incomes by cooperating with each other. When someone in your area wishes to make a payment in the Lübeck region, you get from him the required amount of specie and give him an order on me to give specie to the payee, and I will do so. Then, when someone in my area wishes to make payments in the Genoa region, I will collect from him the required amount of specie and give him an order on you, which I hope you will honor. We will have to ship specie between Lübeck and Genoa only to the extent that the payments I make for your account and the payments you make for my account do not balance out, and I forecast that the net shipments required will be very small indeed relative to the total payments effected by us. In fairness to our customers and in the interest of promoting our business we should not charge for these services as much as it would cost our customers to ship specie equal to the total value of all payments, but in fairness to ourselves and our families our charges should exceed our actual costs.

Such were the motivations that led to the establishment of business relationships among emerging "bankers" in the leading commercial centers. Bills of exchange or orders to pay became an increasingly popular way of effecting payments, and the things transferred were claims against goldsmith-bankers or merchant-bankers.

Up to this point, we have dealt with only two forces that contributed to the evolution of banking: the disadvantages of full-bodied coins because of their liability to theft and robbery and the high cost and risk of transporting them. But these two forces alone were sufficient to concentrate large amounts of the precious metals in the hands of an emerging class of "bankers." At first these were primarily goldsmiths, money changers, or merchants who took on safekeeping of specie and related functions as a side line. Gradually, however, these functions increased in relative importance and profitability, and specialized bankers began to emerge. Note that in this earliest stage, all "deposits" and "bank notes" were fully backed by specie, and the income of the emerging bankers came from charges for safekeeping and for transmitting payments.

Then came a discovery that was to be momentous for the evolution of banking. The emerging bankers discovered that, to meet their promises to pay in specie on demand, they did not need to hold gold and silver equal to 100 percent of their outstanding debts in the form of deposits and bank notes. A banker who was in fact holding specie fully equal to the value of his deposit and bank-note liabilities might have put it this way:

> I do not need to hold all that specie because those people are not all going to demand payment at any one time or even over a short period. Of course, there will be withdrawals. Some will want gold or silver for circulation. Also, I must be prepared to pay gold or silver to other banks who acquire claims against me in the form of deposit and bank note claims that I have issued. But such outpayments will be largely balanced by new inflows of gold and silver. I could meet any net drain that is likely to occur if I held gold and silver equal to only a small fraction—perhaps only a tenth—of my outstanding note and deposit liabilities. To hold more is terribly wasteful. Look at all the gold and silver ·lying there, idle and earning nothing! I think I'll lend out some of it and earn some interest.

And if his conscience was troubled by his contemplated breach of trust, he may have soothed it by replying, "I didn't promise my customers in so many words that I would hold all the gold and silver; I merely promised that I would pay them gold and silver when they asked for it. If I keep the promise why should it be any concern of theirs if I increase my income a little?"

So were banks transformed from mere custodians holding specie reserves equal to 100 percent of the deposit and bank-note liabilities into lenders who held specie equal to only a fraction of their liabilities. Fractional-reserve banking was born. Such banking may indeed have originated as a surreptitious breach of trust. But the secret was soon out, and fractional-reserve banking gained widespread support. A banker could now say in effect to the public:

> It will be to our mutual advantage if you leave most of your gold and silver with me and hold and use as money the bank notes and deposits. The advantage to me as a banker is obvious; I can make loans and earn an income. But I will share this with you by providing valuable services at little or no cost to you. If you want currency that is convenient to hold or transport, I will provide you with bank notes. If you want the convenience of checking facilities I will provide those too. I will hold your funds in safekeeping, provide you with checkbooks, make payments for you over long distances, and do much of your bookkeeping for you.

Many banks also paid interest on deposit balances, an advantage not carried by coins. Moreover, those who were depositors often received preferred treatment when they applied for loans.

In these various ways, the public was persuaded to hold more and more of its money in the form of bank notes and deposit claims against banks. Increasing proportions of the gold and silver money came to lodge in the banks, there to serve as a fractional reserve against the banks' note and deposit liabilities.

The fractional-reserve principle gave banks a great power that will be emphasized in later chapters—the power to increase and decrease the total money supply. Banks did not have this power when they issued bank notes and deposits only in exchange for an equal value of gold and silver; they merely substituted in the hands of the public one type of money for another. Suppose, for example, that the public has entrusted $100 of gold and silver to the banks in exchange for bank notes and deposits. This will appear as follows on the balance sheets of the public and the banks:

BALANCE SHEET OF THE PUBLIC		BALANCE SHEET OF THE BANK	
ASSETS	LIABILITIES	ASSETS	LIABILITIES
Gold and silver .. −$100 Bank notes and de- posits .... +$100		Gold and silver .. +$100	Note and de- posit lia- bilities .. +$100

The public's total holdings of money remain unchanged, its larger holdings of bank notes and deposits being offset by its smaller holdings of gold and silver. And the banks have issued note and deposit liabilities equal to only the $100 of gold and silver surrendered by the public.

Suppose now that, starting from this situation in which both their gold and silver holdings and their note and deposit liabilities are $100, the banks decide they can meet any likely demands for payments if they hold gold and silver reserves equal to only 10 percent of their liabilities. They come to believe that any gold and silver holdings in excess of 10 percent of their liabilities can be used as a basis for lending. Consider two extreme cases:

1. As the banks lend, the borrowers withdraw from the banks gold and silver equal to the full amount of the loans. If the banks lend $90, their holdings of gold and silver will fall by that amount, and they will increase their assets in the form of outstanding loans (debt claims against borrowers) by the same amount. The banks' balance sheets will now appear as follows:

ASSETS		LIABILITIES	
Gold and silver	$10	Note and deposit liabilities	$100
Loans	90		

The effect of this transaction is to increase the public's money supply by $90, the amount of the increase in loans. Thus, in addition to the $100 of notes and deposits still held by the public, the borrowers now have the $90 of gold and silver paid out by the banks. Thus, we find that by making loans or buying other assets, the banks can increase the public's money supply even if borrowers take all their loan proceeds in gold and silver.

However, once the public has become accustomed to using bank notes and deposits as money, borrowers are unlikely to withdraw gold and silver equal to the full amount of their borrowings. They are likely to accept bank notes or deposits instead. Let us therefore consider the other extreme case.

2. As the banks lend, the borrowers take all the loan proceeds in the form of bank notes and deposits, and there is no net drain of gold and silver from the banks. Suppose the banks lend $900, giving note or deposit claims to the borrowers. The balance sheet of the banks will appear as follows:

ASSETS		LIABILITIES	
Gold and silver	$100	Note and deposit liabilities	$1,000
Loans	900		

In this process, the banks have increased the public's money supply by $900, and have done so by issuing new note and deposit liabilities in exchange for debt claims against borrowers. The banks feel secure because their gold and silver reserves are still equal to 10 percent of their liabilities. In a sense, each $1 of gold and silver is supporting, or serving as a basis for, $10 of note and deposit liabilities. But most of these notes and deposits were created as banks purchased assets other than money itself. We shall later analyze these processes in more detail and also review the process through which banks decrease the total money supply by decreasing their holdings of loans and other debt claims. But have a try at explaining this yourself. What would happen to the money supply if, starting from the last situation described above, the banks decreased by $500 their outstanding loans?

In broad outline, such are the processes through which the public came to hold much of its money in the form of claims against banks. Even when full-bodied gold and silver coins were available and the public could have refused to accept or hold anything else, it chose to hold much of its money in the form of bank notes and deposits, and the banks found it profitable to manufacture these claims. Thus, in large part, the development of credit or debt moneys reflected private choices—the public's choices among the various types of money and the choices of bankers as lenders and creators of money.

Government and credit money

Although the composition of the money supply and the trend toward greater use of credit moneys have been greatly influenced by the choices of the public and the bankers, governments have exerted important influences in many ways. We shall mention here only a few of the most important.

1. Governments themselves have been issuers of credit money. In some cases, the purpose has been to provide more convenient types of money, such as token coins or paper money; in others, it has been to remedy an alleged shortage of money; and in still others, it has been to finance government expenditures.

2. Governments influence the establishment and operation of banks in various ways. For example, they have both encouraged the establishment of banks and regulated their operations. At an early stage, they encouraged the issue of bank notes; later they moved toward the abolition of bank notes. And in various ways they regulate the volume of bank deposits.

3. They regulate the availability of full-bodied and representative full-bodied moneys and the redeemability of moneys in precious metals. As noted earlier, the trend has been toward more and more restricted redeemability in gold, thus encouraging the expansion and use of credit moneys.

Most of these points will be developed further in later chapters.

The money supply of the United States

A few facts about the American monetary system as it had developed by the early 1970s will serve as an introduction to more detailed descriptions in the subsequent chapters.

1. All our money is debt or credit money. We have had no full-bodied money or representative full-bodied money since 1933, when gold coins and gold certificates were withdrawn and discontinued.

2. Checking deposits make up almost three-quarters of the money supply, paper money about one-fifth, and coins only about 3 percent. All these types of money, except checking deposits, have full legal-tender powers. That is, they have the legal power to discharge debts; creditors may not insist on payments in any other type of money if the debt is stated in dollars. Although checking deposits are not themselves legal tender, the banks are obligated to redeem them on demand in legal-tender money. This lack of legal-tender power reduces the general acceptability of demand deposits only in periods when people doubt the banks' ability to pay their debts.

3. This distribution of the money supply among coin, paper money, and checking deposits reflects the preferences of the public. The Treasury and the Federal Reserve do indeed regulate the size of the total money supply, and the government determines the specific types of coins and paper money to be made available. But the public itself determines the proportions in which it will hold the various types of money. This is because all types of money are exchangeable for each other on a dollar-for-dollar basis. The Treasury and the Federal Reserve stand ready to exchange all types of coin and paper money for each other at par. The commercial banks are legally required to pay checking deposits at par in coin and paper money, and for reasons of profit, banks will always issue checking deposits in exchange for coin and paper money.

4. There are three types of monetary institutions or issuers of money in the United States: the Treasury, the Federal Reserve, and the commercial banks. Treasury issues, called "Treasury currency," represent the smallest portion, less than 3 percent, of the money supply. The Treasury has a monopoly of coinage and also issues a minor fraction of our paper money. The Federal Reserve issues Federal Reserve notes, which constitute most of our paper money. By far the largest issuers of money are some 13,700 commercial banks, which issue checking deposits. These are privately owned, privately operated, profit-seeking institutions. We shall see later that one of the major functions of the Federal Reserve is to regulate money creation and money destruction by these institutions.

5. Treasury currency, already constituting the smallest share of the total money supply, is likely to become an even smaller share in the future. Coins will almost certainly increase in absolute amount as the economy grows and needs for "small change" increase. But the absolute amount of Treasury paper money is unlikely to increase. The number of United States notes (greenbacks) has remained approximately constant (at about $347 million) since the end of the Civil War, and any proposal to increase or decrease it would probably arouse controversies reminiscent of the late nineteenth century.

Selected readings

Angell, N., *The Story of Money,* New York, Lippincott, 1929.

Board of Governors of the Federal Reserve System, *Banking and Monetary Statistics,* Washington, D.C., 1943, pp. 34–35. (See *Federal Reserve Bulletins* for current statistics on the money supply.)

Del Mar, A., *The Science of Money,* London, Bell, 1885.

Robertson, D. H., *Money,* New York, Harcourt Brace Jovanovich, 1929.

Trescott, P. B., *Money, Banking, and Economic Welfare,* 2nd ed., New York, McGraw-Hill, 1965.

CHAPTER 3

DEBT, CREDIT, AND FINANCIAL INSTRUMENTS

Throughout this book, whether we are dealing with money, commercial banks, central banks, processes of capital formation, or flows of money income, we shall repeatedly refer to debt or credit and the instruments representing them. The purpose of this chapter is to analyze their nature and the principal functions that they perform in the economy.

Debt or credit serves in many ways:

1. All our money is composed of particular types of debt that have somehow achieved the status of general acceptability in payments. Thus, our coins may be looked upon as evidences of debt issued by the federal government; our paper money is, in effect, debt obligations of the Treasury and Federal Reserve; and checking deposits are demand debts of commercial banks.

2. The bulk of our payments is made by transferring bank-deposit debts from payors to payees through the use of credit or debt instruments known as "drafts" or "orders to pay."

3. Our monetary institutions create and issue money predominantly by purchasing assets in the form of debts, and they withdraw and destroy money predominantly by making net sales of assets in the form of debts.

4. Credit or debt creation plays a major role in transferring funds from savers to spenders, thus facilitating transfers of resources from savers to other consumers, capital formation, and maintenance of the circular flow of income.

Although at this stage, we shall confine our attention to debt or credit, we shall later introduce another class of financial claims—ownership or equity claims. These are the claims of owners against the assets and earnings of a business firm that remain after all other claims against the firm have been met. The most important of these equity claims are shares of stock in corporations.

THE NATURE OF CREDIT OR DEBT

Debt and credit are merely the same thing looked at from two different points of view. They are an obligation to pay in the future; and since money is so widely used as a standard of deferred payments, they are usually obligations to pay fixed sums of money. From the point of view of the person to whom the future payment is to be made, the obligation is a credit; it is his claim against another for payment. But from the point of view of the one who is obliged to pay in the future, the obligation is a debt. Since debt and credit are but the same thing looked at from different points of view, it is obvious that the amount of debt outstanding at any time is equal to the amount of outstanding credit.

Credit or debt usually originates in economic and financial transactions in which creditors surrender something of value at one point of time in exchange for debtors' promises to pay in the future. We ignore here debts that may arise out of gifts or promises to pay in the future. The "something of value" surrendered may be money, services, goods, or some sort of financial claim such as stocks or bonds. However, the resulting debt is usually payable in money. We are all familiar with the creation of debt by the sale of goods or services "on credit." For example, Mrs. Jones buys groceries, promising to pay at the end of the month. A corporation gets raw materials from its suppliers with the understanding that it will pay at the end of the quarter. Much of the outstanding debt at any time has arisen from such "extensions of credit" by sellers of goods and services. Most of the remainder has arisen out of money-lending transactions in which creditors surrendered money at one point of time in exchange for promises of debtors to pay later, usually with interest.

ECONOMIC FUNCTIONS OF DEBT

The basic economic functions of debt and financial instruments can be understood most easily and clearly by considering a relatively simple society made up of spending units or households. Each household or unit receives during any income period, such as a month, some flow of money income resulting from the household's or unit's contribution to the value of current output of goods and services. The symbol Y will be used to denote income receipts during a period. During each income period, each unit also spends some amount for the current output of goods and services to be used for consumption purposes. Such consumption expenditures will be denoted by the symbol C. A unit's income and consumption need not be exactly equal during any income period. The difference, $Y - C$ will be called "saving" and will be denoted by the Symbol S. Thus, $S = Y - C$. During any period, therefore, households can be separated into three categories based on their pattern of saving. (1) "Zero savers" are those whose current consumption is exactly equal to their current income. (2) "Positive savers" or simply, "savers," are those who consume less than their current income. Their saving represents the amount of their current income that they do not use to demand goods and services for their own current consumption. (3) "Negative savers" or "dissavers" are people whose current consumption exceeds their current income. Their consumption demands for output exceed their current incomes.

Let us now explore why a household may elect to be a saver or dissaver during a period, and why it may be a saver in some periods and a dissaver in others.

Debt and consumption

One problem faced by each household or unit is that of allocating its consumption through time, recognizing that with given current and expected future incomes "the more we consume in one period the less can we consume in others." To achieve maximum total utility or satisfaction through time, each unit would have to take into consideration its current income, expected future income streams, present needs, and expected future needs. At any given time, different units are likely to attach differing relative values to consumption in the present as against consumption in the future. This may even be true of units with identical present and expected future incomes and present and expected future needs. One unit, lacking foresight and thinking largely of present pleasures, may value present consumption very highly and be willing to sacrifice large amounts of future consumption in order to consume now in excess of its current income. Another, with more foresight and fearful of future deprivation, may place a much lower premium on present consumption and demand little or no reward for consuming less than its current income.

However, differing time patterns of income and needs contribute strongly to differences in valuations of present versus future consumption. For example, some units may have large needs in the present—such as needs for expensive medical care or educational services for their children—but expect their future needs to be lower. And their current income may be well below that expected in the future. Such units are likely to place a high premium on present consumption and to want to consume in excess of their current incomes. One can imagine the head of such a unit saying, "To be able to consume an extra $1,000 worth now I would be willing to give up $1,300 of consumption a year from now. And I would prefer even more present consumption if the premium were lower."

Other units may be in the reverse position. Their present needs may be small relative to those expected in the future when their children reach college age or their parents face retirement. And their present incomes may be high relative to those expected in the future. Such units are likely to place little or no premium on present consumption and to want to consume less than their current incomes. The head of such a unit might say, "If necessary, I would forgo $1,000 of consumption now in exchange for only $900 of consumption a year from now, and I would forgo even more consumption now if I were paid a premium for doing so."

When households place different relative valuations on present and future consumption, all can be made to feel "better off"—to increase their total utility— through exchange or trade of present consumption against future consumption. Those units that place lower premiums on present consumption can transfer their current saving, representing claims on current output, to those units that place a higher premium on present consumption. Later, the borrowing units will return consuming power to the lenders, who can then decide whether to use it immediately for consumption or to save it for later. Thus, all units may be enabled to increase their total utilities through an optimal spreading or allocation of their consumption through time. The "efficiency of consumption" is increased.

In the absence of debt or credit, exchanges of present consumption against future consumption are likely to be inefficient and so limited in extent that large potential increases in utility will fail to be realized. Suppose, for example, that a community has not yet invented consumer credit and has available only two types of assets—physical assets and some form of money, such as coins or paper money, which yields no interest. Households that wished to consume in excess of their current incomes could do so only by drawing down their money balances or by selling their physical assets. However, they may not have any excess money balances or any physical assets that they could sell without serious deprivation or loss. Those who wish to save are faced with only very limited alternative uses of their saving; they can only increase their money balances or buy physical assets. Increased money balances would provide additional liquidity and safety for the saver, but would yield no income. Physical assets might yield an income but be unattractive because of the transactions costs, illiquidity, and risk involved. As a consequence, savers might save less, and, in any case, transfers of their money saving to dissavers would be limited. The situation can be improved by the invention and use of consumer debt or credit. This enables savers to transfer their money saving, representing claims against current output, to dissavers in exchange for their promises to repay in the future.

In some cases, consumer debts are evidenced only by oral agreements. Such "parole credit" may suffice in small transactions among friends or close associates (although even in such cases it often leads to conflicts), but it is inadequate for transactions involving less personal relationships where more formal evidences of debt are needed. In some cases, credit is evidenced only by an entry on the books of the creditor; this is called "book credit." To a greater extent, however, credit is evidenced by a written document in the nature of a promissory note. Such financial instruments not only serve as legal evidence of the amount and terms of a debt, but can also be bought and sold in the market.

Three aspects of consumer credit should be kept in mind.

1. It increases the efficiency of consumption by enabling households to space their consumption optimally through time.

2. It involves the creation of financial instruments that enrich the menu of assets available to savers. At least some asset-holders will consider these promissory notes, which yield an interest income, to be safer and more liquid than physical assets and more desirable than money, which yields no income.

3. It serves to bolster total money demands for output and to maintain the circular flow of income. As already noted, a household's saving during a period is simply that part of its income for the period that is not spent during the period for consumption. Thus saving, considered by itself, is deflationary in the sense that it tends to lower total money demands for output and to shrink the circular flow of income. However, these deflationary effects are offset to the extent that money representing saving is transferred to dissavers who spend it for consumption. We shall discuss this in more detail later.

Debt and investment

Although consumer credit is widely used and the outstanding stock of consumer debt is very large, a much larger part of the total debt outstanding was created in the process of investment or capital formation—the process of adding to the nation's stock of capital goods. The stock of capital goods at any point of time is the accumulated stock of man-made goods that were produced in the past and not yet consumed or "used up." An outstanding characteristic of modern industrial societies, and especially of the United States, is the huge stock of capital, both in the aggregate and in amounts per capita. Some types of capital render services directly to consumers. Outstanding examples are houses and apartments which provide shelter and comfort. However, a larger part of the capital stock renders services as instruments in processes of production. Examples are structures and many types of durable equipment used in mining, manufacturing, transportation, communications, electric and gas utilities, and wholesale and retail trade; office buildings; farm machinery and other equipment; business inventories; and so on. In an industrial economy, this huge stock of capital is a major reason for the high output per capita. Technological advances and increases in the stock of capital relative to labor are the two principal sources of growth of output per capita and of output per man-hour of labor. It is partly because of this that we are so interested in processes of capital formation or investment.

Saving is a necessary condition for capital formation. A society could not add to its stock of capital goods if its members insisted on using for current consumption all of the income or output that its labor and other productive resources could produce. Saving, or abstinence from current consumption, frees some part of available productive resources to produce output to be used to increase the stock of capital. However, although the ability and willingness to save is a necessary condition for capital formation, it is not by itself sufficient to assure that capital formation will occur. The productive resources that are not used to produce output for current consumption may remain unemployed or "go to waste" if no one employs them to produce goods to be added to the stock of capital. Thus investment is another necessary condition for capital formation. *Investment* means the amount spent during a stated period for current output to be used to increase the stock of capital goods of the various types noted above. It is through investment that the amounts of income or output, and more basically the productive resources that are saved, are translated into capital accumulation.

One can imagine an economic system in which each household spent for investment in each period an amount exactly equal to its own saving, no more and no less. Such a system would be highly inefficient, for at least two reasons:

1. Differences in the marginal productivity of capital. For some units, including some with high rates of saving, the marginal productivity of capital—the addition to output resulting from additions to capital stock—may be very low. There may be many reasons for this—lack of interest or ability in entrepreneurship and management, inadequate education or experience, possession of an already large stock of capital assets, and so on. For other units, including some with low rates of saving, the marginal productivity of capital may be much higher because of such things as high interest and ability in entrepreneurship and management, excellent education and experience, an inadequate stock of capital relative to needs, and so on.

2. Diseconomies of small scale. If each household or unit could command only an amount of capital equal to its own accumulated savings, many enterprises would be too small to achieve the greater output made possible by the economies of scale. They would not be able to mass enough capital of specialized types, to command the necessary array of special talents, or to reap the other economies of large-scale production.

It is therefore clear that, if capital is to make its maximum contribution to productivity, ways must be found to transfer savings, and thus the power of investment, to those who can achieve the highest marginal productivity of capital, and that savings must be pooled and used for investment in entities large enough to achieve economies of scale. In some industries, the latter requires the pooling of hundreds of millions or even billions of dollars' worth of assets. In this process, if not earlier, a new type of institution differentiated from households—the specialized business firm—appears.

These purposes can be served by the creation of financial instruments or claims. In effect, savers surrender money savings to those who wish to spend for investment, receiving in return newly created financial instruments or claims which represent claims against both income and the value of assets. Thus, the process of creating real capital usually has its counterpart in the creation of financial claims that are issued to get the money used to buy the capital.

Financial claims are of two broad types: equity claims and debt claims. *Equity claims* are shares of ownership, implying participation in the attributes of ownership of a business firm—control power, claims against income and assets, and risk of loss as well as possibilities of profits. Ownership of a small partnership may be split into only a few shares and held by only a few people. In a large corporation, ownership may be split into tens of millions of shares and held directly or indirectly by millions of shareholders. In some cases, all the shares are homogeneous, carrying the same rights and obligations with respect to control power, amounts and priority of claims against income and assets, and risk. For example, a corporation may issue only one type of equity claims—one class of common stock. In other cases, the firm may issue two or more types of equity claims with differing amounts of control power, differing amounts and priorities of claims against earnings and assets, and differing degrees of risk and prospects of profits. Such differentiation enables the firm to tailor issues to appeal to savers with differing needs and tastes.

In the complex American economy, with its many large business units, the creation and sale of equity or ownership claims is a major method of channeling saving into investment. However, use of this method alone would leave unsolved problems. Some savers dislike the prospect of fluctuating income and the risk of loss of capital value associated with ownership claims, and would buy shares only if offered very high rates of return. These savers prefer claims which offer prospects of a more stable money income and capital value. Moreover, some enterprisers or owners do not want to share their control power, or to pay high returns to bring in other part-owners, or to share with others the high profits that they hope to earn. This problem can be met by the creation of *debt claims* that allow savers to surrender money savings to a business firm in exchange for the firm's promise to pay a stated amount of interest and to repay a stated amount of principal at a later date, and the firm is able to use the money for investment. Thus the saver who wishes it can get a more stable money income and stability of the value of his principal, while the owners of equity claims assume greater risk but also retain control power and claims to profits. Large amounts of business investment are financed through the creation and issue of debt claims.

Debt and other institutions

For almost all other types of institutions in our society, debt and credit serve functions quite comparable to those served for households and business firms. Other such institutions include federal, state, and municipal governments; educational institutions; churches; charitable institutions; country clubs; fraternities; and many others. In any stated period, these institutions receive flows of income and spend for current output. However, many do not wish to spend for output in a period an amount exactly equal to their current income. Some wish to spend for consumption and investment in capital formation an amount less than their current income. They are in a position to extend credit—to transfer to others claims against current output, receiving in return debt or equity claims. Others wish to be deficit units, to buy output to be used for consumption and investment in amounts exceeding their current incomes. Creation of debt claims against themselves enables them to command more output now in exchange for their obligations to repay later.

Debt and income flows

Up to this point, we have concentrated on the contribution of debt to the efficiency of allocation of resources in the economy. Debt increases the efficiency of consumption by facilitating exchange of claims to present consumption against claims to future consumption, thus enabling each unit to space its consumption through time in an optimum way. Debt increases efficiency in production by facilitating investment in units large enough to achieve economies of scale and by allowing the transfer of control and management of capital and enterprises to those who can achieve the highest productivity.

We turn now to the functions of debt and debt creation relative to the rate of flow of national money income. We shall find that the level of income will fall if the rate of debt creation is "too small" and rise if it is "too large." These terms obviously require definition. Suppose we start from a situation in which national income, or expenditures, is flowing at some annual rate, such as $1,200 billion, and this income level is consistent with "full employment without inflation." This entire amount will accrue as income to the units in the society—households, business firms, governmental units, and so on. If every one of these units spent for output for consumption and investment purposes an amount exactly equal to its current income, the flow of national income would proceed at a stable rate. All income receipts flowing from the value of output would return to the market as expenditures for output, thus maintaining the level of output and income. Note that in such a case, the maintenance of a stable flow of income could be achieved without any net creation of debt. Every unit would spend all its own income, and only that.

However, this balance of income and spending is unlikely to occur in the American economy. Some units—such as households, business firms, and governmental units—spend less than their current income for consumption and investment purposes, and thus are called "surplus units." If these surpluses of current income over expenditures for output are not somehow offset, they will cause a decline in the flow of expenditures for output and thus will decrease the level of national money income. If money wage rates and prices were fully flexible downward, the principal result of this declining money demand for output might be falling price levels. However, with money wage rates and prices less than fully flexible downward, some decline of real output and employment will occur.

How, in an economy with surplus units, can such a fall of money income be averted? It can be averted only if there are other units—such as households, business firms, or governmental units—that spend more for consumption and investment than they receive in current incomes. These are called "deficit units." To counterbalance the effect of the surplus units, the deficit units must somehow be enabled and persuaded to purchase the extra output that the surplus units did not purchase. There are two principal ways of achieving this. One is by the creation and sale of ownership claims by deficit units—money savings are surrendered directly or indirectly for shares of ownership. In this way, very large amounts are indeed rechanneled into spendings. However, for reasons suggested earlier, this method by itself is unlikely to be sufficient; the terms that surplus units might require to surrender their total surpluses in exchange for equity claims might not make potential issuers willing to create and issue that value of ownership claims. The second principal method of maintaining flows of national income is by the creation of new debts. By this method, the surpluses of surplus units can be channeled to deficit units to be spent for consumption or investment.

In later sections we shall analyze at length the determinants of the behavior of national money income. Here we shall emphasize only one major point. In an economy like that of the United States, that includes many surplus units during any period, very large total surpluses will be generated when national money income is at a level consistent with "full employment without inflation." This level can be maintained only if there are deficit units able and willing to incur deficits as large as the total surpluses of surplus units. To achieve this requires a high rate of creation of new debt. How high this rate of debt creation must be varies positively with the size of total surpluses and negatively with the rate of creation of new equity claims, the other chief method of maintaining the flow of spending.

The stock of outstanding debt

The preceding sections stressed the role of debt and debt creation in transferring flows of income, or claims against output, from surplus to deficit units, whether these are households, business firms, governments, or others. It was noted that a unit might be a deficit unit in one period and a surplus unit in another. There may indeed be units, such as wealthy households, that are surplus units in every period. And there may be units, such as constantly expanding business firms that are deficit units in every period. More commonly, however, units have deficits in some periods and surpluses in others. When they have deficits they are likely to create debt claims against themselves. And when they have surpluses they are likely to retire debt claims against themselves or buy debt claims against others.

This brings us to the stock of debt or credit outstanding at a stated point of time. This stock is equal to the total of all debt issues in preceding periods minus amounts retired through repayment or default. Table 3–1 presents data relative to the outstanding debt of public and private units in the United States. It includes outstanding debts of all United States entities other than financial institutions. In order to avoid double counting and for other reasons, the table excludes debts of financial institutions, many of which were issued to acquire debts of these nonfinancial units. The totals in the table represent "net debt" in the sense that they include only debt obligations that one entity owes to another; the table excludes debt claims that a unit holds against itself. For example, it excludes certain debts of the federal government such as the social security funds which are held by departments of that government.

Several facts stand out. One is the huge volume of the outstanding debt—approximately $1,700 billion at the end of 1969. Another is the rate of growth of outstanding debt. For the entire period since the end of World War II its annual

Table 3–1 Net public and private debt in the United States (end-of-year figures in billions of dollars)

TYPE OF DEBT	1929	1939	1945	1969
Federal government	$ 16.5	$ 42.6	$252.7	$ 319.8
State and local government	13.2	16.3	13.7	132.4
Corporate debt	88.9	73.5	85.3	692.2
Farm debt	12.2	8.8	7.3	56.7
Total noncorporate, nonfarm debt except consumer debt	53.7	34.8	41.7	375.9
Consumer debt	5.4	7.2	5.7	122.5
Total debt	$190.9	$183.2	$406.3	$1,699.5

SOURCE: *Economic Report of the President,* January, 1971, Washington, D.C., U.S. Government Printing Office, 1971, p. 270.

growth rate has averaged $56 billion, and its annual average growth rate in the 1960s was $77 billion.

To some pessimists, both the size of outstanding debt and its rate of growth are frightening. They lament that we shall never be able to pay off the debt and that as a nation we are borrowing ourselves into bankruptcy. To refute such primitive theses one does not have to argue that the growth rate of debt has been "just right" or that all debt has been wisely incurred. Several facts are relevant:

1. "We owe it to ourselves." Only a small part of this debt is owed to foreigners; most of it is domestically held. Thus the debts of some American units are the assets of others.

2. There is no reason why the outstanding debt should be retired or even reduced in total volume. Some debts will be repaid or reduced and new debt will be created. But attempts to reduce total outstanding debt or even to prevent its increase would inevitably damage investment and deflate national money income.

3. The increase of total debt and of service charges on that debt has been accompanied by increases in ability to pay, whether this is measured in terms of income or in terms of the value of national assets. For example, between 1945 and 1969 gross national product at annual rates and at current prices rose from $212 billion to $931 billion. The rise in corporate debt has been a financial counterpart of a high rate of investment in plant, equipment, and inventories. State and local government debt has been incurred mainly to finance public investment in new schools, streets, sanitary systems, and so on.

The existence of a huge stock of outstanding debt and of the instruments representing this debt, alongside a huge stock of equity claims in such forms as shares of common and preferred stock, has a profound influence on the functioning of the monetary and financial system and of the economic system as a whole. Trading in outstanding claims, both equity and debt, has become a major method of channeling and redistributing funds. Much of this trading occurs as units seek "optimum portfolios"—to adjust and readjust their holdings of assets in the forms of money, debt claims of various types, and equity claims of various types in such ways as to secure what they consider to be, under the circumstances, the most favorable combinations. However, trading in outstanding claims is also an important way of channeling flows of money, directly or indirectly, from surplus to deficit units. A unit that holds a stock of claims against others and wishes to spend in excess of its income during some period can finance its deficit not only by creating new claims against itself but also by selling some of its stock of claims against others. These claims may be purchased by surplus units or by other units. Surplus units may dispose of funds not only by purchasing newly created claims but also by buying outstanding instruments, thus transferring money to sellers who can use it to buy newly created claims or for other purposes.

We shall be especially interested in the role played by the outstanding stock of debt obligations in the functioning of the Federal Reserve, the commercial banks, and other financial institutions. We have already noted that the Federal Reserve and the commercial banks create money primarily by buying assets in the form of debt claims against others and reduce the money supply by reducing their holdings of such assets. In many cases, they do this by acquiring or reducing their holdings of newly created debt claims. However, their dealings are not limited to currently created debt. They often increase their holdings of debt by purchasing already outstanding debt claims from others. And they decrease their holdings of debt not only by requiring debtors to repay outstanding amounts, but also by selling some of their stock of debt claims to others.

FINANCIAL MARKETS

Specialized financial institutions perform such services as gathering and disseminating information about sources and uses of funds and creditworthiness of potential borrowers, serve as middlemen between issuers and ultimate buyers of debt and equity claims, and act as brokers and dealers to facilitate trading in outstanding claims. However, debt, credit, and instruments representing debt and ownership claims could be used even in the absence of these specialized institutions. Deficit units could sell newly created debt or equity claims directly to surplus units, with no go-between. The buyer might then hold the claim until it was redeemed by the issuer. Or if he wished to sell it, he could himself search for someone who would be willing to buy it.

Such a simple set of arrangements could function, but only so inefficiently as to increase the cost and inhibit the development of financial processes. For one thing, it could not produce and disseminate the information and analysis required for rational and efficient valuation of claims. Such instruments are only claims against future asset values and future flows of income, and they can be valued rationally only to the extent that buyers and sellers can forecast what these future values are likely to be and the probabilities that they will be realized. This requires information and analysis concerning many relevant things: the past performance of the issuer in meeting its obligations; forecasts of the future performance of the issues; comparison with other available claims; supply of, demand for, and cost of funds in various geographic areas; and so on. If every buyer and seller had to gather and analyze information for himself the cost would be so high that only very limited amounts of information would be gathered and analyzed; ignorance would remain widespread. This ignorance would limit the scope of markets, inhibit regional mobility of funds, and increase risk. Inefficiency in the allocation of funds and of capital investment would be inevitable.

In such a system the creation and sale of new claims would be inefficient and expensive. The issuer would himself have to seek out buyers, perhaps by ringing doorbells. This might be feasible if he wanted to raise only tens or hundreds of thousands of dollars, but not if he wanted tens or hundreds of millions. Markets would be localized and it would be difficult to move funds from areas of credit plenty to areas of greater scarcity. In the absence of facilities for trading in the stock of outstanding claims, each buyer might hold a security until it matured. If this were necessary, many buyers would be unwilling to acquire claims with longer maturities, or would buy them only at very high yields, because buyers might not want these funds unavailable to them for long periods of time. As an alternative to holding long-term credits, a buyer might seek out other buyers, but this would in many cases be time consuming and the scarcity of prospective buyers might cause the claim to be sold at low prices. The claims would be illiquid and risk of loss of capital value would be high.

To remedy such shortcomings, many types of financial institutions have developed. Here we shall deal with only three of their functions: collection, analysis, and dissemination of financial information; primary distribution of securities; and provision of secondary markets for securities. We concentrate on functions rather than institutions because many financial institutions, like department stores, perform multiple functions.

Financial information

Our financial system now operates on the basis of huge amounts of information concerning large and medium-sized business units; governmental units, domestic and foreign; and many other institutions that are actual or potential participants in financial markets. The basic data come from many sources: published balance sheets and profit and loss statements, reports to the Securities Exchange Commission and other government regulatory agencies, reports to stock exchanges, special investigations, and so on. Such data are collected, compared, analyzed, and disseminated over wide areas by newspapers, specialized financial publications, investment advisory services, brokers and dealers, and others. Similarly, investors are kept informed about interest rates and other financial conditions in the various regions of this country and abroad.

The wide availability of such information greatly increases the mobility of funds. A firm whose issues are widely known need not limit its fund raising to its own locality; it can draw from a national market. And an investor is not limited to locally issued securities; he can buy in a national market. Thus, the issues of many large business firms, governmental units, and others enjoy national and even international markets.

Unfortunately, however, many entities—including very large numbers of farmers, retailers, other small business firms, and households—are known only locally. Distant investors are unaware of these entities and of the quality of the claims they could issue; investors can acquire this necessary information only at considerable cost. Such ignorance and the cost of information constitute an imperfection in financial markets. One effect of this situation is to create some degree of monopoly power for local lenders. Another is to create inefficiency in the allocation of credit and capital; too little capital is made available for use by some units that are not widely known.

Primary distribution of securities

Primary distribution of securities means the initial sale of newly created debt or equity claims. This function is best illustrated by investment banks, which do not buy securities with the intention of holding them, but like any other merchant, buy for the purpose of resale. Suppose some entity—a corporation or a governmental unit—decides to issue $300 million of new securities and to sell them through an investment bank or group of investment banks. It may select the investment bank by competitive bidding or through negotiation. The investment bank performs four functions.

1. Investigation. This involves analysis of the present status and probable future performance of the issuer, the quality of the proposed issue, prices and yields on other comparable securities, and prospective market conditions. This culminates in determining a price and yield for the new issue.

2. Underwriting. The investment bank guarantees the issuer a fixed price and assumes the risk of resale. If the issue is small, a single investment bank may underwrite it. If it is larger, two or more investment banks may form an underwriting syndicate, each assuming a share of the risk. Some underwriting syndicates include 50 or more investment banks.

3. Wholesale distribution. In some cases, the underwriters sell at least a part of the issue to other dealers.

4. Retail distribution. This is the function of selling the new securities to their ultimate buyers. In some cases, the underwriters do this themselves. In others, they sell part of the issue to hundreds of dealers located throughout the nation and even in foreign countries. Their contribution to the regional mobility of funds is evident.

Investment banks are commonly used to distribute issues by many corporations, foreign governments, state governments, municipalities and many types of local authorities, and some agencies of the federal government. In a few cases the federal government has distributed its own direct issues through investment-banking syndicates. Usually, however, this function is performed for federal securities by the Federal Reserve and commercial banks.

Thousands of smaller business firms have not found it feasible to distribute their issues through investment banks. This is primarily because their issues are not widely known and the cost of remedying the situation would be prohibitive. Some other costs, such as registration and legal fees, are also relatively high on small issues.

Commercial-paper houses assist in primary distribution of newly issued short-term claims. *Commercial paper,* in this technical sense, refers to short-term promissory notes issued by finance companies and other corporations of high standing. Much of this is sold by the issuer directly to the ultimate buyer, the latter being primarily financial institutions and nonfinancial corporations with funds to invest for short periods. Some commercial paper is issued to dealers, who pay the issuer and distribute the paper to buyers all over the country. Only well-known firms find it feasible to sell their paper in this market.

We find, then, that institutions engaged in primary distribution of new debt and equity instruments serve, to the extent that they are effective, to reduce the cost of new issues, to increase the mobility of funds over wide areas, and to improve the allocation of investible funds and of investment in real capital.

Secondary markets for securities

By *secondary markets* we do not mean facilities for the initial sale of new issues but facilities for trading in outstanding debt and equity claims. If the term were not derogatory we would call it "the market for second-hand securities." The term *securities* is used here in its broadest sense to include ownership shares and debt obligations of all maturities. Sometimes a distinction is made between "securities markets," in which ownership shares and long-term debt obligations are bought and sold, and "money markets," in which short-term debt obligations are traded. Such a distinction is not necessary for our purposes and would only obscure the similarity of functions performed in these markets.

The secondary securities market in the United States is highly complex, including central securities exchanges and thousands of persons and firms serving as brokers and dealers. A securities dealer buys and sells for his own account; he is like any other second-hand merchant who derives his income from the difference between the price at which he sells and the price at which he buys. However, in serving the brokerage function, a broker does not buy or sell for his own account; he acts as a go-between for buyers and sellers. In some cases, he learns who wants to sell and who wants to buy, and then puts the prospective buyer and seller in contact with each other so they can enter into a transaction. In others, he acts as agent for a buyer or seller. For example, a broker for a seller may as agent sell to a broker who purchases as agent for a buyer. For such services a broker receives a fee or commission. Some brokers and dealers concentrate on only a few types of securities; others are concerned with a wide variety.

Some securities command more efficient secondary markets than others. The *marketability* of a security, its ability to be sold quickly without a large decrease of its price, depends heavily on at least two factors:

1. How widely its issuer and its own qualities are known. If both are widely known, there are likely to be many actual and potential buyers who will stand ready to bid for the security. However, if only a few know about the security, it may be salable only after a considerable delay or decline of price.

2. The amount of the security outstanding and the number of its holders. If a large amount of it is outstanding and it is widely held, transactions are likely

to be frequent and buyers easy to find. But if the amount outstanding is small or most of it is held by only a few, the market for it is likely to be erratic. Many securities meet both these tests and enjoy a continuous market in which individual sellers or buyers can sell or buy considerable amounts quickly with little effect on price. Other less fortunate securities lack marketability and can be sold only after a delay or a significant decline of price.

The existence of a highly efficient secondary market for a security markedly increases its liquidity and safety of principal value. Its quick marketability serves one of the requirements of liquidity—ability to be converted to money quickly. Of course, the other requirement—stability of value—is not assured by the existence of an efficient market. The value of a security may indeed fall because of less optimistic assessments of its issuer, the appearance of more attractive securities, or general changes in financial markets. But the holder is at least assured that there are many potential buyers who will compete for the security at a price commensurate with the prices of comparable issues.

To the extent that secondary markets enhance the expected liquidity and safety of value of securities, buyers are encouraged to hold more of them and at lower yields. Issuers of securities can acquire funds at lower costs, which promotes capital formation. Enhanced marketability of securities also makes it less advantageous for a buyer to purchase only those securities that mature at or before the time when he will want to use his funds for some other purpose; he can buy issues with longer maturities and recover his money at any time by selling in the secondary market—but only by assuming some risk of loss of value, which may or may not be offset by possibilities of capital gains.

Liquidity through marketability thus helps solve a problem that would exist in a system in which buyers of claims would have to hold them to maturity or could sell them only with difficulty—deficit units would want to issue large amounts of long-term claims, considering heavy reliance on short-term financing too risky, while buyers would demand short-term claims because they thought they soon would, or might, want to use their money for other purposes.

Let us now survey briefly a few branches of the secondary market for securities, emphasizing functions rather than institutional detail. We start with the national securities exchanges which include the New York Stock Exchange and the American Stock Exchange in New York City and lesser exchanges in several other cities. The exchanges themselves do not engage in trading. Their functions are to provide physical facilities, including the trading floor; to provide reporting and communications facilities; to determine what issues will be admitted to trading on the exchange; to regulate the conduct of their members; and so on. Actual trading is done by brokers and dealers who are members of the exchanges. These brokers and dealers are interlinked with all parts of the nation and with other countries in various ways: by means of telephone, telegraph, teletype, and cable; through hundreds of branch offices of the member brokers and dealers; through links with brokers and dealers who are not members of the exchanges; through other financial institutions, and so on. Offers to buy and sell flow through this network to the floor of the exchange from all parts of the country and from other countries. These offers meet on the floor of the exchange, where brokers and dealers conduct what is in effect an auction market, with the securities being sold to those who offer the highest prices.

Several thousand of the largest corporations have their issues listed on national securities exchanges. Some corporate bonds are traded on these exchanges, but the great bulk of trading is in ownership shares of listed companies. Stocks listed on such exchanges account for a very large fraction of the total value of all outstanding corporate shares, but the number of corporations that have their stocks listed on national exchanges is only a small fraction of all corporations. Thus, ownership shares in a large majority of corporations and most debt issues of business, government, and others must be traded, if at all, outside the exchanges.

Many of these are traded in what is popularly called the "over-the-counter market." This is not a market in the sense of some central place at which supply and demand meet and at which purchases and sales are consummated. Rather, it is a set of arrangements involving brokers and dealers who are located all over the country and who are linked to each other and to buyers and sellers by telephone, teletype, computers, and written communications (including lists of offers to buy or sell). When an offer to buy or sell is received by a dealer or broker, he may sell or buy for his own account or for a customer, or he may communicate the offer to other brokers and dealers in the network. Some brokers and dealers specialize in a few types of securities; others interest themselves in a wide variety.

Many types of securities are traded in the over-the-counter market: shares of many corporations, corporate bonds and some types of shorter-term corporate debt, debts of foreign governments, debts of the federal government, debts of states and municipalities, and so on. However, there are many corporate stocks and many types of debt issues that are not widely enough known or large enough in value to have access to this market.

We shall later deal further with some branches of the over-the-counter market which play important roles in the functioning of the banking and financial system. Among these are:

1. The market for U.S. government securities, including dealers who maintain continuous markets for marketable issues of the federal government.

2. The market for state and municipal securities, in which issues of all the states and many municipalities and other political subdivisions are bought and sold.

3. The acceptance market, primarily a market for acceptance claims against banks.

4. The market for negotiable certificates of deposit (CDs), which are transferable instruments representing time-deposit claims against banks.

5. The Federal Funds market, in which are bought and sold claims against deposits at the Federal Reserve banks. We shall find that such markets play important roles in enhancing the liquidity of some of these assets, in providing

liquidity for various financial institutions and others, and in increasing the mobility of funds.

ATTRIBUTES OF FINANCIAL INSTRUMENTS

In valuing any financial claim and in choosing among alternative financial claims, actual and potential buyers and holders consider three important attributes or characteristics—liquidity, safety of principal value, and yield.

Liquidity

By the *liquidity* of an asset we mean its capability of being converted into money quickly and without loss of value in terms of money. Money is perfectly liquid; it can be used immediately to pay debts or to spend, and it always remains at a constant value in terms of money. An asset is illiquid to the extent that its conversion into money requires time or entails loss of value either through a decline in its market value or through conversion costs in terms of inconvenience, brokers' fees, dealers' margins, and so on. As we have already seen, the actual liquidity of an asset depends in part on market facilities for it. However, a debt instrument is more likely to achieve a high degree of liquidity to the extent that it possesses two characteristics. First, it is a claim on an issuer with an excellent reputation for meeting its obligations promptly and in full. Second, it is of short maturity—payable on demand or within a few months. With maturity so short, any rise of market rates of interest will reduce its value only slightly.

Most holders consider liquidity to be a desirable characteristic in an asset and are willing to forgo some income to buy some liquidity. However, holders differ widely in the amounts of liquidity demanded in the form of earning assets and in the amounts of yield they are willing to sacrifice in order to obtain liquidity. Some, expecting or fearing large excesses of spending over receipts in the near future, may be willing to forgo considerable amounts of yield in order to demand large amounts of liquidity in this form; this may occur when the alternative is to hold money itself which yields no income. Others, expecting excesses of receipts over payments in the near future, may be willing to sacrifice very little yield to buy liquidity.

To the extent that liquidity requires short maturities, desires of holders may conflict with those of issuers. To the issuer, the short maturity can be a source of illiquidity; it subjects him to the possibility of having to repay inconveniently soon or to refinance in an unfavorable market at higher rates of interest.

Safety of principal

By *safety of principal* we mean freedom from risk that the market value of the debt instrument will decline. "Safety" is used here in its relative sense. Instruments that are highly liquid are also highly safe; they are convertible into money not only quickly but also at a stable price. But some instruments that lack liquidity may be relatively safe; they can be collected or sold without loss over a longer period of time.

Risks of loss of principal value are of two types:

1. Risk of default. This is the risk that promised payments of interest and repayment of principal will not be met fully and on schedule. Default risks on debt instruments obviously differ from one issuer to another; that on debt instruments of the federal government is far below the risk of default on issues of a business concern whose future is doubtful. However, different issues of any given debtor may carry quite different risks of default because of differences in priority of claim against assets or income, or both. Some classes of debt are given prior claim to a debtor's income or assets, while other classes claim only such income and assets as may remain after satisfaction of all other debts. Other things equal, holders prefer instruments with lower default risk to those with greater default risk, but at least some can be induced to hold those with higher default risk if the promised income is higher.

2. Market risk. This is the risk that the market price of a debt instrument will decline in response to a rise in market rates of interest. The market price of an outstanding debt instrument, which is a contract to pay a fixed number of dollars in interest per year and to repay a fixed number of dollars of principal, tends to change inversely with changes in market rates of interest. The market price rises when interest rates fall and falls when interest rates rise. And the longer the remaining term of the instrument to maturity, the more will a given change of interest rates affect its price.[1]

From this it might be inferred that, other things equal, holders will prefer short maturities over long because of their lower market risk, and that they will purchase and hold longer maturities only if rewarded by a higher interest yield. This is sometimes true, but not always. For one thing, longer maturities carry the possibility not only of a larger loss of value if interest rates rise but also the possibility of a larger capital gain if interest rates fall. When interest rates are expected to fall in the future, the interest yield on longer maturities may be below that on shorter maturities, holders will expect to make up the difference, or more than the difference, in capital gains. Moreover, even with given expectations as to the future course of interest rates, different holders are likely to have differing preferences for shorter and longer maturities. Some, expecting to need their funds soon, will prefer short maturities in order to lessen their market risk. Others, looking forward to a very long holding period and wanting an assured rate of return, prefer longer maturities. This also enables them to avoid the expense of buying a succession of shorter maturities. Here again we encounter the important fact of differences among buyers' tastes and preference functions.

Yield

By the *yield* of a debt instrument we mean its annual rate of return over cost, taking into consideration not only annual interest payments but also any difference there may be between its cost and its maturity value. This will be elaborated later.

---

[1] For an elaboration of this point, see p. 63.

Thus, we have seen that financial instruments representing debt vary in many ways—in the creditworthiness of the issuer, in priority of claims against assets and income, in maturity, and so on. These lead to differences in liquidity and safety of principal, which in turn help explain differences in market yields.

INTEREST

We turn now to another subject that we shall encounter repeatedly—interest.

Variety of interest rates

At various times we shall refer to "the" interest rate, which suggests that there is but one interest rate in a given market at a given time. This is a useful device in making the exposition both simple and brief. But we should always remember that this is an oversimplification, and one that can be dangerous for our analysis. The fact is that, at any point of time, there is not just one interest rate, but a complex of rates in the market, and these can differ widely. Moreover, these various rates may not move in a parallel manner through time, although they usually move in the same direction.

How can such differences in rates persist? Why do not lenders shift their funds from debts with low yields to those with higher yields until all yield differentials have been wiped out? A part of the answer is to be found in imperfections in the credit market, which inhibit the mobility of loan funds from one branch of the market to another. Some of the most important of these are lack of knowledge by lenders or borrowers, legal limitations on the types of loans that can be made by some financial institutions, differing degrees of monopoly power in the various branches of the market, and so on. The actual structure of rates cannot be fully understood without reference to such imperfections. But these do not by any means provide a full explanation of the variety of yields; yields would still differ even if the credit market were perfectly competitive, with credit perfectly mobile. This is true because the debts themselves have such differing characteristics.

We have already encountered some characteristics that would cause yields to differ even in a perfectly competitive market—differences reflected in liquidity and safety of principal value. There are also two others:

1. Differences in costs of administration per dollar of loan per year. Interest charges usually include an amount to cover costs of investigating the creditworthiness of the borrower, of holding the loan, and of collecting principal and interest. On some loans, these costs are very low per dollar per year. For example, the annual administrative cost per dollar on a very large loan to a corporation whose credit standing need not be investigated may be almost negligible. On the other hand, such costs per dollar of loan per year may be very high on a small installment loan to a consumer when his credit standing must be investigated and interest and principal collected in weekly or monthly installments.

2. Differences in taxability. An example of such differences is the fact that income on securities issued by states and municipalities is exempt from federal income taxes, which enables these securities to be sold at lower yield rates.

In short, some differences in market yields reflect differences in types and degrees of market imperfections, but because of differences in characteristics of securities such as those described above, we should expect to find differences in yields even in competitive markets.

Yield rates and market values

We return now to two subjects introduced earlier: the calculation of effective interest rates or yields and the relationship between the rate of yield and the market value of a debt obligation.

We can best approach the problem of calculating effective interest rates by distinguishing three different types of yield. The first is the *nominal yield,* which is simply the yield stated on the face of the obligation. Thus, a note promising to pay $100 at the end of a year with interest at 3 percent has a nominal yield of 3 percent. A bond promising to pay $1,000 at the end of 10 years and $30 at the end of each year also has a nominal yield of 3 percent. The nominal yield is of importance primarily in fixing the *dollar amount* of interest to be paid each year. The nominal yield and the effective rate of interest will be the same only if the market value of the debt is equal to its par or stated value, and this may not occur. In fact, the debt may not even have been sold initially at its par or stated value. For example, when the debtor originally issued his promise to pay $1,000 at the end of 10 years and $30 of interest at the end of each year, interest rates in the market on comparable obligations may have been below 3 percent, so that the bond could be sold above par, say, for $1,050. Or, interest rates on comparable obligations may have been well above 3 percent, so that he had to sell the bond below par, say, for $950. In any case, the market value after issue can deviate from par value.

Another type of yield is the *current yield.* This is simply the dollar amount of interest per year divided by the current market price of the obligation. If the bond described above has a market value of $950, its current yield is $30/$950, or 3.16 percent. If its market price is $1,050, its current yield is $30/$1,050, or 2.86 percent. Although current yield is more meaningful than nominal yield, it does not measure accurately the average *net* return per year to be gained if the obligation is purchased at its current market price and held to maturity. This is best reflected by the third type of yield—*average yield to maturity*—which takes into consideration the current market value, annual interest receipts, and the relationship between current market value and the value at which the debt will be paid off at maturity. The general nature of this measure can be explained most easily by an example using simple interest rather than compound interest. Suppose that one buys the 10-year bond described above at $950. He will receive not only $30 a year in interest but also a capital appreciation of $50 over the 10-year period, or an average of $5 per year. Thus, his average return per year will be $35 and his average yield to maturity will be $35/$950, or 3.68 percent. However, if the market price of the 10-year bond is $1,050, the buyer must recognize that his average net return will be $30 a year, *minus* an average of $5 per year because he paid $1,050 for the debt and will collect only $1,000 at maturity. Thus, his average net return per year will be only $25, and the average yield to maturity will be $25/$1,050, or 2.38 percent. This is only approximate because we used simple interest; in practice, buyers would use compound interest, as we shall do later.[2]

When we refer hereafter to yields, to effective interest rates, or simply to interest rates, we shall mean rates of yield to maturity because that is the best measure of the rate of return on debt obligations at any time.

We now deal with the relationship at any point of time between yield rates and the capital value (market value) of a debt obligation or any other income-yielding asset. The present capital value of such an asset is arrived at by a process of *capitalization*, by which we mean "discounting" the expected flow of money receipts. *Discounting* means taking out interest in advance. A buyer who paid the full amount of future dollar returns for an obligation would receive no net interest at all. He usually will not buy an obligation unless the purchase price is such that the yield on the purchase price will be as great as that available to him on other comparable obligations. Of course, he would like to buy at a lower price, but this is likely to be prevented by competition from other purchasers.

The discounting process is easiest to understand when only simple interest or discount is involved. Suppose that, when the market yield on this class of paper is 3 percent, buyers are offered a promise to pay $1,030 one year later. Each buyer will reason as follows: "This piece of paper is of value today only because it represents a claim against money receivable in the future. I will buy it only at such a price that I will receive the going rate of return on my money, and this 'price' is that amount which, if put out at the prevailing yield rate, would be worth $1,030 a year hence." There is some amount of money (P), which, if put out at the current rate of yield (i) on this type of obligation, will be worth $1,030 a year later. Thus,

$$P(1 + i) = \$1,030$$

or

$$P = \frac{\$1,030}{1 + i}$$

If $i = 0.03$, the formula becomes

$$P = \frac{\$1,030}{1.03} = \$1,000$$

---

[2] This example assumes that the debtor does not have the option of paying off the debt before maturity. If the issuer has the option of "calling" it before maturity, at some stated price, the buyer should also compute "yield to call date," to determine what his rate of net return will be if the security is called.

The present value of $1,030 receivable a year hence will be lower if yield rates are higher and higher if yield rates are lower. For example, if the yield rate is 4 percent, the formula becomes

$$P = \frac{\$1,030}{1.04} = \$990.38$$

If, however, the yield rate is 2 percent,

$$P = \frac{\$1,030}{1.02} = \$1,009.80$$

The general formula for simple discount is

$$P = \frac{A}{(1 + i)}$$

where P is the present value, A is the dollar amount receivable at the end of the interest period, and i is the rate of interest for that period stated in hundredths such as 0.02 or 0.04.[3]

The process of arriving at a present capital value for a longer-term obligation such as the bond described above, is based on the same principle, but it is a bit more complicated, for two reasons. First, the obligation is to make a number of payments through time rather than a single payment; second, it involves compound interest or discount. Each prospective buyer will reason as follows: "This obligation is of value only because it represents a claim against $30 at the end of each of the next 10 years and $1,000 at the end of the 10-year period. I will buy it only at such a price that I will receive the going rate of return on my money." The price (P) is the sum of the discounted values of all the individual payments expected in the future. For example, there is some amount of money (P_1) which, if put out at the prevailing yield rate, would be worth $30 a year hence. That is,

$$P_1 (1 + i) = \$30$$

or

$$P_1 = \frac{\$30}{1 + i}$$

There is another smaller amount of money (P_2) which, if put out at compound interest at the prevailing rate, would be worth $30 at the end of two years. Compound interest is used because during the second year, interest would be received on the first year's interest. That is,

[3] Here and later we shall assume that the interest period is one year and that the interest rate is the rate per year. We shall also assume that interest is compounded annually. In some cases, the interest period is less than a year. For example, it may be six months. In such cases the i in our formula will be the interest rate for half a year and the number of interest periods will be twice as large as it would be if the interest period were one year.

$$P_2 (1 + i)^2 = \$30$$

or

$$P_2 = \frac{\$30}{(1 + i)^2}$$

Similarly, there is a yet smaller amount of money (P_3) which, if put out at compound interest, would be worth $30 at the end of three years.

$$P_3 (1 + i)^3 = \$30$$

or

$$P_3 = \frac{\$30}{(1 + i)^3}$$

The present values of the other interest payments can be arrived at in the same way. There remains the $1,000 of principal payable at the end of 10 years. Its present value is $1,000/[(1 + i)^{10}]$. The present value of the bond is the sum of the present values of the various payments to be received on it.

The general formula for arriving at present capital value by discounting is

$$P = \frac{A_1}{1 + i} + \frac{A_2}{(1 + i)^2} + \frac{A_3}{(1 + i)^3} + \cdots + \frac{A_n}{(1 + i)^n} + \frac{F}{(1 + i)^n}$$

where P is the present value, the As are the dollar amounts receivable at the ends of the various interest periods, F is the amount of the principal repayment, i is the rate of discount, and n is the number of interest periods. Fortunately, each potential buyer need not solve such equations for himself; bond tables are easily available, to do this for him.

Columns 5, 6, and 7 of Table 3–2 show the present value of the bond at discount rates of 2, 3, and 4 percent. It will be worth $1,000 if the rate is 3 percent, only $922.94 if the rate is 4 percent, and $1,089.83 if the rate is 2 percent.

One special case is worth noting because of its simplicity: the case of an obligation to pay fixed annual amounts in perpetuity. In this case, the preceding formula becomes simply

$$P = \frac{A}{i}$$

Thus, the present value of the right to receive $30 a year in perpetuity becomes:

$$P = \frac{\$30}{0.03} = \$1,000 \qquad \text{if the discount rate is 3 percent}$$

$$P = \frac{\$30}{0.02} = \$1,500 \qquad \text{if the discount rate is 2 percent}$$

$$P = \frac{\$30}{0.04} = \$750 \qquad \text{if the discount rate is 4 percent}$$

Table 3–2 Discounting and present values

END OF YEAR	FORMULA	VALUES OF COL. (1) AT INTEREST RATES OF:			PERCENT VALUES* OF $30 AT END OF INDICATED YEARS AT DISCOUNT RATE OF:		
		(1) 2%	(2) 3%	(3) 4%	(4) 2%	(5) 3%	(6) 4%
		(2) 2%	(3) 3%	(4) 4%	(5) 2%	(6) 3%	(7) 4%
1	$(1 + i)$	1.0200	1.0300	1.0400	$ 29.412	$ 29.126	$ 28.846
2	$(1 + i)^2$	1.0404	1.0609	1.0816	28.835	28.278	27.737
3	$(1 + i)^3$	1.0612	1.0927	1.1249	28.270	27.454	26.670
4	$(1 + i)^4$	1.0824	1.1255	1.1699	27.715	26.655	25.644
5	$(1 + i)^5$	1.1041	1.1593	1.2167	27.172	25.878	24.658
6	$(1 + i)^6$	1.1262	1.1941	1.2653	26.639	25.124	23.709
7	$(1 + i)^7$	1.1487	1.2299	1.3159	25.605	23.682	21.921
8	$(1 + i)^8$	1.1717	1.2668	1.3686	25.103	22.992	21.197
9	$(1 + i)^9$	1.1951	1.3048	1.4153	26.117	24.393	22.798
10	$(1 + i)^{10}$	1.2190	1.3439	1.4719	24.610	22.323	20.382
Subtotal					$ 269.48	$ 255.90	$243.56
Present value of $1,000 receivable at the end of 10 years					820.35	744.10	679.38
Total					$1,089.83	$1,000.00	$922.94

* The values in columns 5, 6, and 7 are arrived at by dividing $30 by the numbers shown in columns 2, 3, and 4, respectively.

It is important to note that the longer the maturity of an obligation, the greater is the effect of any given change of market rates of interest on its present value. This is illustrated by the following examples:

	PRESENT VALUE IF DISCOUNTED AT		
	3%	2%	4%
An obligation to pay $1,030 at the end of one year	$1,000.00	$1,009.80	$990.38
An obligation to pay $30 annually for 10 years and $1,000 at the end of 10 years	1,000.00	1,089.83	922.91
An obligation to pay $30 a year in perpetuity	1,000.00	1,500.00	750.00

Such is the arithmetic of the negative relationship between the level of market rates of interest and the market values of *outstanding* debt obligations that have maturity values and interest returns that are contractually fixed in terms of dollars. The economic reason for this relationship is that in competitive markets, average yields to maturity on issues already outstanding must be in line with yields on new issues. Thus when yields on new issues are rising, the prices on old issues must fall enough to make their yields equally attractive to investors. And when yields on new issues are falling, investors will bid up the prices of outstanding issues until their yields are no longer higher than those on new issues.

CONCLUSIONS

A few of the major findings in this chapter need to be recalled here.

1. Debt, credit, and financial instruments are interrelated with the functioning of the real economy—with the production of income or output, with the allocation of output among its many potential uses and users, and with the maintenance of the flow of national income.

2. The only way that surpluses of surplus units during a period can return to the market as demand for output for consumption and investment purposes is if they are matched by deficits of deficit units. This process requires the creation of new ownership or debt claims or a transfer of ownership of existing claims from deficit to surplus units.

3. Because of differences of preferences among buyers and among issuers, securities come to be highly differentiated with differing claims on assets and income. These come to be reflected in differences in liquidity, safety of principal value, and yield. Holders are presented with a varied menu from which to choose.

4. Institutions that increase the marketability of securities promote efficiency in the economic system. Those increasing and disseminating financial information provide a sounder basis for rational decisions. Those providing broader and more efficient primary distribution cheapen the cost of new issues and increase the efficiency of allocation of investment. Efficient secondary markets increase the liquidity and safety of principal of securities, make them more attractive, and thus increase the supply of funds made available.

Selected readings

Dewing, A. S., *The Financial Policy of Corporations,* 5th ed., New York, Ronald, 1953.

Graham, B., D. L. Dodd, S. Cottle, and C. Tatham, *Security Analysis,* 4th ed., New York, McGraw-Hill, 1962.

Green, T. F., *Practical Summary of Negotiable Instruments,* New York, McKay, 1938.

Smith, P. F., *Economics of Financial Institutions and Markets,* Homewood, Ill., Irwin, 1971.

CHAPTER 4

FINANCIAL INTERMEDIARIES

The preceding chapter concentrated on financial instruments or claims issued by entities other than financial institutions. Claims issued by financial institutions to acquire funds with which to purchase claims against others were specifically excluded "in order to avoid double counting and for other reasons." This was done to enable us to analyze the functions of ownership and debt claims against households, corporations and other types of nonfinancial business firms, governmental units, universities and other educational institutions, and so on. We shall call claims against such entities "direct securities."

We shall now consider financial intermediaries. A *financial intermediary* is an institution which creates and issues financial claims against itself and uses the proceeds to acquire and hold financial claims against others. Financial claims against itself will be called "indirect securities." In some cases, these are equity claims and in some cases debt claims. The claims acquired and held by the intermediary are usually direct securities, either debt or equity. Among the important types of financial intermediaries in the United States are commercial banks, mutual savings banks, savings and loan associations, credit unions, life insurance companies, mutual investment companies, pension funds, and many others. These have amassed huge amounts of funds, receive a large fraction of total saving each year, and play highly important roles in the functioning of the financial system. Let us now look at some of the economic reasons for their origin and growth.

ECONOMIC BASES FOR FINANCIAL INTERMEDIATION

Households and other ultimate owners of savings can and do acquire and hold very large amounts of direct securities. We have already noted some of the conditions in financial markets which facilitate this: the availability of both equity and debt securities with differing attributes which come to be reflected in differences in liquidity, safety of principal value, and yield; the availability of large amounts of information and analysis concerning great numbers of direct securities; and the availability of trading facilities in both primary and secondary markets to facilitate purchases and sales. The fact that ultimate owners of savings have the alternative of making up their own portfolios of money and many varieties of direct securities raises key questions: How can a financial intermediary make a living? What can it do for ultimate owners of savings that will induce them to pay an amount large enough for its services to cover its operating costs and leave a profit? In general terms, the answer is that, for at least some savers, a financial intermediary can do what the savers cannot do for themselves, or can do only at higher cost.

Especially for those individuals whose total accumulated savings are not large and for those whose current flow of saving is small, as well as for some who are wealthy, the acquisition and holding of direct securities involves high costs and other disadvantages:

1. High cost of information and analysis of direct securities. Many of those who do not acquire expert knowledge about securities in their regular course of business find it costly in terms of time, money, or both to gather and analyze information about any large number of direct securities. This is especially true when people have only small sums to invest.

2. High cost of buying, holding, and selling direct securities. Most brokerage fees and other charges for buying and selling vary inversely in percentage terms with the sums involved. Brokers and dealers commonly impose a minimum flat charge in dollars, plus a diminishing percentage charge on sums in excess of that covered by the flat charge. Thus, transactions costs, in percentage terms, are often prohibitive when the sums involved are small or when the securities are to be held only a short time.

3. High cost of diversification. Safety of principal value can be enhanced by holding a variety of direct securities whose prices do not move in a parallel way. Thus, total default risk can be reduced by holding debt claims against a variety of debtors, and greater stability of value may be achieved by holding a wide variety of ownership shares rather than concentrating on one or a few issues. Wealthy

holders, with millions at their disposal, may achieve a high degree of diversification at relatively low cost, but this is not true of those with a smaller volume of assets. These holders must be content with only a few issues or incur the high transactions costs involved in buying small amounts of large numbers of issues.

4. High costs of liquidity. Most units wish to hold some liquid assets with which to meet foreseen or unforeseen excesses of expenditures over receipts. This can be expensive in terms of forgone income or explicit costs if the only assets available for this purpose are money and direct securities. Money itself yields no explicit income. The holder might buy very short maturities which would mature at or before the time he expected to make payments, but he would still incur the costs of buying and holding, and the yields in such short maturities are often low. He could buy longer maturities and sell them when he needed to make payments, but only by assuming more market risk and incurring costs of buying, holding, and selling.

Such are the principal disadvantages and diseconomies of a financial system containing only money itself and direct securities. These account for the establishment and growth of financial intermediaries. Enterprisers found a source of profit: Members of the community were willing to accept, on the indirect securities issued by financial intermediaries, a rate of return sufficiently below the rates earned on the direct securities acquired by the intermediaries to cover operating costs and yield a net return. Individual financial intermediaries have succeeded in drawing funds from thousands and even hundreds of thousands of ultimate owners of savings, and many have amassed great pools of assets. Intermediaries with total assets in the millions are commonplace; those with assets in the hundreds of millions are numerous; and some have assets in the billions. There are even some intermediaries with assets of over $20 billion.

ECONOMIES IN INTERMEDIARIES

The ability of financial intermediaries to survive and prosper is derived from several types of economies of specialization and scale. An intermediary operating with a large pool of funds can command experts in its various functions; reap the increased productivity and lower costs resulting from a high degree of specialization; employ efficient machinery and equipment, such as computers; and often succeed in purchasing services at prices lower than those charged to individual investors. For example, it can gather and analyze information at low cost per unit by spreading the total cost over a large volume of assets. Some intermediaries claim that they make better decisions than would be made by the ultimate owners of savings. This is undoubtedly true in many cases, but even where it is not true, the intermediary can most likely gather and analyze data at a lower cost than could the individual owner. Also, as will be discussed later in more detail, intermediaries can achieve lower transactions costs in buying, holding, and selling direct securities. The above sources of economics are highly relevant, but we shall stress the importance of "the law of large numbers." This law is basic to both diversification of assets and the principle of offsetting receipts and withdrawal of funds.

Diversification of assets

If relevant future events were always predictable, there would be little or no reason for diversifying one's security holdings. If an investor knew in advance what future returns—including both price changes and current incomes—on all securities would be, the investor would simply put all his funds into the security yielding the highest return. However, perfect certainty is not a characteristic of security markets. No matter how much he may spend in gathering information, analyzing it, and making forecasts, the best that an investor can do is to identify possible outcomes and to estimate a subjective probability distribution for the various possible outcomes. For example, he may estimate the average expected return on a security to be 6 percent, but recognize that there is some probability that the return will be higher and some probability that it will be lower or even negative. Even if he feels confident about the probability distribution, he cannot know which outcome will be realized. Even the improbable can happen. He will, of course, be happy if the actual return is higher than he expected. However, he will hardly welcome the risk that the actual outcome will be lower or even negative. If he holds only a single security, he faces a risk that a lower return or even a negative return will depress by a large percentage his asset value or current income, or both.

Diversification—the holding of more than one security—can decrease the total risk of a portfolio, because lower-than-expected returns on some issues can be offset by higher-than-expected returns on others. However, the extent to which diversification can lower total risk does not depend only on the number of issues held; it is highly dependent on the diversity of behavior of returns on the various securities. Diversification could eliminate risk entirely if returns on different securities were perfectly negatively correlated—if, for example, a fall in the price of one security was always offset exactly by a rise in the price of another. Combining the two risks would completely eliminate the overall risk. Unfortunately, because all securities are subject to some common forces, it is rarely, if ever, possible to find securities whose returns are perfectly negatively correlated. For example, a rise of interest rates tends to lower the prices of all securities, although not all prices are lowered by the same proportion.

At the other extreme, diversification could not reduce total risk at all if returns on all securities were perfectly positively correlated—if, for example, the prices of all securities always rose or fell simultaneously and in the same proportions. Fortunately, returns on all securities are not perfectly correlated; there is some degree of independence and diverse behavior. This is partly because some issues subject to forces that do not affect others and partly because forces impinging on all issuers affect them in different ways and degrees. For example, managements of some companies improve while others deteriorate; demands for products of some companies rise while demands for the products of others remain static or decline; companies in different industries are not affected in the same way and degree by such external events as cyclical fluctuations of business, inflation, and deflation; and so on. It is because of some degree of diversity of behavior of different securities that diversification can reduce total risk.

Thus, financial intermediaries are reducers of risk and manufacturers of safety. Through diversification of assets, they reduce risk to a degree that could not be achieved, or could be achieved only at higher cost, by the individual ultimate owners of savings. Operating with a large pool of funds, an intermediary can acquire and hold a large number of different securities; it can buy each in lots large enough to achieve low transactions costs; and through expert management, it may select a combination or portfolio of securities in which the risks best offset each other.

In short, one basic economic function of financial intermediaries is to reduce risk and enhance safety.

Offsetting receipts and withdrawals of funds

Another fundamental basis for the origin and success of financial intermediaries is the phenomenon of offsetting receipts and withdrawals, which is also related to the law of large numbers. This principle was mentioned briefly in connection with our earlier discussion of commercial banking, but it is also broadly applicable to other types of financial intermediaries. To illustrate the principle, let us assume that some financial intermediary has received funds from a thousand households and has issued to them financial claims against itself, that it stands ready to accept new funds, and that it allows claimants to withdraw funds on demand or after only short notice. The management of the intermediary will expect that during any period some claimants will withdraw funds and that others will bring in additional funds. That all claimants will withdraw funds at the same time is not impossible but highly improbable. In other words, it is quite improbable that withdrawals by all claimants will be perfectly positively correlated. On the basis of its own experience and the experience of other intermediaries and based on its knowledge of the income and expenditure flows of its customers, the management will expect that withdrawals will be at least partially, and perhaps fully or more than fully, offset by inflows of funds. It may even estimate a subjective probability distribution of the possible outcomes. For example, it may estimate that during some stated future period there is an 80 percent probability that net inflows will increase its net assets by at least 5 percent, a 95 percent probability that inflows will be at least equal to withdrawals, only a 5 percent probability that net withdrawals will amount to as much as 5 percent of its assets, and only a 1 percent probability that net withdrawals will amount to as much as 10 percent of its assets.

Operating on the basis of such expectations, an intermediary can create and issue to ultimate owners of savings financial claims against itself that are more liquid than the assets that it acquires and holds. For example, the claims that it issues may be fixed in terms of dollars, payable on demand or on short notice, and thus almost as liquid as money itself. Yet the great bulk of its assets can be in the form of longer-term illiquid securities, such as mortgages or bonds. Expecting that there is only one chance in 20 that net withdrawals will amount to as much as 5 percent of its assets and only one chance in 100 that such net withdrawals will be as high as 10 percent, it will feel secure in holding no more than 10 percent of its assets in liquid form. Even this small fraction need not all be in the form of money; most of it may be in the form of liquid short-term earning assets, such as obligations of the U.S. Treasury or loans to security dealers. Its holdings of liquid assets can be even smaller to the extent that it can confidently rely on borrowing to meet net withdrawals.

The transactions costs incurred by an intermediary can be far below those that would be necessary if ultimate owners of savings managed their liquidity individually. To only a minor extent is this due to the fact that an intermediary, buying and selling in large lots, can buy transactions services at lower prices. It is largely the result of the fact that an intermediary need not engage in as many transactions as the individual owner. If each ultimate owner of savings provided his own liquidity, he would either have to hold money, which yields no income, or pay transactions costs every time he bought a security and every time he sold a security to get money. However, because of the principle of offsetting receipts and withdrawals, an intermediary needs to sell securities only to the extent of net withdrawals. For example, if its receipts are exactly equal to withdrawals, thus leaving total assets unchanged, the intermediary need not sell any securities regardless of how large gross withdrawals may be.

Summary

Financial intermediaries are manufacturers of liquidity and safety. Through the processes described above, the intermediary can create against itself financial claims that have characteristics that differ markedly from those of the assets that they acquire and hold. In these ways, intermediaries create financial claims with combinations of safety, liquidity, and yield that conform more closely to the tastes and preferences of many ultimate owners of savings. For these reasons, intermediaries have been able to attract huge amounts of funds. However, intermediaries also provide important benefits to issuers of direct securities, enabling them to issue at lower costs types of securities conforming more closely to the issuers' needs and preferences. For example, a business firm may wish to issue a long-term security that is itself relatively risky and illiquid, while individual investors place a high premium on safety and liquidity and would purchase and hold the security only if rewarded by a very high yield. An intermediary can help solve such a problem by purchasing the risky and illiquid security conforming to the issuer's preferences and, on the basis of this security, pooled with others, create financial claims conforming to the preferences of investors. It is for this reason that intermediaries are said to intermediate between the preferences of issuers of direct securities and the preferences of asset holders.

Let us now survey briefly some of the principal types of financial intermediaries.

TYPES OF FINANCIAL INTERMEDIARIES

We begin our discussion by citing four types of institutions often called "depository financial intermediaries." They are outstanding manufacturers of liquidity, creating and issuing claims against themselves that are much more liquid than the direct securities that they acquire.

Commercial banks. Since later chapters will deal at considerable length with these institutions, our comments here will be very brief. Some 13,700 commercial banks widely dispersed in every part of the nation command a far larger aggregate volume of assets than any other single type of financial intermediary (see Table 4–1).

Table 4–1 Some important types of financial intermediaries (data, in billions of dollars, relate to end of 1970)

TYPE	TOTAL ASSETS	PRINCIPAL TYPES OF INDIRECT SECURITIES ISSUED	AMOUNTS OUT-STANDING	PRINCIPAL TYPES OF DIRECT SECURITIES HELD
Commercial banks	$499.3	Demand deposits	$183.1	Loans and debt securities of many types
		Savings and time deposits	230.8	
Mutual savings banks	79.0	Savings and time deposits	71.6	Real-estate mortgages and corporate bonds
Savings and loan associations	176.6	Savings and loan shares	146.7	Mortgages
Credit unions	15.4	Saving deposits	15.4	Consumer loans
Life insurance companies	199.0	Life insurance and annuity policies	163.6	Mortgages on real estate and corporate bonds
Private pension funds	107.2	Pension fund reserves	107.2	Corporate bonds, stocks
Investment companies	47.6	Shares of stocks	47.6	Corporate stocks

SOURCE: *Federal Reserve Bulletin,* June, 1971, pp. A71–72.

Their earning assets are largely confined to debt obligations, a major part of which is of short-term and intermediate maturity, although some long-term mortgages and bonds are also included. The financial claims against themselves that they create and issue are largely in the form of deposit liabilities. Demand deposits are so safe and liquid and so widely used as a medium of payments that we include them in the money supply. Various types of savings and time-deposit liabilities are not used as a medium of payments, but are also highly safe and liquid. At most of the commercial banks, the first $20,000 of each account is insured by a federal agency, the Federal Deposit Insurance Corporation [FDIC].

Mutual savings banks. These institutions create and issue claims against themselves in the form of savings and time deposits very much like those of commercial banks. Most of these deposits are insured up to $20,000 for each account, some by the FDIC and some under other insurance arrangements. While the deposit liabilities of mutual savings banks are legally payable on short notice, and in practice are usually repaid when requested, their assets are predominantly of much longer maturity. Real-estate mortgages are the largest component, followed by corporate bonds and U.S. government securities.

Savings and loan associations. Once called "building and loan associations," these institutions are legally of two types. Stock savings and loan associations issue at least two types of claims against themselves—equity claims to their owners and deposit-debt claims to their creditors. In most cases, however, equity claims are very small relative to deposit claims. The other major type—the mutual savings and loan association—is a form of cooperative; it is owned by those who acquire claims against it. Legally, therefore, these claims are equity claims and are often called "shares." In practice, however, they are commonly considered to be the equivalent of deposit-debt claims. They are stated in fixed amounts of dollars, and associations strive to keep them redeemable at face value. Moreover, claims against most of the savings and loan associations are insured up to $20,000 per account by a federally sponsored agency, the Federal Savings and Loan Insurance Corporation (FSLIC).

Some claims against savings and loan associations are comparable to time deposits; they are payable at stated times, some in a year or less, others after a longer period. A larger part of them, however, are comparable to passbook savings deposits in that the association can require prior notice of intent to withdraw. In practice, associations commonly repay on request. Savings and loan associations constitute a prime example of creation of liquidity. While they issue claims against themselves legally payable on short notice and in practice commonly paid on request, their holdings of direct securities are predominantly in the form of mortgages on residential real estate, many of these mortgages being of very long maturity and low marketability.

Credit unions. These credit cooperatives issue what are in effect liquid savings deposit claims to their members. Credit unions' holdings of direct securities are largely in the form of consumer loans. Although credit unions have not yet amassed a great volume of assets, they have grown rapidly on the West Coast and in some other parts of the country during recent years.

Let us now look briefly at some other types of financial intermediaries that do not issue deposit-type claims, but do issue indirect securities with characteristics that differ significantly from those of the direct securities that they hold.

Life insurance companies. By far the most important intermediary in terms of total assets are life insurance companies. They gather funds by issuing claims against themselves in the form of life insurance and annuity policies. Most of these funds are used to acquire long-term direct securities in such forms as real-estate mortgages, corporate bonds and stocks, and government obligations.

Private pension funds. These funds are usually operated by private employers or by employers and employees jointly. Funds are acquired through contributions by employers, employees, or both, and claims for retirement pensions are issued to employees. These funds are used to acquire a wide range of long-term claims, including real-estate mortgages, corporate stocks and bonds, and some government obligations. Private pension funds are among the most rapidly growing financial intermediaries.

Investment companies. Investment companies, or investment trusts, issue ownership claims against themselves and use most of the proceeds to buy a diversified list of common stocks, although some also hold preferred stocks and debt obligations. The holder of investment company shares, therefore, has an equity claim against a diversified portfolio. In some cases, these shares are not redeemable by the investment company but can be bought and sold on a stock exchange or in over-the-counter markets. In other cases, the shares are redeemable on demand at a price equal to the asset value of the shares less a redemption fee.

The institutions described above are the most important of the privately owned financial intermediaries. By the early 1970s they had amassed well over a trillion dollars of assets. Among the other private intermediaries are fire and casualty insurance companies, consumer finance companies, and mortgage companies. Some financial intermediaries are sponsored by the federal government. These gather funds primarily by issuing debt claims against themselves, some of which are guaranteed by the government, and by borrowing from the U.S. Treasury, which in some cases gets the funds by issuing its own debt obligations. Among these intermediaries are: (1) The Government National Mortgage Association which purchases mortgages on residential real estate, (2) The Banks for Cooperatives which make both long-term and short-term loans to various types of farm cooperatives, and (3) The Federal Land Banks which extend long-term loans to farmers. An example of an international financial intermediary is the International Bank for Reconstruction and Development which sells debt claims against itself to investors in several countries and uses the proceeds to make loans in many nations to finance economic development. Still other types of intermediaries are likely to be invented in the future.

SOME PROBLEMS OF FINANCIAL INTERMEDIATION

Because of the very nature of their functions, financial intermediaries present problems of management and regulation. This is especially true of depository types of intermediaries. As we have seen, they issue claims against themselves that are fixed in terms of dollars and have maturities shorter than those of the direct securities that they hold. They "borrow short and lend long." This inevitably creates problems of maintaining solvency and liquidity without undue sacrifice of net income. There is risk that the intermediary will become insolvent—that the value of its assets will fall below the value of its liabilities. And there is risk of illiquidity, or inability to pay promptly and in full, even though the intermediary may be solvent if given a longer period in which to sell its assets.

Insolvency can arise in several ways. One is through a mismatching of types of assets acquired and types of indirect securities issued. For example, it is dangerous for a firm that issues claims fixed in terms of dollars to acquire large amounts of common stock in which prices fluctuate widely. But an intermediary may also become insolvent if its assets are largely in the form of longer-term debt claims, for these are subject to both default and market risks.

The management of an intermediary intent on earning net returns must inevitably assume some risks of insolvency and illiquidity; this is inherent in the nature of their operations. They may, however, take risks that prove to be embarrassing and even disastrous. Management is tempted to make the claims that it issues against itself more liquid in order to acquire more funds more cheaply. Also, it is often tempted to lengthen the maturity of its holdings of direct securities, or to acquire riskier securities, in order to increase its earnings. Moreover, it may be reluctant to forgo much income in order to buy liquidity in the form of money, which yields no explicit income, or highly liquid earning assets, on which the yield is sometimes low.

The management problem of arriving at an optimum balance of liquidity, safety, and income under conditions of uncertainty is indeed difficult. Excessive concentration on liquidity and safety can lower earnings so much as to render the intermediary incapable of attracting and retaining funds; the result may be death through starvation. Excessive concentration on current net earnings to the neglect of liquidity and safety can end in sudden disaster.

The practice of "borrowing short and lending long" also involves the risk that short-term interest rates may rise relative to the average rates earned by an intermediary on its portfolio. For example, in both 1966 and 1969, short-term rates rose sharply above current long-term rates and rose even more relative to the long-term rates that had prevailed during the preceding years. Savings and loan associations and some other intermediaries were faced with difficult choices. To attract new funds or even to avoid losing some of the funds already entrusted to them, they would have to raise the rates that they paid to make them competitive with yields on other comparable short-term assets. To do this would mean losses.

But not to do it would bring large withdrawals. In fact, they raised rates, but not enough to avoid a sharp decrease of inflows and, in some months, net withdrawals.

Government intervention

Because of problems such as these, the government has intervened in many ways to regulate and otherwise influence the creation and functioning of financial intermediaries. Later, we shall discuss in some detail government policies relative to commercial banks. Here it will be sufficient to mention a few of the most important government policies relative to intermediaries.

Portfolio regulation. Regulation of the composition of portfolios and types of claims issued can serve the useful purpose of achieving at least minimum standards of safety and liquidity of institutions through preventing serious mismatching of types of assets acquired and types of claims issued. However, unwise regulations or those that overstress safety and liquidity can jeopardize the growth of intermediaries and reduce their usefulness to the community. For example, if the intermediary is confined to only the safest types of securities, it will not be able to supply funds for useful purposes which necessarily involve risk; the supply of risk funds may be deficient. If the intermediary is largely confined to one type of security, such as home mortgages in the case of savings and loan associations, it is made heavily dependent on only one sector of the economy and prevented from adjusting its loans to changing patterns of demand. And if it is permitted to issue only illiquid types of claims, or claims that are unattractive to potential holders, it may not be able to compete effectively for funds.

Insurance of assets. Some types of assets owned by financial intermediaries are insured by the federal government or its agencies. The most important example is insurance of home mortgages by the Federal Housing Administration and the Veterans Administration. This has increased the liquidity and safety of these mortgages, enabled them to command greater marketability over wider areas, and added to the safety of intermediaries that hold them. Other examples are insurance of loans to farmers on commodities under price-support programs, of loans to contractors producing military supplies for the government, and of loans to finance exports.

Insurance of claims against financial intermediaries. As already indicated, individual accounts are insured by federal agencies up to $20,000 at most commercial banks, mutual savings banks, and savings and loan associations. This has increased the safety and liquidity of these claims, made them more attractive to holders, and enhanced the ability of these institutions to compete for funds. It has also enhanced the geographic mobility of funds; the most striking evidence of this is the ability of insured California savings and loan associations to attract funds from all parts of the country. These results could be enhanced if the $20,000 limit were removed and all deposit-type claims were fully covered by insurance. This proposal has met strong opposition, especially from institutions that believe they enjoy superior prestige. They argue that depositors would then rely on the insurance rather than the quality of the institution for safety, and that this would reduce the incentive for institutions to remain sound. And they deny that official supervision and examination would be adequate to assure soundness under these conditions. It is not clear, however, that this consideration should be allowed to outweigh the benefits of greater safety and geographic mobility of funds that would result from full insurance coverage.

Provision of "rediscount" facilities. Because of the very nature of their operations, involving the issue of claims more liquid than most of their assets, it is almost inevitable that financial intermediaries will, at least occasionally, encounter liquidity difficulties. That is, at some point they will find it difficult or impossible to meet current demands for payment out of their own assets or out of proceeds of loans from other private sources. In some cases, these liquidity difficulties have developed into broad crises and even panics.

It is because of such experiences that we now have federally sponsored institutions to provide liquidity to financial intermediaries by lending to them or by purchasing assets from them. The Federal Reserve supplies funds to the commercial banks that are members of the Federal Reserve System. The Federal Reserve can create the money that is supplied. The Federal Home Loan Banks supply funds to savings and loan associations and to certain other holders of home mortgages. The Federal Intermediate Credit Banks lend to holders of intermediate-term loans to farmers. These last two sets of institutions do not have the power to create money; they get it by selling debt claims against themselves.

The minimum function of these institutions is to assure that a solvent intermediary will not have to close for lack of liquidity. However, once established, they take on broader functions. For example, they provide funds to meet seasonal peaks of demand, to meet demands in areas of acute credit scarcity, and so on. There is no doubt that these federally sponsored sources of liquidity have facilitated growth of financial intermediaries and improved their functioning. However, the existing system is far from perfect. For one thing, many financial intermediaries are not assured access to funds from federally sponsored agencies. Some 7,500 state-chartered commercial banks have elected not to join the Federal Reserve and thus have no assured right to borrow from the Federal Reserve banks. Numbers of savings and loan associations and some mutual savings banks are also without such sources of liquidity. Most of these institutions have deliberately chosen not to meet the conditions required to gain access to such rediscount facilities; they argue that they will meet their liquidity needs out of their own assets or by borrowing from private sources, such as their correspondent banks. These uncovered institutions are a weak spot in the financial system; even if they do not themselves suffer, their customers and the economy may. They may be unable to meet seasonal and other needs of their customers, and their failure for lack of liquidity may harm the whole community. For reasons such as these, many economists believe that all financial intermediaries should be required to have access to funds from some government-sponsored agency, either the Federal Reserve or some other institution.

We find, then, that although some government policies may restrict the growth and functioning of intermediaries, others have been very helpful in this respect.

AN OVERVIEW OF THE FINANCIAL SYSTEM

Having looked at its various parts, we are now in a position to survey the American financial system as a whole. It includes three broad sets of elements.

1. Huge amounts of direct securities of widely varying characteristics issued not only by households, business firms, and governmental units but also by almost every other type of nonfinancial entity. Great stocks of these are outstanding at any point of time and large new issues are generated when the economy is operating near its capacity levels.

2. Market facilities for trading in securities—facilities for primary distribution of newly issued securities and secondary market facilities for trading in securities issued earlier. Many securities, whose issuers are well and favorably known, enjoy national and international markets in which they can be bought or sold quickly at competitive prices. At the other extreme, some securities are still confined to local markets. When they function efficiently, securities markets add significantly to the liquidity and safety of direct securities.

3. A wide variety of financial intermediaries which hold huge amounts of direct securities and issue huge amounts of indirect securities with characteristics differing significantly from those of the direct securities held. Depository types of intermediaries are outstandingly manufacturers of liquidity.

This complex financial system should be kept in mind as we continue our study of processes and institutions. To do so will facilitate understanding of the vital processes of saving, capital accumulation, and determination of the behavior of national income. To be sure, considerable amounts of investment are undertaken by ultimate savers who finance their investment out of their own current flows of saving, without recourse to any branch of the financial markets. However, much investment requires the creation of new securities or trading of old ones. Thus the saving–investment process involves transactions in financial markets; and the behavior of investment, and perhaps also of saving, depends in part on the behavior of prices and yields on securities.

In dealing later with the public's demand for money balances and its relationship to the behavior of spending flows, we shall argue that entities arrive at rational decisions concerning the sizes of the money balances that they will demand by comparing the marginal benefits of holding money with the marginal costs involved in forgoing holding of other assets, most of which yield explicit income. This chapter and the preceding one suggest the length and variety of the list of liquid assets that compete for places in the public's portfolios. As indicated in Table 4–2, the public can choose among money itself; highly liquid but income-yielding claims issued by many financial intermediaries of the depository type; and highly liquid short-term debt claims issued by many well-known and highly regarded governmental units, business firms, and others. In view of the wide availability of such substitutes, it is not surprising that quantities of money balances demanded depend in part on the level of yields on other assets.

Table 4–2 Principal types of liquid assets in the United States

MONEY	OTHER LIQUID CLAIMS AGAINST FINANCIAL INTERMEDIARIES	LIQUID DIRECT SECURITIES
Coins Paper money Checking deposits	Commercial-bank savings and time deposits Mutual savings-bank savings and time deposits Savings-and-loan-association shares Credit-union savings deposits	Treasury bills and other issues of the federal government with short maturities Short-term issues of some state and local governments Short-term commercial paper issued by finance companies and some nonfinancial corporations of high standing Other short-term claims against business firms of high standing

These facts are also relevant in many ways to the operations of the Federal Reserve and commercial banks.

1. The Federal Reserve wields its most powerful instrument for monetary management—open-market operations—by purchasing and selling in two branches of the over-the-counter market, the markets for government securities and acceptances.

2. Individual commercial banks do extend significant amounts of credit directly to their local customers. But they also have access to securities markets of national and even international scope, where they can buy and sell both newly issued and already-outstanding securities. This enables them to acquire securities of types not generated in their local markets and to diversify their portfolios. A large part of their liquidity needs are met by holding *secondary reserves,* which are liquid types of earning assets that gain much of their liquidity through the marketability provided by financial markets. These markets are also a major channel for the geographic mobility of bank funds.

3. As banks seek to acquire earning assets, they meet competition not only from ultimate owners of savings but also from a wide array of other financial intermediaries with huge assets.

4. The volume of demand deposits that the public is willing to hold depends in part on the volume and liquidity of other available claims and on the level of yields on these claims. Thus, when banks are prohibited from paying

interest on demand deposits, they can expect that the quantity of demand deposits demanded by the public will decline if interest rates on other assets rise.

5. In attempting to issue and keep outstanding savings- and time-deposit claims against themselves, commercial banks compete not only with direct securities of varying liquidity and yield, but also with claims issued by other financial intermediaries.

Selected readings

Baumol, W. J., *Portfolio Theory: The Selection of Asset Combinations,* New York, Mc-Caleb-Seiler Publishing Company, 1970.

Brill, D. H., and A. P. Ulrey, "The Role of Financial Intermediaries in U.S. Capital Markets," *Federal Reserve Bulletin,* January, 1967, pp. 18–31.

Goldsmith, R., *Financial Intermediaries in the American Economy Since 1900,* Princeton, N.J., Princeton University Press, 1958.

Gurley, J. G., and E. S. Shaw, *Money in a Theory of Finance,* Washington, D.C., Brookings Institution, 1960

Hester, D. D., and J. Tobin, *Financial Markets and Economic Activity,* New York, Wiley, 1967.

Markowitz, H. M., *Portfolio Selection,* New York, Wiley, 1959.

Moore, B. J., *Introduction to the Theory of Finance,* New York, Free Press, 1968.

Smith, P. F., *Economics of Financial Institutions and Markets,* Homewood, Ill., Irwin, 1971.

PART TWO

COMMERCIAL BANKING

CHAPTER 5

BANKING HISTORY OF THE UNITED STATES

Visitors to the United States are often puzzled by the complexity of the American banking system. In most countries there is a single central bank to perform the functions of monetary management; power to charter and regulate commercial banks is usually concentrated in the central government; and the commercial-banking system typically consists of no more than 20, and in many cases no more than 10, banks with numerous branches. Against such a background, the American system inevitably seems complex, if not confused and confusing. Here, there is not a single central bank but a central-banking system composed of the Board of Governors of the Federal Reserve System located in Washington, 12 separately incorporated Federal Reserve banks located in as many regions, and a total of 24 branches. Even at the federal level, jurisdiction over commercial banks is not concentrated in a single agency but divided among three—the Federal Reserve, the Comptroller of the Currency, and the Federal Deposit Insurance Corporation. Moreover, power to charter and regulate commercial banks is shared in complex and often overlapping ways among federal agencies and the various state governments. A visitor finds the number of separately incorporated commercial banks incomprehensibly large—over 13,700.

No wonder that the visitor asks in bewilderment, "How did it get that way, and why?" No one can understand this system without a knowledge of American banking history, which is closely interlinked with old and continuing political and economic controversies over such issues as the relative roles of the central and state governments in a federal system, concentration of economic and financial power, and conflicts between creditor and debtor areas. Our purpose in this chapter will not be to present a complete history of American banking, but rather to concentrate on those episodes, events, and forces which contribute most to an understanding of the present system and the forces precipitating and impeding change.

To bring out some of the major events in our banking history, we shall divide it into three main periods: (1) from 1781 to the establishment of the National Banking System in 1863; (2) from 1863 to the establishment of the Federal Reserve System in 1914; and (3) since 1914. Each of these periods will be further subdivided for more detailed analysis.

BANKING FROM 1781 TO 1863

In banking, as in most other aspects of American life, this early period from 1781 to 1863 was one of rapid development and widespread controversy. Having gained its independence, the new nation was struggling to determine its social, political, economic, and financial patterns. On all these matters, there were important differences of opinion. By far the largest part of the population lived on farms, most of which were largely self-sufficient; all except a few of the cities were small; manufacturing was still in its infancy; and trade occupied a far less important position than it does today. The nation had virtually no experience with banking of modern types, and there were wide disagreements concerning the contributions that banks could make. Some people were perhaps too laudatory, overestimating the extent to which banks could stimulate capital formation and promote productivity and trade by providing credit and a more generous supply of money in the form of bank notes and deposits. Others denied that banks were productive at all; instead, they insisted that banks merely lowered the quality of the nation's money because issues of bank notes and deposits drove out, or kept out, an equal value of good metallic coins. Alexander Hamilton and others who shared his goal of developing an industrial and commercial type of economy were generally favorably disposed toward banking, believing that banks were an essential part of such an economy. Thomas Jefferson and his sympathizers, who believed that the country should remain largely agricultural, were generally opposed to banks, at least partly because banking was closely related to industry and commerce. The Federalists and others who favored centralization of political power believed that the power to charter and supervise banks should be exclusively federal. They questioned the constitutionality of state activities in this field. On the other hand, the anti-Federalists and their friends, who opposed centralization of political power and championed states' rights, insisted that only the states had the power to create and supervise banks and that such federal activities were unconstitutional. Much of the banking controversy of the period is understandable only as a part of the broader controversy over industrialization versus agrarianism and centralization of political power versus states' rights.

It is important to remember also that bank notes were more important than deposits as means of payment until about the time of the Civil War. Checking deposits were used, especially in the cities, but they were not well suited to a predominantly agricultural country with few towns and slow travel and communication. In fact, during the Colonial period, the word "bank" meant "a batch of paper money." The first bank of a modern type in this country was the Bank of North America, which was established in Philadelphia in 1782 to aid in financing the Revolutionary War. The Bank of New York and the Bank of Massachusetts were established in 1784. These three were the only incorporated banks in the United States in 1790. There were, however, a few unincorporated or private banks, for under the common law everyone had a right to engage in banking as well as in other types of business. Only later, after 1800, did the states begin to limit banking by unincorporated firms.

The First Bank of the United States, 1791–1811

This bank, the first to be authorized by the federal government, received a 20-year charter in 1791. It had a capital stock of $10 million, of which $2 million was subscribed by the federal government with funds borrowed from the bank; the remainder was subscribed by private individuals, some of them residents of foreign countries. By today's standards it was a small bank; in its day it was huge. It was not only by far the largest bank of its day, but also the largest corporation in America. It established its head office in Philadelphia and branches in the other principal cities of the country: Boston, New York, Baltimore, Norfolk, Charleston, Savannah, and New Orleans. It was, in fact, a nationwide bank. Thus, the first federally chartered bank was a nationwide branch bank jointly owned by the federal government and private investors.

The bank made loans and purchased securities; issued both deposits and bank notes; transferred loan funds and payments from one end of the country to the other; and performed useful functions for the government in lending to it, acting as its depository, and transferring funds for it. It also performed some central banking functions, for it regulated the lending and note-issuing powers of state banks. As the largest bank in the system, its own lending policies greatly affected the reserves of other banks. When it expanded its loans, some of the proceeds flowed to other banks, thereby augmenting their reserves in the form of deposits at the First Bank, or gold and silver specie. When the First Bank contracted its loans, it drained reserves from the other banks and limited their lending ability. It could greatly affect their specie reserves and lending power by its disposal of their bank notes that came into its possession. By simply holding these notes or paying them out into circulation, it could permit the banks to retain their species reserves. But by presenting their notes to the issuing banks for redemption, the First Bank could decrease their species reserves. It was in the exercise of its central banking power, and especially in limiting the loans and note issues of state banks, that the First Bank made some of its bitterest enemies.

The First Bank seems to have functioned well, especially so when compared with other banks during the first half of the nineteenth century. Nevertheless, Congress refused to renew its charter when it expired in 1811. Several arguments against recharter were advanced:

1. Much of the bank stock was owned by foreigners. Some people feared that foreigners would exercise excessive control over our economy through the bank, although foreign stockholders had no vote; it was also argued that money was drained out of the country by the payment of dividends to foreign stockholders.

2. Only "hard money" was good money. A large part of the community was still opposed to paper money of any sort, whether issued by banks or by government.

3. The bank was unconstitutional. The Constitution contained no express provision for bank charters. The anti-Federalists contended that no such power was even implied and hence the bank had been unconstitutional from the beginning. Moreover, they feared that it would tend to centralize power in the federal government at the expense of the states, as its foremost proponent, Alexander Hamilton, hoped it would. It was frequently charged, apparently with some justice, that the bank was dominated by Federalists and that it discriminated against anti-Federalists in making loans.

4. The bank discouraged the growth of state banks. It is clear that the First Bank curbed the issue of state bank notes by presenting them regularly for redemption. Some elements of the community, including the owners and officers of state banks as well as other proponents of "easy money," wanted to eliminate the curbing effects of the bank.

Whatever the deciding motives of Congress in refusing its recharter, the First Bank of the United States expired in 1811.

State banking, 1811–1816

Freed from the restraining influence of the First Bank and favored by inflationary financing of the War of 1812, state banks went on a spree. They grew in number from 88 in 1811 to 246 in 1816, and their note issues rose from $45 million in 1812 to at least $100 million in 1817. Virtually all ceased to redeem their notes in gold or silver, and their notes depreciated by varying amounts; the notes of many banks became virtually worthless. All the banking abuses that we shall study later appeared during this period. It was largely because of these gross abuses of the banking privilege by state banks and because of the extreme disorder of the monetary system that the Second Bank of the United States was established in 1816.

The Second Bank of the United States, 1816–1836

The Second Bank of the United States received a 20-year charter from the federal government in 1816. In many respects it resembled the First Bank, but it was much larger and some of its charter provisions were different. Its capital was fixed at $35 million, of which one-fifth was to be subscribed by the federal government and paid for with its bonds. The remaining $28 million was subscribed by individuals, corporations, companies, and states, no one of whom was permitted to subscribe more than $300,000. At least one-fourth of these private subscriptions had to be paid in gold or silver; the remaining three-fourths could be paid in either specie or securities of the federal government. The bank was governed by a board of directors, of whom five were appointed by the President of the United States and 20 were elected by the private stockholders. The amount of property that the bank could hold was limited to $55 million, and its debts, excluding deposits but including bank notes, were limited to $35 million. These limitations did not prevent the bank from being a giant institution as compared with other firms of the period. It established 25 branches to serve all the settled parts of the country.

Like the First Bank, the Second Bank performed both commercial and central banking functions. As a commercial bank, it lent to individuals, business firms, states, and the federal government; it accepted deposits from individuals and business firms as well as from government units; it issued bank notes; it transferred funds from one area to another; and it engaged in foreign-exchange operations. It also performed various functions that are usually entrusted to a central bank. It held government deposits, acted as fiscal agent of the government, and transferred funds from area to area for government account. Moreover, it acted as a regulator of state banks, presenting their notes for redemption, insisting that they redeem their obligations promptly in specie, and limiting in general the amount of credit they created. This was one of the principal purposes for which the Second Bank was created.

By 1833, the Second Bank had become so unpopular with President Andrew Jackson and many of the Jacksonian Democrats that federal deposits were withdrawn from it and placed with selected state banks, and its charter was not renewed on its expiration in 1836. The country was to see no more federally chartered banks until 1863 and was not to have another central banking system until 1914.

To evaluate the success of the Second Bank and the wisdom of Jackson's action in abolishing it is still a difficult task, for most of the contemporary discussions were rabidly partisan, and even some present-day writers are inclined to be apologists for either the bank or Jackson. We shall, however, note some of the reasons for the refusal to recharter the bank. No special attention will be given to charges that it was grossly mismanaged. It is true that mismanagement did appear in its early years and that later the bank performed some of its functions unwisely, or at least clumsily. But the principal objections to it came from deeper sources.

1. Unconstitutionality. Although the power of the strict constructionists had diminished greatly, critics of the bank again alleged that the federal government had no constitutional power to charter a bank. It is unlikely, however, that these people would have raised the question of constitutionality if they had not opposed the bank on other grounds.

2. Opposition to paper money. "Hard-money" men such as Senator Benton opposed paper money of any kind and favored the exclusive use of gold and silver coin. They denied that banks could increase the total quantity of money in a country or that they could "quicken trade," and insisted that bank money merely drove out of circulation an equivalent amount of gold and silver.

3. Opposition by state banks. State banks, especially those that wanted to follow liberal ending and note-issue policies, were much opposed to the Second Bank. In the first place, the bank brought pressure on them to keep their notes redeemable in specie and to limit the quantity of their notes to the amount that they could redeem at par. This had the obvious effect of limiting state-bank earnings. In the second place, the Second Bank competed with state banks in making loans; not only did it take loan business away from state banks, but it also reduced interest rates in some areas, for its discount rate was limited to 6 percent. And in the third place, some state banks, especially those in New York, wanted the large volume of federal government deposits that the Second Bank enjoyed. This opposition by state banks was a potent factor in the Second Bank's undoing.

4. Opposition by others who favored easy-money policies. Realizing that the Second Bank tended to restrict the total amount of money created and the total volume of loans extended by banks, many businessmen, landowners, potential land speculators, and others who felt they would benefit by easier money, worked for the abolition of the bank.

5. Opposition to the concentration of financial and economic power. We have already mentioned that the Second Bank was a giant institution during the period in which it operated. It held about one-third of all the banking assets of the country and was probably larger than any other business firm. Its critics insisted that a free people could ill afford to grant such power to any small group, because with this financial power went the ability to determine the life and death of banks and other business enterprises, the level of employment and prosperity, and even the political freedom of the people. Such critics repeatedly asserted that concentration of economic power in the hands of a few was incompatible with political democracy.

6. Political activity by the bank. Although some attempts were made to secure members of both political parties as directors and officers of the bank, it was well known that the large majority of those in control were opposed to Jackson and his party. Moreover, some of these men were aggressive in their political activities. It is difficult to discover the extent to which the bank's officers

took the political initiative and to what extent their activities were merely defenses against earlier attacks on the bank. But it seems certain that the bank did enter the political arena and that at least some of its branch managers used their lending power to influence votes. The fate of the bank was sealed when its president, Nicholas Biddle, openly but vainly opposed Jackson's reelection in 1832 and made the recharter of the bank one of the principal issues of the presidential campaign. A diplomatic president of the Second Bank might have been able to arrive at a satisfactory *modus vivendi* with the choleric President Jackson. But Biddle was not such a man. "Nicholas Biddle was a man of intense energy, autocratic in temper, and possessing supreme confidence in his own judgment. It was inevitable that he should rule and not merely reign, and the proofs that he did rule are observable everywhere."[1] The inevitable clash between Biddle and Jackson may have altered the entire course of our banking history.

Was President Jackson right in refusing to recharter the Second Bank in 1836? A full answer to this question would require far more space than we can devote to it. Two facts now seem clear, however. In the first place, it is questionable public policy to grant central-banking powers to a corporation which is largely owned and controlled by private individuals and corporations, which is operated by its owners primarily for profit, and which as a profit-seeking enterprise has interests in conflict with those of the banks that it regulates. We now recognize that central banking is a governmental function that can be properly exercised only by institutions with a primary motive that is not profits but financial and economic stabilization. A properly managed central bank must often follow policies that will decrease its profits. In the second place, it is quite clear that the abolition of the Second Bank without establishing another institution to assume its functions was a major blunder. It ushered in a generation of banking anarchy and monetary disorder.

State banking, 1836–1863

From the lapse of the Second Bank's charter in 1836 until the establishment of the National Banking System in 1863, our banking system was made up exclusively of private (unincorporated) banks and of banks operating under corporate charters granted by the various states. We shall not discuss the unincorporated banks except to say that, as a group, they seem to have been neither significantly better nor significantly worse than the incorporated banks as a group. The incorporated banks, operating under widely diverse state laws, varied from good to very bad. Some performed their functions satisfactorily, especially toward the end of the period. At the other extreme, many engaged in practically all the banking abuses known to man.

Prior to 1837, a bank could secure a corporate charter from a state only by a special legislative act. This method of granting bank charters gradually fell into

[1] Davis R. Dewey, *The Second Bank of the United States,* Senate Document No. 571, Washington, D.C., U.S. Government Printing Office, 1912, p. 263.

disfavor for several reasons. It injected banks into politics and politics into banks. Loyal members of the political party in power might receive a bank charter, whereas members of the minority party had little chance of success. The controversy over bank charters threatened to corrupt state governments. Legislators were offered large sums of money to grant new charters and other large sums by existing banks to reject the applications of potential competitors. Furthermore, this method of granting charters often gave monopoly power to the favored banks. This was considered objectionable, both because of its alleged unfairness to those who wished to become bankers and because it was believed to restrict the total amount of credit granted, thereby impeding the economic expansion of the country.

To remedy this situation, Michigan in 1837 and New York in 1838 enacted "free-banking laws." Most of the other states later enacted laws of the same general type. These laws ended the practice of granting charters by special legislative act and provided that anyone might secure a corporate charter and engage in banking by complying with the provisions of a general bank-incorporation law. Banking was made "free" to all enterprisers who met the specified general requirements. The quality of state banks came to depend on how appropriate these general requirements were and on how well they were enforced. In some states, the requirements were strict; banks could issue notes only by depositing with a state official an equivalent amount of high-quality bonds and by meeting adequate capital and reserve requirements. But in the majority of states, the collateral requirements for notes were hopelessly inadequate, and capital and reserve requirements were virtually meaningless.

The relationships between banks and the states varied widely. At one extreme, the banks merely received their charters from the state; they secured all their capital from private sources and made any loans that were permitted within the broad framework of the banking laws. At the other extreme, many banks were wholly owned and operated by states. There were several variations between these two extremes. Thus, some banks were owned jointly by a state and private investors. Others had to pay large sums to the state for the privilege of banking. And still others were permitted to act as banks only if they would lend stipulated amounts to canal companies, railroads, or other enterprises considered meritorious by the state legislature. In a period when "capital" was still scarce, states encouraged and even forced banks to lend large amounts for financing selected projects.

Abuses by the state-chartered banks before the Civil War

Without inferring that all the banks were guilty, we shall now investigate the principal banking abuses during this period. These abuses were so widespread that they greatly influenced both public attitudes toward banks and subsequent banking legislation. Some of the most serious abuses were the following:

1. Violent fluctuations in the amount of money created by the banks in the form of bank notes and checking deposits. With the transfer of federal deposits

from the Second Bank to selected state banks and the removal of the moderating hand of the Second Bank, both the number of state banks and the volume of their credit increased. This is shown in Table 5–1.

Table 5–1 State banks, 1834–1861

YEAR	NUMBER OF STATE BANKS	STATE BANK NOTES OUT-STANDING (MILLIONS)	DEPOSITS AT STATE BANKS (MILLIONS)	TOTAL STATE BANK NOTES AND DEPOSITS (MILLIONS)
1834	506	$ 95	$ 76	$171
1835	704	104	83	187
1836	713	140	115	255
1837	788	149	127	276
1838	829	116	85	201
1839	840	135	90	225
1840	901	107	76	183
1841	784	107	65	172
1842	692	84	62	146
1843	691	59	56	115
1844	696	75	85	160
1845	707	90	88	178
1846	707	106	97	203
1847	715	106	92	198
1848	751	129	103	232
1849	782	115	91	206
1850	824	131	110	241
1851	879	155	129	284
1852	815	161	137	298
1853	750	146	146	292
1854	1,208	205	188	393
1855	1,307	187	190	377
1856	1,398	196	213	409
1857	1,416	215	230	445
1858	1,422	155	186	341
1859	1,476	193	260	453
1860	1,562	207	254	461
1861	1,601	202	257	459

SOURCE: Board of Governors of the Federal Reserve System, *Banking Studies,* Washington, D.C., 1941, pp. 417–418.

This growth was far from steady, however. The banks would expand rapidly for a time and then undergo severe contraction. The principal expansions and contractions during this period are shown in Table 5–2, although the data are admittedly imperfect. Business activity and prices fluctuated widely as banks alternated between: (a) inflationary periods of increased money supplies and liberal loans and (b) periods of shrinking money supplies and reduced loans. The banks' policies were not the sole causes of these fluctuations, but they were unquestionably contributory factors.

Table 5–2 Principal expansions and contractions of state bank notes and deposits, 1834–1860

	PERCENTAGE EXPANSION (+), OR CONTRACTION (−)		
PERIOD	BANK NOTES	BANK DEPOSITS	TOTAL NOTES AND DEPOSITS
1834–1837	+ 56	+ 67	+ 61
1837–1843	− 60	− 56	− 58
1843–1848	+119	+ 84	+102
1848–1849	− 11	− 12	− 11
1849–1854	+ 78	+107	+ 91
1854–1855	− 9	+ 2	− 4
1855–1857	+ 15	+ 21	+ 18
1857–1858	− 28	− 19	− 24
1858–1860	+ 36	+ 37	+ 36

SOURCE: Derived from data in Table 5–1.

2. Inadequate bank capital. Using all the devices described earlier, many banks failed to maintain large enough capital accounts to protect their creditors. Some made no pretense of having adequate capital. Others had a large enough nominal capital, but it was paid for with the promissory notes of the stockholders, many of whom were unable to meet their obligations. Even when bank stocks were initially paid for with gold or silver, stockholders often borrowed back the coin, giving in return their doubtful paper. Furthermore, bank capital was frequently dissipated by excessive dividend payments.

3. Risky and illiquid loans. Many of the banks made highly risk and highly speculative loans without regard for the safety of their creditors, and some lent excessively to their own stockholders and officers. Moreover, many of the loans were highly illiquid. This was especially true of the banks' large loans on real estate, much of which was not in use but was being held for speculative purposes. This combination of inadequate bank capital and highly risky and illiquid loans could lead to but one result: numerous bank failures and serious losses to noteholders and depositors.

4. Inadequate reserves against notes and deposits. In certain of the state banking laws the reserve requirements were either wholly absent or very inadequate, and evasions of existing requirements were widespread. Many banks issued large quantities of notes and deposits with little or no regard for their reserve situation and with little ability to redeem their obligations on demand.

As a result of all these abuses—excessive issues of bank notes, inadequate bank capital, risky and illiquid bank assets, and highly inadequate reserves—bank notes had widely differing values. The notes of some banks were freely redeemed in gold and silver and circulated at their face value. Others circulated at small but varying discounts; still others circulated at only a small percentage of their face value; and many became completely worthless. A "know-your-money" campaign would have been an utter failure in this period.

State bank notes in this period may be divided into four main categories: (1) genuine notes of banks still in operation, (2) genuine notes of failed banks, (3) genuine notes whose denominations had been raised, and (4) counterfeits. The genuine notes of banks still in operation varied greatly in value—for example, around the year 1860 such notes were issued by nearly 1,600 banks operating under the widely diverse laws of some 30 states. Even the banks in a given state varied widely in quality. Some, as we have seen, issued their notes in moderation and redeemed them freely in specie. Others issued notes in great quantity, with virtually no assets behind them, and then employed ingenious devices to avoid redeeming them. For example, an enterpriser would secure a bank charter, pledge virtually worthless securities as collateral for a large volume of bank notes, set up a banking "office" in a remote swamp, put the notes into circulation, and use various ruses to keep his location secret. Only later would some innocent recipient of the bank's notes find that they were virtually worthless.

The period was a counterfeiter's paradise. Each of the hundreds of banks issued notes of its own design and in many denominations; the notes were made of many kinds of paper, mostly of low quality; the workmanship on the genuine notes was usually poor; and no one could be familiar with all the bank notes outstanding. Under these conditions, it was easy to raise the denomination of genuine notes and to issue counterfeits on existent or even nonexistent banks. "Bicknall's Counterfeit Detector and Bank-Note List" of January 1, 1839, contains the names of "54 banks that had failed at different times; of 20 fictitious banks, the pretended notes of which are in circulation; of 43 banks besides, for the notes of which there is no sale; of 254 banks, the notes of which have been counterfeited or altered; and 1,395 descriptions of counterfeited or altered notes [then] supposed to be in circulation, from one dollar to five hundred."[2] That these conditions had not been remedied by 1858 is indicated by the fact that Nicholas's *Bank Note Reporter* gave 5,400 separate descriptions of counterfeit, altered, and spurious notes. There were 30 different counterfeit issues of the Bank of Delaware notes.[3]

The numerous "counterfeit detectors and bank-note reporters" that attempted to warn against counterfeits and to indicate the current values of the various bank notes were of only limited assistance. Even with their supplements they were often out of date, they were beyond the reach of small tradesmen and individuals, and they could not remove the confusion in trade resulting from the fact that the price charged for an article depended on the type of bank note with which payment was to be made.

Although banking abuses during this period were widespread, we must not leave the impression that all state banks were unsound. Some states, notably New York, Massachusetts, and Louisiana, enacted highly protective banking laws and implemented them with bank supervision and examinations. In fact, some of

---

[2] Raguet, quoted by Horace White, *Money and Banking*, Boston, Ginn, 1896, pp. 403–404.
[3] *Ibid.*, p. 398.

these laws, especially those of New York, contributed much to the legislation establishing the National Banking System.

Moreover, it should not be concluded without investigation and analysis that banks that "play it safe" are always more socially beneficial than those that assume large risks in both the types and amounts of their loans. On the one hand, we want banks to be safe, we do not want them to fail, and we want them to keep their bank notes and deposits continuously at parity with other types of money. On the other hand, we want banks to stand ready to finance productive projects, some of which are inherently risky. It may well be that some of the banks that made highly risky loans contributed more to American economic development and growth than some that were overly concerned with safety. It is not always easy to find an optimum balance of these objectives.

THE NATIONAL BANKING SYSTEM, 1863–1914

In 1863, just 27 years after the expiration of the Second Bank of the United States, the federal government again entered the banking field by passing "An Act to provide a national currency, secured by a pledge of United States Stocks, and to provide for the Circulation and Redemption thereof." The 1863 law, which contained a large number of imperfections, was replaced by a new law in 1864. This latter is usually referred to as the National Banking Act.

In providing for a new system of national (federally chartered) banks to be owned and operated by private individuals, Congress had two principal motives: (1) to replace the unsound and unsafe state banking system with new banks that would issue safe and uniform currency, and (2) to secure a new source of loans with which to finance the Civil War. Ever since the demise of the Second Bank, there had been widespread demands for banking reform, and many contended that a satisfactory system of note issue could be achieved only with centralized control and uniform notes. This demand was not successful, however, until reinforced by the exigencies of Civil War finance. Secretary Chase and others believed that they could create an additional market for government bonds by permitting the creation of new banks that could issue notes only on the basis of their holdings of these securities. Thus, the national banking system owes its birth to the demand for safer types of bank money and to the financial embarrassment of the Treasury. But it proved more useful as a means of banking reform than as a source of Civil War funds.

Principal provisions of the National Banking Act

We have already said that the National Banking Act owed much to earlier state banking laws, especially those of New York. The new law provided for "free banking." Anyone meeting the general requirements of the Act was to receive a charter and permission to engage in banking. A new office, the Comptroller of the Currency, was created in the Treasury Department to grant charters and to administer all laws relating to national banks. Some of the principal provisions regulating the establishment and operation of national banks were the following:

1. Capital. To enhance bank safety, several capital requirements were imposed. Minimum capital requirements were fixed as follows:

> $ 50,000 in cities of not over 6,000 inhabitants
> $100,000 in cities with from 6,000 to 50,000 inhabitants
> $200,000 in cities with over 50,000 inhabitants[4]

At least 50 percent of the subscribed capital had to be paid in before a bank could begin business, and the remainder had to be paid within five months. The stock was subject to double liability. In order to expand the market for government securities, each bank was required to deliver to the Treasury of the United States registered bonds amounting to not less than $30,000, or one-third of its capital stock, whichever was larger.[5] These bonds could be used as collateral for issues of national bank notes.

2. Regulation of bank loans. In order to promote safety and liquidity, many restrictions were placed on bank assets. Each national bank was forbidden to lend on real estate or to lend any one borrower an amount exceeding 10 percent of its capital stock.

3. Supervision and examination. In order to ensure compliance with both the letter and the spirit of the Act, national banks were required to supply the Comptroller of the Currency with periodic reports on their financial condition and were made subject to examination by his representatives.

4. Reserve requirements against notes and deposits. In order to enhance bank liquidity and limit the amount of bank money, minimum reserve requirements were specified for both circulating notes and deposits. Banks in reserve and central reserve cities were required to hold reserves of 25 percent and banks in other cities reserves of 15 percent of their outstanding circulating notes and deposits. In 1874, national banks were relieved of the necessity of carrying reserves against their note issues.

5. Protection to note holders. Remembering the sorry record of state bank notes, the framers of the National Banking Act were determined that national bank notes should be perfectly safe. To this end, the Act provided that:

(a) These notes could be issued only against United States government bonds deposited with the Comptroller of the Currency, the amount of notes not to exceed 90 percent of the par value of the bonds or 90 percent of the market value of the bonds, whichever was smaller.

(b) The issuing bank should maintain a redemption fund with the Comptroller equal to 5 percent of its outstanding notes, although this could be counted as part of the bank's required reserve.

---

[4] From 1900 to 1933 the minimum capital requirement was only $25,000 in places with not more than 3,000 inhabitants. This was reestablished at $50,000 in 1933.

[5] This requirement that national banks buy government securities was modified toward the end of the century and dropped after 1900. The double liability was repealed during the depression of the 1930s.

(c) In case a national bank refused to redeem its notes, the Comptroller might sell the pledged bonds and use the proceeds to pay note holders, any remaining claims of note holders to constitute a first claim against the assets of the bank.
(d) No national bank might issue notes in amounts exceeding its capital stock.
(e) The total circulation of national bank notes should not exceed $300 million (this limitation was later revised and was wholly removed after 1875).
(f) Each national bank should accept the notes of every other national bank at par.

Thus, every effort was made to insure the safety and parity of value of national bank notes. In these respects the Act was successful.

State banks

It was hoped that the authorization of national banks would induce state banks to take out federal charters and comply with the requirements of the National Banking Act. When it became evident that few state banks were going to do this, Congress decided to force the issue by levying a 10 percent tax on any bank or individual paying out or using state bank notes. The purpose was to end the issuance of circulating notes by state banks and to force all or most of these banks to become national banks or to cease doing a general banking business. As shown in Table 5-3, the Act did succeed in reducing the number of state banks from 1,089

Table 5-3 State and national banks in the United States, 1864–1914

YEAR	STATE BANKS	NATIONAL BANKS
1864	1,089	467
1868	247	1,640
1870	325	1,612
1880	650	2,076
1890	2,250	3,484
1900	5,007	3,731
1910	14,348	7,138
1914	17,498	7,518

SOURCE: Board of Governors of the Federal Reserve System, *Banking Studies,* Washington, D.C., 1941, p. 418.

in 1864 to 247 in 1868. After 1868, however, the number of state banks again began to expand, and by 1914 they outnumbered national banks by more than two to one.

How were state banks able not only to survive but even to expand greatly in spite of the prohibitive tax on their notes? The first and foremost reason was that note issue had become of much less importance in banking. With the growth of cities and more rapid transportation and communication, people used checking deposits more and more as a means of payment. With the privilege of creating checking deposits, a bank could now operate successfully without issuing notes. But why did many banks prefer to operate under state rather than federal charters when national banks also had the right to create circulating notes? The answer is to be found largely in the fact that many states imposed less rigid restrictions and granted more liberal powers than those contained in the National Banking Act. In general, state banking laws provided lower capital requirements, lower reserve requirements, less supervision by the government, more liberal powers to lend on real estate, greater ability to accept drafts drawn on a bank, and more power to engage in fiduciary activities, such as operating trust departments. This was especially true in the western and southern states, where many of the state banks were located.

Shortcomings of the national banking system

Although the national banking system unquestionably greatly improved the general quality of banking, the system became subject to increasing criticism. Demands for further bank reform swelled during the late years of the nineteenth century and grew still more in the first years of the twentieth, finally ushering in the Federal Reserve System in 1914. Although many aspects of national banks were criticized, the greatest complaint was against their "inflexibility," or "inelasticity." The keynote of the National Banking Act was safety, especially safety of national bank notes. Less attention was paid to the safety of deposits. Critics now complained that the system was too inflexible and that it must be given a greater degree of "elasticity." The meaning of this term was often unclear, but we can discover its general import as we proceed.

Although national bank notes were safe, there was no provisions for appropriate variations in their quantity over the long run, in response to seasonal variations in the need for them, and during crisis periods. We have already seen that these notes could be issued only on the basis of federal bonds, the amount of notes being limited to 90 percent of the par or market value (whichever was lower) of the bonds deposited with the Comptroller. Thus, the supply of national bank notes depended on the government bond market. The supply obviously could not exceed 90 percent of the eligible bonds outstanding. Within this limit, the quantity of notes actually issued by banks depended on the profitability of issuing them. When government bonds could be purchased at or below par, a relatively large volume of national bank notes was issued, since a bank could issue notes equal to 90 percent of the purchase cost of the bonds. But the profitability of issuing notes was decreased, and in some cases eliminated, as the market price of bonds rose above their par value. It was for these reasons that the volume of national bank notes outstanding fell from $352 million in 1882 to $162 million in 1891, a reduction of 54 percent. But they had risen to $175 million by 1914. Critics maintained that a note system of this type based on the government bond market could never supply a properly "elastic" currency that would respond properly to the needs of business. The volume of these notes fluctuated, but not necessarily in ways that were appropriate to economic needs.

National bank notes were also criticized for their lack of seasonal elasticity. The demand for currency for hand-to-hand use showed marked seasonal variations, reaching peaks in the early autumn and around Christmas and dropping to lower levels during other seasons. Yet the volume of outstanding national bank notes remained relatively constant throughout the year; hence, banks could meet seasonal peak demands for currency only by draining funds from their reserves, and the inflow of currency to the banks during slack seasons increased their reserves. Critics complained that the seasonal inelasticity of national bank notes was responsible for seasonal credit stringencies because it forced banks to draw down their reserves to meet peak seasonal demands for cash, and then led to an undue easing of credit in other seasons as currency flowed back into bank reserves. They demanded the creation of a currency that would be seasonally elastic, that would increase and decrease with seasonal demands for coin and currency and would leave bank reserves unaffected.

Critics also complained of the inelasticity of national bank notes during banking crises. They pointed out that there was no existing way in which new currency could be created to satisfy general demands on the banks for cash, and that banks could not meet these demands out of the limited cash in their vaults. They proposed the authorization of a new type of currency whose quantity could be increased to meet crisis demands and then be decreased again as demands for cash subsided. We shall see later that one of the principal purposes of the Federal Reserve Act of 1914 was to supply an elastic currency in the form of Federal Reserve notes.

The disturbing effects of an inelastic bank-note system were intensified by a defective system of reserve requirements. We have already seen that national banks were required to maintain reserves against both notes and deposits (later, against deposits only) equal to 25 percent in central reserve and reserve cities and 15 percent in other places. The banks in a few of the largest cities such as New York, Chicago, and St. Louis, were designated as "central reserve city banks"; those in 47 other cities, as "reserve city banks"; and those in other places, as "country banks." This general classification of banks for the purpose of fixing reserve requirements was carried over into the Federal Reserve Act. Although these reserve requirements appeared large, the form of reserves was defective, as is suggested by the following summary:

TYPE OF BANK	PERCENTAGE RESERVE REQUIREMENT	COMPOSITION OF REQUIRED RESERVES
Country banks	15	Two-fifths of reserve (or 6% of deposits) as cash in vault; remaining three-fifths of reserve (9% of deposits) to be either cash in vault or deposits with reserve city or central reserve city banks
Reserve city banks	25	One-half of reserve (12.5% of deposits) as cash in vault; remaining one-half of reserve (12.5% of deposits) as either cash in vault or deposits in central reserve city banks
Central reserve city banks	25	All cash in vault

This reserve system had three principal weaknesses. The first drawback was that a large part of the nominal reserve was "fictitious" in the sense that it was not available for meeting actual cash drains from the banking system. This was because such a large part of the reserves was in the form of deposit claims against other banks, which in turn held only a small percentage of actual cash as a reserve against their deposit obligations. Suppose, for example, that customers of country banks should demand large amounts of coin or currency. Holding an actual cash reserve equal to only 6 percent of their deposits, the country banks would call on the reserve city banks to send them cash. But the reserve city banks held a reserve equal to only 25 percent of their total deposits, only half of the reserve being in actual cash. To meet the drain, they in turn would call on central reserve city banks for cash; but these banks had reserves equal to only 25 percent of their deposits. Thus, the central reserve and the reserve city banks were in a precarious position; they were liable to drains not only by their own customers, but by all the banks that held "reserves" in the form of deposits with them. The threat of general cash withdrawals by the public or of a suspension of cash payments by the banks in large cities could therefore initiate a banking panic, or at least a general tightening of credit, because it would lead country banks to withdraw their "reserves" from reserve city and central reserve city banks in order to hold their reserves in the form of cash in their own vaults, and the reserve city banks would make similar withdrawals from the central reserve city banks. It is no wonder that the national banking system was susceptible to panics.

The second weakness of the system was that reserve requirements were very inflexible. Each bank was ordered to meet its reserve requirements at all times; it could not legally make any new loans while its reserves were deficient. Thus, when banks had loaned the maximum amount permitted by their reserves, and especially when their reserves had decreased, new lending was suddenly stopped and a scramble to liquidate loans was likely to occur. There arose a general demand that reserve requirements be relaxed by being suspended in periods of crisis or at least by banks' being allowed to meet these requirements on the average over a period of time, deficiencies at one time being balanced by overages at another. This latter method is employed for banks that are members of the Federal Reserve System.

The third shortcoming, which was widely criticized, was the "parcelation of reserves" resulting from the lack of any orderly way of pooling the reserves of individual banks to meet drains of cash from any segment of the banking system. Some compared existing reserve requirements with attempts to fight fires by placing a pail of water in each house; the greater effectiveness of pooling the water and providing a system of pipes to concentrate it at the point of need is obvious. Advocates of bank reform proposed the establishment of a similar system of pooling individual bank reserves so that they could be concentrated at the points of greatest need in time of emergency. This was another purpose of the Federal Reserve Act of 1914.

The inelasticity of national bank notes and the defects, or at least the inadequacy, of bank reserve requirements were dramatized by the recurrent banking panics that occurred under the national banking system before 1914. There were full-fledged panics in 1873, 1884, 1893, and 1907; and serious credit stringencies threatened at other times. Unable to meet their obligations to pay cash on demand, most banks suspended payments for periods of varying lengths; some of them never reopened, a mad scramble to call loans ensued, and business activity suffered. The panic of 1907 was the last straw; popular disgust with recurrent panics made the Federal Act politically possible although the act had objectives beyond the prevention of panics.

BANKING SINCE 1914

The Federal Reserve System

The establishment of the Federal Reserve System in 1914 is one of the great landmarks in American banking history. Then, more than 75 years after the demise of the Second Bank of the United States, the nation again had a set of institutions capable of exercising central-banking powers. We shall see later (1) how the Federal Reserve began with the rather limited objectives of using its powers to create currency and bank reserves, to provide "elasticity," and to prevent or deal with banking crises and panics; and (2) how its objectives became increasingly ambitious, so that it now engages in continuous monetary management to promote selected national objectives.

When the Federal Reserve was established another one of its objectives was to bring under some degree of federal supervision and examination a large percentage of the 18,000 state-chartered banks then in existence. The quality of state regulation of these banks varied from very good to lax and ineffective. However, state-chartered banks were not required, as were the national banks, to join the Federal Reserve and comply with its requirements and regulations. Advocates of states' rights saw to that. In the end, state banks were permitted to join if they wished to do so and could meet entrance requirements. Optimists hoped that a large percentage of these banks would find membership so attractive that they would join voluntarily. This hope has been largely disappointed. At no time have as many as 25 percent of all state banks been members of the Federal Reserve. From 1914 to 1935, the great majority of state banks were not subject to regulation or examination by any federal agency; and large numbers of them were in states where regulation was most lax and ineffective.

The Federal Deposit Insurance Corporation

Another landmark in banking history was the establishment of the Federal Deposit Insurance Corporation following the great surge of bank failures in the early 1930s. A temporary plan was adopted in 1933, which was superseded by a permanent plan in 1935. Initially, the FDIC insured the first $5,000 of each deposit account in an insured bank, but the limit was later raised in several steps to $20,000, where it now stands. For this insurance, the FDIC charges member banks a small annual premium based on the total volume of deposits.

The FDIC has three major purposes:

1. To protect depositors, and especially small depositors, against loss.

2. To protect banks and the economic system as a whole against the results of actual and threatened withdrawals of currency from the banking system. Such currency drains, actual and potential, had been a powerful deflationary force in the early 1930s. Actual currency drains had reduced bank reserves and put banks under pressure to reduce both the volume of credit extended and the money supply. And the fear of further large drains of currency motivated banks to hold idle reserves rather than expand their loans to the maximum. Thus, an insurance system that maintains confidence in the safety of deposits can increase the effectiveness of monetary management, both by protecting banks against reserve losses through currency withdrawals and by encouraging banks to utilize available reserves as a basis for loan and deposit creation.

3. To improve the quality of bank supervision. One might have thought that this objective would have led Congress to require all banks to join the FDIC and become subject to its examination and supervision. But again the advocates of states' rights in banking were victorious. Only members of the Federal Reserve are required to join the FDIC; state banks that are not members of the Federal Reserve have the option. In fact, however, all except about 180 nonmember banks have elected to join in order to get the competitive benefits of deposit insurance.

With the establishment of the FDIC, responsibility for regulating the structure and practices of the banking system became even more widely diffused. Banking commissioners in the 50 states retain power to charter, examine, and supervise state banks in their respective areas. Responsibility at the federal level is not concentrated. The Comptroller of the Currency continues to be empowered to charter, examine, and supervise national banks. The Federal Reserve is empowered to examine and supervise all national banks and state member banks. The FDIC is empowered to examine and supervise all its members, which include all members of the Federal Reserve and some 7,700 nonmember state banks. And, for good measure, the antitrust division of the Department of Justice sometimes intervenes when issues relating to monopoly are involved. Fortunately, there is a considerable degree of cooperation among these agencies. One should not be surprised to hear, however, that there is also competition, conflict, lack of uniformity, and at times even lack of common purpose.

The commercial-banking structure

The commercial-banking structure has undergone sweeping changes during this century, and especially since World War I. Table 5–4 presents relevant data.

A significant change in the commercial-bank structure has been the wide fluctuation in the number of banks. Between 1900 and 1920, the number of banks more than tripled, reaching a peak of more than 29,000. By 1940, toward the end of the Great Depression, it had declined by more than half, falling to 14,344. Since that time it has fluctuated more narrowly, declining a little during the earlier part of the period and showing a slight increase more recently.

Table 5–4 Number of U.S. commercial banks and branch offices on selected dates (end-of-year figures)

YEAR	TOTAL NUMBER OF BANKS	NUMBER OF BANKS WITH BRANCHES	TOTAL NUMBER OF BRANCHES
1900	8,738	87	119
1920	29,087	530	1,281
1930	22,172	751	3,522
1940	14,344	954	3,525
1950	14,121	1,291	4,721
1960	13,472	2,329	10,216
1970	13,688	3,994	21,424

SOURCE: Board of Governors of the Federal Reserve System, *Banking and Monetary Statistics,* Washington, D.C., 1943; *Federal Reserve Bulletin,* various issues.

The organizational structure of the banking system has also undergone, and is still experiencing, great changes, with a strong secular trend toward "multiple-office banking." From an organizational point of view, there are four types of banks:

1. Unit banks. A unit bank is a banking corporation that operates only a single office. An "independent" unit bank is one that is not controlled by an entity that controls any other bank. Most unit banks are independent. However, as will be seen later, some unit banks are controlled by entities that also control at least one other bank.

2. Branch banks. A branch bank is a banking corporation that directly owns and operates two or more banking offices.

3. "Group," or holding company banking. This refers to arrangements under which a corporation has ownership control of two or more separately incorporated banks, which are called its "subsidiaries." The latter may be either unit banks or branch banks. Note that when a bank is acquired by a holding company it continues its corporate existence.

4. Chain banks. This refers to situations in which two or more separately incorporated banks, which may be either unit banks or branch banks, are controlled by the same natural person or group of natural persons. Information concerning the extent of chain banking is quite limited, partly because of the difficulty of determining the degree of interlocking ownership required to establish effective control. It is known, however, that chain banking is important in some areas, such as the midwest, but that it is much less extensive than group banking. We shall say no more about chain banking. The following paragraphs will deal only with unit and branch banking; group banking will be discussed later.

During this century there have been large increases in both the number of banks operating branches and the total number of branches. In 1900, the United States had overwhelmingly a unit-banking system; of the 8,738 banks at that time, only 87 had even one branch office, and the total number of branches was only 119. In 1920, only 530 of the 29,087 banks operated one or more branches, and the total number of branches was 1,281. Since then, branch banking has continued to grow, interrupted only during the Great Depression of the 1930s. Growth has been especially rapid since World War II. For example, between 1950 and 1970, the number of banks operating branches increased from 1,291 to 3,994 and the number of branch offices climbed from 4,721 to 21,424. Despite this increase, unit banks still predominate in numbers, although not in total assets. For example, at the end of 1970, some 9,694 of the 13,688 banks operated only a single office.

In order to explain changes in the number of commercial banks it is necessary to examine new-bank chartering, bank failures, and bank mergers. The net change in the number of banks during any period is equal to the number of new banks created in the period minus the number that disappear through suspension or voluntary liquidation and minus also those that disappear by being consolidated or merged into other banks. For convenience we shall refer to these respectively as new banks, bank failures, and bank absorptions.

Table 5–5 shows that between the end of 1920 and the end of 1970, the

Table 5–5 Changes in the number of U.S. commercial banks during selected periods, 1920–1970

PERIOD	NUMBER AT END OF THE PERIOD	NEW BANKS	BANK FAILURES	BANK ABSORP- TIONS	NET CHANGE DURING PERIOD
1920	29,206				
1921–1929 (inclusive)	23,695	3,253	5,067	3,963	− 5,511
1930–1933 (inclusive)	14,352	674	7,763	2,322	− 9,343
1934–1941 (inclusive)	14,225	890	*	1,127	− 127
1942–1945 (inclusive)	14,011	258	201	327	− 214
1946–1970 (inclusive)	13,688	3,277	252	3,399	− 323
Total, 1921–1970		11,021	13,507	13,978	−15,518

* Data not reliable because of some reopenings of banks which suspended earlier.
SOURCE: Board of Governors of the Federal Reserve System, *Banking and Monetary Statistics,* Washington, D.C., 1943; Federal Reserve Board, various annual reports; and *Federal Reserve Bulletin,* various issues.

number of banks declined by 15,518. More than 11,000 new banks were chartered in this period, but these additions were more than offset by 13,507 failures and 13,978 absorptions of banks through mergers.[6] We turn now to some issues relating to failures, absorptions, and new charters.

---

[6] The careful reader will note some statistical inconsistencies in Table 5–5. These arise partly from discrepancies in the original data and partly from shifts of institutions between the categories of commercial banks and noncommercial banks.

Bank Failures

Even in the nineteenth and early twentieth centuries, the United States had the dubious distinction of possessing one of the highest failure rates, if not the highest, of any important nation with a commercial-banking system. Nearly 3,000 banks failed between 1864 and 1920. But the worst was yet to come. Another 5,067 had suspended operations by the end of 1929 and still another 7,763 were defunct by the end of 1933. The mortality rate was especially high among smaller banks, but many large ones also failed.

To generalize about the reasons for failures of any type of business enterprise is difficult, for the reasons vary from case to case and, even in a particular case, failure usually results not from a single cause but from a combination of conditions. Nevertheless, it is possible to isolate some of the most important factors responsible for high bank-failure rates prior to 1934.

1. Inherent weaknesses in small independent unit banks. Whatever may be the relative merits of large independent unit banks and branch-banking systems, it is clear that small independent unit banks are especially liable to failure. Many are too small to be efficient, their management is often not well trained, and a large percentage of their assets is likely to be in the form of loans to local agriculture, industry, or trade. Thus, they are likely to be weak in the face of unfavorable economic developments, not only those in the economy at large, but also those limited to their own localities.

2. "Overbanking." Because it is difficult to specify the "proper" amount of banking for an area, it is difficult to say precisely when the area is "overbanked." Yet, despite the ambiguity of the term, it is clear that many places were overbanked in the early 1920s, when we had nearly 30,000 banks, and that this situation was remedied only slowly. Some places did not have excessive total amounts of banking resources, but they had too many small banks to achieve efficiency and safety. It was not unusual for a village with 2,000 inhabitants to have three or more banks; many small and medium-sized cities were similarly overbanked. Some banks in overbanked areas would have failed even under favorable economic conditions; adverse economic developments assured disaster.

3. Shifts in the location of business. Thousands of banks were seriously weakened by the revolution in highway transportation during the 1920s and 1930s. Prior to the days of hard-surfaced roads, automobiles, and farm trucks, farmers took much of their business to nearby agricultural villages or small towns. Here they sold many of their products, bought supplies, and did their banking. But as new roads and motor vehicles increased the speed and reduced the cost of transportation, the farmer took his business (including his deposits and borrowing) to the county seat or some other larger city. The smaller village or town was left to wither on the vine; its banks were fortunate if they escaped a less lingering death. Other shifts of business also contributed to the failures of individual banks: shifts of plants from one area to another, the replacement of small firms by larger ones that did their banking business elsewhere, and so on.

4. Deflation and depression. Bank failures and business depressions are mutually aggravating; a depression tends to break banks, and bank failures deepen a depression. Falling prices, incomes, sales, and employment lessen the abilities of debtors to meet their obligations and thereby threaten both the solvency and the liquidity of banks. Many banks were destroyed or seriously weakened during the sharp deflation starting in May, 1920. The failure of agriculture to recover fully during the 1920s injured banks that were heavily dependent on farming. Then came the Great Depression, which started in 1929 and lasted a decade. Thousands of banks failed to survive under its strains, and bank failures and threats of failure played an important role in deepening and prolonging the depression.

Since 1934, bank-failure rates have been much lower than in preceding years. There appear to be many reasons for this, including the protection afforded by the FDIC, better supervision by the FDIC and other supervisory agencies, improved bank management, and more frequent absorptions of weak banks in mergers. However, a basic factor has been the maintenance of high and rising levels of income and economic activity. The mild recessions since World War II have not put banks to the acid test. Many of the bank failures in recent years clearly reflect mismanagement.

Bank absorptions

As shown in Table 5–5, between 1920 and 1970 some 13,978 banks disappeared through absorption in mergers. The absorption rate was high during the 1920s and somewhat lower from 1930 to 1933. After falling sharply from the end of 1933 to the end of World War II, the bank absorption rate again rose to high levels in the postwar period. It would be even higher if not restricted by the banking authorities and the Department of Justice.

What are the reasons for this high rate of bank mergers and for pressures toward even higher rates? Such mergers can occur only if owners of the bank to be absorbed are willing to sell at a price attractive to the owners and management of the acquiring bank. There are many reasons why the owners of an absorbed bank may be willing to sell at such a price. One is the imminence of failure. An unknown number of the absorbed banks would have suspended operations if they had not been bought. The FDIC and other banking authorities have often assisted such mergers. Other reasons for merging include various diseconomies of small scale which come to be reflected in low net earnings, difficulties in providing for management succession at salaries that the bank can afford to pay, and the low liquidity and marketability of shares in a small bank.

There are also many reasons why an acquiring bank is willing to pay an attractive price. One is its desire to establish branch-bank offices. It can do this by creating new branch-office facilities through *de novo* branches or by absorbing a bank and converting its facilities into branch offices. Banks often find it more feasible and economical to branch through absorption than through *de novo* branches. For one thing, they may establish branches only with the permission of the banking authorities, and the latter often permit branching by absorption where they would deny *de novo* branches. Also, branching by absorption often gives access to a highly desirable banking site, it brings with it bank assets and an established banking business, and it eliminates one competitor from the local banking market. Other reasons for bank mergers include a desire for larger assets to increase prestige, to get higher limits on individual loans, and to achieve various economies of larger scale.

New Banks

Table 5–5 indicates that more than 11,000 new banks were chartered between 1921 and 1970. The rate of creation of new banks was high in the 1920s, much lower from 1929 through World War II, and higher again in the postwar period, although still considerably below the rates of the 1920s. The rate of creation of new banks depends directly on the supply and willingness of private investors to establish and finance new banks, which presumably is based on prospective profitability, and on the availability of charters from the banking authorities. Both have undergone wide changes since World War I.

As noted earlier, free banking prevailed in the United States during the latter half of the nineteenth century and through World War I; the Comptroller of the Currency and most state banking authorities were empowered to grant charters to all who met the requirements of the general banking laws. It was under this policy of free banking that the number of banks grew to more than 29,000 in 1920. Many complained of "overbanking"—that there were too many banks and that this was creating banking difficulties and failures. Important modifications of the free-banking principle resulted. Even in the 1920s the Comptroller of the Currency and at least a few state banking authorities denied some applications for charters where they found insufficient need for a new bank in the community. This policy was formalized and made much more restrictive in the Banking Act of 1935, following the banking debacle of the early 1930s. Under this law, a new bank still must meet the requirements of the relevant general banking laws, but the Comptroller of the Currency may issue a charter for a new national bank and the FDIC may insure the deposits of a new state-chartered bank only if they find it in the public interest to do so after investigating such things as the qualifications and experience of the proposed bank directors and officers, the prospects of success of the new bank, and the "need" of the community for additional banking facilities. Most state banking authorities have adopted somewhat similar policies, if only because a new state bank would have but limited chances of success if it were denied deposit insurance.

It would be pleasant to report that chartering policy is now devoted to the purpose of achieving a banking system characterized by efficiency, convenience to customers, and effective competition. Such a report would be inaccurate. Actual decisions are in too many cases influenced by jealousy between state and federal authorities, opposition by existing banks that do not want additional competition, inappropriate criteria of "need," and political activities by bankers. As one studies these decisions, he appreciates better the original reasons for adopting free banking.

The prospective profitability of establishing new banks has also fluctuated widely. It is easy to understand why so few new banks were created during the Great Depression, and also during and immediately following World War II when interest rates were abnormally low. However, one might have expected that the rate of new-bank creation would have increased even more than it has since about 1950 in view of the generally higher level of interest rates, high and rising levels of economic activity, growth of population, and spread of metropolitan areas. A major part of the explanation is to be found in the growth of branch banking. Branch offices have been established in areas that would otherwise have attracted new banks. As one examines the rates of new-bank creation by states, he finds the highest rates in those states that prohibit or severely limit branch banking, and the lowest rates in those states with more liberal branching.

Branch banking would expand even faster in the absence of official restrictions. These are of several types:

1. Prohibitions or limitations by state laws. No bank is permitted to establish domestic branches outside the state in which it is domiciled; only a few states permit statewide branches; a majority that permit branches limit them to the bank's home city or county or to some local region; and several states permit no branching at all. Such limitations apply not only to state-chartered banks, but also to national banks, whose branching powers are limited to those granted to state banks in the state in which the national bank is domiciled.

2. Denials of applications to establish branches on the ground of insufficient need for additional banking facilities in an area.

3. Disapproval of branching through absorption of existing banks because of threatened damage to competition. Although the general trend of public policy is toward liberalization of branching powers, many restrictions remain.

GROUP BANKING

The other principal mechanism for establishing multiple-office banking—group banking—has also expanded greatly since World War II.

By the end of 1970, there were 121 group systems in 35 states and the District of Columbia. These controlled 895 banks that operated a total of 3,260 branches and held more than $78 billion of deposits, or about 15 percent of total commercial-bank deposits. In some states, they were of much greater relative importance. For example, they held more than 50 percent of total deposits in Minnesota, Montana, and Nevada, and more than 40 percent in Florida, Idaho, Maine, Oregon, South Dakota, Utah, Virginia, and Wisconsin.[7] The rapid growth of group banking is attributable both to the same forces that have stimulated the growth of branch banking and to legal limitations on branching. Although not all states

[7] *Federal Reserve Bulletin,* August, 1971, p. A98.

permit group banking, it is permitted by some states that prohibit branching, and some states that permit branching on only a limited basis allow group banking more liberally and over wider geographic areas.

Holding companies used to establish group banking should not be confused with one-bank holding companies, which grew very rapidly during the latter part of the 1960s. The purpose of a one-bank holding company is not to bring two or more banks under common control; instead it is to enable a banking organization to engage in bank-related activities. In a typical case, the shares of a bank—often a large bank—are transferred to a newly created holding company, and the former shareholders of the bank receive in exchange shares of stock in the holding company. The latter then forms subsidiary corporations to provide services to the bank and to others. Among such activities are provision of computer services, selling or writing insurance, provision of investment and management advisory services, extension of real estate credit, equipment leasing, and so on.

Such extensions of services, both directly by banks and through related subsidiaries, have aroused considerable controversy. Some people oppose them, pointing to possible adverse effects on the soundness of banks, conflicts of interest, undue concentration of financial power, and unfair competition with other sellers of the services. Other people contend that such dangers can be averted through appropriate regulation, and that through such extensions of their activities the banks can make valuable contributions to the overall efficiency and competitiveness of the financial system.

CONCLUSIONS

This excursion into American banking history, brief and incomplete as it has been, should have contributed to the reader's understanding of banking structure, public policies toward banks, and current controversies over banking policies and structures. Through our banking history run two themes—change and continuity. Change there has certainly been—changes of many types, sometimes in one direction, sometimes in another. But there has also been continuity, at least continuities of attitudes and of the nature of controversies.

A most important instance of continuity has been the persistence of controversy over the relative powers and responsibilities of the federal and state governments in the banking field. This was illustrated most dramatically in the creation and demise of the First and Second Banks of the United States; in the establishment of the National Banking System, which might have been rejected if some of the strongest supporters of states' rights had not seceded; and in the establishment and determination of the structure and powers of the Federal Reserve. The federal government has achieved more powers over state banks as some have joined the Federal Reserve and most have joined the FDIC. However, the controversy continues with debate over such questions as: Should all state banks be required to join the Federal Reserve? Should all be required to join the FDIC? Should states be permitted to issue charters on terms more liberal than those granted by the federal government? Should branching by national banks be limited by the laws of the states in which they are located? Should national banks be permitted to branch across state lines regardless of state laws?

There also continues to be ambivalence and controversy regarding such related issues as bigness and smallness, concentration and decentralization of economic and financial power, and monopoly and competition. Americans have always been divided on such issues and have often been ambivalent. One may at the same time extol the virtues of smallness and the glories of bigness, or the desirability of decentralization of financial power and the advantages of efficiencies achieved only through some degree of concentration. Such controversies appeared at least as early as 1791, when the First Bank was established; they still persist in debates over group banking, branch banking, and mergers.

Against this historical background, it becomes easier to see why we have a dual banking system, with both national and state banks coexisting; why we have so many banks; why government responsibilities for chartering and regulating banks are so diffused; and why we have not a single central bank but a central banking system.

Selected readings

Board of Governors of the Federal Reserve System, *Banking Studies,* Washington, D.C., 1941.

Dewey, D. R., *Financial History of the United States,* 11th ed., New York, McKay, 1931.

Hammond, Bray, *Banks and Politics in America from the Revolution to the Civil War,* Princeton, N.J., Princeton University Press, 1957.

Sprague, O. M. W., *History of Crises Under the National Banking System,* Senate Document No. 538, Washington, D.C., U.S. Government Printing Office, 1910.

Taus, E. R., *Central Banking Function of the U.S. Treasury, 1789–1941,* New York, Columbia University Press, 1943.

Trescott, P. B., *Financing American Enterprise,* New York, Harper & Row, 1963.

CHAPTER 6

THE COMMERCIAL-BANKING SYSTEM

In Chapter 2, we identified the three sets of monetary institutions in the United States: the Treasury, the Federal Reserve, and the commercial banks. We shall analyze all of these in this text. It will be convenient to start with commercial banks. Commercial-bank debts in the form of demand deposits make up about three-quarters of our money supply; commercial-bank operations account directly for the major part of fluctuations of the money supply through time. However, the functioning of commercial banks is closely intertwined with that of the Treasury and the Federal Reserve, especially the latter. The nature and importance of these interrelationships will be developed as we continue our discussion.

SOME PROBLEMS OF NOMENCLATURE

Although the name "commercial banks" has been used for a long time, it is not accurately descriptive and may be misleading. One way that it is not appropriate is that it does not accurately indicate the scope of commercial-bank lending. The name was originally applied because of a belief that these banks should make only short-term "commercial" loans. That is, their loans should be for no more than one year's duration, and should be made only to *traders* and *merchants* in order to finance the transportation of goods in domestic and international trade and to finance holding of inventories during the relatively short periods required for their sale. It was also believed that banks might properly make similar short-term loans to *farmers* for such purposes as meeting current production costs and marketing their crops. As industry developed, this theory was modified to admit the propriety of short-term lending to *producers* to meet payrolls, finance inventory, and meet other needs for circulating capital. Commercial banks today do indeed make such short-term commercial, industrial, and agricultural loans; in fact, they are by far the largest lenders in this market. And it is also true that the average maturity of their earning assets is shorter than that of most other financial intermediaries. But they have never confined themselves to such loans, and today they hold a wide variety of earning assets. They lend not only to all types of business firms, including other financial institutions, but also to consumers, governmental units, universities, and so on. And the maturities of their earning assets range all the way from one day to long-term mortgages and bonds. Some of these are acquired directly from customers, others in the primary and secondary securities markets.

Another way that the name is misleading is that it fails to highlight the one unique characteristic of these institutions. They are differentiated from other financial intermediaries, not primarily by the types of earning assets that they hold, but by the fact that they are the only intermediaries whose debts circulate as money and who have the power to create and destroy money. We have already seen that in earlier decades they issued money in the form of both bank notes and checking deposits. They have long since lost the legal power of note issue—the state banks in 1865 and the national banks in 1935—but they still create and issue money in the form of demand deposits.

The third weakness of the name "commercial bank" is that it obscures the fact that these institutions perform not just one but many types of functions. Most of them are department-store banks, not specialty shops. They not only issue and transfer checking deposits but also operate savings departments which issue time- and savings-deposit claims in competition with other financial intermediaries. Many operate trust departments, act as agents for their customers in buying and selling securities, underwrite and sell new securities for state and local governments, sell insurance, deal in foreign exchange, and so on. In order to concentrate on the money function of banks we shall largely ignore all of their other functions except those of issuing time- and savings-deposit claims.

For the reasons stated above, we would prefer to call these institutions "checking-deposit banks" or some other name that would highlight their uniqueness. We will bow to popular usage, however, and call them "commercial banks."

COMPOSITION OF THE COMMERCIAL-BANKING SYSTEM

As already noted, our commercial banking system is made up of some 13,700 commercial-banking corporations.[1] These differ in many respects. Nearly 4,600 are national banks, operating under federal charters; 8,949 operate under state charters. All the national banks and 1,138 state banks are members of the Federal Reserve; thus only 5,736 banks, or 42 percent of the total, are in the Federal Reserve System. However, these banks hold about 81 percent of all commercial-bank assets. All members of the Federal Reserve and all except 182 nonmember banks have their deposits insured by the FDIC. About 70 percent are unit banks, operating only a single office. The other 30 percent are branch banks, operating one or more offices in addition to a head office. Some of these operate only one or two branches located close to their head offices; some branch more widely. None operates a domestic office outside its home state.[2]

Banks also vary tremendously in size, ranging all the way from the huge Bank of America with assets well above $20 billion to little banks with assets below $1 million. (See Table 6–1.) In mid-1970, there were 8,387 banks with deposits of less than $10 million each. Although these banks represented almost 61 percent of all United States banks they commanded less than 8.5 percent of

Table 6–1 Size distribution of all commercial banks in the United States, June 30, 1970 (assets in billions of dollars)

SIZE OF BANKS (MEASURED IN MILLIONS OF DOLLARS OF TOTAL DEPOSITS)	NUMBER OF BANKS	PERCENT OF NUMBER OF BANKS*	TOTAL ASSETS*	PERCENT OF TOTAL ASSETS OF ALL BANKS*
Total—all banks	13,690	100.0	$533.0	100.0
Less than $1	359	2.6	0.4	†
$1–$2	1,082	7.9	1.9	0.04
$2–$5	3,499	25.2	13.8	2.6
$5–$10	3,447	25.2	28.1	5.3
$10–$25	3,185	23.2	55.5	10.4
$25–$50	1,111	8.1	44.2	8.3
$50–$100	494	3.6	39.6	7.4
$100–$500	404	3.0	99.6	18.7
$500–$1,000	62	0.5	53.4	10.0
$1,000 or more	47	0.4	196.6	36.9

    * May not add to totals due to rounding
    † Less than $\frac{1}{10}$ of 1%
SOURCE: Federal Deposit Insurance Corporation, *Assets and Liabilities of Commercial and Mutual Savings Banks,* June 30, 1970, pp. 108–109.

    [1] These data relate to mid-1971.
    [2] This is not entirely true; there are a few unimportant exceptions. Also, as will be indicated later, a number of banks have branches in other countries.

total bank assets. At the other extreme, there were 47 banks with deposits of $1 billion or more that held nearly 37 percent of total bank assets. The 513 largest banks, comprising less than 4 percent of the total number of banks, held more than 65 percent of total bank assets.

Because of such differences, banks vary markedly in the variety of banking services performed, in the types of customers served, in the sizes of market areas served, in the compositions of their portfolios, in their financial sophistication, and so on. However, they have enough in common to justify our dealing with them collectively as a system. They all operate on the same general principles and create and destroy money in the same general ways.

In the remainder of this chapter, we shall deal with the commercial-banking system as a whole, largely ignoring relationships among the individual banks and concentrating on the relationships of the commercial banks as a whole with other members of the community. We do this because we are interested here in what the commercial banks do as a group, not in which particular bank does it. As a result, we shall make a number of statements about the commercial-banking system as a whole that may not be valid if applied to an individual bank. Inter-relations among these banks will be discussed later.

BALANCE-SHEET ACCOUNTING

A short discussion of some elementary principles of double-entry accounting will not only illuminate the processes through which the commercial banks issue and withdraw their debts that serve as money but will also prove useful later when we discuss the operations of the Treasury, the Federal Reserve, and other institutions.

In drawing up financial statements for any unit, be it a business firm, a government, or any other organization, an accountant considers the unit to be an entity, separate and distinct from its owners. The entity must therefore account to its owners as well as to other claimants against it. There are two principal types of financial statements. One is the *income statement* or *profit and loss statement*. Such statements summarize, for some stated period of time, all the gross income accruing to the entity and the claims against that gross income—claims of owners as well as others. We shall not use income statements at this point, although we shall later refer back to them.

In contrast to income statements, which refer to flows over a stated period of time, the *balance sheet* refers to a stock at a point in time. One side of the balance sheet, the *assets* side, lists the types and values of everything owned by the entity. These things of value may be money itself, debt claims against others, shares of ownership in other firms, inventories, plant and equipment, and so on. The other side of the balance sheet, *liabilities* and *capital accounts*, lists the types and amounts of claims against the entity's assets. Since double-entry accounting requires that the entity account for the total value of its assets, no more and no less, the total value of claims against assets must be exactly equal to the value of its assets. Any value of assets in excess of other claims against them accrues to the owners. Liabilities are all claims against assets other than ownership claims. Under the law, they have priority over ownership claims. They are mostly debt claims of some sort; they may be evidenced by formal documents such as promissory notes or bills of exchange, or they may be evidenced only by book entries. *Capital account,* or *net worth,* is simply the value of ownership claims against the entity. Since owners have only a residual claim, capital account or net worth is equal to the value of assets minus liabilities.

A highly simplified balance sheet might appear as follows:

ASSETS		LIABILITIES AND CAPITAL ACCOUNT	
		Liabilities	$ 85,000
		Capital account	15,000
Total	$100,000	Total	$100,000

This necessary equality of assets with the sum of liabilities and capital account permits us to write three simple equations that will be useful:

Assets = liabilities + capital account $\quad$ (1)

Capital account = assets − liabilities $\quad$ (2)

Liabilities = assets − capital account $\quad$ (3)

People are sometimes amazed at the accuracy of accountants, noting that no matter how complex the situation or how great the amounts involved, the accountant still manages to make the two sides balance. This becomes less remarkable when we realize how the value of net worth was arrived at.

For most of our purposes it will be sufficient to deal with capital account as a lump sum without further breakdown. However, it is perhaps worth noting that the $15,000 net worth in our example might have been broken down somewhat as follows:

Total net worth	$15,000
Capital (10,000 shares of stock at a par value of $1)	10,000
Surplus	5,000

Capital, or *capital stock,* is the value of ownership claims evidenced by the par or stated value of outstanding shares of stock. *Surplus* is simply the excess of total ownership claims over the par value of outstanding stock. Any other interpretation may be misleading. In some cases, surplus is broken down still further. Thus, the $5,000 in the preceding breakdown could be shown as:

Surplus	$3,000
Undivided profits	2,000

The latter entry suggests that owners have a claim for dividends which will be paid in the near future. This may not occur; firms often carry such an item on their balance sheets for years. Undivided profits are best viewed as only a part of ownership claims.

Since we shall be deeply interested in the behavior of the liabilities of banks in the form of deposits, and especially demand or checking deposits, it will be useful to divide bank liabilities, or debts, into three parts: demand deposits, time and savings deposits, and other liabilities. Thus, we can rewrite as follows our simple equations:

$$\text{Assets} = \text{demand deposits} + \text{time and savings deposits} \\ + \text{other liabilities} + \text{capital accounts} \tag{1}$$

$$\text{Demand deposits} = \text{assets} - \text{time and savings deposits} \\ - \text{other liabilities} - \text{capital accounts} \tag{2}$$

In analyzing the functioning of monetary institutions, we shall emphasize one aspect of the necessary equality of assets and the sum of outstanding claims in the form of liabilities and net worth, namely, that a firm can acquire assets only by creating an equal value of claims against itself. Of course it may change the composition of its assets without changing the other side of its balance sheet at all. For example, it may trade some of its short-term claims against other entities for long-term claims against other entities, and so on. Such exchanges of assets may not disturb either the total value or the composition of outstanding claims against the entity. But an entity can make net additions to its assets only by creating an equal value of claims against itself. And in the process of reducing its total assets, it must withdraw and retire an equal value of claims against itself.

As we proceed, we shall repeatedly find it useful to recall these simple facts:

1. When these monetary institutions make net additions to their assets, they must pay for them by creating and issuing an equal value of claims against themselves.

2. When they make net sales or net reductions in their assets, they must withdraw and retire an equal value of claims against themselves.

A BALANCE SHEET FOR
THE COMMERCIAL-BANKING SYSTEM

Table 6–2 is a simplified consolidated balance sheet for the commercial-banking system. It is simplified in the sense that it eliminates or lumps together some minor items in order to concentrate attention on major variables. It is consolidated to eliminate claims of the various commercial banks against each other, leaving only the claims of the commercial banks as a whole against other members of the community, and the claims of other members of the community against commercial banks.

The information in this balance sheet demonstrates several important

Table 6–2 Consolidated balance sheet for the commercial banking system, December 31, 1970 (billions of dollars)

ASSETS			LIABILITIES AND CAPITAL ACCOUNTS		
	AMOUNT	PERCENT OF TOTAL		AMOUNT	PERCENT OF TOTAL
Cash in vault	$ 7.0	1.4	Demand deposits	$217.3	44.1
Deposits at Federal			Time and savings		
Reserve	23.3	4.7	deposits	231.9	47.1
Loans	295.2	59.9	Capital accounts	43.0	8.8
Securities	147.9	31.0			
Other (net)	18.8	3.0			
Total	$492.2	100.0	Total	$492.2	100.0

SOURCE: *Federal Reserve Bulletin,* June, 1971, pp. A24–A25.

points, some of which relate to the nature and proportions of the claims issued by banks. One point is that banks have acquired only a very small part, less than 9 percent, of their total assets by issuing net-worth or capital-account claims. An even more important point is that the volume of capital-account claims changes only slowly and within narrow limits relative to bank assets. Most of the assets of banks were acquired by creating and issuing bank debts in the form of deposit claims. Moreover, for the most part, banks pay for the acquisition of additional assets by creating additional deposit claims against themselves. And when they make net sales of assets, they collect largely by withdrawing and retiring claims against themselves.

Other points relate to the nature and composition of bank assets. It should be emphasized that banks could, if regulations and business prudence permitted, create or withdraw deposit claims by purchasing or selling assets of any kind. One can even imagine their doing this by buying or selling common stocks, real estate, or double-jointed goobers. However, a look at the asset side reveals that, in practice, they restrict their holdings largely to cash, deposits at the Federal Reserve banks, and debt claims against others, mostly the latter. Assets in the form of cash and deposit claims against the Federal Reserve yield no interest and are held largely to meet legal reserve requirements. Loans and securities do yield interest and make up the major part of total bank assets. Loans include the banks' holdings of debt claims against their borrowers, these being evidenced by acceptances and promissory notes, mostly the latter. The item "securities," sometimes called "investments," includes a small amount of stock, such as stock in the Federal Reserve banks, but it is composed largely of longer-term debt instruments purchased and held by the banks. It includes debt obligations of the federal government, debts of state and local government, corporation bonds, and so on.

As we realize that banks create their own deposit debts primarily by purchasing debt claims against others, we begin to see why these institutions are often referred to as "dealers in debt" and "monetizers of debt."

THE CREATION OF CHECKING DEPOSITS

Let us start our discussion of the creation of checking deposits with the simple case in which banks issue and withdraw claims only in the form of demand deposits. The purpose of this illustration is to show how commercial banks would operate if they were not in the business of issuing time and savings deposits. This latter function of commercial banks will be reintroduced at a later point.

Deposits for cash

The first case to be considered is that in which banks issue deposits in exchange for a net inflow of cash into the banking system. We shall use the term "cash" to include both cash in vault and deposit claims against the Federal Reserve banks. This is justified because banks are free to exchange one of these assets for the other. Thus, they may use a net inflow of coin and paper money from circulation to increase their cash in vault or they may send it along to the Federal Reserve banks to increase their deposits there. Moreover, they can ship cash from their vaults to increase their deposits at the Federal Reserve, and they can write checks on their deposits at the Federal Reserve to get coin and paper money to hold in their vaults. The amount of "cash," in this sense, in the commercial-banking system is equal to all the "money" issued by the Treasury and the Federal Reserve minus that in circulation outside the banking system. Thus, a net inflow of cash to the banking system can result either from new issues of money by the Treasury or the Federal Reserve, or from a net decrease of coin and paper money outside the banks.

Suppose there is a net cash inflow of $1 billion into the commercial-banking system. The direct effect on the banks' balance sheets will be as follows:

ASSETS		LIABILITIES	
Cash	+$1 billion	Demand deposits	+$1 billion

The banks have bought $1 billion of assets in the form of cash by creating their own debt of $1 billion in the form of demand deposits.

It was perhaps injudicious to begin with this case, for it may reinforce popular misconceptions. The reactions of some may be, "Just as I thought! Deposits are nothing but claims on deposited cash; they arise only from the 'deposit' of cash, and anyone leaving cash on deposit can get back that same cash on demand." Such conclusions would be quite wrong because:

1. Only a small part of outstanding deposits was created to pay for net inflows of cash; most deposits were created to pay for other types of assets.

2. The cash holdings of banks are equal to only a small fraction of bank-deposit liabilities.

3. One who "deposits" cash with a bank gets no preferred claim; he gives up title to the cash and takes his place with all other depositors as a creditor of the bank.

Although deposits created to pay for net cash inflows to the banking system become indistinguishable from all other deposits, two characteristics of the process of creating deposits to pay for net inflows of cash should be noted:

1. In this case, and this case only, the transaction that creates deposits also increases the banks' holdings of cash, the latter constituting legal reserves for the banks. Such deposits that arise in transactions which also increase the legal reserves of banks are called *primary deposits*. Those created to pay for other assets that will not serve as reserves are called *derivative deposits;* these are derived from the purchase of such things as loans and securities.

2. When the commercial banks create checking deposits to pay for net cash flows to them, they do not themselves directly increase the total money supply. If the cash flows in from circulation, the increase of money in the form of checking deposits is offset by the decrease of coin and paper money in circulation. If the net cash flow to the bank results from new creations of money by the Treasury or the Federal Reserve, it is these institutions, not the banks, that initially increase the money supply. However, we shall see that net flows of cash into the banks have the very important effect of enabling the banks to create more money by purchasing other assets.

Deposits for debt claims

By far the largest part of outstanding deposits was created to pay for assets in the form of debt claims against others. Suppose the banks increase their loans to customers by $10 billion, giving their customers checking deposits. The effects on the banks' balance sheets are as follows:

ASSETS	LIABILITIES
Loans .... +$10 billion	Demand deposits ..... +$10 billion

By purchasing debt claims, the banks have created $10 billion of money that did not exist before. In effect, the banks traded debts with their customers, presumably to their mutual satisfaction. The banks acquired debts that are not themselves money but which yield income in the form of interest or discount. The borrowers acquired debt claims (deposits) that usually yield no income but which have the advantage of being generally acceptable in payment for all kinds of goods and services. In short, the banks monetized debt.

Banks by no means confine their granting of credit to short-term loans to their customers. They also lend for longer terms to their customers and buy various types of securities in the open market from sellers they do not even know.

Among these are such things as government securities, corporation bonds, and mortgages. We should not be surprised to find that banks create checking deposits in buying such assets. Suppose the banks purchase $10 billion of securities. The effects on their balance sheets will be:

ASSETS	LIABILITIES
Securities .... +$10 billion	Demand deposits ..... +$10 billion

The banking system has created $10 billion of money that did not exist before, and has done so by purchasing debt claims against others. Here, again, it has monetized debt.

Two points that are crucial to an understanding of commercial banking should be emphasized.

1. Most checking deposits are derivative deposits, that is, deposits created in the process of bank purchases of debt claims against others.

2. Checking deposits created to pay for such assets are a net addition to the money supply; there is no offsetting decrease of coin and paper money in circulation.

THE DESTRUCTION OF CHECKING DEPOSITS

Checking deposits are extinguished by processes just the reverse of those that create deposits. They are destroyed as the banking system decreases its assets in the form of cash, loans, and securities.

Net cash drains

The banking system as a whole may suffer a net drain of its cash assets, either through net withdrawals of coin and paper money for circulation outside the banks or because of a net decrease in the amount of money provided by the Treasury and the Federal Reserve. In either case, those withdrawing the cash will probably do so by drawing down their checking deposits at the banks.

Suppose the cash assets of the banking system are reduced by $500 million. The banks' balance sheets will be affected as follows:

ASSETS	LIABILITIES
Cash .... −$500 million	Demand deposits ... −$500 million

In the process of selling $500 million of cash assets, the banks destroyed $500 million of their outstanding deposit liabilities.

Two aspects of this particular process of reducing the volume of checking deposits should be noted. First, when checking deposits are reduced by net out-

flows of cash from the banking system, the banks themselves do not directly decrease the total money supply. If the cash flows out into circulation, the decrease
of money in the form of checking deposits is offset by the increase of coin and
paper money in circulation. If the net cash loss by the banks resulted from a net
withdrawal of money by the Treasury and the Federal Reserve, it is these institutions, not the banks, that initiated the decrease of the money supply. Second, the
drain of cash from the banks may have very important repercussions, for it may
force the banks to decrease the money supply by selling other assets.

Net reductions in bank assets in the form of debt claims

Most reductions in the volume of checking deposits are traceable to net reductions of bank assets in the form of debt claims against others. Suppose that the
banking system reduces its outstanding loans by $5 billion. The former borrowers
usually repay loans by drawing checks against their deposit accounts; bank
liabilities are reduced accordingly. The effects on the banks' balance sheets are:

ASSETS	LIABILITIES
Loans . . . . —$5 billion	Demand deposits . . . . . . −$5 billion

In this process of reducing their outstanding loans, the banks have destroyed $5
billion of money in the form of checking deposits. This is a net reduction of the
money supply; there is no offsetting increase of coin and paper money in circulation. In effect, those who repay bank loans do so by surrendering an equal value
of deposit claims against the banks.

Similar results flow from net reductions of bank holdings of securities.
Suppose the banking system sells $3 billion of its security holdings and the buyers
pay for them by relinquishing checking-deposit claims against the banks. This will
affect the banks' balance sheets as follows:

ASSETS	LIABILITIES
Securities . . . . −$3 billion	Demand deposits . . . . . . −$3 billion

Here, again, the banks have destroyed checking deposits and decreased the total
money supply through net sales of their debt claims against others.

The preceding sections have traced the processes through which the commercial-banking system creates checking deposits by purchasing various types of
assets and destroys checking deposits by net sales of assets. During some periods,
the banks may make net purchases of some types of assets and net sales of others.
It should be evident that the net change in the volume of checking deposits
during any period will equal the net change in total bank assets—still assuming
that the banks issue claims only in the form of checking deposits.

OTHER CLAIMS AGAINST COMMERCIAL BANKS

In the preceding sections we explicitly assumed that commercial banks issued only demand-deposit claims against themselves, and implicitly assumed that all these checking-deposit claims were owned by the public and thus were a part of the public's money supply. We did this to highlight the important point that the banks can indeed increase the public's money supply by purchasing assets and can decrease the public's money supply by making net sales of assets. Now we must consider two facts that will complicate our analysis: (1) that banks issue and withdraw claims other than demand deposits, and (2) some demand deposits are owned not by the public but by the United States government and foreigners. These facts are illustrated in Table 6–3.

Table 6–3 Assets of and claims against all commercial banks in the United States, June 30, 1971* (billions of dollars)

ASSETS		LIABILITIES AND CAPITAL ACCOUNT	
Cash in vault	$ 7.6	Capital account	$ 45.3
Deposits at Federal Reserve	24.1	Other liabilities (net)	18.3
Loans	305.1	Time deposits	254.2
Securities	157.7	Demand deposits owed to:	
		U.S. government	8.4
		Foreigners	2.6
		Public	165.7
Total	$494.5	Total	$494.5

* This is a consolidated balance sheet, omitting claims of commercial banks against each other. The item "Other liabilities (net)" is a net figure reflecting other liabilities minus some minor asset items.
SOURCE: *Federal Reserve Bulletin*, January, 1972, pp. A20–A23.

Note first the other claims against banks. As stated earlier, "capital accounts" is simply the value of ownership claims against banks. "Time deposits," a term that for brevity we shall use to cover both time and savings deposits, are liabilities that banks are not legally required to pay on demand, but only at some future date or some stipulated period after the depositor has given notice of his intention to withdraw. In practice, banks usually waive these legal rights, but they ordinarily do not permit time deposits to be transferred to others in payment. Demand-deposits liabilities to the United States government are like other checking deposits except for their ownership.

Because banks can create and issue these other types of claims, they can acquire and hold larger amounts of loans, securities, and other assets than would be possible if they issued only demand deposits. This was indicated in the equation stated earlier:

Assets = demand deposits + time deposits + other liabilities
+ capital accounts

The banking system can acquire assets equal to the value of all these claims that banks are willing to issue and others are willing to hold. This complicates the relationship between the volume of the banks' assets and the volume of the public's checking-deposit claims against banks. When banks make net purchases of assets, they may pay for them, not by creating new checking deposits for the public, but by creating other types of claims. And when they make net sales of assets, they may withdraw and retire not checking deposits from the public, but other types of claims. Yet it still remains true that the net increases of bank assets will result in increases of the public's holdings of checking deposits to the extent that the assets are not paid for by creating other types of claims on banks. And net sales of assets by banks will decrease the public's holdings of checking deposits to the extent that other claims against the banks are not reduced.

Let us now look more closely at the composition of the claims against banks. The volume of any one type of these claims can be decreased as claimants surrender some of them in exchange for other claims, and can be increased as claimants surrender other claims in exchange for it. For example, the public's holdings of demand deposits can be decreased as the public surrenders some of these deposits to buy ownership claims against banks, to buy time-deposit claims, or to make net payments to the government or foreigners by transferring demand deposits to them. And the public's demand deposits can be increased as the public surrenders time-deposit claims in exchange for checking deposits or has net receipts of checking deposits from the accounts of the government or foreigners.

If we call all these other claims against banks "nonmonetary claims" because we do not include them in the money supply, we get the following relationships:

Demand deposits = assets − nonmonetary claims

This is illustrated in Table 6–4. For example, the $165.7 billion of demand deposits owned by the public on June 30, 1971, resulted from total bank assets of $494.5 billion minus outstanding nonmonetary claims of $328.8 billion. It also follows that the *change* in the volume of the public's demand deposits between any two points of time is equal to the *change* in total bank assets minus the *change* in total nonmonetary claims. Note, for example, the net changes during the 8½-year period from the end of 1962 to mid-1971. The $42.6 billion increase in the public's holdings of demand deposits reflected a $236.7 billion increase in total bank assets minus the $194.1 billion increase in nonmonetary claims against banks. Note also that almost the entire increase in bank assets was in loans and securities. This type of analysis can be used even by those who do not accept our definition of the money supply and would like to include as "money" some other commercial-bank liabilities, such as time deposits or demand deposits owned by the United States government. They need only move the liabilities they wish to regard as money from the status of nonmonetary claims to the same status we have accorded to demand-deposit liabilities to the public.

Recognition of the fact that commercial banks are department stores of

Table 6–4 Changes in assets of and claims against commercial banks (billions of dollars)

	AMOUNT DEC. 28, 1962	AMOUNT JUNE 30, 1971	CHANGE DURING PERIOD
Assets			
Cash in vault	$ 4.3	$ 7.6	+$ 3.3
Deposits at Federal Reserve	17.7	24.1	+ 6.4
Loans	140.1	305.1	+ 165.0
Securities	95.7	157.7	+ 62.0
Total assets	$257.8	$494.5	+$236.7
Minus:			
Nonmonetary claims			
Capital account	24.1	45.3	+ 21.2
Other liabilities (net)	4.8	18.3	+ 13.5
Time deposits	97.8	254.2	+ 156.4
Demand deposits of:			
U.S. government	6.8	8.4	+ 1.6
Foreigners	1.2	2.6	+ 1.4
Total nonmonetary claims	$134.7	$328.8	+$194.1
Equals:			
Demand deposits of the public	$123.1	$165.7	+$ 42.6

finance has complicated our analysis but has been necessary in order to emphasize two important points:

1. The banks can make loans and buy securities by creating not only demand-deposit claims but also claims of other types, principally time deposits. The capacity of the commercial banks to hold loans and securities would be smaller if the banks were not willing to create and others to hold time-deposit claims.

2. To the extent that the volume of these other claims changes, fluctuations in the volume of bank assets will not be accompanied by changes in demand deposits. Yet all this should not be permitted to obscure the fact that the commercial-banking system can and does create money by purchasing debt obligations, and that it can and does destroy money by reducing its holdings of debt obligations.

The fact that commercial banks create money primarily by purchasing loans and securities helps to explain why changes in the money supply are likely to have important effects in the credit markets. As the banks create new money by purchasing loans and securities, the money is injected into the credit market in the first instance. This money may be considered to be either a new supply of loan funds or a new demand for debt obligations. This tends to lower interest rates and raise prices of debt obligations. On the other hand, as the banks reduce the money supply by decreasing their loans and security holdings, the money is in the first instance removed from the credit markets. This may be viewed as either a reduction in the supply of loan funds or a decrease in the demand for debt obligations. It tends to raise interest rates and to lower the prices of debt obligations. However, commercial banks are not the only lenders and do not by themselves determine the behavior of interest rates. The latter depends on the total demand for loan funds and the total supply of loan funds, including the quantities supplied by other lenders, as well as those from commercial banks.

THE VOLUME OF DEPOSITS

The preceding sections concentrated on the processes through which the commercial-banking system creates and destroys deposits by purchasing and selling assets of various kinds. We turn now to questions such as these: What determines the total amount of deposit liabilities that the banking system can create and keep outstanding, and the total amount of assets it can command? What determines the distribution of its liabilities among the categories of demand, time, and savings deposits? One feels intuitively that the answers must somehow involve the public's demand functions for assets in the form of bank deposits. For example, if the public refused to hold any deposits at all, the banks could not keep such claims outstanding and could not acquire assets in excess of their capital accounts. We shall indeed find that the volume of deposits, and the composition of those deposits, are related to the public's demand functions for deposits, which in turn are based on the attractiveness of deposits relative to other assets such as currency, claims against other financial intermediaries, direct securities, and even physical assets. However, the road to this conclusion is somewhat circuitous.

As a first step, we note that the Federal Reserve can and does set and change ceilings on the total amount of deposits that may be created. As we shall see in the next chapter, this involves two elements:

1. Establish a minimum percentage reserve requirement, such as 10 percent, against deposits. This is equivalent to saying, "The banks may not have outstanding more than $10 of deposits for every $1 of reserves at their command."

2. Regulate the dollar volume of reserves available to the banking system. This enables the Federal Reserve to set a ceiling on the total volume of deposits, and to raise or lower that ceiling by manipulating percentage reserve requirements and the available dollar volume of bank reserves. To be more specific, the Federal Reserve can raise the ceiling on total deposits and thus on total bank holdings of loans and securities by lowering the minimum percentage reserve requirement, by increasing the dollar volume of reserves available to the banking system, or both; and it can lower the ceiling on total deposits by increasing minimum percentage reserve requirements, decreasing the dollar volume of reserves available to the banks, or both. The Federal Reserve does not, of course, force the banks to expand their total holdings of loans and securities enough to raise their total deposits to the ceiling. The banks could, if they wished, create only a smaller volume of deposits. This sometimes happens to some extent. In general, however, the profit motive leads the banking system to expand close to the maximum, because to fall short of the ceiling is to keep total earning assets below their

maximum and to hold cash reserves in excess of the amounts required, and such excess reserves yield no interest. Expansion to the maximum is encouraged and facilitated by the availability of highly safe and liquid earning assets in financial markets.

Thus, the first part of our answer to the above questions is that total deposits of the banking system cannot rise above the ceiling imposed by the monetary authority.

However, the ultimate and overriding objective of the Federal Reserve is not to achieve some given level of bank deposits or some rate of change of them; it is rather to promote the achievement of such things as high and growing levels of output, high levels of employment, and stability of price levels. The ceiling on bank deposits, and adjustments of the ceiling, must be consistent with promotion of the more basic objectives. And the volume of bank deposits consistent with these objectives, and therefore the height of the allowable ceiling, depend heavily on the public's demand function for bank deposits. Suppose, to take an overly simple example, that the overriding objective of the monetary authority is to achieve a national income of $1,200 billion in a given year. The volume of bank deposits consistent with this objective, and therefore permitted by the monetary authority, will be very large if, at that level of income, the public demands a large volume of bank deposits, preferring these to other assets such as currency, claims against other financial intermediaries, and direct securities. In fact, the monetary authorities will fail to achieve their ultimate objectives if they do not enable the banks to create a large enough volume of deposits to meet these demands of the public at this income level.

On the other hand, the public might demand, at the target level of income, to hold only a small volume of bank deposits, preferring other assets such as currency, claims against other financial intermediaries, and direct securities. If the monetary authority failed to fix the ceiling on total deposits at an appropriately lower level, inflation would result as the public attempted to spend away its excess deposits.

In short, the volume of deposits that the banking system can issue depends in the first instance on the height of the ceiling on total deposits established by the Federal Reserve through its control of reserve requirements and the dollar volume of reserves available to banks. The public's demand function for deposits enters by determining the height of the deposit ceiling that will be consistent with promotion of the Federal Reserve's selected ultimate objective, such as a full-employment level of income. This is illustrated schematically in Figure 6–1. Suppose the Federal Reserve's ruling objective is to achieve and maintain the level of national income, OA. If the public's demand function for bank deposits is that represented by the lower line, D_1D_1, the appropriate ceiling on total deposits is that represented by the vertical distance, OB. However, if the public's demand function for bank deposits is represented by the higher line, D_2D_2, the appropriate ceiling on deposits is the much higher amount represented by the vertical distance, OC. This suggests that we should investigate some of the deter-

Figure 6–1 The public's demand for bank deposits

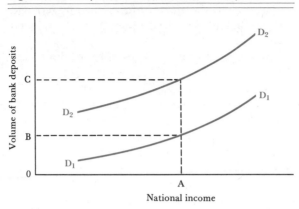

minants of the public's demand for bank deposits. For this purpose, we shall deal separately with demand deposits and with time and savings deposits. Also, in order to concentrate on competitive relationships among the various types of liquid assets, we shall largely ignore the determinant of the public's total demand for liquid assets as a group.

In determining the relative amounts that it will demand of coin, paper money, demand deposits, time and savings deposits at commercial banks, claims against other financial intermediaries, and direct securities, the public presumably considers their relative liquidity and safety and their relative yields net of transactions costs. Bank deposits compete in varying degrees with these other assets for a place in the public's portfolios. Banks can therefore influence the quantity of their deposits demanded by the public by adjusting the safety and liquidity of these claims, by altering service charges on them, and by varying their yields relative to yields on competing assets.

We have already noted some of the characteristics of demand deposits that lead the public to hold them rather than coin and paper money. The public would almost certainly demand more checking deposits relative to coin, currency, and other liquid assets if it received an interest income on these claims. However, the Banking Act of 1935 prohibited the payment of interest on demand deposits and ordered the Federal Reserve and the FDIC to impose ceilings on the rates that their members might pay on time and savings deposits. It was alleged, without persuasive evidence, that in competing for funds banks had driven interest rates on deposits to excessive levels, which tempted them into risky and unsound loans. Another reason for these provisions of the Banking Act was undoubtedly the desire of many banks to enlist the help of government in keeping down their operating costs by limiting price competition among banks for deposits.

It seems unlikely that many banks violate the law by paying explicit interest on demand deposits. But they do reward holders of these deposits indirectly by performing "free" services for them, by reducing service charges, by providing parking spaces, by giving their loan applications preferential treatment, and so on. The value of these services cannot be adjusted flexibly as yields on competing assets change, and to many depositors they are not perfect substitutes for explicit interest. The absence of interest on demand deposits has retarded the secular growth of demands for checking deposits, especially by larger corporations and other owners of large amounts of funds, who "economize on demand deposits" by holding in their place such liquid assets as time deposits at commercial banks, claims against other financial intermediaries, and liquid direct securities such as Treasury bills and commercial paper. The secular growth of demand for checking deposits would almost certainly be greater if banks were permitted to pay interest on demand deposits and in fact did so.

Holding explicit interest rates on demand deposits at zero while yields on competing assets fluctuate also contributes to cyclical and other short-term shifts in the quantity of checking deposits demanded. Rising rates on other assets shift some demand away from checking deposits, and falling rates on other assets have the reverse effect.

As already indicated, the prohibition of interest rates on demand deposits has shifted some of the public's demand toward time and savings deposits at commercial banks, although some of the shift has been toward claims against other intermediaries and toward liquid direct securities. There can now be no doubt that time and savings deposits at commercial banks must compete with claims against other intermediaries and with liquid direct claims for place in the public's portfolio. Substitutability is not perfect, but in many cases it is high. On various occasions, the Federal Reserve and FDIC ceilings on rates paid on time and savings deposits at commercial banks have affected the demanded quantities of these claims. Before 1966, there were no such ceilings on rates paid by other intermediaries or on yields of liquid direct assets. From the end of 1935 to the end of 1956, these ceilings were kept at constant low levels, none above $2\frac{1}{2}$ percent, while rates at other intermediaries, and especially savings and loan associations, were higher. The results should have been expected; these claims against commercial banks grew only slowly while those against savings and loan associations rose rapidly. Since 1956, the ceilings have been adjusted several times and have stood at various levels relative to rates on competing assets. In general, rates of growth of these claims against commercial banks have been high when their rates were high relative to those on other short-term liquid assets and low when their rates were low relative to others. Thus, ceilings have contributed to highly erratic changes in the quantities of these assets demanded.

Many economists are highly critical of the prohibition of interest on demand deposits and of effective ceilings on rates that banks may pay on time and savings deposits. They would either abolish outright these limitations on the freedom of banks to compete for funds with each other, with other intermediaries, and with direct securities, or they would have such powers available only on a standby basis to be used only on those occasions when bank competition for funds became in some meaningful sense "excessive."

Later chapters will discuss further both Federal Reserve control of the volume of bank deposits and the public's demands for such assets.

SOME RELATIONS AMONG BANKS

This chapter has been concerned with the entire commercial-banking system rather than any individual bank. We are concerned with aggregate effects, not with which bank does what. Yet it will be useful to consider here some of the relationships among the 13,700 banks spread over the 50 states, with no bank operating branches beyond the boundaries of its own state.

Interbank payments

We have already noted that the banking system as a whole, as well as an individual bank, may gain or lose cash reserves, owing to net inflows or net outflows of cash. Cash flows into banks continuously in exchange for deposit claims, and cash is continuously withdrawn from banks and deducted from deposit accounts. Ordinarily these cash inflows and outflows largely offset each other, but at times there are net gains or losses. An individual bank within the system may also gain or lose cash reserves through interbank payments, which occur in huge volume. These arise in two principal ways:

1. Through net purchases or sales of other assets by a bank for its own account. For example, a bank may transfer some of its cash reserve (currency or deposits at the Federal Reserve) to buy loans or securities from another bank or from a customer of another bank. Or it may gain cash reserves by selling some of its loans or securities to another bank or a customer of another bank.

2. Through net transfers of deposit claims among banks. Huge amounts of payments are made by transferring, usually by check, deposit claims from payers to payees. Fortunately for banks, only a small fraction of these flows lead to net interbank payments and to net transfers of cash reserves from one bank to another.

For one thing, payers and payees are often depositors at the same bank. For example, both Jones and Whyte may be depositors at Bank A. If Jones gives a $1,000 check to Whyte, Bank A will simply deduct that amount from its deposit liability to Jones and increase equally its deposit liability to Whyte. The bank's assets and total liabilities remain unchanged. But suppose payer and payee are not depositors in the same bank. Suppose Jones writes a $1,000 check on Bank A and gives it to Whyte, who deposits it in Bank B. The latter will add $1,000 to its deposit liability to Whyte and send the check to Bank A, which will deduct this amount from its deposit liability to Jones. Bank A now owes Bank B $1,000, which it will pay by transferring this amount of its cash reserves if there are no offsetting transactions. But there are likely to be some offsetting transactions, which will require Bank B or other banks to pay Bank A.

In the course of every day, large amounts of checks will be drawn on a bank and deposited in other banks, thus creating large liabilities for it to pay those banks. But at the same time, the bank will receive on deposit large amounts of checks drawn on other banks, thus giving it claims for payment by them. Since these will usually be largely offsetting, it would be both confusing and inefficient if each bank had to transfer cash reserves to meet the full value of its liability to pay other banks and to receive cash reserves equal to all its claims for payment by other banks. How much more efficient it would be to offset these flows to the maximum possible extent and transfer cash reserves only to cover net payments or receipts. A complex clearing and collection system has been developed for this purpose. It includes local clearing houses, correspondent banks, and the Federal Reserve banks. At least once a day, and sometimes oftener, these organizations compare for each bank the flow of checks drawn on it and deposited with other banks, with the flow of checks deposited with it and drawn on other banks. Each bank then receives the net amount due it or pays the net amount owed by it. And these net payments are usually made by transferring cash reserves.

As might be expected in a system including thousands of banks, each operating only in a restricted area, net interbank transfers are sometimes large. Some of these are seasonal in character. For example, a bank in a resort area knows that it will gain deposits and reserves in the peak season when its depositors are receiving large payments from visitors from other areas, and that it will lose deposits and reserves in the off season when its depositors' incomes are down and they are buying supplies for the coming season. A bank in a wheat-growing area is likely to gain deposits after harvest and lose them later. In some banks, the receipt and loss of deposits is cyclical in nature. For example, a bank in a steel-producing area is likely to gain deposits when sales of steel are high and to lose them when steel is in the doldrums. Or a bank may lose deposits and reserves simply because the public comes to prefer some other bank.

These interbank transfers of funds are significant for several reasons. In the first place, they help to explain why banks seek to attract deposits away from other banks. A bank that succeeds in this can thereby draw reserves from other banks and increase its lending power. In the second place, they make the "liquidity problem" of an individual bank quite different from that of the commercial-banking system as a whole. An individual bank must be able to meet not only its depositors' demands for coin and currency, but also its payments to other banks. And in the third place, because of these interbank transfers, an individual bank that receives an initial addition to its cash reserves usually cannot expand its loans, investments, and deposits by a multiple amount. The bank must recognize that at least some of the deposits that it creates by making loans or buying securities will be checked out to other banks, thereby necessitating transfer of all or some of the initial increase of cash reserves.

Correspondent relationships

No account of interbank relations would be complete without mention of "correspondent banking" in the United States. This is the arrangement under which some banks hold deposits with other banks and use these banks as agents in various types of transactions, such as check clearing and collection, purchases and sales of securities, purchases and sales of foreign exchange, and participations in large loans. This is our domestic counterpart of international correspondent banking, under which banks located in different countries hold deposits with each other and act as agents for each other in many types of transactions. Nations with only a small number of banks, each operating a nationwide system of branches, have no need for such a highly developed domestic correspondent system. In such cases, each bank has an office in the country's major financial center and can reach all parts of the country through its own branches. The importance of correspondent relationships in the United States derives from the structure of our banking system: the fact that most of our thousands of banks operate only one office, that no branch bank is permitted to have branches outside its home state, and that many of our banks are relatively small.

The center of American correspondent banking is New York City, the nation's great financial center, with its foreign-exchange market, its short-term money market, and its long-term capital markets. Almost every important bank in the country maintains correspondent relations with at least one large bank in that city. Chicago is the next most important center. Each of its two largest banks has more than a thousand correspondents. In addition there are many regional centers, among them Boston, Philadelphia, Atlanta, New Orleans, Cleveland, St. Louis, Kansas City, Dallas, San Francisco, and Seattle. The network of correspondent relations is complex, for many banks hold deposits in more than one center, and correspondent banks in one center often have correspondent relations with banks in other centers. Thus, a bank in a small Missouri town may have deposits in a St. Louis bank and possibly in a Chicago or New York bank, and the St. Louis bank is almost certain to have deposits in Chicago or New York, or both.

These interbank deposits serve several functions. Among these are:

1. To serve as legal reserves. Although members of the Federal Reserve may count as legal reserves only their cash in vault and deposits at the Federal Reserve banks, nonmember banks have more leeway. The relevant state laws permit most nonmember banks to hold at least a part of their legal reserves, usually a large part, in the form of deposit claims against other commercial banks.

2. To facilitate check clearing and collection. Many banks have their correspondent banks pay at least some of the checks drawn on them and collect checks on other banks that are deposited with them. A New Jersey bank may have such an arrangement with the Chase Manhattan Bank of New York. If so, at least some checks drawn on the New Jersey bank and deposited with other banks will be routed to Chase Manhattan, which will deduct them from the New Jersey bank's deposit account. And checks drawn on other banks and deposited with the New Jersey bank will be sent to Chase Manhattan, which will credit the New Jersey bank's deposit account and send the checks along for collection.

3. To facilitate domestic and foreign payments. A customer of the New Jersey bank may want to make payments with a draft drawn on a New York bank

or on some foreign bank. Holding deposits at Chase Manhattan, the New Jersey bank can draw drafts on that bank or on a foreign correspondent of that bank.

4. To facilitate agency operations. The New Jersey bank may use Chase Manhattan as an agent to buy or sell securities, to make loans for it on the Stock Exchange, or to accept or draw drafts. Interbank deposits that can be credited or debited to finance these transactions are helpful.

5. To increase the geographical mobility of credit. Banks with funds in excess of their current needs can increase their deposits at correspondent banks, thereby shifting reserves to them and increasing their lending power. On the other hand, banks that wish to increase their other assets or to meet withdrawals may withdraw some of their deposits from their correspondent banks. Geographical mobility of credit is also promoted, of course, when banks buy securities and other assets outside their own locality, or sell some of their securities and other assets to buyers outside their own locality.

Selected readings

American Bankers Association, *The Commercial Banking Industry,* Englewood Cliffs, N.J., Prentice-Hall, 1962.

Federal Deposit Insurance Corporation, Annual Reports, Washington, D.C.

Shaw, E. S., *Money, Income, and Monetary Policy,* Homewood, Ill., Irwin, 1950.

CHAPTER 7

BANK EXPANSION
AND CONTRACTION

We now return to a topic mentioned briefly in the preceding chapter—the total volume of bank deposits and bank assets. We shall consider such specific questions as: What are the objectives of bankers? What factors determine the maximum volume of loans and securities that the banking system can acquire and hold and the maximum volume of deposit liabilities that it can have outstanding? What factors determine the actual behavior of bank assets and liabilities within these maximum limits? How can the central bank or other monetary authority regulate the volume of bank assets and liabilities?

BANK OBJECTIVES

From the owners' viewpoint, the primary purpose of a commercial bank is to make profits. To say that it strives to maximize profits in either the short or long run is to put the matter too simply; but to say that it deliberately deviates very far or for very long from this purpose would probably be even more misleading. We have found that banks earn gross income when they buy debt claims against others by issuing deposit claims on themselves. Why, then, do they not buy up all the debt instruments in the economy and monetize them? Why should banks stop with monetizing all the debts that they could induce governments, business firms, and individuals to issue? Why should they not proceed to buy up great quantities of real goods that yield an income, paying for them with newly created deposits?

It should not be assumed that banks would find it profitable to expand to such lengths if they were free of official regulation. For one thing, banks do not find it costless to create deposit claims and to entice the public to hold very large amounts of them. They must pay interest to get the public to hold large amounts of time deposits, and it would be prohibitively costly for banks to pay interest rates high enough to attract all funds away from competing claims, such as claims against savings and loan associations, credit unions, and investment companies. They could, of course, create more demand deposits, on which they are presently prohibited by law from paying interest. These are not costless, for the bank must provide services to depositors—such things as checkbooks, accounting services, check clearing and collection, and so on. However, the marginal costs of creating additional demand deposits are probably so low relative to the additional income that would be yielded by the additional earning assets, that this consideration would not be a strong deterrent to money creation. If banks were free of official control, the most powerful deterrent to an unlimited expansion of deposits would be their obligation to keep their deposits redeemable in currency.

In discussing the evolution of fractional-reserve banking, we noted that banks discovered that they could usually keep their liabilities redeemable in currency if they held cash reserves equal to some fraction, such as one-eighth or one-tenth, of their liabilities. In other words, it was relatively safe for banks to create liabilities equal to 10 or 12 times their cash reserves. But to increase the ratio of liabilities to reserves beyond some such multiple becomes increasingly dangerous. If a bank attempted to expand its liabilities too far beyond its reserves, it could so damage the public's confidence in its ability to pay currency on demand that the quantity of liabilities it could keep outstanding would actually be reduced. The bank could even be forced into failure by its inability to honor its promises to pay currency on demand. Unfortunately, many banks have discovered this too late.

There is a real danger that banks would operate in a highly inflationary manner if they were free of official control. Moreover, their money-creating and money-destroying activities might be such as to create and accentuate cyclical fluctuations. In boom periods, when optimism reigns and the demand for bank loans is high, they might create large amounts of new money, thereby "booming the boom." Then, in depression periods, when the outlook is gloomy and risks increasing, they might seriously reduce the money supply, thereby deepening and prolonging the depression. Such dangers are so great that the creation of money by commercial banks is now subject to limitation and regulation in practically every country. In the United States, this is achieved primarily through regulating the *dollar volume of reserves* available to the commercial banks and by imposing *legal minimum-reserve requirements.*

RESERVES AND RESERVE REQUIREMENTS

It must be emphasized that the primary purpose of legal reserve requirements is not to force banks to remain "liquid" enough to be able to meet their obligations to pay. This may indeed have been the original purpose of these requirements. But the purpose now is to serve as a method of regulating the volume of bank deposits and, indirectly, the volume of bank assets.

This involves three steps by the government, central bank, or other monetary authority:

1. Define those particular types of assets that can be counted toward meeting legal reserve requirements. These assets should be of such a type that their dollar value can be regulated by the monetary authority. For commercial banks that are members of the Federal Reserve System (and these account for about 80 percent of all commercial-bank liabilities), only two types of assets can be counted as legal reserves: cash in vault and deposit claims against Federal Reserve banks.[1]

2. Regulate the dollar volume of legal reserves available to the banks. This is one of the major functions of the Federal Reserve.

3. Require the banks to hold legal reserves equal to *at least* some stated fraction of their deposit liabilities. We shall see later that the Federal Reserve is empowered to set such minimum fractional-reserve requirements for member banks and to alter within limits the height of these minimum requirements. Note that to fix a minimum ratio of reserves to deposit liabilities is the same as fixing a maximum ratio of deposit liabilities to reserves. For example, to say to a bank, "You must hold reserves equal to at least 20 percent of your deposit liabilities," is the same as saying, "Your deposit liabilities may not exceed five times the volume of your reserves." And to say, "You must hold reserves equal to at least 10 percent of your deposits," is to say, "Your deposits may not exceed 10 times the volume of your reserves."

Thus, we find that the maximum volume of commercial-bank deposit liabilities that may be outstanding depends on (1) the dollar volume of reserves available to the banks, and (2) the size of the minimum legal ratio of reserves to deposits. This indicates why dollars in bank reserves are often referred to as "high-powered" money; under a fractional-reserve system, each dollar of legal reserves can "support" several dollars for checking deposits. And the lower the required reserve ratio, the "higher powered" is each dollar of reserves.

This also introduces us to the two principal ways in which the Federal Reserve can regulate the behavior of the money supply. Although the Federal

---

[1] From 1917 to 1959, only deposit claims against the Federal Reserve could be counted as legal reserves by member banks.

Reserve uses a number of instruments, all are aimed at regulating either the dollar volume of reserves available to commercial banks or the height of the minimum legal ratio of reserves to deposit liabilities. The Federal Reserve also indirectly regulates the volume of bank loans and security holdings, because changes in these would affect the volume of deposits.

The combination of the dollar volume of bank reserves and the legal minimum-reserve ratio determines only the *maximum* level of deposit liabilities; it does not force the banks to expand their holdings of loans and securities until this ceiling on their deposit liabilities is reached. The only pressure on banks to reach this maximum comes from the profit motive. Dollars of excess reserves yield no interest; loans and securities do. Usually, therefore, banks are impelled to expand their loans and security holdings close to the maximum limit permitted by their reserve positions. However, some banks do hold reserves in excess of legal requirements, at least occasionally. There are several reasons for this: imperfect forecasts of their average deposits or actual reserves during a reserve period, excess reserves are so small and are expected to be retained such a short period that it is not worthwhile to use them to buy other liquid assets, or yields on other liquid assets are extremely low. We shall later return to the case in which banks elect to hold excess reserves. In the meantime, we shall assume that the banking system expands to the maximum permitted by its reserves.

CHANGES IN THE VOLUME OF BANK RESERVES

It should be intuitively plausible that an initial change in the volume of reserves available to a banking system operating on fractional reserves will permit or necessitate a change in bank deposits and assets equal to some multiple of the initial change in reserves. And the size of the multiple will tend to be larger as the fractional-reserve requirement is smaller. Thus, each dollar increase in reserves will permit the banking system to expand deposits and earning assets by some multiple of that dollar. If the banks lose a dollar of reserves when they hold no reserves in excess of legal requirements, they will have to reduce their deposit liabilities and assets by some multiple of the dollar lost. This multiple expansion or contraction of the deposits and assets of a banking system in response to an initial change in the volume of its reserves plays a central role in commercial-banking theory and is of crucial importance to monetary authorities who are responsible for regulating the volume of bank liabilities and assets.

We shall be interested not in just one multiple but in several: those relating to (1) demand deposits; (2) total deposits, including both demand and time; (3) bank earning assets, including both loans and securities; and (4) the money supply, including both changes in demand deposits and changes in currency in circulation outside banks. In some cases, the sizes of these multiples can differ significantly.

Several aspects of our analysis should be considered.

1. In the following section, we shall be dealing with the banking system as a whole. The multiples that will be developed do not apply to an individual bank experiencing an initial change in its reserves. This case will be treated later.

2. The multiples apply to an *initial* change of reserves because a resulting expansion may induce some loss of reserves and a contraction may induce some gain in reserves. Moreover, the multiples apply to initial changes in excess reserves or to a deficiency of reserves relative to requirements.

3. The multiples apply to derivative deposits only and do not include any initial change that occurs in primary deposits.

The last two points require explanation. The banking system can experience a change in its reserves, either through a change in primary deposits or without a change in primary deposits. An example of the latter would be $100 increase in bank reserves resulting from bank borrowings from the Federal Reserve. The initial effects on the balance sheet of the commercial banks would be as follows:

ASSETS		LIABILITIES	
Reserves	+$100	Borrowings from the Federal Reserve	+$100

Since banks are not required to hold reserves against liabilities in the form of borrowings from the Federal Reserve, the entire $100 increase in reserves constitutes an increase in excess reserves, and all these serve as a basis for a multiple expansion of derivative deposits and of bank holdings of loans and securities.

Now consider the case in which the banking system receives a $100 initial increase in its reserves through an increase of primary deposits. This could reflect such events as a net inflow of currency from circulation, an increase in the country's monetary gold stock, or a Federal Reserve purchase of securities from the public. Suppose further that reserve requirements against demand deposits average 15 percent. The initial effect on the banks' balance sheets will be the following:

ASSETS		LIABILITIES	
Reserves	+$100	Demand deposits	+$100
Addenda:			
Required reserves	+$ 15		
Excess reserves	+$ 85		

The $100 of primary deposits have indeed brought a $100 increase in the actual reserves of the banks. But excess reserves are increased only $85 because $15 are required as reserves against the primary deposit. Only this increase of excess reserves can serve as a basis for the multiple increase of derivative deposits and earning assets with which we shall be concerned.

In each of the following cases, we shall assume that the initial change in excess reserves reflects a change in the volume of bank borrowings at the Federal Reserve. This assumption is intended to simplify the accounting and to allow us to deal uniformly with all cases. However, it should be emphasized that the same principles apply to any initial change in excess reserves, regardless of the source.

MULTIPLE EXPANSION—A GENERAL SURVEY

Before analyzing rigorously the factors determining the size of the various multiples of expansion or contraction, let us consider the subject in more general terms.

Suppose the banks receive an initial increase in their excess reserves. Since these funds yield no interest or other income, the banks will feel impelled to use them as a basis for increasing loans or buying securities, or both. Those members of the public who borrow from or sell securities to the banks will usually receive the proceeds in the form of new checking deposits. But regardless of the form in which the proceeds are initially received, the public is free to change the forms and proportions in which it will hold them. According to its preferences, the public may continue to hold all the proceeds in the form of demand deposits, it may hold some or all in time deposits, or it may take at least some to be held in the form of additional currency outside the banking system. The sizes of the various multiples will be affected substantially by the public's choices as to the forms and proportions in which it will hold the proceeds from new bank loans and security purchases.

If all the proceeds continue to be held as demand deposits, all the initial increase of reserves remains in the banks to serve as a basis for additional demand deposits. The size of the multiples will then depend on the size of the fractional-reserve requirement. For example, if the reserve requirement is 0.15, each $1 initial increase of reserves will support a $1/0.15, or $6.67, increase of demand deposits and also of bank loans and securities.

If the public elects to hold at least some part of the proceeds in time deposits, the sizes of the various multipliers are usually different. This is because reserve requirements against time deposits are usually much lower than those against demand deposits, although these requirements are determined by law and by decision of the monetary authorities. For example, when reserve requirements against demand deposits are 0.15, the requirements against time deposits may be only 0.04.[2] In effect, each dollar of reserves will support more time deposits than demand deposits. Thus, the greater the proportions of the proceeds held in

---

[2] As will be seen later, there is strong support for a zero reserve requirement against time deposits. If this were the situation, our point would be strengthened.

time deposits rather than demand deposits, and the lower the reserve requirement against time deposits relative to those against demand deposits, the greater will be the multiple expansion of total deposits, including both demand and time. This is because the greater weight of time deposits with the lower reserve requirement serves to lower the weighted-average reserve requirement against total deposits. Also, the multiple expansion of bank loans and security holdings will be greater, for banks can buy these assets by creating time-deposit claims as well as demand deposits. But the multiple expansion of demand deposits alone will be lower, for the banks must use some part of the initial increase of excess reserves to meet reserve requirements against the increase of time deposits.

All the multiples (those applying to the expansion of demand deposits, total deposits, and bank holdings of loans and securities) will be reduced if some of the proceeds are taken in the form of currency and held as such outside the banking system. We shall call this an "induced cash drain from the banking system." Each dollar withdrawn to serve as currency in circulation removes a dollar of the initial increase of reserves and leaves the banks with a smaller net increase of reserves to support deposit creation. We shall find that induced cash drains can markedly reduce the sizes of the expansion multiples.

In summary, the sizes of the multiples of expansion of demand deposits, total deposits, and loans and security holdings permitted by each dollar of initial increase of reserves in the banking system depend on several things: the height of legal reserve requirements against demand deposits and time deposits, respectively, and the proportions in which the proceeds from the increased bank loans and security holdings come to be held as demand deposits, time deposits, and currency outside banks.

Consider now the reverse process, that is, the multiple contraction of bank deposits and earning assets required in response to an initial loss of reserves. Suppose the banking system suffers an initial net loss of reserves when it holds no reserves in excess of legal requirements. With their actual reserves now deficient relative to the amounts legally required, the banks will be forced to begin to reduce their outstanding loans or to sell securities, or both, in an effort to remedy their reserve deficiencies. Those who buy securities from the banks or repay loans to the banks must surrender something in payment. These net payments to the banks can occur in various forms and proportions. The public might pay the banks entirely by surrendering demand-deposit claims, or it might pay at least in part by surrendering time-deposit claims or currency formerly held outside the banking system. The sizes of the multiples of contraction of bank deposits and earning assets will be substantially affected by the public's choices among the methods of paying the banks.

Suppose the public pays the banks entirely by relinquishing demand-deposit claims. In this case, there is no induced currency flow into the banks to offset any part of the initial loss of reserves. The banks must remedy their reserve deficiency entirely by reducing their loans and security holdings, thus extinguishing demand deposits and lowering the volume of their required reserves. The sizes of the necessary multiples of contraction will then depend on the size of the fractional-reserve requirement. For example, if the reserve requirement is 0.15, each $1 initial loss of reserves will require a contraction of $1/0.15, or $6.67, of demand deposits and also of bank loans and security holdings.

The multiples will be different if the public makes at least some of the necessary payments to banks by relinquishing time-deposit claims. Suppose all the payments are made in this way and that the reserve requirement against time deposits is 0.04. For each dollar of reserves lost, the banks would have to reduce time deposits and also their holdings of loans and securities by $1/0.04, or $25. More generally, the greater the proportion of payments made to the banks with time deposits rather than demand deposits and the lower the reserve requirement on time deposits relative to that on demand deposits, the greater will be the necessary multiple contraction of total deposits. Also greater will be the necessary multiple contraction of bank loans and security holdings. But the necessary contraction of demand deposits alone will be smaller, because the contraction of time deposits reduces the volume of reserves required against them and to this extent lessens the amount of adjustment that must be made by reducing demand-deposit liabilities.

All the multiples of necessary contraction (of demand deposits, time deposits, and bank holdings of loans and securities) will be smaller if the public surrenders in payment to the banks some currency formerly held outside the banking system. We shall call this an "induced cash inflow." Each dollar of induced cash inflow offsets a dollar of the initial loss of reserves and thus reduces the extent to which the banks must repair their reserve deficiency by contracting their deposit liabilities.

We have now described in general terms the multiples of expansion permitted by an initial increase in the excess reserves of the banking system, and the multiples of contraction required by an initial loss of reserves. We have also noted some of the factors determining the sizes of the multiples. Let us now analyze these more closely, using the following symbols:

ΔA = the initial change in the volume of excess reserves of the banking system.

r = the fractional-reserve requirement against demand-deposit liabilities. If reserve requirements against demand deposits are different for various classes of banks, r is the weighted average of these requirements.

b = the fractional-reserve requirement against time deposits.

ΔD = change in the dollar volume of demand deposits. In the case of an initial increase of reserves, ΔD is the maximum permitted expansion. In the case of an initial loss of reserves, ΔD is the minimum required contraction.

ΔT = change in the volume of time deposits. At times, it will be convenient to state this as $\Delta T = n \Delta D$, thus stating ΔT as a fraction or multiple of ΔD.

ΔL = change in the volume of loans and security holdings of the banking system.

ΔC = net induced cash drain from the banking system in the case of bank expansion, and net induced cash inflow in the case of bank contraction. This will sometimes be expressed as $\Delta C = s\,\Delta D$, thus stating ΔC as a fraction, s, of ΔD.

ΔM = change in the money supply. This is equal to $\Delta D + \Delta C$.

We shall now proceed to develop and compare three different cases of multiple expansion and contraction. In order to compare the sizes of the multiplier, we shall in all cases assume that:

ΔA = \$100, reflecting an equal change in bank borrowings from the
  Federal Reserve   (1)
 $r = 0.15$ (2)
 $b = 0.04$ (3)

The reader should find it useful, however, to work through the various cases, using other values for r and b.

CASE I: $\Delta T = 0$ AND $\Delta C = 0$

We start with the simple case in which expansion or contraction by the banking system involves no change in time deposits and no induced cash drain or cash inflow—otherwise expressed, $n = 0$ and $s = 0$. Thus, no part of the initial gain or loss of excess reserves comes to be offset by an induced cash drain or cash inflow, and the banks must adjust to the gain or loss of reserves solely by changing the volume of their demand-deposit liabilities.

Expansion

Suppose the banks receive an initial increase in their excess reserves equal to ΔA. With this accretion to their excess reserves, they can proceed to create additional demand deposits (ΔD) by expanding their holdings of loans and securities (ΔL). They will have expanded to the maximum permitted by ΔA only when they have expanded demand deposits so much that their required reserves ($r\,\Delta D$) have risen by an amount equal to the initial increase of excess reserves. In other words, maximum expansion has been reached when

$$r\,\Delta D = \Delta A$$

or

$$\Delta D = \Delta A\,\frac{1}{r}$$

Substituting our assumed values of ΔA = \$100 and $r = 0.15$, we get

$$\Delta D = \$100 \, \frac{1}{0.15} = \$666.67$$

The net changes on the balance sheet of the banking system will be as follows:

ASSETS		LIABILITIES	
ΔA	+$100	Borrowings from the	
ΔL	+$666.67	Federal Reserve	+$100
		ΔD	+$666.67
Addendum:			
Increase of required reserves			
$= \$666.67 \times 0.15 = \$100$			

The addendum shows that demand deposits have indeed expanded to the maximum permitted, for required reserves have been increased enough to absorb all of the initial increase of excess reserves. For purposes of comparison with the cases that follow, it should be noted that in this case $\Delta L = \Delta D = \Delta M$. In other words, the expansion of bank loans and security holdings was accompanied by an equal increase in checking deposits and an equal increase in the money supply because the volume of currency outside banks remained unchanged.

Contraction

We can deal with contraction briefly because both the process and the reasoning are quite comparable to those above. Suppose that at a time when they hold no reserves in excess of legal requirements, the banks suffer an initial loss of reserves equal to ΔA. Now that their reserves are deficient, the banks must proceed to reduce their demand-deposit liabilities (ΔD) by reducing their loans and security holdings (ΔL). They will have contracted by the minimum necessary amount only when they have reduced deposit liabilities so much that their required reserves ($r \Delta D$) have decreased by an amount equal to the actual loss of reserves. In short, the minimum required contraction has been reached when

$$r \, \Delta D = \Delta A$$

or

$$\Delta D = \Delta A \, \frac{1}{r}$$

Again substituting our assumed values,

$$\Delta D = -\$100 \, \frac{1}{0.15} = -\$666.67$$

The following changes will appear on the balance sheet of the banking system.

ASSETS		LIABILITIES	
ΔA	−$100	Borrowing from the	
ΔL	−$666.67	Federal Reserve	−$100
		ΔD	−$666.67
Addendum:			
Change in required reserves			
= −$666.67 × 0.15 = −$100			

The addendum shows that the decrease of demand deposits has decreased required reserves by an amount equal to the initial deficiency of reserves. Note that here, again, $\Delta L = \Delta D = \Delta M$. By decreasing their loans and security holdings, the banks have destroyed equal amounts of both checking deposits and the money supply.

CASE II: $\Delta C = 0$ $n > 0$

In this case, we shall still assume that in the process of expansion or contraction, the banks experience no net cash drain or inflow, but we recognize that there may be induced changes in time deposits (ΔT). Whether or not such changes in T will occur, and how large they will be relative to changes in demand deposits, depend on many things, such as the nature of service charges on demand deposits, the height of interest rates on time deposits, the characteristics of other available claims and the height of their yields, changes in income levels and rates of saving, and so on. Without delving further into the relevant motivations, we shall assume that time deposits do expand and contract as banks expand and contract their earning assets, and that $\Delta T = n \, \Delta D$. In our numerical example, we shall let $n = \frac{1}{2}$. That is, every $1 of ΔD is accompanied by a 50-cent ΔT.

Expansion

Again suppose that excess bank reserves are increased in the amount of ΔA. On the basis of these new excess reserves, the banks can expand their holdings of loans and securities, thereby creating deposit liabilities. The proportions in which these proceeds will come to be held in demand deposits and in time deposits depend on the public's choices between these two types of assets. The expansion will have reached the maximum only when the sum of the increase in reserves required against the increase of demand deposits $(r \, \Delta D)$ plus the increase in reserves required against the increase in time deposits $(b \, \Delta T$ or $nb \, \Delta D)$ is equal to the actual increase of reserves, ΔA. In other words, maximum expansion is reached only when

$$r \, \Delta D + nb \, \Delta D = \Delta A$$
$$\Delta D \, (r + nb) = \Delta A$$
$$\Delta D = \Delta A \, \frac{1}{r + nb}$$

By substituting our assumed values of $\Delta A = \$100$, $r = 0.15$, $b = 0.04$, and $n = \frac{1}{2}$, we get

$$\Delta D = \$100 \, \frac{1}{0.15 + 0.02} = \$588.23$$

Since we assumed n to be $\frac{1}{2}$, $\Delta T = \frac{1}{2} \, \Delta D$, or \$294.12. And since all the proceeds from the increase of bank loans and security holdings came to be held as demand and time deposits, $\Delta L = \Delta D + \Delta T$, or \$882.35. The balance sheet on the table below shows how the changes would appear in the balance sheet of the banking system.

ASSETS		LIABILITIES	
ΔA	+\$100.00	Borrowings from the Federal Reserve	+\$100
ΔL	+\$882.35	ΔD	+\$588.23
		ΔT	+\$294.12

Addenda:
Change in reserves required against

Demand deposits	$= 588.23 \times 0.15$	\$ 88.24
Time deposits	$= 294.12 \times 0.04$	11.76
Total	....	\$100.00

A glance at the addenda to the table above shows that the banks have indeed expanded to the maximum, for the entire \$100 initial increase of excess reserves is now "used up" in meeting the \$88.24 of reserves required against the expansion of demand deposits and the \$11.76 increase of reserves required against the new time deposits.

A comparison of the results in this case with those in Case I highlights some important points. If not all the proceeds from an expansion of bank loans and security holdings are held as demand deposits, but some are instead reflected in an increase of time deposits, the sizes of the various multiples will be affected as follows:

1. The total deposit multiple will be greater. This is because b is lower than r. And the size of the multiple will be greater as n is larger and as b is smaller relative to r.

2. The multiple of expansion of loans and security holdings will also be greater, for the banks can acquire earning assets by creating both time- and demand-deposit liabilities.

3. The multiple expansion of demand deposits alone will be smaller. This is because some part of the initial increase of reserves is "used up" to meet reserve requirements against the additional time deposits. Of course, if reserve requirements against time deposits were zero, this would not be true.

4. The multiple expansion of the total money supply, as we define it, will also be smaller, for we exclude time deposits from the money supply.

Contraction

Because contraction and expansion are such comparable processes, we ask the reader to review the discussion immediately above, and to develop the process of contraction on his own. Assume that at a time when they hold no reserves in excess of legal requirements, the banks suffer an initial loss of reserves equal to ΔA. Then, as the banks decrease their loans and security holdings, the public pays in part by surrendering time-deposit claims. Let $\Delta T = n \Delta D$. Then solve for the minimum necessary contraction of $D, D + T, L,$ and M. *Suggestion:* Check your results by computing the changes in the volume of reserves required against ΔD and ΔT and comparing the sum with the actual initial change of reserves, ΔA.

CASE III: EXPANSION AND CONTRACTION WITH INDUCED CASH DRAINS AND INFLOWS

In the first two cases, we assumed that, as banks expanded, they induced no net currency drain from the banking system and therefore lost none of the initial increase of reserves. And when they contracted, they induced no net currency flow into the banks and were not able to gain reserves in this way to offset some of the initial loss. In some cases, these assumptions are realistic, especially when the expansion or contraction is relatively small. But frequently (and even usually when expansions or contractions are large) net cash drains or inflows are induced. When these do occur, they can markedly reduce the sizes of the various multiples of expansion or contraction.

Why does the public tend to hold more currency as the banks increase the total money supply, and to hold less currency when the banking system contracts? The answers most frequently given are of two general, although not necessarily conflicting, types. One emphasizes that, given the state of institutional arrangements and public preferences, there will be some more-or-less fixed ratio of currency and checking deposits that the public considers to be most advantageous. When the total money supply is increased, the public will elect to hold a major part of it in the form of deposits, but will take some part in additional currency. And when the total supply of money is decreased, the public will give up some currency as well as relinquish deposits.

The other approach emphasizes the behavior of the types of payments for which currency is widely held and used. These include payrolls and consumer expenditures to retail stores, restaurants, transportation companies, nightclubs, parking meters, gasoline stations, and so on. The amounts of currency that the public demands to hold will most likely vary in the same direction if not in strict proportion with these expenditures. When the banking system expands its loans and security holdings to any considerable extent, the result is likely to be an expansion of expenditures in general, including payrolls and spendings of a retail nature. The public is therefore likely to demand more currency. But a sizeable contraction of bank credit is likely to bring the opposite results, that is, a decrease of spendings in general, including payrolls and retail trade, and a net relinquishment of currency by the public.

Although both these approaches lead to the same qualitative conclusion—that large changes in bank deposits and asset holdings are likely to be accompanied by changes in the same direction of the public's demand for currency—they need not imply the same quantities or timing. In fact, the second explanation seems more realistic because it implies that changes in the public's demand for currency will change only as the effects of bank expansion or contraction are reflected in changes in income, payrolls, and retail trade. However, for reasons of simplicity we shall assume that as banks expand they do induce a net drain of currency into circulation (ΔC). And as banks contract, they induce a net inflow of currency from circulation. In both cases, ΔC will be expressed as a fraction s times ΔD. In our numerical example, we shall let $s = 0.23$. Thus, $\Delta C = 0.23\,\Delta D$.

Expansion

Again we start with the assumption that the banking system enjoys an initial increase in its excess reserves (ΔA) and that it proceeds on this basis to expand its loans and security holdings. The public will hold the proceeds in the desired proportions in the form of additional demand deposits (ΔD), additional time deposits $(n\,\Delta D)$, and additional currency $(s\,\Delta D)$. In this case, the initial increase of reserves is "absorbed," or "used up," in three ways: as required reserves against the additional demand deposits $(r\,\Delta D)$; as required reserves against the additional time deposits $(bn\,\Delta D)$; and to meet the net induced drain of currency from the banking system $(s\,\Delta D)$. The banks will have expanded to the maximum only when all the initial increase of reserves has been "absorbed" in these three forms. In short, maximum expansion is reached when

$$r\,\Delta D + nb\,\Delta D + s\,\Delta D = \Delta A$$
$$\Delta D\,(r + nb + s) = \Delta A$$
$$\Delta D = \Delta A\,\frac{1}{r + nb + s}$$

Substituting our assumed values of $A = \$100$, $r = 0.15$, $b = 0.04$, $n = 0.5$, and $s = 0.23$, we get

$$\Delta D = \$100\,\frac{1}{0.15 + 0.02 + 0.23} = \$100\,\frac{1}{0.40} = \$250$$

We can also use this formula and our assumed values to compute other magnitudes in which we are interested.

1. ΔT, which is stated as nD, is $\frac{1}{2}\,\Delta D$, or $\$125$.
2. The increase of total deposits, $\Delta D + \Delta T$, may be stated as $(1 + n)\,\Delta D$. In this case, it is $(1 + 0.5)\,\$250$, or $\$375$.
3. The net drain of currency into circulation, ΔC, is $s\,\Delta D$. In this case, it is $0.23\,\Delta D$, or $\$57.50$. Note that this represents both the amount of the initial increase of reserves that the banking system loses through the induced currency drain and

the part of the increased money supply that the public elects to hold in the form of increased currency outside the banks.

4. The increase of bank loans and security holdings is equal to the sum of $\Delta D + \Delta T + \Delta C$. This reflects the fact that the banks can buy claims against others by creating demand- and time-deposit claims and also by paying out some of its cash reserves to those who borrow from or sell securities to them. ΔL may also be expressed as $(1 + n + s) \Delta D$. In this case, $\Delta L = (1 + 0.5 + 0.23)$ \$250, or \$432.50.

5. The increase of the public's money supply (ΔM) is equal to the increase in demand deposits plus the net induced drain of currency from the banks into circulation (ΔC). Since the latter is equal to $s \Delta D$, $\Delta M = (1 + s) \Delta D$. In this case, it is $(1 + 0.23)$ \$250, or \$307.50.

The final effects on the balance sheet of the banking system will be as shown on the table below. The addenda indicate that the banks have expanded to the maximum, because the entire \$100 initial increase of excess reserves has been "used up" to meet the induced cash drain and to serve as required reserves against the additional demand and time deposits.

ASSETS		LIABILITIES	
Initial ΔA	+\$100.00	Borrowings from the Federal	
Less: cash drain	57.50	Reserve	+\$100
		ΔD	\$250
Remaining increase of		ΔT	\$125
reserves	\$ 42.50		
ΔL	\$432.50		

Addenda:
"Absorption" of the initial \$100 increase of reserves:

Loss of reserves through cash drain	\$ 57.50
Increase of reserve required against new demand deposits	37.50
Increase of reserve required against new time deposits	5.00
Total	\$100.00

As one compares the results in this case with those in Cases I and II, he cannot fail to be impressed by the powerful force of an induced cash drain in reducing the sizes of the various multiples of expansion. A cash drain has this effect because each dollar it removes from the banks is a dollar of reserves which, if it had remained in the banks, would have "supported" several dollars of expansion of bank deposits and of bank holdings of loans and securities. This is a fact of great importance to anyone who would understand banking and also to monetary authorities charged with responsibility for regulating the money supply and the quantity of credit supplied by banks through their acquisition of loans and securities.

Contraction

Suppose that the banks suffer an initial loss of reserves, ΔA, at a time when they have no excess reserves, and that the ensuing bank contraction induces a net flow of currency into the banks. You are invited to trace through the process and to calculate the minimum necessary contractions of demand and time deposits, bank loans and security holdings, and the money supply. Test your understanding by considering these questions:

1. Why are all the multiples of minimum necessary contraction so much smaller than in Cases I and II?
2. Why is ΔL greater than $\Delta D + \Delta T$?
3. Why is ΔM greater than ΔD?
4. How do you know that the banks have contracted by the necessary minimum when they have contracted by the amounts that you calculated?

The general case

We developed our analysis through three cases, both to proceed from the simplest to the more complex and also to emphasize the importance of the values of the variables in determining the sizes of the various multiples of maximum expansion and minimum necessary contraction. It should be clear, however, that the formulas used in Case III apply generally. Case I is simply the special case in which $n = 0$ and $s = 0$. Case II is the special case in which $s = 0$. Thus, the general formulas are

$$\Delta D = \Delta A \, \frac{1}{r + nb + s} \tag{1}$$

$$\Delta T = n \, \Delta D \tag{2}$$

$$\Delta D + \Delta T = (1 + n) \, \Delta D \tag{3}$$

$$\Delta C = s \, \Delta D \tag{4}$$

$$\Delta L = \Delta D + \Delta T + \Delta C = (1 + n + s) \, \Delta D \tag{5}$$

$$\Delta M = \Delta D + \Delta C = (1 + s) \, \Delta D \tag{6}$$

It should be remembered that this analysis assumes that the entire initial change in reserves represents a change in excess reserves, and the deposit multiples refer only to derivative deposits. When the initial change of reserves occurs as a result of primary deposits, excess reserves change only by an amount equal to the initial change of reserves minus the additional reserve required against the primary deposit.

COMPARISON OF CASES OF
MULTIPLE EXPANSION AND CONTRACTION

Table 7–1 enables us to compare easily the various multiples of expansion in the three cases resulting from a given initial increase of excess reserves and given levels of reserve requirements. (In all three cases the multiples of minimum necessary contraction are the same as those for maximum expansion.)

The largest multiple of expansion of demand deposits and the money supply is achieved in Case I, where there is no induced increase in either time deposits

Table 7–1 Summary of expansion in three cases
($\Delta A = \$100$, $r = 0.15$, $b = 0.04$)

	CASE I $n = 0$ $s = 0$	CASE II $n = 0.50$ $s = 0$	CASE III $n = 0.50$ $s = 0.23$
ΔD	$666.67	$588.23	$250.00
ΔT	0	294.12	125.00
$\Delta D + \Delta T$	666.67	882.35	375.00
ΔL	666.67	882.35	432.50
ΔC	0	0	57.50
$\Delta M = \Delta D + \Delta C$	666.67	588.23	307.50

or currency outside banks. Case II illustrates the effects when some part of the proceeds of bank net purchases of loans and securities comes to be held in the form of time and savings deposits. The effects are to increase the expansion multiples of total deposits and of loans and security holdings, but to decrease the multiples of expansion of demand deposits and the money supply. Case III illustrates how sharply an induced currency drain from the banks can decrease all the multiples of expansion.

In forecasting the monetary effects that will flow from changing the volume of reserves available to the banking system and in determining the appropriate amount of new reserves to be injected or amounts to be withdrawn, the Federal Reserve needs to consider the factors determining the sizes of these multiples. It knows, of course, the height of legal reserve requirements against the various classes of deposits. The other factors it must forecast as well as it can and try later to offset any errors in its forecasts by further adjustments in the volume of reserves. At least three questions are involved.

1. How much of the change in excess reserves will banks use as a basis for expansion and how much will they elect to hold idle?

2. How large will be the induced change of currency in circulation? They may be unable to forecast this accurately, but econometric studies of past experience throw considerable light on the subject.

3. As the banks expand their loans and security holdings, what part will come to be held as demand deposits and what part as time and savings deposits? This question is difficult to answer; the authorities must rely on past experience and on projections based on analyses of the level of yields on time and savings deposits as compared with those on other competing assets.

Perhaps the most puzzling questions that the Federal Reserve faces in this area are questions of interpretation. Which of these variables is most relevant to the behavior of interest rates; to aggregate demand for output; and to the behavior of output, employment, and price levels? Is it the money supply, narrowly defined; the sum of currency in circulation, demand deposits, and time and savings deposits at commercial banks; or the total loans and security holdings of commercial banks?

The issues can be sharpened by comparing Cases I and II above. Some economists believe that of all these variables, the money supply exerts the most potent influence on interest rates and aggregate demand, and that the money supply should be defined narrowly. They would say that Case I, in which the money supply thus defined rose $667, was more expansionary than Case II, in which this variable rose only $588. Milton Friedman and others who emphasize the key role of the money supply but also include time and savings deposits at commercial banks in their definition of the money supply would reply that Case II is the more expansionary in its effects on the economy, because in it the money supply, broadly speaking, increased by $882. Still others, who believe that it is the volume of bank loans and security holdings rather than the money supply that is crucial would also say that Case II is the more expansionary in its effects because in it the volume of bank credit rose $882 as compared with only $667 in Case I.

Time and savings deposits and their effects obviously play a key role in such controversies for they represent the difference between two definitions of the money supply and a major part of the difference between the volume of loans and securities in the two cases. The role of these deposits has received extensive theoretical and empirical analysis in recent years as their volume has risen relative to demand deposits and as their rate of growth has varied widely relative to that of demand deposits.[3] Such studies have clarified some of the issues but have not yet produced empirical findings to enable us to estimate reliably the economic effects of changes in these deposits.

A simple, perhaps overly simple, example will illustrate a few of the critical issues. Suppose we start from an equilibrium situation in which the banking system is fully expanded to the limit permitted by its reserves, that the Federal Reserve does not allow the total volume of reserves to change, and that the public has the combination of assets in the forms of demand deposits, time deposits, and direct securities that it desires at the prevailing yields on time deposits and direct securities. Suppose now that the public demands $100 more of time deposits. We shall present two extreme cases.

1. A pure substitution of time deposits for demand deposits. The public does not decrease its demand for direct securities at all; it merely decreases its demand for demand deposits by $100. This creates excess reserves in the banking system, the amount depending on the difference between the requirements on demand and time deposits. Suppose the requirements are 15 and 4 percent, respectively. Reserves required against demand deposits are decreased by $15 while those against time deposits are increased only $4. Thus, the banks gain $11 of excess reserves on the basis of which they can expand their holdings of direct securities, the amount of the expansion depending on the factors already analyzed. However, since the public's demand for direct securities did not decrease, any

[3] See Lyle E. Gramley and Samuel B. Chase, Jr., "Time Deposits in Monetary Analysis," *Federal Reserve Bulletin,* October, 1965, pp. 1380–1406.

increase of demand by the banks will increase the total demand for direct securities, raise their price and lower their yields, and stimulate investment spending. In this case of pure substitution of time for demand deposits, the effect of the increase of time deposits is clearly stimulative.

2. A pure substitution of time deposits for direct securities. In this case, the public does not decrease its demand for demand deposits; it decreases its demand for direct securities by an amount fully equal to its increased demand for time deposits. Suppose banks initially buy the $100 of direct securities by issuing an additional $100 of time-deposit claims. This will increase their required reserves by $4, and since we assumed they were already fully "lent-up," their reserves will now be deficient by $4. To remedy this deficiency they will have to reduce their holdings of direct securities by some multiple of this amount. Thus, the net purchases of direct securities by banks would be less than $100 and not sufficient to offset the $100 decrease of the public's demand for direct securities.[4] The result would be a decrease in the total of public and bank demand for direct securities, a fall in the price and a rise in the yield on these securities, and some restrictive effect on investment spending.

Thus, the two extreme cases yield opposite results when total bank reserves are kept constant. If the public's increased demand for time deposits reflects an equal decrease of its demand for demand deposits, the effects on the economy are expansionary. At the other extreme, the effects on the economy are restrictive if the public's increase of demand for time deposits reflects an equal decrease of its demand for direct securities. Between these extremes, increases of the public's demand for time deposits can reflect various combinations of decreases of its demands for demand deposits and for direct securities. Thus, whether an expansion of time deposits is expansionary or restrictive, and just how expansionary or restrictive it will be, will vary from case to case.

EXPANSION AND CONTRACTION BY AN INDIVIDUAL BANK IN THE SYSTEM

At several points in the preceding sections, we emphasized that we were dealing with multiple expansion or contraction by the *banking system as a whole* in response to an initial change in its reserve. Although the same analysis can be applied to an individual bank, it can be applied only with very important modifications, because an individual bank is subjected to "induced reserve losses" and "induced reserve gains" that do not apply to the banking system as a whole. An individual bank, like the banking system, may experience an induced drain of currency into circulation or an inflow of currency from circulation. In addition, however, the individual bank is subject to induced reserve losses to make net payments

---

4 Suppose, for example, that the reserve requirement against demand deposits is 15 percent and that as the banks sell direct securities the public pays entirely by relinquishing demand deposits. The necessary decrease of demand deposits and of bank holdings of direct securities will be $4/0.15 = $26.67. Thus, the net increase of bank holdings of direct securities will be $100 − $26.67 = $73.33.

to other banks and to induced reserve gains as other banks make net payments to it. It is because of these induced reserve losses or gains through payments to, or receipts from, other banks that an individual bank receiving an initial increase of its reserves usually cannot expand its deposit liabilities and earning assets by a multiple and it need not contract its deposits and earning assets by a multiple because of an initial loss of reserves.

Expansion

To illustrate this, let us consider an individual bank, which we shall call "the first bank," and make the following assumptions:

1. The first bank receives a $10 million addition to its reserves through a primary deposit. This may, for example, result from an inflow of currency, gold inflows, or a Federal Reserve purchase of securities from the public.
2. All proceeds of bank loans are held in demand deposits; there is no change in time deposits and no induced cash drain.
3. All banks operate under a reserve requirement of 20 percent.

The initial effects on the balance sheet of the first bank are these:

ASSETS		LIABILITIES	
Reserves	+$10 million	Deposits	+$10 million
Addenda:			
Required reserves ..	+$ 2 million		
Excess reserves	+$ 8 million		

Now that it has $8 million of excess reserves, can the first bank proceed to increase its loans and security holdings by $8 million/0.20, or $40 million? It could if all the derivative deposits remained with it. In this case, all of the initial increase of reserves would remain in the first bank, available to support additional derivative deposits. But this is most unlikely to occur in a system with more than 13,000 banks. It is much more likely that a large part of the derivative deposits will be checked out to other banks, thus requiring the first bank to transfer reserves and thereby reducing its ability to expand its own loans and security holdings. Table 7–2 shows the expansion for individual banks and for the banking system as a whole on the extreme assumption that *all* derivative deposits created by one bank are checked out to the next bank and that an equal amount of reserves must be paid over to the transferee bank.

After receiving the $10 million addition to its deposits and reserves, the first bank "sets aside" the $2 million of additional required reserves, and expands its loans and security holdings by $8 million. These loan-created deposits are checked out to the second bank and an equal amount of reserves transferred to it. (We know that, for the banking system, these are derivative deposits; but to the second bank they will appear as primary deposits, because they brought with them an equal amount of reserves.) The second bank "sets aside" the $1.6 million of required reserves (20% of $8 million) and expands its loans and security holdings

Table 7–2 Deposit expansion on new reserves by a banking system

	ADDITIONAL DEPOSITS RECEIVED	ADDITIONAL RESERVES RETAINED AGAINST DEPOSITS RECEIVED (20%)	ADDITIONAL LOANS MADE (80%) *
First bank	$10,000,000	$ 2,000,000	$ 8,000,000
Second bank	8,000,000	1,600,000	6,400,000
Third bank	6,400,000	1,280,000	5,120,000
Fourth bank	5,120,000	1,024,000	4,096,000
Fifth bank	4,096,000	819,200	3,276,800
Sixth bank	3,276,000	655,360	2,621,440
Seventh bank	2,621,440	524,288	2,097,152
Eighth bank	2,097,152	419,430	1,677,722
Ninth bank	1,677,722	355,544	1,342,178
Tenth bank	1,342,178	268,436	1,073,742
Total, first ten banks	$44,630,492	$ 8,926,258	$35,705,034
Other banks in turn	5,369,508	1,073,742	4,294,966
Grand total	$50,000,000	$10,000,000	$40,000,000

* The deposits created by these loans are all checked out to the next bank.
SOURCE: Adapted from Board of Governors of the Federal Reserve System, *The Federal Reserve System—Its Purposes and Functions,* 1939, p. 73.

by $6.4 million. The resulting derivative deposits and an equal amount of reserves are transferred to the third bank, which continues the expansion, as do the others in turn. Thus, the $50 million expansion of deposits in the system as a whole ($40 million of which was created by bank loans and security purchases) represents increases at many banks.

This example illustrates some important points:

1. Every individual banker could properly say, "I certainly didn't engage in multiple expansion. All I did was to accept deposits, set aside the required reserve, and then lend an amount equal to the remainder." Yet for the system as a whole, there was indeed a multiple expansion of deposits and earning assets, and most of the new deposits were derivative deposits.

2. Most of the expansion occurred not at the bank initially receiving the increase of reserves, but in other banks to which most of the reserves came to be transferred.

3. This illustrates the process through which initial injections of additional reserves in only one or a few banks can lead to increased reserves and credit expansion throughout the banking system.

Contraction

Using comparable assumptions, suppose that an individual bank, the first bank, loses $10 million of reserves through a withdrawal of currency. The process, results, and conclusions are symmetrical with those above. Table 7–2 can be used to illustrate this if the column headings are changed. Change the first column to read, "Decrease in deposits and reserves"; the second to, "Decrease of required reserves because of loss of deposits"; and the third to, "Decrease in loans (this is equal to 80 percent of deposits lost)."

Now that its reserves are deficient, the first bank will decrease its loans and security holdings, receive in payment checks drawn on the second bank, and gain reserves from the latter. The second bank will decrease its loans and security holdings, receive in payment checks on the third bank, and gain reserves from it. And so the contraction process spreads and continues until the system has contracted by the minimum amount required to repair the reserve position of its members.

The general case

In order to emphasize the difference between an individual bank and the banking system as a whole, the preceding examples assumed that when an individual bank experienced an initial increase in its excess reserves and proceeded to expand its holdings of loans and securities, all of the resulting derivative deposits and an equal amount of reserves would be transferred to other banks. Thus, it could expand its loans and securities only by an amount equal to the initial addition to its excess reserves. This is an approximation of what often happens to an individual bank in a system of thousands of banks. However, in some cases a part of the derivative deposits created by an individual bank remains with it, at least for a time, so that its loss of deposits and reserves to other banks is less than depicted above. For example, a borrower from the bank may voluntarily leave some of the proceeds on deposit with the bank, or the bank may require him to do so as a condition for granting the loan. Or the borrower may pay some of the derivative deposits to others who are depositors at the same bank. In such cases, an individual bank may expand its loans and securities more than was indicated in the earlier example. However, the distinction between the individual bank and the banking system as a whole remains valid. Failure to make this distinction has in the past led to muddled thinking and policy mistakes and to needless controversies between bankers and economists.

CONCLUSIONS

Several of the major points in this chapter will be essential in our later analysis, especially when we deal with monetary management by the Federal Reserve.

1. Each dollar of bank reserves is indeed "high-powered" money, capable of supporting several dollars of deposits. Thus, by creating an additional dollar of reserves for the banks, the Federal Reserve can enable them to create several dollars of bank credit. And by depriving the banks of a dollar of reserves, the Federal Reserve can force them to reduce bank credit by some multiple.

2. The volume of deposits and also of bank loans and holdings of securities that can be supported by each dollar of reserves depends greatly on the height of legally required reserve ratios. Thus, the Federal Reserve's power to increase and decrease reserve requirements is a potent instrument.

3. The Federal Reserve or any other central bank that wishes to forecast the size of the effects that will flow from its own actions must use the type of analysis presented in this chapter.

Selected readings

Angell, J. W., and K. F. Ficek, "The Expansion of Bank Credit," *Journal of Political Economy*, 1933, pp. 1–32, 152–193.

Crick, W. F., "The Genesis of Bank Deposits," *Economica*, June, 1927.

Phillips, C. A., *Bank Credit*, New York, Macmillan, 1926.

Shaw, E. S., *Money, Income, and Monetary Policy*, Homewood, Ill., Irwin, 1950.

CHAPTER 8

COMMERCIAL-BANK POLICIES

Until now, our discussion of the commercial-banking system has primarily involved the commercial-banking system as a whole because, as we said earlier, "We are interested in what the commercial banks do as a group, not in which commercial bank does it." Now, however, we shift our attention to the individual bank—to its functions, its problems, its decision making, and its policies. One result of this approach should be to provide the reader with a better understanding of some basic problems and principles of managing an individual bank. However, by studying the policies of the basic decision-making units—the individual commercial banks—we shall also broaden and deepen our understanding of the system as a whole, because the behavior of the system is a result of the varying degrees and types of competition among the various units, all operating within the broader financial framework. We shall concentrate largely on the functioning of a bank as a financial intermediary and shall pay little attention to other functions that may be performed by a bank, such as dealing in foreign exchange, operating a trust department, and underwriting issues of state and municipal securities.

A BANK AS A FINANCIAL INTERMEDIARY

The individual banker will probably look at the relationship between bank deposit liabilities and bank assets in a different way than we did when we looked at the banking system as a whole. In the last two chapters, we emphasized that the great bulk of deposits were created through bank purchases of assets, although it was also noted that the banking system could not create and keep outstanding a larger volume of deposits than people were willing to acquire and hold. A banker is likely to view the relationship with the roles reversed—that is, the banker may feel that bank deposits give rise to bank acquisitions of assets. He might put it this way: "My bank is a member of the family called 'financial intermediaries.' As such, it gathers funds from people by issuing and selling financial claims against itself. It can acquire assets to the extent, and only to the extent, that it is supplied with funds in exchange for financial claims against it."

Thus a bank participates in financial markets in two principal roles—as a buyer of funds through issues of claims against itself and as a seller of funds or purchaser of financial claims against others.

Bank liabilities

A bank that seeks to attract funds by issuing financial claims against itself realizes that these claims must compete with many other types of financial claims for a place in the portfolios of asset holders—for example, these claims must compete with currency, with claims against other commercial banks, with claims against other types of financial intermediaries, and with direct securities of varying maturities and varying degrees of safety and liquidity. Thus the volume of claims against itself that a bank can persuade others to hold depends in part on both its "price policy"—the yields that it offers—and the characteristics of these claims in terms of safety, liquidity, and conformity to the preferences of various types of asset holders. A banker's freedom in determining the price and characteristics of these claims is to some degree restricted by laws and official regulations, but the banker still has considerable leeway within the regulatory framework. For example, although payment of explicit interest on demand deposits is prohibited by law, bankers have developed many nonprice methods of competing for these deposits. Also, although the Federal Reserve and the FDIC place ceilings on rates that banks may pay on time and savings deposits, these ceilings are sometimes high enough to permit considerable variation of actual rates beneath the ceilings, and, in any case, banks can adjust other characteristics of such deposits to make them more attractive.

For reasons to be discussed later, issues of equity or ownership claims usually provide a bank with only a minor portion of its total funds. Its net worth or capital account is rarely much above 10 percent of its total assets and is usually somewhat less. The bank relies largely on issues of debt claims, the great bulk of which are deposit liabilities of some type. From the mid-1930s until about the mid-1950s, most banks relied largely on demand deposits as sources of funds. However, since the mid-1950s banks have become increasingly aggressive in promoting their issues of time and savings deposit claims, and by the early 1970s these claims exceeded demand deposits at many banks.

To establish a policy for attracting demand deposits, a bank must first determine the nature and extent of the market from which it can expect to draw such deposits. For example, a small bank in a small or medium-sized town is unlikely to find it feasible to draw demand deposits from long distances or from large corporations; most of its funds of this type are likely to come from households, small and medium-sized business firms, and governmental units within its own locality. To attract deposits of these types, the small-town bank must usually compete only against a few local banks. At the other extreme, huge banks located in major financial centers find it feasible to attract demand deposits not only from their own localities but also from all over the nation and even from foreign countries. To attract depositors in such an expansive market, these banks must compete against many more banks than does its small-town counterpart.

The characteristics of time and savings deposit claims can be varied in many different ways. A major purpose of such differentiation is to tailor the claims to the differing preferences of asset holders. However, at least an incidental effect is to enable a bank to practice price discrimination—to attach differing yields to the various classes of claims. *Passbook savings deposits* are evidenced only by entries on the bank's books and in the depositor's passbook and bear no stipulated maturity date. The bank is legally empowered to require prior notice for withdrawal—usually at least 30 days—but, in practice, banks permit withdrawals at any time, the only penalty being a forfeiture of accrued interest. The interest rate is set by the bank and can be changed at any time. These deposits are held primarily by individuals and households. The principal attraction of these accounts is the immediate availability of the funds; however, their yields are often appreciably below those paid on some types of time deposits.

Time deposits have stipulated maturity dates, are evidenced by a written instrument, and bear a rate of interest that remains fixed during the life of the deposit contract. The shortest initial maturity is 30 days, but many have maturities of 60, 90, or 180 days, or even longer. Historically, most maturities have been a year or less, but in recent years many banks have offered longer maturities, some running for 5 or even 10 years. Time deposits are often classified in two categories—consumer type and business type. The consumer type is offered in denominations of less than $100,000 and is meant to appeal primarily to individuals and households. The written instruments representing these deposits are given various names, such as "certificates of deposit," "savings certificates," and "savings bonds." Holders of these claims are expected to hold them to maturity, but many banks stand ready to redeem them before maturity, imposing a penalty in the form of a loss of interest, or to make loans to the holders. The business type of time deposit is issued in denominations of at least $100,000, and some may have dollar amounts in the millions. Aside from their larger denominations, most business-type deposits are similar to consumer-type time deposits. However, a major event in commercial banking since the early 1960s has been the rapid development of the "large-denomination negotiable certificate of deposit." These are popularly known as "negotiable CDs." They have fixed denominations, fixed maturity dates, fixed rates of interest, and they are not payable by the issuing bank before their maturity. However, prior to maturity, they can be transferred freely from holder to holder by means of endorsement. If they are made out "to bearer," they do not even require endorsement. A group of dealers and brokers stand ready to facilitate the marketability of these instruments. Thus, while the issuing bank need not redeem the CD before its maturity, any holder can exchange it for money at any time in the secondary market.

The negotiable CD has assumed an important role in short-term money markets. It appeals to many types of investors, including nonfinancial business corporations, as a prime, liquid, earning asset. And for many banks, and especially for larger banks, it is an important source of funds. By 1971, the volume of outstanding negotiable CDs had passed $22 billion. The great bulk of these had been issued by banks with assets of $100 million or more, but some had been issued by smaller banks.

In issuing savings- and time-deposit claims, a bank encounters widely differing types and degrees of competition in different segments of the market. For example, some individuals and households have only small amounts of funds, are not sophisticated in their knowledge and appraisal of financial alternatives, and would find it costly and inconvenient to explore distant opportunities. These units may be willing to hold passbook savings accounts even at relatively low yields. At the other extreme, are large corporations with millions of dollars of investible funds and expert money managers who are fully aware of all financial alternatives. These corporations are likely to hold time-deposit claims against banks only if their yields are fully competitive with those available from other alternatives. In view of such differences, it is hardly surprising that banks practice price discrimination and attach different yields to claims tailored to appeal to different classes of investors.

Although deposit liabilities constitute the great bulk of bank debt, banks do create some other types of liabilities. We shall later discuss the types of debt that banks create as they borrow to meet temporary liquidity needs. In recent years, however, some banks have tended to rely more heavily and continuously on other debt to meet longer-term needs. For example, some banks have issued promissory notes or bonds that run for several years. And bank-holding companies, or non-bank subsidiaries of these holding companies, have issued commercial paper and transferred the proceeds to subsidiary banks. Such practices may well develop further in the future.

Bank assets

In its other role as a participant in financial markets, a bank acts as a seller of funds or a purchaser of financial claims against others. In this role it faces various types and degrees of competition from other lenders—such as other commercial banks, other types of financial intermediaries, and individual lenders and purchasers of direct securities. The asset policies of banks will be discussed later in more detail. At this time it is sufficient to indicate that a bank faces difficult policy decisions in determining the composition of its diversified portfolio—how much of its total assets should be allocated to holdings of cash, how much to loan to its various customers, and how much to each of the many other types of earning assets available in financial markets.

Interrelations between asset and liability policies

Although bank asset policies and bank liability policies were separated for expositional purposes, these two sets of policies are interdependent in various ways. For example, the yields that a bank can profitably pay on its deposit liabilities depend in part on the yields realized on its assets, which is influenced by the composition of its portfolio. Disaster may follow if assets and liabilities are seriously mismatched—if, for example, a bank issues liabilities that are denominated in fixed amounts of dollars and acquires assets, such as common stocks, that have values that fluctuate widely. Various other examples could be mentioned. However, at this point we are especially interested in the fact that the terms on which a bank supplies one type of service affects demands for its other types of services. We have all seen bank advertisements extolling the advantages of "one-stop, full-service banking," by which a bank may proclaim: "This bank stands ready to meet all your financial needs; it will supply all your reasonable requests for consumer, housing, and business credit; it provides the best of convenient and cheap checking services; and its savings department offers a wide choice of deposits, all safe and liquid and carrying good returns." Such a bank can offer any one of its services on favorable terms as a means of stimulating demand for its other services. We shall stress a bank's use of its lending policies to customers as a means of attracting deposits.

Bank earnings, safety, and liquidity

Banks are, of course, profit-seeking institutions. If they operated in a world of perfect certainty, their motive would probably be to maximize their long-run profits. However, as we have already seen, neither a bank nor any other financial intermediary operates under such conditions. It faces uncertainties, and therefore risks, of many kinds—uncertainties as to its future volume and costs of funds and uncertainties as to the future incomes and prices on the various types of earning assets that it may acquire. A bank does not, therefore, consider earnings alone; instead, it seeks some optimum combination of earnings, liquidity, and safety. And to secure more of one, the bank must often sacrifice some of the others. For example, to get higher earnings, it may have to incur more risk and illiquidity and to get more safety and liquidity, it may have to sacrifice some earnings.

Safety of assets

As noted earlier, there are two types of risks that a debt obligation will decline in value.

1. The market risk—the risk that the price will decline because of a rise in market rates of interest. On some occasions this risk is estimated to be very small because interest rates are expected to remain stable or even to fall, which would create capital gains.

2. Default risk—the risk that the debtor will not meet promptly and fully his promise to pay interest and to repay principal.

Each banker faces difficult problems in determining the types and amounts of risk to assume. If he goes to the extreme of purchasing and holding only the safest assets, his earnings are likely to be very low. Moreover, he may fail to meet his customers' reasonable demands for loans, may acquire the reputation of being an undependable and inadequate source of credit, and may lose customers and their deposits to other banks. On the other hand, there are real dangers in assuming "too much" risk. For one thing, the bank may suffer such large losses on risky assets that their net return will be less than that on safer assets. Moreover, large losses, or even the prospect of such losses, can endanger the future of the bank.

Commercial banks are especially limited in their ability to assume risks because of the very high ratio of their fixed-dollar liabilities to their total assets. As noted earlier, the net worth of banks is equal to only about 9 percent of their total assets. The other 91 percent of claims are liabilities, mostly deposits, that are fixed in terms of dollars. Thus, if the assets of a bank with these ratios depreciated by more than 9 percent, the bank would be insolvent; the value of its assets would be less than its liabilities to depositors and others. The bank might have to be closed. But the bank may face serious consequences long before its assets depreciate enough to wipe out its net worth and make it insolvent. As its net worth shrinks, depositors may become distrustful, and the bank may face serious problems in attracting deposits and even in retaining existing deposits. This has obvious deleterious effects on the bank's lending power.

A bank can attempt to maintain an adequate degree of solvency in two different ways: (1) by increasing its net worth and (2) by maintaining safety of its assets. One way to increase net worth is to retain profits. This method has obvious limitations. If profits are low, net worth can be built up only slowly even if the bank pays no dividends to shareholders. And to the extent that a bank reduces dividends in order to retain earnings, it may depress the market price of its outstanding shares. The bank may also increase its net worth by selling additional stock. As it does this, it may feel justified in acquiring a larger proportion of risky assets, thereby increasing its earnings. But there is a limit to the extent that this can be done profitably. Experience indicates that banks can achieve a profit rate on net worth comparable to profit rates in other industries only if they have a large "leverage factor"; that is, only if total earning assets are a large multiple of net worth. At some stage, therefore, a bank finds it unprofitable to expand further its net worth relative to its assets. It must therefore limit the amount of risk that it assumes.

Thus, in determining the composition of his portfolio, a banker faces difficult problems in balancing safety against earnings. He must estimate the amounts of risks attached to the various types of available assets, compare estimated risk differentials against interest differentials, consider both long-run and short-run consequences, and strike a balance. If he veers too far toward safety, he may face not only inadequate profits in the short-run but also charges that his aversion to risk prevents him from serving adequately the needs of his customers and the economy. But if he veers too far in the direction of risk bearing, he may face disaster or at least endanger his ability to attract or even to retain deposits. He must also consider his need for liquidity, a problem to which we now turn.

Bank liquidity

By the *liquidity* of a bank is meant its capacity to meet promptly demands that it pay its obligations. As noted earlier, commercial banks must pay more attention to liquidity than must many other types of financial institutions, such as life insurance companies. This results from the very high ratio of their debt liabilities. A large part of the gross outpayments by a bank is met from current gross receipts of funds in the normal course of business. We have already noted that deposit withdrawals are expected to be offset, at least in large part, by inflows of new deposits. A bank also receives inflows of funds as income on its assets, as repayment of principal on maturing assets, and as weekly or monthly repayments on installment loans. In many cases, such gross inflows are at least sufficient to meet gross payments by a bank. Nevertheless, each bank must be prepared to make net payments of two types: (1) payments to meet net withdrawals of currency into circulation, and (2) payments to cover adverse clearing balances with other banks. Some of these are of such a regular seasonal or other cyclical nature that they can be predicted with fair accuracy and prepared against. Others are more erratic and less predictable. Inability to meet these drains promptly means failure or at least an impairment of confidence in the bank.

A bank could, of course, elect to "play it safe" and remain completely liquid by holding cash equal to all its liabilities. But the effects on its income would be disastrous. At the other extreme, the bank could select assets solely with an eye to income, ignoring liquidity. This, too, can lead to disaster, perhaps to sudden death rather than slow starvation. Thus, in determining its portfolio composition, a bank must balance its desire for income against its desire for liquidity. And it usually tries to buy any given amount of liquidity at the lowest possible cost in terms of sacrifice of net earnings. An individual bank has two principal sources of liquidity: borrowings from others and sales out of its asset holdings.

How much liquidity a bank will seek in its asset holdings depends in part on the availability and cost of borrowings. If a bank is assured that it can borrow large amounts at any time without onus and at a low interest cost relative to yields on its assets, it may rely largely on this source for liquidity and hold few liquid assets. But if the availability of borrowings is uncertain or if borrowing carries an onus or if borrowing costs are high relative to yields on the bank's assets, the bank will seek more liquidity in its asset portfolio.

A bank has access to several types of loans:

1. Borrowings from the Federal Reserve. A Federal Reserve bank rarely refuses to lend to a member bank with deficient reserves, but it does not conceal the fact that this source should be used sparingly. It emphasizes that such borrowing is a privilege and not a right, reminds banks of the tradition against continuous borrowing, uses moral suasion to discourage "excessive" borrowing and to encourage repayment, and sometimes raises its discount rate to make borrowing more expensive.

It should be noted that when a bank borrows from the Federal Reserve it increases its reserves without decreasing the reserves of any other bank. This is not true of the other types of borrowing described below; in all these cases the reserves that are borrowed by one bank come out of the reserves of other banks.

2. Federal funds. The Federal Funds market operates through brokers and dealers, including a few very large banks which operate Federal Funds departments. What is bought and sold, or borrowed and lent, are deposits at the Federal Reserve banks. In effect, banks with reserves in excess of legal requirements lend them to other banks. These are one-day loans, but they can be renewed if both borrower and lender agree. Rates on these loans are usually at or below the Federal Reserve discount rate, but they sometimes rise above the discount rate in periods of credit restriction when some banks are willing to pay a premium to avoid facing Federal Reserve lending officers. In earlier years, borrowing and lending in this market was largely confined to big banks; more recently, however, many smaller banks have participated.

3. Other loans by commercial banks. Many banks borrow from their correspondent banks and sometimes from others.

4. Borrowing under repurchase agreements. This is an arrangement under which a bank sells some asset, such as a government security, to a purchaser with an agreement to repurchase it at some stipulated time in the future at a stipulated price. The bank pays interest in the form of the difference between the repurchase and sale prices.

5. Borrowing through negotiable certificates of deposit. As we have seen, these are written instruments representing a time-deposit liability of a bank which can be freely traded in the market. Many large banks use this instrument extensively as a means of borrowing funds from large corporations and others. Some smaller banks have also employed it, but less extensively.

6. Borrowing Eurodollar deposits. Eurodollar deposits are dollar-denominated deposit claims against banks domiciled outside the United States. The prefix "Euro" is somewhat misleading because not all the banks issuing these claims are located in Europe; some are in Canada, Japan, and even in Southeast Asia and the Bahamas. Eurodollar deposits are issued by the foreign banks in exchange for deposit claims against banks in the United States, these claims being relinquished by either Americans or foreigners. Borrowers of Eurodollars receive in return deposit claims against banks in the United States. American banks first borrowed large amounts in the Eurodollar market during the periods of domestic

credit restriction in 1966 and 1969. At one time in 1969 the amount of these borrowings exceeded $15 billion. An example will clarify the mechanics of such borrowing. Suppose that the Chase Manhattan Bank borrows $100 million through its branch in London or through some other foreign bank. It will promise to repay $100 million at a stated time and receive in return a check for $100 million drawn on a bank in the United States. If, as is likely, the check is drawn on another bank, Chase Manhattan will collect reserves from that bank. If the check is drawn on a deposit account at the Chase Manhattan, that bank will deduct the $100 million from its deposit liabilities, thereby lowering its required reserves. Thus bank borrowings of Eurodollars constitute a circuitous but effective way of reallocating reserves among American banks. Needless to say, this form of borrowing is unavailable to many small banks. Some other aspects of the Eurodollar market will be discussed later.

Many banks rely heavily on these various types of borrowing as a source of liquidity. However, for various reasons—such as fear that they will be unable to borrow, the tradition against continuous borrowing, and fear that borrowing will be expensive—banks hold some fraction of their assets in highly liquid form.

Available to banks are many types of assets with varying degrees of liquidity. Among the most liquid are cash in vault; deposits at the Federal Reserve; deposits at other banks; demand or call loans to other banks, brokers, dealers in government securities, and others; Treasury bills and other short-term obligations of the federal government; acceptances; and open-market commercial paper issued by large firms of unquestioned credit rating. Among the less liquid are loans to customers, longer-term bonds, and mortgages. Generally speaking, the higher the degree of liquidity, the lower the yield on an asset. Holders are willing to forgo some yield to buy liquidity, and they demand more income to offset illiquidity. Each banker therefore faces the problem of balancing his desire for income against his desire for liquidity. His demand curve for liquidity usually slopes downward. Some liquidity is so important that he will, if necessary, sacrifice large amounts of income to buy it. He will buy further amounts only if the cost is lower. But he will always try to buy liquidity at the lowest possible cost in terms of forgone earnings.

We have already noted that legally required reserves are not an important source of liquidity to banks. Cash in vault and deposits at the Federal Reserve that banks are legally required to hold are not available to make payments to others. Only reserves in excess of legal requirements are available for this purpose. But even legally required reserves can supply liquidity for a few days. This is because a bank need not meet its legal reserve requirements every day but only on the average over a "reserve period," which is one week. Thus, a bank can indeed use some of its legally required reserves to make net payments for a few days in a reserve period. But if it does so, it must balance out by holding reserves in excess of requirements during the remainder of the period, and to acquire these reserves it must have other sources of liquidity.

Suppose a bank must make payments, either as currency for circulation or as payments to other banks, because of a net loss of deposits. It can finance these payments out of its legally required reserves only to the extent that the amount of its required reserves is thereby reduced, which is equal to the loss of deposits times its required reserve ratio. For example, if this ratio is 15 percent, each dollar loss of deposits will reduce required reserves only 15 cents and will free only this amount for payments. The other 85 cents must come from other sources, and the lower the required reserve ratio, the larger the proportion of funds needed for payment that must come from other sources.

A bank could, of course, hold liquidity in the form of cash in vault and deposits at the Federal Reserve in excess of legal requirements. Or it could hold large amounts of deposits at other banks. These highly liquid assets have one serious disadvantage: They yield no income. Bankers are therefore impelled to hold a major part of their liquidity in the form of liquid assets that yield an income.

It should not be assumed that the ratio of liquid assets to total bank assets remains constant. For example, banks may maintain a high degree of liquidity if yields on liquid assets are almost as high as those on more illiquid assets, and they may become less liquid if yields on liquid assets are relatively much lower. They may also allow their liquidity to decline in order to satisfy an upsurge of customer loan demands.

SURVEY OF BANK ASSETS

Having examined some of the policy problems of banks relating to earnings, solvency, and liquidity, we are now in a better position to understand the types and proportions of assets acquired and held by banks. Table 8–1 shows the composition of total commercial bank assets as of a recent date. This is a *combined balance sheet,* simply an addition of the asset sides of the balance sheets of all commercial banks. Thus, it includes the claims held by banks against other commercial banks as well as claims against others. It should be remembered that such large aggregates hide important differences among banks, but the proportions reflect a sort of weighted average.

Several types of assets are conspicuous for their absence or scarcity. Outstanding in this respect are physical assets in the form of land, buildings, and equipment. Few banks own many more assets of this type than are needed for banking purposes. Even smaller, are bank holdings of common stock; and most of these are in the form of stock in the Federal Reserve banks, which member banks are required to hold. Currency and deposits at the Federal Reserve are more prevalent, but are usually kept close to the minimum necessary to meet reserve requirements. Balances at other banks arise out of the system of correspondent-banking relationships described earlier. The great bulk of bank assets, about 90 percent, is composed of loans and securities, which are debt claims against others. Table 8–1 suggests the great variety of these claims.

Table 8–1 Commercial-bank assets, December 31, 1970 (millions of dollars)

	AMOUNT	PERCENT OF TOTAL ASSETS
Cash in vault	$ 7,046	1.4
Deposits at the Federal Reserve	23,319	4.7
Balances with domestic banks	23,136	4.6
Loans		
Commercial and industrial	$112,486	22.5
Agricultural	11,155	2.2
For purchasing and carrying securities		
To brokers and dealers	6,332	2.7
To others	3,536	0.7
To financial institutions		
To banks	2,660	0.5
To others	15,855	3.2
Real estate	72,492	14.5
Other loans to individuals	65,807	13.2
Other loans	7,574	1.5
Total loans (gross)	$297,900	59.7
Securities		
U.S. government	$ 61,742	12.4
State and local government	69,637	13.9
Other securities	16,481	3.3
Total securities (gross)	147,860	29.6
Total assets	$499,261	100.0

SOURCE: *Federal Reserve Bulletin,* September, 1971, pp. A24–A25.

Commercial and industrial loans

Let us start with the type of loan that gave commercial banking its name. The *commercial-loan* theory of banking, which has been highly influential but never wholly accepted by either bankers or economists, holds that banks should confine themselves exclusively to this type of credit. They should make only short-term, self-liquidating loans based on the production, distribution, or sale of goods and services. The basic idea is that a bank should lend only on the basis of a specific transaction or process that is short-term in nature and which at its termination will provide the borrower with funds that he can use to pay off the loan. For example, it is held that a merchant may properly borrow to buy an inventory of merchandise that can be sold in a few months for enough money to retire the loan. Or a manufacturer may borrow to buy raw materials and components and to meet payrolls in order to turn out a product that can soon be sold and the proceeds used to pay off the loan. Or a farmer may properly borrow to finance the planting, tending, and marketing of a crop that will be sold in a few months. On the negative side, the commercial-loan theorists contend that banks should not make long-term loans and should not lend on the basis of a project or process that will bring in proceeds only over a long period. For example, a bank should not lend money to a merchant to buy a store, to a manufacturer to buy plant and durable equipment, or to a farmer to buy land. Most economists now reject the commercial-loan theory, and few bankers are guided exclusively, or even largely, by it.

Some of the loans included in "commercial and industrial loans" in Table 8–1 conform to the commercial-loan theory, but many do not. For one thing, some are not short-term (they do not mature within a year), but are "term loans" that may run for three to five years or even longer. Perhaps more important, many of these loans, short-term as well as term loans, are not based on a specific transaction or process. Rather, they are based on the general credit rating of the borrower as reflected by his past and prospective income and expenses; the ratio of his assets to his total liabilities; and the ratio of his short-term assets to his short-term liabilities. A borrower whose rating in these respects is satisfactory may get a short-term or term loan from a bank without specifying any particular project, mix the proceeds with his other funds, and use the funds as he sees fit, including perhaps the purchase of real estate or durable equipment.

The term "commercial banks" is appropriate in the sense that these institutions are by far the largest source of short-term, and even of term, commercial and industrial loans. In many areas and for many business firms, there is no other source of short-term loans that can compare in convenience, adequacy, and cheapness. But it remains true that these loans represent only a fraction of total commercial-bank credit.

Other loans

Commercial banks constitute one of the largest sources of both installment and noninstallment consumer credit. Banks extend much of this credit directly to consumers, but they also provide such credit indirectly through sales finance companies, consumer finance companies, and others who lend to consumers. Banks do this by lending directly to these institutions and by purchasing in the open market the short-term or longer-term promissory notes that these institutions issue to get funds.

A smaller but rapidly growing amount of consumer credit is extended through bank credit cards and arrangements given such names as "instant credit" or "check credit." These credit systems became economically feasible as computers became available to handle the large amounts of record keeping involved. Some banks issue their own individual credit cards, but the trend is toward cards that are also issued by many other banks and are acceptable over wide geographic areas. Two of the most widely used are "Bankamericard" and "Master Charge." A bank customer who establishes his creditworthiness receives, in effect, a line of credit which he can use to purchase goods and services from merchants who have joined the plan or to get cash advances from any bank that is a member of the plan. "Instant credit" or "check credit" is, in effect, an arrangement for overdrafts. After establishing a line of credit at his bank, the customer can get credit automatically by writing checks in excess of his deposit balance. Such methods of extending consumer credit will probably become increasingly important in the future.

Some of the loans on real estate are short-term construction loans, which are paid off when a building is finished and sold. But most of them are long-term mortgages on farms, on residential properties, and less often on commercial and industrial properties. Banks feel justified in holding these long-term mortgages primarily because of their time and savings deposits.

Loans on securities are for various purposes, but have the common characteristics that securities are used as collateral. Some are a type of business loan to enable security dealers to carry inventories. For example, dealers in United States government securities have to carry large inventories relative to their net worth and borrow heavily for this purpose, usually on a very short-term basis. Banks are an important source of such credit and also lend to dealers who hold inventories of other types of securities. Loans to brokers are primarily for the account of the brokers' customers who buy securities "on margin." In effect, the broker gets a loan on the basis of the customer's securities and uses the proceeds to pay the sellers of the securities. Individuals and others sometimes borrow directly from banks on the basis of securities and clearly use the proceeds for "purchasing or carrying securities." But the proceeds from loans backed by securities are often used for other purposes, securities being used as collateral simply because the lending bank finds them acceptable. For example, you might pledge as collateral some shares of General Motors and use the proceeds to buy a car, finance a marriage, or buy business inventory In many cases, there is no relation between the nature of the collateral and the use of loan proceeds. This is well expressed in the observation, "I once knew a fellow who pawned his overcoat to buy beer."

We need not discuss the other types of bank loans to establish the fact that commercial banks lend to many types of borrowers, for widely varying lengths of time, on many bases, and for a wide variety of stated purposes.

U.S. government obligations

For several years after World War II, these securities made up 40 percent or more of total commercial-bank assets. More recently they have declined in absolute amount and even more as a percentage of total assets as banks have increased their holdings of private debt. However, they still have such an important role as bearers of safety and liquidity that we should pay special attention to their various types. *Treasury bills* have the shortest original maturity. They used to run no more than 3 months, but many of the later issues have been longer, some as long as a year and a half. They carry no coupon or stated interest; the holder receives income by purchasing them at a discount from the face value at which they will be paid at maturity. All other issues pay interest at a stated percentage of face value. *Certificates of indebtedness* usually have an initial maturity of 9 to 12 months, *Treasury notes* run one to seven years, and *bonds* run seven years or more. It should be noted that these are initial maturities. As time elapses, what were originally longer-term securities become shorter-term and are treated as such by banks and other investors.

The banks acquire some of these securities directly from the Treasury, and they sometimes dispose of these securities directly to the Treasury. But a larger part of the banks' transactions in these securities is not with the Treasury or the Federal Reserve but with other types of buyers and sellers. Federal obligations are held in large amounts by many types of holders: by mutual savings banks, savings and loan associations, insurance companies, other financial institutions, nonfinancial corporations, individuals, pension funds, state and local governments, foreign investors, and so on. As we saw earlier, all these buyers and sellers are interlinked in a national and even international market through a small group of government-security dealers. These dealers maintain a continuous market by standing ready to buy and sell, exacting only a small gross margin. Thus, one can usually buy or sell any quantity that he wants very quickly and at small cost. And the prices of the shorter maturities vary only within narrow limits.

Owing both to the nature of the securities themselves and to the efficiency and cheapness of the market mechanism, these securities, and especially Treasury bills and other short-term issues, have become a highly important instrument for adjusting cash, liquidity, and portfolio positions. We shall later see how commercial banks buy these securities when they have excess reserves or wish to shift funds from other uses, and how they sell these securities to repair reserve deficiencies or to get funds for other purposes. Other financial institutions and nonfinancial holders act in comparable ways.

Thus, net purchases or net sales of government securities by the banks do not necessarily supply money to the Treasury or withdraw money from it. When banks buy these securities from others, the result is to supply others with money, which they can use as they see fit. For example, when banks buy these securities from insurance companies or other financial institutions, these sellers are provided with money which they can use to buy other types of assets, to pay debts, or to hold idle. When they buy securities from nonfinancial business firms, the latter can use the money to hire workers, buy inventory, construct plants, or for any other purpose. And when banks sell government securities to other financial institutions or others, they withdraw funds and reduce the amount of money available to the former holders. The banks may then use the funds to acquire other types of assets, or they may simply reduce the money supply.

Other securities

Among the other types of securities held by commercial banks, obligations of the states and their subdivisions are by far the largest. Some of these are acquired directly from their issuers, others in the open market. Their special attraction to banks is the exemption of their income from the federal income tax.

In summary, banks hold a wide variety of earning assets. Far from restricting themselves to short-term business loans, banks hold debt claims of widely varying maturities against other financial institutions, government at all levels, consumers, and others. Thus, they are involved in many branches of the markets for savings and financial claims and can bring about widespread effects as they expand or contract their credit.

Yet we must not overstate the point. We do find differences when we compare bank portfolios with those of other important financial institutions. Perhaps most obvious, they are on balance in shorter maturities. And they tend to be more liquid and less risky. Certainly commercial banks contrast sharply with mutual savings banks (which hold largely long-term mortgages and bonds), with mutual investment companies (which are mostly in common stocks), and life insurance companies (which are largely in mortgages, long-term bonds, and some real estate and common stock).

OPEN-MARKET AND CUSTOMER RELATIONSHIPS

As a further step in explaining the behavior of bank portfolios, it will be useful to distinguish between customer loans and earning assets acquired and sold in the "open market." As do most classifications, this one presents troublesome borderline cases, but it does highlight some motivations and market differences that strongly influence a banker's decisions relative to his portfolio.

The very term "customer" suggests a relationship that is customarily of a continuing nature and that at least one of the parties involved would be reluctant to break. "Open market" suggests a quite different sort of relationship: impersonal, not necessarily continuing, and "open to all comers."

Open-market assets

The clearest examples of open-market relationships are those in which the bank that buys or sells a debt claim does not deal directly with the ultimate debtor. Thus, a bank may buy or sell, through a broker or dealer, United States government securities, state and municipal obligations, acceptances, open-market commercial paper, brokers' loans, and so on. In many cases, the banker knows the debtor only by reputation, and the debtor does not know who holds the claims against him.

Open-market relationships usually have the following characteristics:

1. The bank decides whether to buy or sell a particular debt claim solely on the basis of the asset's attractiveness relative to other available open-market assets, and is not influenced by considerations concerning other possible relations with the debtor. For example, it does not assume that by purchasing a particular debt claim, it will attract deposits from the debtor.

2. The bank is not impelled to buy or is not constrained from selling a particular debt claim by any feeling of "loyalty" or "responsibility" to the debtor.

3. The individual bank has no significant monopoly power in the open market as a whole, or even in the market for the particular type of debt claim. From the individual banker's point of view, conditions in the open market approach the "purely competitive." Each bank controls only such a small part of the

total demand that its own actions in buying or selling an open-market asset is assumed to have no significant effect on the price of the asset. Each banker assumes that he can buy or sell as much of the asset as he wishes at the going price.

This is not to say that conditions in the open market conform completely to those required for pure competition. But they come much closer than do conditions in customer-loan markets.

Customer loans

Relations between a bank and its borrowing customers are quite different in several respects. For one thing, the lender-borrower relationship is intertwined with other bank-customer relationships. The customer usually holds checking deposits, and sometimes time deposits, at the bank, and he may also be a customer of the trust or foreign-exchange departments. The customer is made fully aware that the amount of loans that he can get depends in part on the bank's experience with him as a depositor. And the banker is equally aware that the amount of deposits that he can attract and retain, and therefore his lending power, depends in part on his reputation for "taking care of the legitimate credit needs of customers," even in periods of credit tightness. This is important partly because of the limited degree of price competition among banks in a local market. Banks are legally prohibited from paying interest on demand deposits, and they are reluctant to compete aggressively on rates paid on time deposits and those charged on loans. Where price competition is thus restricted, nonprice competition comes to the fore. This takes many forms: reputation for soundness, convenience of location, decor, courtesy, and so on. Not the least of these is the bank's reliability as a loan source. The advertising slogan, "You have a friend at Chase Manhattan," referred to a loan officer, but it was not meant to be ignored by potential depositors.

As already implied, there are many imperfections of competition in customer-loan markets, and each bank has some degree of monopoly power relative to its customers. The amount of this power depends on many things, including the nature of the customer. No bank may have much monopoly power relative to a huge corporation of well-known credit rating that has access to banks all over the country and can easily secure funds by selling short- or long-term claims in the open market. In fact, a huge corporation can often dominate even a very large bank by threatening, in effect, "If you do not give us the money we need at a rate of interest as low as that charged your most-favored customer we shall find it necessary to move our multi-millions of deposits to banks that are more sympathetic." At the other extreme is the small firm that is virtually unknown to any bank other than its own and that could issue securities in the open market only at prohibitive cost. For such reasons, there are wide differences among customers' price elasticities of demand for loans at an individual bank. It is not surprising, therefore, that banks practice price discrimination.

To illustrate our points, let us consider the intermediate case of a small or medium-sized business firm that is a good credit risk but whose credit rating is not widely known. Such a firm finds it costly and inconvenient to shift its banking business to distant banks. To hold all its deposits at distant banks is possible but usually costly in time and convenience. To borrow at distant banks is even more costly, even when possible, because of the time and expense incurred by those banks in investigating his creditworthiness. Thus, there are strong forces tending to confine the firm's borrowing to banks in its own area, but as it surveys the local banking structure, the firm finds a situation of banking oligopoly (few sellers) of customer credit. There are only a few local banks, all charging about the same rate of interest, and afraid to compete aggressively for loans by lowering interest rates. Each bank knows that if it lowers its rates its competitors will soon do the same, so it will gain a differential advantage for no more than a short period. If the firm tries to "shop around" at the various banks, it is likely to meet responses of this sort: "Why don't you borrow at your own bank, where you do your other banking business? They know you, understand your credit needs, and are in a position to take care of you. It isn't sound policy to change frequently from one bank to another. Of course, if you decide to switch banks and bring all your banking business here, we can talk about the loan. Our first obligation is to meet the borrowing needs of our own customers." Such imperfections of competition gives each bank some degree of monopoly power over its customers. But the attachment of customers to other banks works to the disadvantage of a given bank, for that bank finds it harder to attract the business of those customers.

Comparison of open market and customer-loan market

Much can be learned from observing differences between conditions in the open market and those in customer-loan markets. For one thing, this comparison helps to explain differences in the behavior of interest rates and yields in the two branches of the market. Like prices in most other highly competitive markets, interest rates in the open market change frequently and quickly in response to changes in demand-supply relations. They often change every day and even several times during a day. In contrast, rates on customer loans change less frequently and more slowly. Like other "administered prices," they often go unchanged for a considerable period, even though supply-demand relationships have clearly changed.

The basic rate on bank loans to customers is called the *prime rate*. This is promulgated by a very large bank, usually one in New York City, but sometimes by a bank in another major financial center, which assumes the role of "price leadership." This is the rate charged to "prime" customers, usually very large customers with unquestioned credit rating and a favorable competitive position. Rates to other customers range upward from the prime rate, those to customers who are almost "prime" being only a little higher, and so on. The prime rate is changed only infrequently and usually only after pressure for change has accumulated. For example, suppose bank lending power is increased markedly relative to the demand for customer loans. Instead of lowering the prime rate quickly, banks seek to expand their credit in other ways. For one thing, they increase their holdings of open-market paper. In the customer-loan market they become more generous in meeting loan requests, give some nonprime customers rates closer to the prime rate, and so on. Only after a delay, when downward pressures have already lowered rates in the open market, do they lower the prime rate. Suppose, on the other hand, that the supply of credit is decreased relative to the demand for it and that this is reflected in rate increases in the open market. Here again, banks may delay in raising the prime rate, perhaps partly because each bank fears that if it raises the rate, other banks will not follow suit. For some time they ration loans to customers, not by raising the interest rate, but by scaling down loan requests and otherwise limiting the availability of credit. Only after pressures for increases of rates have accumulated and open-market rates have already risen is the prime rate increased.

An innovation in October, 1971 may lead to more frequent changes in the prime rate and to a closer relationship between it and yields on short-term assets in the open market. At that time one of the largest banks announced that in the future it would adjust its prime rate weekly, floating it 1/2 percent above the average yield on prime open-market commercial paper during the preceding week. However, it is not clear that the new policy will persist and that banks will not return to something like their old practices.

Differences in conditions in the open market and in customer-loan markets also help to explain why, other things equal, a bank is likely to prefer customers' loans over assets acquired in the open market. One reason for this preference is that a given initial amount of excess reserves is likely to enable a bank to lend more to customers than it could lend in the open market. If a bank lends in the open market, the entire amount of the loan is likely to be deposited in other banks, thereby draining off an equal amount of reserves. But if the bank lends to customers, some of the proceeds are likely to be kept on deposit with it, thereby lessening its loss of reserves. Customers may hold some of the deposits voluntarily; the lending bank also has ways of encouraging the customer to be a depositor. For example, it may require "compensating deposit balances" from its borrowers, and let them know that the availability of loans will depend on the amount of their deposits.

Perhaps more important, a banker knows that his total lending power is not independent of his lending policies to customers. If he acquires a reputation of meeting all reasonable loan demands of customers, he will be able to attract and retain more deposits, and thus to lend more. But if he becomes known as a banker who is niggardly in meeting customers' needs, he will be able to attract and retain only a smaller volume of deposits, and his total lending power will shrink. The extent to which this consideration will influence the composition of a bank's portfolio depends in part on the size of customers' loan demands relative to the total lending power of the bank. If customers' demands are relatively small, the bank can feel free to hold a large fraction of its portfolio in open-market assets. But if customers' demands for loans are very large relative to its total lending power, the bank is under heavy pressures to hold most of its portfolio in this form. The extent of these pressures vary from bank to bank, and they can also change markedly at a given bank as customers' loan demands rise and fall.

Thus, other things equal, a bank is strongly impelled to meet customers' loan demands rather than acquire open-market assets. But "other things," such as interest rates and degrees of safety and liquidity, may not be equal. For example, open-market assets may be safer, more liquid, or higher yielding. The bank's desire to make customer loans must therefore be balanced against its demand for safety, liquidity, and, in some cases, earnings. It should be emphasized, however, that what a bank considers to be an optimum portfolio composition in one set of circumstances may not be optimum under other circumstances. The optimum can be shifted by such things as changes in the banker's estimates of the amount of safety and liquidity needed, changes in the general level of interest rates and in the relative heights of the various types of interest rates, and changes in customers' demands for loans. Let us illustrate some of these with two examples.

Increase in customers' demands for loans

Assume that we start from a situation in which bankers in general consider their portfolios to be close to their optimum composition under existing conditions. Suppose now that there occurs a sharp increase in customers' demands for bank loans, and that the Federal Reserve does not supply additional reserves and does not provide excess reserves by reducing reserve requirements. The banks will be strongly impelled to supply at least a part of the increase in customers' demands for loans, but to do so, they will need funds to meet the increased reserves required against the newly created deposits and perhaps also to cover induced cash drains. They can seek these funds from three sources: any excess reserves that they may have, borrowings, and sales of assets. If they have excess reserves, they are likely to use them first. Whether they turn next to borrowing or to sales of assets will depend in part on the cost of borrowing as compared with the yield sacrificed on the assets that might be sold. They may borrow from other banks, either directly or through the Federal Funds market. But as this continues, the rate of interest charged will tend to be forced up, both because the demand for such loans has increased and because the amount of excess reserves available for lending has declined. At some stage, therefore, the banks will begin selling assets, probably such liquid open-market assets as short-term government obligations, acceptances, call loans to security dealers, and so on. As some banks sell these assets to other banks, they do not increase either total bank reserves or the total lending power of the banking system; they merely transfer reserves from the buying banks to the selling banks.

If the rise of demand for customers' loans is general, there are likely to be fewer banks who are willing to be net purchasers of these open-market assets. Even when banks sell open-market assets to nonbank buyers—such as other financial institutions, business corporations, or individuals—they usually do not increase the total reserves of the banking system, for the buyers ordinarily pay by relinquishing deposit claims. But the reduction of deposits reduces the required reserves of banks enough to enable them to expand their customers' loans by an equal amount. For example, if the public surrenders $100 million of deposits to pay for Treasury bills purchased from the banks, this reduces the banks' required reserves and adds enough to excess reserves to enable the banks to increase customers' loans by $100 million.

In some cases, this is merely a way of channeling some of the nation's current saving into loans to bank customers. For example, the public uses some of its current saving to buy Treasury bills from the banks, and the banks lend to customers. In other cases, it may be a way of "activating idle deposits." A buyer pays for a Treasury bill by relinquishing a deposit that he would otherwise have held idle. This lowers the banks' required reserves and creates excess reserves, and the banks are thereby enabled to increase their customers' loans. A newly created "active deposit" replaces the old "idle deposit," but, in any case, bank sales of open-market assets tend to raise interest rates in the open market, which represents an increase in the cost of acquiring funds to lend to customers. Banks are thereby impelled to raise interest rates on customer loans, although perhaps only after a delay.

Thus, the banks do indeed increase the proportion of customers' loans in their portfolios in response to marked increases in customers' demands for loans. But as the process continues, the banks become increasingly reluctant to make further increases in their loans to customers. This is because of the impairment of their liquidity and perhaps also their safety. They become less liquid as they increase their borrowings and sell off their most liquid assets. And they become less safe to the extent that customers' loans are riskier than the assets sold. The banks may seek to reduce the impairment of their liquidity and safety by selling off not their most liquid and safe assets but some of their longer-term, riskier, open-market assets such as long-term bonds. This usually involves capital losses, for the rise of interest rates will have lowered the market prices of longer-term securities. Increasingly, therefore, banks will resist further increases of customers' loans. They will ration loans to some extent by raising interest rates. They may also reduce the availability of credit by nonprice rationing methods, that is, by trying to convince customers that they should reduce their loan requests, by granting only a fraction of the loans requested, and by outright denial of loan applications. Such methods of nonprice rationing of loans are likely to have quite uneven impacts on borrowers, with the most generous treatment being accorded to customers considered by the bank to be "most valuable."

Increase in bank reserves

Suppose now that the Federal Reserve provides banks with a considerable amount of additional reserves at a time when customers' loan demands are not rising and may be falling. The immediate effect is to increase bank liquidity in the form of excess reserves, which yield no income. These funds may be used for three purposes: to pay off bank borrowings from the Federal Reserve and others, to purchase open-market assets, and to expand loans to customers. How the funds will be distributed among these uses will depend on existing conditions, such as the liquidity of the banks and the amount of unsatisfied demands for customers' loans. If the banks have been rationing loans, they may relax their restrictions and expand customers' loans at an early stage. But they are most unlikely to lower interest rates on these loans at an early stage. Rather they will pay off borrowings and purchase assets—especially highly liquid assets—in the open market. As they do this, interest rates in the open market will fall. At first, the decline of interest rates may be largely limited to short-term maturities, but as these yields decline relative to yields on longer-term obligations, both banks and other buyers will be impelled to switch their purchases to the longer maturities, thereby tending to lower their yields.

Thus, the initial response of banks to an increase of their excess reserves may be to purchase assets in the open market and to lower interest rates there. But, as the banks become more liquid and face lower yields in the open market, they will try to expand their loans to customers. At first they may try to do this solely by relaxing restrictions and encouraging customers to borrow, but at some stage, interest rates on customers' loans will be reduced.

These two examples illustrate some of the forces that influence the composition of bank portfolios. We shall discuss more of these later in connection with Federal Reserve policies.

Selected readings

Crosse, H. D., *Management Policies for Commercial Banks*, Englewood Cliffs, N.J., Prentice-Hall, 1962.

Hodgman, D., *Commercial Bank Loan and Investment Policy*, Champaign, University of Illinois Press, 1963.

Reed, E. W., *Commercial Bank Management*, New York, Harper & Row, 1963.

Robinson, R., *The Management of Bank Funds*, 2nd ed., New York, McGraw-Hill, 1962.

Smith, P. F., *Economics of Financial Institutions and Markets*, Homewood, Ill., Irwin, 1971.

PART THREE

CENTRAL BANKING

CHAPTER 9

THE FEDERAL RESERVE SYSTEM

In passing the Federal Reserve Act in late 1913 and actually establishing the Federal Reserve banks in November, 1914, the United States was one of the last of the great economic powers to provide itself with a central bank. The Bank of Sweden was founded in 1656, the Bank of England in 1694, the Bank of France in 1800, the Netherlands Bank in 1814, and the Bank of Belgium in 1835; most of the other leading European countries established central banks well before the end of the nineteenth century. In general outline, the functions of the Federal Reserve are similar to those of central banks in other countries. Like other central banks, its primary function is to regulate monetary and credit conditions. To this end, it creates and destroys money and regulates the creation and destruction of money by commercial banks. It also performs many other similar functions, including check clearing and collection, acting as fiscal agent for the government, engaging in operations in the foreign-exchange market, and so on.

Despite these similarities, there are also important differences in the structure, control, and functioning of the various central banks. For example, most countries have only one central bank, with control clearly concentrated in a central authority. The United States has 12 separately incorporated Federal Reserve banks located in as many Federal Reserve districts, with control power divided among the 12 banks and the Board of Governors of the Federal Reserve System located in Washington. This arrangement seems sprawling indeed to those accustomed to a single central bank under centralized control.

Differences among various central banks arise from many sources, only a few of which can be mentioned here.

1. Differences in geographical area. In small countries without pronounced regional variations, there was little reason to establish more than one central bank. But in the United States, with its large geographical area and differing economic and financial conditions in the various regions, it was at least plausible to argue in 1913 that each broad region should have its own central bank, which could adapt its policies to the peculiar conditions of the region.

2. Differences in allocations of jurisdiction over banking. In countries where the central government enjoyed exclusive jurisdiction over chartering, supervision, and regulation of commercial banks, there was little opposition to a single central bank. This was not true in the United States, with its dual banking system.

3. Differences in commercial-banking structures. In countries with only a few banks, each operating a nationwide system of branches, it was clear that the banking system could best be regulated by a centralized management in the nation's financial center. This did not seem feasible in the United States, with its thousands of banks, most of them operating only a single office and none with branches outside its home state.

BACKGROUND

To understand the original structure and control of the Federal Reserve System and its evolution since 1914, it is helpful to recall some aspects of American monetary history before 1913 and the objectives of those responsible for the passage of the Federal Reserve Act. The major point to be emphasized is that the purposes of the Federal Reserve System as conceived by its originators were far different from those of today. Almost everybody now believes that the primary purpose of the Federal Reserve is to manage money deliberately and continuously. We believe that "money will not manage itself; it must be managed." And we expect the Federal Reserve to use its powers continuously and positively to promote the achievement of selected objectives, such as high levels of employment, economic growth, and stable price levels.

Such ideas were alien and unacceptable to those who conceived and established the Federal Reserve System. They did not want a "managed money"; they were well pleased with the international gold standard then in operation. After decades of controversy over bimetallism, greenbackism, and other "unsound" proposals, the nation had reasserted its loyalty to the international gold standard by adopting the Gold Standard Act of 1900. The following decade of rising gold production, rising price levels, and prosperity seemed to confirm the wisdom of the decision. There would almost certainly have been no Federal Reserve System if its advocates had heralded it as an instrument for continuous monetary management. This function of the Federal Reserve developed only several years later when the international gold standard had broken down and the nation had, for the first time in its history, accumulated a large volume of excess gold reserves.

Thus, the original purpose of the Federal Reserve was not the ambitious one of introducing a high degree of monetary management, but the much more limited one of remedying a number of shortcomings in the existing system of state and national banks. The Federal Reserve Act sought to replace the slow and expensive system of check-clearing and collection with one that would be faster and more efficient; to provide a more satisfactory fiscal agent for the federal government; to achieve a better coordination of state and national banks, and especially to secure more effective supervision of state banks; to promote the development of an acceptance market in the United States; and to provide more liberal powers for national banks, such as those of establishing trust departments and lending on real estate, to enable them to compete more effectively with state banks and trust companies, many of which enjoyed more freedom of action. These reforms were important, but they were secondary. The primary purpose of the new banking reform was to end recurrent banking panics and crises. The panic of 1907, following similar events in 1893, 1884, and 1873, and serious credit stringencies on several other occasions, was the last straw; banking reform became politically feasible. As Carter Glass told the House of Representatives:

> Financial textbook writers in Europe have characterized our banking as "barbarous," and eminent bankers of this country . . . have not hesitated to confess that the criticism is merited. . . . The failure of the system in acute exigencies has caused widespread business demoralization and almost universal distress. Five times within the last thirty years financial catastrophe has overtaken the country under this system; and it would be difficult to compute the enormous losses sustained by all classes of society—by the banks immediately involved; by the merchants whose credits were curtailed; by the industries whose shops were closed; by the railroads whose cars were stopped; by the farmers whose crops rotted in the fields; by the laborer who was deprived of his wage. The system literally has no reserve force. The currency based upon the nation's debt is absolutely unresponsive to the nation's business needs. The lack of cooperation and coordination among the more than 7,300 national banks produces a curtailment of facilities at all periods of exceptional demand for credit. This peculiar defect renders disaster inevitable.[1]

Many other observers agreed with Glass that the primary problem was that the existing system had no "reserve force," no "elasticity" in time of strain. No existing institution was motivated to hold large excess reserves for use in time of strain, none had the power to create new bank reserves in such periods, and none was empowered to create additional currency in time of need. The remedy followed from the diagnosis; new institutions should be created to provide a "reserve force," to provide "elasticity." Some part of the nation's gold reserve should be

[1] *The Congressional Record,* September 10, 1913, p. 4642.

concentrated in the new institutions, which would be empowered to create new currency and new bank reserves "as needed." "Elasticity" was the central theme of the new "reserve system."

Even among those who favored banking reform, and many did not, there were widely differing opinions as to the proper control and structure of any new institutions that might be established. Some thought they should be regarded as cooperative or mutual aid societies formed by banks to enable banks to function more safely and effectively. To those holding this view, it seemed only natural that banks should contribute the capital of the new institutions and exercise exclusive control over them. Others thought that the new institutions should be regarded as regulators of banks and that to allow bankers to regulate themselves would be absurd. This was properly a function of the government or its appointees. Opinions as to the proper structure of the new system also differed. Some insisted that the United States, like most other countries, should have a single central bank with centralized control. Such a single institution could most effectively pool the nation's gold reserves, make its resources available at the points of greatest need, and effectuate a national credit policy. Others thought such centralization both unnecessary and undesirable. It would bring a dangerous concentration of financial power, invite domination of the entire country by Wall Street or Washington, and ignore regional differences in economic and financial conditions. One congressman thought that 50 such regional institutions would be about the right number.

The Federal Reserve Act represented a compromise among such conflicting views. The country was divided into a number of districts, each with its own Federal Reserve Bank, and a central authority was established in Washington to supervise the various Reserve banks and to coordinate their policies while permitting some degree of regional autonomy.

STRUCTURE OF THE FEDERAL RESERVE SYSTEM

The 12 Federal Reserve Banks and their branches

The Federal Reserve Act provided that the continental United States should be divided into not less than eight nor more than 12 Federal Reserve districts, each to have a Federal Reserve Bank. The maximum number of districts and Reserve banks was established at the outset, so we have 12 Federal Reserve banks and 12 Federal Reserve districts. The boundaries of these districts are shown on the map in Figure 9–1. Each Federal Reserve bank is named after the city in which it is located; thus, there is the Federal Reserve Bank of Boston, the Federal Reserve Bank of New York, and so on. To facilitate their operations, some of the Federal Reserve banks have established branches in their districts. There are now 24 of these branches distributed unequally among the various Federal Reserve districts.

It is interesting to note, as is shown in Table 9–1, that the Federal Reserve banks differ greatly as to both size and influence on credit and monetary conditions. The Federal Reserve Bank of New York, which is by far the largest, holds

Figure 9-1 Federal Reserve districts, Federal Reserve banks, and branches of Federal Reserve banks

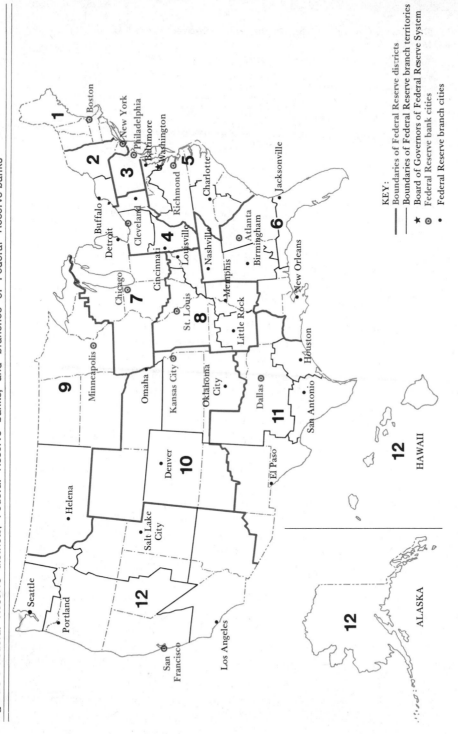

KEY:
— Boundaries of Federal Reserve districts
— Boundaries of Federal Reserve branch territories
★ Board of Governors of Federal Reserve System
◎ Federal Reserve bank cities
• Federal Reserve branch cities

Table 9–1 Relative sizes of the 12 federal reserve banks, May 31, 1971

FEDERAL RESERVE BANK OF	ASSETS (BILLIONS)	PERCENT OF TOTAL FEDERAL RESERVE BANK ASSETS
Boston	$ 4.6	5.0
New York	22.1	24.2
Philadelphia	4.8	5.3
Cleveland	6.9	7.6
Richmond	6.7	7.4
Atlanta	5.8	6.4
Chicago	14.7	16.1
St. Louis	3.4	3.8
Minneapolis	2.0	2.2
Kansas City	3.9	4.3
Dallas	4.9	5.4
San Francisco	11.4	12.5
Total	$91.2	100.0

SOURCE: *Federal Reserve Bulletin,* June, 1971, p. A13.

nearly a quarter of the total assets of all the Reserve banks. The predominance of the New York bank is even greater than these statistics imply, for it is the principal point of contact with foreign central banks; it has a direct influence on international financial transactions; and it is located in the midst of the great New York money market, which draws funds from and dispatches funds to every part of the country. Its member banks (especially the giant banks in New York City) greatly influence banks in all parts of the nation through their correspondent relationships. At the other extreme, the relatively small Federal Reserve Bank of Minneapolis holds only 2.2 percent of all the assets of the Reserve banks, and its actions have much less influence on nationwide credit and monetary conditions.

Each Federal Reserve bank has many *member banks,* which are those commercial banks in the district that have met at least the minimum requirements and have been accepted for membership in the Federal Reserve System.[2] As a member of the Federal Reserve, a commercial bank has both obligations and privileges. It must continue to meet various requirements for membership, submit to supervision and examination by Federal Reserve authorities, subscribe to stock in its Federal Reserve bank, and hold all its legal reserves in the form of cash in vault or deposits at its Federal Reserve bank. On the other hand, it enjoys the privilege of borrowing from its Federal Reserve bank and of using the other facilities of the System.

Before the establishment of the Federal Reserve System, there were wide differences of opinion as to which commercial banks should be required or per-

[2] Morris Plan banks and certain other incorporated banking institutions engaged in a similar type of business may also petition for membership.

mitted to become members. At one extreme, those who were opposed to further "regimentation" of banks would have made membership in the System optional with each bank. At the other extreme, some would have forced every commercial bank in the country to become a member or cease to perform commercial-banking functions. Here, again, the issue was settled by compromise. Every national bank must become and remain a member of its Federal Reserve bank or forfeit its federal charter. Each state bank may, at its option, become a member if it can meet the minimum requirements for membership.

Table 9–2 shows the number of members and nonmembers of the Federal Reserve System on various dates.

Table 9–2 Member and nonmember commercial banks

DATA AS OF JUNE 30	NUMBER OF COMMERCIAL BANKS	MEMBER BANKS			NON-MEMBER STATE BANKS	NUMBER OF MEMBER BANKS AS A PERCENTAGE OF ALL COMMERCIAL BANKS	DEPOSITS AT MEMBER BANKS AS A PERCENTAGE OF TOTAL DEPOSITS
		TOTAL	NATIONAL	STATE			
1915	25,875	7,715	7,598	17	18,260	29.4	49.4
1925	27,858	9,538	8,006	1,472	18,320	34.2	72.8
1935	15,478	6,410	5,425	985	9,068	41.4	84.5
1945	14,003	6,840	5,015	1,825	7,163	48.8	86.6
1950*	14,121	6,873	4,958	1,915	7,248	48.7	85.7
1955*	13,719	6,543	4,692	1,851	7,176	47.7	85.2
1962*	13,429	6,049	4,505	1,544	7,380	45.0	83.7
1970*	13,686	5,767	4,620	1,147	7,919	42.1	80.0

* Data as of end of the year.

In 1970, there were 5,767 member banks, of which 4,620 were national banks and 1,147 were state banks. Thus, 42.1 percent of all commercial banks, holding 80 percent of total deposits in commercial banks were members. Some 7,919 state banks, or 87 percent of all state banks, were nonmembers. However, most of these institutions are relatively small, as is indicated by the fact that although they comprise 57.9 percent of all commercial banks, they account for only 20 percent of total bank deposits. Some Federal Reserve officials are disturbed by the fact that membership in the Federal Reserve has declined in recent years—with members accounting for decreasing percentages of both the number of banks and total deposits.

There are several reasons why many state banks have failed to become members of the Federal Reserve System.[3] Many of them cannot qualify for

[3] For an excellent discussion of this subject, see B. Magruder Wingfield, "Deterrents to Membership in the Federal Reserve System," in Board of Governors of the Federal Reserve System, *Banking Studies*, Washington, D.C., 1941, pp. 273–292.

membership because of their inability to meet its minimum-capital requirements. But many state banks with sufficient capital for membership have failed to join for various reasons:

1. The Federal Reserve requirement of par clearance by its members. No member of the System may make "exchange charges" on checks forwarded to it for payment through the Reserve banks. That is, the member bank on which a check is drawn must pay the full face amount of the check to the payee or to the agencies taking the check for clearance and collection; it may not deduct any amount to cover costs of making payment.[4] But many state banks refused to pay checks at par, preferring to remain outside the System. The importance of this reason for nonmembership has declined in recent years as several states outlawed exchange charges. Only 501 banks remained on the nonpar list at the end of 1970.

2. Lower reserve requirements under state laws. The fact that reserve requirements for member banks are higher than those prescribed by some state laws makes some banks unwilling to join.

3. Unwillingness to comply with other regulations applicable to member banks. Many state banks operating under more lenient state banking laws are unwilling to comply with member bank regulations, such as the Clayton Anti-Trust Act prohibitions against interlocking bank officers, directors, and employees; restrictions on affiliates of member banks; limitations as to the types of assets acquired; limitations on a bank's loans to its executive officers; and reports required.

4. Availability of Federal Reserve services without membership. With certain limitations, nonmember banks may use the Federal Reserve clearing system and various other Federal Reserve facilities. A less-generous policy toward nonmembers would probably force more banks into the System.

OWNERSHIP OF THE FEDERAL RESERVE BANKS

Another controversial question prior to the passage of the Federal Reserve Act was, "Who shall provide the capital for the Federal Reserve banks?" Some wanted government ownership. Others wanted the stock to be sold to the general public, and still others wanted all stock to be sold to member banks. The solution was a compromise. Each member bank is required to subscribe to the stock of its Federal Reserve bank in an amount equal to 6 percent of its own paid-up capital and surplus. If insufficient capital was obtained from this source it was provided that stock would be offered to the public; and if subscriptions by the banks and the public were insufficient, stock would be sold to the federal government. In reality,

---

[4] It must be noted that these "exchange charges" differ somewhat from the service charges with which we are now familiar. A member of the Federal Reserve may still charge its customers for the services it performs for them, including charges for cashing checks that are drawn on other banks. But it may not remit less than the face amount of a check drawn on it and presented to it by a Federal Reserve bank for payment.

no stock of the Federal Reserve banks has been sold to either the public or the government, and even the member banks have been required to pay in only half of their subscriptions. Thus, the Federal Reserve banks are owned wholly by their member banks, each member bank having paid in to its Federal Reserve bank an amount equal to 3 percent of its own paid-up capital and surplus.

It is important to note, however, that in this case, ownership does not carry with it control of the corporation and enjoyment of all its earnings. (The distribution of control is discussed in the next section.) Annual dividends to stockholders of the Reserve banks are limited to 6 percent of the paid-in capital stock. The remainder of Reserve-bank earnings has been used to build up the surplus accounts of the Reserve banks and to provide revenue for the Treasury. Prior to 1933, each Reserve bank was required by law to pay the Treasury a franchise tax equal to 90 percent of its net earnings in excess of dividends after it had accumulated a surplus equal to its subscribed capital. By the end of 1932, the Reserve banks had accumulated surplus accounts amounting to $278 million and had paid $149 million in franchise taxes to the Treasury. The Banking Act of 1933 required the Reserve banks to pay half of their accumulated surplus, or $139 million, as a subscription to the capital stock of the Federal Deposit Insurance Corporation; in return, the Act repealed the franchise tax in order to enable the Reserve banks to use all their earnings in excess of dividend requirements to replenish their surplus accounts. By the end of 1946, the Reserve banks had built up their combined surplus accounts to nearly $440 million. Partly because of this, the Board of Governors in April, 1947, voluntarily put into operation a plan to channel into the Treasury most of the Reserve-bank earnings in excess of their dividend requirements.[5] In recent years all Federal Reserve earnings in excess of dividend requirements have been transferred to the Treasury through an interest charge on outstanding Federal Reserve notes levied by the Board of Governors. These have recently averaged over $2.5 billion a year.

CONTROL OF THE FEDERAL RESERVE SYSTEM

Closely related to the heated controversies over the structure of the Federal Reserve System were those concerning its control. The most widely debated questions were: (1) Who should control the Federal Reserve? (2) Should control be centralized or decentralized? Three principal groups wanted a voice in control—the federal government, member banks, and businessmen who were customers of member banks. Some, arguing that central banking is essentially a governmental function and that one of its principal objectives is the regulation of member banks, demanded full government control. On the other hand, many bankers who considered the new Reserve banks to be essentially cooperative institutions for member banks demanded that full control be placed in the hands of bankers,

---

[5] *Federal Reserve Bulletin,* May, 1947, pp. 518–519. The authority for this action by the Board is found in Section 16, paragraph 4, of the Federal Reserve Act.

although small banks feared domination by their larger competitors. Others argued that businessmen as customers of banks should be given a voice. No less heated were the discussions concerning the degree of centralization of control. Some wanted almost complete centralization, whereas others demanded a large degree of regional autonomy.

Here, too, the issue was settled by compromise. All the competing groups were given representation, and control was divided between a central authority in Washington and the regional Federal Reserve banks. In the succeeding sections we shall describe the present system of control. It should be remembered, however, that the original division of authority proved unsatisfactory in many respects and that it has been changed in several ways since 1914. In general, the evolution has been toward greater centralization of authority and a greater degree of control by the federal government.

The Board of Governors of the Federal Reserve System

The central controlling authority, which has its offices in Washington, is the Board of Governors of the Federal Reserve System. This Board is composed of seven members (each called a governor) appointed by the President of the United States with the advice and consent of the Senate. Each member devotes his full time to the Board, is appointed for a term of 14 years, and is ineligible for reappointment if he has served a full term.[6] No more than one member of the Board may be selected from any one Federal Reserve district, and in making appointments, the President is to "have due regard to a fair representation of the financial, agricultural, industrial, and commercial interests, and geographical divisions of the country." The President designates one of the members as chairman of the Board and another as vice-chairman.

Although the actual location of control has in the past depended greatly on economic and political conditions and on the forcefulness of the various personalities involved, the Board of Governors is now clearly the most powerful controlling force in the entire Federal Reserve System. Among its most important powers are the following:

1. To exercise general supervision over the Federal Reserve banks, to examine their accounts and affairs, and to require reports by them.
2. To approve or disapprove appointments to the positions of president and first vice-president of each Federal Reserve bank and to suspend or remove any officer or director of any Federal Reserve bank.
3. To supervise the issue and retirement of Federal Reserve notes by each Federal Reserve bank.
4. To serve as a majority of the members of the Federal Open Market Committee.
5. To permit one Reserve bank to lend to another, and by a vote of at least five members of the Board to require it to do so.

---

[6] Prior to 1935, this body was known as the Federal Reserve Board. Both the Comptroller of the Currency and the Secretary of the Treasury were ex-officio members of the old Board. The Board was reconstituted in 1935, its members being given higher salaries and longer terms in order to strengthen it and centralize control to a greater degree.

6. To determine, within the broad limits prescribed by law, the types of loans that the Reserve banks may make.
7. To approve or disapprove discount rates established by the Reserve banks.
8. To fix, within the limits established by law, member-bank reserve requirements.
9. To regulate loans on securities.

Although this list is far from complete, it indicates the general scope of the Board's authority.

Federal Open Market Committee

As we shall see later, one of the most powerful instruments of control in the hands of the Federal Reserve System is its power to buy and sell government securities, acceptances, and other obligations in the open market. The Reserve banks can create additional member-bank reserves by purchasing obligations in the open market and can contract member-bank reserves by selling securities. The original Federal Reserve Act was vague as to who should control this function, with the result that the individual Reserve banks sometimes followed conflicting policies, and sharp controversies arose within the System. Attempts were made to solve the problem in the 1920s by creating an informal open-market committee made up of representatives of the Federal Reserve banks, but these efforts were only partially successful. Some Reserve banks complained that they were not adequately represented; others ignored the decisions of the informal committee; and the Board in Washington felt that it should have more control of this function.

The Federal Open Market Committee was created by amendments to the Federal Reserve Act in order to clarify the location of authority and to centralize the control of Federal Reserve open-market operations.[7] It is composed of 12 members; seven of these (a majority) are members of the Board of Governors of the Federal Reserve System and five are representatives of the Reserve banks. The latter are elected annually, must be either presidents or vice-presidents of Reserve banks, and are elected by the board of directors of the various Reserve banks, each board having one vote. The distribution of the five Reserve bank representatives is as follows:

One from the Federal Reserve Bank of New York
One from the Federal Reserve Banks of Boston, Philadelphia, and Richmond
One from the Federal Reserve Banks of Atlanta, Dallas, and St. Louis
One from the Federal Reserve Banks of Minneapolis, Kansas City, and San Francisco
One from the Federal Reserve Banks of Cleveland and Chicago

Because of its key position, the New York Bank is always represented on the Committee.

The Federal Reserve Bank of New York occupies a unique position with respect to the Federal Reserve System, the Treasury, and the banking system of the country. Its

[7] The first Federal Open Market Committee was established by amendment to the Federal Reserve Act in 1933. The Committee was reconstituted by further amendments in 1935, and minor changes have been made since that time.

resources total approximately 40 percent of the aggregate of the twelve Federal Reserve Banks. It is located at the central money market and at the principal market for Government securities; its operations as fiscal agent of the United States and its transactions with foreign governments, foreign central banks and bankers, as well as its operations in foreign exchange, are in far greater volume than those of any other Federal Reserve Bank. It is clearly in the public interest that the Federal Open Market Committee be given at all times the benefit of counsel of the Federal Reserve Bank which is in constant touch with the domestic and international money and capital markets and has had long experience in these fields.[8]

The Federal Open Market Committee has full control of all open-market purchases and sales by the Reserve banks. No Reserve bank may engage or decline to engage in open-market operations except in accordance with the regulations adopted by the Committee. The Committee was also given jurisdiction over Federal Reserve purchases and sales of foreign exchange soon after these began in the early 1960s.

Federal Advisory Council

The Federal Advisory Council is composed of 12 members, one being selected by the board of directors of each Reserve bank. The sole function of this Council is to act in an advisory capacity to the Board of Governors. The only sources of its power are its eloquence and the prestige of its members, most of whom are prominent men.

Control of individual Federal Reserve banks

Control of each of the 12 Federal Reserve banks is divided among the member banks in the district, businessmen in the district, and the Board of Governors of the Federal Reserve System. Each Reserve bank has a board of directors with nine members. Three of these are known as Class A directors, three as Class B directors, and three as Class C directors. The Class A directors represent the member banks of the district and are chosen by them. To prevent domination of the Reserve bank by any one banking group, the member banks of the district are divided into three groups based on size, and each group elects one Class A director. The Class B directors represent industry, commerce, and agriculture in the district and must be actively engaged in one of these pursuits at the time of their election. They may not be officers, directors, or employees of any bank. They are, however, elected by the member banks of the district in the same way as the Class A directors. All three of the Class C directors are appointed by the Board of Governors. One of these, who must be "a person of tested banking experience," is chairman of the board of directors and Federal Reserve Agent at the bank. As Federal Reserve Agent, he acts as official representative of the Board of Governors in carrying out its legal functions. Another Class C director at each Reserve bank acts as deputy chairman of the board of directors.

The chief executive officer of each Reserve bank is its president, who is

[8] *Federal Reserve Bulletin*, August, 1942, pp. 740–741.

Table 9–3 Present structure of the Federal Reserve System

Board of Governors	Located in Washington, composed of seven members appointed by the President.
Federal Open Market Committee	12 members, including the Board of Governors and five representatives of the Reserve banks.
12 Federal Reserve banks	Each separately incorporated, each located in an important city, each with a board of directors of nine members, and each with its president and other officers.
24 Branches of the Federal Reserve banks	To facilitate the functioning of the Federal Reserve banks of their districts.
Member banks	About 5,800 banks (mostly commercial banks), of which about 4,600 are national banks and about 1,200 are state banks. These banks hold about 80 percent of all commercial-bank assets and by their magnitude can dominate commercial-banking operations in this country. It is largely through its effects on member banks that the Federal Reserve can control the credit policies of nonmember commercial banks.

appointed by its board of directors with the approval of the Board of Governors. The first vice-president of each Reserve bank is appointed in the same way. Other Reserve bank officers and employees are appointed by the bank's board of directors, although they may, of course, be removed by the Board of Governors.

After a long period of doubt as to the proper location of authority in the Federal Reserve System, it is now clear that the Board of Governors occupies the dominant position. Some power still rests with the representatives chosen by member banks, but the Board of Governors has many sources of power:

1. Exclusive regulation of many Federal Reserve and commercial-bank functions is in the hands of the Board.
2. Its members make up a majority of the members of the powerful Federal Open Market Committee.
3. The Board appoints three members of the board of directors of each Reserve bank, one of its appointees at each bank being chairman of the board of directors and Federal Reserve Agent.
4. The Board may disapprove appointments of presidents and first vice-presidents of the Reserve banks and remove directors, officers, and employees.

PROPOSALS FOR FUTURE CHANGES

It would be rash indeed to assume that the evolutionary development of the Federal Reserve has now ended and that the System will continue unchanged for an indefinite period. There are still heated controversies over both the structure and the control of the System, and these tend to center around membership and control. Most Federal Reserve officials, and probably a majority of monetary economists, believe that all commercial banks should be required to become members of the Federal Reserve, or at least be required to hold reserves equal to those of comparable classes of member banks. They contend that monetary management is a responsibility of the federal government and that the freedom of state-chartered banks to abstain or withdraw from membership tends to weaken the Federal Reserve in performing the functions delegated to it by Congress. This is especially true when the Federal Reserve attempts to raise member-bank reserve requirements considerably above those of nonmember banks, but it applies to some other Federal Reserve actions as well. Such actions tend to put member banks at a competitive disadvantage relative to nonmembers, to create discontent and threats of withdrawal among members, and to lessen the willingness of Federal Reserve officials to apply appropriate restrictive measures to members. For these reasons, it has been proposed several times that nonmembers should be required to hold reserves at least as high as those of member banks, and there is considerable support for legislation to require all commercial banks to join the Federal Reserve.

There is strong opposition to these proposals, especially from bankers and state bank commissioners. These opponents bolster their position with several arguments:

1. The Federal Reserve already has adequate credit-control powers, since its members hold about 80 percent of total commercial-bank assets and deposits. Moreover, the presence of nonmembers is disadvantageous only when the Federal Reserve tries to increase reserve requirements of members to excessive levels, and this should not be done anyway.

2. Such an extension of federal power would violate states' rights, in this case the right of states to regulate the banks that they charter.

3. The ability of banks to abstain from Federal Reserve membership or to withdraw if already in the System is a desirable part of our governmental system of "checks and balances"; it acts as a check on the severity of Federal Reserve actions.

4. A requirement that all banks hold their reserves in the form of deposits at the Federal Reserve would cause some of the bigger banks to lose at least part of their profitable interbank deposits. The opposition to both universal membership and the extension of federally determined reserve requirements to all commercial banks is by no means confined to bankers whose institutions are now outside the System.

The location of control over Federal Reserve activities also continues to be a subject of intense controversy. Involved here are both the relation of the Federal Reserve to the executive branch of the government and the distribution of control within the System. The Federal Reserve is based on the principle of "independent central banking." It is, of course, responsible to Congress; it was created by Congress, must make reports to Congress, and Congress can at any time change its basic legislation, give it directives, or even abolish it. It is not, however, responsible to the executive branch. This "independence" from the executive branch is based on several considerations.

1. The administration in power is likely to have an easy-money inflationary bias, partly because easy money and mild inflation tend to be popular and to increase the ability of the incumbent political party to remain in power, and partly because the Treasury is likely to insist on easy money and low interest rates to keep down interest charges on the national debt and to facilitate its refunding and new borrowing operations.

2. Control of the central bank is likely to inject "politics" into that bank's operations: patronage, discrimination on the basis of party affiliation, and so on.

3. Successful monetary management requires greater continuity among top officials than would be likely to result from responsibility to a President, whose tenure will be only four to eight years.

4. The existing arrangement elicits more confidence and cooperation from the commercial banks than they would give to a "politically dominated" institution.

On the other hand, several arguments are advanced for terminating the "independence" of the Federal Reserve and for making it responsible to the executive branch:

1. Monetary policy, like other governmental policies, should be controlled by people responsible to the electorate.

2. The present arrangement makes the appropriate coordination of monetary policy with the other economic policies of the government difficult. It is intolerable that the Federal Reserve should follow policies in conflict with those determined by the elected representatives of the people.

3. Especially serious are the overlapping of powers and the conflict of interest between the Federal Reserve and the Treasury during inflation periods. At such times, the debt-management policies of the Treasury, when it emphasizes low interest rates, are in conflict with the Federal Reserve objective of curbing inflation. Some people would resolve this conflict between institutions, if not between objectives, by making the Federal Reserve responsible either to the Treasury or to the President. Others, however, would secure coordination by instructing the Treasury to adjust its debt-management policies to the monetary policies of the Federal Reserve.

It is still too early to forecast the outcome of this controversy over the relationship between the Federal Reserve and the executive branch. Some method of achieving better coordination of monetary, debt-management, and other economic policies is clearly needed. But it is to be hoped that the tradition of an "independent" central bank will not be discarded without full consideration of the resultant dangers.

Less intense, but nevertheless important, are the continuing controversies over the location of control within the Federal Reserve System. Some who believe that centralization has gone too far would transfer some power back to the Reserve banks, or at least from the Board to the Federal Open Market Committee on which the Reserve banks are represented. Others would concentrate still more power in the Board.

Proposals such as the following have been advanced in recent years.

1. Reduce the number of members of the Board of Governors from seven to no more than five. The primary purpose of this would be to increase the prestige of the Board and attract more able people to it. Other possible benefits are a greater concentration of responsibility and more flexible decision making.

2. Abolish the Federal Open Market Committee, remove from the Reserve banks their last vestige of control over discount policy, and vest in the Board of Governors complete authority over discount policy, open-market policy, foreign-exchange policy, and member-bank reserve requirements. The boards of directors and executive officers of the 12 Reserve banks would then be responsible for carrying out the policies laid down by the Board of Governors, but their role in policy making would be purely advisory.

3. Retire the Federal Reserve stock now held by member banks, and with it, all the power of member banks to elect members of the boards of directors of the Reserve banks. This, it is expected, would leave the banks with no more control over monetary policy than they could achieve as members of the community.

None of these proposals has been adopted, and all remain controversial. If all were adopted, we should have in fact, if not in form, a single central bank.

FEDERAL RESERVE "CHORES"

Having examined the structure and control of the Federal Reserve System, we can now begin to study its functions. We shall look first at its functions other than those of monetary and credit management. For brevity these will be called "chores." But these chores are not merely incidental or unimportant functions. Collectively, they account for the great bulk of work within the Federal Reserve. And in performing these chores, the Federal Reserve has contributed greatly to the efficiency and convenience of the banking system.

Banking supervision

The supervision and examination of banking in this country are not exclusively a Federal Reserve function, but are shared with several other authorities. The Comptroller of the Currency has jurisdiction over all national banks. State banking authorities have jurisdiction over state banks. And the Federal Deposit Insurance Corporation has jurisdiction over all banks with deposit insurance, which includes all members of the Federal Reserve System and most nonmembers. Each Reserve bank has its staff of bank examiners, and member banks must periodically report their condition. In addition to requiring reports and examining member banks, the Federal Reserve exercises other important supervisory powers, among which are the powers to:

1. Fix maximum rates of interest that member banks may pay on time and savings deposits.[9]

---

[9] Banks are not allowed to pay interest on demand deposits.

2. Remove officers and directors of member banks for continued violation of banking laws or for continued unsafe or unsound banking practices.
3. Suspend a member bank's borrowing privileges at the Federal Reserve if it is found to be making undue use of bank credit for speculation in securities, real estate, or commodities.
4. Permit national banks, where appropriate, to exercise trust powers.
5. Permit holding companies, when it is not against the public interest, to vote the stocks of member banks controlled by them.
6. Permit member banks to establish branches in foreign countries.

Although by its supervision and examination the Federal Reserve has undoubtedly helped improve the quality of banking, its success has been limited. One reason for this is the principle of optional membership for state-chartered banks, which has permitted 85 percent of these banks to remain nonmembers. Unfortunately, many of these banks are located in states in which banking laws and supervision are least satisfactory and improvement most needed. Thus, federal efforts to improve bank supervision were seriously hampered until after the banking collapse in 1933. The situation was much improved by the establishment, in the mid-1930s, of the Federal Deposit Insurance Corporation, which insures deposits of only those banks that submit to its jurisdiction, supervision, and examination. Fortunately, less than 200 banks, most of them small, have remained noninsured.

Overlapping jurisdictions of the chartering, supervisory, and examining authorities remain a problem despite the degree of cooperation achieved. These agencies sometimes conflict with each other, differ in their administrative interpretations if not in basic principles, and enable banks to "play off one agency against another." To eliminate the overlapping of federal and state jurisdictions may be politically infeasible. But many think it desirable, and perhaps politically possible, to eliminate at the federal level the overlapping jurisdictions of the Comptroller of the Currency, the Federal Reserve, and the Federal Deposit Insurance Corporation. Some suggest that all supervisory and examination powers should be vested in one of the existing agencies. Others think they should be concentrated in a newly created agency, which might also have jurisdiction over other types of financial institutions.

Clearing and collection of checks

The Federal Reserve System has greatly enhanced the speed, convenience, and cheapness of clearing and collecting checks and other similar items. Before 1914, a check might spend two weeks or more in the process of being cleared and collected, especially if it had to move long distances. The maximum time now required is only a few days, and banks that clear checks through the Federal Reserve receive payment in two days or less. The whole process is completed with virtually no shipment of coin or currency. Deposit accounts at the Federal Reserve banks play a central role in this process. All member banks hold deposit claims against their Federal Reserve banks to meet their legal reserve requirements, although cash in vault also counts as legal reserves. Many nonmember banks have deposits at the Federal Reserve for clearing purposes. This permits banks to make or receive net payments through the transfer of deposit credits on the books of the Federal Reserve.

To illustrate the high development of the clearance and collection system for checks and other similar instruments, let us look at the process in a few typical situations. The processes often vary in detail from those described below, but the principles involved are similar. Let us suppose that Smith deposits with the First Hartford Bank in Connecticut a check for $100 given him by Jones. If Jones's check is drawn on the First Hartford Bank, the process of clearance is simple; the bank merely adds $100 to Smith's deposit account and deducts $100 from Jones's account.

Suppose, however, that Jones had written the check on another bank in the same city, the Second Hartford Bank. After Smith has deposited the check with the First Hartford Bank, it may be cleared in either of two general ways. The two banks may informally exchange their claims against each other at the end of the day, the net debtor then paying the other bank with a check drawn on another bank, probably the Federal Reserve bank of the district. Final payment is thus made by transferring a deposit credit at the Federal Reserve from the account of the Second Hartford Bank to that of the First Hartford Bank. Or the banks may clear and collect checks through a local clearing house. At an appointed time each day, each bank in the area takes to the clearing house all the checks and other matured claims that it has against the other members of the clearing house. There, clearing-house officials compare the total amounts of checks presented by each bank against all other banks with the total amount of checks presented by all other banks against it, and then pay each bank the net amount due it or collect the net amount owed by it. These net payments are usually made with checks, often with checks drawn on the Reserve bank of the district. Actual coin or currency is almost never used to pay net differences at a clearing house.

If the check Jones gives to Smith is drawn on a bank located in another city in the same Federal Reserve district (say, in Springfield, Massachusetts), the clearance and collection procedure is somewhat as follows: Smith deposits the check with the First Hartford Bank, which credits his account and sends the check along with others to the Federal Reserve Bank of Boston for clearance and collection. The Boston Reserve bank then sends the check to Springfield, and the Springfield bank deducts the amount of the check from Jones's deposit account. After the lapse of sufficient time for notification if the check is not good, the Boston Reserve bank deducts the amount of the check from the Springfield bank's reserve account with it and adds the same amount to the Hartford bank's reserve account. Payment of the check has been achieved quickly and with no shipment of coin or curency.

The procedure is only slightly more complicated if Jones's check is drawn on a bank in another Federal Reserve district, say, on the Los Angeles Commercial Bank. Smith deposits the check with the Hartford bank, which credits his deposit account and sends the check along with others to the Federal Reserve Bank of

Boston. The latter then sends the check along with others via air mail to the Federal Reserve Bank of San Francisco, which then sends it to the Los Angeles Commercial Bank. If the San Francisco bank is not notified within an appointed time that the check is bad, it deducts the amount of the check from the Los Angeles bank's reserve account with it. At or about the same time, the Boston Reserve bank adds the amount of the check to the Hartford bank's reserve account. At this point Smith has been paid, Jones has paid, Smith's bank has been paid, and Jones's bank has paid. But the San Francisco bank still owes the Boston bank the amount of the check, if it has not been offset by counterclaims. How is a net balance paid between Reserve banks? This is accomplished without any shipment of coin or currency by the simple expedient of book entries in the Interdistrict Settlement Fund, which is maintained by the Board of Governors in Washington. Each Reserve bank establishes a credit in the Interdistrict Settlement Fund. Any net balance due a Federal Reserve bank at the end of a day is added to its account in the Fund, and any net claim of another Reserve bank against it is deducted from its account.

It is through arrangements of this type that payments can be made to all points within the country quickly and without the inconvenience and expense of shipping coin or currency. Federal Reserve facilities for clearing and collection are available without charge to all member banks and to all nonmembers who will remit the par value of checks drawn on them. The Federal Reserve will not, however, clear and collect checks drawn on nonmembers who refuse to pay the full face amounts of checks drawn on them. The "nonpar banks" are still an inconvenience in the banking system.

Wire transfers

In addition to providing a rapid and efficient system for clearing and collecting checks, the Federal Reserve transfers funds and certain types of securities by wire. Until the early 1970s, the wire-transfer system consisted of telegraphic linkages among the Board of Governors, the 12 Federal Reserve banks, and the 24 branches of the latter. This system was replaced in the early 1970s by a system of interconnected computers. The new system has far greater capacity than the old one and can accomplish in minutes what might earlier have required hours. Partly because of the rapidly rising burden of handling checks and other paper instruments, the Board of Governors encourages the use of wire transfers. To this end, it has lowered charges for such transfers, lowered the minimum amounts that may be transferred by wire, and requested the Reserve banks to promote uses of the system. Almost all large payments are now transferred by wire. At some time in the future, perhaps not too far distant, the present computer interconnections of the Board and all the Reserve banks and their branches is likely to become the center of a nationwide electronic-payments system. All, or at least the great bulk of commercial banks, will have their computers linked into the computers of their Reserve banks, either directly or through a correspondent. Orders to pay will typically be communicated electronically, not by a written instrument. The result may not be a "checkless society," but it is almost certain to be a society with fewer checks.

Through the wire-transfer system, the federal government, banks, and customers of banks can transfer funds from one end of the country to another almost instantaneously. Suppose, for example, that Jones in Los Angeles wishes to transfer by wire $1 million to Smith in Hartford, Connecticut. Jones gives his bank a check for that amount, and his bank wires the Federal Reserve Bank of San Francisco, asking it to transfer the funds. The San Francisco Reserve bank deducts the amount from the reserve account of the Los Angeles bank and wires the Federal Reserve Bank of Boston, telling the latter to transfer the funds to Smith at the First Hartford Bank. The Boston Reserve bank adds the amount to the First Hartford Bank's reserve account and wires the Hartford bank to credit Smith's account. The whole process is completed within minutes. The San Francisco Reserve bank settles with the Boston Reserve bank through a transfer on the books of the Interdistrict Settlement Fund at the Board of Governors.

Through its wire-transfer system, the Federal Reserve can also transfer federal government securities over long distances within a few minutes. Suppose, for example, that a bank in Seattle wishes to transfer $10 million of Treasury obligations to a New York dealer in government securities. The bank will take the securities to the Seattle branch of the Federal Reserve Bank of San Francisco, indicating the identity of the dealer to whom they are to be delivered. The Seattle branch will retire the $10 million of certificates and wire the Federal Reserve Bank of New York to issue and deliver to the buyer new Treasury obligations of the same issue and in the same amount. After the dealer has sold these securities, he may pay the Seattle bank through the wire-transfer system.

In some cases, such transfers of claims against the government debt are even simpler than the process described above. This is because at least some of a member bank's debt claims against the Treasury may not be evidenced by certificates or any other paper document, but only by book entries at its Federal Reserve bank. This claim at the Federal Reserve indicates the particular Treasury issues against which the bank has claims, and the amounts of each. If a bank wishes to sell some of these claims, it simply sends the relevant information to the Federal Reserve, which makes the transfer on its books.

FISCAL-AGENCY FUNCTIONS

As noted earlier, one purpose of the Federal Reserve Act was to provide the United States Treasury with a more satisfactory fiscal agent. Before that time, the Treasury relied on commercial banks and on the so-called Independent Treasury System, which consisted of a number of regional suboffices of the Treasury. Both were unsatisfactory. Banks were unsatisfactory because some were unsafe, check clearing and collection were slow, and the limited geographic scope of each bank was not conducive to rapid regional transfers of government funds. The Independent Treasury System was unsatisfactory, partly because its offices were so expensive to operate. Much more serious was that net movements of coin and paper money into and out of its vaults sometimes had undesirable effects on general credit conditions. Net collections of coin and currency from the public served to reduce bank reserves and restrict bank credit, whether or not this was desirable. And net outpayments of coin and currency tended to increase bank reserves and ease credit, sometimes when such results were not wanted. Treasury officials gradually learned how to avoid such undesirable results and even to use these powers in a stabilizing way. Nevertheless, it became clear that a more efficient mechanism was needed.

In acting as fiscal agent, the Federal Reserve banks do an enormous amount of work for the federal government and its various offices and corporations. At some of the Reserve banks, the amount of work done for the government is comparable to, and even greater than, that done for the bank itself as principal. Among the functions performed by the Federal Reserve as "principal banker to the government" are:

1. Financial advisor
2. Depository and receiving and paying agent
3. Agent for issuing and retiring Treasury securities
4. Agent in other transactions involving purchases and sales of securities for Treasury account
5. Agent for the government in purchasing and selling gold and foreign exchange
6. Lender to the Treasury

Financial advisor

The Treasury and other government departments do not, of course, rely solely on the Federal Reserve for financial information and advice; they have their own staffs and many other sources. Yet the Federal Reserve, which is so intimately and continuously in contact with the money, securities, and foreign-exchange markets, is in a position to be especially helpful to the government in its debt management and foreign-exchange transactions.

Depository

The Federal Reserve banks, collectively, are in one sense the principal depository of federal government funds, for most government payments are made out of the Treasury's deposit accounts at the Federal Reserve. Yet the Treasury ordinarily holds only a small fraction of its deposit balances at the Federal Reserve; the remainder are held in thousands of commercial banks. This system was evolved to minimize disturbances to bank reserves and the general credit situation that would otherwise result as the government had large net receipts or made large net payments. During some periods, especially at the peak of tax collections or when the Treasury has sold a large issue of securities, the Treasury has large net receipts, mostly in the form of checks. If all these were put into deposits at the Federal Reserve banks, the Federal Reserve would add them to its deposit liability to the Treasury and deduct them from its deposit liabilities to the banks on which the checks were drawn. Thus the banks would lose reserves and the supply of money and credit would tend to be restricted, whether or not this was desired. At other times, especially when tax collections are small relative to expenditures, the Treasury must make large net payments to the rest of the community. If it made these payments with checks drawn on deposits built up earlier at the Federal Reserve, the payees would deposit the checks in their banks, which would in turn send them to the Federal Reserve, which would subtract them from Treasury deposits and add them to reserve accounts of the banks. This increase of bank reserves would tend to expand credit, which might or might not be desirable. We shall see later that the Federal Reserve can attempt to offset such disturbances by sales and purchases of government securities in the open market. But to do this smoothly and effectively when the disturbances are large presents difficulties.

It is largely to avoid such difficulties that the Treasury ordinarily holds most of its deposits in tax and loan accounts at more than 10,000 qualified commercial banks. These banks are those that want to hold Treasury deposits, have pledged government securities to assure the safety of these deposits, and have met certain other requirements. The system works as follows: A bank, or customers of a bank, send checks to the Treasury to pay taxes or to pay for securities purchased from the Treasury. The Treasury records the amounts received and routes the checks back through the Federal Reserve to the bank on which they are drawn, and the latter adds the amounts of the checks to its deposit liability to the Treasury. Note that at this stage, the bank has lost no reserves; it has merely increased its deposit liability to the Treasury, and if the checks were written by customers, has reduced its deposit liabilities to the public. In the meantime, the Federal Reserve maintains complete records of the amounts of Treasury deposits at every bank. Later, a few days before the Treasury wishes to use the deposits for payment, the Federal Reserve in its capacity as fiscal agent announces the date when a stated percentage of Treasury deposits will be called. The call states, in effect, "On the specified date, X percent of Treasury deposits will be withdrawn from your bank. On this date we shall deduct this amount from your reserve account at the Federal Reserve and you shall deduct this amount from your deposit liability to the Treasury." This tends, of course, to reduce bank reserves. However, meanwhile, the Treasury checks drawn on the Federal Reserve will have been sent to payees. As these are deposited with banks and sent by banks to the Federal Reserve, the effect is to restore bank reserves. If the timing is perfect, there will be no net change in the total volume of bank reserves, although there may be some redistribution of reserves among the banks.

Agent for the Treasury in securities transactions

The Federal Reserve does a tremendous amount of work for the Treasury in issuing and retiring securities and in purchasing and selling securities for trust funds and other accounts controlled by the government. When the Treasury offers new securities for sale, the Federal Reserve publicizes the issue, receives bids and subscriptions, decides which to accept and which to reject in accordance with

Treasury instructions, and collects on behalf of the Treasury. As paying agent for the Treasury, it pays interest on the federal debt and redeems maturing securities. When, as sometimes happens, the Treasury offers an issue through an investment-banking syndicate, the Federal Reserve serves as agent for the Treasury in making arrangements.

Agent for the Treasury in gold and foreign-exchange transactions

As already indicated, and as will be discussed more fully at a later point, the Treasury is sole custodian of the nation's monetary gold and buys and sells gold for monetary purposes. In almost all these transactions, the Federal Reserve acts as agent for the Treasury. The Federal Reserve also buys and sells foreign exchange (claims against foreign moneys) both on its own account and as agent for the Treasury. Many of these transactions are for the purpose of influencing the behavior of the exchange rate on the dollar. Others are merely to assist the Treasury in making or receiving international payments.

Lender to the government

To be able to borrow directly from the central bank is a great convenience to the Treasury. But it is also dangerous, for the Treasury may insist on borrowing unduly large amounts from the central bank, thereby increasing bank reserves, despite potentially inflationary consequences. It is largely because of this danger that the power of the Federal Reserve to lend directly to the Treasury is limited by law. The Federal Reserve may not at any time hold more than $5 billion of federal securities acquired directly from the Treasury, and even this authorization is extended by Congress only on a year-to-year basis. However, this limitation removes neither the danger of undue Treasury pressure nor the power of the Federal Reserve to facilitate Treasury finance, for the Federal Reserve can purchase federal debt that has been sold to others and can otherwise create a liberal supply of credit that will be favorable to Treasury borrowing.

Selected readings

Bach, G. L., *Federal Reserve Policy Making,* New York, Knopf, 1950.
Board of Governors of the Federal Reserve System, Washington, D.C.:
  The Federal Reserve System, Its Purposes and Functions, 2d ed., 1947.
  Banking Studies, 1941.
  Banking and Monetary Statistics, 1943.
  Federal Reserve Bulletins (monthly).
  Annual Reports.
Burgess, W. R., *The Reserve Banks and the Money Market,* New York, Harper & Row, 1946.
Chandler, L. V., *Benjamin Strong, Central Banker,* Washington, D.C., Brookings Institution, 1958.
Commission on Money and Credit, *Money and Credit,* Englewood Cliffs, N.J., Prentice-Hall, 1961.

Glass, Carter, *Adventure in Constructive Finance*, New York, Doubleday, 1927.

Goldenweiser, E. A., *American Monetary Policy*, New York, McGraw-Hill, 1951.

Hardy, C. O., *Credit Policies of the Federal Reserve System*, Washington, D.C., Brookings Institution, 1932.

Harris, S., *Twenty Years of Federal Reserve Policies*, Cambridge, Mass., Harvard University Press, 1933.

U.S. Congress, Joint Committee on the Economic Report:

Subcommittee on Monetary, Credit, and Fiscal Policies,

Statements on Monetary, Credit, and Fiscal Policies, 1949.

Hearings on Monetary, Credit, and Fiscal Policies, 1949.

Report on Monetary, Credit, and Fiscal Policies, 1950.

Subcommittee on General Credit Control and Debt Management,

Replies to Questions and Other Materials, 1952.

Hearings, 1952.

Report, 1952.

(All published by the U.S. Government Printing Office, Washington, D.C.)

Wicker, Elmus R., *Federal Reserve Monetary Policy, 1917–1933*, New York, Random House, 1966.

CHAPTER 10

FEDERAL RESERVE CREDIT AND BANK RESERVES

Although its service functions are highly useful, the primary function of the Federal Reserve, as well as other central banks, is monetary management; that is, regulation of the supply of money and of the supply and availability of loan funds for business, consumer, and government spending. Federal Reserve powers in this area are inescapably great; by its very existence the System inevitably affects the behavior of not only financial markets but also real output, employment, and price levels. If these powers are used in an appropriate manner, the Federal Reserve can act as a powerful stabilizing force; if they are used in other ways, the System can be a potent destabilizer.

The monetary or credit-management activities of the Federal Reserve are of two broad types: (1) general monetary or credit controls, and (2) selective credit controls. The immediate objective of the general controls is to regulate the total supply of money and credit; it is not to determine the allocation of the total supply of credit among the various types of borrowers or among its various possible uses, although some allocative effects may occur as an unintended by-product. The function of allocating credit is left to the private market. On the other hand, the immediate purpose of selective controls is to regulate the amount of credit used (or the terms on which credit is available) for selected purposes, such as credit extended for consumer purchases, to purchase or carry securities listed on the national exchanges, or for new residential construction. The deliberate purpose of such selective controls is to interfere with the allocative functions of private credit markets. Selective controls may also affect the total supply of credit, but this is a secondary effect. Further discussion of selective controls will be postponed to a later chapter; the remainder of this chapter will discuss general monetary and credit controls.

GENERAL CONTROLS

In an earlier chapter, we found that the volume of deposits that commercial banks can create and have outstanding, and also the volume of earning assets that they can acquire and hold, depend on (1) the dollar volume of legal reserves available to the banks, and (2) the height of their legal fractional reserve requirements against deposits. Every dollar of legal reserves is "high-powered money" in the sense that each dollar of reserves can support several dollars of commercial-bank deposits. But how "high powered" each dollar of reserves is depends on the height of legal reserve requirements.

To carry out its function of general monetary and credit management, the Federal Reserve has powers to control both the height of reserve requirements and the volume and cost of bank reserves. As we have already seen, the Federal Reserve Act provides that only two types of assets can be counted as legal reserves for member banks: deposits at the Federal Reserve and cash in vault. Moreover, it empowers the Board of Governors to alter, within specified limits, the percentage reserve requirements against deposits in member banks. By raising the level of these requirements, the Board can inhibit the creation of money by the banking system and exert an anti-expansionary or even a contractionary influence. By lowering these requirements, the Board can permit and even encourage an expansion of money and credit. We shall see later that this is a powerful instrument which the Board sometimes uses.

However, the Federal Reserve relies more continuously on its power to regulate the volume and cost of reserves available to the commercial-banking system. The remainder of this chapter will discuss the factors determining the volume of bank reserves and the processes through which the Federal Reserve creates and destroys these reserves. We shall emphasize Federal Reserve control of the money-creating and money-destroying activities of the commercial banks. However, it should be noted that in this process, the Federal Reserve can itself create and destroy money. For example, when the Federal Reserve makes net purchases of assets, it creates and issues funds that usually appear somewhere in the money supply. And when it makes net sales of assets, it can directly decrease the money supply.

FEDERAL RESERVE BALANCE SHEETS

An analysis of the consolidated balance sheets of the 12 Federal Reserve banks will help us understand the processes through which the Federal Reserve increases or decreases the reserves of the commercial-banking system. We start with basic balance sheet equations of the type developed in Chapter 6:

$$\text{Assets} = \text{liabilities} + \text{capital accounts} \tag{1}$$

$$\text{Liabilities} = \text{assets} - \text{capital accounts} \tag{2}$$

Assets include everything of value owned by the Federal Reserve banks at the stated point of time. *Liabilities* are debt claims against the Federal Reserve banks. *Capital accounts,* or net worth, are the ownership claims against the Federal Reserve banks. At any point of time, the Federal Reserve banks must have outstanding a total of debt claims and ownership claims exactly equal to the value of their assets. If they make net increases in their assets, they must pay for these assets by creating and issuing an equal net increase in debt and ownership claims against themselves. And if they decrease their total asset holdings, they must withdraw and retire an equal amount of outstanding debt and ownership claims against themselves.

An examination of the Federal Reserve balance sheet in Table 10–1 reveals that the Reserve banks have paid for only a very small fraction, less than 2 percent, of their assets by issuing capital-account, or net-worth, claims. Moreover, the

Table 10–1 Balance sheet of the Federal Reserve banks, May 26, 1971 (millions of dollars)

ASSETS		LIABILITIES AND CAPITAL ACCOUNTS	
Gold certificates	$10,075	Federal Reserve notes	$50,517
SDR certificates	400	Deposits due to:	
Foreign exchange	94	Member banks	25,985
Cash	276	U.S. Treasury	887
Discounts and advances	1,274	Foreign	156
Acceptances	102	Other	671
U.S. government securities	64,971	Total deposits	$27,699
Cash items in process of collection	9,929	Deferred availability cash items...................	7,441
Other assets	777	Other liabilities	542
		Capital accounts	1,699
Total assets	$87,898	Total liabilities and capital accounts	$87,898

Addenda: Cash items in process of collection	$ 9,929
Minus: Deferred availability cash items	7,441
Equals: Float	$ 2,488

SOURCE: *Federal Reserve Bulletin,* June, 1971, p. A12.

total of these net-worth claims rises only slowly through time, reflecting mostly new stock subscriptions by member banks equal to about 3 percent of increases in the paid-up capital and surplus of member banks. Thus, the Reserve banks pay for their assets largely by issuing debt claims against themselves, and they withdraw and retire debt claims when they decrease their total assets.

FEDERAL RESERVE NOTES AND DEPOSITS

Federal Reserve liabilities are largely of two types: Federal Reserve notes and deposit liabilities. As indicated earlier, Federal Reserve notes make up the great bulk of paper money in the United States. Although impressively engraved and endowed by law with full legal-tender powers, they are nothing but debt claims against the Federal Reserve banks. Deposits at the Federal Reserve banks are also merely debts owed by the Federal Reserve. They are evidenced by book entries. Table 10–1 indicates that the Federal Reserve issued deposit claims against itself to only a few types of holders. It will not accept deposits from individuals, businesses, or state and local governments. Most of its deposit liabilities are to member banks. These serve both as legal reserves for member banks and as a medium for clearing and collection, as noted earlier. Smaller deposit liabilities are owed to the federal government, to nonmember banks for check-clearing purposes, and to foreign central banks and the International Monetary Fund. It should be evident that member-bank deposits at the Federal Reserve may be decreased as these deposits are shifted to the ownership of other depositors at the Federal Reserve, and that member-bank deposits at the Federal Reserve may be increased as other deposits at the Federal Reserve are transferred to the ownership of member banks.

Changes in the volume of Federal Reserve notes outstanding reflect changes in the demand for paper money to be held in commercial-bank vaults or to be used as currency in circulation, predominantly the latter. Whenever the public wants more currency, the commercial banks are the first to feel the impact. Customers write checks on their deposit accounts and withdraw cash. The banks may supply the currency out of their cash in vault, thereby losing legal reserves in this form, or they may get it by drawing down their deposits at the Federal Reserve. In the latter case, the increase in Federal Reserve notes outstanding is at the expense of member-bank deposits at the Federal Reserve. On the other hand, when the public wishes to hold less paper money, it deposits the excess at commercial banks, which may either add it to their legal reserves in the form of cash in vault or send it along to the Federal Reserve. In the latter case, the Federal Reserve retires the net inflow of Federal Reserve notes and adds an equal amount to its deposit liabilities to banks.

This demonstrates several important points. First, it indicates how the volume of Federal Reserve notes is made responsive to the public's demand for paper money. Second, it shows that increases in Federal Reserve notes outstanding tend initially to be at the expense of bank deposits at the Federal Reserve, and that decreases in Federal Reserve notes outstanding tend initially to increase the volume of bank deposits at the Federal Reserve. Third, it suggests why we are justified in assuming that when the Federal Reserve makes net purchases of assets, it initially pays for them by creating deposit claims against itself; and when it makes net sales of assets, it initially collects by withdrawing an equal value of its deposit liabilities. For simplicity of exposition we shall assume in the succeeding sections that when the Federal Reserve purchases assets, it makes payment by adding to the reserves of commercial banks; and that when it sells assets, it collects by deducting from the reserve balances of commercial banks.

FEDERAL RESERVE ASSETS

It should be emphasized that the Federal Reserve banks can create or destroy their own deposit liabilities by purchasing or selling any kind of asset whatsoever. Thus, they can create deposit liabilities to pay for land, buildings, equipment, services, or any type of claim against others. Or they can withdraw their deposit liabilities by making net sales of any kind of asset. This point should be borne in mind, because even now the Federal Reserve makes several kinds of purchases and sales, and in the future it might broaden the categories of assets in which it deals.

It will be useful to distinguish between two types of Federal Reserve purchases and sales of assets:

1. Transactions with member banks. When the Federal Reserve purchases assets from a member bank, it pays that bank by adding to its reserve account. When it sells an asset to a member bank, it collects payment by reducing the bank's reserve account.

2. Transactions with the "public." When the Federal Reserve buys an asset from the "public"—from an individual, business firm, or state or local government—it usually pays with a check drawn on a Federal Reserve bank. The seller of the asset usually deposits the check at a commercial bank, receiving in return a deposit credit there, and the commercial bank then sends the check to its Federal Reserve bank, which adds the amount of the check to the commercial bank's reserve account. Thus, Federal Reserve purchases of assets from the "public" tend to increase directly both the public's money supply and commercial-bank reserves. Federal Reserve sales of assets to the public have the reverse effects. When a member of the public buys an asset from the Federal Reserve, he usually pays with a check drawn on a commercial bank. The Federal Reserve deducts the amount of the check from the commercial bank's reserve account and sends the check to the commercial bank, which deducts its amount from the customer's deposit account. Thus, a Federal Reserve sale of an asset to the public tends to reduce directly both the public's money supply and commercial-bank reserves. The effect on commercial-bank reserves is, of course, the more important, for each

dollar of change in commercial-bank reserves may induce, or even force, several dollars of change in the commercial banks' loans, investments, and deposit liabilities.

Although the Federal Reserve can create or destroy commercial-bank reserves by buying or selling assets of any kind, Table 10–1 indicates that, in practice, Federal Reserve purchases and sales are largely confined to a few types of assets. We shall now examine these assets, and the ways in which they are acquired and sold by the Federal Reserve.

INTERNATIONAL RESERVE ASSETS OF THE FEDERAL RESERVE

We start our discussion with three types of Federal Reserve assets closely related to international monetary transactions—gold certificates, SDR Certificates, and foreign exchange. Gold certificates are Federal Reserve claims against monetary gold held by the Treasury. As we shall see later, these usually are approximately equal to the value of the nation's monetary gold stock. SDR Certificates are Federal Reserve claims against Special Drawing Rights (SDRs) held by the Treasury. They are the part of the nation's holdings of SDRs that have been monetized. Federal Reserve assets in the form of foreign exchange are claims denominated in foreign currencies. These are in various forms—such as deposit claims against foreign, central, and commercial banks; short-term claims against foreign governments and business firms; and so on.

These Federal Reserve assets have several important characteristics in common:

1. They are all components of, or claims against components of, the nation's international monetary reserves.

2. Purchases and sales of these assets are not made for the primary purpose of affecting the reserve positions of American banks and domestic monetary conditions. Instead, the primary purpose is to influence the behavior of exchange rates between the dollar and foreign moneys, and both the timing and amounts of purchases and sales of these assets depend on the state of the nation's balance of international payments and on its exchange-rate objectives. For example, suppose that an excess supply of dollars in foreign-exchange markets tends to lower the exchange rate on the dollar to an undesired extent. The authorities can prevent or limit the decline by purchasing the excess dollars in exchange markets. To pay for the dollars, they can surrender some of their assets in the form of gold, SDRs, and foreign exchange. Suppose, on the other hand, that a deficient supply of dollars in the foreign-exchange market tends to raise the exchange rate on the dollar to an undesired extent. The authorities can prevent or limit the extent of the rise by supplying more dollars in exchange markets. They can create and supply the dollars by purchasing assets in the form of gold, SDRs, and foreign exchange.

3. Although the primary purpose is to affect exchange rates, purchases and sales of these assets also affect the supply of bank reserves for the American banking system, and these latter effects are sometimes undesired. For example, purchases or sales of these assets to meet exchange-rate objectives may tend to increase or decrease bank reserves when no such change is desired. Fortunately, as we shall see later, the Federal Reserve can prevent such unwanted increases or decreases of bank reserves by making offsetting sales or purchases of other types of assets, such as securities of the United States Treasury.

In early 1972, almost all aspects of American international monetary policies were in a turmoil. President Nixon had announced dramatically on August 15, 1971 that, at least temporarily, ties between the dollar and gold had been severed. The United States monetary authorities would neither buy nor sell gold, not even in transactions with international monetary institutions or with foreign central banks and governments. He also stated his determination that the dollar should depreciate in terms of other major national currencies. Since the dollar had been a significant factor in the international monetary system, these actions necessitated basic readjustments in the world's monetary systems and raised many policy questions which possibly may not be answered for many years. Among the major types of policy questions most directly relevant to our interests at this point are the following:

1. Exchange-rate policies. Will the United States again purchase and sell some type of international asset in such a way as to hold within narrow limits exchange rates between the dollar and other major currencies? Will it go to the other extreme and allow exchange rates to be determined by market forces without any official purchases and sales to influence exchange-rate behavior? Will it follow some intermediate policy, allowing fairly wide variations of exchange rates but with some official purchases and sales to influence exchange-rate behavior?

2. Gold policies. Will the United States continue to refuse to buy any gold for monetary purposes or to sell any of its existing stock of monetary gold? If it does sell some of its monetary gold, to whom will it sell, for what purposes and in what amounts, and at what prices? If it resumes purchases of gold for monetary purposes, from whom will it buy, for what purposes and in what amounts, and at what prices?

3. SDR policies. At least two years before President Nixon's announcement in August, 1971, nations had agreed through the International Monetary Fund that SDRs should play an increasing role as a component of international monetary reserves. Because the president's action will almost certainly precipitate a decreased role for claims against United States dollars as a component of international monetary reserves, the future role of SDRs is likely to be even greater than was earlier contemplated, although it is possible that SDRs will be supplemented or even supplanted by a new type of international reserve asset. Several questions are relevant. For example, at what rate will SDRs or other similar reserve assets be created, and how will they be allocated among the various

nations? What will be American policies with respect to purchasing, selling, and holding SDRs?

4. Foreign-exchange policies. What will be the policies of American monetary authorities with respect to purchasing sales and holdings of claims against foreign currencies?

All of these questions are directly relevant to Federal Reserve purchases, sales, and holdings of international reserve assets. Since we cannot foresee what future policies will be, and since these are likely to change through time, we shall describe the policies followed in the recent past, indicate the direction of recent changes, and suggest some possible lines of development in the future.

Gold and gold certificates

We shall first describe American monetary gold policies during the period of more than 34 years from January, 1934 to mid-March, 1968.

Prior to 1933, the United States was on an unlimited gold-coin standard. All types of money were freely convertible into gold coins, gold certificates, or gold bullion on demand, and there were no legal restrictions on holding or dealing in gold. The Federal Reserve held large amounts of gold and gold certificates, far in excess of the small amounts demanded by the public. These policies were changed markedly in 1933 and by the Gold Reserve Act of 1934. Several aspects of the new arrangements are relevant to our present purposes.

1. All gold and gold certificates, including Federal Reserve holdings, were nationalized at the old official price of $20.67 per ounce of fine gold. The Federal Reserve was paid with a new type of gold certificate, and others were paid with checking deposits. Since 1934, only the Treasury has been permitted to hold monetary gold and only the Federal Reserve may hold gold certificates. The amount of the latter outstanding has been approximately equal to the value of the nation's monetary gold stock. When the Treasury purchased gold, usually employing the Federal Reserve as its agent, it would issue an equal amount of gold certificates to the Federal Reserve banks, which would create a deposit for the Treasury, and the deposit would be used to pay the gold seller. When the Treasury sold gold, it normally used the proceeds of the sale to retire an equal value of gold certificates held by the Federal Reserve.

2. The Treasury's purchase price for gold was $35 an ounce less a ¼ percent service charge, or a net price of $34.9125. At this price it stood ready to buy all gold offered to it.

3. The Treasury's sale price for gold was $35 an ounce plus a ¼ percent service charge, or a total price of $35.0875. At this price, the Treasury sold gold freely to the International Monetary Fund and to foreign central banks and governments. However, it would not sell to other foreigners, and it would sell only limited amounts to Americans to meet their "legitimate" needs for professional, industrial, and artistic purposes.

These arrangements existed for more than 34 years until they were modified in mid-March, 1968, when the United States government and other major nations announced that henceforth they would only buy gold from and sell gold to other official monetary institutions. They would not sell to other buyers and would buy no gold not already in official monetary reserves. Then, as we have already mentioned, President Nixon announced in mid-August, 1971 that the United States had terminated all purchases and sales of monetary gold.

Although we do not know what American gold policies will be in the future, we can analyze the domestic monetary effects of changes in the nation's monetary gold stock. We shall start with Treasury purchases of gold from, and sales of gold to, Americans. Such transactions have occurred in the past and they might occur in the future, although the probability of the latter is small. Gold transactions with foreign central banks will be discussed later.

Suppose that an American gold miner or melter of scrap offers $10 million of gold, which is purchased by the Federal Reserve for the account of the Treasury. Let us trace the direct effects in two steps. Step 1: The gold becomes an asset of the Treasury, which issues $10 million of gold certificates to the Federal Reserve, which adds $10 million to the Treasury's deposit account at the Federal Reserve. At this stage, the gold purchase has not yet affected either the volume of bank reserves or the money supply. Step 2: The Treasury writes a check for $10 million on its deposit at the Federal Reserve and sends the check to the gold seller; the latter deposits the check in a commercial bank, which sends it to the Federal Reserve, which deducts $10 million from the Treasury's deposit and adds it to the bank's deposit account at the Federal Reserve. All this appears on the various balance sheets as follows:

STEP	TREASURY		FEDERAL RESERVE BANKS		COMMERCIAL BANKS	
	ASSETS	LIABILITIES	ASSETS	LIABILITIES	ASSETS	LIABILITIES
1	Gold stock .. +$10	Gold cert. .. +$10	Gold cert. .. +$10	Treas. dep. ... +$10		
2	...	...	...	Treas. dep. ... −$10 Due banks ... +$10	Reserve .. +$10	Deposits due public ..... +$10
Net direct effects	Gold stock .. +$10	Gold cert. .. +$10	Gold cert. .. +$10	Deposits due banks ... +$10	Reserve .. +$10	Deposits due public ..... +$10

Thus, the normal direct effects of a net purchase of gold by the Treasury are to increase by equal amounts (1) the public's money supply, (2) commercial-bank reserves, and (3) Federal Reserve holdings of gold certificates. Note that these are only the direct effects; further effects may be induced by the increase of commercial-bank reserves.

Net sales of gold by the Treasury to Americans normally have exactly the opposite direct effects. Suppose, for example, that a jeweler buys $5 million of gold from the Treasury, paying with a check drawn on a commercial bank. The

Treasury will send the check to the Federal Reserve to retire $5 million of gold certificates; the Federal Reserve will deduct $5 million from its deposit liability to the bank on which the check is drawn and send the check to the bank; and the bank will deduct $5 million from the jeweler's deposit account. Thus the direct effect of the $5 million net sale of gold by the Treasury to Americans has been to decrease by equal amounts (1) the public's money supply, (2) commercial-bank reserves, and (3) Federal Reserve assets in the form of gold certificates. The reader should verify this by tracing the effects on the balance sheets of the commercial banks, the Federal Reserve, and the Treasury.

Let us now consider Treasury purchases of gold from and sales of gold to official foreign and international institutions. Suppose that the Federal Reserve, acting as agent for the Treasury, purchases $100 million of gold from a foreign central bank, perhaps the Bank of France. Again, let us analyze this in two steps. Step 1: The Treasury adds the gold to its assets, creates and issues an equal amount of gold certificates to the Federal Reserve, and the latter adds $100 million to its deposit liabilities to the Bank of France. On the balance sheets this will appear as follows:

	TREASURY		FEDERAL RESERVE		COMMERCIAL BANKS	
STEP	ASSETS	LIABILITIES	ASSETS	LIABILITIES	ASSETS	LIABILITIES
1	Gold stock .. +$100	Gold cert. .. +$100	Gold cert. .. +$100	Deposits due Bank of France .. +$100		
2	....	....	....	Deposits due Bank of France .. −$100 Deposits due U.S. banks .. +$100	Reserves .. +$100	Deposits .. +$100
Net direct effects	Gold stock .. +$100	Gold cert. .. +$100	Gold cert. .. +$100	Deposits due U.S. .. +$100	Reserves .. +$100	Deposits .. +$100

Note that as long as the Bank of France continues to hold the proceeds of the gold sale as a deposit at the Federal Reserve, there will be no effect on either the public's money supply or on the volume of bank reserves, though there will be an increase in the Federal Reserve's gold-certificate holdings. In effect, the rise in foreign deposits at the Federal Reserve offsets the expansionary effect of the Treasury gold purchase. Ordinarily, however, foreign central banks keep their deposits at the Federal Reserve to relatively low levels, partly because they yield no return. Thus, there is likelihood of Step 2, in which the Bank of France transfers the funds to Americans. This can happen in several ways. For example, the Bank of France may sell checks on its deposits at the Federal Reserve to Frenchmen who wish to make payments to Americans. Or it may, on its own account, buy Treasury bills or other investments in the American markets. In any case, the recipient of the check is likely to send it to his bank to be added to his deposit account, his bank will send it to the Federal Reserve, and the Federal Reserve will deduct $100 million from the deposit account of the foreign central bank and add $100 million to deposits due to the commercial bank. Thus, the direct effects of Treasury net purchases of gold from foreign central banks are normally to increase by equal amounts the public's money supply, the volume of commercial-bank reserves, and gold-certificate holdings by the Federal Reserve.

The direct effects of Treasury net sales of gold to foreign central banks or international institutions are normally the reverse of those described above. Suppose that the Bank of England uses checks drawn on American banks to buy $50 million of gold from the Treasury. The latter will send the checks to the Federal Reserve with instructions to retire an equal amount of gold certificates; the Federal Reserve will substract $50 million from its deposit liabilities to the banks on which the checks were drawn and send the checks to the banks; and the banks will deduct $50 million from the deposits of their customers. Thus, the direct effects of the Treasury's net sales of gold are to reduce by $50 million the public's money supply, commercial-bank reserves, and Federal Reserve holdings of gold certificates.

As shown in Table 10–2, the size of the nation's monetary gold stock has varied over a wide range, thereby tending to have large direct effects on the

Table 10–2 Monetary gold stock of the United States on selected dates (millions of dollars)

DATE	MONETARY GOLD STOCK	CHANGE FROM PRECEDING DATE
August, 1917	$ 2,896	—$
November, 1924	4,230	+ 1,334
January, 1934	4,036	— 194
November, 1941	22,786	+ 18,750
December, 1945	20,065	— 2,721
October, 1949	24,584	+ 4,519
June, 1963	15,797	— 8,787
December 31, 1967	12,436	— 3,361
August 31, 1971	10,132	— 2,304

SOURCE: Various Federal Reserve publications.

volume of bank reserves and the nation's money supply. Because of the magnitude and importance of these Treasury transactions, several points must be emphasized.

1. Net purchases or sales of gold by the Treasury serve to increase or decrease by equal amounts the public's money supply, bank reserves, and Federal Reserve holdings of gold certificates. Note that these are only the direct effects; the induced effects flowing from the changes in the volume of bank reserves may be much larger.

2. The Treasury has no direct control over the size of its monetary gold stock because this depends heavily on the nation's balance of international payments and on the amounts of gold that foreign central banks wish to sell to or buy from the United States. However, as we shall see later, the Federal Reserve and the Treasury have various indirect ways of influencing the amounts of gold offered or demanded.

3. Also, as we shall see later, gold purchases and sales affect the behavior of the exchange rate on the dollar.

SDR Certificates

These are quite similar to gold certificates except that they are issued against "paper gold." An earlier section described the system of Special Drawing Rights that was initiated at the beginning of 1970. These unconditional drawing rights are created by the IMF and issued to participating countries in proportion to their quotas in the Fund. The American portion is issued to the Treasury, whose holdings at any time are equal to the total issues received from the IMF, plus those received in payment from other countries minus amounts of them paid to other countries. In contrast to its normal practice with respect to gold and gold certificates, the Treasury does not issue to the Federal Reserve a volume of SDR Certificates equal to all its holdings of SDRs; instead, it holds some of its SDRs inactive or "unmonetized" and issues or "monetizes" only enough of them to cover its probable needs for such funds for some time in the future. For example, in mid-1971, when total Treasury SDR holdings exceeded $1,200 million, it had issued only $400 million of SDR Certificates to the Federal Reserve.

The normal effects of issuing SDR Certificates, which are very similar to the effects of gold purchases, are to increase directly Federal Reserve holdings of SDR Certificates, the dollar volume of commercial-bank reserves, and the public's money supply. For example, suppose the Treasury decides to monetize $400 million of its holdings of SDRs. Step 1: It issues this amount of SDR Certificates to the Federal Reserve, receiving in return a deposit claim against Federal Reserve banks. At this stage there is no effect on either the volume of bank reserves or the money supply. Step 2: To buy foreign currencies or for other purposes, the Treasury writes a check on its deposit at the Federal Reserve and sends it to the seller, who deposits it at a bank, which then sends the check to the Federal Reserve to be deducted from the Treasury's deposits and added to the bank's reserve account. The direct effects of a decrease of Federal Reserve holdings of SDR Certificates are just the reverse—to decrease directly both bank reserves and the money supply.

Foreign-exchange holdings

Before the early 1960s, the Federal Reserve and the Treasury held the exchange rate on the dollar within narrow limits by the sole method of purchasing and selling gold. They supplied dollars to other countries by purchasing gold, and they removed excess dollars from the exchange market by selling gold for dollars. Beginning in the early 1960s, however, they began to buy and sell foreign exchange for this purpose. By *foreign exchange* we mean claims denominated in foreign currencies. These include such things as deposit claims against foreign banks, short-term claims against foreign governments, and short-term claims against foreign private debtors. The Federal Reserve and the Treasury can supply dollars in exchange markets by purchasing foreign exchange, thereby tending to hold down the exchange rate on the dollar. And they can remove excess dollars from exchange markets by selling foreign exchange, thereby tending to support the exchange rate on the dollar. We shall see later that this can be an important device for influencing not only the dollar-exchange rate but also the amounts of gold offered to, or demanded from, the Treasury.

At this point, however, we are concerned only with effects on domestic monetary and credit conditions when the Federal Reserve makes net purchases or sales of foreign exchange. These are almost exactly the same as those resulting from net purchases or sales of gold.[1] When the Federal Reserve buys foreign exchange, it pays with checks on itself, and these are added to the money supply of the seller and to bank reserves. And when it sells foreign exchange, it withdraws funds from both the money supply and bank reserves.

Discounts and advances

We come now to three types of assets that the Federal Reserve can buy and sell at will and whose volume can be increased and decreased to regulate the supply and cost of bank reserves. These are discounts and advances, acceptances, and United States government securities. All these Federal Reserve assets are debt claims against others. *Discounts and advances* are simply outstanding Federal Reserve loans to borrowers, mostly member banks. Most of the Federal Reserve holdings of acceptances and government securities are purchased in the open market.

Both the theory and form of Federal Reserve credit have changed markedly since the inception of the Federal Reserve System. The framers of the Federal Reserve Act seem to have assumed that the new Reserve banks would be guided by two principles in extending their credit.

---

[1] Treasury purchases and sales of foreign exchange usually do not have these domestic effects when the Treasury uses dollars acquired through taxation or borrowing. The effects may be the same, however, if the Treasury pays for foreign exchange by decreasing its deposits at the Federal Reserve and if it uses the proceeds from sales of foreign exchange to increase its deposits at the Federal Reserve.

1. They would provide credit largely, if not exclusively, by lending to member banks. They would act as "banker's banks," lending to their members much as commercial banks lend to their own customers. They might occasionally buy or sell securities in the open market, but these operations would be limited and of minor importance.

2. They would extend their credit largely on the basis of private debt obligations. In lending to members, they would either discount paper acquired by banks in lending to their own customers or would make advances to banks on the basis of collateral consisting of these private debt obligations. They were to provide credit to only a limited extent, if at all, on the basis of the debt of the federal government.

All of this is now reversed. The Reserve banks still lend to member banks, but most of their funds are provided by purchasing securities in the open market. Moreover, most of their credit is based not on private debt but on the debt of the federal government. The debts that they buy and sell in the open market are largely federal debt obligations, and even their loans to member banks are largely collateralized by Treasury obligations. Of the many factors accounting for this reversal, two should be emphasized:

1. Changes in the composition of outstanding debt. Most of the debt outstanding just prior to World War I was private debt. The federal debt had shrunk to less than a billion dollars and nearly three-quarters of it was pledged at the Treasury as collateral for national bank notes. Banks had few free government securities that they could pledge as collateral for loans, and the volume of "floating" government securities in the market was far too small to permit large Federal Reserve purchases and sales even if the System had wished to make them. Two world wars and a great depression changed all this. By the end of World War I, the federal debt had grown to $26 billion. After falling about $9 billion during the 1920s, it grew to more than $55 billion during the Great Depression. After the end of World War II, federal debt outside the Treasury amounted to more than $200 billion and was widely held by banks and almost all other types of investors. As banks increased their holdings of federal securities, they tended to pledge them as collateral for loans from the Federal Reserve. Even in the 1920s, collateral for more than half of all member-bank borrowings at the Reserve banks was in the form of Treasury obligations; since the mid-1930s almost all their borrowings have been of this type. Moreover, the very large growth of the federal debt and its wide ownership have made possible large Federal Reserve open-market operations in these securities.

2. Changes in concepts of Federal Reserve responsibilities. The original theory of the Federal Reserve was one of "passive accommodation." The theory was that the Reserve banks should "accommodate commerce, industry, and agriculture" by assuring that their "legitimate" needs for credit were met. As long as this theory prevailed, it was plausible (if not valid) to argue that the volume of Federal Reserve credit should be made passively responsive to the member banks' demands for loans, because these demands would faithfully reflect in-

creases and decreases in the economy's "needs" for credit. Gradually, however, it became apparent that such a policy of passive accommodation could seriously destabilize the economy. A policy of passively supplying rising demands for credit during periods of high prosperity could "boom the boom," and a policy of passively accepting repayment of outstanding Federal Reserve loans in periods of declining business activity could "depress the depression." The Federal Reserve therefore shifted from a philosophy of passive accommodation to one of positive control. The new policy called for resistance to undesirable changes in the supply of money and credit and for efforts to achieve selected objectives. This shift of philosophy encouraged a substitution of Federal Reserve open-market operations for Federal Reserve lending, since by undertaking open-market operations on its own initiative, the Federal Reserve could more accurately control the volume of bank reserves. It no longer had to depend on member banks to take the initiative in increasing or decreasing their demands for Federal Reserve credit.

Although by far the largest part of its loans is to member banks, the Federal Reserve sometimes makes small direct loans to the Treasury, nonmember banks, foreign central banks, and business. Congress so fears that the Treasury might abuse its power to borrow directly from the Reserve banks that it extends the enabling legislation only one year at a time and provides that at no time shall the Reserve banks hold more than $5 billion of securities acquired directly from the Treasury. Only rarely does the Treasury borrow directly from the Federal Reserve. Federal Reserve loans to nonmember banks are largely limited to periods of war and national crisis. It is felt that, in more normal times, these banks should not have the privilege of borrowing if they will not assume the obligations involved in becoming members of the Federal Reserve. Loans to foreign central banks are usually small, but extremely useful when these banks need additional gold and foreign-exchange reserves. The Reserve banks never lent directly to business firms until the mid-1930s. However, complaints that worthy borrowers were unable to secure credit led to an amendment to the Federal Reserve Act providing that Reserve banks might lend directly to a business firm if that firm could prove both that it was creditworthy and that it could not secure credit from its normal sources at reasonable rates. Federal Reserve loans of this type were never large even during the Great Depression. This power of the Reserve banks to lend to business was repealed by Congress in 1958.

Although the distinction has little economic significance, Federal Reserve loans to member banks are of two principal types: discounts (sometimes called rediscounts) and advances. When a bank secures Federal Reserve credit by discounting, or rediscounting, it simply endorses some of its customers' paper and sends it to a Reserve bank for "discount." In effect, the Federal Reserve subtracts interest at its prevailing discount rate and credits the remainder to the borrowing bank's reserve account. Advances are simply loans to a bank on its own promissory note, although some sort of acceptable collateral is required. In recent years, most Federal Reserve loans have been in the form of advances.

What types of paper should be eligible for discount or to be used as collateral for Federal Reserve advances to member banks? This long was a controversial subject. The original Federal Reserve Act was based on the theory that the Reserve banks should take only "short-term self-liquidating agricultural, industrial, or commercial paper which was originally created for the purpose of providing funds for producing, purchasing, carrying or marketing of goods." They should not take paper whose proceeds were "used to finance fixed investments of any kind; or any investments of a purely speculative character; or for carrying or trading in stocks and bonds except obligations of the United States; or to finance relending operations except relending by cooperative marketing associations and factors." The theory that this short-term, self-liquidating paper should be given preferential status still survives in the provision that the Reserve banks may discount (or rediscount) only paper of this type. But this provision is now of only limited importance, because most Reserve-bank loans take the form of advances, and other types of bank assets may be used as collateral for these advances.

The so-called commercial-loan theory of banking, on which the lending provisions of the original Federal Reserve Act were based, has lost most of its adherents since 1914 and has virtually ceased to serve as a guide to Reserve-bank lending. There are several reasons for this:

1. The mechanical difficulties of discounting customers' paper or of using it as collateral for advances to commercial banks. Reserve-bank advances to banks with government securities as collateral are much simpler.

2. Inadequacy of member-bank holdings of eligible commercial paper. Because of changes in the business structure and in commercial-bank lending practices after World War I, bank holdings of high-quality commercial paper declined markedly. The decline was especially great during the depression following 1929. As a result, it was necessary to make other types of bank assets eligible as a basis for borrowing if the Reserve banks were to be of maximum usefulness to their members and to the economy.

3. The basic fallaciousness of the commercial-loan theory. With the passage of time, it became increasingly evident that the restriction of commercial-bank and Reserve-bank loans to "commercial paper" could not attain any of the objectives claimed for it. It could not automatically adjust the volume of credit to the amount that is socially desirable, for harmful inflations and deflations of the volume of credit can occur even if both commercial banks and Reserve banks make only "commercial loans." Moreover, it has become increasingly clear that "commercial paper" is often less liquid than some other types of assets, especially call loans on securities and short-term government obligations. An individual commercial bank can achieve "liquidity" more easily by selling highly marketable securities than by calling its commercial loans. The liquidity of any asset for the commercial-banking system as a whole depends on the ability and willingness of the Reserve banks to buy it or lend on it and to issue currency or bank reserves in exchange. Thus, the liquidity of the commercial-banking system as a whole is enhanced by broadening the Reserve banks' lending powers, not by limiting the types of paper on which they can lend. It is hard to see how any asset can be

"illiquid" for the Reserve banks if it can be used as a basis for issuing Federal Reserve notes which have full legal-tender powers.[2]

Because of the factors indicated above, the types of assets on which the Reserve banks may lend have been greatly broadened. The present powers of the Federal Reserve to lend to member banks may be summarized as follows:

1. The Reserve banks may discount (or rediscount) for member banks only short-term commercial paper of the type described above. Only infrequently, however, do banks borrow in this way.

2. By far the greater part of Reserve-bank loans take the form of advances to banks, with collateral in the form of eligible short-term commercial paper or United States government securities. Most of these advances have government securities rather than commercial paper as collateral.

3. Although virtually all Reserve-bank loans to banks take the above forms, the Banking Act of 1935 provides that a Reserve bank can also make advances to a member bank on its note "secured to the satisfaction of the Federal Reserve Bank" and complying with rules and regulations prescribed by the Board of Governors. The effect of this provision is to give the Federal Reserve System almost complete freedom to determine the types of collateral it will accept. But loans made under this provision must bear interest at a rate not less than $\frac{1}{2}$ percent above the highest rate applicable to loans of the types under (1) and (2) above. As a result, banks usually do not borrow under this section as long as they have an adequate supply of eligible commercial paper and government obligations.

In short, the trend has been toward greater freedom for the Federal Reserve to determine the types of loans it will make. It is difficult to see why this trend should not be extended by eliminating from the Federal Reserve Act all its complex eligibility requirements and stating simply that the Federal Reserve may lend to member banks on any assets it deems acceptable. This would not only enable the Reserve banks to be of maximum help in time of strain, but would also end forever the implication that there is any necessary relationship between the type of paper offered to the Reserve banks for discount or as collateral and the type of use to which the borrowed funds will be put.

It should be clear that the Federal Reserve can create or destroy bank reserves by increasing or decreasing its outstanding loans. Case I indicates that when the Federal Reserve expands its loans to banks, it creates for them an equal increase in their reserves. Case II shows that when the Federal Reserve decreases its outstanding loans, it collects by reducing bank reserves.

Acceptances

Before the passage of the original Federal Reserve Act, acceptances were not widely used in the United States. National banks were not permitted to accept

[2] For a good, short criticism of the commercial-loan theory as applied to Reserve banks, see W. R. Burgess, *The Reserve Banks and the Money Market,* New York, Harper & Row, 1936, pp. 41–67.

	FEDERAL RESERVE BANKS		COMMERCIAL BANKS	
	ASSETS	LIABILITIES	ASSETS	LIABILITIES
Case I	Loans .. +$100	Deposits due banks .. +$100	Reserves .. +$100	Borrowings from the Federal Reserve .. +$100
Case II	Loans .. —$ 50	Deposits due banks .. —$ 50	Reserves .. —$ 50	Borrowings from the Federal Reserve .. —$ 50

time drafts drawn on them for the benefit of their customers, and there was no well-developed acceptance market. Critics found many faults with this situation. They complained that banks were deprived of legitimate business, that America's growth as an international financial center was inhibited, that industry was deprived of a convenient and cheap method of short-term finance, and that temporarily available short-term funds tended to be diverted into security speculation rather than channeled into the financing of commerce and industry. To remedy this situation, the Federal Reserve Act empowered national banks to accept drafts drawn on them, thereby promoting a supply of acceptances; it also provided that the Reserve banks might purchase acceptances in the open market, thereby helping to create a market for them.

The importance of Federal Reserve open-market operations in acceptances has varied widely. During the period prior to the Great Depression, Federal Reserve holdings of this paper were often large, sometimes larger than its holdings of government securities. The volume of outstanding acceptances declined sharply during the Great Depression and remained very low until after the end of World War II. Federal Reserve operations in acceptances were negligible during this period. More recently, however, there has been a renewed increase in the volume of acceptances and the Federal Reserve has resumed its purchases and sales of them. These operations are still very small, but they could grow in the future.

Net Federal Reserve purchases and sales of acceptances have the same effects on bank reserves and the money supply as do similar transactions in government securities. These will be discussed in the next section.

United States government obligations

By far the largest volume of Federal Reserve assets is in the form of debt claims against the United States government, including fully guaranteed obligations of federal agencies. Table 10–1 showed that in May, 1971 these amounted to nearly $65 billion, or 74 percent of total Federal Reserve assets. This asset is of special importance not only because it is so large but also because it has become the principal medium through which the Federal Reserve regulates the volume and cost of bank reserves. The Federal Reserve creates bank reserves by purchasing government securities, and it destroys bank reserves by selling government securities. It buys and sells very frequently, sometimes almost continuously, and its net purchases or sales are often very large.

As already indicated, Federal Reserve purchases and sales of acceptances, foreign exchange, and government securities are under the jurisdiction of the Federal Open Market Committee and are executed for the System account through the Federal Reserve Bank of New York. The manager of the account buys and sells through government-security dealers, of which there are less than 20. These, in turn, deal with every type of investor that buys and sells government securities—commercial banks, all other types of financial institutions, nonfinancial business firms, individuals, foreign central banks, and others. The manager of the open-market account usually does not know the ultimate source of the securities he buys or the ultimate buyers of the securities he sells. It will further our analysis, however, to distinguish two types of transactions: (1) Federal Reserve purchases from, and sales to, commercial banks; and (2) Federal Reserve purchases from, and sales to, nonbank investors.

Consider first the case in which the Federal Reserve purchases $500 million of government securities from commercial banks. As shown in case I, the effect is to increase bank reserves by $500 million. The Federal Reserve pays for its additional assets by creating additional deposit liabilities to the selling banks. The total assets of commercial banks are not directly changed; the banks have simply exchanged $500 million of earning assets for an equal amount of legal reserves. The public's money supply is not directly affected. However, with the addition of $500 million to the excess reserves of banks, an expansion of bank credit and deposits becomes likely. Case II shows that a Federal Reserve sale of

| | FEDERAL RESERVE | | COMMERCIAL BANKS | |
	ASSETS	LIABILITIES	ASSETS	LIABILITIES
Case I	Government securities .. +$500 million	Deposits due banks .. +$500 million	Reserves .. +$500 million Government securities .. −$500 million	
Case II	Government securities .. −$700 million	Deposits due banks .. −$700 million	Reserves .. −$700 million Government securities .. +$700 million	

$700 million of government securities to banks will decrease bank reserves by that amount. In effect, the Federal Reserve collects from the buying banks by subtracting from their reserve accounts. There is no direct effect on the public's money supply, but a reduction may be induced by the decrease in bank reserves.

Let us now consider the case of Federal Reserve purchases of securities from any ultimate seller other than a bank. Case III assumes that you, as an insurance company executive, a manufacturer, or an individual, sell $500 million of government securities to the Federal Reserve. As shown in the balance sheets, the direct effect is to increase by $500 million both the public's money supply and bank reserves. When you, as the seller of securities, receive the $500 million check, you deposit it in your bank, which adds its amount to your deposit account and then sends the check to the Federal Reserve, which adds the amount to your bank's reserve account.

A comparison of Cases I and III shows that all Federal Reserve purchases of securities add to the volume of bank reserves, but that only purchases from

	FEDERAL RESERVE		COMMERCIAL BANKS		PUBLIC	
	ASSETS	LIABILITIES	ASSETS	LIABILITIES	ASSETS	LIABILITIES
Case III	Government securities .. +$500 million	Deposits due banks .. +$500 million	Reserves .. +$500 million	Deposits .. +$500 million	Deposits .. +$500 million Government securities .. −$500 million	
Case IV	Government securities .. −$700 million	Deposits due banks .. −$700 million	Reserves .. −$700 million	Deposits .. −$700 million	Deposits .. −$500 million Government securities .. +$700 million	

nonbank sellers add directly to the public's money supply. The total effects on the public's money supply and on the supply of credit may be the same in the two cases when both the direct effects and the induced expansion of commercial-bank loans and security holdings are taken into account. In Case I, where the banks receive increased reserves without any increase in primary deposits, the entire $500 million is added to excess bank reserves and becomes the basis for creating new derivative deposits through an expansion of commercial-bank loans and security holdings. In Case III, however, the banks receive the $500 million of reserves in a transaction that increases their primary deposits. Some part of the increase of reserves must therefore be used to meet reserve requirements against the primary deposits, and only the remainder becomes excess reserves that can serve as a basis for creating derivative deposits.

Separation of Cases I and III nevertheless serves to emphasize some important points.

1. The Federal Reserve can buy securities even when commercial banks do not want to sell; it can buy them from nonbank sellers who are depositors at banks.

2. The Federal Reserve can itself directly increase the public's money supply and need not rely solely on the willingness of banks to expand their loans and security holdings. Quantitatively, this direct effect of Federal Reserve purchases is usually much smaller than the expansion of commercial-bank credit induced by the increase in their reserves. At times, however, it is important.

3. The Federal Reserve can directly contribute to the supply of lendable and spendable funds. Nonbank financial institutions, business firms, and others who sell securities to the Federal Reserve are provided with funds that they can lend, spend, or use in any other way they wish.

We shall emphasize the effects of Federal Reserve purchases and sales on the volume of commercial-bank reserves, and thus on the ability of the banks to create credit and money, because these are usually so much larger. But the other effects should not be forgotten.

The effects of Federal Reserve sales of securities to purchases other than commercial banks are exactly the reverse of those in Case III. As shown in Case IV, Federal Reserve sales of $700 million of securities to you, a nonbanker, would reduce by that amount both the public's money supply and commercial-bank reserves. When the Federal Reserve received your check, it would deduct its amount from the reserve balance of your bank and send the check to your bank, which can be relied on to deduct it from your deposit account. You and other nonbank purchasers of securities from the Federal Reserve would have less funds to lend to others, to spend, or to use otherwise.

Later sections will discuss at length the policy problems faced by the Federal Reserve as it must decide when, to what extent, and on what terms it will purchase or sell acceptances and government securities in the open market.

Federal Reserve float

Only one other Federal Reserve asset requires consideration here. This is Federal Reserve float. This is actually a net-asset item arrived at by subtracting a liability called *deferred availability cash items* from an asset called *uncollected cash items*. Both arise out of the Federal Reserve function of clearing and collecting checks and other such claims. Checks worth billions of dollars flow into the Federal Reserve banks every day and require some time to be cleared, paid to the reserve accounts of the banks that deposited them, and deducted from the reserve accounts of the banks on which they are drawn. As a result, at any point of time, the Federal Reserve owns a great volume of checks that it has not yet collected and has not yet paid. The asset "uncollected cash items" indicates the value of checks in its possession on which it has not yet collected by deducting from its deposit liabilities to banks. The liability "deferred availability cash items" indicates the value of checks it has not yet paid by adding to its deposit liabilities to the banks that sent the checks to it.

If the Federal Reserve paying and collection schedule were to work out perfectly, these asset and liability items would balance out exactly, because the Federal Reserve attempts to pay banks depositing checks at the same time that it collects from the banks on which the checks are drawn. As checks flow into the Reserve banks, they are classified as payable "today," "tomorrow," or "the day after tomorrow," the date depending on the estimated time required for the checks to reach the banks on which they are drawn. On the appointed day, the amounts of the checks are credited to the reserve accounts of the depositing banks. Ideally, they would on the same day be deducted from the reserve accounts of the banks on which they are drawn. In this case "deferred availability cash items" would be exactly equal to "uncollected cash items"; the Federal Reserve would not have paid depositing banks before it collected from others. In the process of clearing and collection, it would have neither created nor destroyed bank reserves but would have only shifted reserves from some banks to others.

In practice, however, the Federal Reserve sometimes pays depositing banks before it collects from the banks on which checks are drawn. To this extent, it contributes to total bank reserves. This source of bank reserves is called *Federal Reserve float*. At any point of time, it measures the net amount the Federal Reserve has contributed to bank reserves because it has paid some banks before it collected from others. For example, on the date to which Table 10–1 refers, Federal Reserve float amounted to $2,448 million. In most of the Federal Reserve balance sheets that we shall use later, we shall enter float as a net asset item and omit the two items from which it has been derived.

Several factors account for the existence of Federal Reserve float:

1. Unrealistic collection schedules. In at least a few cases, checks could not reach the banks on which they are drawn within the appointed time even if their flow were unimpeded. For example, checks drawn on banks located in remote sections of Utah and Nevada and deposited at the Federal Reserve Bank of Boston are credited two days later to the reserve accounts of the banks that deposited them, even though the checks cannot within that time reach the bank on which they are drawn.

2. Delays in the transit departments of the Federal Reserve banks. The time of paying a check is determined at the time of its receipt at a Federal Reserve bank. If the process of clearing is delayed because of inadequate staff, or an unusually heavy flow of work, or for any other reason, the collection of checks may be delayed.

3. Delays in transportation. Anything that delays the transportation of checks after they have been received by a Reserve bank and their dates of payment have been determined can increase float. For example, a heavy fog over the eastern half of the United States could delay air mail and the collection of checks from the banks on which they are drawn and thereby increase Federal Reserve float and bank reserves by several hundred million dollars.

Once the Federal Reserve has determined its time schedules for clearing any collection, it has no direct control over the volume of float. It must passively pay and collect checks in accordance with its announced schedules. Unfortunately, Federal Reserve float fluctuates widely over short periods. Sometimes it rises by several hundred million dollars, owing to such things as delays or large increases in the value of checks in transit. This, of course, tends to increase bank reserves and to ease credit conditions. Float falls by several hundred millions at other times, owing to such things as a reduction in the value of checks in transit or a reduction in the backlog of uncollected checks. This tends to reduce bank reserves and to tighten credit conditions. We shall see later that one function of the Federal Reserve is to prevent fluctuations in the volume of float, and in other things capable of altering the reserve positions of the banks, from exerting unwanted influences on monetary and credit conditions.

LIMITS ON FEDERAL RESERVE LIABILITIES

What, if anything, limits the extent to which the Federal Reserve can create Federal Reserve note and deposit liabilities by purchasing assets of various kinds? One type of limit has been in the form of legal-reserve requirements. Prior to 1945, the Federal Reserve Act required Reserve banks to hold reserves equal to at least 35 percent of their deposit liabilities and 40 percent of the outstanding Federal Reserve notes. By the middle of 1945, the actual reserve ratio had fallen to 45 percent, and it was feared that the Federal Reserve would soon have to choose between suspending its reserve requirements and ceasing to expand its loans and security holdings to facilitate war finance. Congress, wanting a continuance of easy-money policies, lowered the reserve requirements to 25 percent, requiring that these be in the form of gold certificates. By the mid-1960s, as a result of both gold losses and expansion of Federal Reserve notes and deposits, the actual reserve ratio was approaching the new legal minimum; and it appeared that the Federal Reserve would have to suspend the requirements or follow restrictive policies. Congress responded by repealing the reserve requirement against Federal Reserve deposits but retaining the 25 percent requirement against outstanding Federal Reserve notes. By 1968, the actual ratio of gold certificates to outstanding Federal Reserve notes had fallen below 30 percent and it was apparent that this would be reduced to 25 percent or below within a few years by a normal rate of expansion of Federal Reserve notes, and sooner if the nation's monetary gold stock fell further. In March, 1968, Congress responded by repealing the reserve requirement against Federal Reserve notes.

Most students of monetary management hope that legal-reserve requirements will not be restored against either Federal Reserve deposits or Federal Reserve notes. They believe that: (1) Such requirements are usually inoperative, and if they do become operative, it is likely to be in a period of stress or crisis when their restrictive effects are undesirable; (2) discretionary management is likely to yield more beneficial policies than will such mechanical guides as legal-reserve requirements.

DETERMINANTS OF MEMBER-BANK RESERVES

While pointing out that the Federal Reserve can create or destroy member-bank reserves by purchasing or selling assets of any type, we stressed the fact that it has direct control over only two types of its asset holdings: its loans in the form of discounts and advances and its holdings of acceptances and United States government securities acquired in the open market. It can buy or sell these assets at its discretion. It has no direct control over the volume of its holdings of other assets, notably gold certificates and float, although these affect the volume of member-bank reserves. There are also several other factors that have important effects on the volume of member-bank reserves and over which the Federal Reserve has no direct control. To understand fully either the operation of the monetary and banking system or several aspects of Federal Reserve policy, one must have a thorough understanding of all these major determinants of the volume of member-bank reserves.

To aid our understanding and to facilitate its own operations, the Federal Reserve has developed an excellent statistical series entitled, "Member Bank Reserves and Related Items." These statistics, which are issued weekly by the Board of Governors, are carried in the major newspapers on Thursday afternoon and Friday morning, in the monthly *Federal Reserve Bulletin,* and in several other periodicals. Table 10–3 presents such a statement for the week ending May 26, 1971.[3]

All these items are derived from the balance sheets of the United States Treasury and the Federal Reserve. The column on the left, labeled "Factors supplying reserve funds," includes all the sources of funds that are capable of being used as member-bank reserves. If there were no competing uses for these funds, the volume of member-bank reserves at any time would be equal to the sum of these sources. We have already discussed the first principal source, total Federal Reserve credit. This is simply the volume of funds that has been created by the Federal Reserve in the process of acquiring and holding assets in the form of United States government securities, acceptances, discounts and advances, float, and other Federal Reserve assets. This source accounted for about 80 percent of all these funds. The second major source is the monetary gold stock, which represents the volume of funds supplied as the Treasury bought and held gold. The third source is the amount of SDRs monetized by the Treasury. The fourth source, Treasury currency outstanding, indicates the amount of funds supplied by the outstanding coin and paper money issued by the Treasury.

The right-hand column of Table 10–3, labeled "Factors absorbing reserve funds," shows the various uses of the total funds provided by the sources, and the

---

[3] For back figures and an excellent description of this series and of the method of deriving it, see Board of Governors of the Federal Reserve System, *Banking and Monetary Statistics,* Washington, D.C., 1943, pp. 360 ff., or *Federal Reserve Bulletin,* July, 1935.

Table 10–3 Bank reserves and related items for the week ending May 26, 1971 (weekly average of daily figures, in millions of dollars)

FACTORS SUPPLYING RESERVE FUNDS		FACTORS ABSORBING RESERVE FUNDS	
Federal Reserve credit:		Currency in circulation	$57,155
U.S. government securities ..	$64,714	Treasury cash holdings	506
Discounts and advances	330	Deposits at Federal Reserve	
Float	2,688	due to:	
Other F.R. assets	1,076	Treasury	1,112
Total F.R. Credit	68,910	Foreign	173
Gold stock	10,448	Member banks	25,235
SDR Certificate account	400	Other	690
Treasury Currency		Other F.R. liabilities and	
outstanding	7,357	capital	2,244
Total	$87,115	Total	$87,115

Addendum: Member-bank reserves
Member-bank deposits at the Federal Reserve $25,235
Plus: Cash in vault 5,173
Equals: Total $30,408

amounts absorbed in each use. It is immediately apparent that large amounts of the funds supplied by the sources are not available for use as member-bank reserves because they are absorbed in competing uses. The volume of member-bank reserves at any time is equal to the total volume of funds supplied by the sources in the left column minus the amounts of these funds absorbed in competing uses, shown in the column on the right. This can be put in equation form:

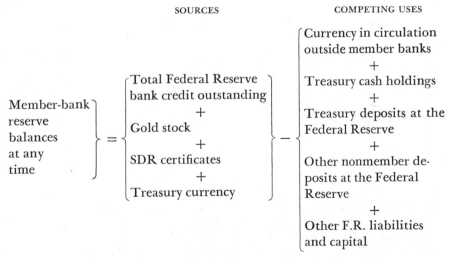

For example, Table 10–3 shows an average of $30,408 million of member-bank reserves during the week of May 26, 1971. These were equal to the $87,115 million supplied by the various sources at that time, minus the $56,707 million absorbed by competing uses.

The preceding discussion related to the factors that determine the size of member-bank reserves as of a given date. Changes in these factors over any stated period of time determine the change in the volume of member-bank reserves during that period. Increases or decreases in the source items tend to increase or decrease member-bank reserves. On the other hand, increases in the amounts of funds absorbed in competing uses tend to reduce bank reserves, and decreases in the amounts of funds employed in competing uses tend to increase bank reserves. This is illustrated in Table 10–4, which compares member-bank reserves and

Table 10–4 Bank reserves and related items, December, 1969 and week ending May 26, 1971 (averages of daily figures in millions of dollars)

BANK RESERVES AND RELATED ITEMS	DECEMBER, 1969	MAY 26, 1971	CHANGES IN ITEMS DURING THE PERIOD TENDING TO:	
			INCREASE BANK RESERVES	DECREASE BANK RESERVES
Sources				
Federal Reserve credit:				
U.S. government securities	$57,500	$64,714	+$7,214	
Discounts and advances	1,086	330		−$ 756
Float	3,235	2,688		− 547
Other F.R. assets	2,204	1,076		− 1,128
	$64,025	$68,808		
Gold stock	10,367	10,448	+ 81	
SDR Certificates	0	400	+ 400	
Treasury currency	6,841	7,357	+ 516	
Total sources	$81,233	$87,013		
Minus: Competing uses				
Currency in circulation	53,591	57,155		+ 3,564
Treasury cash holdings	656	506	− 150	
Treasury deposits at F.R.	1,194	1,112	− 82	
Foreign and other non-member deposits at F.R.	604	863		+ 259
Other F.R. liabilities and capital	2,192	2,244		+ 52
Total competing uses	$58,237	$61,880		
Equals: Member-bank deposits at F.R.	$23,071	$25,235		
Plus: Member-bank cash in vault	4,960	5,173		
Equals: Total member-bank reserves	$28,031	$30,408		

SOURCE: *Federal Reserve Bulletin,* August, 1971, p. A6.

related items during the week ending May 26, 1971 with those in December, 1969. Some factors tended to increase and some to decrease bank reserves during this period, but the net effect was an increase of $2,377 million. The factors tending to decrease bank reserves were decreases of Federal Reserve discounts and advances, Federal Reserve float and other Federal Reserve assets, and increases in amounts absorbed by competing uses in the forms of currency in circulation, foreign and other nonmember deposits at the Federal Reserve, and other Federal Reserve liabilities and capital. On the other hand, the factors tending to increase bank reserves were increases in Federal Reserve holdings of government securities, the gold stock, SDR Certificates, and Treasury currency, and decreases in amounts absorbed by Treasury holdings of cash and Treasury deposits at the Federal Reserve. The large net purchases of government securities by the Federal Reserve during this period were for the immediate purpose of offsetting all the factors that tended to decrease bank reserves and to achieve a net increase.

COMPETING USES OF FUNDS

No further description of the various sources should be necessary here; a review of earlier sections should clarify the processes through which increases or decreases in these items tend to increase or decrease the volume of bank reserves. However, some of the items under "competing uses" in the preceding equation require comment.

Currency in circulation

Of all the competing uses of funds supplied by the sources, currency in circulation outside member banks is by far the largest. It also shows the largest increases and decreases. As noted earlier, when the public wishes to hold more coin and paper money, it withdraws these forms of money from the banks, which thereby lose reserves in the form of cash in vault or deposits at the Federal Reserve. On the other hand, when the public surrenders some of its holdings of coin and paper money to the banks, the latter receive an addition to their legal reserves. As indicated in Table 10–4, the official Federal Reserve tables handle this item in a somewhat clumsy way. They first include as a competing use all currency outside the Federal Reserve and the Treasury, including the cash held in member-bank vaults. Then, at the end, they add back as a component of member-bank reserves, that amount of currency held by the member banks. At some time in the future the Federal Reserve may simplify this table by subtracting as a competing use only currency in circulation outside member banks.

Treasury cash holdings and
Treasury deposits at the Reserve banks

Because they are so closely related and because their fluctuations have the same effects on the general monetary and credit situation, we shall consider together the Treasury cash holdings and Treasury deposits at the Federal Reserve banks. Both compete with member-bank reserves for funds supplied by the sources. In-

creases in both tend to decrease bank reserves, and decreases in both tend to add
to bank reserves.

The Treasury can alter both the size of its money balance and the form
in which it is held. It holds its money balance in three principal forms: (1) as
cash in its own vaults, (2) as deposits at the Reserve banks, and (3) as deposits
with commercial banks. As noted earlier, the last are usually called "tax and loan
accounts." To illustrate the process through which increases in Treasury cash
holdings or in Treasury deposits at the Federal Reserve tend to reduce member-
bank reserves, let us consider two cases.

1. The Treasury deposits at the Federal Reserve $100 million of checks it
has received from the public. These checks may represent payments of taxes or
payments for securities bought by the public. On receiving the checks, the Federal Reserve will add $100 million to Treasury deposits and deduct the same
amount from the reserve accounts of the banks on which they are drawn. The
checks will then go to the banks on which they are drawn, which will deduct
them from the public's deposit accounts. Thus, the effects are to decrease by $100
million both the public's money supply and member-bank reserves.

2. The Treasury increases its deposits at the Federal Reserve by withdrawing $100 million of deposits from commercial banks. On receiving the checks,
the Federal Reserve will add them to Treasury deposits and subtract them from
member-bank reserves.

When the Treasury draws down its cash in vault or its deposits at the Federal
Reserve, it produces the reverse effects:

1. Suppose the Treasury pays to the public $100 million in checks drawn
on the Federal Reserve. The public will deposit the checks at commercial banks
and the latter will send them to the Federal Reserve, which will deduct them
from Treasury deposits and add them to member-bank reserve balances. Thus, the
effects are to increase by $100 million both the public's money supply and mem-
ber-bank reserves.

2. Suppose the Treasury pays out to commercial banks $100 million of
checks drawn on the Federal Reserve banks. When the commercial banks return
the checks to the Federal Reserve, the latter will deduct them from Treasury
deposits and add them to bank reserves.

We shall see later that fluctuations in the size of Treasury holdings of cash
and deposits at the Federal Reserve often tend to have important effects on the
reserve positions of commercial banks, especially in periods of large net receipts
or net payments by the Treasury, and the Federal Reserve often takes action to
prevent their having undesired effects on the general credit situation. We shall
also see that the Treasury itself may engage in monetary management by regulating the size and location of its cash and deposit holdings.

Foreign deposits at the Federal Reserve

These are largely deposits owed by the Federal Reserve to foreign central banks.
As do Treasury deposits at the Federal Reserve, foreign deposits compete with

member-bank reserves for funds supplied by the sources. Increases in this item tend to decrease member-bank reserves, and decreases in it tend to add to member-bank reserves. Suppose, for example, that foreign central banks pay out to the United States public $100 million of checks drawn on the Reserve banks. This will tend to increase by $100 million both the public's money supply and member-bank reserves, because the public will deposit the checks at commercial banks, which will send them to the Federal Reserve to be added to their reserve accounts. If foreign central banks deposit at the Federal Reserve $100 million of checks received from the United States public, the effects will be just the reverse: decreases in both the public's money supply and member-bank reserves.

Other deposits at the Federal Reserve

These are largely deposits that nonmember banks maintain at the Federal Reserve to facilitate check clearing and collection. They are usually relatively small and fluctuate narrowly. Nevertheless, they are competitive with member-bank reserves for funds supplied by the sources. Increases in this item tend to reduce member-bank reserves, largely because they reflect net losses of reserves by member banks to nonmembers. On the other hand, decreases in this item, usually reflecting gains of reserves by members from nonmembers, tend to increase member-bank reserves.

Other Federal Reserve liabilities and capital

This item is made up largely of the Federal Reserve net worth or capital account, with adjustments for minor liability items not accounted for elsewhere and competes with member-bank reserves for funds supplied by the sources. To the extent that the Federal Reserve acquires assets by issuing ownership claims, it does not have to issue liability claims. This item usually fluctuates only narrowly over short periods.

CONCLUSIONS

In carrying out its monetary policy, and especially its open-market operations in acceptances and government securities, the Federal Reserve relies heavily on the type of analysis developed above. As Robert V. Roosa has pointed out, Federal Reserve open-market purchases and sales are of two principal types: dynamic and defensive. *Dynamic purchases* or sales are those undertaken to effect net increases or net decreases in member-bank reserves. *Defensive purchases* or sales are those undertaken to prevent other factors from bringing about unwanted changes in bank reserves. In effect, they are offsetting operations. These defensive operations can be in the right direction and in the right magnitude only to the extent that the Federal Reserve can forecast the behavior of the various determinants of member-bank reserves. The manager of the open-market account therefore seeks not only to detect changes as they occur but also to forecast future changes.

For this purpose, he has several sources of information. To help him forecast the behavior of Federal Reserve float, he has elaborate studies of its seasonal behavior in the past and reports from the various Reserve banks concerning any unusual conditions that might cause it to rise or fall. The behavior of float has proved difficult to forecast with accuracy. With respect to current and prospective changes in the monetary gold stock, the open-market account manager has several sources of information. The Reserve banks themselves, and especially the Federal Reserve Bank of New York, report purchases or sales of gold for Treasury account. The Treasury also reports its own transactions. Moreover, foreign central banks sometimes report several days in advance any plans they may have for buying or selling gold in the United States market. The Treasury reports any significant changes that it plans in the volume of its outstanding currency and in the size and location of its money balance. Studies of past seasonal patterns are used in predicting the volume of currency in circulation. Instructions from foreign central banks assist in forecasting the behavior of foreign deposits at the Federal Reserve. The Reserve banks also report changes in their deposit liabilities to non-member banks and any large transactions that would affect significantly the size of other Federal Reserve accounts.

In short, an understanding of the nature and behavior of the various determinants of member-bank reserves is essential for both the student and the practioner of monetary management.

Selected readings

Board of Governors of the Federal Reserve System, Washington, D.C.:
"Supply and Use of Member Bank Reserve Funds," *Federal Reserve Bulletin,* July, 1935.
Banking and Monetary Statistics, 1943, pp. 360–402.
Banking Studies, 1941.
Federal Reserve Bulletins.
Annual Reports.
Goldenweiser, E. A., *American Monetary Policy,* New York, McGraw-Hill, 1951.
Roosa, R. V., *Federal Reserve Operations in the Money and Government Securities Markets,* Federal Reserve Bank of New York, 1956.

CHAPTER 11

INSTRUMENTS OF MONETARY MANAGEMENT

In this chapter, we shall analyze the various instruments of monetary management in the hands of the Federal Reserve and a few instruments that are under the control of the Treasury. "General" monetary or credit controls—those directed toward regulating the total supply of money or credit without necessarily regulating the allocation of credit among its various possible borrowers or uses—will be discussed first. Selective controls, those intended to regulate or influence the allocation of credit, will be considered later.

As already indicated, the Federal Reserve's powers to regulate the total volume of money and bank credit are of two broad types: (1) power to determine and alter member-bank reserve requirements, and (2) various powers to regulate the volume and cost of member-bank reserves. These will be discussed in order.

MEMBER-BANK RESERVE REQUIREMENTS

Prior to 1935, member-bank reserve requirements were rigidly set by the Federal Reserve Act and could not be altered by Federal Reserve officials. This legislation provided that nothing other than deposits at Reserve banks would count as legal reserves. Minimum-reserve requirements against time and savings deposits were set at 3 percent for all member banks.[1] In fixing reserve requirements against demand deposits at member banks, the Federal Reserve Act carried over the classifications used in the National Banking Act. Central Reserve city banks are those located in New York and Chicago; reserve city banks are those located in about 60 other specified large cities; country banks are those located elsewhere.[2] The minimum percentages of reserves required against demand deposits were fixed at 13 percent for central reserve city banks, 10 percent for reserve city banks, and 7 percent for country banks.

The Banking Act of 1935 empowered the Board of Governors to alter the reserve requirements of any class or of all classes of member banks. However, it placed limits on these alterations, providing that the percentages required should not be fixed below those already prevailing or at more than twice those already prevailing. Thus, the Board of Governors could vary member-bank reserve requirements as shown in Table 11–1.

Table 11–1 Member-bank reserve requirements, 1935

RESERVES REQUIRED AGAINST	PERCENTAGE AT WHICH REQUIREMENTS COULD BE SET	
	LOWEST LEVEL	HIGHEST LEVEL
Net demand deposits at		
Central reserve city banks	13	26
Reserve city banks	10	20
Country banks	7	14
Time deposits at		
All member banks	3	6

Legislation enacted in 1959 and the 1960s changed these arrangements in four principal ways:

1. It empowered the Board of Governors to allow member banks to count cash in vault as legal reserves. Since November 24, 1960, all member-bank cash in vault has been included in legal reserves.
2. It ordered the Federal Reserve to discontinue the "central-reserve-city" category and to apply to member banks in those cities (New York and Chicago) the reserve requirements applicable to member banks in reserve cities. This was done on July 28, 1962.
3. It provided that the Board of Governors should set reserve requirements against demand deposits in banks in reserve cities at not less than 10 percent nor more than 22 percent.

---

[1] This discussion relates to the legislation in effect from June, 1917, to 1935. We shall not discuss here the earlier arrangements.

[2] In some cases, banks in the outlying areas of large cities are placed in a category with lower reserve requirements. Thus, a bank located in an outlying area of New York or Chicago may be classified as a reserve city bank or even as a country bank.

4. Legislation in September, 1966 empowered the Board to set and change requirements against time and savings deposits within a range of 3 to 10 percent. Since
these changes were made, the Board's powers to set and change member-bank reserve requirements are those shown in Table 11–2.

Table 11–2 Member-bank reserve requirements, since 1966

RESERVES REQUIRED AGAINST	PERCENTAGE AT WHICH REQUIREMENTS COULD BE SET	
	LOWEST LEVEL	HIGHEST LEVEL
Net demand deposits at		
Central reserve and reserve city banks	10	22
Country banks	7	14
Time deposits at		
All member banks	3	10

The ranges within which the Board is legally enpowered to set and alter
reserve requirements against the various types of deposits at the different classes
of member banks are indicated in Table 11–2. The Board has repeatedly indicated
its unhappiness with differential reserve requirements based on the location of a
member bank and has strongly advocated a system in which reserve requirements
would be graduated on the basis of the amount of deposits in a bank regardless
of the bank's location. After Congress had ignored several recommendations that
such changes be enacted into law, the Board began to initiate the principle
within the percentage limits embodied in the existing law. For example, reserve
requirements in effect in August, 1972 were as shown in Table 11–3. Note that
reserve requirements against time and savings deposits depended only on the
amount of such deposits in a bank, and not on the location of the bank. However,
reserve requirements against net demand deposits depended on both the location of a bank and the amount of its demand deposits.

Table 11–3 Member-bank reserve requirements in effect in August, 1972

RESERVES REQUIRED AGAINST: NET DEMAND DEPOSITS AT	PERCENTAGE OF REQUIRED RESERVES	
	ON FIRST $5 MILLION OF DEPOSITS	ON DEPOSITS IN EXCESS OF $5 MILLION
Reserve city banks	17	17½
Country banks	12½	13
Time deposits (all classes of banks)	3	5
Savings deposits (all classes of banks)	3	3

SOURCE: *Federal Reserve Bulletin,* June, 1972, p. A10.

In the summer of 1972 the Board announced further changes, to become
effective in two steps in late September and early October. (1) Thereafter, reserve
requirements on net demand deposits would be based solely on the volume of

such deposits at a member bank, not on the location of the bank. These requirements are shown in Table 11–4. This action reduced total required reserves

Table 11–4 Reserve requirements against net demand deposits at member banks, October, 1972

AMOUNT OF NET DEMAND DEPOSITS	RESERVE PERCENTAGES APPLICABLE
First $2 million or less	8
Over $2 million to $10 million	10
Over $10 million to $100 million	12
Over $100 million to $400 million	13
Over $400 million	17½

against demand deposits by more than $3 billion, which, in the absence of off-setting actions, would be highly expansionary. (2) Simultaneously, check collections would be accelerated enough to reduce Federal Reserve float by at least $2 billion, thus lowering member-bank reserves by this amount. (3) The Federal Reserve would sell enough government securities to mop up any remaining amount of unwanted excess reserves.

Though this action made an important change in the pattern of member-bank reserve requirements, there is no reason to expect that further changes will not be made.

Changes in member-bank reserve requirements are a powerful instrument for monetary management. A change of one percentage point, or even of one-half percentage point, can have a marked effect on monetary and credit conditions. To illustrate this, let us start with a situation in which member banks have neither excess reserves nor a deficiency of reserves, their deposits subject to reserve requirements total $340 billion, their average reserve requirement is 10 percent, and their actual reserve balances are $34 billion. Suppose now that the Board lowers average reserve requirements to 9 percent. This will reduce required reserves by $3.4 billion, thereby initially creating that amount of excess reserves. The latter will serve as a basis for multiple expansion by the banking system, which will tend to lower interest rates and increase the availability of bank credit.

Suppose, on the other hand, that the Board raises average reserve requirements from 10 to 11 percent. This will raise required reserves by $3.4 billion, thus creating a reserve deficiency of that amount. If the banks are unable to secure additional reserves, they will have to reduce by some multiple both their earning assets and their deposits. This would decrease the availability of bank credit and raise market rates of interest.

Change in reserve requirements is an instrument well adapted to two purposes. The first is to absorb large excess reserves or to offset large losses of reserves by the banking system. For example, in the late 1930s, owing largely to huge gold inflows, member banks accumulated several billions of excess reserves, far more than the Federal Reserve could have eliminated by selling all its government securities and other earning assets. Large increases in member-bank reserve requirements absorbed most of these excess reserves and reduced the potential expansion of bank credit on the basis of the excess reserves that remained. Reductions of reserve requirements might be similarly useful if the banks should at some time suffer large losses of reserves. A second purpose for which this instrument is well adapted is for announcing important policy decisions to both the public and the banks. Changes in reserve requirements are overt and well-publicized actions that the public can understand and that immediately affect the reserve positions of thousands of banks. They are, therefore, an effective way in which the Board of Governors can in effect say, "This is the direction our policy is taking and we really mean it!"

In general, this instrument is employed infrequently, and then only to bring about relatively large changes in the reserve positions of banks; it is not used for day-to-day or week-to-week adjustments. In part, this is because it has acquired the reputation of being "more like an ax than a scalpel." This reputation, which dates largely from the late 1930s when requirements were changed several percentage points at a time, is not wholly justified. More delicate adjustments can be made if the changes are smaller, announced well in advance, and made effective in steps. Nevertheless, Federal Reserve officials prefer to rely largely on open-market operations and discount policy for their finer and day-to-day adjustments.

Of all the restrictive measures available to the Federal Reserve, increases in member-bank reserve requirements are by far the most unpopular with member bankers. Bankers view required reserves as sterile assets that yield no return, and they resent any requirement that a larger percentage of their assets be held in this form. The resentment of member bankers is increased by their feeling that their higher reserve requirements place them at a competitive disadvantage. They point out that nonmember banks generally have lower reserve requirements against both demand and time deposits, and they complain bitterly that their higher reserve requirements against time and savings deposits place them at a competitive disadvantage with mutual savings banks, savings and loan associations, and credit unions in bidding for savings. Federal Reserve officials are somewhat influenced by these attitudes of member bankers and also by the danger that higher reserve requirements might influence some member banks to withdraw from the System and some nonmembers to refrain from joining.

Most, though not all, economists agree that the power of the Federal Reserve to alter member-bank reserve requirements is a useful instrument of monetary management. However, several reforms are widely advocated, among which are the following:

1. Discrimination should be eliminated by applying the same reserve requirements to the same types of liabilities, regardless of the institutions issuing them. One way of eliminating discriminatory reserve requirements against demand deposits is to require all commercial banks to become members of the Federal Reserve. Another method is to require all commercial banks, whether member or

nonmember, to meet the same reserve requirements. Some have also proposed that all savings accounts, whether at the commercial banks or elsewhere, should be subject to the same reserve requirements.

2. The present classification of member banks for purposes of fixing reserve requirements should be eliminated and the same reserve requirements against demand deposits should be applied to member banks in all locations. The present system, based on the outmoded theory that the purpose of required reserves is to provide liquidity, has no rational basis.

In summary, the power of the Board of Governors to alter reserve requirements is a powerful and useful instrument of monetary management. It is especially useful for offsetting very large changes in the volume of bank reserves and for announcing important changes in the direction of Federal Reserve policy. However, it is not likely to be used frequently or for day-to-day adjustments.

OPEN-MARKET OPERATIONS

We turn now to the instruments used by the Federal Reserve to regulate the cost and dollar volume of member-bank reserves. The most important of these are open-market purchases and sales of acceptances and government securities; the same principles apply to Federal Reserve purchases and sales of acceptances.

Some mechanics

As noted earlier, Federal Reserve open-market operations are controlled by the Federal Open Market Committee (hereafter referred to as the FOMC), which is composed of the seven members of the Board of Governors, the president of the Federal Reserve Bank of New York, and four other presidents of Reserve banks. The FOMC meets in Washington at least once every 3 weeks, and its members communicate with each other much more frequently, usually daily, by telephone. This body determines open-market policy, sets its objectives, and prescribes, in a general way, the nature and magnitude of the actions to be taken. Actual purchases and sales are made by the manager of the open-market account, who is a vice-president of the Federal Reserve Bank of New York, but is accountable to the FOMC. Because New York is the nation's great financial center, almost all transactions occur there. In buying and selling, the manager deals with about 18 government-security dealers, who, as noted earlier, are at the center of a national and even international market for government securities. The manager of the open-market account is thus in a position to use open-market operations in a highly timely and flexible manner. He can buy or sell quickly, change his rate of purchases or sales quickly, and shift quickly from buying to selling, or vice versa.

When the manager of the open-market account purchases government securities from a dealer, he pays the dealer with a check on the Federal Reserve Bank of New York. The dealer must, of course, pay these funds to the seller of the securities. If the seller is a commercial bank, the immediate effect is to increase the volume of bank reserves. If the seller is someone other than a bank, the effect is to increase directly both the public's money supply and the dollar volume of bank reserves, because the seller will deposit the check with his bank, which will deposit it at a Reserve bank. Sales of government securities by the manager of the open-market account have the opposite effect. The dealer who sells the securities to the Federal Reserve pays for them, in effect, with funds that he receives from the buyer to whom he sells the securities. If the buyer is a commercial bank, the effect is to reduce bank reserves. If the buyer is someone other than a bank, the effect is to reduce directly both bank reserves and the public's money supply. In effect, the dealer pays the Federal Reserve with a check received from a customer of some bank, the Federal Reserve deducts the check from the bank's reserve account and sends the check to the bank, which deducts it from the customer's deposit account.

Although these transactions occur in New York City, their effects are by no means confined to that area. Those who sell the government securities purchased by the Federal Reserve and thereby gain Federal Reserve funds may be located at any place within the country. So may those who buy the government securities from the Federal Reserve and thereby lose Federal Reserve funds. Moreover, the effects will be spread throughout the banking system and the financial markets regardless of the geographic location of the institution or person selling securities to, or buying securities from, the Federal Reserve. This happens because the banks that receive the reserves created by Federal Reserve purchases will lose reserves to other banks as they expand their own loans and security holdings. And banks that lose reserves because of Federal Reserve sales will draw reserves from other banks as they contract their credit. These processes may, of course, require some time.

Federal Reserve open-market operations are of two principal types: (1) outright purchases and sales, and (2) acquisitions under repurchase agreements. *Outright purchases and sales,* which make up by far the larger part of the total, are ordinary transactions in which neither the buyer nor the seller commits himself to resell or rebuy. The transaction is final. In some cases, however, the Federal Reserve buys securities from a dealer with an agreement that the dealer will repurchase the securities within a stipulated period, which never exceeds 15 days. This is much like a short-term loan to the dealer. A sort of interest charge is made, approximately equal to the discount rate at the Federal Reserve Bank of New York, by paying the dealer a price below that at which he is obliged to repurchase the security. Federal Reserve officials regard money created in this way as "dollars with strings on them," for the very purchases that involve the issue of the dollars make provision for return of the dollars on a stipulated date.

Acquisitions under *repurchase agreements* are a useful instrument for at least two purposes. For one thing, they are a convenient way of supplying funds to meet a temporary need, and of withdrawing funds when the need has passed. For example, the Federal Reserve may acquire securities under repurchase agreements during the week before Christmas when currency is being drained from the banks, arranging for dealers to repurchase the securities just after Christmas when large amounts of currency flow back into the banking system. This device is also useful for avoiding disorderly changes in the market price of government securities. Dealers in these securities ordinarily hold inventories far larger than they can finance with their own capital funds. They rely heavily on borrowed money. If at some time they could not borrow sufficient funds, or could do so only at very high rates of interest, they might dump large amounts of their inventory on the market, thereby seriously disturbing not only government security prices but also money-market conditions in general. Judicious Federal Reserve acquisitions under repurchase agreements can help prevent such occurrences.

Federal Reserve outright open-market operations are either "regular way" or "cash." Purchases or sales in the *regular way* call for payment and delivery of the securities on the day following the transaction. Such purchases or sales thus involve a one-day delay in putting money into the market or taking it out of the market. However, in purchases or sales for *cash,* the securities are delivered and payment is made or received on the day of the transaction. The availability of these various arrangements contributes to the timeliness and flexibility of open-market operations.

Effects of Federal Reserve purchases or sales

Federal Reserve purchases or sales of government securities may have three types of direct effects: (1) effects on the dollar volume of bank reserves, (2) impact effects on the price and yield of the particular type of security bought or sold, and (3) effects on expectations concerning the future behavior of security prices and yields. In some cases, one or more of these effects may fail to appear, but when they do, they may be powerful or weak, desired or undesired, anticipated or unanticipated.

Effects on the volume of bank reserves appear in every case and are usually the most powerful, for every change of one dollar in bank reserves is the basis for a change of several dollars in the money supply and bank credit. It is for this reason that throughout we shall stress the effect of open-market operations on the reserve position of the banking system. However, it would in some cases be a mistake to ignore the other effects.

When the Federal Reserve buys or sells a particular type of government security, the impact or initial tendency is to change the price and yield of that particular security. This effect may be negligible if the amount purchased or sold is very small relative to the total supply, but it may be significant if the operation is larger relative to the supply. Suppose, for example, that the Federal Reserve purchases a large amount of government securities in the 10-year maturity range. This may be described as an increase in the demand for that type of security. Or it may be described as a decrease in the supply available to meet private demands. In any case, the initial tendency is to raise the price of the security and lower its yield. This impact effect is likely to be moderated and spread to other securities through private arbitrage. Private investors will tend to shun this security, and even to sell it, until its yield is as attractive as yields on other securities. However, this process may be time consuming and imperfect, especially if the impact effects were very large. Comparable processes may be involved if the Federal Reserve sells large amounts of a particular security.

Federal Reserve attitudes toward the impact effects of its purchases and sales on the prices and yields of particular securities or groups of securities have varied widely. During much of its history, the Federal Reserve has sought to avoid, or at least to minimize, them. To this end, it has often confined its operations to short maturities, where the impact effects are expected to be small, and has spread its purchases or sales over time. At other times, it has consciously used this power to influence directly the prices of particular securities or groups of securities. For example, it has often bought or sold to prevent or ameliorate "disorderly movements" of security prices. From 1942 to 1951, it even went so far as to "peg" the prices and yields on long-term government securities within narrow limits. It has also engaged in "swap operations," sales of securities in one maturity range offset by purchases of securities in another maturity range. For example, in the early 1960s it sold Treasury bills and other short-term securities in order to hold down their prices and support their yields, at the same time buying long-term securities in order to support their prices and hold down their yields. We shall see later that some Federal Reserve efforts to affect directly the behavior of the prices and yields of securities have jeopardized its ability to control the volume of bank reserves.

Federal Reserve open-market operations may also influence the behavior of security prices and yields by influencing private expectations. These are often called "announcement" effects. Suppose, for example, that private investors see that the Federal Reserve has begun to purchase large amounts of securities with the apparent purpose of easing credit. If they come to believe that the policy will continue and will succeed, private investors will be impelled to increase their demands for securities, thereby increasing the flow of loanable funds, supporting the rise of security prices, and reinforcing the decline of yields. On the other hand, large Federal Reserve sales of securities may create expectations of higher interest rates in the future, which will tend to decrease private demands for securities and tighten credit further.

Patterns of open-market operations

The Federal Reserve can use its powers to buy and sell in the open market in many different ways, with quite different consequences for financial markets and the economy. We shall explore only a few of the possible patterns. The first is one in which the Federal Reserve retains precise control of the amount of securities held. Members of the FOMC might describe it this way: "We shall determine the amount of securities that we hold, the types and amounts that we buy and sell, and when we buy and sell. We retain the initiative and will not buy or sell simply because others wish to sell to us or buy from us." Under such a policy, the Federal Reserve can accurately control both the volume of its holdings and the volume of bank reserves, but the prices and yields on securities can fluctuate in response to changes in demand-and-supply relationships in the market.

Another and very different pattern is the one in which the Federal Reserve passively buys and sells some security or group of securities at a fixed price and yield. For example, the FOMC might say, "At this price and yield on long-term government securities we shall buy all offered to us and shall sell all demanded from us." While such a policy is in effect, the price of the selected security or group of securities obviously cannot fall below the price at which the Federal Reserve will buy nor can it rise above the price at which it will sell. However, the Federal Reserve, in adopting such a policy, loses control over both the volume of its security holdings and the volume of bank reserves. It must hold all the securities that others issue and that others do not want to hold at the fixed price and yield levels. As passive buyer and seller it surrenders control over the volume of its holdings.

We shall later consider other patterns of open-market operations and some of the problems faced by the Federal Reserve in determining which pattern to follow. However, two points should be emphasized here.

1. The System must choose between accurate control of the volume of its holdings of government securities on the one hand and stabilization of interest rates on the other. If it is to control accurately the volume of its holdings, it must allow the prices and yields of government securities to fluctuate in response to changes in the supply of, and demand for, these obligations. If it is to stabilize their prices and yields, it must abandon accurate control of the volume of its holdings and passively buy or sell all the securities offered to it, or demanded from it, at the selected level of prices and yields. In this case, the initiative is with other investors, for it is they who determine the volume of securities offered to, or demanded from, the Federal Reserve. This means, of course, that they also determine the volume of bank reserves.

2. As long as investors can shift freely between government securities and other obligations, the Federal Reserve can dominate the entire structure of interest rates by regulating yields on the federal debt. This debt now makes up over one-fifth of all the outstanding interest-bearing debt of the country, and is equal to many times the annual increase in total debt. If the Federal Reserve buys and sells these securities freely in such a way as to maintain a certain structure of yields on them, and also establishes, within narrow limits, the structure of yields on other debts. The reason for this is that private investors are free to arbitrage among the various branches of the debt market, to sell in one and buy in another until they see no further advantage in shifting their funds. This applies not only to banks but to other investors as well. In short, Federal Reserve operations in the government-securities market can dominate the entire money market. However, we shall see later that if this power is used to stabilize interest rates, the effect may be to destabilize the rest of the economy.

Defensive and dynamic open-market operations

As noted earlier, *defensive open-market operations* are those undertaken by the Federal Reserve to prevent other factors, such as changes in the gold stock or in currency in circulation outside the banks, from bringing about unwanted changes in the reserve positions of banks. *Dynamic operations* are those aimed at altering the reserve positions of banks. This distinction is useful in emphasizing that not all Federal Reserve purchases and sales are designed to bring about net increases or decreases in bank reserves. In fact, many of them are purely defensive.

However, it would be misleading to overemphasize the distinction. The two operations are closely related, and some actual transactions are partly defensive and partly dynamic. For example, suppose the monetary gold stock decreases by $500 million, lowering bank reserves by that amount. The Federal Reserve must decide how to respond. If it wants restriction of credit, it may do nothing. In fact, if the gold outflow had not occurred, it might have engaged in a dynamic open-market sale of securities to restrict credit. However, if it wants easier credit conditions, it may buy $750 millions of securities. Perhaps $500 million of these purchases should be called defensive; the other $250 million, dynamic. This illustrates the point that, in practice, it is often difficult to distinguish clearly between dynamic and defensive transactions.

DISCOUNT POLICY AND DISCOUNT RATES

We have already noted that the Federal Reserve can create bank reserves by increasing its loans and discounts and can destroy bank reserves by decreasing its outstanding loans and discounts. Although the Federal Reserve now relies primarily on open-market operations to regulate the volume of bank reserves, its discount policy, which refers to the terms and conditions on which it will lend, remains important. It has two major components:

1. Discount-rate policy. As noted earlier, the discount rate is simply the interest rate charged by the Reserve banks on their loans. Increases in discount rates raise the cost of acquiring reserves by borrowing, whereas decreases in discount rates make it cheaper for banks to acquire reserves in this way.

2. A wide array of "nonprice" methods are used to influence the amount of discounting—these range from moral suasion to quantitative rationing and even to outright denial of loans.

Central banks differ greatly in the extent to which they rely on discount rates and on other methods to regulate the volume of their loans and discounts. Also, the role of the discount rate and the effects of discount-rate changes are strongly influenced by the extent to which other methods of control are used.

Under certain conditions, a central bank's discount rate could regulate with accuracy the level of market rates of interest, or at least of short-term interest rates. Suppose, for example, that two conditions obtain: (1) The central bank stands ready to lend freely at its established discount rate; it uses no other rationing methods and relies on the discount rate alone to regulate the volume of its loans. (2) Commercial banks have no inhibitions against borrowing from the central bank. Intent on maximizing their profits, they borrow from the central bank and lend whenever market rates of interest exceed the discount rate by an amount sufficient to cover the cost of risk-bearing and loan administration. They also withdraw loans from the market and repay their borrowings at the central bank whenever market rates of interest are not sufficiently higher than the discount rate. Under such conditions, the central-bank discount rate could dominate market rates of interest. Increases and decreases in the discount rate would almost automatically raise or lower market rates of interest. Moreover, discount rates would be the central bank's sole method of regulating the volume of bank reserves that it created by lending.

These are not the conditions in American banking, and the Federal Reserve discount rate is not the only method used to regulate the volume of bank borrowing. Many observers have pointed out that even before the establishment of the Federal Reserve there was, among American banks, a "tradition against continuous borrowing," a feeling that it was "unsound" for a bank to borrow "continuously" or "excessively." Although such a tradition undoubtedly did exist, it would probably be far weaker and less powerful as a deterrent to borrowing if Federal Reserve officials had not worked so hard and continuously to strengthen it. Perhaps it would be more accurate to say that the Federal Reserve developed "a tradition against continuous and excessive lending to an individual bank," and that the banks are well aware of this. Federal Reserve officials have repeatedly stated that borrowing is a privilege and not a right, that a member bank should not borrow simply because it is profitable to do so, and that a bank should borrow only to meet the drains it could not forsee, and even then only for short periods except under "unusual and exceptional circumstances." The following statement was issued by the Board of Governors in 1955 in a foreword to its regulations governing member-bank borrowing.

> Federal Reserve credit is generally extended on a short-term basis to a member bank in order to enable it to adjust its asset position when necessary because of developments such as a sudden withdrawal of deposits or seasonal requirements for credit beyond those which can reasonably be met by use of the bank's own resources. Federal Reserve credit is also available for longer periods when necessary in order to assist member banks in meeting unusual situations, such as may result from national, regional or local difficulties or from exceptional circumstances involving only particular member banks. Under ordinary conditions, the continuous use of Federal Reserve credit by a member bank over a considerable period of time is not regarded as appropriate.
>
> In considering a request for credit accommodation, each Federal Reserve bank gives due regard to the purpose of the credit and to its probable effects upon the maintenance of sound credit conditions, both as to the individual institution and the economy generally. It keeps informed of and takes into account the general character and amount of the loans and investments of the member bank. It considers whether the bank is borrowing principally for the purpose of obtaining a tax advantage or profiting from rate differentials and whether the bank is extending an undue amount of credit for the speculative carrying of or trading in securities, real estate, or commodities, or otherwise.

A Reserve Bank rarely refuses to lend to a member bank that is facing an actual or prospective deficiency in its reserves. But after making a short-term loan to a bank, it studies the situation carefully. If it finds that the bank has borrowed too often, too continuously, too much, or for improper reasons, it may advise the bank to contract its loans or sell securities in order to reduce or retire its borrowings. It may even go as far as to refuse to renew the loan, and, in extreme cases, it may suspend the bank's borrowing privilege.

Federal Reserve officials could, of course, attempt to regulate the volume of member-bank borrowing by varying their own attitudes toward lending—being very strict on some occasions and more liberal on others. Although this method is used to some extent, it is not a very flexible or effective instrument.

This combination of member-bank inhibitions against large and continuous borrowing from the Federal Reserve and the latter's unwillingness to make such loans to a member helps to explain several aspects of monetary policy in the United States.

1. When member-bank borrowings from the Federal Reserve are large, credit is usually "tight." Credit is, of course, less tight than it would have been if the banks had not been able to borrow and secure reserves, but it is tighter than it could have been if the banks had had the same volume of reserves without borrowing.

2. The role of discount rates in regulating the volume of bank reserves is reduced in importance. The Federal Reserve does not rely solely on increased discount rates to limit member-bank borrowing. And because of the tradition against continuous borrowing, decreases in discount rates may not be very effective in inducing larger member-bank borrowings.

It would be a mistake to dismiss changes in discount rates as ineffective and useless and to rely solely on the tradition against continuous borrowing and on Federal Reserve admonitions to regulate the amount of member-bank borrowing. Changes in discount rates remain important and influence the economy in several ways:

1. They do have some effect on the volume of member-bank borrowings from the Federal Reserve. A member bank with an actual or prospective deficiency in its reserves can repair its reserve position in either of two general ways: by borrowing or by selling some of its earning assets, such as short-term government obligations. It is tempted, despite the tradition against continuous borrowing, to repair its reserves in the cheapest way. If the Federal Reserve discount rate is lower than the yield it would have to sacrifice by selling some of its earning assets, a member bank may elect to borrow from the Federal Reserve and may be in no hurry to repay its borrowings. This is especially true of banks that have not been borrowing continuously and therefore fear no early chastisement by Federal Reserve officials. The result can be a significant increase in member-bank borrowings and reserves and a minimum of pressure toward credit restriction. However, if the discount rate is higher than the yields on assets that the banks might sell to repair their reserve positions, many banks will not borrow and will repay their borrowings quickly. They will attempt to repair their reserve positions by calling loans or selling securities. The result may be to decrease member-bank borrowings and to enhance restrictive pressures.

2. Changes in discount rates can be an effective way of announcing to both the banks and the public the direction of Federal Reserve policy. Open-market operations are not well suited to this purpose, partly because they are not widely

understood and partly because dynamic operations are often obscured for some time by defensive operations. On the other hand, changes in discount rates are widely publicized as soon as they occur, and are generally believed to be important. In fact, many people exaggerate their importance. An increase in discount rates is generally interpreted as meaning that the Federal Reserve is moving toward tighter credit and higher interest rates. This may induce some lenders to restrict their loans in anticipation of higher interest rates in the future. A reduction of discount rates, presaging an easier monetary policy and lower interest rates, may induce some lenders to increase immediately their willingness to lend. Of course, there is the possibility that changes in discount rates will have perverse announcement effects. For example, if an increase in discount rates is interpreted to mean that Federal Reserve officials believe inflation is coming, such an action might encourage people to borrow and spend, thereby increasing the danger of inflation. If a decrease in discount rates is taken as a forecast of business recession, it could encourage a reduction of spending and hasten a business decline. However, such perverse announcement effects are likely to occur only if changes in discount rates create expectations about the trend of business that the public would not have had anyway, and if the public believes the Federal Reserve will not be able to achieve its objectives. The public has so many other sources of information that it would usually know about dangers of inflation or recession even if the Federal Reserve did nothing to announce its intention of combating such disturbances.

3. Changes in discount rates affect market rates of interest in various ways. We have already noted that increases or decreases in this rate may affect lenders' expectations about future rates and immediately cause them to lend less liberally or more liberally. There are other effects as well. A few (but only a few) long-term debt contracts escalate their interest rates with the Federal Reserve discount rate. The other principal effects are less direct, but nevertheless important. For example, an increase in the discount rate increases the bargaining power of lenders relative to borrowers. A banker can argue, "I have to charge you more because I have to pay more when I borrow." Nonbank lenders may insist that, "even the Federal Reserve recognizes that credit is scarcer and interest rates should go up." Reductions in discount rates generally increase the bargaining power of borrowers and tend to bring down "sticky" rates of interest, such as those on loans by banks to their large and medium-sized customers. They are less effective in reducing rates to small borrowers.

MORAL SUASION

In many countries with only a handful of commercial banks, the central bank relies heavily on moral suasion to accomplish its objectives. It can confer informally with responsible officials of the five or ten important commercial banks and persuade them to follow policies that it considers appropriate. For example, it may get them to agree to limit their borrowing from the central bank, to refrain from expanding their loans or even to contract them, or to lend less liberally for some purposes than for others. Such techniques of monetary management are not well adapted to the American system with its thousands of widely scattered banks, more than half of which are not members of the Federal Reserve. Nevertheless, Federal Reserve officials often use moral suasion to supplement their other policies. At times, they use publicity, interviews, and other devices to persuade banks to borrow less and to tighten their credit policies. On a few occasions, as in 1947 and in 1951, they have encouraged banks and other lenders to follow "voluntary credit-restraint programs" to curtail "nonessential credit." At other times, they attempt to persuade banks to follow more liberal lending policies.

Moral suasion can be a useful supplement to other Federal Reserve actions, but it is unlikely to be an effective substitute for them.

COORDINATION OF THE INSTRUMENTS OF GENERAL MONETARY MANAGEMENT

We have now discussed the three major Federal Reserve instruments of general monetary management: changes in member-bank reserve requirements, open-market operations, and discount policy. We now consider the interrelationships of these instruments and the coordination of their use.

Methods of coordination

If one looks only at the legal provisions of the Federal Reserve Act, he may fear that these instruments will not be used in a coordinated way, for authority over them is not fully centralized. Member-bank reserve requirements are set by the Board of Governors alone. Open-market operations are controlled by the FOMC. Discount-rate changes are usually initiated by the 12 Federal Reserve banks, subject to approval by the Board of Governors. Loan offices at the 12 Reserve banks decide whether or not to make specific loans to member banks, although they operate under general regulations prescribed by the Board of Governors. In practice, there is far more coordination than this dispersion of legal authority suggests, and it is achieved in many ways, both formal and informal. In this process, the Board of Governors plays a central role. With full authority over member-bank reserve requirements, a majority of the members of the FOMC, power to approve or disapprove discount rates, and authority to prescribe regulations for lending to member banks, its legal powers are formidable. It is also in a position to persuade other Federal Reserve officials to cooperate. Officials of the various Reserve banks also confer frequently among themselves and with the Board, exchanging information and points of view.

In this process, the meetings of the FOMC, held in Washington about once every 3 weeks, are very important. These meetings are attended not only by the members of the FOMC, but also by the seven presidents of Reserve banks not currently members of the FOMC, the principal economists on the Board's staff, and an economist from each of the Reserve banks. The presidents who are not members of the FOMC are free to participate in the meeting, but not to vote. For two days, those assembled analyze current and prospective financial and economic conditions and discuss various policy alternatives. By the end of the meeting, they all know what the open-market policy will be, probably also the Board's intentions with respect to member-bank reserve requirements, the Board's attitude toward discount rates, and even the intentions of the various presidents with respect to the discount rates they will recommend to their boards of directors. In these and various other ways, a high degree of coordination is achieved. However, a greater degree of centralization of authority is often advocated to achieve even greater coordination.

Importance of coordination

The various instruments of monetary policy may be used singly or in various combinations, and they may supplement each other or tend to weaken each other. For example, if the Federal Reserve wishes to restrict credit, it may take one or various combinations of the following actions raising reserve requirements, selling securities in the open market, increasing discount rates. The net effects of using one instrument depend in part on current policies with respect to the others. Suppose the Federal Reserve increases member-bank reserve requirements enough to absorb existing excess reserves and put many banks in a deficient reserve position. Banks may be forced to restrict credit sharply if the Federal Reserve refuses to create additional reserves by purchasing securities and if it raises discount rates to discourage borrowing. However, the restrictive effects may be largely negated if the Federal Reserve stands ready to buy at fixed prices and yields all the government securities offered to it. And the degree of restriction will be lessened if the Federal Reserve fails to raise discount rates or to take other actions to restrict member-bank borrowing.

To take another example, suppose that the Federal Reserve, faced with actual or threatened inflation, sells enough securities in the open market to absorb any existing excess reserves and to put some banks in a deficient reserve position. The degree of credit restriction will be greater if the Federal Reserve keeps its discount rates high relative to market rates than it would be if discount rates were left unchanged while market rates rose.

These examples indicate the importance of proper coordination in the use of the various instruments. Proper coordination does not require that all the instruments be used in every case. It requires only that the instruments not be used in such a way as to prevent the achievement of desired results. In many cases, the Federal Reserve can achieve its objectives by using only one or two of these instruments. Open-market operations are often used alone, especially for defensive purposes or where only small dynamic effects are desired. For larger operations, they are ordinarily combined with changes in discount rates. In some cases, and especially when much easier monetary conditions are desired, both will be combined with changes in member-bank reserve requirements. Although there is no invariable sequence in its use of these instruments, the Federal Reserve usually "leads off" with open-market operations and then adjusts its discount rate as market conditions are changed.

In a later chapter we shall describe in detail the purposes for which the Federal Reserve has used its powers and the ways it has used its instruments. The succeeding examples will illustrate a few of the patterns of Federal Reserve restrictive and expansionary policies.

Restrictive policies

Suppose that to avoid an actual or threatened inflation—due to an excessive rate of increase in the total of government and private money demands for output— the Federal Reserve decides to implement a "restrictive" monetary policy. Only in the most extreme cases of inflation will the Federal Reserve take actions to achieve an actual decrease in the flow of spending for output. In an economy with a productive capacity that is rising because of increases in the labor supply and a rising stock of capital and advancing technology, some positive rate of increase in the flow of spending for output is consistent with inflation control and is in fact necessary if excessive unemployment is to be avoided. Thus, a restrictive Federal Reserve policy usually has the more modest purpose of restricting the rate of growth of spending for output, and, to this end, restricting the rates of growth of the stock of money and the stock of bank credit in the face of rising demands for them.

Suppose, for example, that the Federal Reserve decides that for some time it will permit no increase whatsoever in the money supply. Sometimes it can achieve this by simply refraining from further purchases of securities. At other times, it will actually sell some government securities to reduce bank reserves and force banks to borrow or to sell assets in order to repair their reserve positions. On rare occasions, it may raise reserve requirements for the same purpose. Commercial banks, facing shortages in their reserves and probably also continued increases in customers' demands for loans, try in various ways to adjust. One way that a bank can improve its position is by seeking more loans from the Federal Reserve. At this stage, if not before, the Federal Reserve will raise its discount rates and may also admonish banks that seek to "borrow too much or too frequently." Banks also try to borrow more from others—in the Federal Funds market, from correspondent banks, in the Eurodollar market, and so on. Moreover, they sell earning assets, such as Treasury bills and commercial paper, to repair their reserve positions and meet customers' demands for loans. Both the banks' increased demands for borrowings and their sales of assets tend to raise interest rates. At first, the rise of yields may be largely confined to short-term assets, but the rise spreads to longer maturities as banks make few, if any, net purchases of them and may be net sellers. Eventually, banks will restrict their loans to customers by raising interest rates and by various types of nonprice rationing.

It is through such processes that restrictive Federal Reserve policies restrict the growth of credit supplies, raise interest rates, and slow down the rate of increase of spending for output.

Expansionary policies

Suppose now that the country is slipping into a recession, following a prosperity period in which interest rates, including discount rates, were relatively high and member-bank borrowings were large. Such recession periods are usually characterized not only by declining business activity and rising unemployment, but also by declining demand functions for credit, which tend to lower market rates of interest. If the Federal Reserve neither lowers discount rates nor takes other positive action, it will encourage decreases in the money supply. Faced with declining demands for credit and falling interest rates, banks that were willing to borrow and lend when interest rates were high relative to discount rates will now seek to repay their debts to the Federal Reserve. Some banks may also want to hold some excess reserves if they think lending is becoming riskier. Thus, the Federal Reserve must take some positive liberalizing action if it is to prevent an actual decrease in the volume of money and bank credit, and still more positive action if it is to induce an expansion.

Which instruments the Federal Reserve will use, the sequence in which it will use them, and the scope of its actions will depend on its estimate of the strength and probable duration of the depressive forces. If it fears that the recession will be serious and prolonged, it may at an early stage reduce reserve requirements. If it does, the banks will add some of the released reserves to their excess reserves and use some to repay borrowings at the Federal Reserve. Usually, however, the Federal Reserve "leads off" with either decreases in discount rates or open-market purchases, more often the latter. As the Federal Reserve purchases securities, banks add some of the proceeds to their excess reserves and use some to retire thir debts to the Reserve banks. During recession periods, the Federal Reserve often buys enough securities to enable banks to retire practically all their borrowings and to accumulate large excess reserves. As their reserve positions improve, and especially as they receive excess reserves, banks seek to "put the money to work." At first they may buy large amounts of short-term government securities and other open-market assets, thereby depressing short-term interest rates. Gradually, however, interest rates will fall in almost all parts of the market. At some point, usually early, the Federal Reserve will begin to lower discount rates. In a prolonged recession, these are usually decreased several times as market rates decline. After practically all banks are out of debt to the Federal Reserve and most have large excess reserves, further decreases of discount rates may be of little significance except for their effect on expectations, which may also be weak.

GUIDES TO FEDERAL RESERVE POLICY ACTIONS

Federal Reserve officials face major policy decisions in determining their ultimate goals or objectives and also in developing operating guides, or intermediate guides, for their policy actions. Their ultimate goals or objectives relate to the behavior of such things as real output, employment, price levels, and the balance of payments. For example, Federal Reserve officials have often stated, in effect, "Our objectives are to promote the highest sustainable rate of real economic growth, continuously high levels of employment and low levels of unemployment, reasonable stability of domestic price levels, and an improvement in our balance of international payments." As is well known, multiple objectives often prove to be less than fully compatible, so that some individual goals may have to be compromised. However, even if all Reserve officials agreed on some compromise of ultimate objectives, they would still face the problem of developing or selecting operating guides for their policy actions.

A Federal Reserve official might state the problem this way: "We have selected our goals and know what we want to accomplish. But how do we achieve these goals? None of the instruments at our disposal permits us to intervene directly in either the market for output or the market for labor to influence directly demands for output or labor. Instead, all of our instruments are designed to affect the reserve positions of the banks. Thus, we face the problem of assessing the relationships between the reserve positions of banks and the behavior of demands for output and labor. Moreover, we realize that our policy actions do not achieve their effects immediately. We may take a specific policy action today, but time is required for it to achieve its full effects in financial markets and perhaps even longer to achieve its full effects on demands for output and labor. In the meantime, we face the problem of issuing specific instructions to the manager of the Open Market Account. What guide should we prescribe? Should it be the behavior of interest rates, or the money supply, or total bank credit, or the reserve positions of banks?"

Here, we shall concentrate on two related sets of questions: (1) What have been some of the Federal Reserve's "operating guides" to policy actions—not ultimate objectives, but criteria for current operating actions? (2) How are outsiders to assess and interpret the nature of current Federal Reserve policies—whether they are "restrictive" or "liberal," or how "restrictive" or "liberal"? Financial reporters and the public have tried to find some single operating guide, preferably one to which a number can be attached, and Federal Reserve officials have at times yielded to the same temptation. In general, however, Federal Reserve officials have insisted that there is no single reliable operating guide; they must look at several. Among these are interest rates, the money supply, total bank credit, and the reserve position of the banking system. Unfortunately, these guides do not always counsel the same policy actions.

Interest-rate behavior

One of the worst mistakes that a Federal Reserve official or outside observer can make is to equate rising market rates of interest with a "deflationary" monetary policy and falling interest rates with an "expansionary" monetary policy, without any reference to whether the change in interest rates reflects shifts in demand functions for funds, or in the supply functions of funds, or both. This can lead to absurd conclusions. For example, rising interest rates in a boom period are often initiated and supported by large upward shifts in demand functions for loanable funds. Should one conclude that the Federal Reserve is following a restrictive or deflationary policy if it allows bank credit and the money supply to increase markedly, but not enough to prevent some rise of interest rates? On the other hand, declining interest rates in a recession period are often initiated by downward shifts of demand functions for loanable funds. Should one conclude that the Federal Reserve is following an expansionary policy if it allows the money supply and bank credit to decline, but not enough to prevent some fall of interest rates? Unfortunately, erroneous conclusions of this nature were drawn by Federal Reserve officials during the earlier years of the System, and some outside observers are still making similar mistakes.

However, the behavior of interest rates can be a useful operating guide if used with care and sophistication, because the Federal Reserve exerts its principal influence on the behavior of aggregate demand for output through its effects on interest rates and the availability of credit, and thence on investment demands for output. The Federal Reserve does use interest rates as one of its operating guides—though seldom as its only guide—comparing the actual behavior of market rates with some target level it believes would best promote its objectives. For example, the manager of the Open Market Account is told to prevent disorderly movements of rates, or to keep rates at about their present level, or to move toward higher or lower rates.

The money supply

Milton Friedman and others have proposed that the Federal Reserve should have one and only one operating guide—the behavior of the money supply—and that its invariable rule should be to increase the money supply at a steady rate approximating the rate of potential growth of real output—about 3 to 4 percent a year.[3] Although Friedman includes time and savings deposits at commercial banks in his definition of the money supply, some who support his policy prescription do not. Friedman believes that there is a highly stable and reliable relationship between the size of the money supply and the level of aggregate demand for output, and that the money supply is a more appropriate and reliable guide than any other guide or group of guides that the System has used.

Federal Reserve officials do use the behavior of the money supply as one of their policy guides, but they reject the idea that this should be their sole or dominating guide. Basically, this is because they reject Friedman's hypothesis of a stable relationship between the money supply, however defined, and the level of aggregate demand for output. They believe that the quantities of money demanded relative to national income are unstable, rising at some times and falling at others in response to such things as changes in the general level of interest rates and changes in relationships among the various types of interest rates. Thus, a

---

[3] See especially Milton Friedman, *A Program for Monetary Stability,* New York, Fordham University Press, 1959.

constant rate of increase of the money supply would not assure an acceptable behavior of aggregate demand.

The existence and erratic behavior of time and savings deposits at commercial banks pose special problems for any mechanical rule. These deposits are included by Friedman in his definition of the money supply; he thus implies that one dollar of time and savings deposits exerts the same influence on the level of aggregate demand as would a dollar of demand deposits or currency. This is almost certainly wrong. For example, at some times when rates paid by banks on time and savings deposits have been high relative to rates on competing assets, these deposits have grown at annual rates of 10 percent or more, while demand deposits grew very little. At least to some extent this represented a shift of public holdings away from claims against other types of intermediaries and from direct securities, not a shift of demand away from demand deposits. Yet Friedman's rule would call for action to restrict the growth of total deposits to an annual rate of 3 or 4 percent. At other times, especially when rates paid by banks are low relative to those on competing assets, the public has demanded smaller increases of time and savings deposits and larger amounts of other earning assets. Friedman's rule would prescribe a compensating higher rate of increase of demand deposits and currency on every such occasion.

The rule cannot be saved by defining the money supply to include only currency and checking deposits. For one thing, the relationship between the money supply so defined and the level of aggregate demand is not stable; it shifts in response to such things as changes in the general level and structure of interest rates, including rates paid on time and savings deposits. Moreover, the Federal Reserve's control over the money supply, thus narrowly defined, is far from precise, especially over short periods. The Federal Reserve can indeed regulate the reserve positions of banks, thus putting them in a position to provide more or less funds by purchasing loans and securities. But the public determines the proportions in which it will distribute its holdings among currency, demand deposits, and time and savings deposits; and these shift in response to such things as shifts in the level and structure of interest rates.

Total bank credit
Another operating guide that the Federal Reserve has long used is the behavior of total bank credit—the sum of bank holdings of loans and securities. Variations in this total are parallel to changes in total deposits at banks—the sum of demand, time, and savings deposits—the principal difference between the two totals being the amount of bank reserves. However, the Federal Reserve has never used total bank credit as an exclusive guide.

Member-bank reserve positions
Since the Federal Reserve exercises its powers of general monetary management by operating on the reserve positions of banks, it was almost inevitable that its officials would seek an operating guide in the form of some measure of the reserve

position of banks, and that instructions to the manager of the Open Market Account would come to be couched in terms of the effects of his operations on the reserve position of the banking system as a means of affecting such things as the money supply, bank credit, and interest rates. For such purposes, several measures of the reserve position of the banking system are available, as indicated in Table 11–5. No one of these is considered to be, by itself, an accurate indicator of either

Table 11–5 Measures of the reserve position of member banks, May, 1971 (monthly average of daily figures in millions of dollars)

Total reserves:	$30,408
Less: Borrowed reserves	330
Equals: Unborrowed reserves	$30,078
Total reserves:	$30,408
Less: Required reserves	30,113
Equals: Excess reserves	295
Less: Borrowed reserves	330
Equals: Free reserves	−$ 35

SOURCE: *Federal Reserve Bulletin,* June, 1971, p. A6.

the current reserve position of the banks or of any existing pressures toward bank expansion or contraction. For example, "total reserves" does not by itself indicate what quantity resulted from bank borrowing at the Federal Reserve and what quantity was acquired from other sources; nor does it indicate the amount of excess reserves, if any, that the banks hold, and so on. The Federal Reserve searched for some one composite figure which would serve as an indicator of the current reserve position of the banks and of the direction and strength of pressures for expansion or contraction. The result is a statistical series on "free reserves" of member banks, which is published weekly by the Federal Reserve and receives much attention in the financial press. *Free reserves* are equal to total member-bank excess reserves minus total outstanding member-bank borrowings from the Federal Reserve. Free reserves are obviously positive when excess reserves exceed borrowings and negative when borrowings exceed excess reserves. Negative free reserves are often called *net borrowed reserves.* The volume of free reserves in selected periods is shown in Table 11–6. *Restrictive periods* are those in which the Federal Reserve was trying to slow down bank expansion, and *liberal periods* those in which it was trying to encourage expansion.

Let us deal first with a naive view of the meaning and significance of free reserves. This is the view that the free-reserve figure is an accurate and reliable index of the amount of pressure for expansion or contraction of the supply of money and bank credit. When excess reserves are much greater than bank borrowings from the Federal Reserve, banks are under strong pressure to expand and

Table 11–6 Free reserves of all member banks for selected periods
(monthly averages of daily figures in millions of dollars)

PERIOD	EXCESS RESERVES	BORROWINGS AT FEDERAL RESERVE BANKS	FREE RESERVES
Liberal periods			
June, 1958	$626	$ 142	$484
April, 1963	416	121	295
November, 1969	735	142	593
Restrictive periods			
December, 1957	577	710	− 133
August, 1959	472	1,007	− 535
September, 1966	398	766	− 368
November, 1969	253	1,241	− 988

SOURCE: *Federal Reserve Bulletin,* various issues.

are likely to do so; but when their borrowings from the Federal Reserve are much greater than their excess reserves they are under strong pressure to contract. These conclusions flow from two assumptions: (1) Because of the tradition against borrowing, banks always feel under pressure to repay their debt to the Federal Reserve, and the greater their outstanding debt of this type, the greater will be the pressure for contraction. (2) Banks either do not want to hold reserves in excess of legal requirements or the amount of excess reserves demanded does not change.

This single free-reserve figure has several shortcomings as an index of pressures toward expansion or contraction.

1. It does not indicate the behavior of the total volume of reserves available to banks. Excess reserves could be increased by decreases of deposits which lower required reserves, and they could be decreased by increases of deposits which raise required reserves.

2. It assumes implicitly that the expansionary effect of a dollar of excess reserves is equal to the contractionary effect of a dollar of outstanding borrowings. Any given amount of free reserves can result from many different combinations of excess reserves and borrowings, and it is not clear that all these combinations will exert the same pressures for expansion or contraction.

3. It ignores the distribution of excess reserves and borrowings among the various classes of member banks. Some classes appear to be more sensitive than others. For example, smaller country banks almost always hold considerable amounts of excess reserves and adjust only sluggishly. On the other hand, big city banks usually hold only small amounts of excess reserves and adjust quickly.

4. It does not take into account changes in member-bank demands for excess reserves, changes in the amount of borrowings at the Federal Reserve that the banks are willing to maintain, and therefore changes in bank demands for free reserves. Bank demands for free reserves are likely to show important cyclical changes.

The most basic objection to the naive view is its assumption that banks demand some constant quantity of free reserves—i.e., some constant difference between their excess reserves and their borrowings at the Federal Reserve. In fact, the quantities of free reserves demanded by banks undergo broad changes. For example, in periods of prosperity when both customers' loans and interest rates are high, banks are likely to demand only small amounts of excess reserves, and also to be perfectly willing to remain heavily in debt to the Federal Reserve if they can lend at rates profitably above Federal Reserve discount rates. On the other hand, bank demands for free reserves are likely to rise during recession periods when both demands for bank credit and interest rates are falling. They usually demand more excess reserves, both because this costs less with lower interest rates and because demands for loans are less insistent. And they demand a smaller amount of borrowings at the Federal Reserve, especially if market rates of interest have fallen relative to the Federal Reserve discount rate. Thus, they demand a larger volume of free reserves and will feel under pressure to expand only if the actual amount of free reserves exceeds the amount they want to hold under existing circumstances.

Federal Reserve officials now recognize the fallacies of this naive view and use free reserves as an operating guide in a more sophisticated way. They recognize that the quantities of free reserves demanded by banks can change, that a given amount of free reserves may exert more pressure for expansion or contraction under some circumstances than under others, and that they must watch carefully the way banks respond to initial changes in their free reserves and be ready to modify their actions if banks do not respond in the desired way.

As indicated earlier, Federal Reserve officials have not been willing to be guided exclusively by any one of the proposed guides; instead, they consider several, including interest rates, the money supply, total bank credit, and the reserve positions of the banking system. The relative weights attached to the various guides appear to change from time to time. By the early 1970s, increased attention was being given to the money supply and bank credit, but the other guides continued to receive close attention.

TREASURY INSTRUMENTS OF MONETARY MANAGEMENT

The Treasury influences monetary and credit conditions in many ways: through its revenue and expenditure policies, its debt management policies, its policies relative to the size and location of its money balance, and so on. At this point, we shall deal only with its policies relative to the size of its money balance and the distribution of this balance among its three possible forms: Treasury cash in vault, Treasury deposits at the Federal Reserve, and Treasury deposits at commercial banks. Owing to the magnitude of Treasury operations, these policies can have marked effects on monetary and credit conditions, especially over short periods. Ordinarily, the Treasury does not use these powers for deliberate and continuous monetary management; this is the primary responsibility of the Federal Reserve. However, it does try to use its powers in such a way as to avoid creating serious problems for the Federal Reserve, and on occasion it uses them deliberately to supplement Federal Reserve policies.

We shall build here on some of our findings in the preceding chapter, that is, generally speaking, that increases or decreases in the size of the Treasury's money balance tend directly to restrict or liberalize the supply of money and credit to the public. Moreover, shifts of the Treasury balance from deposits at commercial banks to Treasury cash in vault or Treasury deposits at the Federal Reserve tend to reduce member-bank reserves, and shifts in the opposite direction tend to increase member-bank reserves. We shall now see how these actions can be used for restrictive or liberalizing purposes.

Restrictive actions

Let us deal with three major cases:

1. The Treasury increases its money balance $1 billion by taxing the public or selling securities to the public. When the Treasury cashes the checks, the public will lose $1 billion of its deposits. If the Treasury holds these deposits at commercial banks, this is the extent of the effect; the reserve positions of the banks are unaffected. But if the Treasury uses the $1 billion to build up its cash in vault or its deposit at the Federal Reserve, member-bank reserves will be reduced by $1 billion.[4]

2. The Treasury increases its balance $1 billion by borrowing from commercial banks. In this case, there is no direct effect on the public's money supply. If the Treasury continues to hold the balance at commercial banks, there is no change in the dollar volume of bank reserves; nevertheless, credit conditions tend to be tightened because the banks must hold reserves against the Treasury deposit, and therefore they have fewer reserves to support deposits owed to the public. If the Treasury transfers the deposit to the Federal Reserve or converts it to cash in vault, member-bank reserves will be reduced.

3. The Treasury builds up its money balance by borrowing from the Federal Reserve banks. This action cannot restrict credit. If it holds the increased balance in the form of cash in vault or deposits at the Federal Reserve, there is no effect on either the public's money supply or bank reserves. But if it transfers the funds into a deposit at a commercial bank, the effect is actually to increase member-bank reserves and to ease credit conditions.

In short, we find that an increase in the Treasury's money balance tends to be restrictive unless the Treasury acquires the extra money by borrowing from the Federal Reserve. If it acquires the money balance by taxing the public or selling securities to it, the public's money supply is directly decreased. If it acquires the money by selling securities to commercial banks, the public's money supply is not directly decreased, but the ability of the banks to create deposits for the public is reduced because they must use some of their reserves to support the Treasury deposit. However, given the size of any increase in the Treasury's bal-

---

4 Here we are neglecting the income effects of tax collections.

ance, the degree of restrictiveness depends on the form in which it is held. The effects are least restrictive if the balance is held in the form of deposits at commercial banks, and are most restrictive if it is held as cash in vault or deposits at the Federal Reserve.

Liberalizing actions

The Treasury can ease monetary conditions by taking actions that are just the reverse of those described above; that is, by decreasing its money balance and by shifting it from the forms of cash in vault or deposits at the Federal Reserve into deposits at commercial banks.

The most liberalizing action that it can take is to draw down its balance in the form of cash in vault or deposits at the Federal Reserve to make payments to the public or to retire debt held by the commercial banks. If it uses these funds to make payments to the public, it directly increases both the public's money supply and commercial-bank reserves. The banks can then expand their loans and security holdings by a multiple of the additional reserves not required to support the initial increase of the public's deposits. If the Treasury uses the funds to retire debt held by commercial banks, the effect is to increase by that amount both the actual and excess reserves of commercial banks.

Less powerful liberalizing actions are those of using Treasury deposits at commercial banks to make payments to the public or to retire Treasury debt held by the commercial banks. If these deposits are transferred to the public, the effect is to increase the public's money supply without changing the banks' reserve positions. If they are used to retire Treasury debt held by the commercial banks, there is no direct effect on either the public's money supply or the dollar volume of bank reserves. However, the reduction of Treasury deposits reduces required reserves and enables the banks to create new deposits by lending or buying securities. If the Treasury uses some of its deposits at commercial banks to retire debt held by the Federal Reserve, the effect is to reduce the dollar volume of bank reserves.

The Treasury sometimes uses these powers in a positive way to restrict or ease credit to supplement Federal Reserve actions. More often, however, it uses them to avoid creating conditions that would make the job of the Federal Reserve more difficult. For example, it avoids large shifts of its balance among the categories of cash in vault, deposits at the Federal Reserve, and deposits at commercial banks unless the Federal Reserve would welcome the resulting tendency toward ease or restriction. When it has large net tax receipts, it often seeks to minimize restrictive effects by using the funds to retire debt held by the public or the commercial banks, rather than to increase its money balance. And if it does increase its money balance, it holds the extra funds at commercial banks.

SELECTIVE CREDIT CONTROLS

We have emphasized that the purpose of general monetary management is to regulate the total supply of money and bank credit and the general level of interest rates; it is not to determine the allocation of credit among its many possible users and uses. This allocative or rationing function is left to the private market. Those who believe in a predominantly free-market economy generally favor primary reliance on general monetary management because the allocation of credit helps to allocate real resources, which they believe should be allocated through competition in the market place. However, many persons, including some who favor primary reliance on general measures, believe that these measures should be supplemented by *selective controls;* that is, by measures that would influence the allocation of credit, at least to the point of decreasing the volume of credit used for selected purposes without the necessity of decreasing the total supply and raising the cost of credit for all purposes.

Selective credit controls can be either negative or positive. *Negative controls* seek to decrease the supply or increase the cost of credit for certain specified purposes. *Positive controls* seek to increase the supply or lower the cost of credit for specified purposes. Although our central interest is in selective controls by the Federal Reserve, it should be noted that many actions by other govenment agencies significantly affect the allocation of credit among its potential uses and users. A few examples will suggest the range of these policies.

1. Low-cost government loans to rural electric and telephone cooperatives, to finance exports, and for certain types of housing.

2. Limitations on types of assets that may be acquired by savings and loan associations. A major purpose of this action is to increase the supply of credit for housing.

3. Government guarantees of loans for such purposes as storing farm products or housing.

4. Tax policies, such as exemption from the federal income tax, which lower the rates that state and local governments must pay on their borrowings.

These examples suggest that even when selective credit controls are justified it does not necessarily follow that they should be wielded by the Federal Reserve.

We now turn our attention to some of the forms of selective credit controls that have been administered by the Federal Reserve.

MORAL SUASION

The Federal Reserve sometimes employs moral suasion as an instrument of general monetary management—to influence total borrowings at the Federal Reserve and the behavior of the total supply of money and bank credit. Moral suasion is also used for selective purposes, especially with banks currently borrowing from the Federal Reserve. For example, in the late 1920s, and especially in early 1929, the Federal Reserve urged banks to curb their "speculative loans on securities" and to favor "loans for legitimate business purposes." In the spring of 1951, during the Korean conflict, the Federal Reserve sponsored a "voluntary credit-restraint program," which encouraged banks and some other financial institutions to restrict "nonessential, nonproductive loans" while continuing to make "essential productive loans." In 1966, the Federal Reserve urged banks to curb the rate of expansion of business loans and to reduce their sales of government securities. Also, in the mid-1960s, as a part of a program to improve the nation's balance of payments, banks were first urged, and then legally required, to refrain from increasing their total loans to foreigners.

Let us now look at some of the more formal types of selective controls.

Margin requirements on security loans

This selective control arose out of the Federal Reserve's unhappy experience with stock-market speculation in the late 1920s. At that time there was nothing in the basic economic situation that called for a policy of very tight money. Employment was not overly full, commodity prices were steady, and the objective of promoting recovery and prosperity abroad called for easy money. However, the stock market was booming, and the rapid rise of prices was supported in part by large increases of loans on stock collateral. Federal Reserve officials were convinced that this was "unsound" and that less credit should be available for stock purposes. However, they then had only two methods of dealing with the situation— moral suasion and general credit restriction. They attempted moral suasion, exhorting banks not to make speculative loans on stocks while borrowing at the Federal Reserve. This did not work, partly because most of the banks were not in debt to the Federal Reserve, and partly because of the huge and rising volume of nonbank loans on stock. They also invoked general credit restriction, which seemed to dampen business activity more than stock-market speculation. The outcome is now famous; stock speculation climbed until the great crash in October, 1929, and the Federal Reserve's policy of general credit restriction came to be blamed in part for the ensuing Great Depression.

In 1934, largely because of this experience, Congress gave the Board of Governors power to fix, and to alter at its discretion, minimum margin requirements on security loans. These apply where two conditions are met. (1) The loan is collateraled by a security listed on a national securities exchange and not exempted—government obligations and some others are exempted. And (2) the purpose of the loan is for purchasing or carrying such securities. Minimum margin requirements are, in effect, minimum downpayments stated as a percentage of the market value of the security. To set a minimum margin requirement is an indirect way of setting a maximum loan value. The latter, in percentage terms, is equal to 100 percent minus the minimum margin requirement.

As shown in Table 11–7, the Board of Governors has changed margin requirements several times, sometimes lowering loan values to discourage borrowing and lending for these purposes, and at other times raising loan values to reduce the degree of restriction. On one occasion, in 1946, it raised margin requirements to 100 percent. Since early 1968, margin requirements have also been applied to loans on convertible bonds.

Several aspects of this selective control are worth noting.

1. It applies to borrowers as well as to lenders. It is just as illegal for a borrower to borrow in excess of the maximum loan value as it is for a lender

Table 11–7 Margin requirements and maximum loan values

PERIOD	MARGIN REQUIREMENT (PERCENT)	MAXIMUM LOAN VALUE (PERCENT)
Oct. 1, 1934–Jan. 31, 1936	25–45*	55–75*
Feb. 1, 1936–Mar. 31, 1936	25–55*	45–75*
Apr. 1, 1936–Oct. 31, 1937	55	45
Nov. 1, 1937–Feb. 4, 1945	40†	60
Feb. 5, 1945–July 4, 1945	50	50
July 5, 1945–Jan. 20, 1946	75	25
Jan. 21, 1946–Jan. 31, 1947	100	0
Feb. 1, 1947–Mar. 29, 1949	75	25
Mar. 30, 1949–Jan. 16, 1951	50	50
Jan. 17, 1951–Feb. 19, 1953	75	25
Feb. 20, 1953–Jan. 4, 1955	50	50
Jan. 5, 1955–Apr. 22, 1955	60	40
Apr. 23, 1955–Jan. 15, 1958	70	30
Jan. 16, 1958–Aug. 4, 1958	50	50
Aug. 5, 1958–Oct. 15, 1958	70	30
Oct. 16, 1958–July 27, 1960	90	10
July 28, 1960–July 9, 1962	70	30
July 10, 1962–Nov. 5, 1963	50	50
Nov. 6, 1963–June 7, 1968	70	30
June 8, 1968–May 5, 1970	80	20
Effective May 6, 1970	65	35

* Maximum loan value was either 75 percent of current market value or 100 percent of lowest price since July 1, 1933, whichever was smaller, but it could always be at least 55 percent of current market value (45 percent after February 1, 1936) .

† Fifty percent for short sales.

SOURCE: *Federal Reserve Bulletin,* various issues.

to make such loans. Thus, this control limits the demand for such credit as well as limiting the supply for this purpose.

2. It applies not only to member banks but also to lenders of every type. Thus, for this purpose, it extended the jurisdiction of the Board of Governors. This precedent was followed in later selective controls.

3. It not only enables the Federal Reserve to restrict the volume of credit used for this purpose without restricting the supply or raising the cost of credit for other purposes, but it may actually ease credit for other purposes. To the extent that less credit is demanded or supplied for this purpose, more credit tends to be made available for other uses.

It is very difficult to assess precisely the effectiveness of this regulation in curbing the amount of credit used for purchasing and carrying securities. It certainly has some overall effect, and is especially effective in curbing such borrowing by those persons who could borrow little without pledging the securities as collateral. However, many people have found ways of evading the intent of the regulation. For example, they buy and carry these securities with funds acquired by borrowing on their general credit standing, on exempt securities, on their houses, on their businesses, and so on.

Consumer-credit controls

Selective controls of consumer credit, which were administered under Federal Reserve Regulation W, have had a checkered career. They were first instituted in the autumn of 1941, under an Executive Order, and remained in effect until 1947, when they were withdrawn. They were reinstated in September, 1948, under a temporary authorization by Congress, and expired in June, 1949. After the outbreak of war in Korea, they were imposed again, but were withdrawn in 1952. Since that time, the Federal Reserve has not been empowered to use this type of control.

This selective control employed two devices: minimum downpayments and maximum periods of repayment. Both applied to consumer loans on listed articles. Raising the required downpayment (which is, of course, the same as lowering the maximum loan value) tended to reduce the demand for credit for this purpose as well as to reduce the amount that could be legally supplied for it. Shortening the maximum period of repayment, which increased required monthly payments, also tended to reduce the demand for such loans. Only the latter device applied to consumer loans for unlisted purposes.

Consumer-credit control proved to be almost impossible to administer and enforce. Since this control applied not only to banks but also to other providers of consumer credit, a very large number of lenders had to be kept under surveillance, and the Federal Reserve was not adequately staffed for the job. Consumers who were offered credit terms more liberal than those permitted by the regulations were not inclined to file complaints, and many suppliers of consumer credit, especially those who sold goods and services on credit, either ignored the regulations or violated them frequently.

Real-estate credit controls

From 1950 until 1952, as a part of the anti-inflation program initiated after the outbreak of war in Korea, Congress authorized the Board of Governors to exercise selective control over credit extended to finance new residential construction. This it did under Regulation X. It utilized the same devices as Regulation W: minimum downpayments and maximum periods of repayment. Also, its terms like those of Regulation W, were not uniform for all loans of this general type. Instead, Regulation X was designed to favor low-cost housing and housing for veterans. It therefore required larger downpayments and shorter periods of repayment for higher-cost housing and on loans to nonveterans. This regulation was in effect for only a short time and even then it did not apply to many construction projects that were already in progress or in the planning stage. For these reasons, it is difficult to predict its effectiveness over a longer period. However, there are reasons to expect that it would be difficult to enforce.

Interest-rate ceilings and legal-reserve requirements

As we have already seen, these measures were not originally considered to be instruments for selective credit control. The major reason given by the Federal Reserve for imposing ceilings on rates that banks may pay on time and savings deposits was to prevent banks from paying such high rates on funds that they would be led to make unsafe loans, but banks viewed the ceilings as a way of keeping down their costs. And the primary function of legal-reserve requirements is to regulate the total volume of bank deposits and credit. Yet both of these instruments were used to some extent for selective credit-control purposes in 1966 and 1969 and may play similar roles in the future.

As will be remembered, both 1966 and 1969 were years of price inflation, highly restrictive Federal Reserve policies, and the highest interest rates in over 100 years. In fact, general credit restriction was so severe that some feared a credit "crunch" or crisis. Two special aspects of the situation led to consideration of some type of selective controls. One was the rapid expansion of bank loans to business, which was helping finance inflationary levels of business expenditures for investment. The other was the plight of savings and loan associations and some other types of financial intermediaries. They could not afford to pay much higher rates for savings because the average rate of earnings on their existing assets was dominated by the lower levels of long-term interest rates that had prevailed in earlier years. Yet, yields on competing open-market assets, such as Treasury bills, rose to historically high levels, and it was clear that banks would also raise their rates on time and savings deposits to high levels if the Federal Reserve would raise the ceilings. Savings and loan associations first suffered a decrease in the flow of funds to them and then the danger of large net withdrawals. The effects would be not only a shortage of mortgage funds, with further depressing effects on housing, but perhaps also wide distress among these financial institutions.

Several actions were taken to deal with these special situations.

1. The Federal Home Loan Banks sold very large amounts of their own bonds, carrying a government guarantee, and loaned the proceeds to savings and loan associations to help them meet withdrawals and purchase some mortgages. This positive selective control was very helpful to the savings and loan associations, but it did not, of course, serve to slow down the expansion of bank loans to business.

2. The Board of Governors raised the legal-reserve requirements from 4 to 6 percent against time deposits at each bank in excess of $5 million. One purpose of this action was general credit restriction. The other was to decrease bank demands for time-deposit funds. It was believed that banks would compete less aggressively for funds and pay only lower interest rates if they could lend an amount equal to only 94 percent instead of 96 percent of such time deposits. It is very doubtful that this small increase in required reserves appreciably reduced bank demands for time deposits. After all, the banks were by this time paying much more for funds from other sources.

3. The Board refused to raise rate ceilings on time and savings deposits even though rates on competing assets in the open market rose to much higher levels. This action was effective in checking flows of funds into time and savings deposits at banks; in fact, some banks suffered large net withdrawals, especially in the form of large denomination CDs.

The refusal to raise ceilings on rates that banks might pay only partially achieved its basic objectives. It did not stop withdrawals from other financial intermediaries. It did inhibit shifts of funds to commercial banks, but it did not stop customers of other intermediaries from withdrawing funds in order to buy Treasury bills and other high-yielding assets in the open market. Also, the refusal to raise ceiling rates was only partially successful in slowing the expansion of bank loans to business. Banks, and especially large banks, showed great ingenuity in devising other ways of getting funds for this purpose—by selling government securities, selling participations in their portfolios, issuing commercial paper through holding companies or their subsidiaries, borrowing federal funds, borrowing Eurodollars, and so on.

It is still debatable whether interest-rate ceilings can be used effectively to create selective credit control in periods of unusual financial stress. There is a general agreement, however, regarding two matters related to interest-rate ceilings. One is that they should not be regarded as a substitute for basic reforms that would make real-estate credit less vulnerable in periods of high interest rates. The other is that if such ceilings are effective over a long period or are used frequently, the efficiency of the financial system can be impaired because the ceilings may inhibit the survival and growth of the most efficient financial institutions and practices.

Attitudes toward selective controls

Attitudes toward selective controls differ widely. Few people object to their use in time of war or rapid military mobilization when the government will in any case intervene heavily to regulate the allocation of resources and output. At such times, selective credit controls may serve a useful purpose, both in diverting resources away from nonessential uses and in inhibiting inflation. But their use in noncrisis peacetime periods is another matter. As might be expected, they are often opposed by those whose economic interests may be diversely affected. Thus, some stock-exchange members and officers are not friendly toward margin requirements on security loans, automobile manufacturers and dealers have criticized regulation of consumer credit, and the construction industry and realtors opposed restrictions on credit for residential purposes.

Many economists have opposed selective controls on several grounds: (1) that they may interfere unduly with the freedom of borrowers and lenders, (2) that they prevent an allocation of resources and output in line with buyers' wishes, (3) that they are unnecessary because general monetary management and fiscal policies are sufficient, (4) that they may come to be looked upon as a substitute for more general and more widely effective measures, and (5) that they are likely to become unenforceable or enforceable only with a very large staff. Other economists contend that selective controls can be a useful supplement to general monetary controls, especially when the misbehavior of credit is limited to only one or a few sectors of the economy.

Selected readings

Fousek, Peter G., *Foreign Central Banking: The Instruments of Monetary Policy*, Federal Reserve Bank of New York, 1957.

Meigs, A. J., *Free Reserves and the Money Supply*, Chicago, University of Chicago Press, 1962.

Tamagna, Frank M., "Processes and Instruments of Monetary Policy: A Comparative Analysis," in Commission on Money and Credit, *Monetary Management*, Englewood Cliffs, N.J., Prentice-Hall, 1963, pp. 1–174.

CHAPTER 12

THE MONETARY SYSTEM: AN OVERALL VIEW

The purpose of this brief chapter is not to present new materials but to summarize some of our findings, to bring them into focus, and to enable us to visualize more clearly the functioning of the United States monetary system as a whole. We shall concentrate primarily on those types of transactions that directly increase or decrease the public's money supply, but will devote some attention to effects on the reserves of the commercial-banking system. A balance-sheet analysis will account for the size of the money supply at a point of time and its changes through time. However, as an exercise in *ex post* accounting, we shall not explain why the money supply behaved as it did. To do this requires an analysis of the determinants of all the relevant variables.

Several of our earlier findings are essential to this analysis:

1. By *money supply* we mean the amount of coin, paper money, and checking deposits owned by the United States "public"; that is, by all individuals and entities of the United States other than the federal government, the Federal Reserve, and the commercial banks.

2. All these types of money are *debt money;* they are debt claims against their issuers. They may also be called the *monetary liabilities* of the issuing institutions.

3. Only the Treasury, the Federal Reserve, and the commercial banks have the power to create debts that serve as money.

4. In general, these institutions create and issue monetary liabilities in the process of purchasing assets, and they withdraw and destroy monetary liabilities when they decrease their assets.

THE MONETARY EQUATION

Our analysis will be based on a consolidated balance sheet for the commercial banks, the Federal Reserve banks, and the monetary operations of the Treasury. Three points should be emphasized:

1. The balance sheet will not include all the many aspects of Treasury operations; it will include only those related to the money-supply function, which we shall call the *monetary operations* of the Treasury.

2. The balance sheet is not simply a summation of the three separate sets of balance sheets; it is a partially consolidated balance sheet. Because we are interested primarily in the relation of these institutions to others, we eliminate many of their claims against each other.[1]

3. Although we shall use balance-sheet accounting, our central interest is not in the accounting itself, but in identifying and analyzing the factors that determine the size of the money supply at any time and changes in its size through time.

We start with the following fundamental balance-sheet equation:

$$\text{Assets} = \text{liabilities} + \text{capital accounts} \tag{1}$$

The asset side of the balance sheet for a stated point in time shows the total value of assets that have been acquired and that are owned by the entities at that time; the other side shows the types and amounts of claims that have been issued to acquire those assets. "Liabilities" represent the value of outstanding debt claims; "capital accounts," or "net worth," represents the value of ownership claims. Debt and ownership claims together must be exactly equal to the value of assets. Moreover, the above monetary institutions can acquire an increased value of assets during any period only by creating and issuing an equal increase of debt and ownership claims. If they decrease their assets, they must reduce by an equal amount the value of outstanding debt and ownership claims against themselves.

---

[1] Although it differs from them in several respects, the analysis in this chapter borrows very heavily from both of the following: Morris A. Copeland and Daniel H. Brill, "Banking Assets and the Money Supply Since 1929," *Federal Reserve Bulletin,* January, 1948, pp. 24–32 (statistical tables based on this formulation appear monthly in the *Federal Reserve Bulletin*); Edward S. Shaw, *Money, Income, and Monetary Policy,* Homewood, Ill., Irwin, 1950, Chaps. 2 and 3.

For our purposes, it is necessary to divide total liabilities into two categories: nonmonetary liabilities and monetary liabilities. In nonmonetary liabilities we include all of the types of debt liabilities issued by these institutions that are not money. Thus, we may rewrite our fundamental equation as follows:

$$\text{Assets} = \text{monetary liabilities} + \text{nonmonetary liabilities} \atop + \text{capital accounts} \tag{2}$$

This is the same as Equation 1 except that it makes the distinction, essential for our purposes, between debt liabilities that serve as money and those that do not.

By transposing in Equation 2, we get the following:

$$\text{Monetary liabilities} = \text{assets} - \begin{cases} \text{nonmonetary liabilities} \\ + \\ \text{capital accounts} \end{cases} \tag{3}$$

This equation shows that the value of the money supply (monetary liabilities) at any time is equal to the total value of assets held by these institutions, minus the value of their outstanding nonmonetary liabilities and capital or net-worth accounts. And through time, the size of the money supply varies directly with the value of these assets and inversely with the value of nonmonetary liabilities and capital accounts.

In Equation 3, by listing the principal types of assets actually held by these institutions and the types of nonmonetary liabilities issued by them, we get Equation 4, which we shall use in the remainder of this chapter.

$$\begin{matrix} \text{Monetary} \\ \text{liabilities} \end{matrix} = \text{assets} - \begin{matrix} \text{nonmonetary} \\ \text{liabilities} \\ + \text{capital} \\ \text{accounts} \end{matrix} \tag{4}$$

$$\begin{Bmatrix} \text{Checking deposits} \\ + \\ \text{Currency outside} \\ \text{banks} \end{Bmatrix} = \begin{Bmatrix} \text{monetary gold} \\ \text{stock} \\ + \\ \text{SDR Certificates} \\ + \\ \text{Treasury currency} \\ + \\ \text{Federal Reserve} \\ \text{holdings of loans} \\ \text{and securities} \\ + \\ \text{commercial-bank} \\ \text{holdings of loans and} \\ \text{securities} \end{Bmatrix} - \begin{Bmatrix} \text{foreign deposits} \\ + \\ \text{time deposits} \\ + \\ \text{Treasury holdings} \\ \text{of cash and} \\ \text{deposits} \\ + \\ \text{capital accounts} \end{Bmatrix}$$

Table 12–1 applies this analysis to the situation on May 26, 1971. It shows that the money supply of $209.6 billion on that date resulted from the acquisition

Table 12–1 The money supply and related items, May 26, 1971 (billions of dollars)

Assets

Monetary gold stock	$ 10.7	
Treasury currency	7.4	
Federal Reserve holdings of loans and securities	66.3	
Commercial-bank holdings of loans and securities	468.1	
Total assets		$552.5

Less:

Nonmonetary liabilities

Foreign deposits, net	$ 2.3	
Treasury holdings of cash and deposits	9.9	
Time deposits at commercial banks	250.8	
Total		$263.0

Less:

Capital accounts* .... | | $ 79.9

Equals:

Monetary liabilities

Demand deposits	$160.2	
Currency and coin outside banks	49.4	
Total		$209.6

* Also contains some miscellaneous liabilities and statistical discrepancy.
SOURCE: Derived from data in *Federal Reserve Bulletin,* June, 1971, p. A19. As used here, the item "capital accounts" is a balancing item. It is simply total assets minus the sum of nonmonetary liabilities and monetary liabilities as shown. This was done to escape the laborious job of accounting for a number of minor items in the balance sheets of the Treasury, the Federal Reserve, and the commercial banks.

and holding of $552.5 billion of assets by these monetary institutions, less the $342.9 billion of outstanding claims against them in the form of nonmonetary liabilities and capital accounts.

ASSETS

To isolate the effects of purchases and sales of assets by these institutions, we shall assume that when they buy assets, they pay for them by issuing coin, paper money, or checking deposits to the public, and that when they sell assets, they withdraw an equal amount of money from the public. The cases in which nonmonetary debts and capital accounts are involved will be considered later.

Monetary gold stock and SDR Certificates

As we did earlier, we shall lump together as assets the monetary gold stock and Treasury issues of SDR Certificates. When the Treasury buys gold or issues SDR Certificates, it usually issues an equal amount of gold or SDR Certificates to the

Federal Reserve banks, receiving in return a deposit credit. When the Treasury writes checks on these deposits, the receiver deposits the check at his bank, which sends it to the Federal Reserve to be added to the bank's reserve account and deducted from the Treasury's deposit account. Thus, the effects are to increase by equal amounts the public's money supply and member-bank reserves.

Net sales of gold by the Treasury have the opposite effects. Gold buyers usually pay the Treasury with checks on their banks, thereby giving up deposits. The Treasury retires an equal amount of certificates, and the Federal Reserve deducts an equal amount from the reserves of the bank on which the check is drawn.

Treasury currency outstanding

This source of money includes all coins in the United States and paper money issued by the Treasury. Increases of this item tend to increase not only the public's money supply but also the volume of member-bank reserves. Consider two cases:

1. The Treasury issues additional currency to the public when there is no increase in the demand for currency in circulation. The public will return the excess currency to its banks in exchange for increased deposits, and this cash will increase bank reserves.

2. The Treasury issues additional currency equal to an increase in the public's demand for currency. In this case, the public has an increase in its money supply in the form of currency, and the banking system is spared the loss of reserves it would have suffered in the absence of the increased Treasury issue.

Federal Reserve holdings of loans and securities

These are obviously earning assets of the Federal Reserve banks. In general, Federal Reserve purchases of earning assets tend to increase both the public's money supply and member-bank reserves, and Reserve net sales of assets have the opposite effect. But two cases need to be distinguished:

1. It lends to the public or buys assets from the public. In this case, it pays with checks on itself, the public deposits the checks at banks, and the banks send them along to be added to their reserve accounts.

2. It lends to banks or buys assets from them. In this case the banks receive additional reserves, but there is no direct addition to the public's money supply. However, the increase of Federal Reserve assets has prevented the public's money supply from being decreased by the decrease of commercial-bank assets or by the rise of commercial-bank nonmonetary liabilities in the form of debt to the Federal Reserve.

Net sales of assets by the Federal Reserve tend to have the opposite effects, but here, again, the two cases need to be distinguished. Net sales to the public tend to decrease both the public's money supply and bank reserves. But net sales of assets to commercial banks or net decreases of loans to commercial banks decrease bank reserves without directly decreasing the public's money supply. However, these decreases in Federal Reserve assets offset the increase of commercial-bank assets, or the decrease of commercial-bank nonmonetary liabilities in the form of debt to the Federal Reserve, and prevent them from being reflected in an increase of the public's money supply.

Commercial-bank holdings of loans and securities

When commercial banks buy assets in the forms of loans and securities, they pay for them by creating deposit credits or by paying out coin and currency, usually the former. When they sell these assets, they decrease their deposit liabilities or withdraw coin and currency from the public, mostly the former.

Thus, we find that the assets in the consolidated balance sheets of the three sets of monetary institutions are of four types: (1) monetary gold stock, (2) Treasury currency, (3) Federal Reserve holdings of loans and securities, and (4) commercial-bank holdings of loans and securities. In purchasing these assets, the monetary institutions tend to issue debt money to the public; and in selling these assets, they tend to withdraw and destroy money formerly held by the public. Increases or decreases in the first three also tend to increase or decrease the dollar volume of member-bank reserves.

Nonmonetary liabilities and capital accounts

The size of the money supply depends not only on the total volume of assets of the monetary institutions, but also on the volume of their nonmonetary liabilities and capital accounts. The nonmonetary liabilities are foreign-deposit claims against the Federal Reserve and commercial banks, Treasury holdings of cash and of deposit claims against the Federal Reserve and commercial banks, and time-deposit claims against commercial banks. The item, capital accounts, is the value of ownership claims against the Federal Reserve and commercial banks. All these claims have the following points in common:

1. They are not a part of the money supply as we have defined it.

2. They are alternatives to, and compete with, monetary liabilities as claims against assets.

3. When considered by themselves, increases or decreases in these claims tend to produce opposite variations in the money supply.

The monetary institutions can acquire assets by issuing nonmonetary liabilities or ownership claims. For example, they may acquire assets by issuing claims to the Treasury, to foreign depositors, to time depositors, or to their owners. In this way, they can secure assets without increasing the supply of money. On the other hand, they may reduce their assets without decreasing the money supply to the extent that they reduce their other liabilities and ownership claims against themselves.

Moreover, the money supply can be decreased or increased by an exchange of monetary liabilities for other claims, or vice versa. Thus, the public's holdings of money can be reduced as it relinquishes money in exchange for time deposits at commercial banks or to make net payments to the accounts of foreigners or the Treasury. Its holdings of money can be increased if it converts its time-deposit claims against commercial banks into monetary claims or receives net payments out of foreign deposits or out of Treasury holdings of cash and deposits.

The various types of developments that tend directly to increase or decrease the money supply are summarized in Table 12–2.

Table 12–2 Factors of money supply

FACTORS TENDING TO EXPAND THE MONEY SUPPLY	FACTORS TENDING TO CONTRACT THE MONEY SUPPLY
Increases of assets	**Decrease of assets**
1. Increase of the monetary gold stock	1. Decrease of the monetary gold stock
2. Increase of Treasury currency outstanding	2. Decrease of Treasury currency outstanding
3. Increase of Federal Reserve holdings of loans and securities	3. Decrease of Federal Reserve holdings of loans and securities
4. Increase of commercial-bank holdings of loans and securities	4. Decrease of commercial-bank holdings of loans and securities
Decreases of nonmonetary liabilities	**Increases of nonmonetary liabilities**
5. Decrease of foreign deposits	5. Increase of foreign deposits
6. Decrease of Treasury holdings of cash and deposits	6. Increase of Treasury holdings of cash and deposits
7. Decrease of time deposits	7. Increase of time deposits
DECREASE OF CAPITAL ACCOUNTS	**INCREASE OF CAPITAL ACCOUNTS**

It is important to remember that the first three asset items also appeared in our analysis of "member-bank reserves and related items" as determinants of the dollar volume of member-bank reserves, as did also some of the liability and capital-account items.

BEHAVIOR OF THE MONEY SUPPLY

Table 12–3 shows the size of the money supply and related items on selected dates beginning with 1929. The wide fluctuations of the money supply during this period are particularly striking.

From mid-1929 to the low point of the Depression in mid-1933, the money supply declined from $26.1 billion to $19.2 billion, for a drop of 26 percent. From that time to the end of 1939, it rose 89 percent. During the defense and war period from the end of 1939 to the end of 1945, it rose $66.2 billion, or 183 percent. From that time to May, 1971 it rose another $107.2 billion, or over 100 percent. Thus in May, 1971, the money supply was 8.03 times its level at the end of 1929, 10.9 times its level at the bottom of the Great Depression, and 5.8 times its level at the end of 1939. The money supply is certainly not a static quantity.

Table 12–3 also indicates the relative quantitative importance of the various factors directly relevant to the money supply. By far the most important source of money has been commercial-bank holdings of loans and securities. These did not comprise less than 63.8 percent of total assets in the consolidated balance

Table 12–3 Direct determinants of the money supply (billions of dollars)

	JUNE 29, 1929	JUNE 30, 1933	DEC. 30, 1939	DEC. 31, 1945	MAY 26, 1971
Assets					
Monetary gold stock	$ 4.0	$ 4.0	$17.6	$ 20.1	$ 10.7
Treasury currency	2.0	2.3	3.0	4.3	7.4
Federal Reserve holdings of loans and securities	1.3	2.2	2.5	24.4	66.3
Commercial-bank holdings of loans and securities	49.2	30.4	40.7	124.0	468.1
Total assets	$56.5	$38.9	$63.8	$172.8	$552.5
Less:					
Nonmonetary liabilities					
Foreign deposits, net	$ 0.4	$ 0.1	$ 1.2	$ 2.1	$ 2.3
Treasury holdings of cash and deposits	0.6	1.1	3.9	27.9	9.9
Time deposits at commercial banks	19.6	10.8	15.3	30.1	250.8
Total	$20.6	$12.0	$20.4	$ 60.1	$263.0
Less:					
Capital accounts	$ 9.8	$ 7.7	$ 7.2	$ 10.3	$ 79.9
Equals:					
Monetary liabilities					
Demand deposits	$22.5	$14.4	$29.8	$ 75.9	$160.2
Currency and coin outside banks	3.6	4.8	6.4	26.5	49.4
Total	$26.1	$19.2	$36.2	$102.4	$209.6

SOURCE: Computed from data in the *Federal Reserve Bulletin,* various issues.

sheet on any of the dates shown in Table 12–4, and on most of the dates they accounted for an even larger share of the total.

Moreover, changes in the volume of commercial-bank loans and security holdings were by far the largest single source of changes in the money supply.

Table 12–4 Commercial-bank loans and security holdings and the total assets of the monetary system

DATE	TOTAL ASSETS IN CONSOLIDATED STATEMENT (BILLIONS)	COMMERCIAL-BANK HOLDINGS OF LOANS AND SECURITIES (BILLIONS)	COMMERCIAL-BANK HOLDINGS OF LOANS AND SECURITIES AS PERCENTAGE OF TOTAL ASSETS
June 29, 1929	$ 56.5	$ 49.2	87.1
June 30, 1933	38.9	30.4	78.1
December 30, 1939	63.8	40.7	63.8
December 31, 1945	172.8	124.0	71.8
May 26, 1971	542.5	468.1	86.3

The other assets should not be neglected. Both the monetary gold stock and Federal Reserve holdings of loans and securities directly contribute significant amounts to the money supply, and their changes contribute directly to changes in the money supply. However, these two items are far less important as direct determinants of the money supply than they are as determinants of the volume of bank reserves, which is a major determinant of commercial-bank loans and security holdings. The volume of Treasury currency outstanding is much smaller and fluctuates within narrower limits.

Of the nonmonetary liabilities that also help to determine the behavior of the money supply, time deposits at commercial banks are the largest and show the widest changes. Especially noteworthy is the very large increase since the end of World War II, which absorbed $221 billion of the funds provided by the increase of assets. Most of this increase occurred after the late 1950s when the Federal Reserve raised ceiling rates on these deposits and the banks began to compete more aggressively for such funds. The capital accounts of the commercial and Federal Reserve banks show an upward trend, but do not change much in short periods. Changes in foreign deposits and in Treasury holdings of cash and deposits are not major direct determinants of secular changes in the money supply, but they are sometimes important determinants of short-run changes. For example, the Treasury sometimes tends to add several billions to the public's money supply by drawing down its holdings of deposits; at other times it tends to decrease the money supply by increasing its own holdings of deposits.

The purpose of this chapter has been the modest one of summarizing the principal types of transactions that directly affect the size of the money supply, not to present a theory of the behavior of the money supply. The latter would require analyses of all the principal determinants of the behavior of the factors discussed above.

Selected readings

Copeland, Morris A., and Daniel H. Brill, "Banking Assets and the Money Supply Since 1929," *Federal Reserve Bulletin,* January, 1948, pp. 24–32.
Shaw, Edward S., *Money, Income, and Monetary Policy,* Homewood, Ill., Irwin, 1950.

PART FOUR

MONETARY THEORY

CHAPTER 13

THE NATIONAL-INCOME ACCOUNTS

The preceding chapters were largely concerned with the supply, or stock, of money—its nature and composition, the process of increasing and decreasing it, techniques of managing its size, and so on. In contrast, the primary purpose of the several chapters that follow this one will be to explore monetary theory—the relationships between the stock of money and the behavior of other selected economic variables, such as rates of real output, levels of employment, price levels, and interest rates. One important variable that will receive much attention in those chapters will be *money flows,* or rates of money expenditures per unit of time. Whether or not money flows vary proportionally with the stock of money need not concern us at this point; our primary concern is to point out that they are different phenomena and that it should not be assumed that money flows are necessarily proportioned to the money stock.

Flows of money expenditures are usually stated at annual rates, although they can be measured over any unit of time—such as days, weeks, or months. Some concepts of money flows or expenditures are very comprehensive, including every expenditure of money for other things during a stated period—for all types of financial instruments; for existing physical assets, such as real estate and personal property; and for purchases of currently produced goods and services at every stage of their production and distribution. We shall concentrate on a much narrower measure of flows of expenditures—"expenditures on national-income and product account." We concentrate on money demands for the current output of goods and services because it is this flow of expenditures that is most relevant to the behavior of the rate of real output, employment, and price levels of output.

NATIONAL-INCOME ACCOUNTING

It should be emphasized from the outset that this chapter does not pretend to offer any "income or monetary theory." It presents no behavioral hypotheses concerning the determinants of the level, or changes in the level, of output or income. It does not attempt to explain why income was a certain amount, rather than any other amount during a stated period. Instead, it concentrates on national-income accounting—on *ex post* accounts of what happened during each stated period. Nevertheless, a clear understanding of at least the basics of national-income accounting will greatly facilitate our later theoretical analysis. This chapter will identify the various components of national output or income, force us to define each of them clearly, and suggest some of the relationships among the totals and among components.

In earlier sections, we employed double-entry balance-sheet accounting to deal with the stock of assets of the various monetary institutions and claims against those assets at stated points in time. We began with the simple balance-sheet identity: Assets = liabilities + capital accounts. Then we found it useful to explore the various components of the equations. Now we shall use double entry income accounting to deal with flows of income or output over stated periods of time. We begin with an accounting identity: Value of output (or expenditures for output) = sum of income shares accruing to all claimants. This identity means simply that whether output is large or small its entire value during a period, must accrue to someone, and that the sum of all accruing income shares must be equal to the value of output. This conclusion may seem less than earthshaking, but we shall find that by analyzing the components of the equation we can cast much light on the processes involved in income flows. In valuing national output or income, we shall use gross national product (or expenditure). However, the same basic principles apply if any other consistent basis for valuation is used.

THE NATURE OF GROSS NATIONAL PRODUCT

Gross national product or *expenditure,* popularly known as GNP, is the market value of the output of goods and services produced by a nation's economy during a stated period of time before deduction of depreciation charges and other allowances for business and institutional consumption of durable capital goods.[1] It is usually stated at an annual rate. It avoids double counting and includes the nation's entire output once and only once. Thus, it does not add together the values of autos produced and sold by the manufacturer to the dealer and by the dealer to consumers; it includes only their value at the point of final sale. It does not add together the values of the flour and other components of the bread produced and the values of bread sold by the baker to the merchant and by the merchant to the final buyer; it includes only the value of the bread at its point of final sale. Thus, GNP includes the value of all output at its point of final sale, and this value includes all the values added at earlier stages of processing and handling.[2]

Table 13–1 presents data relating to the behavior of GNP during the years following 1928. Column (1) shows the value of GNP in each year, with output valued at the average level of prices prevailing during that year. Thus, its changes reflect the behavior of both real output and the prices of output. Column (2) shows the value of GNP for each year at constant (1958) prices. In effect, the real output of each year is valued at the average level of prices prevailing in 1958. Since the effects of changes in the price level are eliminated, this is an indicator of the behavior of real output. The implicit GNP price deflator, shown in column (3), is an index of average prices of all goods and services included in GNP. It states the average level of prices for each year as a percentage of the average level that prevailed in 1958. For convenience of comparison, columns (4) and (5) show GNP in both current and constant prices as percentages of their levels in 1958.

Several facts stand out in Table 13–1.

1. Real GNP shows a strong upward trend. For example, in 1970 it was 3.6 times its level in 1929, twice its level in 1950, and nearly 50 percent above its level in 1960. There is no reason to believe that growth of the productive capacity of the economy is at an end. A policy implication is that real demands for output must also grow if growth potentials are to be realized.

2. The growth of real GNP was seriously interrupted during the Great Depression of the 1930s. From 1929 to the nadir of the Depression in 1933, GNP

---

[1] For excellent descriptions of GNP and other income concepts, as well as a wealth of statistical materials relating to GNP and its components since 1929, see U.S. Department of Commerce, *U.S. Income and Output,* U.S. Government Printing Office, 1959, and *The National Income and Product Accounts of the United States, 1929–1965,* U.S. Government Printing Office, 1966. For later data, see the *Survey of Current Business* for July of each year.

[2] When concentrating on the welfare aspects of national income, many economists prefer to use the concept "net national product," which is GNP minus depreciation charges and other allowances for business and institutional consumption of durable capital goods. It is net national product that measures the value of output available for private and public consumption and for making net additions to the stock of capital goods. We shall use the GNP measure because we shall employ a saving-investment analysis to explain the behavior of output and income, and capital consumption allowances make up a major part of gross saving in the United States. It is therefore helpful to keep this element of gross saving in plain sight.

Table 13–1 Gross national product, 1929–1971 (billions of dollars)

	(1)	(2)	(3)	(4)	(5)
		GNP AT	INDEXES, 1958 = 100		
	GNP AT	CONSTANT	IMPLICIT GNP	GNP AT	GNP AT
CALENDAR	CURRENT	(1958)	PRICE	CURRENT	CONSTANT
YEAR	PRICES	PRICES	DEFLATION	PRICES	PRICES
1929	$103.1	$203.6	50.6	23.0	45.5
1930	90.4	183.5	49.3	20.2	41.0
1931	75.8	169.3	44.8	16.9	37.8
1932	58.0	144.2	40.3	13.0	32.2
1933	55.6	141.5	39.3	12.4	31.6
1934	65.1	154.3	42.2	14.6	34.5
1935	72.2	169.5	42.6	16.1	37.9
1936	82.5	193.0	42.7	18.4	43.1
1937	90.4	203.2	44.5	20.2	45.4
1938	84.7	192.9	43.9	18.9	43.1
1939	90.5	209.4	43.2	20.2	46.8
1940	99.7	227.2	43.9	22.3	50.8
1941	124.5	263.7	47.2	28.8	59.0
1942	157.9	297.8	53.0	35.3	66.6
1943	191.6	337.1	56.8	42.8	75.4
1944	210.1	361.3	58.2	47.0	80.8
1945	211.9	355.2	59.7	47.4	79.4
1946	208.5	312.6	66.7	46.6	69.9
1947	231.3	309.9	74.6	51.7	69.3
1948	257.6	323.7	79.6	57.6	72.3
1949	256.5	324.1	79.1	57.3	72.5
1950	284.8	355.3	80.2	63.7	79.4
1951	328.4	383.4	85.6	73.4	85.7
1952	345.5	395.1	87.5	77.2	88.3
1953	364.6	412.8	88.3	81.5	92.3
1954	364.8	407.0	89.6	81.6	91.0
1955	398.0	438.0	90.9	89.0	97.9
1956	419.2	446.1	94.0	93.7	99.7
1957	441.1	452.5	97.5	98.6	101.1
1958	447.3	447.3	100.0	100.0	100.0
1959	483.7	475.9	101.7	108.1	106.4
1960	503.7	487.7	103.3	112.6	109.0
1961	520.1	497.2	104.6	116.3	111.2
1962	560.3	529.8	106.8	125.3	118.4
1963	590.5	551.0	107.2	132.0	123.2
1964	632.4	581.1	108.9	141.4	129.9
1965	684.9	617.8	110.9	153.1	138.1
1966	749.9	658.1	114.0	167.7	147.1
1967	793.9	675.2	117.6	177.5	151.0
1968	865.0	707.2	122.3	193.4	158.1
1969	931.4	727.1	128.1	208.2	162.6
1970	976.5	724.1	134.8	218.3	161.9
1971	1,046.8	739.4	141.6	234.0	165.3

SOURCE: *Economic Report of the President*, February, 1971, pp. 197–201; *Federal Reserve Bulletin*, various issues.

at constant prices fell nearly 30 percent. Since the average prices of output declined about 22 percent, the decline of GNP at current prices was nearly 46 percent. At that point, nearly one-quarter of the labor force was wholly unemployed and many others had only part-time jobs. After 1933, the recovery was sluggish and incomplete until the nation entered World War II.

3. Since World War II, growth of real GNP has not been interrupted by a major depression. However, there have been several recessions—in 1946, 1949, 1954, 1958, 1961, and 1970. By historical standards, these recessions have been relatively short and minor. Real GNP actually declined in only four of the recessions—those of 1946, 1954, 1958, and 1970; in 1949 and 1961 it failed to grow as fast as productive capacity. That the nation has escaped major depressions since World War II is indeed fortunate. However, large amounts of employment and potential output have been lost during the recessions and during some other years of only sluggish real growth.

4. In general, the post-World War II period has been one of price inflation. For example, the price level of output in 1970 was about 125 percent above that in 1945. Nearly three-quarters of this increase was associated with wars. Over one-quarter of the increase occurred in the three years immediately following World War II, about one-eighth during the Korean conflict of 1950–1953, and well over one-third during the Vietnam War in 1965–1970. However, the rate of price increases during some other years was uncomfortably high.

These data suggest that we are still far from the ideal of "continuously full employment without inflation."

Let us now look at the various components of GNP at current prices, stating them as values of output or expenditures for output.

GNP AS EXPENDITURES FOR OUTPUT

GNP is composed of four main categories of expenditures for output: (1) personal-consumption expenditures, (2) gross private domestic investment, (3) net exports of goods and services, and (4) government purchases of goods and services. GNP for any given period is therefore equal to the sum of these four types of expenditures, and it varies with their total. This is shown in Table 13–2.

Personal consumption

Personal-consumption expenditures include all purchases of current output by consumers. These include durable consumer's goods, nondurable consumer's goods, and consumer's services. The durables include such things as new automobiles, TV sets, refrigerators, and furniture. The nondurables include food, beverages, clothing, tobacco, and so on. Consumer's services embrace a wide variety of services such as shelter, medical care, barber and beauty services, domestic service, and admissions to theaters and professional sporting events. All of these are, of course, valued at their market prices.

Table 13–2 Gross national product as expenditures for output, 1950–1970 (billions of dollars at current prices)

YEAR	GROSS NATIONAL PRODUCT	PERSONAL CONSUMPTION	GROSS PRIVATE DOMESTIC INVESTMENT	NET EXPORTS OF GOODS AND SERVICES	GOVERNMENT PURCHASES OF GOODS AND SERVICES
1950	$284.8	$191.0	$ 54.1	$1.8	$ 37.9
1951	328.4	206.3	59.3	3.7	59.1
1952	345.5	216.7	51.9	2.2	74.7
1953	364.6	230.0	52.6	0.4	81.6
1954	364.8	236.5	51.7	1.8	74.8
1955	398.0	254.4	67.4	2.0	74.2
1956	419.2	266.7	70.0	4.0	78.6
1957	441.1	281.4	67.9	5.7	86.1
1958	447.3	290.1	60.9	2.2	94.2
1959	483.7	311.2	75.3	0.1	97.0
1960	503.7	325.2	74.8	4.0	99.6
1961	520.1	335.1	71.7	5.6	107.6
1962	560.3	355.1	83.0	5.1	117.1
1963	590.5	375.0	87.1	5.9	122.5
1964	632.4	401.2	94.0	8.5	128.7
1965	684.9	432.8	108.1	6.9	137.0
1966	749.9	466.3	121.4	5.3	156.8
1967	793.9	492.1	116.6	5.2	180.1
1968	865.0	535.8	126.5	2.5	200.2
1969	931.4	577.5	139.8	1.9	212.2
1970	976.5	616.7	135.7	3.6	220.5

SOURCE: *The National Income and Product Accounts of the United States, 1929–1965, Statistical Tables,* August, 1966, pp. 2–5, 158–159; *Federal Reserve Bulletin,* various issues.

Gross private domestic investment

Every word in this title is important. The term "investment," as used here, has nothing directly to do with buying stocks, bonds, or any other type of financial instrument. We use it here and in the succeeding sections to mean simply expenditures for the current output of goods and services for the purpose of maintaining and increasing the stock of capital goods. The term "domestic" indicates that we include here only expenditures for the purpose of maintaining or increasing the stock of capital goods at home, not those for maintaining or building up capital abroad. "Private" means that only private expenditures for these purposes are included, not those by the government. The term "gross" indicates that we include expenditures for output to offset the depreciation of capital goods as well as to make net additions to the stock. If we deduct from gross private domestic investment for any period the depreciation or "using up" of capital during the period, we arrive at net private domestic investment, the net increase in the stock of these goods during the period.

Gross private domestic investment is made up of three broad classes of expenditures for output.

1. New construction, both residential and nonresidential. Residential construction is the value of output of new dwelling units during the stated period, both single and multiple units. Nonresidential construction embraces the output of such things as new farm, industrial, commercial, public utility, and other private buildings, and new dams by privately owned public utilities.

2. Producers' durable equipment. This includes the output of such things as farm machinery, manufacturing equipment, scientific instruments, railroad rolling stock, accounting machines, store fixtures, and all other types of equipment used for production.

3. Net changes in the size of business inventories.

The term "net changes in business inventories" requires further clarification. Business inventories in existence at any point in time are, of course, a part of the community's stock of capital goods; they are raw materials, goods in process, and finished goods held by business firms to facilitate their operations. Some of these are held by the firms that produced them; others are held by firms in later stages of the production-distribution process, such as fabricators of raw materials, wholesalers, or retailers, who purchased them from their producers. A net increase in business inventories during a given period is *investment* because it is an addition to the stock of capital goods. A net decrease of business inventories during a period is *negative investment,* or *disinvestment,* because it represents a decrease in the stock of capital goods. The net change of business inventories during any period is equal to total output minus final sales, because output tends to increase inventories, and sales to reduce them.

Changes in the volume of output used to increase or decrease inventories are an important source of fluctuations in GNP and employment over short periods. To illustrate this point, let us assume that the rate of final sales remains constant but that the rate of change of inventories varies. Suppose that in the first period, business is increasing its inventories at an annual rate of $4 billion. GNP will be equal to final sales plus the $4 billion of output used to effect the net increase of business inventories. This rise of inventories represents expenditures for output, either expenditures by firms that bought the output from other firms or production expenditures by firms that produced the goods and held them. It also provided employment. Suppose that in the next period, business firms reduce their output enough to decrease their inventories at an annual rate of $4 billion. GNP will be equal to final sales minus $4 billion. Thus, the shift by business from increasing its inventories at a rate of $4 billion a year to decreasing its inventories at a rate of $4 billion a year tends directly to lower GNP by $8 billion and also to lower employment. By reducing the incomes of producers and workers, it may induce still further declines of GNP by decreasing consumption expenditures.

In the example above, where final sales were assumed to continue at a constant rate, fluctuations in the rate of change of inventories were a source of fluctuations of GNP. But this item can be a stabilizing force, at least in the short run, if it moves counter to changes in the rate of final sales. Suppose, for example, that the rate of final sales falls by $5 billion. GNP may remain constant, at least temporarily, if business maintains its rate of output and increases its rate of inventory accumulation. However, if this increase of inventory is "unwanted," business may later reduce output sharply, to draw down its inventories. The adjustment of output to the decline of final sales is delayed, but it may be magnified. Suppose, on the other hand, that the rate of final sales rises by $5 billion. This need not be reflected in the current rate of output if business offsets it by allowing its inventories to be drawn down. But when inventories fall below desired levels, business may try to increase output sharply in order to replenish them.

Net exports of goods and services

American exports during any period represent the amount of our output of goods and services taken by the rest of the world. Our imports of goods and services represent the amount of the output of the rest of the world taken by us for use by our private and public sectors. Thus, our net exports represent the net amount of our output taken by other countries. We can, of course, have net imports, although, in fact, we have had net exports during most of the recent years.

Suppose that during some year there are $60 billion of exports and $55 billion of imports:

$$\text{Net exports} = \$60 \text{ billion} - \$55 \text{ billion} = \$5 \text{ billion}$$

The $5 billion of net exports can be looked at in two ways: (1) as the net value of our output taken by the rest of the world, and (2) as the net amount of income shares created for Americans in transactions with other countries. Americans use a part of their income to buy imports. On the other hand, foreign purchases of our output create value of output and income shares for Americans producing that output. Thus, our net exports represent net contributions to demands for our output by the rest of the world.

Net U.S. exports during any stated period are equal to the sum of (1) net private and government transfer payments to the rest of the world, and (2) net foreign investment. The first is made up of private and government gifts and grants to foreigners; in effect, we give this part of our national income to foreigners. They can return it to spending for American output by purchasing our exports.[3] Net foreign investment represents that value of our output and of our exports used during a stated period to increase our net claims against the rest of the world. This part of our exports, like gross private domestic investment, is a part of the total demand for our output. Also, like gross private domestic investment, it is an offset to saving; it is a way that saving can be reinjected into the spending stream for our output.

---

[3] Since we are interested here primarily in explaining domestic factors influencing our national income, we shall assume that any transfer payments that may be made to foreigners will be returned in the form of demands for our exports; in other words, net transfers to foreigners do not represent any leakage in the circular-flow process.

Because both are offsets to saving and tend to increase our national wealth, we shall add together gross private domestic investment and net foreign investment and call them "gross private investment."

Government purchases of goods and services

Government purchases include the expenditures of the federal, state, and local governments for the current output of goods and services. These are of two major types:

1. Direct expenditures for the services of productive factors, primarily for labor. In this category are the services of both military and civilian government personnel. These services are valued at the prices paid for them by the government.

2. Expenditures for the output of business firms. These are large and diverse; they include government expenditures for construction materials and services, military equipment and supplies, red tape, and the tens of thousands of other items purchased by government from private producers.

Business firms provide employment and produce in response to government demand much as they would if the demand emanated from private sources.

We find, then, that GNP for any period is the sum of expenditures for output in the form of personal consumption, gross private domestic investment, net exports of goods and services, and government purchases of goods and services. GNP therefore fluctuates with the sum of these four types of expenditures.

For convenience, we shall denote these expenditures by the following symbols:

C = personal consumption
I = total gross investment; it is the sum of gross private domestic investment and net foreign investment
G = government purchases of goods and services
Y = GNP, or gross national product

Thus, for any period,

$$Y = C + I + G$$

The reader will find it instructive to study carefully Table 13–2, noting the size and variability of GNP, the relative sizes of its various components, and their variability.

GNP AS GROSS NATIONAL INCOME

We noted earlier that GNP may be viewed not only as the value of output or expenditures for output but also as the sum of gross-national-income shares accruing to the members of the community, including the government. We also noted that the sum of these shares accruing to the community during any period must be exactly equal to the value of output or expenditures. On reflection, this becomes almost obvious. Value created must accrue to someone; it cannot disappear in thin air. Nor can the community as a whole receive values that are not created. To state this observation in another way, expenditures made must be received by someone, but no one can receive expenditures that are not made.

This is shown in Table 13–3. For each period, the sum of the distributive shares of gross national income indicated by the column heads is determined by,

Table 13–3   Gross national product as the sum of gross income shares, 1960–1970 (billions of dollars)

YEAR	TOTAL GROSS NA- TIONAL PRODUCT	IN- DIRECT BUSI- NESS TAXES	BUSI- NESS CAPITAL CON- SUMP- TION ALLOW- ANCES	COM- PENSA- TION OF EM- PLOYEES	RENTAL IN- COME OF PERSONS	NET INTER- EST IN- COME	EARN- INGS OF UNIN- CORPO- RATED BUSI- NESS*	CORPO- RATE PROF- ITS*
1960	$503.7	$45.2	$43.4	$294.2	$15.8	$ 8.4	$46.2	$49.9
1961	520.1	47.7	45.2	302.6	16.0	10.0	48.4	50.3
1962	560.3	51.5	50.0	323.6	16.7	11.6	50.1	55.7
1963	590.5	54.7	52.6	341.0	17.1	13.8	51.0	58.9
1964	632.4	58.4	56.1	365.7	18.0	15.8	52.3	66.3
1965	684.5	62.5	59.8	393.8	18.2	17.9	57.3	76.1
1966	747.6	65.3	64.1	435.6	20.8	20.2	60.7	83.9
1967	789.7	69.6	69.2	468.2	23.3	22.4	60.7	80.4
1968	864.2	78.6	74.5	514.6	21.2	26.9	64.2	84.3
1969	929.1	85.7	81.1	565.5	22.6	29.9	67.0	78.6
1970	974.1	92.9	87.6	601.9	23.3	33.0	66.9	70.8

* After inventory valuation adjustment. Items may not add to totals shown, partly because of rounding and partly because of omissions of minor adjustment items.
SOURCE: *The National Income and Product Accounts of the United States, 1929–1965. Statistical Tables,* August, 1966, pp. 12–15; *Survey of Current Business,* July, 1971, pp. 15–17.

and equal to, total expenditures for output. A part of these expenditures accrues to the government as income in the form of indirect business taxes, by which we mean all business taxes except those on corporate net income. These include taxes on production and sales by business, license fees of business, taxes on business property, and so on. The remainder of GNP accrues to private business and individuals as gross money income before any taxes except indirect business taxes. One part accrues to business in the form of depreciation and other capital-consumption allowances. This is not net income, but it is a part of the expenditures for output received by business and at its disposal. Another part accrues as compensation of employees, in the form of wages, salaries, commissions, and so on. Another part accrues as rental incomes of persons, and another in the form of interest. All the remainder accrues as profits of business enterprises—as earnings of unincorporated enterprises and as corporate profits. This is a residual claim; all the value of business output not claimed by others accrues to the owners of business.

These relations between expenditures for output and income receipts suggest both the interrelatedness of the various sectors of the economy and the nature of the circular flow of income. Suppose we divide the economy into three major sectors: consumer households, business, and government. The interrelationships are so numerous and complex that we can mention only a few. The government receives income in the form of taxes from both households and business. It creates income for both by purchasing goods and services. Its expenditures for labor directly create income for households; its expenditures for the output of business create income for both business and households. Households pay income to the government in the form of taxes and create income for business by their expenditures; in turn, they receive income from both the government and business. Business, too, both receives income from, and pays income to, the other sectors.

As already noted, the flow of income is a circular flow. Expenditures for output become income receipts, these income receipts are spent for output, these spendings create income receipts, and so on. If this circular flow continued at a constant rate, GNP would, of course, remain constant. But we know that the circular flow sometimes slows down and lowers GNP, and at other times it speeds up and increases GNP. This raises several important questions. Through what processes do these rises and falls occur? How are they related to the ways that income recipients dispose of their incomes? Which types of income disposal tend to maintain or increase expenditures for output; which types tend to lower expenditures? As a first step toward answering these questions, we shall analyze the disposal of income receipts.

DISPOSAL OF INCOME AND THE CIRCULAR FLOW

For the purpose of analyzing the disposal of income receipts, the classification of income shares used in Table 13–3 is inadequate. In the first place, it shows income shares by functional type rather than by type of recipient. In the second place, it shows income shares before any taxes, except indirect business taxes, and also before transfer payments. For our analysis of income disposal, we shall divide income recipients into three classes—government, business, and persons or households—and consider their *disposable incomes*, by which we mean the amounts of money income left at their disposal after taxes and all transfer payments.

As indicated in Table 13–4, the total disposable gross national income for any period must be exactly equal to GNP for that period, and it must fluctuate with GNP. It is equal to the sum of disposable government income, disposable business income, and disposable personal income. Let us look at each of these in turn.

Disposable government income

We start with total government receipts, as shown in column (1) of Table 13–5. These include all revenues accruing to federal, state, and local governments—not only indirect business taxes but also personal and corporate income taxes, property

Table 13–4 Disposable gross national income, 1960–1970 (billions of dollars)

	(1)	(2)	(3)	(4)	(5)	
YEAR	TOTAL GROSS DISPOSABLE INCOME (= GNP)	DISPOSABLE INCOME OF GOVERNMENT	DISPOSABLE BUSINESS INCOME	DISPOSABLE PERSONAL INCOME*	TOTAL DISPOSABLE PRIVATE INCOME [(3) + (4)]	STATISTICAL DISCREPANCY*
1960	$503.7	$103.3	$56.8	$342.2	$399.1	−1.3
1961	520.1	103.3	58.7	356.3	415.0	−1.8
1962	560.3	114.2	66.3	376.6	442.9	−3.2
1963	590.5	124.3	68.8	394.9	463.7	−2.5
1964	632.4	127.3	76.2	427.4	503.6	−1.5
1965	683.9	139.1	83.7	460.3	544.0	−0.8
1966	743.3	157.5	89.7	495.7	585.4	−0.4
1967	785.1	163.6	90.4	530.3	620.7	−0.7
1968	864.2	192.7	95.4	575.9	671.3	−0.2
1969	929.1	217.2	95.6	617.5	713.1	+1.2
1970	974.1	206.3	99.3	666.9	766.2	−1.6

* Disposable personal income as used here is disposable personal income excluding interest paid by consumers and personal transfers to foreigners. Net transfers to foreigners are not shown explicitly in the table. The column, "statistical discrepancy" is a combination of this item from the national income accounts and net transfers to foreigners. It is equal to GNP minus the sum of disposable income shares.

SOURCE: *The National Income and Product Accounts of the United States, 1929–1965, Statistical Tables,* August, 1966, pp. 149–150; *Survey of Current Business,* July, 1970, p. 40.

Table 13–5 Government income and its disposal, 1960–1970 (billions of dollars)

	(1)	(2)	(3)	(4)	(5)
YEAR	TOTAL GOVERNMENT RECEIPTS (T)	TRANSFER PAYMENTS (P)	GOVERNMENT DISPOSABLE INCOME (T_n)	GOVERNMENT PURCHASES OF GOODS AND SERVICES (G)	GOVERNMENT SAVING [(3) − (4)] (S_g)
1960	$139.8	$36.5	$103.3	$ 99.6	$ 3.7
1961	144.6	41.3	103.3	107.6	− 4.3
1962	157.0	42.8	114.2	117.1	− 2.9
1963	168.8	44.4	124.3	122.5	1.8
1964	174.1	46.7	127.3	128.7	− 1.4
1965	188.8	49.7	139.1	136.4	2.7
1966	213.0	55.5	157.5	154.3	3.2
1967	227.3	63.7	163.6	176.3	− 12.7
1968	263.5	70.7	192.8	199.6	− 6.8
1969	295.6	78.4	217.2	209.8	7.4
1970	300.5	94.2	206.3	219.4	− 13.1

SOURCE: *The National Income and Product Accounts of the United States, 1929–1965, Statistical Tables,* August, 1966, pp. 149–150; *Survey of Current Business,* July, 1971, p. 40.

taxes on households, license fees, contributions for social insurance, and so on. In recent years, total taxes have taken more than one-quarter of the GNP. Taxes obviously tend to reduce the disposable income—incomes after taxes—of households and business. However, the government uses some of its total receipts to make transfer payments, designated as P, by which we mean all expenditures for which the government does not receive goods and services in return. These are not a part of the government's demand for output. They consist chiefly of social security benefits, relief payments, bonuses and other benefits to veterans and their dependents, interest on the federal debt, and net subsidies. Most of these go to households, although some accrue to business. These transfer payments by government obviously contribute to the disposable incomes of recipients. Column (2) of Table 13–5 shows that these have become very large.

We shall define the government's disposable income for any period (T_n) as its total receipts minus its transfer payments (P). Thus, $T_n = T - P$. How does the government dispose of its disposable income (T_n)? One way is to spend for goods and services (G). If G is exactly equal to T_n, the government tends to maintain the circular flow constant, because its spendings create money income equal to the net income extracted from others. But G may be either smaller or larger than T_n. We shall call $T_n - G$ *government saving* and designate it by S_g. Thus,

$$S_g = T_n - G$$

S_g is, of course, positive when G is less than T_n and negative when G exceeds T_n. When S_g is negative, it will be called *government dissaving*.

We call the quantity $(T_n - G)$ government saving because it is so comparable, both in nature and in effects, with private saving. As we shall see, private saving is simply that part of private disposable income that is not returned to the market for output as expenditures for consumption during the stated period. It also represents that part of private disposable income available to finance gross private domestic investment and net foreign investment. Similarly, S_g is that part of the government's disposable income that it does not return to the market as expenditures for output. Moreover, S_g, like private saving, is a potential source of funds to finance gross private domestic investment or net foreign investment. For example, suppose that, during some period, S_g is $5 billion. The government may use at least some part of these funds to lend to foreigners, thereby helping finance net exports of goods and services; or it may use at least some of the funds to retire debt held by American financial institutions or individuals. The recipients of the money are thus put in a position to spend for investment or to lend to others for such purposes. The government may, of course, fail to make its savings available for use, or the savings may for other reasons fail to find their way into investment spending, but the same is true of private saving. Government dissaving, an excess of G over T_n, has effects on the level of money income similar to those of private investment expenditures, for it too is an offset to saving, a way of converting private saving into expenditures for output. The simplest example is that in which the government borrows private savings and uses them to finance its deficit spending for output.

Several points about government fiscal operations should be emphasized because of their importance to our later analysis:

1. Government expenditures are an important determinant of both the total demand for output and private disposable incomes. Increases of G directly increase the total demand for output and also contribute to the private disposable incomes of those who produce for the government. Decreases of G have the opposite effects.

2. Total private disposable incomes (the sum of business and household disposable incomes) for any period are equal to total GNP minus T_n. If we use Y to designate gross national product and Y_p to designate total private disposable income, we can state this as follows:

$$Y_p = Y - T_n$$

Since $T_n = T - P$, we can also state this as follows:

$$Y_p = Y - T + P$$

This suggests that at any given level of Y, the government can increase private disposable incomes by decreasing T or by increasing P.

3. We have now identified the three broad classes of fiscal actions that the government can use to influence the behavior of gross national product: G, T, and P. It tends to raise Y by increasing G, by increasing P, or by decreasing T. Increases of G directly increase the total demand for output and contribute to private disposable incomes. Increases of P and decreases of T do not directly affect the demand for output, but they do tend to increase private disposable income, which usually tends to increase private demands for output. On the other hand, the government can tend to lower Y by decreasing G, by decreasing P, or by increasing T. Decreases of G directly decrease the demand for output and also decrease private diposable income. Decreases of P and increases of T do not directly decrease the demand for output, but by lowering private disposable incomes, they tend to reduce private demands for output.

4. Government saving (S_g) is quite comparable in nature and effects to private saving. It is that part of the gross national income taken by the government in taxes and not spent as domestic transfer payments and as government purchases of goods and services. It also represents a part of national money income available to finance private investment and net exports. Government dissaving (an excess of G over T_n) is an offset to private saving, a way of channeling a part of private saving into expenditures for output.

Disposable business income

Disposable business income is the amount of gross money income left at the disposal of business after all taxes and transfer payments. As shown in Table 13–6, disposable business income is made up of two parts.

Table 13–6 Disposable business income, 1960–1970 (billions of dollars)

YEAR	TOTAL DISPOSABLE BUSINESS INCOME (S_b)	CAPITAL-CONSUMPTION ALLOWANCES	UNDISTRIBUTED CORPORATE PROFITS*
1960	$56.8	$43.4	$13.4
1961	58.7	45.2	13.5
1962	66.3	50.0	16.3
1963	68.8	52.7	16.1
1964	76.2	56.1	20.1
1965	83.7	59.9	23.8
1966	89.7	63.5	26.2
1967	90.4	67.0	23.4
1968	95.4	74.5	20.9
1969	95.7	81.2	14.5
1970	99.3	87.6	11.7

* After inventory valuation adjustment.
SOURCE: *The National Income and Product Accounts of the United States, 1929–1965, Statistical Tables*, August, 1966, pp. 78–79, 149–150; *Survey of Current Business*, July, 1971, pp. 33, 40.

1. Capital-consumption allowances. As indicated earlier, a part of expenditures for output accrues to business firms as depreciation and other allowances for declines in value of capital goods during a period. This is not net income, but it is a part of gross national income that remains at the disposal of business firms. Because of the huge stock of depreciable assets held by business and the widespread practice of charging off depreciation annually, these flows are very large. In the early 1970s, their total dollar value exceeded $80 billion, and they accounted for considerably more than half of total gross saving in the United States.

2. Undistributed corporate profits, or the part of corporate net profits after taxes that are retained by corporations and not paid to stockholders. These fluctuate widely. During periods of unusually high profits, corporations often retain a large fraction of their net earnings after taxes. But in periods of low profits or losses, they may pay out more than their current net earnings; their undistributed profits may be negative.

How does business dispose of its disposable income? All of it is "saved"; none of it is spent for consumption. To emphasize this aspect of disposable business income, we shall refer to it also as gross business saving and denote it by the symbol S_b. A business firm may, of course, use some of its own S_b to finance its own current expenditures for output to maintain or increase its stock of capital goods. But this need not occur; a firm may use such savings in ways that do not directly contribute to expenditures for output: to add to its money balances, to retire debt or other claims against itself, to buy securities, and so on. Even if these savings are transferred to others, they, like personal savings, may fail to find their way into expenditures for output.

Disposable personal income

Disposable personal income during a stated period is the money income remaining at the disposal of persons (or households) after all taxes and transfer payments.[4] We can arrive at personal disposable income in either of two ways:

1. We can compute it by adding the components of personal income and subtracting personal taxes. Thus, it is equal to the sum of wages, salaries, and other income received for labor, net incomes of proprietors of unincorporated business enterprises, personal rental incomes, dividends, personal interest income, and net transfer payments received from government and business, minus personal taxes.

2. We can also compute it by subtracting the disposable incomes of government and business from total gross national income or product. Thus,

$$\text{Disposable personal income} = Y - T_n - S_b$$

We shall have many occasions to emphasize that by no means all of gross national income accrues to persons or household as disposable personal income; some of it remains at the disposal of government and business. Business may increase personal disposable incomes at any given level of GNP by retaining less disposable income and disbursing more to households. Thus, it may retain only smaller depreciation allowances or declare more dividends and retain only a smaller amount of its net earnings. And it may lower personal disposable incomes by retaining more as depreciation allowances or by retaining more of its net earnings and declaring less as dividends. The govenment may also raise disposable personal income at any given level of GNP by reducing personal taxes or by increasing its transfer payments to households, and it may lower disposable personal income at any given level of GNP by increasing personal taxes or by lowering its transfer payments to households.

Disposable personal income is disposed of in two ways:

1. As personal consumption expenditures, which we denote by the symbol C. This is the same C that we used in the equation showing GNP as the sum of expenditures for output. This method of disposing of disposable personal income clearly tends to maintain the circular flow of spendings for output.

2. As personal saving, which we shall denote by the symbol S_p. Personal saving is simply that part of disposable personal income that is not spent for consumption. Such an act obviously does not itself create expenditures for output; it is simply "not spending" for consumption.

Since personal saving is that part of disposable personal income not spent for C, it should be obvious that total personal disposable income is equal to $C + S_p$.

---

[4] The reader is warned that the definition of disposable personal income used here differs slightly from the official definition, although neither the logic nor the final figures are changed. For an explanation, see the Appendix to this chapter.

Disposable private income

In later sections, we shall find it convenient to deal with the total disposable private income. The value of this item may be derived in two principal ways:

1. We may consider it as total GNP minus T_n. This view emphasizes the fact that at any given level of GNP, the government may increase disposable private income by reducing T_n, either by lowering its tax collections or by raising its transfer payments. Or it may lower total disposable private income by increasing T_n, either by raising its tax collections or by reducing its transfer payments.

2. It may be viewed as the sum of disposable business income (S_b) and disposable personal income ($C + S_p$).

A close study of Table 13–7 reveals several facts about the behavior of private disposable income in recent years, which will be relevant to our later analysis:

Table 13–7 Disposable private income and its disposal, 1960–1970 (billions of dollars)

YEAR	DIS-POSABLE PRIVATE INCOME (Y_p)	DIS-POSABLE PERSONAL INCOME ($C + S_p$)	PERSONAL CON-SUMPTION (C)	PERSONAL SAVING (S_p)	GROSS BUSINESS SAVING (DIS-POSABLE BUSINESS INCOME) (S_b)	TOTAL PRIVATE GROSS SAVING ($S_p + S_b$)
1960	$399.1	$342.3	$325.2	$17.0	$56.8	$ 73.8
1961	415.0	356.3	335.2	21.2	58.7	79.9
1962	442.9	376.6	355.1	21.6	66.3	87.9
1963	463.7	394.9	375.0	19.9	68.8	88.7
1964	503.6	427.4	401.2	26.2	76.2	102.4
1965	544.0	460.3	433.1	27.2	83.7	110.9
1966	585.4	495.7	465.9	29.8	89.7	119.5
1967	620.7	530.3	491.6	38.7	90.4	129.1
1968	671.3	575.9	536.2	39.8	95.4	135.2
1969	713.2	617.5	579.6	37.9	95.7	133.6
1970	766.2	666.9	612.8	57.1	99.3	153.4

SOURCE: *The National Income and Product Accounts of the United States, 1929–1965, Statistical Tables*, August, 1966, pp. 149–150; *Survey of Current Business*, July, 1971, p. 40.

1. About 84 to 86 percent of total private disposable income accrues to households; the other 14 to 16 percent remains with business as gross business saving.

2. Households use about 93 to 95 percent of their disposable income for consumption and about 5 to 7 percent for personal saving. Moreover, it appears that when households enjoy an increase in disposable income, they generally use a major part of it to increase their consumption and a small part to increase their rate of saving. And when they suffer a decline of disposable income, they reduce both their consumption and their saving. In the face of very large decreases in income, such as those in the early 1930s, personal saving can become negative.

3. Total private gross saving is equal to about 17 to 20 percent of total private disposable income. Well over half of this is in the form of gross business saving.

Summary

We can now trace in a general way the processes involved in the circular flow of income. We start with some rate of money-income creation or expenditures for output composed of $C + I + G$. Some of these expenditures for output are claimed directly by government in the form of indirect business taxes. All the remainder is claimed initially by business and households. However, the government extracts large amounts from private incomes through tax collections, T. Then it returns some of these funds to the private sectors through transfer payments, P. The remainder, T_n, is the government's disposable income. The government can reinject these net receipts into the spending stream by purchasing goods and services, G. If G is exactly equal to T_n, the government itself does nothing to change the rate of flow of income. If G is greater than T_n, the government tends to make a net contribution to the flow of income. But if G is less than T_n, so that S_g is positive, the government fails by that amount to reinject into the income stream as much as it received from that stream.

A major part of $C + I + G$ accrues initially to business firms as receipts for output. A large part of these receipts must then be transferred to the government and household sectors. Taxes must be paid to the government. Much larger amounts must be paid to households as compensation for labor, interest, rentals, dividends, and other distributed profits. However, business does retain at its disposal considerable amounts in the form of capital-consumption allowances and retained net earnings. These are gross business saving, S_b. They are a part of the gross national income that is not returned as spending for output in the form of consumption.

Members of households receive a large part of total expenditures for output as compensation for their labor and for use of their property, and they also receive transfer payments from government and business. Out of this they must meet their personal tax liabilities; the remainder is personal disposable income. A large part of this is reinjected into the spending stream as consumption expenditures, C. However, the remaining part used for personal saving, S_p, is not so reinjected.

We find, then, that the circular flow of income and the level of demand for output tend to be maintained to the extent that disposable-income receipts are spent as G and C. But what about the amounts used for government saving (S_g), business saving (S_b), and personal saving (S_p)? They represent shares of income not spent for either consumption or government purchases. Viewed alone, an act of saving, or not spending, tends to shrink the circular flow of income and to lower demands for output.

We shall use the symbol S to designate total gross saving. The value of S may be derived in two different ways (that yield similar results).

$$S = S_p + S_b + S_g$$

or

$$S = Y - C - G$$

SAVINGS AND INVESTMENT

By now we should begin to suspect that processes of saving and investment play crucial roles in the circular flow of income and in determining the level, and changes in the level, of GNP. Saving is a necessary condition for gross investment —using the latter term to mean gross private domestic investment plus net foreign investment. If the nation used the entire value of its output for consumption and to supply goods and services to the government, no output and no productive factors would be available for these investment purposes. Saving serves to make available a part of output, or potential output, for investment use. But "not spending" for consumption and government use does not assure that the potential output so released will actually be used for investment. The result can be merely a decline in the demand for output and a decrease in actual output and employment. Saving can be "offset," demands for output sustained, and acts of saving converted into actual investment only to the extent that there are demands for output to be used for gross investment. Thus, actual investment requires not only a willingness of the nation to save some part of its income and output, but also the enterprise and courage to spend for investment purposes.

Table 13–8 shows the behavior of gross saving and gross investment during

Table 13–8 United States gross saving and gross investment, 1960–1970 (billions of dollars)

	SUPPLY OF SAVING				GROSS INVESTMENT			
YEAR	PER-SONAL SAV-ING (S_p)	GROSS BUSI-NESS SAV-ING (S_b)	GOVERN-MENT SAV-ING (S_g)	TOTAL SAV-ING (S)	GROSS PRIVATE DOMES-TIC IN-VEST-MENT	NET FOR-EIGN INVEST-MENT	TOTAL GROSS INVEST-MENT (I)	STATIS-TICAL DISCREP-ANCY $(I - S)$
1960	$17.0	$56.8	$ 3.7	$ 77.5	$ 74.8	$1.7	$ 76.5	−1.0
1961	21.2	58.7	− 4.3	75.5	71.7	3.0	74.7	−1.0
1962	21.6	66.3	− 2.9	85.0	83.0	2.5	85.5	0.5
1963	19.9	68.8	1.8	90.5	87.1	3.1	90.3	−0.3
1964	26.2	76.2	− 1.4	101.0	94.0	5.7	99.7	−1.3
1965	27.2	83.7	2.7	113.5	107.4	4.1	111.5	−2.0
1966	29.8	89.7	3.2	122.7	118.0	2.2	120.2	−2.6
1967	38.7	90.4	− 12.7	116.4	112.1	2.0	114.1	−2.3
1968	39.8	95.4	− 6.8	128.4	126.0	− 0.4	125.6	−2.8
1969	37.9	95.7	7.4	140.9	138.8	− 0.9	136.9	−4.0
1970	54.1	99.3	− 13.1	140.3	135.3	1.3	136.6	−3.7

SOURCE: *The National Income and Product Accounts of the United States, 1929–1965, Statistical Tables*, August, 1966, pp. 78–79, 149–150; *Survey of Current Business*, July, 1971, p. 33.

recent years. Note that these are merely *ex-post* accounting figures; that is, they show what did, in fact, result, but not how or why. A close study of the data for each year reveals something that may at first seem surprising: In every year, total gross saving was equal to total gross investment in the form of gross private investment and net exports, except for a statistical discrepancy which reflects problems of valuation. This was true when GNP was very low and also when it was very high. In fact, there is nothing remarkable about the *ex post* equality of S and I. It follows from our national-income accounting. We saw that, in terms of income created during any stated period, and therefore the amount of income available for disposal,

$$Y = C + I + G$$

In terms of the disposal of that income,

$$Y = C + S_p + S_b + G + S_p$$

Subtracting C and G from both equations, we get

$$I = S_p + S_b + S_g$$

or

$$I = S$$

In later chapters dealing with national-income analysis, we shall explore the behavior of consumption, saving, and investment functions and the processes through which these functions affect the level, and changes in the level, of national output and income.

SUMMARY AND CONCLUSIONS

This chapter has concerned itself largely with what is usually called "national-income accounting," showing the nature of national income (in this case GNP), the components of GNP, and some of their relationships to the total and to each other. We have devoted little attention to "national-income analysis," by which we mean the determination of the level of national income at any time and of its fluctuations through time. For example, we did not consider such questions as: "Why did Y have a particular value at a particular time, rather than a higher or lower value? Why and through what processes did Y change from one level to another?" Such questions will be discussed later.

Nevertheless, we have made many useful discoveries:

1. Expenditures for output, and only expenditures for output, create money income for the nation. Money income must, therefore, vary with the level of expenditures.

2. The income flow is a circular flow involving flows of expenditures into the market for output, into income receipts, back again into the market for output, and so on.

3. Saving and investment play crucial roles in the flow of income. Saving can be reinjected as spending for output only through investment spending. However, government dissaving is comparable to investment as an offset to private saving. Private saving can be reinjected into demand for output by government purchases in excess of its disposable income.

4. During any period, the nation as a whole can succeed in saving only an amount just equal to investment expenditures for output.

5. The government can directly affect the flow of incomes by altering its rate of expenditures for output, the amount of its tax collection at each level of Y, and its rate of transfer payments.

Appendix

Disposable personal income

The concept of disposable personal (or household) income employed in this book differs slightly from the concept of the same name in the official national-income and product accounts: Our concept is exactly the same as that appearing in the official accounts under the name, "Disposable personal income excluding interest paid by consumers and personal transfers to foreigners."

Relationships among these concepts are illustrated in the table below which gives the official accounts for the calendar year 1970.

	BILLIONS
Disposable personal income	$687.8
Less: Interest paid by consumers and personal transfers to foreigners	17.9
Equals: Disposable personal income excluding interest paid by consumers and personal transfers to foreigners	669.9
Less: Personal consumption	612.8
Equals: Personal saving	$ 57.1

SOURCE: *Survey of Current Business,* July, 1970, p. 40.

Selected readings

Ackley, G., *Macroeconomic Theory,* New York, Macmillan, 1961.

Ruggles, R., and N. D. Ruggles, *National Income Accounts and Income Analysis,* New York, McGraw-Hill, 1956.

Smith, W. L., *Macroeconomics,* Homewood, Ill., Irwin, 1970.

CHAPTER 14

AN INTRODUCTION TO MONETARY THEORY

We now turn our attention to monetary theory—to an analysis of the relationships among money and the behavior of such other economic variables as the rate of real output, levels of employment and unemployment, price levels, and levels of interest rates. A knowledge of such relationships is essential not only for those who wish to understand the overall functioning of the economy but also for those who make relevant economic policies.

MONETARY THEORY AND POLICIES

Rational policy making involves at least three essential elements:

1. Selection of objectives or ends. This is both difficult and controversial because there are many different objectives toward which monetary actions can be directed, not all of which are likely to be compatible with each other. It is therefore necessary not only to identify the possible objectives, but also to analyze and evaluate the extent to which they are or can be made compatible, to weigh against each other those that appear to be in conflict, and to make choices.

2. Design and use of instruments to promote the selected objectives. As we have already seen, the principal instruments available to the Federal Reserve are discount operations, open-market operations, and changes of reserve requirements.

3. Theory of relationships among variables. As a guide to the appropriate use of the instruments of policy making to promote its selected objectives, it must have some theory—implicit or explicit, but preferably explicit—concerning relationships among the relevant economic variables, and especially of relationships between the actions that might be taken and the effects that would flow from them, is desirable. By sheer coincidence and rare good luck, a policy maker might do the thing most conducive to the promotion of his chosen objectives, even if his actions were not guided by an explicit valid theory. But such a happy outcome would indeed be sheer coincidence and rare good luck, unlikely to be often repeated.

Some of the many ways in which theory is inescapably involved in policy making can be illustrated by an example. Suppose the Federal Reserve has selected as its dominant objectives the simultaneous promotion of continuously high levels of employment and output, the highest sustainable rate of economic growth, stability of price levels, and stability of the exchange rate on the dollar. The Federal Reserve is not empowered to control or regulate directly any of these important variables. Its powers are largely limited to actions relating to discounting, open-market operations, and reserve requirements of the banks. It is immediately involved in important theoretical questions on several levels. If it takes, or fails to take, some specific action, what will be the effects on the stock of money? On the supply of credit? On interest rates? On the behavior of aggregate money demands for output? On the responses of employment, real output, money wage rates, and prices?

It would indeed be misleading to claim that either central bankers or economists have developed fully satisfactory answers to these and many other important theoretical questions. Yet, it is clear that rational policy must be guided by some type of theory. And it is unlikely that policy can for long be better than the theory on which it is based. It is partly for this reason that we shall devote so much attention to monetary theory.

Much of our theory will deal with the effects of money and monetary policy on other economic variables in which we are interested. In effect, we shall ask: How will this specific monetary action affect such things as the aggregate demand for output, employment, real output, interest rates, and prices? How will the results differ from those that would have prevailed if this action had not been taken or if some other action had been taken? This type of analysis is highly important to the monetary authority, which must be concerned with, and be responsible for, the effects attributable to its own action or inaction.

However, monetary theory has another related but broader function, which is to analyze all the determinants, or at least the most powerful determinants, of the behavior of the economic variables in which we are interested. It is clear that the behavior of such things as employment, output, and prices is determined not by money and monetary policy alone, but also by many other forces. The monetary authority needs to understand these if its policy actions are to be appropriate. Much of monetary policy is of a defensive nature, designed to offset or compensate disturbances from other sources. If the roles of these other determinants of economic behavior are not understood, the monetary authority is not in a position to prescribe the appropriate compensating or offsetting action. More generally, we need to analyze all important determinants in order to view monetary policy in an overall context and to assess realistically the role that it can play.

ELEMENTS OF MONETARY THEORY

As will become evident in the remainder of this chapter and in several later chapters, the interrelationships analyzed by monetary theory are both numerous and highly complex. To facilitate exposition, we shall divide these into three groups:

1. Relationships between monetary policy actions and the stock or supply of money.

2. Relationships between the stock of money and aggregate demands for output.

3. Relationships between aggregate demands for output and the behavior of real output, employment, prices, and money wage rates.

It should be constantly remembered, however, that this grouping is an oversimplification in which we indulge only to facilitate exposition, and that there are interrelations among the variables in the three different categories.

The first category has already been discussed at some length. The second will command our attention in several of the chapters that follow this one. The present chapter will deal largely with the third category—responses to given changes in aggregate money-demand functions for output. It is concerned with questions such as: "Suppose that the aggregate money-demand function for output increases or decreases by some specified amount. To what extent will this be reflected in price changes? In changes in money wage rates? In the rate of real output? In the level of employment?"

Although this is but a part of aggregative theory, it is an important part, because effects on economic welfare depend heavily on response patterns. For example, it does matter whether a decline of money demands for output is reflected almost entirely in decreased price levels or largely in decreased real output and employment. And it does matter whether an increase in money demands for output is reflected solely in price inflation or in large increases in real output and employment.

It should be intuitively plausible that response patterns to a given change of aggregate money demands for output depend heavily on the structures of markets for the various types of output and labor. Suppose, for example, that conditions in every market approximated those of pure competition, in which no individual seller or buyer had any significant power to affect prices by changing the amounts he offered or purchased. Under such circumstances, prices would adjust quickly and flexibly, and each producer would adjust both his output and the amount of labor employed to the point at which his marginal cost was equal to the market price of his product. Suppose now that various types and degrees of market imperfections and monopoly power are introduced into at least some of the markets. For example, collective bargaining through unions replaces atomistic competition in labor markets, and producers achieve some degree of monopoly power through smallness of numbers in each industry, differentiation of products, explicit or implicit price collusion, and so on. Under such conditions, both prices and money wage rates are likely to be less flexible downward and perhaps also upward, and a larger part of the response to a given change in money demands for output is likely to be reflected in changes in real output and employment. However, where buyers or sellers have some degree of monopoly power, the outcome will be affected by the nature of their price-output-employment policies.

In fact, of course, structures of individual markets differ widely, and so do their response patterns. It is partly for this reason that it is so difficult to generalize about response patterns.

DEMAND AND SUPPLY

As the next step toward understanding the responses of output, employment, and prices to demand conditions and to changes in demand conditions, it will be useful to recall some aspects of general economic theory relating to the output, sales, and prices of a particular commodity that is produced and sold under conditions approximating those of pure competition. Theory tells us that these factors are all determined simultaneously by demand and supply conditions. Suppose, for example, that the demand and supply conditions for this commodity are represented by the demand function (DD) and the supply function (SS) in Figure 14–1. Price (denoted by P) is measured along the vertical axis. The quantities de-

Figure 14–1 Demand for, and supply of, a commodity

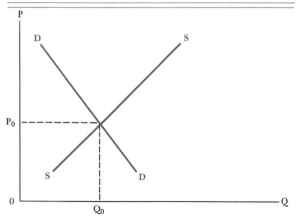

manded and supplied per period of time, such as per year, are measured along the horizontal axis (designated by Q). We find that as long as demand and supply conditions for this commodity continue to be those represented by the DD and SS curves, the market for this commodity can be in equilibrium only if the quantities actually supplied and demanded are at Q_0 and the price is P_0. Only this combination of P and Q will exactly clear the market, leaving no excess supply or excess demand.

This example illustrates at least two simple points that will be useful for our later analysis. First, market equilibrium is not determined by demand conditions alone, nor by supply conditions alone, but by a combination of both. Second, both price and the actual rate of output and sales are determined simultaneously. Thus, demand and supply conditions together determine price, rate of real output and sales, and the total money value of output and sales, P_0Q_0. If we knew more about the production functions of the industry (the amounts of the various types of inputs required to produce the various rates of output), we could also determine the quantities of productive factors employed in producing the commodity at the equilibrium rate of output Q_0.

This type of analysis is often referred to as *statics;* it involves those equilibrium, or "balance," conditions that tend to be established and maintained with static demand and supply conditions reflected in given demand and supply functions. Since we shall at times use this type of analysis, two of its characteristics should be noted: (1) Its attention is centered on equilibrium conditions; it deals with disequilibrium conditions only to show that they are unstable and cannot be maintained. And (2) it has no time dimension; it does not indicate the length of time required to achieve or to restore equilibrium. Because of miscalculation or for other reasons, price-quantity relationships can obviously depart from those of equilibrium. Yet static analysis specifies neither the time required to restore equilibrium nor the time path followed by prices and quantities before they again reach equilibrium.

The type of analysis, called *comparative statics,* compares two sets of equilibrium conditions: those existing before and after a shift of a demand or supply function. It attempts to determine how equilibrium will be changed if the demand function or the supply function shifts in a specified way. For example, we have already noted that price will remain at P_0 and actual real sales at Q_0 as long as demand and supply conditions continue to be those represented by the DD and SS curves. Suppose, as in Figure 14–2, that, for some reason, the demand function increases from DD to D_1D_1. That is, the community demands more of the commodity at each price or will pay a higher price for each quantity. This increase of the demand function will tend to raise the price, to increase the quantities actually supplied and purchased, or to raise both prices and quantities produced and sold. The actual effects of any given increase of demand will depend on supply conditions, and more specifically on the responsiveness of quantities supplied to changes in price.

Suppose supply is completely unresponsive or inelastic to price, as indicated

Figure 14–2 Shifts in demand

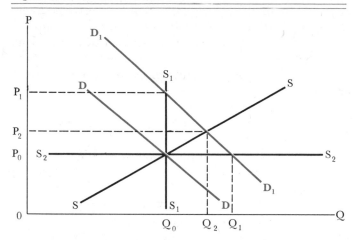

by the supply curve S_1S_1 (Figure 14–2). In this case, the entire effect of the increase in demand is to raise the price from P_0 to P_1. Quantities produced and sold and the quantities of productive factors employed in producing the commodity remain unchanged. Suppose, to go to the other extreme, that supply is completely responsive or elastic to price, as indicated by the supply function S_2S_2. That is, suppliers stand ready to supply at price P_0 any quantity that may be demanded, but will supply nothing at a lower price. In this case, the increase of demand will not raise price at all; its entire effect will be to increase quantities produced and sold and to increase the quantity of productive factors employed in producing the commodity. Usually, the responsiveness of supply to price will lie somewhere between these extremes. This is illustrated by the supply function *SS*. In these situations, an increase of demand will increase price, quantities actually produced and sold, and the quantities of productive factors employed in producing the good. The more responsive supply is to price, the less will a given increase of demand raise price, and the more will it increase quantities.

The reader will find it useful to trace the effects of a decrease of demand, such as a shift from D_1D_1 to *DD,* noting the relevance of the responsiveness of supply to the effects on price and output. He may also wish to trace the effects of a decrease of supply, by which we mean a decrease in the quantity supplied at each price, and of an increase in supply, by which we mean an increase in the quantity supplied at each price.

In the remainder of this chapter, we shall adapt this type of analysis, which was originally developed to explain the prices and output of individual commodities, to the economy as a whole. Our supply function will relate to the economy's aggregate output of goods and services, and our demand function will relate to the quantities of that output demanded at various levels of prices. However, as we adapt this kind of analysis, we shall have to alter certain assumptions relating to demand and supply functions and their relationships to each other.

In the first place, the responsiveness of supply to changes in demand and price is likely to be greater for an individual commodity than for the total output of the economy. Consider first the case of an individual commodity, such as copper, cotton shirts, or rice, which constitutes only a small part of total output and employs only a small fraction of the total labor force and other inputs. Suppose now that, starting from equilibrium conditions, the demand for the commodity rises. The first response may be to expand output by reemploying labor, capital, and other productive factors already committed to that industry. Output of the commodity can be expanded still further by drawing labor, materials, and other factors away from other industries. If this industry employs only a small fraction of the productive factors in the economy, it may be able to hire many more at no more than a modest increase in cost and to expand output greatly with only a small increase in price.

Contrast with this the responsiveness of the supply of total output. Suppose that the aggregate-demand function for total output increases. Business firms can indeed respond by using unemployed labor and unutilized capacity to expand output. But they obviously cannot expand total output further by drawing labor and other productive factors away from each other. As full employment of labor and existing capacity is approached, the responsiveness of output to demand and price necessarily becomes very low, and further increases of demand must necessarily be reflected largely in prices. What is possible for each industry singly is impossible for all together.

In the second place, it is dangerous to assume that shifts in the aggregate-demand function for total output will leave the supply function of total output unchanged. Such assumptions are usually permissible in the case of a particular commodity. Suppose, for example, that the demand function increases for a commodity that constitutes only a small fraction of total output and whose production requires only a very small fraction of the labor force and other productive factors. The rise of demand for this commodity will indeed increase this industry's demand for labor and other factors. But the rise of this demand may increase the total demand for factors so little as to have practically no effect on the general levels of money wage rates and the prices of other inputs that enter into costs of production.

Increases of the demand function for total output may have quite different effects. From branches of economic theory dealing with the pricing of inputs and the functional distribution of income, we learn that demand functions for labor and other inputs are *derived demands;* that is, demands derived from the value of the outputs produced by those factors. Firms hire or buy inputs only because they can produce output, and the amounts of inputs they will buy and the prices they will pay depend on the amounts the factors can add to the value of output.

Suppose that, starting from an equilibrium situation, there is a sharp increase in the demand function for total output and that this tends to raise the prices of output. This increase in the money value of output will raise the marginal value product of labor and other inputs and increase demand functions for these inputs. The result is likely to be increases of money wage rates and the prices of other inputs. Thus, the rise of demand for output indirectly raises wage rates and other elements of cost. Increases of prices, wage rates, and costs of production can be so interrelated as to make it almost impossible to disentangle causal relationships. To some it may appear that price increases were caused by rising costs of production; others proclaim that increases in costs were induced by rising prices for output, which in turn were induced by excessive demands for output.

In a comparable way, decreases of the demand function for output decrease demand functions for labor and other inputs. If wages and the prices of other inputs are flexible downward, cost levels will also fall. But if money wage rates and prices of other inputs will not fall, a given decrease of demand for output may be reflected fully in decreased employment of inputs.

These are only a few examples of the interrelations of aggregate-demand and supply functions. More will be encountered later.

STATICS, COMPARATIVE STATICS, AND DYNAMICS

As noted earlier, we shall rely largely on types of economic analysis known as statics and comparative statics. Two characteristics of these types of analysis should be kept in mind. First, they concentrate on equilibrium conditions. Second, they do not explicitly take time into account. They do not indicate the length of time required to reach equilibrium, or the time required to move from one set of equilibrium conditions to another, or the time path followed by variables in their journey toward equilibrium.

Another type of analysis, which we shall use very little, is called *economic dynamics*. As one writer defines it, "Economic dynamics is the study of economic phenomena in relation to preceding and succeeding events."[1] Dynamic analysis explicitly takes time into account, analyzes the process of change, and attempts to trace out the time path followed by variables. The conclusions yielded by dynamic analysis can differ from those of statics and comparative statics, but they need not. In many cases, these types of analysis supplement each other.

One type of relationship between comparative statics and dynamics can be illustrated by returning to the case already considered (see Figure 14–2) in which the demand function for a particular commodity increased from DD to D_1D_1, with the constant *long-run* supply function SS. Comparative statics indicates that the effects of the increase of demand are to raise price from P_0 to P_2, and the quantities produced and sold, from Q_0 to Q_2. However, it would be too much to expect that the adjustment will occur instantaneously or even that prices and quantities will move steadily toward the new equilibrium point. To increase quantities supplied may require time. In the first period, the quantity supplied may not increase at all, so that price rises above P_2 to P_1. But this high price will attract additional production, and as quantities supplied increase from period to period,

---

[1] W. J. Baumol, *Economic Dynamics*, 2nd ed., New York, Macmillan, 1959, p. 4.

the price will fall. Producers may even overshoot the mark and increase quantities so much as to drive price below P_2. Only later, as excess production disappears, may prices rise back toward P_2. Thus, the time required for the adjustment may be short or long, and the time path followed by the variables may be highly complex.

Ideally, we should make liberal use of dynamics as well as statics and comparative statics in our monetary theory. For one thing, time is important in monetary policy. It is not enough to know what the final effects of the monetary action will be; we would also like to know the amount of time required to achieve those effects and the time path of the responses. Moreover, monetary policy must deal with disequilibrium conditions and disequilibrating processes, such as business cycles. Although our analysis will be largely in terms of statics and comparative statics, we shall use some elements of dynamics to analyze forces that produce change and processes of change.

The following sections will illustrate, with a few simple models, some patterns of response of output, employment, and price levels of output to autonomous shifts of the aggregate-demand function for output. Unless otherwise indicated, the time period considered will be short enough to justify our assumption that the total labor supply, the available stock of capital, and the state of technology are given and constant. To facilitate our exposition, we shall use graphs of the general type depicted in Figure 14–3. Part A relates to output. The average price per unit of output, or the price level of output, is measured on the vertical axis (denoted by P). The rate of real output (O) is measured on the horizontal axis.[2] The horizontal distance O_F is of special interest because it indicates the level of output that could be achieved with full employment of labor. The line DD represents the aggregate-demand function for output, showing the quantities of real output that would be demanded at various levels of P. Several types of aggregate-supply functions will be introduced later.

Part B of Figure 14–3 relates to the supply of and demand for labor. Quantities of labor supplied and demanded are measured on the vertical axis (denoted by N). We measure N in terms of man-hours rather than in numbers of people

---

[2] In what unit is this real output measured? The usual physical measures, such as pounds, tons, gallons, barrels, or dozens are unacceptable for aggregating diverse types of output such as coal, petroleum, and eggs. For one thing, the choice of units is quite arbitrary; we could measure coal in pounds or bushels as meaningfully as in tons. Moreover, physical measurements of different commodities have little or no economic meaning. For example, a ton of gravel is usually not considered economically equivalent to a ton of rubies. For such reasons, our unit for measuring real output is that amount of each commodity that sold for $1 in some selected base period. For example, if the price of coal in the base period was $20 a ton, our unit of measurement is $\frac{1}{20}$ of a ton of coal. If the price of wheat was $3 a bushel, our unit is $\frac{1}{3}$ of a bushel of wheat, and so on. Our reason for using this unit is that quantities of the various commodities that in the base period sold for the same price must in some sense have been considered economically equivalent to each other, at least in that period. These quantities change, of course, as the relative prices of the commodities change. Since we measure real output in units of one dollar's worth in the base period, P, the average price per unit of output at any given time is the average number of dollars required to buy the quantity of output that $1 bought in the base period.

Figure 14–3 Demand functions for output and labor

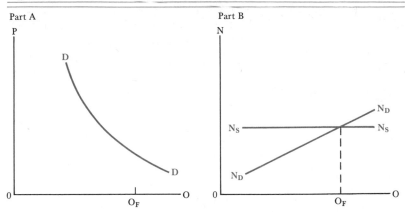

because underemployment can be reflected not only in the number of people without jobs but also in part-time unemployment. The supply of labor is assumed to be constant (indicated by the horizontal line, $N_S N_S$). The demand function for labor (indicated by the line $N_D N_D$) is a positive function of the level of output. Roughly speaking, the amount of labor demanded at each level of real output is equal to that rate of real output divided by the average real output per man-hour of work. Only at the full-employment level of output, O_F, will the quantity of labor demanded be equal to the available supply. As real output falls below O_F, the quantity of labor demanded will fall in rough proportion. This is, of course, a great oversimplification of supply and demand conditions in labor markets, but for our present limited purposes it will suffice.

SHIFTS OF MONEY DEMAND FOR OUTPUT WITH OUTPUT COMPLETELY UNRESPONSIVE

It will be convenient to start with a model in which an upward shift of the demand function for output, stated in terms of money, leads only to changes in the price level, not to significant changes in the level of output or employment.

Increase in demand for output

One case in which these results are approximated is that in which there is an upward shift of the demand function for output when the economy is already operating at practically "capacity levels." This is illustrated in Figure 14–4. Suppose we start from a situation in which the demand function is DD and the rate of output is at the full-employment level, O_F. The price level is P_0 and the value of national income is $P_0 O_F$. Suppose now that, because of an increase in the money supply, or for any other reason, the demand function for output doubles in the sense that the community becomes willing to pay twice as high a price for each level of output. This is indicated by the upward shift of the demand curve

Figure 14–4 Shifts of demand with supply unresponsive

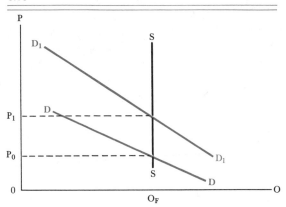

from DD to D_1D_1. The supply of output must be unresponsive to the rise of demand and prices because it was already at its full-employment level. The effect must therefore be to double the price level of output, raising it from P_0 to P_1. The total money value of output or income must also double, rising from P_0O_F to P_1O_F.

We may be sure that such a rise in demands for output and in the prices of output will be accompanied by increases in money wage rates and in the prices paid for the use of other productive factors, because the demand for these factors is based on the money value of their output. The rise of money wages may occur quickly or slowly, but it will occur as employers, enjoying a marked increase in the prices of their output, bid against each other for labor and other productive factors. If these rises occur very rapidly and closely parallel the rise in the prices of output, the community may engage in bitter arguments as to whether the increase in prices caused the rise of costs, or vice versa.

This phenomenon of rising prices with no change in real output or real income may be called *pure price inflation*. Such an inflation cannot harm everybody in the community, because the total real income or output available for sharing remains unchanged, and the stock of real wealth in the form of land, buildings, equipment, and other improvements is not diminished. But pure price inflation can bring about important shifts in the distribution of real income and wealth. When the price level doubles, all those whose money incomes fail to double suffer a decrease in their real purchasing power over income goods. Those whose money incomes remain constant lose half of their real incomes. Among the many types of money income that remain constant while price levels change are: interest on debt holdings, building or land rentals fixed by long-term contracts, and pensions and annuities. Some other types of money income may rise, but at a lower rate than the rise of prices. Among these are likely to be salaries of government employees, teachers, and employees of religious and charitable institutions. On the other hand, those whose money incomes rise more rapidly than prices gain real income. Among these are likely to be recipients of business profits and highly volatile types of wages.

It is difficult to generalize about the behavior of money wage rates in periods of pure price inflation. In some periods they have lagged seriously behind the rise of prices, so that real wages fell during the period of the lag. More recently, however, labor has found ways of reducing or eliminating the lag; it has used escalator clauses and other devices to increase wages as fast as prices rise. Nevertheless, some types of wages and salaries still lag.

Pure price inflation also redistributes real wealth. If the price of an asset rises at a lesser rate than the general level of prices, its holder loses real purchasing power. If an asset's price remains constant, its purchasing power is reduced by half when the price level doubles. Among such assets are money itself; savings accounts; mortgages, bonds, and other debt obligations; and accrued values of annuities and life insurance policies. Huge amounts of wealth are held in these forms and are subject to erosion by inflation. On the other hand, some assets will increase in real purchasing power because their price increases at a greater rate than the general price level. Among these assets are likely to be ownership claims against real estate, commodities, and business firms. In times of inflation, gains are likely to be especially large for those owners who are heavily in debt, because they can repay their debts with dollars that have lost part of their purchasing power. It is small wonder that creditors and debtors have different attitudes towards inflation.

Decrease in demand for output

Let us turn now to the reverse case, in which the demand function for output shifts downward. Suppose that we start from a situation in which the demand functions for output is D_1D_1, the rate of real output is at the capacity level O_F, and the price level is P_1. Suppose now that the demand function falls by half, in the sense that the community is now willing to pay only half as much for each rate of output. This is shown in Figure 14–4 as a downward shift of the demand function from D_1D_1 to DD. Are the results likely to be *pure price deflation* with no significant decline of either real output or employment? Under the conditions that actually prevail in markets for labor and output this is most unlikely; all three elements (price, output, and employment) are likely to fall, and a major part of the response may be in the form of decreases in output and employment. We shall return to this case after investigating the "classical model," which assumed, among other things, complete flexibility of money wage rates and prices.

THE CLASSICAL MODEL

John Maynard Keynes applied the term "classical" to those economists who dominated economic thought, at least in England and the United States, from the latter part of the 19th century until the early 1930s. It is difficult to describe precisely and fairly the economic theory and policy prescriptions of the members of this school, partly because there was not full agreement among them and partly because some aspects of their theory were not developed fully and clearly. However, the following description indicates at least the general nature of their arguments and conclusions. Two of their major conclusions were:

1. A free-enterprise economy contains within itself strong forces toward the achievement and maintenance of full employment. These forces serve to prevent departures from full employment, and any unemployment that may occur invokes automatic adjustments that restore full employment. Equilibrium at less than full employment is impossible.

2. Changes in the level of money expenditures for output do affect price levels, but are not important determinants of the behavior of output and employment.

One line of reasoning behind these conclusions was expressed in Say's Law—the idea that "supply creates its own demand." In one interpretation, this is simply an identity, quite similar to the income-accounting identity discussed earlier:

Value of output = sum of income shares accruing to all claimants

Thus, the value of output creates enough income to buy all the output if all of the income is returned to the market as demands for output. An identity does not, of course, argue that this will in fact occur. However, the classical economists made the behavioral assumption that all income would be spent for output. They considered hoarding of money to be irrational because it seemed to them that a rational person would not use any part of his money income to increase his money balances. Instead they thought that he would spend some part for goods and services for consumption purposes, and that even the part that he saved would not be hoarded, but would either be spent for investment or loaned to others. Market rates of interest would adjust in such a way as to equate saving and investment. For example, any tendency of saving to exceed investment would lead to a fall of interest rates. In response to this, income receivers would consume more and save less, and more would be spent for investment.

Say's Law, even if valid, states only that a level of real output or income that is achieved will tend to be maintained; it does not state that this must be a full-employment level of output. However, the classical economists added the further argument that price and wage adjustments in output and labor markets would force output and employment toward full-employment levels.

Three basic assumptions are essential for the operation of the classical model:

1. All markets for output and labor are purely competitive and all enterprises seek to maximize their profits.

2. Decisions relating to output and employment are not based on absolute levels of prices and money wage rates; instead, they are based on relative wages and prices. Thus, each producer bases his output decisions not on the absolute price of his product, but on its price relative to its cost. In equilibrium, his production is such that the price of his product is equal to marginal cost. Equipro-

portionate changes of price and of his marginal-cost function will not alter his equilibrium rate of output. The quantity of labor demanded by an employer does not depend on the absolute money wage rate, but on the level of wages relative to the marginal value product of labor. Equiproportionate changes of money wage rates and of the marginal value product of labor will not affect the quantity of labor demanded. Similarly, the quantities of labor supplied depend not on the absolute level of money wage rates, but on real wages or real money wage rates. We shall designate this by W/P. The supply of labor was assumed to be a positive function of W/P. Note that the quantity of labor supplied is assumed to be unaffected by equiproportionate changes of money wage rates and the price level.

3. Both prices of output and money wage rates are perfectly flexible and can fluctuate both upward and downward. They change to the extent necessary to secure equilibrium levels of relative prices and wages.

Let us now see how such wage and price flexibility, under the market conditions described above, was supposed to remedy any departure from full employment. We start from a situation in which the money-demand function for output is at some level that produces full employment and equilibrium relationships between prices and money wage rates. Now, suppose that the money-demand function for output shifts downward. In competitive markets this will lower prices of the various types of output. Producers will eliminate those parts of their output whose marginal costs now exceed their lowered prices. The fall of prices also lowers the marginal value product of labor, leading employers to decrease the quantity of labor demanded at the old level of money wage rates. Some unemployment will occur, at least initially. However, the unemployed will bid against each other for jobs, thereby lowering money wage rates. Such decreases of money wage rates lower money costs of production, including marginal costs, and with each decrease of their marginal costs, producers lower the prices of their output. Such declines of money wage rates and prices will continue so long as unemployment persists.

Is it inevitable that decreases in money wage rates and prices will again make it profitable for producers to employ the entire labor supply? A decrease of money wage rates has at least two types of effects. On the one hand, as we have already seen, it serves to lower costs of production. This appears favorable to an expansion of output and employment. On the other hand, it lowers the amount of money income received by labor for each hour of work. Thus it is possible, at least in principle, that the favorable effects of reductions in money costs of production will be fully offset by reductions of money demands for output. The classical economists contended that this would not occur; the deflationary spiral of money wage rates and prices would be stopped and recovery of real output and employment would be induced by a phenomenon that has been called variously "the Pigou effect," "the real-balance effect," and "the real-wealth effect." The real-wealth effect is based on two propositions:

1. Real demands for output depend not only on real income, but also on real wealth. The latter is defined as (*money value of assets*/price level) . Thus, it

can be increased either by a rise of assets in money terms or by a fall in the price level. In general, the greater the community's real wealth, the greater will be the level of its real consumption relative to its real income.

2. A fall of the price level raises the real wealth or purchasing power of the community's assets that are fixed in terms of monetary units. No net expansionary effect may result from the rise of purchasing power of debts owed by the private sector and held in the private sector. Holders of these claims are indeed made wealthier in real terms, but the private debtors are made poorer. There remain, however, debt claims against the government that are held directly or indirectly by the private sector. The government's expenditures may not be affected by the increase of its real debt. But members of the private sector, feeling richer in real terms because of the increased purchasing power of their claims against the government, increase their real demands for output, thereby pushing output and employment back toward full-employment levels.

Such are the processes through which, in the classical model, any departure from full employment was supposed to generate forces that would automatically return the economy to full employment. Note the key role of the downward flexibility of wages and prices in this process. It both adjusts relative wages and prices to equilibrium levels and creates the real-wealth effects that end the deflationary spiral and induce real recovery.

However, the automatic forces might not restore full employment even if pure competition prevailed in all markets for output and labor and all money wage rates and prices were fully flexible downward.

1. The real-wealth effect may be too weak to overcome unfavorable forces. Small declines of prices and wages are likely to generate only weak expansionary effects, and very large declines may generate depressing effects that outweigh their expansionary effects.

2. Price declines may generate price expectations that are unfavorable to recovery of demands for output. Effects are likely to be favorable if consumers are confident that a price decline will be followed later by price increases. However, effects will be unfavorable if each price decline creates expectations of still further price decreases in the future, because potential buyers will be encouraged to postpone their purchases. This applies especially to consumer's durable goods and to capital goods.

3. The process of price deflation decreases the net worth and creditworthiness of business firms and may discourage investment. As both their money incomes and the prices of their assets fall, business firms with outstanding debts suffer at least some deterioration in their net worth positions, and some are forced into bankruptcy. Unfortunately, their reduction of capital makes them less willing to undertake investment projects and less able to secure funds from others on acceptable terms.

In summary, even in an economy conforming to all the assumptions of the classical model, there would be no assurance that automatic forces would restore full employment reliably, quickly, and at minimum social cost. However, actual conditions and policies in markets for labor and output depart significantly from those assumed in the classical model.

DEPARTURES FROM THE CLASSICAL MODEL

Rigid money wages

It will be remembered that the classical model assumed that the supply of labor was a function of real wages rather than money wage rates, and that wage rates were freely flexible both upward and downward. As one looks at labor markets in the United States and other industrialized countries, he is forced to conclude that these conditions are not met. Money wage rates are often rigid, sometimes for long periods. For example, when unemployment appears or increases in amount, money wage rates do not fall, or they begin to fall only after a long delay. On the other hand, even large increases in demands for labor often fail to raise money wage rates, or raise them only after a considerable delay, especially if there remains a significant amount of unemployment.

Let us see how the conclusions of the classical model are altered if we drop the classical assumptions concerning the behavior of labor and assume that money wages are rigid, at least during the period under consideration. In Figure 14–5, the money wage rate is shown on the vertical axis and the amount of employment is shown on the horizontal axis. The line WW represents the supply function of labor with perfectly rigid wages; labor will be supplied at the prevailing money wage, but none at a lower wage. It is implicitly assumed that all markets for output are purely competitive and that enterprises attempt to maximize their profits. Each enterprise produces up to the point at which the price of its product is equal to its marginal cost. And each hires labor up to the point at which the marginal value product of labor is equal to its wage rate. The marginal value product of labor $[(MPL)P]$ is the marginal product of labor *times* the price of each unit of the marginal product of labor.

Suppose we start with the situation in which the aggregate-demand function

Figure 14–5 Rigid wages

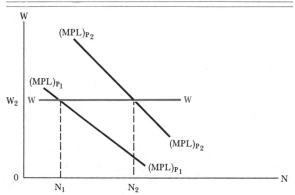

for output, stated in money terms, is such as to yield the price level for output P_2. The marginal value product of labor function is represented by the line $(MPL) P_2$. The amount of employment of labor will be N_2, which will produce some level of total output (not shown) O_2. Suppose now that, because of a reduction of the nominal money supply or for any other reason, the aggregate demand function for output, stated in terms of money, declines so much as to lower the price level of output from P_2 to P_1. The effect will be to lower the level of employment from N_2 to N_1, and to reduce the level of real output. The reason for this can be stated two ways. Stating it in real terms, we can say that the fall of the price level from P_2 to P_1, while the money wage rate remained rigid, increased the real wage from W/P_2 to W/P_1, which reduced the quantity of labor demanded. Or, stating it in money terms, we can say that the fall of prices shifted downward and to the left the $(MPL) P$ function, which is the demand function for labor. With the money wage rate rigid, less labor is demanded.

Thus, the effects in the model with rigid wage rates differ markedly from those in the classical model. A shift of the aggregate-demand function for output, stated in terms of money, can indeed change the level of employment and real output. Moreover, once a decline of output and employment has been induced by a decrease of the aggregate demand for output, there are in this model no forces that automatically tend to restore output and employment to their full-employment levels. The result is what Keynes called an "underemployment equilibrium."

On the other hand, a rise of money demands for output can increase employment and real output. Suppose that, starting from a situation in which the price level is P_1 and the level of employment is N_1, money demands for output rise enough to raise the price level from P_1 to P_2 (refer to Figure 14–5). The demand function for labor will increase from $(MPL) P_1$ to $(MPL) P_2$ and employment will rise from N_1 to N_2 if the money wage rate remains constant. However, we shall see later that wage rates may begin to rise before full employment is reached.

Rigidity of prices of output

We found in the preceding section that rigidity of wage rates can limit the flexibility of prices even if all markets for output meet all the requirements of pure competition. When we relax the assumption that all output markets are purely competitive and recognize various types and degrees of *imperfect competition* and monopoly power, we find still other limitations on price flexibility. The imperfections of competition emanate from several sources—from a scarcity of sellers, from explicit or implicit collusion among sellers, from differentiated rather than homogeneous products, and so on.

Such imperfections of competition have at least one effect in common: They give each seller some degree of control over the price of his product. Under pure competition, the individual seller has no such power; he faces a perfectly elastic demand function for his output at the prevailing market price. However, the individual seller under conditions of imperfect competition does not face a perfectly elastic demand function for his output; he faces a downward-sloping demand curve. The price that he can get depends in part on how much he offers for sale. He can, therefore, to some degree, set and administer a price policy. He can maintain a high price, but only at the cost of restricting the quantities that he sells. Or he can sell more, but only by lowering his price. He also has some power to determine, in response to a shift of the demand function for his output, the extent to which he will respond by changing his price and the extent to which he will respond by changing his output.

To illustrate this, let us assume that, starting from an equilibrium situation, there occurs a downward shift of the aggregate-demand function for output, and that a part of this decrease is seen by sellers in imperfectly competitive markets as decreased demand functions for their respective outputs. Each faces this set of questions: "How should I respond? How should I adjust my prices, if at all? What are the implications for the quantity that I can sell?" If the objective of each seller is to maximize profits, the answer will depend heavily on his estimate of the price elasticity of the demand function that he now faces. If he estimates the price elasticity of demand to be very high, he will be impelled to reduce prices to reap the benefits of much larger sales. However, if he thinks that the price elasticity of demand for his product is low he will consider it more profitable to maintain his price rather than to cut it and reap only a small increase in sales. Unfortunately, many such sellers estimate the price elasticity of demand for their products to be low. This is in part because they believe or fear that price decreases by them would be at least matched by their rivals. They reason this way: "It would indeed be profitable for me to cut my price if my competitors would leave theirs unchanged. In that case I could increase my sales greatly by taking business away from them. However, I fear (or know) that if this happened they would respond by matching, or more than matching, my price cuts, which would end my competitive advantage. We could all sell some more at a lower price, but the price elasticity of demand for the output of all of us together is so low as to make a general price cut unprofitable for all of us. So I won't cut my prices."

Such imperfections of competition contribute importantly to the inflexibility of prices in response to decreases in aggregate-demand functions for output. This is not to say that such prices are completely inflexible downward in such situations. They do fall, especially if the decrease of demands is large and prolonged. However, price decreases are often long delayed and limited in extent. One effect is that a given decline of aggregate-demand functions for output is reflected to a greater extent in decreased employment and output. Another is that the delay and limited extent of price decreases limits the efficacy of downward price flexibility as a means of increasing real wealth and of raising real aggregate demands for output.

Just as imperfections of competition delay and limit downward price flexibility, they can also decrease the extent to which a given upward shift of aggregate-demand functions for output will be reflected in price increases. This is especially true when large numbers of firms are operating far below capacity levels. Under such conditions, upward shifts of demand functions are often reflected largely in increases of output and employment rather than in price increases. One reason for this is that output can be increased with little increase in marginal cost. Another is that sellers desist from increasing their prices for fear that their competitors will not follow suit. However, this fear usually diminishes as output approaches capacity levels.

Some policy implications

If actual conditions in the economy corresponded to those assumed in the classical model, it would not be wholly unreasonable to argue that monetary policies, fiscal policies, and other deliberate measures to control the behavior of aggregate money demands for output are of relatively little importance. Fluctuations of aggregate demands for output would change price levels and money wage rates but not employment and real output. The complete flexibility of wages and prices might be relied on to restore full employment. However, even under these conditions, measures to regulate aggregate money demands for output could improve the functioning of the economic system. For one thing, the required adjustments of prices and money wage rates could not be achieved instantaneously; they would require time. Monetary and fiscal policies might do the job faster. Also, pure price inflation and deflation have their evils; they redistribute real wealth and income, often in inequitable ways.

The case for deliberate management of aggregate money demands for output becomes compelling in an economy with many imperfections of competition in output and labor markets, with money wage rates that are rigid or adjust only after a long delay and then to only a limited extent, and with incompletely flexible prices. In such an economy, fluctuations of aggregate money demands for output affect not only prices and money wage rates but also employment and output. In addition, it can not be expected that a departure from full employment will be corrected automatically, quickly, and effectively by quick and complete flexibility of prices and money wage rates.

In such an economy, monetary, fiscal, and other policies that regulate aggregate money demand for output can indeed be used to regulate total employment and output. For example, an increase of aggregate demand can increase total employment and output if the economy is operating below capacity levels. As a part of the process of adjustment, it can adjust real wage rates to equilibrium levels; to the extent that money wage rates are rigid, real wages can be lowered by increases of demand that raise prices.

To say that output and employment can be regulated by the control of aggregate money demands for output is not to say that this method can make total output and employment behave optimally or that it can simultaneously achieve optimum behavior of output, employment, or price levels. For one thing, control of aggregate demand is not that precise. Also, relationships between aggregate-demand functions and the behavior of supply functions of labor and output may not be conducive to the simultaneous achievement of full employment and price-level stability. We turn now to some of these issues.

COMPATIBILITY OF OBJECTIVES

Since World War II, authorities charged with responsibility for regulating aggregate demand have commonly pursued at least two objectives simultaneously: full employment and stability of price levels. For example, Federal Reserve officials have often stated that their major domestic objectives are to promote the highest sustainable rate of economic growth, continuously low levels of unemployment, and reasonable stability in the purchasing power of the dollar. This immediately raises questions relating to the compatibility of these multiple objectives. Are employment and price-level objectives fully compatible in practice? Will the level of aggregate demand required for an optimum behavior of output also produce an optimum behavior of price levels? If the objectives are incompatible, what are the "trade-offs"? For example, to lower unemployment by a percentage point, how much would it cost in terms of price increases? Or to reduce price increases by some stated amount, how much would it cost in terms of increased unemployment? Most of the answers to these questions are to be found in the relationships between the level of aggregate demand, and changes in this level, and the behavior of the supplies of labor and output.

The conditions most favorable to compatibility of price-level stability and very low levels of unemployment are the following:

1. The average level of money wage rates does not rise so long as there remains any significant amount of unemployment in the economy. Any excess supplies of labor in some sectors flow freely into sectors with excess demand for labor, and no general increase of wage rates occurs until the pool of unemployed has been virtually exhausted. This would require a high degree of mobility of labor. Also, it would be necessary for the existence of unemployed labor to act as an effective brake on wage increases. The absence of wage increases would serve to prevent an upward shift of cost-of-production functions.

2. Sellers of output raise their prices only to the extent necessary to match increases in their marginal costs as they expand production. They may indeed encounter rising marginal costs as they push employment and output toward their full-employment levels, even though the prices of labor and other inputs do not rise. This is because of diminishing marginal productivity of labor as more labor is used with a virtually constant stock of capital and natural resources, recourse to less productive labor and less efficient capital equipment, and so on. However, if price increases do not exceed such increases of marginal costs, a high degree of price stability may be compatible with a very low level of unemployment.

Price stability and low levels of unemployment become less compatible as responses in labor and output markets depart from the patterns described above.

1. Wage rates begin to rise while there is still a considerable amount of unemployment and rise faster as unemployment declines. The existence of an excess supply of labor is not an effective brake on wage increases. One reason for this is the limited mobility of labor. For such reasons as ignorance of employment op-

portunities elsewhere, unwillingness to move to other areas, lack of requisite skills, race discrimination, and limitations on freedom of entry, the unemployed may fail to move to areas of excess demands for labor. Thus, workers in areas of excess demand can get wage increases more easily. Another related reason is the lack of pure competition in labor markets. Typically, each worker does not bargain individually, taking whatever wage he feels is necessary for him to get a job. Instead, workers bargain collectively for groups including all in a skill, a plant, a company, or an industry. Rarely, if ever, does a bargaining group have the objective of setting wages at such a level as to provide employment for all workers in the economy. Each group is concerned with its own welfare and may demand and get wage increases even though many would-be workers remain unemployed.

2. Sellers of output increase prices more than enough to match increases in their marginal costs. As demands for their output increase, at least some sellers with a degree of monopoly power find it most profitable to raise their prices by a greater amount than the increase in their marginal costs.

Because of such behavior patterns in labor and output markets, attempts to achieve, simultaneously, low levels of unemployment and a high degree of price stability by regulating aggregate demand for output present serious policy problems. A higher rate of increase of aggregate demand to promote output and employment brings a higher rate of increase of money wages and prices, while a lower rate of increase of aggregate demand to promote price stability has its cost in terms of a lower rate of increase of employment and real output.

Unhappiness about such "trade-offs" has led to widespread interest in measures to improve behavior patterns in labor and output markets. Virtually everyone is now agreed that achievement of acceptable behavior of output, employment, and price levels requires appropriate control of the aggregate demand for output through monetary and fiscal policies. However, many now believe that control of aggregate demand needs to be supplemented by measures aimed at improving the supply function of output—measures that will increase the extent to which a given increase of demand will increase real output rather than prices. Various measures for this purpose have been proposed. One such program aims at improving the mobility of labor by improved employment exchanges and more widely disseminated information about employment opportunities, assistance in moving to areas where employment opportunities exist, job training and retraining, elimination of racial discrimination in employment, lowering of barriers to entry, and so on. Among the objectives of this program are to open "labor bottlenecks," to lessen the extent to which unemployment and excess demand for labor can coexist, and to lower the rate of wage increases while considerable amounts of unemployment persist.

Other measures are aimed at compelling or persuading those in labor and output markets to use their monopoly power more responsibly. These measures have been given various names, such as "wage-price guidelines" in the United States and "the incomes policy" in Great Britain. Their general nature is indicated by the wage-price guidelines adopted by the Council of Economic Advisers in the early 1960s, but abandoned during the Vietnam War. The general principle of the wage guideline was that annual increases in money wage rates should be equal to the average annual increase in output per man-hour in the economy as a whole. For example, if average output per man-hour in the entire economy rose by 3 percent a year, it would be appropriate for money wages to rise by the same percentage. This means that labor cost per unit of output would remain unchanged in industries where the increase in labor productivity was equal to the economy-wide average, would fall where the rise of productivity was above average, and would rise where the rise of productivity was below average. Exceptions to this general wage guideline were envisaged. For example, larger wage increases would be appropriate where the guideline wage was not high enough to attract sufficient labor or where this wage was "inequitably low."

The general principle of the price guideline is that prices should be changed only by a percentage equal to the change in labor cost per unit of output. This means that prices would remain unchanged where the rise of labor productivity was equal to the national average, would fall where the rise of productivity was above the national average, and would rise where the rise of productivity was below the national average.

Although the old wage-price guidelines were abandoned in the late 1960s during the inflation associated with the Vietnam War, conditions in 1970 and the first 7½ months of 1971 created demands that something be done to reconcile the objectives of high employment and price stability in a more satisfactory way. By the early months of 1970, what had previously been a clear case of "demand-pull inflation" had become largely a "cost-push inflation." While unemployment was at excessive levels and excess plant capacity was evident, money wage rates rose far faster than productivity, labor costs per unit of output were increasing, and price inflation continued. During the summer of 1971, prices rose at an annual rate of about 5 percent, while the unemployment rate hovered around 6 percent. Under these conditions, there were widespread proposals that "something be done," such as restoring some type of wage-price guidelines or establishing a wage-price review board. Until August 15, President Nixon flatly rejected all such proposals. Then, in a dramatic reversal, he imposed a 90-day freeze on wages, prices, and rents. This was followed in mid-November by "Phase II," which provided more flexible government controls over increases of wages, prices, and rents.

These controls were still in effect in early 1972, but at that time it was impossible to predict how long they would remain in effect, how successful they would prove to be with the passage of time, or what their sequel would be. One should not be surprised, however, if some type of direct intervention in wage- and price-making processes persists long after Phase II is ended.

CONCLUSIONS

This chapter has had only a limited objective: to explore the effects of changes in the aggregate money demand for output on such variables as the rate of real output, employment, and prices. There was no attempt to explain either the behavior of aggregate demand or complex interactions among the variables. These will be subjects of later chapters.

Selected readings

Ackley, G., *Macroeconomic Theory,* New York, Macmillan, 1961.

Bowen, W. G., *The Wage-Price Issue: A Theoretical Analysis,* Princeton, N.J., Princeton University Press, 1960.

Smith, W. L., *Macroeconomics,* Homewood, Ill., Irwin, 1970.

CHAPTER 15

QUANTITY THEORIES

The preceding chapter explored the responses of such economic variables as employment, output, and price levels to changes in aggregate money demands for output, but did not analyze the behavior of the latter. Now we turn our attention to an analysis of the determinants of aggregate money demands for output, which will usually be stated as flows of money expenditures at annual rates. We shall arrive at what may be called a synthetic or eclectic theory, which is a combination of two branches of theory, each of which has a long history. One is the quantity theory, which in its analysis of flows of money expenditures concentrates on the supply (stock) of money and the demand for money balances. Variants of this approach have been used for hundreds of years. The other is the income and expenditure approach, which analyzes expenditure flows in terms of consumption, saving, and investment. Elements of this approach also have deep roots in the history of economic thought, but they were not combined into a coherent model until the publication, in 1936, of John Maynard Keynes' monumental *General Theory of Employment, Interest and Money*. A combination of these two approaches will highlight four functions as determinants of aggregate demand for output: (1) the supply function of money, (2) the demand function for money balances, (3) the supply function of saving, and (4) the investment demand function for output. Equilibrium can exist only if two conditions are met simultaneously: The demand for money balances is equal to the money supply, and investment demand is equal to the supply of saving.

This chapter will concentrate on the quantity-theory approach.

THE NATURE OF QUANTITY THEORIES

As might be expected, in view of their long history and widespread use, quantity theories have appeared in many versions, differing in terminology, in degree of sophistication, and in the relative weights attached to the different variables. However, all versions have had at least two characteristics in common: They all consider the quantity (stock) of money to be a significant determinant of the rate of flow of money expenditures; and they all face the problem of explaining the linkage between the stock of money on the one hand and the rate of money flows on the other. Only the most naive persons failed to distinguish between stocks and flows or assumed that some law of nature decreed a constant ratio of flows to stocks. Some versions of the quantity theory have been concerned with expenditure flows in the most comprehensive sense, including all money expenditures for other things. For the reasons indicated earlier, we shall use an income variant, including only money expenditures for output. These expenditures are represented by GNP at current prices.

Two principal concepts have been used to express the linkage between the stock of money and the flow of money expenditures. One is the "velocity of money"—in this case the "income velocity of money." This is the average number of times each dollar of the money stock is spent for output during a year. To facilitate exposition, those who employ this approach often begin with an identity:

$$MV = OP = Y \qquad \text{Identity} \qquad (1)$$

where M = the stock of money
           V = the income velocity of money; the average number of times per year that each dollar of M is spent for output
           O = real output, stated at an annual rate
           P = average price per unit of output or the price level of output
           $Y = OP$ = GNP at current prices

This is often called a *Fisherine type of equation* because a similar type was used by Irving Fisher, the great Yale economist. Note that this is not a "theory"; it is only an identity asserting the necessary *ex post* equality between the flow of expenditures for output (MV) and the money value of output purchased by that flow (OP or Y).

The other concept used to express the linkage between the stock of money and the flow of money expenditures is the "demand for money balances." Users of this concept also employ an identity to facilitate exposition:

$$M = KOP = KY \qquad \text{Identity} \qquad (2)$$

where $M, O, P,$ and Y are defined as in (1)

$K =$ fraction of OP that the community demands to hold in the form of money balances

This is often called the *Cambridge equation* because it was used by Alfred Marshall and other economists at Cambridge University. The left side of the equation shows the supply (stock) of money; the right side depicts the quantity of money balances demanded (KOP). The K on the right side, often called the *Marshallian K*, states the demand for money balances as a fraction of the nation's annual money income or expenditures for output. For example, if $K = \frac{1}{4}$, the community demands to hold money balances equal to $\frac{1}{4}$ of its annual rate of expenditures for output.

Arithmetically, V and K are reciprocals; that is, $V = 1/K$ and $K = 1/V$. For example, if $V = 4$, $K = \frac{1}{4}$. If we divide the Fisherine equation by $1/V$ we get the Cambridge equation, $M = (1/V)\,Y$, or $M = KY$. And if we divide the Cambridge equation by $1/K$ we get the Fisherine equation, $M\,(1/K) = Y$, or $MV = Y$.

Table 15–1 shows the behavior of V and K during recent decades. Column (3) shows the behavior of income velocity, which is simply GNP/M. Column (4) shows the behavior of K, which is $M/$GNP, or $1/V$. This equation assumes that in each year the public had adjusted its money balances to desired levels relative to GNP. During the Great Depression and World War II, V had fallen by nearly half from its level in the late 1920s; it was still low by historical standards in 1947. Since that time it has shown a marked upward trend, rising from 2.07 in 1947 to 4.64 in 1970. K has shown a marked downward trend, falling from more than 48 percent of GNP in 1947 to less than 22 percent in 1970. Thus, V and K are not constant through time, but neither do they fluctuate widely over short periods. In general, V declines or rises less rapidly during recessions and rises more rapidly during periods of prosperity. Some of the reasons for this will be discussed later.

It should be emphasized that both the Fisherine and Cambridge equations are only identities; they express only the necessary *ex post* equalities between the left and right sides of the equations. They do not explain how expenditure flows behave, nor why. To arrive at a theory of the behavior of expenditure flows we must analyze the determinants of the behavior of M and of K or V.

The behavior of V and K is determined by the choices of the community, not by the monetary authority. Even if the latter has firm control of the stock of money, the community is free to decide its rate of expenditures relative to M. In terms of the velocity approach, members of the community may elect to hold money balances only briefly before spending them, in which case V will be high. Or, they may elect to hold money balances longer before spending, which will be

Table 15–1 The income velocity of money and ratio of the money supply to GNP (money values in billions of dollars)

CALENDAR YEAR	(1) GNP AT CURRENT PRICES	(2) AVERAGE MONEY SUPPLY*	(3) INCOME VELOCITY OF MONEY [(1) ÷ (2)]	(4) RATIO OF MONEY SUPPLY TO GNP [(2) ÷ (1)]
1947	$231.3	$111.8	2.07	0.483
1948	257.6	112.3	2.29	0.437
1949	256.5	111.2	2.31	0.433
1950	284.8	114.1	2.50	0.400
1951	328.4	119.2	2.76	0.362
1952	345.5	125.2	2.76	0.362
1953	364.6	128.3	2.84	0.352
1954	364.8	131.3	2.78	0.360
1955	398.0	134.4	2.96	0.338
1956	419.2	136.0	3.08	0.325
1957	441.1	136.8	3.22	0.311
1958	447.3	138.4	3.23	0.310
1959	483.7	143.3	3.38	0.296
1960	503.7	141.6	3.56	0.281
1961	520.1	143.9	3.61	0.277
1962	560.3	147.0	3.81	0.262
1963	590.5	151.3	3.90	0.256
1964	632.4	157.2	4.02	0.249
1965	684.9	163.8	4.18	0.239
1966	749.9	171.0	4.39	0.228
1967	793.9	177.8	4.47	0.224
1968	864.2	190.4	4.54	0.224
1969	929.1	201.8	4.60	0.217
1970	974.1	210.0	4.64	0.216

* Average money supply in annual average of daily figures.
SOURCE: *Economic Report of the President*, February, 1971; *Federal Reserve Bulletin*, December, 1970, and various other issues.

reflected in a lower V. In terms of the K approach, members of the community may choose to hold only small balances relative to their rate of expenditures, which will be reflected in a high rate of expenditures relative to the stock of money. Or they may choose to hold larger balances relative to their expenditures, in which case Y will be smaller relative to M. A major concern of monetary theory is to analyze and explain the behavior of V or K. We shall use the latter concept, couching our analysis in terms of the supply function of money and the demand function for money balances.

In broad outline, we shall argue as follows:

1. The rate of expenditures for output depends on both the supply function of money and the demand function for money balances.

2. The rate of expenditures can be in equilibrium only if the demand for money balances is exactly equal to the supply of money available for holding.

3. If the supply of money exceeds demanded balances, members of the community try to dispose of the excess supply by increasing their rate of expenditures for other things.

4. If actual balances are below the demanded level, they try to repair the deficiency by decreasing their rate of expenditures.

SUPPLY OF MONEY

Since the money supply has already been discussed at some length, only a few comments will be added here. Unless otherwise indicated, the following sections will assume that the size of the stock of money is firmly and precisely controlled by the monetary authority, and that M is not allowed to respond passively to increases or decreases in demands for money balances. In short, M is a policy-determined independent variable. One consequence of this assumption is that to achieve equilibrium, the demand for money must be brought into equality with the available supply by means of adjustments in the quantities demanded. Excesses of the supply of money over the demand for it must be eradicated by developments that increase the quantity demanded. And excesses of quantities demanded over the available supply must be corrected by some sort of development lowering the quantity demanded.

It should be recognized, however, that the assumption that the monetary authority has and exercises precise control over the size of M is in some cases unrealistic. For one thing, the Federal Reserve may be unable to control the size of M precisely, even if it tries to do so. There may be slippages between the instruments under its control—open-market operations, discount policy, and member-bank reserve requirements—and the size of M. Also, the intermediate policy guide that dominates Federal Reserve actions may not be that of achieving a certain size or rate of change of M, but rather a specified behavior of some other economic variable, such as interest rates. For example, the objective may be to stabilize interest rates, or to achieve some other pattern of behavior of interest rates. In such cases the Federal Reserve would have to allow M to respond to the extent necessary to achieve its other intermediate objectives, and M would itself be determined, at least in part, by factors determining the behavior of demands for money balances. Some cases in which M is allowed to respond passively will be treated later.

DEMAND FOR MONEY

The theory of the demand for money balances is best viewed as but one part of the theory of choice in the allocation of scarce resources. Each member of the community has at his command only limited resources in the form of current income and total accumulated assets. He must, therefore, make choices concerning their allocation. If he chooses more consumption, he must hold fewer total assets. And, if he chooses to hold more of one type of assets, he must hold less of others. He must constantly balance the advantage of holding more of one against the disadvantage of holding less of others. Putting the matter this way raises the question of why people elect to hold any money balances at all. Money usually yields no explicit income, or at most, only a low rate of return relative to yields on other assets. But holding money costs something; the cost is the satisfaction or income forgone by holding money rather than devoting this amount of resources to other uses.

The fact that people do choose to hold some money balances at the cost of attractive alternatives suggests that holding money must yield some sort of utility, satisfaction, or advantage. It does, and these result from the qualities of money—its general acceptability in payments, its perfect liquidity, and its safety in the sense that it does not depreciate in terms of money. However, for each individual or business firm, money balances, like most other goods, are subject to the law of diminishing utility. Some amount of money balances is highly advantageous. But beyond some point, further additions to money balances yield only decreasing advantages per dollar. This helps explain why people elect to hold some balances, but do not hold all their assets in this form. We shall now investigate some of the reasons for holding money.

Motives for holding money

Two of the functions of money discussed in the first chapter were to serve as a medium of exchange or means of payments, and to serve as a store of value. One motive for holding money is the *transactions motive*—to hold something with which to make payments. Households and business firms hold money balances for transactions purposes because they think they will, or may, want to make expenditures before they enjoy a sufficient inflow of money receipts. They might hold little or no money if they were assured that money would flow to them in sufficient volume just a moment before they wanted to spend. Usually, they have no such assurance. Therefore, they elect to hold some money to cover the excess of their expenditures over their receipts during some period. This is true even if they can forecast perfectly and confidently both the amounts and timing of their expenditures and receipts. For example, a household may know exactly what it is going to spend during the remainder of the month, and also that it will receive no further income until the end of the month. Or a business firm may forecast perfectly both its flow of cash receipts and its flow of expenditures, and know that for some time its expenditures will exceed its receipts. However, forecasts of cash receipts and expenditures can rarely be made with such precision and confidence. Expected receipts may fail to materialize, or highly important expenditures may be earlier or larger than anticipated, or unusually attractive bargains may become available. Some money balances are held against such contingencies.

Another motive for holding money may be called the *store-of-value motive*. The community may elect to hold balances in excess of its projected needs for transactions purposes because of its desire to hold assets that are perfectly liquid and perfectly free from risk of depreciation in terms of money. Money balances demanded for this purpose will be called the *asset demand for money*.

To separate the amounts of money balances demanded for transactions purposes and those demanded for store-of-value or asset purposes is impossible empirically, and to do so even conceptually presents difficulties. For example, the distinction between the two motives is fuzzy; even if a dollar is to be spent for output in the near future it serves as a store of value while it is held. Nevertheless, it will be useful for analytical purposes to divide the total demand function for money balances into the demand function for transactions purposes and the demand function for store-of-value or asset purposes. That is,

$$L = L_1 + L_2 \tag{3}$$

where L = the total demand function for money balances

   L_1 = the demand function for money balances for transactions purposes

   L_2 = the demand function for money balances for store-of-value or asset purposes

We shall argue that the L_1 function is of the following general form:

$$L_1 = JOP = JY \tag{4}$$

where $O, P,$ and Y are defined as above.

   J = the demand for money balances for transactions purposes stated as a fraction of OP, or Y

The fraction J in this equation should not be confused with the Marshallian K. The latter relates the total demand for money balances (L) to the level of Y, whereas J relates only the transactions demand for money balances (L_1) to the level of Y. Thus, J is generally smaller than K. L_1 is assumed to be a positive function of O, P, and Y. The community demands L_1 balances sufficient to purchase some fraction, J, of its annual rate of real output. Thus, if J is given, increases of O and of P will tend to increase money balances demanded for L_1 purposes, and decreases of O and of P tend to decrease L_1 demands for money balances. The principal determinants of the size and behavior of J will be discussed later.

The L_2 function is of the following general form:

$$L_2 = AP \tag{5}$$

where A = the amount of real purchasing power for store-of-value or asset purposes that the community demands to hold in the form of money balances

   P = the price level, as defined above

The basic idea here is that what the community desires to hold for store-of-value purposes is some amount of real purchasing power in the form of money balances. Thus, the quantities of L_2 balances demanded tend to vary directly with the price level (P).

To get the total L function, we insert into Equation (3) the L_1 and L_2 functions in Equations (4) and (5).

$$L = JOP + AP \tag{6}$$

or

$$L = P(JO + A)$$

In other words, the community demands to hold money balances sufficient to purchase some fraction, J, of its rate of real output plus some amount of real purchasing power (A) for asset purposes.

DETERMINANTS OF THE L FUNCTION

As already indicated, the quantities of money balances demanded tend to vary positively with levels of real output and prices if J and A are given and constant. That L is positively related to the levels of O, P, and Y should be intuitively plausible. However, in order to understand the size of L at each level of O and Y we must analyze the determinants of J and A. We must consider such questions as these: What factors determine the size of the fraction J at any time? Why may it be only $\frac{1}{6}$ rather than $\frac{1}{2}$ or some larger figure? What factors are capable of effecting shifts in the size of J? What factors determine the size of A—the amount of real purchasing power demand in the form of money balances for asset purposes? What factors can shift the public's preferences and result in increases or decreases in the size of A?

Some of the most important determinants of the behavior of J and A are the following:

1. The nature and variety of substitute assets. The demand for money is likely to be high if the only other assets available for holding are highly illiquid and risky. However, the demand for money is reduced as more liquid and safer substitutes become available. We have seen that a wide variety of highly liquid and safe substitutes are available in American financial markets. These include short-term Treasury obligations, open-market commercial paper, bankers' acceptances, time and savings deposits at commercial banks, and claims against a wide variety of nonbank financial intermediaries.

2. The wealth of the community. One would expect that the richer the community, the greater will be the quantity of money that it will demand. However, with such a wide variety of highly liquid and safe earning assets available, there is no logical reason why any large part of any increase of wealth should come to be reflected in an increase of demand for money balances.

3. *The ease and certainty of securing credit.* If credit were unavailable, or were available only uncertainly and on onerous terms, both households and business firms would find it advantageous to hold larger money balances relative to their expenditures. However, as financial institutions and the use of credit become more highly developed, the community finds it advantageous to hold smaller balances relative to expenditures. Consumers need not accumulate large balances to pay for an expensive item, such as a car or a TV set; they buy it "on credit" and pay so much each payday. They need not hold balances to cover their expenditures between paydays; they can "charge it" and pay when they receive income. This also applies to business; it need not hold so much money relative to expenditures if it is assured of credit to meet excesses of expenditures over receipts. Thus, the development of such things as credit cards, instant credit, and confirmed lines of credit serve to reduce the demand for money balances.

4. *The system of payments in the community.* Several aspects of the system of payments affect the quantity of money demanded relative to the rate of expenditures. One is the frequency of income receipts. In general, the quantity of money demanded relative to expenditures tends to be smaller as the length of the period between income receipts is shortened.

> To illustrate this, let us consider a family that has income receipts and expenditures of $7,200 a year, and spends its income at a constant rate of $20 a day. (We neglect the other five days of the year; they would complicate our arithmetic.)
> a. Suppose the family receives all its income at the beginning of the year, that its money balance is $7,200 just after it receives its income, and that its balance is zero at the end of the year. Its average balance during the year is $3,600.
> b. Suppose it receives $600 at the beginning of each month and spends all of it during the month. Its average balance will be $300. Shortening the income period to a week would reduce the demand for money still further.

Another determinant is the regularity of receipts and disbursements. If people and business firms receive predictably stable amounts of money at regular intervals, they are likely to feel free to spend most of it before the next date on which they are to receive money. But if receipts are highly unstable and unpredictable, they are likely to feel a need to hold more money to tide them over lean periods.

A widespread use of barter tends to decrease the quantity of money demanded relative to the value of output. When goods and services are bartered directly for each other, less money is needed. But as barter declines and the economy becomes more and more a "money economy," the transactions need for money tends to rise relative to the value of output. Changes in this factor are usually small in the short run, but may be important over longer periods of economic development.

The more often that currently produced goods and services are sold for money in the process of production and distribution, the larger is the demand for money likely to be. Suppose, for example, that in producing a certain product, all the processes of producing the raw material, fabricating, jobbing, wholesaling, and retailing are carried out by different firms, and that all payments among them are made with money. The demand for money relative to the final value of output is likely to be large. But the demand for money is likely to be smaller if all these processes are combined within vertically integrated firms with no money payments among the departments of each firm.

The more rapid the transportation of money, the lower the demand for money tends to be. For example, the demand may be large if money does not reach its receiver until two weeks after it left the spender; in the meantime, it is not available for respending. But the demand may be much smaller if money is received within a day or so and is available quickly for respending.

5. Expectations as to future income receipts. The demand for money is also affected by the community's expectations as to the certainty and size of its future income receipts. Suppose, for example, that at some time the community comes to fear that its future income receipts will be less certain and may decline seriously. Community members may try to build up their money balances to tide them over the feared or expected lean period. But if they come to believe that the flow of income receipts will rise markedly in the future, they may decrease their money holdings relative to their current rate of expenditure; that is, they may increase their current rate of expenditures relative to their money balances.

6. Expectations as to prices. Expectations concerning the future behavior of prices are also relevant. If the members of a community believe that the prices of the things they intend to buy will remain stable, that a dollar will buy in the future just what it will buy today, they may elect to hold one quantity of money relative to their expenditures. They are likely to increase this quantity if they expect prices to fall. Both business and consumers may postpone purchases and hold larger balances relative to expenditures. They may elect to hold money, which they expect to increase in purchasing power, rather than hold inventories of goods that they expect to depreciate relative to money. They try to do this by decreasing their expenditures. Expectations of higher prices have the reverse effects; the members of the community are likely to try to hold smaller balances relative to their expenditures. They try to buy before prices rise. In hyperinflations, such as that in Germany after World War I, the quantity of money demanded relative to expenditures falls to very low levels. When members of the community come to fear that each monetary unit will lose half or more of its purchasing power in a day or two, they try to avoid holding money. They refuse to accept money for their goods and services, resorting to barter instead, or if they sell for money, they race to get rid of it immediately.

7. Levels of interest rates. Quantities of money balances demanded tend to be negatively related to the level of interest rates, because the latter may be viewed as the cost of holding money balances. If the holder is in debt, the cost of holding money is the *interest cost* that he would avoid if he used the money to retire that amount of his debt. If he is not in debt, the *opportunity cost* of holding money is the interest forgone by failing to exchange the money for earning assets.

This can also be viewed another way. While interest is the income or benefit received for holding earning assets, there are costs involved in acquiring, holding, and selling such assets. These include not only explicit transactions costs, but also inconvenience and sacrifice of liquidity and safety. We saw earlier that such costs, stated in percent of principal value per year, can be high if only small amounts are involved or if the earning assets are held for only a short period. If interest rates are quite low, the community is likely to want to hold more money because the costs of holding some types and amounts of earning assets exceed the income that they yield. However, as interest rates become higher, only smaller money balances will be demanded because it becomes less profitable to hold money than to hold earning assets.

Such, then, are some of the principal factors that determine the behavior of J and A. Some of these are institutional in nature and change only slowly. Others, such as expectations relative to the future behavior of income and prices, are more volatile.

EQUALITY OF L AND M

We noted earlier that a necessary condition for equilibrium of the rate of expenditures for output (Y) is that the quantity of money balances demanded (L) be exactly equal to the stock of money (M), and that any inequality of L and M would generate forces that would force Y to an equilibrium level. We shall now elaborate on this, illustrating the general principles involved by using very simple M and L functions. In Figure 15–1, the money-supply function (MM) is assumed to be fixed by the monetary authority. The L function, $L = KY$, is in the Marshallian tradition, with K as a constant fraction. The level of Y is measured on the vertical axis and quantities of M and L are plotted on the horizontal axis.

With these L and M functions, the unique equilibrium level of Y is Y_e, because it is only at this level of Y that $L = M$. At any lower level of Y, such as Y_1, M would exceed L, and the excess supply of money would raise expenditures for output. The excess supply of money can operate through two principal channels

Figure 15–1 Income determination by L and M functions

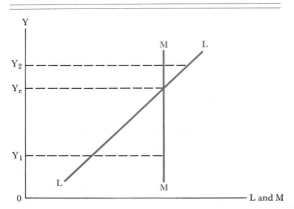

to raise expenditures for output: It can be used directly to increase expenditures for the current output of goods and services; or, at least some of it, can be used to increase demands for financial claims. Those persons who are in debt can use some of their excess money to repurchase their outstanding obligations, thus decreasing demands for credit and tending to lower interest rates. Or they can use some of their excess balances to increase their demands for financial claims against others, thus tending to raise prices and lower yields on these claims. In turn, the fall of interest rates and the increased availability of credit serve to stimulate investment spending, thereby directly increasing expenditures for output and increasing money income for the community. With higher incomes, members of the community increase their consumption spending. Such expansionary forces will continue until the level of Y is raised to Y_e and L is brought into equality with M.

On the other hand, any level of Y above Y_e, such as Y_2, would be one of disequilibrium, because at such a level L would exceed M; members of the community would consider their actual money balances deficient relative to amounts demanded. This deficiency can be repaired by the reduction of expenditures for current output or through operations in financial markets. Some people may try to borrow more to add to their money balances, thus tending to raise interest rates, and some may decrease their demands for claims against others, or actually sell some of their holdings of such claims, thus tending to lower their prices and raise their yields. Such increases of interest rates and decreased availability of credit discourage investment spending, thereby directly decreasing expenditures for output and lowering money incomes. With lower incomes, the community decreases its consumption spending. Such contractionary forces will continue until the level of Y is lowered to Y_e and L no longer exceeds M.

Although the model above is very simple, one of our findings is valid for every model that we shall consider. In every model, a necessary condition for equilibrium is that $L = M$. Also in every model, an excess of M over L tends to lower interest rates, to increase Y, or both; and an excess of L over M tends to raise interest rates, to lower Y, or both. The reader should therefore understand clearly and constantly keep in mind the nature of the adjustment processes involved. However, one outcome of this simple model is not of general applicability; it is not always true that the L and M functions are by themselves sufficient to establish a unique equilibrium level of Y. We shall later deal with models in which $L = M$ is a necessary, but not a sufficient, condition for a unique equilibrium level of Y.

STABILITY OF V OR K

A crucial question for the quantity-theory approach is: "How stable and predictable is the ratio of the level of expenditures for output (Y) to the stock of money (M)?" In other words, how stable and predictable are V and K? Answers to such questions are important for both the theory of aggregate demand and monetary policy. For example, suppose V and K are both stable and predictable. In this case, the stock of money is the major determinant of aggregate demand and the level of Y can be managed precisely through control of M. To the extent that V and K are unstable, the stock of money loses explanatory power over the behavior of Y and more weight must be given to the determinants of the behavior of V and K. However, if V and K remain predictable it is still possible to regulate the behavior of Y through appropriate offsetting changes of M unless each change in M induces opposite offsetting changes in V and K. If V and K are both highly unstable and unpredictable, M loses importance as a determinant of the behavior of Y, and monetary policy loses its effectiveness as an instrument for regulating aggregate demand.

In general, quantity theorists before the 1930s considered V and K to be relatively stable and predictable. This general view is shared by the modern Monetarists, led by Milton Friedman. This is not to say that these economists considered V and K to be either completely stable or completely predictable. However, they considered them to be constant enough for M to remain the most important determinant of the behavior of aggregate demand, and thought both of them constant enough and predictable enough to enable monetary policy to regulate aggregate demand through controlling the stock of money.

One basis for their belief in the relative stability of V and K was their assumption that demands for money balances are not affected significantly by the level of interest rates. Thus, they believed that even a large rise of interest rates would not significantly decrease either the amount of money balances demanded for transactions purposes or the amount demanded for asset or store-of-value purposes. And even a large decline of interest rates would not significantly increase demands for money balances for either transactions or asset purposes; it would not lower V or raise K. One implication of this assumption is that changes in interest rates to bring saving-investment relationships into equilibrium are not inhibited by "hoarding" or "dishoarding." For example, suppose savings tends to rise relative to investment demands, so that interest rates tend to decline. Each fall of interest rates will not induce the community to use some of the funds it has saved to increase its money balances held for asset purposes. Instead, all the funds will be offered in loan markets, which will drive down interest rates and stimulate investment and, perhaps also, consumption spending.

Since the 1930s, and especially since the development of Keynesian hypotheses and theories, this view has been strongly challenged. Most monetary economists now believe that demands for money balances are sensitive to the level of interest rates, tending to fall as interest rates rise and to rise as interest rates fall. We shall see later that such a responsiveness of demands for money balances to interest rates not only contribute to instability of V and K but also lessen the adjustability of interest rates. However, before elaborating further on this model, let us look at some further aspects of the model in which V and K are relatively constant and not affected significantly by changes in the level of interest rates.

QUANTITY THEORY AND THE PRICE LEVEL

As noted earlier, the quantity theory is essentially a theory of the behavior of aggregate money demands for other things. To proceed from this theory to the behavior of such variables as output, employment, and prices, we must add an analysis of responses in output and labor markets. However, many economists have believed that the primary function of the quantity theory is to explain the behavior of price levels or the purchasing power of money, and they have concluded that "normally" the price level tends to vary proportionally with the stock of money. It is therefore important to note carefully the methodology and assumptions on which their analysis and conclusions were based. Their method of analysis was that of comparative statics—a comparison of equilibrium conditions before and after a shift of the money-supply function. Their assumptions were basically those of the classical model discussed earlier—pure competition in labor and output markets, full flexibility of money wage rates and prices, strong forces in the economy tending to maintain output at full-employment levels, and relatively constant V and K. Employing comparative statics and these assumptions, it is valid to conclude that the price level tends to vary proportionally with the stock of money.

To elucidate their argument we shall use Equation (6): $L = P (JO + A)$. The community demands to hold in the form of money balances an amount of purchasing power equal to $JO + A$. The fraction J is constant, O is constant at its full-employment level, and A is constant in total purchasing power. Thus, quantities of money balances demanded vary proportionally with the price level and are equal to $P(JO + A)$. This is represented by the LL line in Figure 15–2, where L is stated as a function of P. Suppose the money supply is at the level represented by the line M_0M_0. The equilibrium price level is P_0, because only at

Figure 15–2 Price-level determination by L and M functions

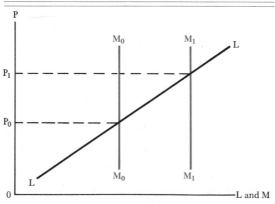

that level of P will $L = M$. At any lower level of P, M would exceed L, and at any higher level L would exceed M. Suppose that the money supply was doubled, as represented by the line $M_1 M_1$. The price level P_0 is now one of disequilibrium because M exceeds L. A new equilibrium can be established only when the price level has doubled, rising from P_0 to P_1, because only at that level of P will L equal M. Note that it was the rise of M that stimulated the higher rate of expenditures which served to raise the price level. But the extent to which prices can rise is limited, because increases of prices increase the quantities of money balances demanded. At any price level above P_1, L would exceed M.

At least the more sophisticated quantity theorists recognized the extent to which their conclusion that "P tends to vary proportionally with M" depended on their use of comparative statics and on the nature of their assumptions, and they were careful to point out that this conclusion does not necessarily hold under other types of analysis and under other conditions. Irving Fisher was a member of this group. He was careful to distinguish between "permanent or ultimate effects" and "temporary effects during the period of transition."[1] By "the period of transition" he meant the period required to make the transition from one state of equilibrium to another. During such periods the economy is in a state of disequilibrium. His analysis proceeded essentially as follows: Suppose we start from a situation in which the money supply is $M_0 M_0$, the price level is in equilibrium at P_0, and interest rates are at equilibrium levels. Now increase the money supply by some amount. The initial effect is an excess of M over L. This will induce a decline of interest rates, which will increase investment expenditures. If the economy has been operating below a full-employment level, the initial response to increased expenditures may be largely in the form of a rise of real output. However, as full employment is approached, the response to further increases in the rate of money expenditures must be largely in price increases. If the rise of prices is large or prolonged, each price increase is likely to generate expectations of still further price increases. Such inflationary expectations have two important effects. For one thing, they tend to increase expected rates of profit on business investment. Businessmen come to expect not only the "normal profits" that they would make with stable price levels, but also "something extra" resulting from further increases in the prices of their assets and output. For example, they may come to expect not only their "normal" profit rate of 6 percent, but also an additional 4 percent from expected price increases in the future. They, therefore, increase their demands for loan funds for investment purposes; their demand functions for loan funds shift upward and to the right. Owners of savings, fearing that the purchasing power of their money will be eroded, may become willing to lend only at higher rates of interest. Thus, both the rise of demands for loan funds and the change in supply conditions tend to increase market rates of interest. However, for at least some time, the rise of market rates of interest is likely

---

[1] *The Purchasing Power of Money,* New York, Macmillan, 1926, pp. 55–56.

to lag behind the rise of expected profit rates. This is because businessmen are more likely than savers to expect future price increases, and because many savers are not aware of, or do not have access to, attractive uses for their funds other than lending. In any case, the lag of market rates of interest behind expected profit rates serves to stimulate further increases in spending.

Another consequence of the generation of inflationary expectations is an increase in the velocity of circulation of money. When people come to expect future price increases that would erode the purchasing power of their money, they seek to reduce their money balances relative to their expenditures. As stated by Fisher, "We all hasten to get rid of any commodity which, like ripe fruit, is spoiling on our hands. Money is no exception; when it is depreciating, holders get rid of it as fast as possible."[2]

Thus the rise of expenditures and prices, initiated by the increase of the money supply, is continued and supported by the lag of market rates of interest behind expected profit rates and by the rise of velocity. Prices might even rise temporarily above their longer-term equilibrium level. However, if the money supply is not allowed to rise further, the inflationary process will be brought to an end. This occurs as the rise of prices raises the quantity of demanded money balances relative to the available money supply. As L comes to equal or exceed M, market rates of interest will rise faster than expected profit rates, inflationary expectations will subside, and velocity will fall. The price level may climb to its new long-term equilibrium and stabilize there. More likely, however, it will rise temporarily above that level, then overreact and fall below it, and stabilize only after oscillations.

Fisher's treatment of developments during transition periods following a decrease of the money supply was essentially symmetrical to that described above. However, because he assumed downward flexibility of money wage rates and prices he tended to understate the depressing effects on levels of output and employment.

Fisher also stated clearly that only by coincidence would P remain proportional to M through historical time. To make this point, he divided both sides of his equation by O, thus converting it into the form $P = MV/O$. In other words, the price level varies directly with M and V and inversely with O, the rate of real output available for purchase. Fisher discussed at some length various factors, mostly institutional in nature, that are likely to change through time the size of money balances demanded by a community relative to its rate of expenditures. He also dealt with numerous factors that change through time an economy's capacity to produce.

This brief account of some aspects of the quantity-theory approach should at least dispose of the facile assertion: Quantity theorists contended that the price level is always proportional to the stock of money.

2 *Ibid.*, p. 63.

INTEREST RATES AND DEMANDS FOR MONEY BALANCES

We noted earlier two conclusions that follow from the assumption that demands for money balances are not affected significantly by the level of interest rates: (1) L and M functions are by themselves sufficient to establish a unique equilibrium level of Y. And (2) changes in interest rates to bring saving-investment relationships into equilibrium are not inhibited by net additions to demanded money balances (hoarding) or by net withdrawals (dishoarding) from demanded money balances. Neither conclusion is valid if the quantities of demanded money balances are affected significantly by changes in the level of interest rates.

Most economists now believe, on the basis of both economic theory and empirical research, that both L_1 and L_2 demands are negatively related to the level of interest rates, although the same economists emphasize the responsiveness of L_2 demands to interest rates. To facilitate exposition, we shall include all interest-rate effects in the L_2 demand.

In explaining why demands for money balances should be negatively related to the level of interest rates, many economists stress the fact that an interest rate is both a cost of holding money balances and a reward for holding earning assets. Therefore, increased interest rates encourage the community to economize on money balances and to hold a larger fraction of its total assets in the form of earning assets. Reduced interest rates have the opposite effect. Keynes added a further reason for expecting such a negative relationship: Expected losses on earning assets increase as interest rates are lower. He reasoned essentially as follows: First, he cited the familiar fact that increases of interest rates lower prices of outstanding debt obligations, and decreases of interest rates increase such prices. Second, he hypothesized that members of the community have some concept of "a normal level" of interest rates, which is based on experience, and especially on recent experience. This level is "normal" in the sense that the interest rates are expected to return to this level after each significant departure from it. Thus, if actual rates are well above the normal level, the community will consider further increases of rates less likely than future declines and capital losses less likely than capital gains. It will therefore demand to hold more earning assets and only smaller money balances. However, as actual interest rates fall well below the normal level, the community considers future rate increases to be more likely than rate decreases and capital losses more likely than capital gains. It therefore demands larger money balances and less earning assets.

Keynes extended this idea to its pessimistic extreme in developing his concept of a "liquidity trap"—an idea that at some positive rate of interest that is low by historical standards, the demand for money balances becomes infinitely elastic. In this model, Keynes assumed that only two types of financial instruments were available—money itself and homogeneous perpetual bonds. In Figure 15–3, the liquidity trap is represented by the section of the L_2 line to the right of point

Figure 15–3 The liquidity trap

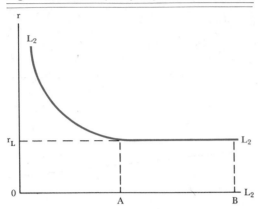

A. At the low level of the interest rate, r_L, the demand for money balances is infinitely elastic. The community will not hold any bonds at yield rates below r_L because it expects that income from holding bonds will be more than offset by capital losses resulting from future increases of interest rates.

The liquidity-trap hypothesis has pessimistic implications for the adjustability of interest rates and for the efficacy of monetary policy. Interest rates could not fall below r_L, but that level of interest rates may at times be too high to elicit enough investment spending to offset the supply of saving at a full-employment level of income. Under such conditions, output and employment would be "trapped" at levels below full employment. Moreover, increases of the money supply could not lower interest rates below r_L or stimulate spending. Suppose that the money supply is raised from A to B. All of the increase would be "trapped" in L_2 balances. In terms of the velocity approach, the increase of M would be offset by a decline of V. On the other hand, any tendency for interest rates to rise above r_L would lead the community to decrease markedly its demands for balances for L_2 purposes, thus freeing large amounts for spending. This would be reflected in a rise of V. Even a decrease of the money stock from B to A might have no effect on Y.

Few economists now accept the liquidity-trap hypothesis in the extreme form described above. For one thing, a model including only two types of financial instruments—money itself and perpetual bonds—bears little resemblance to a modern economy with a wide array of earning assets of all maturities. In such an economy, a person who is unwilling to hold long-term bonds because he fears a rise of interest rates need not increase his holdings of money balances. Instead, he can buy earning assets of short maturities, which have prices that would be affected but little by a rise of interest rates. Such shifts to short maturities tend to lower at least short-term interest rates. Also, expectations concerning the future behavior of interest rates are neither so homogeneous nor so unalterable as is implied by the horizontal section of the L_2 curve. Some members of the community are likely to expect lower rates than others; this would give some negative slope to the L_2 curve. Moreover, the L_2 curve can be shifted upward or downward to some extent. For example, the monetary authority may shift the community's expectations downward by adopting an aggressive easy-money policy and by announcing its determination to lower interest rates.

However, rejection of the extreme version of the liquidity trap does not mean that Keynes' ideas are without merit. Demands for both earning assets and money balances are affected by the community's expectations concerning the future behavior of interest rates and asset prices, and, on at least some occasions, these expectations are such as to change the quantities of money balances demanded for L_2 purposes. And fears of rate increases in the future may cause even an aggressive expansionary monetary policy to lower long-term interest rates only slowly and to a limited extent. Thus, the assumption that L_2 demands for money balances are negatively related to the level of interest rates seems realistic, both for the reasons advanced by Keynes, and because an interest rate is both the cost of holding money balances and the reward for holding earning assets.

Equality of M and $L_1 + L_2$

In the remaining parts of our theoretical analysis, we shall employ the following types of L functions. For simplicity, we assume that the functions are linear; that is, we assume that they have constant slopes. As before, the total demand function for money balances is the sum of demands for transactions and asset purposes:

$$L = L_1 + L_2 \tag{3}$$

L_1 is a positive function of income, as developed earlier.

$$L_1 = JOP = JY \tag{4}$$

This is illustrated in Part A of Figure 15–4. L_2 is a negative function of interest rates, such that

$$L_2 = P\ (A - er) \tag{7}$$

where $P =$ the price level

$A =$ a positive constant, stated in billions of dollars of constant purchasing power

$e = \dfrac{\Delta L_2}{\Delta r} =$ the "slope," stated as the number of billions of change in

L_2 with each change of one percentage point in r.

$r =$ the interest rate, stated in whole numbers, such as 2 or 6

The shape of the L_2 function is indicated in Part B of Figure 15–4. The quantity of money balances demanded varies negatively with interest rates; a 1-percent rise of r will decrease demanded balances by e billions, and a 1-percent fall of r

Figure 15–4 L_1 and L_2 functions

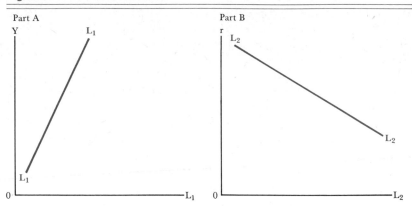

will increase demanded balances by e billions. Inserting Equations (4) and (7) into Equation (3), we get the total demand function for money:

$$L = JOP + P(A - er) \tag{8}$$

or

$$L = P(JO + A - er)$$

Since $OP = Y$, we can also write:

$$L = JY + P(A - er)$$

As in the models considered earlier, a necessary condition for equilibrium is that the demand for money balances (L) be exactly equal to the money stock (M). Any excess of M over L would serve to increase Y, to lower r, or both. And any excess of L over M would serve to lower Y, to raise r, or both. In contrast to the earlier models, however, L and M functions are not by themselves sufficient to determine a unique level of Y when demands for money balances are significantly affected by the level of interest rates. In this case, there are many combinations of levels of Y and r that will equate L to a given stock of M. Figure 15–4 suggests that $L_1 + L_2$ can be equated to a given M by a high level of Y, at which L_1 would be large, together with a high level of r, at which L_2 would be small; or by lower levels of Y, at which L_1 would be smaller, together with lower levels of r, at which L_2 would be larger. This can be clarified further by using a numerical example, as is done in Table 15–2. M is assumed to remain constant at $250 billion, $L_1 = 1/5Y$, and $L_2 = \$110$ billion $-$ ($\$10$ billion $\times r$). In other words, each 1-percent increase of r decreases by $10 billion the amount of balances demanded for L_2 purposes.

The table shows nine of the many combinations of Y and r at which $L_1 + L_2$ is equal to $250 billion, the size of M. This occurs at $Y = \$1,150$ billion and $r = 9$ percent; at $Y = \$1,000$ billion and $r = 6$ percent; and so on. This is

Table 15–2 Equality of L and M with given L and M functions (amounts in billions of dollars)

(1)	(2)	(3)	(4)	(5)	(6)
			r (IN	$L_2 =$	TOTAL L
M	Y	$L_1 = 1/5Y$	PERCENT)	$110 - 10r$	$[(3) + (5)]$
$250	$ 750	$150	1	$100	$250
250	800	160	2	90	250
250	850	170	3	80	250
250	900	180	4	70	250
250	950	190	5	60	250
250	1,000	200	6	50	250
250	1,050	210	7	40	250
250	1,100	220	8	30	250
250	1,150	230	9	20	250

depicted graphically in Figure 15–5. If M is constant and the L function to be that described above, the $L = M$ line represents all combinations of Y and r that will equate L to M. An equilibrium combination of Y and r must therefore lie somewhere on this line. Any combination off the line will be one of inequality of L and M, which will create pressures for adjustment. Any combination above the line, such as point A, is one at which M exceeds L. We know this because there is a point on the line vertically below A, at the same level of income, at which $L = M$. At the same level of Y and a higher r, L will be smaller, and the excess supply of money will create pressures for a decrease of r.

On the other hand, at any combination below the line, such as point B, L exceeds M. We know this because there is a point vertically above B, at the same level of income, at which $L = M$. At the same level of Y and a lower r, L will be greater, and the excess demand for money balances will bring pressure for an increase of r.

We shall see later that shifts of the L and M functions shift the $L = M$ line. For example, an increase of M shifts the $L = M$ line to the right, leading to a fall

Figure 15–5 An $L = M$ line

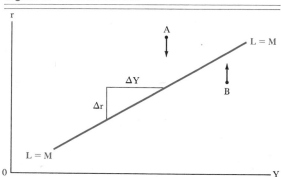

of r, a rise of Y, or both. And a decrease of M shifts the $L = M$ line to the left, leading to an increase of r, a decrease of Y, or both.

CONCLUSION

From the quantity-theory approach we get two elements—the money-supply function and the demand function for money balances—that are necessary to explain the behavior of the rate of expenditures for output and the level of interest rates. These functions determine the $L = M$ line on which equilibrium must lie, and shifts of these functions shift the $L = M$ line. However, these functions alone are not sufficient to determine unique equilibrium levels of Y and r. To determine the unique point of equilibrium on the $L = M$ line, we need further information. That will be supplied by consumption, saving, and investment functions, which will be explored in the next chapter.

Selected readings

Friedman, M., *A Theoretical Framework for Monetary Analysis,* New York, National Bureau of Economic Research, 1971.

Smith, W. L., *Macroeconomics,* Homewood, Ill., Irwin, 1970.

CHAPTER 16

CONSUMPTION, SAVING, AND INVESTMENT

The other branch of theory that our synthetic or eclectic theory will draw on is "the income and expenditure approach," which is stated in terms of consumption, saving, and investment. Elements of this approach were involved in centuries-old questions such as: Does saving enrich a nation by permitting and inducing capital formation, thereby raising production and incomes? Or does it impoverish a nation by depressing total demand for output and creating unemployment of labor and other resources? Can the market mechanism be relied on to convert a nation's thrift into real wealth in the form of capital? Or is there a "flaw in the price system?" Is thrift a private virtue or a private vice; when practiced collectively, is frugality a national blessing or a national curse?

Elements of this approach have also played prominent roles in various types of business-cycle theories, especially those emphasizing "oversaving," "undersaving," "overinvestment," and "underinvestment." However, this type of theory remained fragmentary and unsystematic until the 1930s. It suffered from lack of national-income accounts that would permit quantification of its concepts and also from lack of a comprehensive and logically consistent theory of income determination. Both deficiencies have now been largely remedied. Almost all countries have developed national-income accounts, varying in amount of detail and degree of reliability. Theories of national-income determination have also developed rapidly, especially since the publication, in 1936, of John Maynard Keynes' monumental *General Theory of Employment, Interest and Money*. We are indebted to modern versions of the income approach for such concepts as the consumption function, supply of saving function, and investment-demand function for output as determinants of aggregate demand. The income approach emphasizes that one necessary condition for equilibrium of income and interest rates is that the supply of saving be equal to investment demand for output.

For the remainder of this chapter we shall concentrate on consumption, saving, and investment. Several characteristics of the following analysis should be borne in mind:

1. It is essentially short run in nature. That is, it does not attempt to analyze changes in the productive capacity of the economy through time; instead, it is concerned with the behavior of income and output within given capacity levels.

2. Unless otherwise indicated, it assumes that price levels of output are constant, so that the money value of output is an index of the behavior of real output.

3. It assumes that the government engages in no economic activity, so there are no taxes, government transfer payments, or government purchases. Thus, private disposable income is equal to GNP, which is the sum of $C + I$. By making this assumption, we can decrease the number of variables and describe the principles involved more clearly. The government will be restored to the picture in a later chapter.

4. Our central interest is in aggregate, or total demands for output. In this chapter, aggregate demand for output is the sum of consumption demands and gross investment demands.

Our first task will be to develop consumption and saving functions and state them as functions of GNP.

CONSUMPTION AND SAVING

The following symbols will be used:

$Y = $ GNP
$C = $ personal-consumption expenditures for output
$S_p = $ personal saving
$S_b = $ gross business saving $=$ capital-consumption allowances $+$ undistributed corporate profits
$S = $ total saving $= S_p + S_b = Y - C$
$I = $ gross private investment $=$ gross private domestic investment $+$ net foreign investment
$Y_H = $ personal or household disposable income

All these flows are stated at annual rates in billions of dollars.

Also, assuming no government economic activities, we have the following accounting identities, which are always true by definition:

$$Y \equiv C + I$$

$$Y_H \equiv Y - S_b$$

$$S_p \equiv Y_H - C$$

$$S \equiv (S_b + S_p) \equiv Y - C$$

The functions

The most powerful determinant of private consumption and saving is the **level of private disposable income**, which in the absence of government is equal to **total income**. Both consumption and saving are positive functions of the level of income. That is, at higher levels of income, the private sectors will both consume more and save more; at lower levels of income, they will both consume less and save less. This is shown schematically in Figure 16–1. The level of income created $(C + I)$ is measured on the horizontal axis. The amount of private disposable income $(C + S)$ is measured on the vertical axis in Part A. As an expositional device, we draw a line at a 45° angle through the origin. If a line is dropped vertically from any point on the 45° line, the vertical distance to the base is exactly equal to the horizontal distance from the origin to the point of intersection on the base. This illustrates the fact that the amount of disposable income $(C + S)$ must be exactly equal to the amount of income created $(C + I)$.

The CC line represents the *consumption function*. That is, it states consumption as a function of the level of income. The consumption function can also be stated algebraically:

$$C = B + \left(\frac{\Delta C}{\Delta Y} Y \right) \tag{1}$$

Figure 16–1 Private disposable income and its disposal

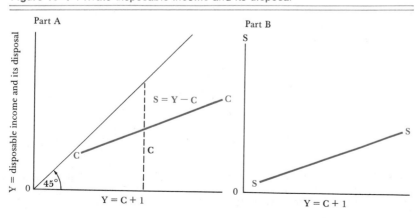

$B = $ a positive constant, stated in billions of dollars. It is the height of the intercept on the vertical axis, and its size establishes the height of the consumption function

$\frac{\Delta C}{\Delta Y} = $ the "slope" of the consumption function

$= $ the marginal propensity to consume

$= $ MPC

The slope of the consumption function ($\Delta C/\Delta Y$) indicates the marginal responsiveness of consumption to changes in the level of income. This is called the *marginal propensity to consume,* or MPC. A basic hypothesis of income theory is that the marginal propensity to consume ($\Delta C/\Delta Y$) is greater than zero but less than one. That is, in response to a rise (or fall) of disposable income, the community will increase (or decrease) its consumption, but by an amount less than the change in income. For example, a $\Delta C/\Delta Y$ of 0.8 indicates that a given change of disposable income will change consumption by an amount equal to eight-tenths of the income change.[1]

The saving-supply function is shown in Part A of Figure 16–1 as the vertical distance from the 45° line to the amount of consumption at that level of income. This necessarily follows from the fact that $S = Y - C$. For convenience, the saving-supply function, represented by the line SS, is shown separately in Part B of Figure 16–1. It, too, is a positive function of income. Its slope ($\Delta S/\Delta Y$) measures the marginal responsiveness of saving to income. This is called the *marginal propensity to save,* or MPS. The value of MPS is obviously related to the value of MPC. In fact, since $Y \equiv C + S,$

$$\Delta Y = \Delta C + \Delta S$$

and, dividing both sides of the equation by ΔY, we get

$$1 = \frac{\Delta C}{\Delta Y} + \frac{\Delta S}{\Delta Y} \qquad \text{or} \qquad \frac{\Delta S}{\Delta Y} = 1 - \frac{\Delta C}{\Delta Y}$$

Thus, if $\Delta C/\Delta Y = 0.8$, then, $\Delta S/\Delta Y = 0.2$. Any change in income must be equal to the changes in consumption and saving; any part that is not used to change consumption must be reflected in a change in saving.

It is important to remember that when we define either the consumption function or the saving-supply function, we are actually defining both functions because each function is simply Y minus the other function. For example, we obtain the saving-supply function by subtracting the consumption function from Y:

$$S = Y - (B + \frac{\Delta C}{\Delta Y}Y) \tag{2}$$

---

[1] It is, of course, possible that the value of $\Delta C/\Delta Y$ will be different at different levels of income. We use a linear consumption function partly because of its simplicity and partly because empirical studies suggest that linear functions fit the data as well as other types of functions.

$$= Y - \frac{\Delta C}{\Delta Y} Y - B$$

$$= Y \left(1 - \frac{\Delta C}{\Delta Y}\right) - B$$

Since $1 - \Delta C/\Delta Y = \Delta S/\Delta Y$, we can also express the saving-supply function as:

$$S = Y \frac{\Delta S}{\Delta Y} - B$$

A basic hypothesis in our theory of income determination is that the supply of saving is greater at higher levels of income than at lower levels. The saving-supply function can be stated two ways, but both amount to the same thing.

1. The supply of saving is the value of output produced but not demanded for consumption $(S = Y - C)$. This view emphasizes that, with given consumption and saving functions, larger amounts of output will be "left over" after consumption demands at higher levels of income.

2. The supply of saving is equal to gross business saving (S_b) plus personal saving (S_p). These represent that part of private disposable income that is not returned to the market as consumption demand. Both S_b and S_p tend to be positive functions of income. Let us look at them in turn.

Gross business saving, S_b

As already indicated, gross business saving is composed of two parts: depreciation and other capital-consumption allowances, and undistributed ("plowed in") corporate profits. These comprise a major portion of total private saving. The first component, capital-consumption allowances, is rather insensitive to the level of Y. It depends instead on two factors that are not very responsive to changes in the level of income (especially not in the short run); these factors are the stock of depreciable assets in the hands of business and the policies of business firms relative to writing off and retaining allowances for depreciation. However, the other component, undistributed corporate profits, is usually quite responsive to income levels. One reason why is that total corporate profits after taxes are very responsive to changes in Y, especially to cyclical changes. Short-run increases in Y usually increase corporate profits more than proportionally, and decreases in Y decrease corporate profits more than proportionally. Also, changes in corporate dividend payments are usually less than changes in corporate profits and taxes. When these profits rise, corporations usually increase dividends but not by the full amount; some part is used to increase undistributed profits. A fall of corporate profits is reflected in large degree in a reduction of undistributed profits, and only belatedly in a decline of dividends.

Thus, S_b is a positive function of Y. The marginal responsiveness of business saving to Y will be designated by $\Delta S_b/\Delta Y$. Since the disposable income of households (Y_H) is equal to total disposable private income minus gross business saving, Y_H does not change by the same absolute amount as Y. That is,

$$\Delta Y_H = \Delta Y - \Delta S_b$$

When Y rises, some part of the increase is retained by business in the form of ΔS_b, and does not accrue to households. On the other hand, a fall of Y brings a fall of S_b, so that the impact on the disposable income of households is smaller. The significance of this will be developed later.

Personal consumption and saving

We shall assume, as already stated, that both consumption and personal saving are positive functions of the disposable income of households (Y_H). The marginal propensity to consume $(\Delta C/\Delta Y_H)$ is positive and less than one. The marginal propensity to save $(\Delta S_p/\Delta Y_H)$ is also positive and less than one, and is equal to $1 - \Delta C/\Delta Y_H$. We concentrate on the effects of income on the levels of consumption and saving because both a priori reasoning and empirical investigations indicate that income is the most powerful determinant, given our social structure and attitudes.

This is not to say that the amounts of consumption and saving depend solely on the level of disposable household income; many other factors help determine how any given level of household disposable income will be divided between consumption and saving. Moreover, changes in these other factors can shift the consumption function up or down; that is, they can lead to more or less consumption at each level of income. Some of the more important of these factors are the following:

1. Social attitudes toward current consumption versus saving for the future.

2. Distribution of total household income by size of household income. For example, total saving out of a given level of total household income is likely to be higher if a greater part of the total income accrues to high-income classes, rather than to low-income groups.

3. Age composition of the population. Both elderly and young families have higher propensities to consume than families in their middle years. A shift in age composition could shift consumption and saving functions.

4. The stock of wealth. Other things equal, a wealthy community might be expected to consume a larger part of its income than a population with the same income but less wealth. "Windfall" capital gains or losses can increase or decrease the consumption function.

5. Expectations concerning future levels of income relative to current income levels. When future levels of income are expected to be higher than present levels, the community is likely to consume more out of its current income.

These are some of the factors that determine the height and shape of the consumption and saving functions. When we state consumption and personal saving as functions of disposable household income, thus isolating the effects of this income on C and S_p, we implicitly assume that such other factors are constant in their effects.

The following analysis will draw heavily on our previous findings concerning the consumption and saving functions.

1. Both consumption and saving are positive functions of the level of national income. Thus, consumption is higher at higher income levels but so also is the supply of saving.

2. Both gross business saving and personal saving are positive functions of income. The higher business saving is at any level of income, the smaller disposable household income will be at that level of Y, for $Y_H = Y - S_b$.

3. Consumption and personal saving are assumed to be positive functions of Y_H. Despite this, however, it will facilitate exposition to relate them to total disposable private income, Y. Thus,[2]

$$\text{MPC} = \frac{\Delta C}{\Delta Y}$$

$$\text{MPS} = \frac{\Delta S}{\Delta Y} = \frac{\Delta S_b}{\Delta Y} + \frac{\Delta S_p}{\Delta Y} = 1 - \frac{\Delta C}{\Delta Y}$$

INVESTMENT-DEMAND FUNCTIONS

Since the saving-supply function developed earlier related to gross saving, the investment-demand function used here will relate to gross investment, which includes gross private domestic investment and net foreign investment. An investment-demand function indicates the values of output demanded at various possible rates of interest. The latter will be denoted by r. Net foreign investment is included to make the model correct, but its analysis will be deferred to a later chapter.

[2] The marginal propensities to consume and save out of total private disposable income (Y), are arrived at in the following way when S_b is a function of Y, and C and S_p are assumed to be functions of disposable household income.

$$\Delta Y_H = \Delta Y - \Delta S_b$$

Dividing by ΔY,

$$\frac{\Delta Y_H}{\Delta Y} = \left(1 - \frac{\Delta S_b}{\Delta Y}\right) = \text{fraction of } \Delta Y \text{ accruing as } \Delta Y_H$$

$$\frac{\Delta C}{\Delta Y} = \frac{\Delta C}{\Delta Y_H}\left(1 - \frac{\Delta S_b}{\Delta Y}\right)$$

$$\frac{\Delta S}{\Delta Y} = \frac{\Delta S_b}{\Delta Y} + \frac{\Delta S_p}{\Delta Y_H}\left(1 - \frac{\Delta S_b}{\Delta Y}\right)$$

For example, suppose

$$\frac{\Delta C}{\Delta Y_H} = 0.9 \quad \text{and} \quad \frac{\Delta S_b}{\Delta Y} = 0.1$$

$$\frac{\Delta C}{\Delta Y} = 0.9 \times 0.9 = 0.81$$

and

$$\frac{\Delta S}{\Delta Y} = 1 - \frac{\Delta C}{\Delta Y} = 1 - 0.81 = 0.19$$

This emphasizes two points: First, that $\Delta C/\Delta Y$ is smaller than $\Delta C/\Delta Y_H$; and second, that the size of $\Delta C/\Delta Y$ can be altered by anything that alters the fraction of ΔY accruing as ΔY_H.

Gross private domestic investment includes expenditures for new construction, both residential and nonresidential; producers' durable equipment; and desired net changes in business inventories. Note that because we are interested in determining an equilibrium level of Y, we include in investment demand only "wanted" or desired changes in business inventories. An "unwanted" actual increase of inventory would be followed by a decrease of Y as business tried to dispose of its excess inventory. On the other hand, an "unwanted" decrease of inventory would be followed by an increase of Y as business stepped up its output to restore inventories to the desired level.

Most of the components of investment demand (I) are demands by business for output with which to maintain or increase stocks of capital goods. These demanders are presumably motivated by a desire for profits, perhaps a desire to maximize their profits. For this purpose they compare the expected returns from new investment with the costs involved. However, some of investment demand, notably expenditures by homeowners for new residential construction, may not be profit motivated. However, even these demanders presumably arrive at decisions by balancing expected benefits and costs; and, other conditions being constant, they will presumably buy less when the cost to them is higher. Interest costs are an important part of the carrying charges of a house.

An investment-demand function, such as that illustrated in Figure 16–2, is a typical demand curve showing the relation of quantity demanded to price. In this case, the price of loan funds, or the interest rate on investable funds, is measured along the horizontal axis. The values of output demanded for investment are measured along the vertical axis. The II curve depicts the size of investment demand at the various possible levels of r. From the point of view of the spender for investment, r is a cost. If he gets the money to finance investment by borrowing from others, r is the annual interest rate he must pay to lenders. If he finances his investment spending by using his own money, r is his opportunity cost; it is the interest rate he sacrifices by using the money himself rather than by lending it to someone else. It is therefore plausible to assume that, other things remaining

Figure 16–2 An investment-demand function

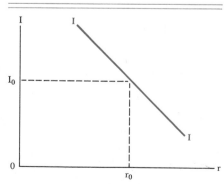

the same, a rise of interest rates will decrease the actual investment demand for output and a fall of interest rates will stimulate it.

The investment-demand function can also be stated in algebraic terms:

$$I = D - \frac{\Delta I}{\Delta r} \qquad (3)$$

$D =$ a positive constant in billions of dollars. It is the intercept on the horizontal axis and establishes the location of the I function.

$\Delta I / \Delta r =$ the "slope" of the function. It is the marginal responsiveness of investment to interest rates.

$r =$ the interest rate, stated in whole numbers, such as 5 or 7

We are engaging in oversimplification in assuming a single interest rate in the market. There are, of course, many rates. Moreover, other terms of lending and borrowing may change: the length of time for which lenders will make funds available, the risks that they will take at any given interest rate, the amount of security demanded for loans, and so on. Nevertheless, it will be convenient to let r represent the height of the structure of interest rates and the annual cost per dollar of borrowed funds.

In drawing any demand curve, we have to assume that all other conditions affecting demand are given and unchanged. But it is important to know what determines the position of the demand curve. We need to answer questions such as: Why is the demand curve neither higher nor lower at each level of interest rates? What forces can shift I upward at each rate of interest? What forces can shift the curve downward? To answer such questions, we need to know the motivations of those who spend for investment, and the nature of the benefits they balance against interest costs in arriving at decisions as to whether and how much to spend for investment.

Marginal efficiency of investment

The great bulk of investment expenditures are made by business firms intent on making net profits. Hence, in determining whether or not to make a capital expenditure, they ask, "Will the acquisition of this capital good add at least as much to my revenues as it adds to my costs?" This applies to purchases for replacement as well as to net additions to capital. Decisions as to the amount of new investment therefore depend on a comparison of interest costs and the expected annual rate of return on new investment. The latter has been given many names, including "marginal revenue product of capital" and "marginal efficiency of investment." We shall use the latter term and define it as the annual amount (stated as a percentage of the cost of the capital goods) that the acquisition of the new capital goods is expected to add to the enterprise's net revenues after deduction of all additional costs of operation except interest costs on the money used. For our purposes, we shall view the marginal efficiency of investment as a schedule or function showing the various amounts of new investment that are expected to yield at least various rates of return. The demand for investment is derived from the marginal-efficiency-of-investment schedule. Enterprisers intent on maximizing their profits tend to buy those types and amounts of capital that they expect to yield a rate of return in excess of the interest cost of the money used to purchase them. Presumably, they will not buy capital whose expected rate of return is below the interest rate.

Note that we have emphasized that the "expected" annual rate of return is a prime consideration in the selection of a new investment. Enterprisers select their investments on the basis of their expectations as to future yields—their decisions are based on the best forecasts they can make. They cannot be certain that the returns will meet their expectations because many types of capital yield their returns only over a long period and much can change in the interim. But they must make decisions, even if they recognize the fallibility of their forecasts.

Of the many factors that affect the schedule of the marginal efficiency of investment some of the more important are listed below.

1. Size and composition of stock. If the existing stock of capital goods is largely obsolete and too small to produce most economically the rate of output currently demanded, large amounts of new investment may be expected to yield high rates of return. But if the existing stock of capital goods is very large relative to the current demand for output and if this stock includes the most efficient types of capital that man knows how to make and utilize, only small amounts of new investment will be profitable. If there is already excess capacity, business firms may refrain from replacing some of their equipment when it wears out.

2. Rate of innovation. If the rate of innovation is high, it may be profitable to undertake much new investment in order to produce the new types of products or to use new and more economical processes of production. If the rate of innovation is low, the profitability of new investment goods for this purpose may be smaller.

3. Expected future behavior of demands for output. If demands for output are expected to rise rapidly, much new investment may be expected to yield high profits. If demands for output are expected to remain at existing levels and the present stock of capital goods is adequate, the demand for new capital goods may be largely a replacement demand. And if demands for output are expected to decline, many potential spenders for investment may not replace their capital equipment when it wears out.

4. Cost expectations. Expectations as to future wages, other costs, taxes, and government policies also determine investment efficiency. Estimates of the profitability of new investment may be greatly affected by expectations regarding the future course of these factors.

5. State of "business psychology." In view of the scarcity and vagueness of our knowledge about the future and the precariousness of any forecast based on that knowledge, it is not at all surprising that expectations concerning the future should be greatly affected by prevailing conditions and the trends of the immediate past. The late John Maynard Keynes put it as follows.

It would be foolish, in forming our expectations, to attach great weight to matters which are very uncertain. It is reasonable, therefore, to be guided to a considerable degree by the facts about which we feel somewhat confident, even though they may be less decisively relevant to the issue than other facts about which our knowledge is vague and scanty. For this reason the facts of the existing situation enter, in a sense disproportionately, into the formation of our long-term expectation; our usual practice being to take the existing situation and to project it into the future, modified only to the extent that we have more or less definite reasons for expecting a change.[3]

This convention of projecting the present situation into the future—and particularly the practice of extending the trend of the immediate past so that it applies to the future—is an aggravating factor in the business cycle. In the period of upswing, an original increase in the profitability of production is likely to give birth to expectations of still greater profits, whereas in the downswing, an original decline is likely to breed expectations of continued contraction.

Partly because of the paucity and uncertainty of our knowledge concerning future events, expectations are inordinately influenced by waves of excessive optimism and pessimism. Realizing the untrustworthiness of his own opinions with respect to the future, each person relies heavily on the opinions of others, which may be as undependable as his own. By a process that only a social psychologist can explain, the public temperament fluctuates from exultation to melancholia. At one time, it exhibits the exuberance and optimism of a "new era." Then it lapses into dark discouragement and despair. In these alternating periods of over-optimism and overpessimism, enterprisers are prone to overestimate and underestimate the returns to be realized from new investment.

It is an essential characteristic of the boom that investments which will in fact yield, say, 2 percent in conditions of full employment are made in the expectation of a yield of, say, 6 percent, and are valued accordingly. When disillusion comes, this expectation is replaced by a contrary "error of pessimism," with the result that the investments, which would in fact yield 2 percent in conditions of full employment, are expected to yield less than nothing; and the resulting collapse of new investment then leads to a state of unemployment in which the investments, which would have yielded 2 percent in conditions of full employment, in fact yield less than nothing.[4]

It is difficult to assess the relative importance of the state of "business psychology" as a determinant of the marginal efficiency of investment. It can easily be overstressed as a determinant of expectations. We should be quite suspicious of explanations based solely on mob psychology and ignoring such basic factors as the supply of capital goods relative to other factors of production, the state of technology and its rate of advance, the rate of growth of population, and so on. On the other hand, explanations based solely on these basic factors and their rates of change cannot deal adequately with short-run and cyclical shifts of the marginal efficiency of investment.

[3] J. M. Keynes, *The General Theory of Employment, Interest and Money*, New York, Harcourt Brace Jovanovich, 1936, p. 148.

[4] *Ibid.*, p. 322.

In any case, the schedule of the marginal efficiency of investment is capable of wide shifts. This should be borne in mind for two reasons:

1. When we draw an investment-demand schedule to show the effects of interest rates on investment demand, we are assuming that the schedule of the marginal efficiency of investment is given and constant.

2. We shall later want to deal with upward and downward shifts of the investment-demand schedule and their effects on Y. An upward shift of the II curve, an increase of investment demand at each interest rate, may be brought about by any force that raises the marginal efficiency of investment schedule. The II curve may be shifted downward at each level of interest rates by anything that lowers the marginal-efficiency-of-investment schedule.

MARGINAL RESPONSIVENESS OF INVESTMENT DEMAND TO INTEREST RATES

Let us now return to the investment-demand curve that is drawn on the assumption that the marginal efficiency of investment is given and constant, and which therefore enables us to consider the effects of interest rates on the size of the investment demand for output. In determining the equilibrium level of Y, it is sometimes sufficient to know that I tends to be larger when r is lower, and lower when r is higher. For some purposes, however, it is useful to try to quantify this relationship, to ask how much a given change of interest rates would alter the size of the investment demand. We shall call this the *marginal responsiveness of investment to interest rates*. By this we shall mean the dollar change in the annual rate of investment expenditure for output in response to a change of 1 percent in the interest rate. This can be denoted by $\Delta I/\Delta r$, where ΔI is the change in the investment demand for output, and Δr is a change of 1 percent in the interest rate. In Figure 16–3, $\Delta I/\Delta r$ is clearly larger on the I_0I_0 investment-demand curve than it is on the I_1I_1 curve.[5]

In our later analysis of income determination we shall employ investment-demand functions that are negatively related to interest rates. However, at this point we use a simpler investment-demand function to accomplish two purposes: (1) to establish the generally applicable principle that a necessary condition for equilibrium is that investment demand be exactly equal to saving supply, and (2) to elucidate the nature of "the multiplier." Until further notice, we shall assume that investment demand is not at all responsive to interest rates. This is illustrated by the II line in Figure 16–4.

EQUALITY OF *I* AND *S*

The one major point to be made here is that income and output can be at an equilibrium level only if investment demand is exactly equal to the supply of

---

[5] An investment-demand curve need not, of course, be a straight line, and the value of $\Delta r/\Delta I$ may be different at different ranges of interest rates.

Figure 16–3 The marginal responsiveness of investment to the interest rate

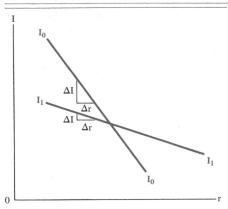

saving. Given the *II* and *SS* functions, the only equilibrium level of *Y* is Y_0. Only at this level of *Y* is the investment demand for output exactly equal to the supply of output represented by the supply of saving, that is, to the supply of output in excess of the amount taken off the market by *C*. Only at this level of *Y* is the market just cleared of output, with neither excess demand nor excess supply. Any level of *Y* greater than Y_0 would be a level of disequilibrium, because the supply of output represented by saving would exceed investment demand; some part of the supply would not be cleared from the market. If such a situation occurred, producers might immediately respond by reducing their rate of output, thus lowering *Y*. If they did not respond quickly enough, some of their output would pile up in "unwanted" inventories, which would lead them to cut production so that they could dispose of their excess stocks. In this process, they might temporarily reduce their output below Y_0 until their excess inventories had been sold off.

Any level of output below Y_0 would be a level of disequilibrium, because at lower levels of *Y*, the investment demand for output would exceed the supply of output represented by saving. Faced by such a situation of excess demand, pro-

Figure 16–4 The equality of investment demand and the supply of saving

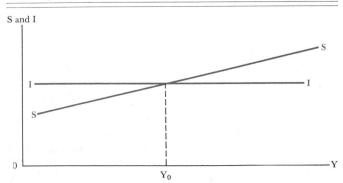

ducers might immediately increase their rate of output, thereby raising the level of Y. If they did not increase the output rate fast enough, they would experience an "unwanted" depletion of their inventories, which would lead them to accelerate production in order to rebuild their stocks. In this process, they might temporarily raise their rate of output above Y_0 until their inventories had been replenished.

Thus, equality of investment demand and saving supply is always a necessary condition for an equilibrium level of Y. If investment demand were completely unresponsive to r, an investment-demand function and a saving-supply function together could establish a unique equilibrium level of Y with no help from the money-supply function and the demand for money-balances function. But this becomes impossible if investment demand is responsive to interest rates. In this case, there are many combinations of interest rates and income levels that will equalize I and S, as we shall see later.

THE MULTIPLIER

The multiplier is one of the key concepts in Keynesian models of income determination. It refers to the fact that an autonomous increase or decrease of expenditures for output can increase or decrease total expenditures for output by some multiple by inducing a change of consumption expenditures in the same direction. This effect results from the positive slope of the consumption function, which posits that the community will increase its consumption expenditures by a fraction, equal to $\Delta C/\Delta Y$, or MPC, of each increase in its disposable income. The total effect on the level of expenditures for output (ΔY) is equal to the autonomous rise of expenditure (designated by ΔE) plus the induced change of consumption (ΔC).

An autonomous change in expenditures can take any one of several forms. For example, an autonomous increase can be in the form of a rise of investment demand (ΔI), a rise of government purchases of goods and services (ΔG), a rise of foreign demand for American exports (ΔX), or an upward shift of the consumption function, which is the same as a downward shift of the saving-supply function. To illustrate the principles involved, let us assume that the autonomous change is an increase of investment demand (ΔI), that $\Delta I = \$100$, and that investment demand remains at this higher level. This increase of investment will directly increase Y by $\$100$ and also raise the community's income by the same amount. The community can be expected to use some part of this increase of income to increase its consumption expenditures. Suppose that $\Delta C/\Delta Y = 0.8$ and $\Delta S/\Delta Y = 0.2$. Those persons whose incomes were increased by the rise of I will increase their consumption expenditures by $\$80$, which will increase by that amount the incomes of others, who will in turn increase their consumption by 0.8 times $\$80$, or $\$64$. And so the process of increased income and increased consumption will be continued until consumption reaches a new plateau. At the end of the process, Y will have been increased by $500, of which $100 represents the rise of investment and $400 the induced rise of consumption.

The outcome is summarized by the Keynesian multiplier:

$$\Delta Y = \Delta E \; \frac{1}{1 - (\Delta C/\Delta Y)}^{6}$$

where ΔE = the autonomous change of expenditures

$$\frac{1}{1 - \Delta C/\Delta Y} = \text{the multiplier}$$

Since $1 - \Delta C/\Delta Y = \Delta S/\Delta S$, the multiplier can also be expressed as $1/(\Delta S/\Delta Y)$. In our numerical example, the size of the multiplier is 5, and

$$\$500 = 100 \; \frac{1}{1 - 0.8} = \frac{100}{0.2}$$

It should be clear that as $\Delta C/\Delta Y$ increases (that is, as $\Delta S/\Delta Y$ grows smaller), the multiplier will become larger. It should also be clear that the multiplier operates downward in response to an autonomous decline of expenditures. For example, trace the effects on Y if investment falls by $50 and remains at the lower level, and $\Delta C/\Delta Y = 0.8$.

The multiplier process can also be explained in terms of saving-investment relationships. For example, suppose that, starting from the equilibrium-income level, Y_0, at which $I = S$, I rises by $100 and remains at this higher level (see Figure 16–5). Y_0 is no longer an equilibrium level, because at that level of income

Figure 16–5 Multiplier effects of an increase of investment

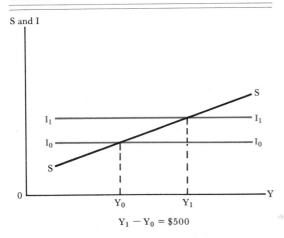

S and I

$Y_1 - Y_0 = \$500$

---

6 This is the sum of an infinite geometric series of type: $1 + r + r^2 + r^3 + \cdots$, where r is the common ratio. The formula for the sum of such an infinite series reduces to $1/(1 - r)$. In our case, r is $\Delta C/\Delta Y$. In the long form, the sum of the series would be $100 + 100 \, (0.8)^2 + 100 \, (0.8)^3 + 100 \, (0.8)^4 + \cdots$.

there will now be a $100 excess of I over S, which will drive income upward. If I remains at its new higher level, a new equilibrium will be reached only when S is also increased by $100. But with a constant saving-supply function, S can be increased only by an increase of Y. How much Y will have to rise to increase S by $100 varies reciprocally with the marginal responsiveness of S to Y. Suppose $\Delta S/\Delta Y = 0.2$. In this case, Y must rise by $500 to increase S by $100.

Let us consider this in steps:

1. Since I has risen $100 and remains at the new level, S must rise by the same amount if a new equilibrium is to be established.

2. With a constant saving-supply function, only a rise of Y can increase S, and each rise of Y will increase S by an amount equal to $\Delta S/\Delta Y$.

3. Since the required rise of $S = \$100$, we can write

$$\$100 = \Delta Y \frac{\Delta S}{\Delta Y}$$

Dividing both sides of the equation by $\Delta S/\Delta Y$ to find the required increase of Y, we get

$$\Delta Y = \$100 \times \frac{1}{\Delta S/\Delta Y}$$

If $\Delta S/\Delta Y = 0.2$,

$$\Delta Y = 100 \frac{1}{0.2} = \$500$$

Only if Y rises by this amount can it be in equilibrium with $I = S$. Any smaller rise of Y would leave S smaller than I, and the excess demand for output would continue to increase Y. On the other hand, any larger rise of Y would make S larger than I, and excess supply of output over the total demand for output would serve to depress Y.

To clarify the multiplier principle, we have employed a very simple model and made some simplifying assumptions. One of the latter is that "the full multiplier effect" will actually be realized. However, we shall see later that the very process of expansion or contraction following an autonomous change of expenditures may generate changes in interest rates that will modify the outcome. The actual outcome is not independent of the behavior of L and M.

AN I = S LINE

In an earlier model, which assumed that investment demand is unaffected by the level of interest rates, we found not only that equality of I and S is a necessary condition for equilibrium, but also that I and S functions alone were sufficient to determine a unique equilibrium level of Y. The latter conclusion is not valid when I is responsive to the level of r. In this case, there are many combinations

Figure 16–6 Investment demand and the supply of saving

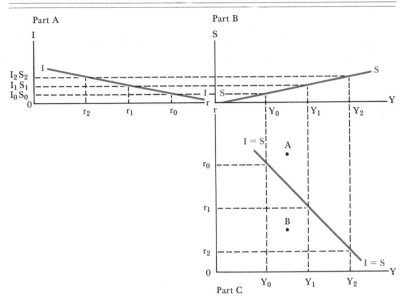

Part C

of Y and r that satisfy the necessary condition for equilibrium, $I = S$. This is shown graphically in Figure 16–6.

The vertical scales in Parts A and B of Figure 16–6 are the same, so that the same vertical heights indicate equal amounts of S and I. Even a casual inspection of the two upper graphs reveals that there are various combinations of interest rates and income levels that will produce the condition $I = S$. For example, $S = I$ at the low vertical level $I_0 S_0$ if r is at the high level r_0, thereby holding I to a low level, and if Y is at the low level Y_0, thereby generating only a low supply of S. $I = S$ at the somewhat higher level $I_1 S_1$ if the rate of interest is at the lower level r_1, thereby stimulating I, and if Y is at the higher level Y_1, thereby generating a larger supply of saving. $I = S$ at the very high level $I_2 S_2$ if the rate of interest is at the very low level r_2 and income is at the high level Y_2. We might thus note all the possible combinations of interest-rate levels and income levels that would produce the condition $I = S$.

This is done in Part C of Figure 16–6. The line $I = S$ plots out all those combinations of r, measured on the vertical axis, and Y, measured on the horizontal axis, at which S and I would be equal. The $I = S$ line slopes downward to the right because the supply of S would be larger at higher levels of income, and with a given investment demand function, I can be made correspondingly larger only by a fall of r.

The same conclusions emerge from the numerical example in Table 16–1. This table is based on the types of consumption, saving, and investment functions presented above in Equations (1), (2), and (3). The following values are assumed, with all flows stated in billions of dollars at annual rates.

$$C = 130 + 0.8Y$$

$$S = 0.2Y - 130$$

$$I = 130 - 10r$$

Table 16–1 Equality of I and S with I responsive to r

r (PERCENT)	Y	C	S	I
1	1,250	1,130	120	120
2	1,200	1,090	110	110
3	1,150	1,050	100	100
4	1,100	1,010	90	90
5	1,050	970	80	80
6	1,000	930	70	70
7	950	890	60	60
8	900	850	50	50
9	850	810	40	40

It will be noted that $I = S$ at every combination of Y and r shown in the table. For example, $I = S = \$120$ at $Y = \$1,250$ and $r = 1$ percent. $I = S = \$70$ at $Y = \$1,000$ and $r = 6$ percent, and so on. Note also that when $I = S$, $Y = C + I$. Thus we could also analyze total demand for output by adding together the consumption and investment-demand functions.

Let us return to Part C of Figure 16–6. No point representing a combination of r and Y that is off the $I = S$ line can represent equilibrium conditions. For example, consider any point A that lies above the $I = S$ line. At any such point, I would be less than S. We know this because at the same level of Y, there is some lower rate of interest directly below A on the $I = S$ line at which I is exactly equal to S. If, by some chance, the combination of r and Y represented by point A should occur, the excess of S over I could be remedied only by a fall of interest rates to stimulate I, a decline of Y to reduce S, or some combination of changes of r and Y to a point on the $I = S$ line. On the other hand, at any point such as B, below the $I = S$ line, I would be greater than S. We know this because at the same level of Y, there is some higher rate of interest directly above B on the $I = S$ line at which I is exactly equal to S. A disequilibrium combination such as B could be remedied only by a rise of r to reduce I, an increase of Y to increase S, or a combination of changes of r and Y to a point on the $I = S$ line.

Any combination of Y and r that is off the $I = S$ line is not only one of disequilibrium but also creates pressures serving to return the level of Y to some point on the $I = S$ line. For example, a combination above the line with saving supply exceeding investment demand indicates that there is an excess of the total supply of output over the total demand for output $(C + I)$. This deficiency of demand will lead producers to reduce output and employment. On the other hand, a combination below the line with I exceeding S indicates an excess of total

demand for output $(C + I)$ over the total supply of output, thus inducing producers to expand output and employment. However, the point on the $I = S$ line
to which Y returns need not be a point of full employment.

When we recognize that I is responsive to the level of interest rates, we must
somewhat modify our explanation of the multiplier, although the basic principles
remain unchanged. In the simple model with I unresponsive to interest rates, we
could use comparative statics to explain the multiplier effect—comparing the
unique equilibrium levels of Y before and after an autonomous change of expenditures (ΔE) (see Figure 16–5). With I responsive to interest rates, this type
of presentation becomes inapplicable because I and S functions alone cannot
determine unique equilibrium levels of Y; they determine only $I = S$ lines. In this
case, the multiplier effect appears as a right or left shift of the $I = S$ line. A rise of
autonomous expenditures shifts the $I = S$ line to the right, and a fall of autonomous expenditures shifts it to the left.

This is illustrated in Figure 16–7. Assume that the initial situation from
which we start is represented by $I_0 = S_0$, which is derived from the investment-
demand function I_0I_0 and the saving-supply function S_0S_0. Assume further that
the equilibrium level of interest rates is r_0 and the equilibrium level of income is
Y_0. Suppose now that the investment-demand function shifts upward at each level
of interest rates by \$100, rising to I_1I_1, while the saving-supply function remains
unchanged. The various combinations of Y and r that formerly equated S and I
will no longer do so; at each such combination I now exceeds S by \$100. At any

Figure 16–7 Shift of investment demand

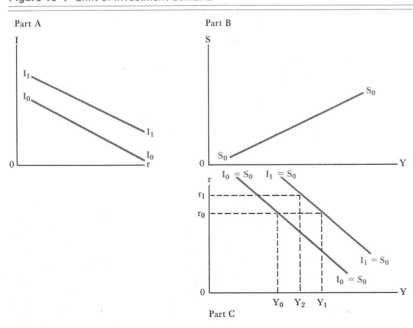

Part A

Part B

Part C

given level of interest rates, S can be raised to the level of I only by a rise of Y. As before, the amount by which Y must rise to increase S by \$100 varies reciprocally with $\Delta S/\Delta Y$. If $\Delta S/\Delta Y = 0.2$,

$$\Delta Y = \$100 \; \frac{1}{0.2} = \$500$$

The new line, $I_1 = S_0$, lies to the right of the old $I_0 = S_0$ line at each level of interest rates by this amount. The new equilibrium-income level must lie somewhere on this line, for it includes all combinations of Y and r which would equate I and S.

If interest rates remain unchanged at the level r_0, the full multiplier effect on income will be realized, with income rising from Y_0 to Y_1. Suppose, however, that in this process interest rates are increased, perhaps from r_0 to r_1. As will be seen in the next chapter, this is quite likely to happen if monetary policy is not such as to prevent a rise of rates. In this case, the full multiplier effect will not be realized. Some of the rise of investment expenditures that would have occurred if interest rates had remained constant will be "snubbed" by the rise of interest rates.

Similarly, a downward shift of the I function at each level of r will shift the $I = S$ line to the left by an amount equal to the downward shift of I times the multiplier. The full downward-multiplier effect will be realized if the interest rate remains unchanged. If, however, the process of decline generates a fall of interest rates, this will "snub" the decline of I and Y.

Multiplier analysis is an essential element in the theory of income determination. The forces and tendencies with which it deals are potent. However, it would be a mistake to assume that a given autonomous change of expenditures will in fact change Y by exactly the amount indicated by the multiplier. Multiplier analysis assumes that the process does not generate or encounter any change in interest rates or in the availability of funds that would "snub" the expansion or contraction. However, something like this will probably occur unless prevented by monetary policy. This point will be elaborated later, but enough has already been said to indicate the danger of using any form of income theory that does not take into account the money supply and demand-for-money functions.

CONCLUSIONS

This chapter has presented three functions that will be essential elements in the synthesis of monetary and income theories to be presented in the next chapter— the consumption function, the saving-supply function, and the investment-demand function. Although these are necessary elements in explaining equilibrium levels of Y and r, they are not by themselves sufficient to determine unique equilibrium levels of Y and r. To do this, they must be supplemented by our old friends—the money-supply function and the demand function for money balances.

Selected readings

Ackley, G., *Macroeconomic Theory*, New York, Macmillan, 1961.

Allen, R. G. D., *Macroeconomic Theory: A Mathematical Treatment*, London, Macmillan, 1968.

Smith, W. L., *Macroeconomics*, Homewood, Ill., Irwin, 1970.

CHAPTER 17

A SYNTHESIS
OF MONETARY
AND INCOME THEORY

The analysis presented below combines elements from the quantity-theory approach with elements from the income and expenditure approach. From the quantity-theory approach it borrows the concepts of a money-supply function and a demand function for money balances. The money supply (M) is assumed to be determined by the monetary authority. Thus,

$$M = \text{stock of money} = \text{a policy-determined variable} \tag{1}$$

The demand function for money balances (L) is the sum of the demand function for money for transactions purposes (L_1) and the demand function for money balances for asset or store-of-value purposes (L_2). L_1 is a positive function of Y, such that $L_1 = JOP = JY$. L_2 is a negative function of interest rates, such that $L_2 = P(A - Er)$. Thus,

$$L = L_1 + L_2$$

$$L = JOP + P(A - Er)$$

or

(2)

$$L = P(JO + A - Er)$$

A necessary condition for equilibrium is that $L = M$. However, with L responsive to interest rates, M and L functions alone are not sufficient to determine unique equilibrium levels of Y and r. They can determine only $L = M$ lines, at some point on which an equilibrium combination of Y and r must lie.

From the income and expenditure approach we borrow the concepts of a consumption function, a saving-supply function, and an investment-demand function. Consumption is a positive function of income, such that

$$C = B + \frac{\Delta C}{\Delta Y} Y \tag{3}$$

$\Delta C / \Delta Y$ (or MPC) is a positive fraction, with a value greater than zero but less than one. Saving supply is also a positive function of income, such that

$$S = Y \frac{\Delta S}{\Delta Y} - B \tag{4}$$

It will be remembered that $\Delta S / \Delta Y = 1 - (\Delta C / \Delta Y)$. Investment demand is a negative function of interest rates, such that

$$I = D - \frac{\Delta I}{\Delta r} r \tag{5}$$

If we wished, we could analyze the total demand for output (Y) by adding the consumption function to the investment-demand function:

$$Y = B + \frac{\Delta C}{\Delta Y} Y + D - \frac{\Delta I}{\Delta r} r$$

This reduces to

$$Y = \frac{B + D - (\Delta I / \Delta r) r}{1 - (\Delta C / \Delta Y)} \tag{6}$$

However, we get the same results by using the S and I functions. A necessary condition for equilibrium is that $I = S$. However, I and S functions alone are not sufficient to determine unique equilibrium levels of Y and r. They can determine only $I = S$ lines, at some point on which an equilibrium combination of Y and r must lie.

Combining the two approaches, we shall discover that:

1. Unique equilibrium levels of Y and r are determined simultaneously by the four functions, $M, L, S,$ and I. Equilibrium is determined not by any one or two of the functions but by all of them together, and a shift of any one of the functions will shift the equilibrium.

2. Equilibrium can exist only if two conditions are met simultaneously: $L = M$ and $I = S$.

Until further notice, we shall assume that the price level remains constant, so that money values also indicate the behavior of "real" values. Complications accompanying changes in price levels will be discussed later.

SIMPLE STATICS

We begin with the determination of equilibrium levels of income and interest rates with four given and constant functions: saving-supply, investment-demand, money-supply, and demand-for-money balances. "Equilibrium" does not necessarily signify "full employment" or "desirable"; it indicates only the levels that will tend to be established and maintained by the given and constant functions.

It will be convenient to assume that the $L = M$ line in Figure 17–1 results from the values given to the M and L functions in Table 15–2 (see p. 000) and that the $I = S$ line results from the values given to the S and I functions in Table 16–1 (see p. 364).

Given these functions, interest rates and income can be in equilibrium only at the point of intersection, r_e, Y_e, of the $I = S$ and $L = M$ lines. Only this combination satisfies simultaneously the two necessary conditions for equilibrium: $I = S$ and $L = M$. Any other combination of r and Y would be a disequilibrium combination and would create pressures for change. We found earlier that at any combination above the $L = M$ line, M would exceed L, and the excess supply of money would serve to lower interest rates. This pressure toward lower interest rates is indicated in Figure 17–1 by the downward-pointing arrows from points A and B, both of which lie above the $L = M$ line. On the other hand, at any combination of Y and r below the $L = M$ line, L would exceed M, and the excess demand for money balances would serve to raise interest rates. This is indicated in Figure 17–1 by the upward-pointing arrows from points C and D. We also found that at any combinations of Y and r above the $I = S$ line, S would exceed I, and that the excess of supply of output over total demands for it would induce reductions of output and employment. This is indicated in Figure 17–1 by the left-pointing arrows from points A and D, both of which lie above the $I = S$ line. However,

Figure 17–1 $L = M$ and $I = S$ lines

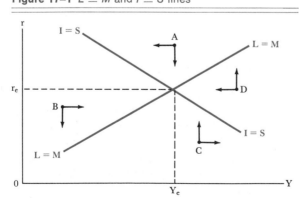

at any combination below the $I = S$ line, I would exceed S, and the excess of total demand over the supply of output would lead producers to increase output and employment. This is indicated in Figure 17–1 by the right-pointing arrows from points B and C. Only at the point of intersection of the $L = M$ and $I = S$ lines, Y_e, r_e, is there no pressure for change.

COMPARATIVE STATICS

Let us now use comparative statics to analyze the effects of shifts of the four functions. We shall shift the functions one at a time, leaving the other three unchanged, and compare equilibrium conditions before and after the shift.

Increase of the investment-demand function

Suppose that, starting from the equilibrium situation illustrated in Figure 17–1 there occurs an upward shift of the investment-demand function, and that the function remains at the higher level. For example, investment expenditures might be increased by $10 billion at each level of interest rates. This is indicated in Part A of Figure 17–2. The combination r_e, Y_e is no longer an equilibrium combination because at those levels of r and Y investment demand now exceeds saving supply by $10 billion. The rise of investment spending increases directly the total demand for output and also increases the community's disposable income, which will induce a rise of consumption spending. This is the multiplier process discussed earlier. A new equilibrium can be established only when I and S are

Figure 17–2 Shift of investment demand

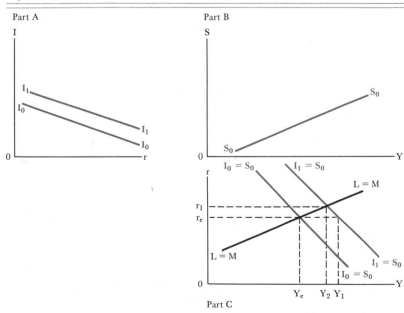

again equated. Given the constant saving-supply function and the new investment-demand function, I and S can be equated only by a rise of Y that will increase S, a rise of r that will decrease I, or some combination of the two. S can be raised by $10 billion to match the rise of I at each level of interest rates only by an increase of Y, such that

$$\Delta Y \frac{\Delta S}{\Delta Y} = \$10 \text{ billion}$$

If we assume that $\Delta S/\Delta Y = 0.2$,

$$\Delta Y = \frac{\$10 \text{ billion}}{0.2} = \$50 \text{ billion}$$

This is illustrated by the horizontal shift to the right of the $I = S$ line to $I_1 = S_0$ in Figure 17–2. The new equilibrium must be somewhere on this line, because only at the combinations of r and Y represented by this line can $I = S$.

Figure 17–2 indicates that if interest rates remain unchanged at the old equilibrium level, r_e, the full multiplier effect on income levels can be achieved. Actual investment expenditures will increase by an amount equal to the upward shift of the function, $10 billion, and the multiplier effect will be

$$\Delta Y = \$10 \text{ billion} \frac{1}{0.2} = \$50 \text{ billion}$$

However, if the money supply remains constant and the L function is of the type assumed here, neither the full $10 billion increase of I nor the full multiplier effect on income is likely to be realized. This is because the rise of Y serves to increase the quantity of money demanded, so that the total demand for money can be equated to the constant supply only if interest rates rise, and the rise of interest rates will "snub" the increase of investment. How much the rise of actual investment will be snubbed depends on the extent of the rise of r and on the marginal responsiveness of investment to interest rates $(\Delta I/\Delta r)$.

It is clear, therefore, that the consequences of the upward shift of the I function depends in part on the slope of the $L = M$ line $(\Delta r/\Delta Y)$. If the $L = M$ line is nearly vertical—that is, if $\Delta r/\Delta Y$ approaches infinity—the outcome will be a large rise of r and virtually no increase of actual investment or income. However, if the $L = M$ line approaches a horizontal position—that is, if $\Delta r/\Delta Y$ approaches zero—there will be virtually no rise of r and almost the full multiplier effects will be realized.

The value of $\Delta r/\Delta Y$ depends on both the size of J and on the degree of responsiveness of L_2 to r, or $\Delta L_2/\Delta r$. The reasoning is as follows: Each rise of Y will increase the quantity of money demanded for L_1 purposes by an amount equal to $J\Delta Y$. With total M constant, the quantity of money demanded for L_2 purposes must decline by an offsetting amount to maintain the necessary equilibrium condition, $L = M$. But with L_2 a constant negative function of r, the quantity of money demanded for L_2 purposes can be reduced only by a rise of r. If the responsiveness of L_2 to r approaches zero, very large increases of r will be required to reduce L_2 demands enough to offset each increase of L_1 demands, and the $L = M$ line will be nearly vertical. This is illustrated by the $(L = M)_a$ line in Figure 17–3. However, if L_2 demands for money are almost infinitely responsive to r only a very small rise of r will be required to offset each increase of L_1 demands, and the $L = M$ line will be almost horizontal. This is illustrated by the $(L = M)_b$ line in Figure 17–3.

Two extreme cases will be instructive.

1. The marginal responsiveness of L to r is so small as to approach zero. That is, a rise of interest rates brings no decrease in the quantity of money demanded, so none is freed to satisfy the increased demand for money that would be generated by a rise of Y. In this extreme case, the upward shift of the investment-demand function increases neither actual investment nor the level of income; it is reflected solely in a rise of interest rates.

2. The responsiveness of L to r approaches infinity; that is, even a minute rise of r will decrease by huge amounts the quantity of money demanded, and this will be available to meet the increased demand for money generated by a rise of Y; the $L = M$ line will be virtually horizontal. In this extreme case, there will be no rise of interest rates, investment will rise by the full amount of the upward shift of the investment function, and the full multiplier effects on Y will be achieved.

In the usual case, the $L = M$ line will be neither vertical nor horizontal; it will have a positive slope between these two extremes. From this case of an upward shift of the investment-demand function we can draw several conclusions:

1. It is dangerous to discuss the magnitude of multiplier effects without considering the money-supply and demand-for-money functions. The very process of increasing the level of income generates an increase in the quantity of money demanded which, in the absence of a compensating increase of the money supply, will tend to raise interest rates and snub the increases of investment and income.

2. To hold the money supply constant in the face of an upward shift of the investment function will usually not suffice to prevent some rise of total expenditures for output. The ensuing rise of r will free some part of the money stock to

Figure 17–3 Some slopes of the $L = M$ line

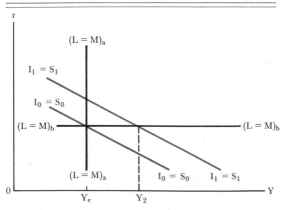

satisfy the increased demands for money generated by the rise of the money value of output.

We need not trace in detail the effects of a downward shift of the investment-demand function. In brief, at the old equilibrium levels of r and Y, the supply of saving will exceed investment demand, and a downward multiplier process will begin. This can be represented by a shift to the left by the $I = S$ line. However, the very decline of Y will serve to reduce the quantity of money demanded, and the excess supply of money will tend to reduce r, which will snub the decline of I and Y. Here again, the extent of the actual changes of I and Y will depend in part on the shape of the $L = M$ line in the relevant range. If L_2 demands for money are very highly responsive to each reduction of r, the $L = M$ line will be nearly horizontal, interest rates will fall but little, and nearly the full downward multiplier effects will result. But if L_2 demands for money are less responsive to each decline of interest rates, a larger decrease of r will result and the declines of I and Y will be snubbed.

Decrease of the saving-supply function

Suppose now that, starting from the initial equilibrium situation with $Y = Y_e$ and $r = r_e$, there occurs what may be viewed as either an upward shift of the consumption function or a decrease of the saving-supply function. For example, consumption demand may rise by $10 billion at each level of income, which is the same as saying that the supply of saving declines by $10 billion at each level of income, for $S = Y - C$. In many respects, although not all, the process and the results are the same as those following an upward shift of the investment-demand function. At the old equilibrium levels of Y and r, investment demand will exceed saving supply and the total demand for output (including the rise of consumption) will exceed the total supply of output by $10 billion. Thus an upward multiplier process is initiated. S and I can again be equated only by a rise of Y that will increase S, a rise of r that will reduce I, or some combination of the two. This is illustrated in Figure 17–4 by the shift to the right of the $I = S$ line to $I = S_1$. The amount of the shift to the right is, of course, equal to the $10 billion upward shift of the consumption function times the multiplier, $1 \div (\Delta S/\Delta Y)$. The new equilibrium must lie somewhere on this line.

However, the actual outcome in this case, as in the preceding ones, depends in part on the M and L functions. As Y rises, it increases the quantity of money demanded and tends to create an excess demand for money, which serves to raise interest rates. Any rise of r that occurs tends to decrease I and thus to snub the rise of income. How much I will be decreased and how much the rise of income will be snubbed depends on the amount of the rise of interest rates and on the marginal responsiveness of investment to interest rates $(\Delta I/\Delta r)$.

Up to this point, we have stressed the similarities of the case in which the investment-demand function shifted upward and the present case in which the consumption function shifted upward or the saving-supply function shifted downward. In both cases, there is an upward multiplier effect on income; and in both

Figure 17–4 Shift of saving supply

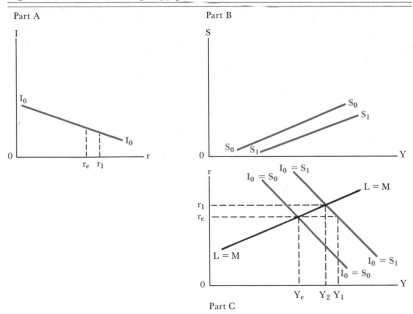

Part A

Part B

Part C

cases, the actual outcome depends in part on the slope of the $L = M$ line. However, there is an important difference between the two cases, and this relates to the composition of the increased output. In the general case in which the investment-demand function shifted upward, the resulting increase of output is composed in part of increased investment and in part of increased consumption. Only in the extreme case in which the $L = M$ line is vertical, is there no rise of I and C. In all other cases, there is some rise of Y, and this includes both some rise of I and an induced rise of C. However, if the upward thrust on income emanates from an upward shift of the consumption function (a decline of the saving-supply function), there will occur no rise of investment if investment remains a constant function of interest rates. In the extreme case in which the $L = M$ line is completely horizontal, so that there is no rise of interest rates, investment remains unchanged and the entire increase in output is in the form of consumption goods. However, to the extent that r rises and I is responsive to interest rates, I will actually decline.[1] This serves, of course, to reduce the extent of the rise of Y.

The reader is invited to trace the effects of a downward shift of the consumption function or upward shift of the saving-supply function. Note the initial autonomous decline of consumption demand, the downward multiplier effect on income illustrated by a shift to the left of the $I = S$ line, and the relevance of the

---

[1] These conclusions depend heavily on the assumption followed throughout this chapter that changes in the level of income do not shift the investment-demand function in the same direction.

slope of the $L = M$ line to the outcome. The outcome is, of course, some decline of output, income, and employment. This is often referred to as "the paradox of thrift"; an increase in the thriftiness of a community, in the sense of an upward shift of its saving function, can make it less prosperous. The outcome seems less paradoxical when we remember that this is a downward shift of the consumption function and note the implicit assumption that there is neither an offsetting rise of the investment-demand function nor a fall of interest rates sufficient to stimulate I enough to offset the fall of C.

Increase of the money supply

Again, starting from an initial equilibrium situation in which $Y = Y_e$ and $r = r_e$, suppose that the money supply is increased by some amount, such as \$10 billion, with all the other functions remaining constant. At the old equilibrium levels of Y and r, M will now exceed L, and the excess supply of money will serve to raise demands for securities and to lower interest rates. With the demand function for money constant, L can again be equated to M only when it is increased by \$10 billion by a rise of Y, a decline of r, or some combination of the two. At a constant level of interest rates, L could be increased \$10 billion by some increase of Y such that $J\Delta Y = \$10$ billion. For example, if

$$J = \frac{1}{5}$$

the rise of Y required to equate L and M would be

$$\frac{\$10 \text{ billion}}{1/5} \quad \text{or } \$50 \text{ billion}$$

This is shown in Figure 17–5 as a horizontal shift to the right of the $L = M$ line to $L = M_1$. L could also be increased \$10 billion by some decrease of r such that

$$\Delta r \frac{\Delta L}{\Delta r} = \$10 \text{ billion}$$

Suppose, for example, that $\Delta L/\Delta r = 5$; that is, each decline of r by 1 percent increases L by \$5 billion. In this case, the decline of r required to equate L and M would be

$$\frac{\$10 \text{ billion}}{\$5 \text{ billion}} = 2 \text{ percent}$$

In Figure 17–5 this is shown as a vertical downward shift of the $L = M$ line to $L = M_1$.

The new equilibrium must lie somewhere on the $L = M_1$ line, which includes all combinations of Y and r that equate L to M. At any combination lying below and to the right of this line, L would exceed M and the excess demand for money balances would serve to reduce demands for securities, and to raise interest rates. At any combination lying above and to the left of the $L = M_1$ line, M

Figure 17–5 Shift of the money supply

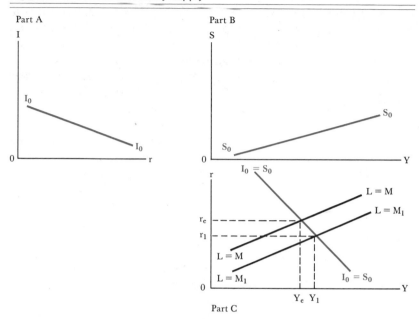

Part A

Part B

Part C

would exceed L, and the excess supply of money would serve to increase demands for securities and to lower interest rates.

However, as shown in Figure 17–5, the effects of a given increase of the money supply depend not only on the demand function for money balances but also on the saving-supply and investment-demand functions, which determine the location and shape of the $I = S$ line. For example, if the $I = S$ line is virtually horizontal, there will be little change of r but an increase of Y approximating the shift to the right of the $L = M$ line. However, if the $I = S$ is virtually vertical, the principal effect will be to lower r with little increase of Y. It is imperative, therefore, to investigate the determinants of the shape of the $I = S$ line. For this purpose, it will be convenient to deal not with the slope of the line but rather with its reciprocal, $\Delta Y/\Delta r$. This is a measure of the flatness of the line.

If, from some point on the $I = S$ line, r is lowered by some amount, Δr, this will increase I by an amount equal to $\Delta r (\Delta I/\Delta r)$. Thus, I will exceed S. With a constant saving-supply function, S can be increased to match the increase of I only by some rise of Y such that

$$\Delta Y \frac{\Delta S}{\Delta Y} = \Delta r \frac{\Delta I}{\Delta r}$$

Dividing both sides of the equation by Δr and $\Delta S/\Delta Y$, we get

$$\frac{\Delta Y}{\Delta r} = \frac{\Delta I}{\Delta r} \times \frac{1}{\Delta S/\Delta Y}$$

Thus, the flatness of the $I = S$ line $(\Delta Y/\Delta r)$ varies directly with the marginal responsiveness of investment to interest rates $(\Delta I/\Delta r)$ and reciprocally with the marginal propensity to save. Since $1 \div (\Delta S/\Delta Y)$ is our old friend, the multiplier, we can say that $\Delta Y/\Delta r$ varies directly with $\Delta I/\Delta r$ and the size of the multiplier. For example, if investment is completely unresponsive to interest rates—if $\Delta I/\Delta r = 0$— an increase of the money supply will not increase Y even if it succeeds in lowering interest rates. However, the more responsive investment is to interest rates, the greater will be the response of Y.

We are now in a position to visualize the processes through which a given increase of the money supply influences interest-rate and income levels and some of the factors that determine the nature and extent of the effects. We shall assume that the monetary authority increases the money supply by purchasing securities of various types from the public, and that spending for output is affected only through effects on the prices and yields on securities. The following processes are involved:

1. In creating the additional money, the monetary institutions—the central bank and the commercial banks—increase their demands for securities and loans. This increase of their demands tends to raise the prices of debt obligations and to lower their yields. As the public sells debt obligations to the monetary institutions and acquires more money, it finds that money constitutes a large fraction of its total assets and is impelled to buy more debt obligations, which tends to decrease interest rates still more.

2. As interest rates fall, the public demands larger quantities of money balances. How much a given increase of the money supply can depress interest rates varies inversely with the marginal responsiveness of the demand for money to interest rates $(\Delta L/\Delta r)$. If $\Delta L/\Delta r$ is large—if each fall of interest rates greatly increases the quantity of money demanded—the increase of the money supply can lower interest rates but little. However, if $\Delta L/\Delta r$ is very small, interest rates can be lowered more.

3. The size of the increase of investment demand depends not only on the size of the decrease of interest rates but also on the marginal responsiveness of investment to interest rates $(\Delta I/\Delta r)$. The greater is $\Delta I/\Delta r$, the greater will be the expansionary effects on I.

4. The size of the expansion of Y depends not only on the rise of I but also on the value of the multiplier, which varies directly with the marginal propensity to consume.

5. The rise of Y increases the quantity of money demanded; and as the expansion of Y continues, interest rates will rise. At some point the rise of r will bring the expansion to an end. This is the point of intersection of the $I = S$ line and the new $L = M$ line. How large this expansion will be depends in part on J.

We find, then, that the effects on Y of a given increase in the money supply depend on a number of factors: on $\Delta L/\Delta r$, which determines how much interest rates can be lowered; on $\Delta I/\Delta r$, which determines how much each decline of interest rates will stimulate investment; on $\Delta C/\Delta Y$, which determines the size of the multiplier; and on J, which reflects the amount by which the demand for money balances will be increased by each increase of Y. The smaller is J, the larger will be the increase of income that can occur before a rise of interest rates ends the expansion.

The case of a decrease of the money supply is symmetrical with that of an increase of the money supply. With the decrease of M, L exceeds M, and the excess demand for money balances decreases demands for securities and raises interest rates. The effects of Y and r depend on all of the factors described above. The reader is invited to trace out the effects, noting that the decrease in M will be evidenced by a horizontal leftward shift of the $L = M$ line.

Shifts of the L function

A decrease of the demand function for money, in the sense of a decrease in the quantity of money balances demanded at each combination of Y and r, has effects exactly comparable to those of an equivalent increase of the money supply. At the old equilibrium levels of Y and r, M will exceed L, and the excess supply of money tends to lower r and stimulate spending. This is reflected in a right and downward shift of the $L = M$ line. The outcome depends on the factors discussed in the case of an increase of the money supply.

On the other hand, an increase of the demand function for money balances, in the sense of an increase in the quantity of money balances demanded at each combination of Y and r, has effects exactly comparable to those of an equivalent decrease of the money supply. It creates an excess of L over M, and the excess demand for money serves to depress demands for other things.

CONCLUSIONS

The behavior of interest rates and of the level of income or output within the capacity levels of the economy depend, of course, on innumerable things. However, these can be summarized in four functions:
1. The consumption function and the saving-supply function
2. The investment-demand function
3. The money-supply function
4. The demand function for money

Equilibrium levels of income and interest rates depend not on just one or two of these functions but on all of them together. This was illustrated in the case of static equilibrium; the equilibrium would have been different if any one of the functions had been different. It became clearer in the cases of comparative statics, in which we shifted the functions one at a time, leaving all other functions constant. The outcome depended not only on the function that was shifted but also on its interactions with the other functions.

PRICE LEVELS AND EQUILIBRIUM

Up to this point, we have assumed that the price level was given and constant so that changes in Y, I, and S represented changes in real output and income. This assumption of a stable price level may be realistic if all the levels of Y under consideration are below those corresponding to full employment and if money wage rates and prices are inflexible upward and downward. Under such conditions, increases and decreases in demand may indeed be reflected largely, if not wholly, in changes in the level of real output or income. However, we must now recognize that increases or decreases in demands for output can increase or decrease the price level of output. In fact, further increases of demand after full employment has been reached must be reflected in price increases. This raises a series of questions, such as: What determines the equilibrium price level? How do changes in the price level affect r and other economic variables?

To explore such questions, we shall assume that demands for output are so large that actual output is at its full-employment level, so that further increases in demand would be reflected in higher prices. We shall state all the functions in "real" terms. That is, we shall state them in constant dollars, or at the price level prevailing in some base period. It will be convenient to state this price level as $P = 1$. In Figure 17–6, real income (Y/P) is measured on the horizontal axis. $(Y/P)_F$ is the highest achievable level of real output. The investment-demand function in real terms (I/P) is a negative function of interest rates. The saving-supply function in real terms (S/P) is a positive function of the level of real income Y/P. As before, a necessary condition for equilibrium is $I/P = S/P$. With given I/P and S/P functions, there is some rate of interest, such as 7 percent, which will equate I/P to the real supply of saving at the full-employment level of output $(Y/P)_F$. At any interest rate above this level, S/P would exceed I/P and the supply of output would exceed total demands for output. This deficiency of demand would lower P if prices are flexible downward and would lower real output below the full-employment level if prices are inflexible downward. At any level of interest rates below the equilibrium level, I/P would exceed S/P and would be reflected in excess demand for output. With Y/P already at its full-employment level, the excess demand would increase P.

Figure 17–6 Income determination in real terms

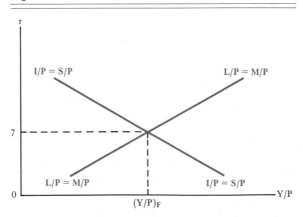

The demand for money balances in real terms (L/P) is a positive function of real income $(O$ or $Y/P)$ and a negative function of interest rates, such that

$$\frac{L}{P} = J \frac{Y}{P} + + A - er$$

At the full-employment level of output and at the equilibrium interest rate of 7 percent, L/P is a fixed quantity equal to $J(Y_F/P) + (A - 7e)$. This is indicated by the vertical L/P line in Figure 17–7. In this model we shall assume that the nominal money supply (M) is fixed and constant at some level, such as $250. With M constant, the real supply of money (M/P) varies inversely with the price level (see the M/P line in Figure 17–7). For example, measured in dollars of constant purchasing power $(1/P_1)$, M/P would be $250 with $P = 1$, only $125 with $P = 2$, and only $83\frac{1}{3}$ with $P = 3$. With the constant L/P function and a constant nominal money supply (M), there is only one price level consistent with the necessary condition for equilibrium: $M/P = L/P$. In Figure 17–7, it is assumed that this price level is $P = 2$. At any lower price level, M/P would exceed L/P, the excess supply of real balances would lower interest rates, and the fall of interest rates would increase investment spending and induce a rise of consumption spending. But with output already at its full-employment level, the higher demands would raise the price level. Excess demands would continue so long as the price level remained below $P = 2$.

On the other hand, at any level of prices above the equilibrium level, L/P would exceed M/P, the excess demand for money would tend to raise interest rates, and the rise of rates would reduce spending for investment. This, together with the induced lower level of consumption, would serve to lower P, or the rate of real output, or both. Thus the only equilibrium price level is that at which M/P is equated to L/P.

Two conclusions emerge from this model in which the nominal money supply is constant and the other functions are constant in real terms.

Figure 17–7 L/P and M/P with constant M

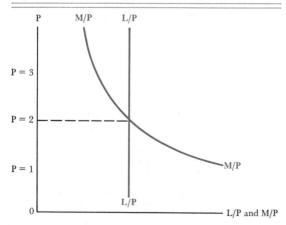

1. It is through adjustment of the price level that the real money supply (M/P) is equated to the constant demand for real money balances (L/P). For example, the price level cannot be in equilibrium above $P = 2$ because a higher level of P would reduce M/P below L/P.

2. The higher the price level, the higher will be the level of interest rates. This is because higher price levels reduce the real money supply.

Let us now use comparative statics to analyze the effects of an increase of the money supply after full employment has been reached. We start from an equilibrium situation in which the nominal money supply is $250, P is in equilibrium at 2, and r is in equilibrium at 7. Now we double the nominal money supply to $500, while the other functions remain constant in real terms. A new equilibrium will be reached only when the price level has also doubled. Adjustments will occur somewhat as follows:

1. At the old level of prices, $P = 2$, the real money supply will be doubled and will far exceed L/P. An excess of M/P over L/P will continue until a doubling of P has reduced M/P to its original level.

2. The excess of M/P over L/P will initially depress interest rates below their equilibrium level, thereby increasing investment spending, which will, in turn, induce a rise of spending for consumption.

3. With output already at full-employment levels, further increases in spending will be reflected in increases of the price level.

4. The rise of prices reduces M/P and tends to raise interest rates. This process will continue until prices have doubled, M/P is reduced to the level of L/P, and interest rates have risen to their old equilibrium level.

5. Prices cannot be in equilibrium at more than double their former equilibrium level because at such higher prices M/P would be smaller than L/P and r would be pushed above its equilibrium level, thereby tending to lower expenditures for output.

One conclusion from this model may be surprising: We conclude that the equilibrium level of interest rates is unaffected by a doubling of both the nominal money supply and the price level. This leads to more general questions concerning the relationships between the size of the money supply and the level of interest rates.

THE MONEY SUPPLY AND THE LEVEL OF INTEREST RATES

How does a change in the supply of money affect the equilibrium level of interest rates? In one set of cases we concluded that an expansion of the nominal money supply would lower the equilibrium level of interest rates, but in the last case we concluded that even a doubling of the nominal money supply would leave the equilibrium level of interest rates unchanged. This difference in conclusions results from differences in assumptions concerning the response of the price level following an increase in the nominal stock of money. In the first set of cases, we assumed that price levels remained constant; the induced increase of expenditures was reflected wholly in an expansion of real output. The real money supply remained proportional to the increased nominal money supply, and the larger real money supply depressed the equilibrium level of interest rates. The outcome is modified to the extent that the rise of expenditures induced by the increase of the nominal money supply is reflected in price increases. Each rise of P causes M/P to rise less than proportionally with M and correspondingly reduces the downward pressure on the equilibrium level of interest rates. If P rises proportionally with M, the real money supply is unchanged in the new equilibrium, and the equilibrium level of interest rates is also unchanged. Thus it does not at all follow that increases of the nominal money supply after full employment has been reached will lower equilibrium levels of interest rates.

In fact, as has been proved repeatedly, attempts to hold interest rates below their equilibrium level by increasing the nominal money supply are likely to generate accelerating price inflation. Suppose that an economy is operating at, or very close to its full-employment level and that the monetary authority decides to increase the nominal money supply to the extent necessary to hold interest rates below their equilibrium level. The initial increase of M will initiate a rise of P, which will tend to lower M/P and increase interest rates. So, more M will be created. At some stage, as Irving Fisher pointed out, price increases will create expectations of still more price increases in the future, thus raising demand functions for loan funds. Still more money would have to be created to prevent interest rates from rising. Such a policy is a perfect recipe for continuing, and probably accelerating, price inflation. In fact, once inflationary expectations become widespread, a level of interest rates that would have maintained price stability under conditions of noninflationary expectations will actually encourage inflation. Suppose that the old equilibrium rate was 7 percent, but that the annual rate of expected price inflation increases to 20 percent. A market rate of 7 percent is now a negative rate in real terms. For example, suppose you lend $100 at the beginning of a year and receive $107 at the end of the year, but in the meantime prices have risen 20 percent. The purchasing power of the $107 will be equal to only 89 percent (or 107/120) of the purchasing power of the money that you loaned. The borrower is, of course, the beneficiary. Once inflationary expectations have become firmly entrenched, very large increases in market rates of interest are required to halt the inflationary process.

Appendix A

Effects of income levels on investment demand

The preceding chapter emphasized many times the effects of the investment-demand function on income levels, but it did not deal in any systematic way with the effects of income levels on the investment-demand function. Implicitly, any shift of the investment-demand function was considered to be autonomous. This raises troublesome issues. It is quite clear that a change of income levels can indeed shift investment-demand functions. However, we considered this relationship so variable and unreliable that we did not assume investment to be a function of income as well as interest rates.

Some economists think otherwise and employ models in which investment is a negative function of interest rates and a positive function of the income level. In effect, they assume that any increase or decrease of income (ΔY) will shift the investment-demand function in the same direction by an amount equal to $\Delta Y\,(\Delta I/\Delta Y)$, where $\Delta I/\Delta Y$ is the marginal responsiveness of investment to income. Thus, a rise of income would shift the I function upward at each level of interest rates, and a fall of income would shift it downward.

Those who use this model take $\Delta I/\Delta Y$ into account by making it a determinant of the size of the multiplier. In our model, the multiplier is $1 \div (\Delta S/\Delta Y)$, with $\Delta S/\Delta Y$ considered to be in itself a "leakage" from the spending stream. In this model, however, any change in S because of a change in Y is at least partially offset by a change of I in the same direction. Thus, the "net leakage" is not ΔS but $\Delta S - \Delta I$. And the multiplier is

$$\frac{1}{(\Delta S/\Delta Y) - (\Delta I/\Delta Y)}$$

It is evident that the larger is $\Delta I/\Delta Y$, the larger will be the multiplier.

Note that in this model, at any given level of interest rates, the rate of investment is a function of the level of income, not of the rate of change of income. No reference is made to the stock of capital, or to the relationship between that stock and the size of the stock demanded. Yet at any specified level of income the actual capital stock could be either far below or far above demanded levels.

This model differs importantly from "accelerator" models, which seek to explain the level of investment as a function of the rate of change of output or income. In the simpler accelerator models, the rate of investment in any given period is stated as a positive function of the difference between the stock of capital demanded at the end of the period and the actual stock at the beginning of the period. All of the following will be measured in dollars of constant purchasing power. Let

$K_A =$ the stock of capital at the beginning of period t
$K_D =$ the stock of capital demanded for the end of the period
$I_t =$ investment during period t
$f =$ function of

Then

$$I_t = f\,(K_D - K_A)$$

As $(K_D - K_A)$ increases, I_t will become higher. An essential assumption of this model is that the quantity of capital stock demanded is some positive function of real output (Y). Thus $K_D = \alpha Y$, where α represents the "optimum" or demanded ratio of the capital stock to output, and Y is the level of real output. The size of α

depends in part on the level of interest rates; the lower the level of interest rates, the larger will be the demanded capital stock relative to the rate of output. This should be borne in mind, but in the following we ignore interest-rate effects, or assume interest rates to remain unchanged. We can rewrite equation (1) as

$$I_t = f(\alpha Y - K_A)$$

Consider now three cases:

1. The actual stock of capital (K_A) at the beginning of the period was exactly equal to the stock demanded at the level of Y prevailing at that time. In this case, the increase in the stock demanded is related to the increase of income during the period by the relation $\alpha \Delta Y$. If buyers succeed in bringing their stock of capital up to the desired level during the period,

$$I_t = \alpha \Delta Y$$

Note that if income does not rise at all (if $\Delta Y = 0$), there will be no net investment. The latter becomes positive only if ΔY is positive.

2. The actual stock of capital at the beginning of the period exceeds the amount demanded at that time. This excess stock of capital is likely to retard investment even though output rises during the period. For example, this can occur when business activity is recovering, but output has not yet regained the high levels to which the capital stock was earlier adapted.

3. The actual stock of capital at the beginning of the period was deficient relative to demands at that time, which will serve to stimulate investment during the period.

For reasons such as these it is dangerous to employ models in which investment is made a function of the level of income without reference to the rate of change of income or to the relationship between actual and demanded stocks of capital.

Selected readings

Ackley, G., *Macroeconomic Theory,* New York, Macmillan, 1961.
Branson, W. H., *Macroeconomic Theory and Policy,* New York, Harper & Row, 1971.

CHAPTER 18

GOVERNMENT FISCAL OPERATIONS AND POLICIES

The two preceding chapters deliberately ignored government expenditures and receipts, and in effect assumed both to be zero, so that the number of variables could be reduced and the reader could concentrate on the behavior of private consumption, saving, and investment. Now we shall add the government to our model. Specifically, we shall consider government expenditures for goods and services (designated by G), government transfer payments (designated by P) and government tax receipts (designated by T). Our central purpose will be to analyze the effects of government expenditures and taxes on the behavior of output, employment, and price levels. Used responsibly and appropriately, government fiscal actions can be powerful instruments for promoting economic stability; used irresponsibly and inappropriately, they can be even more powerful sources of instability.

GOVERNMENT PURCHASES OF GOODS AND SERVICES (G)

As already indicated, G includes all expenditures by federal, state, and local governments for currently produced goods and services. Table 18–1 shows that

Table 18–1 Government expenditures, 1970 (billions of dollars)

	FEDERAL	STATE AND LOCAL	TOTAL
Purchases of goods and services	$ 97.2	$122.2	$219.4
Transfer payments	83.5	10.7	94.2
Federal grants-in-aid to state and local governments*	24.4	–	–
Total	$205.1	$132.9	$313.6

* In order to avoid double counting and to measure expenditures to the public, total expenditures exclude the $24.4 billion of federal grants-in-aid to state and local governments.

SOURCE: *Survey of Current Business*, July, 1971, pp. 25–26.

in 1970 these amounted to more than $219 billion, or approximately 22 percent of GNP. Nearly half of these expenditures were in the form of compensation of civilian and military employees for their services. The remainder was for new public construction and the thousands of other types of goods and services used by modern governments. Like any other form of expenditure for output, G is both a part of the aggregate demand for output and a contributor to the total of national-income shares.

We shall assume that G is exogenously determined by the government and is not responsive to changes in the level of Y. The government can, of course, increase or decrease the level of G. Our earlier analysis suggests immediately that upward or downward shifts of G will serve to induce upward or downward multiplier effects, just as would similar shifts of the I or C functions.

GOVERNMENT TRANSFER PAYMENTS (P)

During any period, these include all government payments to others on income account for which the government does not receive goods or services in return. These represent neither a government demand for output nor a value of output used by the government itself. However, they do represent a contribution by the government to the incomes of others. As shown in Table 18–1, these amounted to more than $94 billion in 1970. The great bulk of these were in the form of social security payments of various types—old-age benefits, unemployment-insurance benefits, health benefits, direct relief, and so on. Also included, however, are net interest payments on government debt and net subsidies to business.

Some of these payments do not appear to be responsive to changes in the level of Y. Some are responsive, however, and tend to rise when Y falls and to decline when Y rises, especially to the extent that changes in Y are accompanied by changes of unemployment in the opposite direction. This is clearest in the case of unemployment benefits. These benefits differ from state to state and with the wage or salary levels of workers, but they average between 30 and 35 percent of the recipients' full-time labor incomes. Thus, a rise of unemployment increases total unemployment-benefit payments, which serve to cushion the decline of private incomes; and a decline of unemployment reduces these payments. Some other transfer payments are also responsive to changes in income levels and employment opportunities. For example, when employment opportunities are scarce for the elderly, some retire earlier and draw old-age benefits. Direct relief payments also tend to vary directly with the amount of unemployment.

Our analysis will therefore assume that, with a given government program for transfer payments, the volume of P is a negative function of Y. When Y falls, some part of the impact on private disposable income will be offset by a rise of P; and when Y rises, a decline of P will occur, thus snubbing the rise of private disposable incomes. Quantitatively, however, this is less important than the automatic responses of total tax collections to Y, which we shall investigate later.

The government can, of course, shift its transfer-payment function. That is, it can increase or decrease the amount of its transfer payments at each level of Y. This can be an important tool of fiscal policy. By increasing P at each level of Y, it can increase private disposable incomes at each level of Y, thus tending to raise C as a function of Y. By reducing P at each level of Y, it can produce the reverse effects.

GOVERNMENT RECEIPTS OR TAXES (T)

These include all receipts by federal, state, and local governments on income and product account. Thus, they include not only taxes in the narrow sense of the term but also various types of license fees and contributions by employers and employees to governmentally sponsored social-insurance programs. Table 18–2

Table 18–2 Government receipts, 1970 (billions of dollars)

	FEDERAL	STATE AND LOCAL*	TOTAL	PERCENT OF TOTAL RECEIPTS
Corporate profits taxes	$ 30.6	$ 3.5	$ 34.1	11.4
Personal taxes	92.2	23.6	115.8	38.5
Indirect business taxes	19.3	73.6	92.9	30.9
Contributions for social insurance	49.3	8.3	57.6	19.2
Total	$191.4	$109.0	$300.4	100.0
Addendum:				
Personal income taxes (net)	$ 88.4	$ 11.1	$ 99.5	

* In order to avoid double counting and to measure receipts from the public, federal grants-in-aid to state and local governments are excluded from state and local receipts.
SOURCE: *Survey of Current Business,* July, 1971, pp. 25–26.

shows that in 1970 total government receipts amounted to $300 billion, or more than 30 percent of total GNP. These tax collections (T) served to lower private disposable incomes.

Total yields of the American tax system are highly responsive to changes in the level of GNP. With a given tax program on the books, defining both the things subject to tax and applicable tax rates, total yields rise and fall sharply with increases and decreases of Y. This is not true of all types of taxes. For example, total yields of property taxes and certain types of fees do not respond automatically to changes in Y in the absence of action by the tax authorities. It is, however, true of taxes that account for the great bulk of government receipts. Corporate profits usually vary directly with Y, and, in recent years, these have been subject to marginal tax rates fluctuating around 50 percent. Yields of personal income taxes, which exempt certain amounts of household income and tax the remainder at graduated rates, are highly sensitive to changes in Y. So are total contributions for social insurance, which are based on payrolls. Total revenues from various taxes on production and sales, included in indirect business taxes, also vary with Y.

Our later analysis will emphasize the importance of this "automatic" fluctuation of total tax receipts. A given tax system, with defined tax bases and applicable tax rates, produces total revenues that are highly responsive to Y. We shall use $\Delta T/\Delta Y$ to denote "the marginal responsiveness of total tax receipts to Y." The value of $\Delta T/\Delta Y$ depends, of course, on the nature and rates of taxes. However, in the early part of the 1970s, $\Delta T/\Delta Y$ appears to be at least 30 percent. That is, each \$1 increase or decrease of GNP raises or lowers T by at least 30 cents.

The government can shift its tax-collection function upward or downward at each level of Y. For example, by broadening tax bases, or raising applicable tax rates, or both, it can increase T at each level of Y, thus serving to lower private disposable incomes at each level of Y.

GOVERNMENT DISPOSABLE INCOME (T_n) AND ITS DISPOSAL

By "the government's disposable income" (T_n) we mean its total taxes (T) minus its transfer payments (P). T_n measures the amount of income at the disposal of the government to use for purchases of goods and services (G) and for government saving (S_g). Thus,

$$T_n = T - P$$
$$S_g = T_n - G \qquad \text{or} \qquad T - P - G$$

We found that, with a given tax system, T is a positive function of Y, and with a given transfer-payment program, P is a negative function of Y. For both these reasons, T_n is a positive function of Y. A rise of Y serves to increase T_n both by increasing T and by lowering P, and a decrease of Y lowers T_n both by lowering T and increasing P. This is illustrated in Part B of Figure 18–1.

This fact is of great significance for the behavior of private disposable income. As we saw earlier, total private disposable income at any level of GNP is equal to $Y - T_n$. Thus, the higher the level of Y, the greater will be the difference between Y and private disposable incomes. This is often referred to as an "automatic-stabilizer effect," although "automatic-snubber effect" would be a more accurate description. These are the effects that follow automatically from

Figure 18–1 T, P, T_n, and G

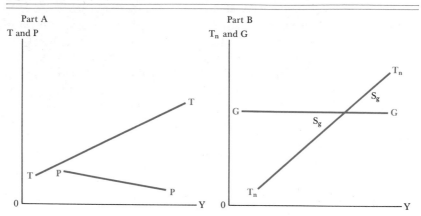

an initial decline of Y even if the government makes no change in G, in its tax system or in its transfer-payment program. If there is an initial decline of Y and no change at all in total T, P, and T_n, the full impact of the decline of Y will fall on private disposable incomes. However, to the extent that the decline of Y is reflected in a decrease of T_n, reflecting a fall of T or a rise of P, the impact on private disposable incomes is reduced, with a corresponding decrease of pressures for further reductions of private spending. The decline of Y is snubbed.

On the other hand, an increase of expenditures for output may occur when the economy is already operating at virtually full-employment levels and an undesirable rate of price inflation threatens. If total T_n remained constant, the full increase of Y would be reflected in private disposable incomes. To the extent that the rise of Y is absorbed by an increase of T_n, the rise of private disposable incomes is snubbed.

Such automatic-snubber effects are powerful and often contribute to stability at approximately full-employment levels. However, they sometimes militate against recovery of economic activity. For example, in the early 1960s when unemployment remained excessive, the large increases of T_n with each rise of Y snubbed the rise of aggregate private demands for output and slowed recovery. There was an automatic "fiscal drag." This was remedied by a tax reduction in 1964—a downward shift of the T function. Similar effects on aggregate demand could have been achieved by upward shifts of the G or P functions.

Government saving (S_g)

In the national-income accounts $(T_n - G)$ or $(T - P - G)$ is called "the government's surplus or deficit on income and product account." We call it "government saving" (S_g) because of its comparability to private saving. For example, like personal saving, it is a part of disposable income that is not used by its recipient to purchase output for current consumption purposes.

With a given level of government expenditures for output (G) and given

T and P functions, government saving (S_g) is a positive function of the level of income (Y). We shall use $\Delta S_g/\Delta Y$ to denote the "marginal responsiveness of S_g to Y." When G is constant, this is equal to $\Delta T_n/\Delta Y$. This is illustrated in Part B of Figure 18–1. At some level of Y, $S_g = 0$. That is, $T_n = G$. Above that level of Y, S_g becomes increasingly positive. Below that level of Y, S_g becomes increasingly negative. Thus, changes in Y generate changes in the value of S_g in the same direction. Under the tax system in effect in the late 1960s, the value of $\Delta S_g/\Delta Y$ was at least 0.30. This large value has important implications for the behavior of total saving, government plus private, and for the size of the multiplier.

THE MODEL, INCLUDING GOVERNMENT

We now extend our model to the entire economy, including the government as well as the private sectors. Much of the analysis developed in previous chapters remains unchanged. For example, our analysis of the money-supply function and the demand-for-money function remains unaltered, as does the necessary condition for equilibrium, $L = M$. Also, we continue to assume that gross private investment (I) is a negative function of interest rates.

However, introduction of the government does require some important changes. For one thing, we introduce another type of expenditures for output, G, so that total demand for output becomes $C + I + G$. As already indicated, we shall assume that G is exogenously determined by the government and is not responsive to changes in Y. Also, the introduction of taxes (T) and government transfer payments (P) alters the relationship between GNP and total private disposable income; these two items would be the same in a system without taxes or government transfer payments. However, under actual conditions, private disposable incomes are equal to total GNP (or Y) minus T_n. This is illustrated in Figure 18–2. At any level of Y, measured horizontally, private disposable income, measured vertically, is equal to Y minus the government's net tax collections at

Figure 18–2 Private disposable income

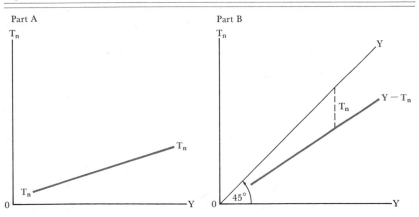

that level of Y. With given tax and transfer-payment programs, T_n will be larger at higher levels of Y. This is because T is a positive function of Y, and P is a negative function of Y.

We are especially interested in the relationship between personal or household disposable income (designated by Y_H) and Y because of its relevance to the behavior of personal consumption and saving. Y_H is equal to GNP minus T_n and minus also business disposable income (S_b). That is,

$$Y_H = Y - T_n - S_b$$

We found earlier that both T_n and S_b are positive functions of Y. Thus a change of Y will bring not an equal change of Y_H, but a change equal to only $\Delta Y - \Delta T_n - \Delta S_b$. That is,

$$\Delta Y_H = \Delta Y - \Delta T_n - \Delta S_b$$

Dividing both sides of the equation by ΔY to get the ratio $\Delta Y_H/\Delta Y$, we get

$$\frac{\Delta Y_H}{\Delta Y} = \left(1 - \frac{\Delta T_n}{\Delta Y} - \frac{\Delta S_b}{\Delta Y}\right)$$

For example, suppose that $\Delta T_n/\Delta Y = 0.30$ and $\Delta S_b/\Delta Y = 0.05$. Then

$$\frac{\Delta Y_H}{\Delta Y} = (1 - 0.30 - 0.05) = 0.65$$

In this case only 65 percent of any change of GNP would be reflected in a change in household disposable income.

This has important implications for the relationships between GNP and personal consumption. As already indicated, it is most reasonable to assume that personal consumption and personal saving are positive functions of personal disposable income. Households base their decisions to consume or save on their incomes after taxes and transfer payments, not on any knowledge they may have about the behavior of GNP. Thus, the marginal propensities to consume and to save that are related to household decision making are the marginal propensities to consume out of household disposable income $(\Delta C/\Delta Y_H)$ and the marginal propensity to save out of household disposable income $(\Delta S_p/\Delta Y_H)$. As a numerical example, assume that these are 0.9 and 0.1 respectively.

Although C and S_p are most directly related to the level of personal disposable income, it will facilitate our exposition to relate them to the level of total income, Y. Thus, $\Delta C/\Delta Y$ equals the marginal responsiveness of consumption to GNP. This is arrived at as follows:

$$\frac{\Delta C}{\Delta Y} = \frac{\Delta C}{\Delta Y_H}\left(1 - \frac{\Delta T_n}{\Delta Y} - \frac{\Delta S_b}{\Delta Y}\right)$$

For example, if

$$\frac{\Delta C}{\Delta Y_H} = 0.9 \quad \text{and} \quad 1 - \frac{\Delta T_n}{\Delta Y} - \frac{\Delta S_b}{\Delta Y} = 0.65$$

then

$$\frac{\Delta C}{\Delta Y} = 0.9 \times 0.65 = 0.585$$

This emphasizes two points:

First, $\Delta C/\Delta Y$ is smaller than $\Delta C/\Delta Y_H$. To the extent that changes in GNP are absorbed by changes in T_n and S_b, consumption is made less responsive to changes in GNP. Since the multiplier is $1 \div (1 - (\Delta C/\Delta Y))$, this means a smaller multiplier effect.

Second, the size of $\Delta C/\Delta Y$ can be increased or decreased by anything that increases or decreases the fraction of ΔY accruing as ΔY_H. For example, this can be done through changes in tax or transfer policies that alter the value of $\Delta T_n/\Delta Y$.

Similarly,

$$\frac{\Delta S_p}{\Delta Y} = \frac{\Delta S_p}{\Delta Y_H} \left(1 - \frac{\Delta T_n}{\Delta Y} - \frac{\Delta S_b}{\Delta Y} \right)$$

For example, if

$$\frac{\Delta S_p}{\Delta Y_H} = 0.10 \qquad \text{and} \qquad 1 - \frac{\Delta T_n}{\Delta Y} - \frac{\Delta S_b}{\Delta Y} = 0.65$$

then

$$\frac{\Delta S_p}{\Delta Y} = 0.10 \times 0.65 = 0.065$$

The saving-supply function and the multiplier

Introduction of the government into our model also requires modifications of both the definition of the supply of saving and estimates of the responsiveness of total saving supply to changes in Y. In the earlier model, in which government had been omitted, total saving supply was defined alternatively as the sum of personal saving (S_p) and gross business saving (S_b) or as $Y - C$. Now we introduce government saving (S_g), which is equal to $T_n - G$. Thus, total saving supply (S) is defined alternatively as:

$$S = S_g + S_b + S_p \qquad \text{or} \qquad S = Y - C - G$$

The first equation views saving as that part of total disposable income shares not used for personal consumption or government purchases of output. The second equation views saving supply as that of value of total output not demanded for personal consumption or government use.

Introduction of government saving also increases markedly the responsiveness of saving supply to changes in the level of GNP. We have already seen that both personal saving and gross business saving are positive functions of Y; that is, both $\Delta S_p/\Delta Y$ and $\Delta S_b/\Delta Y$ are positive fractions. The marginal responsiveness of government saving to Y (that is, $\Delta S_g/\Delta Y$) is even greater. This is because of the high value of $\Delta T_n/\Delta Y$. If G is not at all responsive to Y, then $\Delta S_g/\Delta Y = \Delta T_n/\Delta Y$. As noted earlier, $\Delta S_g/\Delta Y$ has a value of about 0.30 under the tax and transfer-payment programs in effect in the late 1960s. Thus, the marginal responsiveness of saving supply to GNP is

$$\frac{\Delta S}{\Delta Y} = \frac{\Delta S_g}{\Delta Y} + \frac{\Delta S_b}{\Delta Y} + \frac{\Delta S_p}{\Delta Y}$$

A numerical example will suggest the significance of such a high value of $\Delta S_g/\Delta Y$. Let

$$\frac{\Delta S_g}{\Delta Y} = 0.30$$

$$\frac{\Delta S_b}{\Delta Y} = 0.05$$

$$\frac{\Delta S_p}{\Delta Y} = 0.065$$

$$\frac{\Delta S}{\Delta Y} = 0.30 + 0.05 + 0.065 = 0.415$$

Thus 40 percent or more of each change of the level of GNP may be reflected in a change in total saving.

This has obvious implications for the size of the multiplier, which is $1 \div (\Delta S/\Delta Y)$ or

$$\frac{1}{(\Delta S_g/\Delta Y) + (\Delta S_b/\Delta Y) + (\Delta S_p/\Delta Y)}$$

Suppose there is an exogenous increase in expenditures for output, whether in the form of a rise of investment demand, an increase of foreign demands for our exports, an upward shift of the consumption function, or a rise of G. As Y rises, "leakages" will occur not only in the form of larger business and personal saving but also in the form of larger government saving. The high value of $\Delta S_g/\Delta Y$ lowers markedly the value of the multiplier. In the numerical examples employed in the remainder of this chapter we shall assume that $\Delta S/\Delta Y = 0.40$ and that the multiplier is $1/0.40 = 2.5$.

FISCAL POLICIES

We shall now investigate the government's three principal instruments of fiscal policy—its expenditures for goods and services, its taxes, and its transfer policies. In doing this we shall employ comparative statics. We start in each case from an equilibrium situation, in which $I = S$ and $L = M$. Then we shift one of the functions, leaving all others unchanged, and compare the new equilibrium situation with the old. We start by shifting the government's demand for output, G.

Increase of G

Suppose that the government raises G by $10 billion and maintains this higher level of expenditures while leaving its tax and transfer programs unchanged. The direct impact effect is to increase by $10 billion both aggregate demand for output in the form of $C + I + G$ and also the total of gross income shares accruing to the nation. The subsequent effects can be traced in two ways, with both methods producing the same results. One way is to view the $10 billion rise of G as an exogenous rise of expenditures for output which, to the extent that it leads to increases in household disposable incomes, will induce upward multiplier effects via increased consumption. For example, if $\Delta G = \$10$ billion and $\Delta S/\Delta Y = 0.4$, $\Delta Y = \$10$ billion $(1/0.4) = \$25$ billion. Of the $25 billion increase of Y, $10 billion will reflect ΔG and $15 billion the induced rise of C.

The other approach, which will be developed more fully, is to view the rise of G as a $10 billion downward shift of the saving-supply function at each level of Y, the downward shift reflecting a decrease of the S_g function. Since $S = Y - C - G$, S declines by $10 billion at each level of Y if G increases while C is unchanged at the level of Y. The decrease of the saving-supply function is illustrated in Part B of Figure 18–3 by the downward shift from S_0S_0 to S_1S_1.

The original equilibrium levels of income and interest rates, before the rise of G, is represented by $Y_e r_e$, at which $L = M$ and $I_0 S_0$. After the rise of G, reflected in the downward shift of the saving-supply function, this is no longer an equilibrium situation; I exceeds S by $10 billion. A new equilibrium can be

Figure 18–3 Rise of government expenditures

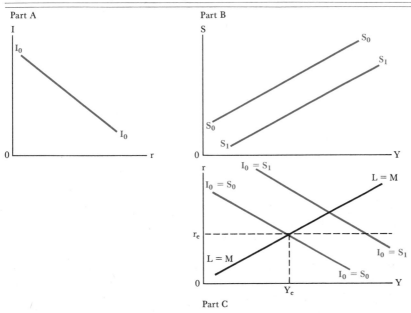

Part A

Part B

Part C

established only by a rise of interest rates which would lower I, a rise of income which would raise S, or some combination of the two. At any level of interest rates, equilibrium of I and S could be reestablished by a rise of Y such that $\Delta Y \, (\Delta S/\Delta Y) = \$10$ billion. If $\Delta S/\Delta Y = 0.40$, this becomes

$$\Delta Y \times 0.40 = \$10 \text{ billion}$$

or

$$\Delta Y = \frac{\$10 \text{ billion}}{0.40} = \$25 \text{ billion}$$

This is represented in Figure 18–3 by a $25 billion shift to the right of the $I = S$ line from $I_0 = S_0$ to $I_0 = S_1$. This will be recognized as the "full multiplier effect," including the $10 billion rise of G and an induced $15 billion rise of C.

Will Y actually rise by "the full multiplier effect"? It may if the process of expansion induces no rise of interest rates which would tend to reduce the rate of investment. However, interest rates are likely to rise if the money supply remains unchanged. The increase of Y increases the quantity of money demanded, which tends to make L exceed M. Equality of L and an unchanged M can be maintained only by a rise of interest rates which will serve to reduce the quantity of money demanded. The rise of r will tend to reduce I, and thus to snub the rise of Y. This illustrates several important points:

1. A rise of G tends to increase Y, not only by its direct increase of total demand for output but also by inducing increases of consumption demand.

2. Even with given values for $\Delta C/\Delta Y$ and $\Delta S/\Delta Y$, the actual change of Y resulting from a given ΔG is not independent of monetary policy. If M remains unchanged, the rise of Y will lead to an increase of interest rates which will tend to lower investment demand, thus snubbing the rise of Y. If the full expansionary effects of the rise of G are desired, M should be increased in order to shift the $L = M$ line downward and to the right, thus avoiding a rise of interest rates. To prevent an increase of G from raising Y, the money supply would have to be reduced, thus shifting the $L = M$ line upward and to the left, to raise interest rates and reduce I enough to offset the rise of G.

The above discussion assumes that the increase of G and the ensuing rise of Y left the investment-demand function unchanged. This may occur, especially if the economy is operating significantly below capacity levels. However, the rise of Y may increase the expected profitability of investment and shift the investment-demand function upward at each level of interest rates. In such cases, a rise of interest rates may reduce I less or not at all; in fact, the upward shift of I could be so large that I would be increased despite the rise of interest rates.

Decrease of G

The effects of a decrease of G are just the reverse of those discussed above. The reader is invited to trace these effects and to note the initial decline of demand for output, the induced decrease of consumption, and the relevance of monetary policy to the outcome.

A decrease of the tax-collection function or an increase of the government transfer-payment function

We now explore the case in which the government lowers its T_n (or $T - P$) function; that is, it lowers its net tax collections at each level of Y, leaving its rate of expenditures for output unchanged. This result could be achieved in either or both of two ways: (1) by decreasing tax yields at each level of Y by reducing tax bases, or tax rates, or both; or (2) by increasing transfer payments at each level of Y. Suppose that the reduction of T_n is $10 billion at each level of Y. This does not directly affect aggregate demand for output; it does, however, increase total private disposable income by $10 billion at each level of Y, because private disposable income equals $Y - T_n$. With greater disposable incomes, the private sectors could be expected to spend more at each level of GNP.

There are two ways of tracing the expansionary process and both yield the same results. The first way is to trace the effects on consumption. With an additional $10 billion of disposable income at the existing level of GNP, the private sectors are likely to increase both their saving and their consumption—to shift both upward at each level of GNP. Some part of the tax rebate is likely to be used to increase business saving at each level of Y, and some to increase personal saving. However, a major part is likely to be used to increase consumption at each level of Y. Let us assume that of the $10 billion of tax relief, $8 billion is used to increase consumption and $2 billion is used to increase private saving. This can be viewed as an $8 billion upward shift of the consumption function at each level of GNP. This exogenous rise of consumption will bring multiplier effects of a type that should now be familiar. The initial rise of consumption expenditures will increase incomes of those in the consumer-goods industries, who will increase their consumption expenditures, which will increase incomes still further, and so on. Note that the multiplier that is relevant here is the one that not only includes S_b and S_p but also takes into account "leakages" in the form of increases of S_g as Y rises. If the upward shift of the consumption function is $8 billion and $\Delta S/\Delta Y = 0.4$, then $\Delta Y = \$8$ billion $(1/0.4) = \$20$ billion.

The other way of tracing the expansionary process is by noting the effect of the $10 billion decrease of T_n on the total saving-supply function. The $10 billion decrease of T_n while G remains unchanged lowers S_g by the same amount. This decrease is likely to be offset in part by a rise of S_b and S_p at each level of Y as private disposable income is increased. Suppose that the combined rise of S_b and S_p is $2 billion. The net downward shift of the saving-supply function at each level of Y will be $8 billion. At the old equilibrium level of Y and r, I will now exceed S by $8 billion. A new equilibrium can be established only by a rise of interest rates which would lower I, a rise of Y which would raise S, or a combination of the two. At any level of interest rates, equilibrium of I and S could be reestablished by a rise of Y such that $\Delta Y\,(\Delta S/\Delta Y) = \$8$ billion. Thus, if $\Delta S/\Delta Y = 0.40$,

$$\Delta Y \times 0.40 = \$8 \text{ billion} \qquad \text{or} \qquad \Delta Y = \frac{\$8 \text{ billion}}{0.40} = \$20 \text{ billion}$$

This can be represented by a $20 billion shift of the $I = S$ line to the right. This is the "full multiplier effect."

Again we ask, "Will Y actually rise by the full multiplier effect?" Again the answer is that it may if the process of expansion induces no rise of interest rates that would tend to reduce the rate of investment. However, the rise of Y is likely to induce a rise of interest rates and to discourage investment if the money supply remains unchanged. This assumes again that neither the tax reduction nor the ensuing rise of Y shifts the investment-demand function upward.

Increase of T_n

An increase of the T_n function has effects that are the reverse of those described above.

Increase of G versus decrease of T_n

We find, then, that the government can raise Y by increasing G or by lowering its T_n function through reducing taxes or raising its transfer-payment function. A comparison of the effects of a given increase of G and an equal reduction of T_n brings out some interesting similarities and contrasts.

1. Both serve to increase Y. However, the rise of Y resulting from a given increase of G will be greater than that resulting from an equal decrease of T_n. This is because all of an increase of G is reflected in an exogenous rise of demand for output whereas an equal decrease of T_n will not increase the consumption function by the full amount; some of the tax rebate will be used to increase S_b and S_p.

2. Both are likely to increase interest rates if the money supply is not increased. This will inhibit investment if the rise of G, the decrease of the T_n function, and the ensuing rise of Y do not raise the investment-demand function sufficiently to offset the rise of interest rates.

3. Effects on the composition of the increased output are different. If the expansion results from a decrease of the T_n function, all of the increased output is in the form of consumer goods. If it results from an increase of G, the increased output is partly in the form of additional goods and services for the government and partly in the form of additional consumer goods.

DEBT-MANAGEMENT POLICIES

These refer to the government's policies concerning the composition of its debt—the characteristics of financial claims against it. Actions affecting the size of the government debt are not in the realm of debt-management policy; they are a part of fiscal policy. We have already seen that the instruments of fiscal policy—T, P, and G—have "income effects." G is both a component of demands for output and a creator of money income for the community. P and T affect the disposable incomes of the private sectors. However, when these three components of fiscal policy are combined, they also have "wealth effects," because they determine whether, during a period, the government will have a balanced budget, a deficit which will have to be covered by an increase in the government debt, or a surplus which will permit a net decrease of the government debt. For example, suppose that government expenditures $(G + P)$ exceed government revenues (T) during some period. Additional financial claims against the government must be created to cover the deficit, and these will be viewed by the private sectors as an increase in their financial wealth. This increase in the stock of financial wealth will remain even after the government's budget is brought into balance. On the other hand, a surplus of government revenues (T) over its expenditures $(G + P)$ during a period enables the government to reduce its debt, thereby reducing the financial wealth of the private sectors. This reduction remains even after surplus is eradicated.

Thus the behavior of the size of the government debt is in the realm of fiscal policy, but determination of the composition of the debt is in the province of debt-management policy. This policy is concerned with both the composition of a government debt of constant size and with the changes in composition of the debt that accompany net increases or net decreases of the debt resulting from current deficits or surpluses. Decisions involving the composition of the government's debt obviously affect the public's selection of these types of financial claims and hence affect the composition of the public's portfolios. In this respect, debt-management policies are similar to monetary policies, which also affect the composition of the public's financial portfolios. In fact, we shall find it useful in some cases to include the central bank's actions in our discussion of debt-management policies.

In determining the characteristics of its debt instruments and the proportions in which the various types of instruments will be issued, debt managers have a wide range of choice as to maturities, interest rates, and other characteristics. For example, the maturities of interest-bearing debt can range from very long to very short. At one extreme, most interest-bearing debt can be in the form of perpetual bonds or bonds of very long maturities. At the other extreme, most of the interest-bearing debt can be in very short maturities, such as Treasury bills. Also, the debt manager can vary the proportions of interest-bearing and non-interest-bearing debt. Governments have often issued debt that pays no interest and that serves as money. American greenbacks are but one example. In recent times, instead of issuing noninterest-bearing debts, governments have often accomplished much the same results by selling their debt obligations to their central banks, which create and issue money in exchange.

The effects of debt-management policies on financial markets and on the economy can be illustrated by shifts in the composition of a government debt of constant size. We begin this illustration with shifts in the maturities of the interest-bearing debt. Suppose that the government creates and issues a large amount of long-term debt, retiring an equal amount of short-term debt. At least initially, this will tend to lower the prices and raise the yields on long-term bonds and to raise the prices and lower the yields on short maturities. Such a differential may persist if investors do not consider long and short maturities to be close substitutes, but it will later narrow to the extent that the differing maturities are considered to be close substitutes. Such a shift of maturities is likely to have more important and persistent effects by means of its altering the overall liquidity and safety of the public's portfolios. Longer maturities are less liquid and more susceptible to loss because of the chance of future increases of interest rates. Thus, the shift from short to long maturities reduces the overall liquidity and safety of investors' portfolios. To restore its liquidity and safety, the public is likely to demand larger money balances and to reduce its demands for other risky assets. In the absence of an increase in the money supply, interest rates tend to be raised; this is especially true of the interest rates on less safe and less liquid assets.

An increase of short-term debt offset by a decrease of long-term debt has the opposite effects.

Shifts between interest-bearing and noninterest-bearing debt can have powerful effects on financial conditions. For example, suppose that the government issues to the public a large volume of noninterest-bearing debt, or fiat money, to retire an equal value of long-term interest-bearing debt. The effects are essentially the same as those of an equal Federal Reserve purchase of government securities from the public: direct equal increases of high-powered money, of bank reserves, and of the public's money supply, and a decrease of the public's holdings of earning assets. This, as we have already seen, would lower interest rates and increase the rate of expenditures for output. On the other hand, issues of additional interest-bearing debt in exchange for noninterest-bearing debt would have the opposite effects.

Debt-management problems inevitably arise when the size of the government's debt is increased or decreased by its current deficit or surplus. Suppose that, starting from a balanced-budget situation, the government increases its expenditures or decreases taxes so that a deficit results. The government must decide what types and proportions of debt to create and sell to cover the deficit. Many alternatives are available, of which the following are only a few examples.

1. Cover the entire deficit by the creation and sale of interest-bearing debt and allow no increase in the money supply. Interest rates will be increased. This is partly because the rise of Y induced by the expansionary fiscal actions will increase the quantity of money demanded for L_1 purposes, leaving only a smaller part of the constant money supply to satisfy L_2 demands, and partly because only at a higher level of interest rates will the community be willing to hold a larger fraction of its portfolio in the form of earning assets and a smaller fraction in the form of money balances. The rise of interest rates will discourage private invest-

ment spending, thereby offsetting at least a part of the expansionary effects of the fiscal-policy actions, and the full multiplier effects of the fiscal actions will not be realized. Such a debt-management policy is appropriate if the government wishes to minimize the net expansionary effects of its fiscal actions, but not if it desires larger expansionary effects.

2. Cover a part of the deficit by creating and selling interest-bearing debt but allow the money supply to rise just enough to prevent any rise of interest rates. The latter may be achieved through government issues of noninterest-bearing debt or through purchases of government securities by the central bank. In this case, the expansionary fiscal actions have no discouraging effects on private investment, and the full multiplier effects are realized.

3. Cover the entire deficit by issuing noninterest-bearing debt (fiat money) or by creating and selling interest-bearing debt to the central bank, which will pay for the securities by creating and issuing high-powered money. In either case, the increase of high-powered money increases bank reserves, enables the banking systems to expand bank credit and the money supply by some multiple, lowers interest rates, and stimulates private investment. This combination of fiscal, debt-management, and monetary policies is clearly more expansionary than either of the two policies described above. It may be appropriate if the economy is deep in depression. However, it is a recipe for inflationary disaster if pursued when the economy is operating at or near its full-employment level. Imagine the consequences if, during every period, the volume of high-powered money and bank reserves were allowed to rise by an amount equal to the government's continuing deficit!

When the government has a current surplus of revenues over expenditures, and is therefore in a position to reduce its total outstanding debt, it must decide on what types of debts to retire and in what proportions. The most contractionary uses of surplus receipts are to retire noninterest-bearing debt (fiat money) or to retire debt held by the central bank without offsetting purchases by the central bank. In both cases, the stocks of high-powered money and bank reserves are reduced, banks are forced to contract credit, interest rates rise, and private investment is discouraged. The least contractionary use of surplus receipts is to retire interest-bearing debt held by the public and to allow no decline of the money supply. In this case, the money representing the government's surplus, or positive saving, is used to retire interest-bearing securities, thereby reducing the supply of earning assets available to private holders and tending to raise prices and lower yields on securities. The decline of interest rates, in turn, tends to encourage private investment. Thus, the contractionary effects of collecting the surplus taxes from the private sectors are offset to at least some extent by a stimulation of investment.

One conclusion suggested by all of this discussion is that an efficient overall stabilization policy requires coordination of fiscal, debt-management, and monetary policies.

OPTIMUM MIXES OF MONETARY AND FISCAL POLICIES

We have found that for purposes of managing the behavior of aggregate money demands for output two major classes of policies are available: monetary policies and fiscal policies. We also noted that for the purpose of achieving a specified behavior of aggregate demand these instruments are substitutable for each other to at least some extent; they can be used in various proportions or "mixes." This leads to basic policy questions: What are the optimum policy mixes under various economic conditions? Should we rely only on fiscal policies for stabilization purposes? If so, what should be the relative roles of government expenditure and tax policies? Should we rely only on monetary policies? If so, what should be the relative roles of the various monetary instruments? If both monetary and fiscal policies are to be used, what should be the specific mix?

We shall not attempt to prescribe the specific mix to be used in each type of economic situation, but we shall suggest some major considerations.

1. Political and institutional limitations on the substitution of instruments. Even though instruments may be technically substitutable for each other to achieve a specified behavior of aggregate demand, actual substitutability may be limited by political and institutional arrangements. For example, Congressional action on taxes and expenditures has frequently been long-delayed and dominated by considerations other than economic stabilization. Monetary actions, which can be taken quickly, have often been used to a greater extent when fiscal actions would have been more efficient.

2. Technical limitations on substitutability of instruments. Under some conditions and in some ranges of the mix, the substitutability of instruments to achieve a desired behavior of aggregate demand may be virtually zero or at best very small. A classic case is the Keynes liquidity-trap situation, in which the interest rate is trapped at a level too high to produce a level of investment sufficient to offset a full-employment level of saving. In this case, a more expansionary monetary policy cannot substitute for a more expansionary fiscal policy as a means of restoring aggregate demand. Substitutability may be low even in less extreme conditions. For example, suppose that the country is in a recession from which it wishes to recover as quickly as possible. Even if a strongly expansionary monetary policy could achieve recovery, it might not be able to do so as quickly as could a mix of a somewhat less expansionary monetary policy together with tax reductions, an increase of government expenditures, or both. Another example of low substitutability may arise when the total of government and private demands for output is so large as to produce very strong inflationary pressures. In principle, it would be possible to curb demands sufficiently by using only a restrictive monetary policy. However, if fiscal policies remain highly expansionary, the degree of monetary restriction required to halt the inflation may be so great as to produce an actual or threatened financial crisis. On the other hand, if monetary policy remains strongly expansionary, the magnitude of the fiscal re-

striction required to halt the inflation may be greater than is politically achievable.

3. Differential economic effects of various mixes capable of achieving the same specified behavior of aggregate demand. Although a desired behavior of aggregate demand may be achievable through a number of different policy mixes, the various mixes may have significantly different effects on other economic variables and obectives that are considered to be socially important. One of the most important of these differences relates to the allocation of productive resources and output among their various alternative uses and users. Maximum economic welfare depends not only on the rate of real output or income but also on the efficiency of its allocation, and the latter is affected significantly by the nature of the policy mix. For example, suppose that at a time of underemployment, it is decided to raise the level of aggregate demand by some specified amount. This total increase could be achieved by many different combinations of ΔC, ΔI, and ΔG. Let us compare the results of a few different policy mixes. (a) Sole reliance for increasing aggregate demand is placed on increased government purchases of goods and services. In this case, the entire increase in output is likely to be absorbed by the government and by the induced rise of consumption. Investment will not rise unless the adverse effect of the induced rise of interest rates is more than offset by an upward shift of the investment-demand function resulting from the increase of aggregate demand. (b) Sole reliance is placed on a tax reduction or on an increase of government transfer payments. In this case, the entire increase in output is likely to be absorbed by increased consumption. None of the increase is taken for government use, and investment will increase only if the stimulative effects of the rise of consumption demand more than offset the adverse effects of the induced rise of interest rates. (c) Sole reliance is placed on an expansionary monetary policy. In this case, all of the increase of output is absorbed by the increase of investment and the induced rise of consumtpion. None of the increases is taken by the government. Many other policy mixes, with differing allocation effects, could be used.

Similar issues arise when it is decided that, in order to combat inflation, aggregate demand should be reduced, or its rise should be limited, by some specified amount. How should the limitation be allocated among C, I, and G? Whose demands should be limited, and by how much? Members of the community may have widely differing judgments on the nature of a socially optimum allocation of resources and real income, but few will contend that allocation effects are unimportant.

The optimum policy mix is also influenced at times by considerations relating to a nation's balance of international payments. Only one example will be noted at this point. Suppose that a nation is simultaneously concerned about domestic underemployment and about an actual or threatened deficit in its balance of payments. It wishes to increase aggregate demand by some amount to increase domestic output and employment, and to do this with minimum adverse effects on its balance of payments. No matter what policy mix is used, the rise of aggregate demand and national income will increase imports, and thus have adverse effects on the balance of payments. However, the nature of the policy mix will affect the response of domestic interest rates and the behavior of international flows of funds on capital account. If the nation relies only on an expansionary monetary policy to raise domestic demands, interest rates will fall and large amounts of funds may flow to other countries if interest rates in foreign financial centers are higher. The outflow of funds can be minimized, and perhaps prevented entirely, by relying largely on expansionary fiscal policies, which can raise domestic demands for output without lowering interest rates. In fact, an aggressively expansionary fiscal policy could even raise interest rates enough to attract inflows of funds from abroad and to offset, at least in part, the adverse effects of the rise of imports on the nation's balance of payments.

CONCLUSIONS

We have now completed our survey of monetary, income, and fiscal theories, which are essential elements in the making of policies to regulate the behavior of aggregate demand. We have also surveyed the various monetary and fiscal instruments that have been developed. We have not, however, had much to say about the monetary and fiscal policies that have actually been followed—what their objectives have been and how these objectives have changed through time, how the various instruments have been used, how successful they have been, and so on. This deficiency will be remedied in Part Six. However, before embarking on this task we must consider another essential element—international aspects of money and monetary policies.

Selected readings

See list at end of Chapter 17.

PART FIVE

INTERNATIONAL MONETARY RELATIONS

CHAPTER 19

THE INTERNATIONAL MONETARY SYSTEM

Most of the discussion up to this point has concentrated on domestic aspects of money and monetary policy. This somewhat isolationist approach was necessary to simplify the exposition. However, we cannot afford to ignore international aspects—even if our central interest remains in the functioning of the domestic economy—because the behavior of domestic employment, output, price levels, and interest rates is influenced markedly by such factors as the nature of the international monetary system and the behavior of real incomes, price levels, and interest rates abroad. Moreover, monetary, financial, and economic policies and developments in the United States, the world's greatest economic and financial power, have profound effects on the rest of the world. For these reasons, we shall broaden our perspective and explore such topics as:

1. Functions of money in international transactions
2. Mechanisms of international payments
3. Exchange rates among national moneys
4. International effects of domestic monetary policies
5. International monetary policies and monetary cooperation

At the beginning, we shall assume a system of free multilateral payments: that all individuals and business firms are permitted to make international payments as they see fit and to exchange at will any national money for any other. The various types of official restrictions on international payments will be considered later.

FUNCTIONS OF MONEY IN INTERNATIONAL TRANSACTIONS

The basic function of money in international trade is the same as in domestic trade; that is, to facilitate specialization and exchange. Like domestic trade, international trade is essentially barter; in the final analysis, goods and services are exchanged for goods and services. But barter would be at least as clumsy and inefficient in international transactions as in domestic trade, and probably more so in view of the greater distances that are usually involved. The use of some type of money as a medium of exchange or payments is essential to the full development of international trade, lending, and specialization.

Moreover, international payments, like domestic payments, are facilitated by using types of money that can be transferred from payer to payee quickly, cheaply, and safely. It would, of course, be possible to make all international payments by shipping precious metals in the form of coin or bullion or by shipping paper money. This would be costly and inconvenient. Freight costs would be high, the risk of loss would be ever present, and the speed of transferring payments would depend on the speed of transport facilities. To avoid such costs and inconveniences, international payments are, as domestic payments are, generally made by transferring debt (or credit) claims from payers to payees. The debts so transferred are usually deposit liabilities of banks. Many of these deposit transfers are made, as in domestic payments, by written orders. Some of these are ordinary checks written by bank customers. Some are certified checks. Some are checks or drafts drawn by a cashier or other bank official on his own bank or some other bank. Many payments, especially very large ones, are made with orders on banks transmitted by telegraph or cable.

BANKS AND INTERNATIONAL PAYMENTS

The process of making international payments is greatly facilitated by a network of banking offices within each country and by interrelationships among the banks of the different countries. We have already seen how the thousands of banks in the United States are intertwined in a nationwide system for clearing and collection and in a correspondent-banking system. Practically every bank in the country has a correspondent relationship with a bank in New York or with some larger bank that, in turn, has a correspondent in New York. Thus, virtually every bank, large or small, is enabled to provide its customers who wish to make payments abroad with checks drawn on a well-known New York or other metropolitan bank and even with checks drawn on foreign banks with which its city correspondent maintains close relations. In most other countries, similar results are achieved through nationwide branch-banking systems. Even small villages are served by branches of banks that have important offices, if not their head offices, in the nation's principal financial centers. Some countries have domestic correspondent-banking systems similar to that in the United States.

The financial centers and commercial-banking networks of the various countries are interconnected in two principal ways.

1. Foreign branches. A number of the larger banks in this country, such as the Chase Manhattan Bank, the First National City Bank, the Bank of America, the Continental Illinois Trust, and the Guaranty Trust Company, operate foreign branches. Several British banks maintain branches in various parts of the world, as do banks in France, Holland, Canada, and some other countries. Foreign branches usually become members of the clearing and collection system of the country in which they are located, establish relations with banks in that country, and engage in banking activity insofar as the laws of the country permit it. For the head office and its correspondents and customers, foreign branches perform many types of services. They supply credit and market information, draw and sell drafts, collect drafts, pay drafts, accept drafts, and so on. In addition to their foreign branches, some American banks have established subsidiaries for the primary purpose of financing international trade. These finance not only trade between the United States and other countries but also trade among foreign countries. Also, some American banks have joined with banks of other countries in establishing and operating banks abroad.

2. International-correspondent relationships. The nature of these international-correspondent relationships can be illustrated by a hypothetical example in which the Chase Manhattan Bank of New York and the Midland Bank, Ltd., of London become correspondents of each other. Under such arrangements, each performs many services for the other, compensation being fixed by prior agreement or by later negotiation. Each acts for the other and for the customers and correspondents of the other in paying and collecting checks and other items, in presenting bills of exchange for acceptance, in buying and selling securities, and so on. At least one of the banks maintains a deposit account with the other, and each may hold deposits with the other. For example, Midland may hold deposits with Chase, and Chase may hold deposits with Midland. Each may agree to lend to the other up to a stipulated maximum amount. Suppose, for example, that you wish to buy £100,000 at a time when the exchange rate is £1 = $2.40. Chase may sell you such a draft on the Midland Bank even though its deposit account with Midland is depleted at the time, and Midland will pay the draft. Chase may continue to owe Midland for a time, or it may immediately purchase claims against sterling and send them to Midland to replenish its deposit account, or it may pay Midland by crediting $240,000 to the latter's deposit account in New York.

It is easy to see how this vast network of correspondent relationships facilitates international payments. Americans are enabled to make payments abroad with written, telegraphic, or cable orders drawn by their banks on American banks or on foreign-correspondent banks. And foreigners can make payments in the United States with written, telegraphic, or cable orders drawn by foreign banks on foreign- or United States-correspondent banks. It is interesting to note that a United States bank is even enabled to sell orders drawn on foreign banks with which it has no direct correspondent relationship. Suppose that you wish to make a £10,000 payment in Sydney, Australia, but neither Chase nor any other United States bank has a correspondent there. Chase might nevertheless sell you a £10,000 draft on a Sydney bank, informing that bank that when it makes payment, its account with Midland in London will be credited an equivalent amount. In effect, you pay Chase, Chase pays Midland, Midland pays the Sydney bank, and the Sydney bank pays the Australian payee. All of these payments can be made by crediting and debiting deposit accounts.

In some cases, international payments are made with money of the payer's country. For example, most United States payments abroad are made with orders drawn on United States banks and stated in dollars. The recipient of these dollars may have deposit accounts in the United States to which the dollars can be added, and he may use them directly to make payments in the United States or elsewhere. Much more commonly, however, he sells the dollars in the exchange market— probably to his own bank or to the central bank or exchange authority of his country—in exchange for the money of his own country. In some other cases, international payments are made in the money of the payee's country. For example, a Swedish merchant would usually make payments to Britain in terms of sterling. If the payer does not himself have a sterling deposit in Britain, he will have to offer his own national money in the exchange market to buy claims on sterling.

A very large volume of international payments is made with the money of a third country. Two of the principal moneys used in this way are the United States dollar and the British pound sterling. For example, payments from Argentina to France may be made by transferring deposit credits on the books of New York banks. In effect, the Argentinian payer uses pesos to buy an order on a New York bank and sends the order to pay dollars to the French payee, who sells the dollars for French francs. Someone in France may then buy the claims against dollars and use them to make payments to still other countries. It is partly to make payments to other countries as well as to the United States that foreign banks maintain large deposit accounts in this country. In a similar way, many countries make payments to each other by transferring sterling claims against British banks. This includes not only most members of the British Commonwealth, but also the Scandinavian countries and many others as well. For this and other purposes, these countries maintain large accounts in London. Because of their widespread use in international payments, the dollar and the pound are often referred to as the great international currencies.

FOREIGN-EXCHANGE MARKETS

International payments involve a huge volume of exchanges of national moneys. For example, an American who receives a claim against French francs and who does not want to spend in France or to hold French francs will offer them in exchange for dollars or for some other nation's money that he wants to spend or hold. Other Americans who want to spend or hold moneys of other nations offer dollars in exchange for them. Similar transactions occur all over the world. The term *foreign-exchange market* refers to all the facilities and processes involved in the exchange of claims against the various national moneys. The things bought and sold include small amounts of coin and larger amounts of paper money, but the great bulk of trading is in claims against banks denominated in the various national moneys. Some of these are payable on demand; others, only after a lapse of time. Short-term claims against nonbank debtors are also exchanged in these markets.

Like all efficient markets, foreign-exchange markets have their middlemen. These are of several types. In some cases, as in New York, most of the business is done by the foreign-exchange departments of commercial banks, which buy and sell on their own account. Some countries have types of banks that specialize in foreign-exchange operations. Most have at least some nonbank dealers, who buy and sell on their own account, and brokers who bring buyers and sellers together. Moreover, as will be stressed later, central banks often participate in these markets, as also do exchange-stabilization funds in countries that have them.

Virtually all countries have some type of foreign-exchange market; some markets are more highly developed than others. Among the largest and most active are those in New York, London, Paris, Amsterdam, Brussels, Zurich, Frankfurt, and Rome. These are closely interlocked through international branch-banking and correspondent-banking systems and by telephone, telegraph, and cable. Very large purchases in one market and sales in another can be effected quickly and cheaply. Thus, in the absence of official restrictions, exchange rates in the various markets can differ only slightly. *Exchange arbitrage,* the simultaneous purchase in one market and sale in another, prevents wide differences.

A foreign-exchange market has two major branches, although these are interrelated in complex ways. One is the *spot market.* In this market a transaction and an exchange rate are agreed on at a certain time and delivery is made immediately, or "on the spot." The other branch is the *forward market,* which is essentially similar to futures markets for commodities. In this market, a transaction and an exchange rate are agreed on at a certain time but actual exchange or delivery of the currencies occurs at some time "forward," such as after 30, 60, 90 days or longer. A large part of purchases and sales in forward markets is for the purpose of *hedging*—of reducing or eliminating risks. For example, suppose that an American, Joe Jones, owns a claim to receive £100,000 at the end of 90 days. Jones may have acquired the claim on sterling by selling goods or services on credit, by lending in foreign financial centers, or in any other way. If he waits for 90 days to collect the sterling and sell it in the spot market, he runs the risk that the dollar price of sterling will have fallen. He can avoid this risk by selling sterling immediately at a fixed price for delivery 90 days forward. On the other hand, Sid Smith is obligated to pay £100,000 at the end of 90 days. This obligation may have arisen from Smith's purchases of goods and services on credit, from his borrowing abroad, or for any other reason. If he waits for 90 days to buy the sterling, he runs the risk that the dollar price of sterling will have risen. Smith can avoid this risk by purchasing sterling immediately at a fixed price for delivery 90 days hence.

It should be evident that Jones and Smith can eliminate their risks by "marrying" them. Jones escapes the risk that the dollar price of sterling will fall by selling to Smith £100,000 for delivery 90 days hence, and Smith avoids the risk that the dollar price of sterling will rise. A large part of purchases and sales in forward-exchange markets are of this type. However, some are for purposes of *speculation*. Speculative transactions in exchange markets, like those in commodity markets, are those undertaken to derive profit from expected differences in prices at different points in time. Suppose that you are an exchange speculator dealing in dollars and sterling and that you observe in the market the 90-day forward rate on sterling. If you think the spot rate 90 days hence will be above the present forward rate, you will buy sterling now at the forward rate, hoping to sell it later at a higher price. If you think the future rate on sterling will be lower, you will sell sterling now for forward delivery. In its details, exchange speculation is complex and, some people think, exhilarating.

The facilities of forward-exchange markets perform important functions in enabling traders to reduce exchange risks involved in their international commercial transactions and in facilitating international movements of funds on capital account, especially movements of short-term funds. For example, one who lends in terms of a foreign currency can reduce or eliminate his exchange risk by selling that currency for forward delivery. And one who borrows in terms of a foreign currency can reduce or eliminate his exchange risk by purchasing that currency for forward delivery.

MULTILATERAL PAYMENTS AND MULTILATERAL TRADE

In the first chapter, we noted that one of the great advantages of using money in trade is that it enables each person or firm to sell to those who offer the highest price and to buy from those who offer the best bargain. This not only enables each entity to make the most of his available resources, but also promotes maximum output by helping each person, firm, and region to specialize in the production of those things in which it has the greatest comparative advantage. This is just as true internationally as it is domestically. To make its maximum contribution to world trade and world productivity, an international monetary mechanism must enable buyers to purchase and sellers to sell in the most favorable markets; it must not force Nation A to buy from Nation B simply because the latter bought from it or lent to it.

Let us see how unrestricted exchange markets facilitate multilateral trade and multilateral payments. Suppose that the United States exports £1 million worth of wheat to England and receives sterling in return. Our exporters will sell the sterling claims to banks for dollars, and the banks are thus put in a position to sell sterling to others who wish to make payments abroad. The United States may not want to buy in England, but may want Brazilian coffee, and may therefore buy checks or drafts on sterling deposits in London and remit them to Brazilian coffee exporters. These exporters sell their sterling claims to their banks for cruzeiros, and thus the Brazilian banks have sterling for sale. Brazilian importers may buy the sterling and use it to buy women's clothing in France. French exporters sell the sterling to French banks, which may then sell it to French importers, who use it to buy British industrial products. This example, admittedly simpler in its explanation than in many actual cases, illustrates the principles of multilateral trade and multilateral payments. No two of the countries balanced their trade with each other; England bought from us, we bought from Brazil, Brazil bought from France, and France bought from England. Through an unhindered exchange of money, each nation was enabled to sell in the most favorable market and to buy in the most favorable market the things it wanted most. This freedom of buyers also tended to cause producers to adjust their production to the desires of buyers and to locate the production of each commodity in the area or areas that could produce it most cheaply.

Free-exchange markets also permit borrowers to use the proceeds of international loans in ways that they consider most advantageous and which will promote the most efficient types of specialization and production. Suppose, for example, that a French public-utility company borrows $50 million in New York because interest rates are relatively low there. This company may wish to buy only domestic labor and equipment and may therefore sell the dollar proceeds of the loan for francs. Other Frenchmen may remit the dollars to Argentina for needed foodstuffs and raw materials, and an Argentina railroad may use the dollars to buy United States locomotives. In the final analysis, the loan enabled France to increase its imports, but it imported what it wanted most and from the most favorable world market. Our loan to France increased our exports, but to Argentina rather than to France. We shall see later how various types of exchange control inhibit the multilateral-payments system, discourage multilateral trade, and impede international specialization.

INTERNATIONAL FLOWS OF RECEIPTS AND PAYMENTS

As already noted, each nation makes most of its payments to other countries by transferring to them deposit claims against banks. But how do the members of a nation acquire these deposit claims with which to pay other countries? The answer is that they rely largely on a flow of receipts from other countries. To explain this, consider first the case of a country which has a currency that other nations are not willing to hold in large quantity, and which receives in payment claims against foreign banks, and which pays with claims against foreign banks. As will be seen later when we study balances of international payments, each nation enjoys a flow of receipts from other countries. A major part of these receipts is usually in payment for a nation's exports of goods and services, but a nation may supplement these receipts by selling securities to the rest of the world, by borrowing, or by receiving gifts and grants. This flow of receipts provides the nation with deposit claims against other countries and is the major source of its ability to pay other countries.

The same is true in essence of a nation whose money is an important international currency. For example, the United States pays other countries by giving them, primarily, dollar-deposit claims against American banks and it receives payment from other countries primarily in the form of claims against American banks. Other countries are willing to hold very large amounts of claims against dollars, but unhappily this amount is not unlimited. As we make payments to the rest of the world, in the form of deposit claims against American banks, we build up our stock of short-term debts in this form to the rest of the world. But our flow of receipts from the rest of the world transfers ownership of these deposits from foreigners to Americans, thus tending to decrease our short-term debts to other nations. Thus we, too, rely largely on our flow of receipts to make payments to others, because it is primarily this flow of receipts that prevents our stock of short-term debts to other countries from rising above the amounts they are willing to hold.

In short, the major source of each nation's capacity to make payments to others is its flow of current receipts from them. However, the members of a nation might find it inconvenient, or worse, if this were the only source of its capacity to make international payments so that in each period the amount it could spend in the rest of the world would be no greater than its current flow of receipts. These receipts may at times dwindle because of failure of the nation's principal export crops, or unfavorable conditions in export markets, or for other reasons. To decrease its international purchases and payments quickly to match the decline of receipts may create hardships. Or, internal mishaps, such as crop failures, may cause a nation to increase its expenditures abroad at the same time that its exports are lessened.

Thus, over a limited period of time, the members of a nation collectively need to be able to spend more abroad than they receive in payments from abroad. This is comparable to an individual's need for a stock of money balances to bridge the gap of an excess of expenditures over receipts during some future period. In this case, however, the nation requires command over something that will be acceptable in payment in other countries. It needs some source of liquidity in addition to its flow of receipts.

INTERNATIONAL "LIQUIDITY"

This need for something with which to bridge a possible or expected excess of payments to other nations over receipts from them during some future period raises some of the most difficult and controversial questions in the field of international monetary policy. These include:

1. How much international liquidity do nations need, both individually and collectively? This obviously depends in part on the behavior of flows of

receipts and payments, because these determine the size of the "payments gap" that will need to be bridged. The amount of "needed liquidity" may be small indeed if a nation is willing, when faced with an excess of payments over receipts, to take quick and effective action to increase its receipts, decrease its payments, or both. However, needed liquidity may be very large if a nation takes no steps to remedy an excess of payments, and especially if it follows policies that tend to enlarge and prolong the excess payments. The remedies for an excess of payments over receipts often present serious problems, because they involve such actions as lowering the exchange rate on the nation's money, raising interest rates, or lowering domestic income or price levels.

2. On what sources of liquidity should nations rely? To what extent should they rely on holdings of assets in the form of foreign money or things that can be readily exchanged for foreign money, and to what extent on arrangements for borrowing foreign money when needed? What forms of assets should they hold and in what proportions? What types of borrowing arrangements should be made?

3. Who should manage the international liquidity positions of nations individually and collectively? To what extent should this be done by private sectors, by individual central banks and governments, by central banks in cooperation, and by international institutions?

Sources of international liquidity

As suggested above, a nation may prepare against a future excess of its international payments over its receipts in two principal ways: (1) by holding a stock of assets in the form of claims against foreign moneys or other things that can be readily exchanged for foreign moneys, and (2) by arranging facilities to borrow foreign moneys when needed.

Gold has long been a popular form of international reserves. This may be largely for historical reasons, and if history had been different, some other asset or group of assets might have served as well or better. In fact, however, gold does represent generalized purchasing power over the moneys of almost all nations because the monetary authorities of those countries stand ready to buy it in unlimited quantities, giving their money in exchange. Moreover, they rarely decrease the price they will pay for gold and they sometimes raise it. These facts make gold an attractive form of international reserve. However, gold does have some disadvantages for its holders. Perhaps most important, it yields no interest or other explicit income. Also, its shipment to make payments is expensive and requires time. It should not be surprising, therefore, that nations have sought some form of asset that would be as good as gold, or almost as good, in terms of acceptability, and that would be better than gold in the sense that it would not be inconvenient or costly to ship and would yield an income.

Many countries now hold at least some part of their international reserves in the form of claims against foreign moneys. The United States dollar is by far the most important "international-reserve currency"; next in importance is the

British pound sterling. Smaller amounts of the moneys of several other countries are held for this purpose, and these may increase in the future. These claims against dollars and other reserve currencies take several forms: deposit claims against the central bank, demand deposits at commercial banks, time deposits, Treasury bills and other short-term government securities, acceptances, and so on. Their owners usually hold in the form of demand deposits and other nonearning claims only such amounts as they need for working purposes, and the remainder in earnings assets.

Thus, income-yielding claims against a foreign money may be considered superior to gold as an international reserve as long as that money is freely convertible or exchangeable into the moneys of other nations and there is confidence that it will not depreciate in terms of gold or of other moneys. But, if fears arise that the money will depreciate in terms of gold or of other moneys, foreign holders of claims against it may exercise their right to demand gold, thereby subjecting the gold-losing country to deflationary pressures and decreasing the total international reserves of the world. Thus, an international-reserve system depending heavily on claims against national moneys can create problems not only for the country whose money is used as a reserve but also for the world's monetary system.

Ability to borrow foreign moneys when needed can be at least a partial substitute for holding assets as an international reserve. It may be a very attractive substitute if a nation is assured that very large amounts can be counted upon, that interest costs will be low, and that no onerous terms will be imposed. However, it becomes an inferior substitute to the extent that prospective loans of foreign money are limited in amount, unreliable, expensive, and may be offered on onerous terms. We shall later study several existing and proposed schemes for lending foreign moneys to countries with deficits in their balances of payments and shall find that important policy problems are involved in determining what amounts, for what purposes, for what periods, at what interest rates, and on what other terms a nation should be permitted to borrow.

We now come to this question: Who should serve as custodian and manager of international reserves and take responsibility for borrowing foreign moneys when needed for international payments? Private banks and other parts of the private sector usually do this to some extent. Thus, banks often hold some claims against foreign moneys, and in the past they sometimes held gold. Moreover, banks and other business firms may have some capacity to borrow foreign moneys. However, most countries do not rely heavily on the private sectors for this purpose, for two principal reasons. First, private banks and other business firms are likely to find it unprofitable to hold gold and claims against foreign moneys in amounts sufficient to meet the needs of the nation as a whole. Second, it often proves difficult to mobilize private holdings and to use them to make international payments in time of need, and especially in time of crisis. For such reasons, the functions of serving as custodian of international reserves and as manager of international-reserve positions has fallen largely on central banks, governments, and international institutions.

ROLES OF CENTRAL BANKS

One of the earliest functions of central banks was to serve as custodian of the nation's international reserves and as manager of its international-reserve position. The central bank held a gold reserve and sometimes claims against foreign moneys, and used these to regulate the behavior of the exchange rate on the nation's money. If the exchange rate on its money tended to fall below desired levels (that is, if exchange rates on other moneys tended to rise above desired levels), the central bank would provide more foreign money to limit or stop the rise. One way of doing this was to sell some of its claims against foreign moneys or to sell gold to other countries and then sell the foreign moneys that it received. Another was to sell gold to banks or others who would sell the gold abroad and then sell the foreign-money proceeds. On the other hand, when the exchange rate on the nation's money tended to rise above desired levels, the central bank provided more of the nation's money in exchange markets by purchasing gold or claims against foreign moneys.

Before the 1930s, the central bank was usually the principal, and often the sole, custodian of a nation's centralized international reserves. Since that time, many countries have transferred at least a part of this function to a government agency known by such names as "exchange-stabilization funds" or "exchange-equalization accounts." These agencies hold at least some part of the nation's gold and foreign-currency reserves, and buy and sell in exchange markets. In most cases, however, central banks manage these agencies.

The responsibility of a central bank usually does not end with serving as custodian of a nation's international reserves and using these for operations in exchange markets. It also includes managing the size of the nation's international reserves and the state of its international-reserve position. A common responsibility is that of assuring that its international-reserve position is adequate to meet demands for foreign payments without an undesired decline of the exchange rate on its money. For example, if its international reserves threaten to become inadequate, the central bank may restrict credit and raise interest rates. This serves to decrease credit outflows and even to attract inflows, and perhaps also to increase exports relative to imports by lowering domestic price and income levels. We shall later encounter several instances in which such policies conflict with the promotion of domestic objectives of promoting high levels of employment and high rates of growth.

Central banks and central bankers have also played important roles as agencies for international monetary cooperation. Prior to the 1930s, when governments themselves were unwilling to assume much responsibility in this field, central banks were almost the sole agencies of monetary cooperation. Under the leadership of Montagu Norman of the Bank of England and Benjamin Strong of the Federal Reserve Bank of New York, central-bank cooperation became frequent and useful, although not always successful. After the 1930s, the relative role of central bankers in this field declined somewhat as governments assumed more responsibility and as new international monetary institutions were established. Since the early 1960s, there has been a resurgence of central-bank cooperation. Now, however, central bankers operate closely with governments and international monetary institutions, and especially with the Bank for International Settlements and the International Monetary Fund.

Central-bank cooperation takes many forms. For example, central banks sometimes attempt to adjust their domestic monetary and credit policies in such a way as to help other countries, insofar as this can be done without undue sacrifice of their domestic interests and objectives. They also cooperate in certain types of operations in both spot and forward-exchange markets, which will be discussed later. Here we shall concentrate on two closely related forms of cooperation. One relates to central-bank holdings of claims against foreign moneys and the terms and conditions under which the central-bank holders will demand payment in gold. Although full information is not available, it is clear that central banks sometimes agree to continue to hold claims against foreign moneys, and even to increase their holdings of these claims, instead of exercising their legal right to demand payment in gold. In other words, they agree to continue lending and even to increase their lending to the country or countries against whose money they hold claims. This is clearly a source of liquidity to the beneficiary country.

Central banks also make other types of loans to each other. In some cases, these are bilateral transactions; in others, large numbers of central banks are involved. For example, 10 or even more central banks sometimes participate in a loan to a country experiencing or threatened with a crisis in its balance of payments. Central banks also enter into "reciprocal currency" or "swap" agreements, in which one agrees to give to the other a certain amount of its own money in exchange for an equivalent amount of the money of the other and in which each allows the other free use of the swapped money as it is needed. In early 1971, the Federal Reserve had swap agreements aggregating $11.2 billion with 14 foreign central banks and the Bank for International Settlements (see Table 19–1). During the preceding 15 months it had drawn about $1.7 billion of foreign currencies under these agreements.

All these loans and agreements to lend are important sources of international liquidity. They can become even more important if countries agree to increase the amounts that they will lend and to make firm commitments to lend. They could even make it unnecessary for countries to hold large amounts of assets as international reserves. Suppose, for example, that every financially important country agreed that when it had an excess of international receipts over its international payments, it would lend the excess to countries in the reverse situation. Under these conditions, the world's trade and payments could be carried on with a minimum of international reserves in the form of assets. We have yet to see how far these lending agreements among central banks and governments will develop and what limitations will be imposed on borrowers.

Table 19–1 Federal Reserve reciprocal currency arrangements as of March 16, 1971 (millions of dollars)

INSTITUTION	AMOUNT OF FACILITY
Austrian National Bank	$ 200
National Bank of Belgium	500
Bank of Canada	1,000
National Bank of Denmark	200
Bank of England	2,000
Bank of France	1,000
German Federal Bank	1,000
Bank of Italy	1,250
Bank of Japan	1,000
Bank of Mexico	130
Netherlands Bank	300
Bank of Norway	200
Bank of Sweden	250
Swiss National Bank	600
Bank for International Settlements	1,600
Total	$11,230

SOURCE: *Federal Reserve Bulletin,* March, 1971, p. 190.

Let us now examine the role of the principal international monetary institution.

THE INTERNATIONAL MONETARY FUND

The International Monetary Fund is one of two international financial institutions established in 1946, following plans agreed upon in July, 1944, by experts from 44 nations meeting in Bretton Woods, New Hampshire. The other is the International Bank for Reconstruction and Development, popularly known as the World Bank. The major purpose of the World Bank is to promote and supplement the international flow of long-term funds for construction and development. Its emphasis in the early postwar years was on reconstruction of areas damaged by the war. In more recent years, it has emphasized long-term loans to underdeveloped countries. It operates in two principal ways. The first, which has turned out to be the more important, is by selling its own bonds in the principal money centers and lending the proceeds. The second is by guaranteeing loans made by others.

The Fund has many purposes, of which the following are the most important:

1. Reestablishment of a system of free multilateral payments and reduction of other barriers to trade and payments. During the Great Depression, many countries had adopted various types of exchange restrictions—limitations on freedom to make payments to other countries. Many of these limited not only the

total amounts of payments that could be made abroad, but also the types of payments, the countries to which they could be made, and the types of goods and services that could be bought. Some countries, and especially the belligerents, tightened their exchange controls during World War II. Other restrictions on trade were also widespread—not only tariffs but also various types of quantitative controls. One purpose of the Fund, therefore, was to eliminate exchange restrictions as quickly as possible, with the exception of those restrictions on abnormal capital movements, and to work toward lowering other trade barriers. Progress in removing exchange restrictions was very slow during the first decade following the war, but rapid thereafter. Since 1958, a system of relatively free multilateral payments has prevailed.

2. Provision of an orderly system for setting and altering exchange rates. During the Great Depression, exchange rates fluctuated widely, sometimes in a disorderly manner; and some countries engaged in competitive exchange-rate depreciation in efforts to increase their exports, decrease their imports, and achieve economic recovery at home in a true "beggar-my-neighbor" fashion. Many feared that exchange-rate behavior in the postwar period would again be chaotic. The Fund agreement provided that each member country establish with the Fund an initial exchange rate, and that the exchange rate should thereafter be kept within narrow limits except when the Fund gave permission for a change "to correct a fundamental disequilibrium." It is important to note that the Fund agreement rejected the principles of floating or freely flexible exchange rates and of frequently changing pegged rates, and adopted the principle of stable exchange rates with adjustments only when necessary "to correct a fundamental disequilibrium." The importance of this decision will become apparent as we consider exchange-rate theory and policy.

3. Provision of financial aid to member countries needing assistance to meet actual or threatened deficits in their balance of payments. It is in this function of the Fund as a source of international liquidity that we are especially interested here.

Financial aid by the Fund

The transactions through which the Fund makes foreign moneys available to a member are not called "lending"; they are called "sales of currencies," or "drawings on the Fund." The drawing country obtains foreign money in return for an equal amount of claims on its own money. Nevertheless, this is in effect a loan transaction, because the claims the Fund receives against the country are only debts. We shall find later that the IMF creates the SDRs that it makes available, much as would an international central bank. However, in its other operations, which are our concern at this point, it does not create the currencies that it sells or lends; it only lends the gold and national moneys that are contributed to it by its member countries. Each member country has its "quota." These quotas are important for three reasons. In the first place, a country's quota indicates the amount of that country's gold or money put at the disposal of the Fund. In the second place, its quota is a basis for determining the amount of the moneys of other countries that a country can draw from the Fund. In the third place, a country's quota determines its voting power in the Fund.

By 1971, the Fund had 118 members and had received from them more than $28 billion in total resources. Countries normally pay 25 percent of their quotas in gold and the remainder in claims against their own moneys. Table 19–2 shows

Table 19–2 International Monetary Fund quotas and sales of currencies as of March 31, 1971 (millions of dollars)

COUNTRY	QUOTA	DRAWINGS ON THE IMF, 1947 THROUGH MARCH, 1971	TYPES OF CURRENCIES SOLD BY THE IMF, 1947 THROUGH MARCH 31, 1971 (CURRENCY OF COUNTRY SHOWN ON LEFT)
United States	$ 6,700	$ 2,240	$ 7,911
United Kingdom	2,800	7,284	1,032
Germany	1,600	880	3,817
France	1,500	2,250	1,473
India	940	1,090	–
Canada	1,100	726	1,567
Japan	1,200	249	805
Italy	1,000	688	1,872
Netherlands	700	–	1,197
Australia	665	159	300
Belgium	650	200	1,034
Argentina	440	425	107
Brazil	440	578	32
Spain	395	216	136
Sweden	325	–	263
Denmark	260	114	263
All other countries	7,718	5,242	532
Total	$28,433	$22,341	$22,341

SOURCE: *International Financial Statistics*, May, 1971, pp. 8–12. International Monetary Fund.

that the quota of the United States is by far the largest, making up more than 25 percent of the total. Next in size is the quota of the United Kingdom, which makes up about 10 percent of the total. From its inception in 1947 through March, 1971, the Fund has loaned more than $22 billion. The largest single drawer was the United Kingdom. A total of 74 countries have drawn on the Fund at least once.

The Fund sold currencies on only a modest scale during its early years. From its inception in 1947 through 1956, its total sales were only $1.9 billion. However, from that time through March, 1971, it sold another $20.4 billion. Sales were especially large during years of crisis and near crisis in the 1960s and early 1970s. For example, it sold $1.5 billion in 1961, $1.8 billion in 1964 and again in 1965, $2.8 billion in 1968, $2.4 billion in 1969, and $1.3 billion in 1970.

There have also been important changes in the proportions of the various national moneys sold. Through 1957, almost all of these sales were of United States dollars. Since then, large amounts of other currencies have been supplied, especially Deutsche marks, Italian lire, Canadian dollars, French francs, Netherlands guilders, and Belgian francs. In part, this reflects changes in the international positions of the various currencies. During the early period, the dollar was in greatest demand, the United States was still in a very strong international-reserve position, many important currencies were not yet freely convertible or exchangeable into other currencies, and many countries were in weak reserve positions. In contrast, the reserve position of the United States is now weaker, most of the other important currencies have become freely convertible into other moneys, and some countries (notably Germany, France, Italy, and the Netherlands) have achieved strong reserve and balance-of-payments positions. In part, however, the changed composition of its sales represents a change in policy by the Fund. It now tends to sell, not the particular national currency that a borrowing country wants to hold or spend, but the freely convertible currency of some country that is in a highly favorable reserve and balance-of-payments position. Thus, the Fund is becoming an important medium for channeling the moneys of countries with a surplus in their balances of payments to countries with deficits.

Under what terms and conditions will the Fund provide foreign moneys to a country? This has presented serious policy problems. From the beginning, there has been agreement on these general principles:

1. The Fund should not provide long-term funds, but should confine itself to making shorter-term loans to help a country meet deficits in its balance of payments and to give it time to eliminate those deficits. Borrowings should be repaid within three to five years, if not sooner.
2. Borrowing from the Fund is a privilege and not a right, and the Fund should lend only when the borrower is following, or promises to follow, sound policies that will eliminate its deficit.

In its earlier years, the Fund tended to be very strict in determining both the amounts it would lend and the conditions under which it would lend. Its policies are now much more liberal. For one thing, it will now lend to a country to meet abnormal capital outflows, whereas this was forbidden in the earlier years. Since 1952, it has stood ready to enter into standby agreements with countries, in effect giving them a line of credit on which they can draw if needed. The mere existence of a widely publicized standby agreement tends to restore confidence in the exchange rate on a money and to retard capital outflows. Perhaps the most important change, however, is in the general attitude of the Fund, which is to give applicant countries more benefit of any doubts concerning their requests.

Stated in general terms, a member's drawing rights on the Fund are as follows:

1. It may draw "essentially automatically" an amount not in excess of its "gold tranche" position, normally 25 percent of its quota.
2. It is given "the overwhelming benefit of the doubt" on requests for amounts not in excess of its quota. If the Fund has made net sales of the nation's currency, the

nation may draw under this provision an amount equal to its quota plus these net sales.

3. It may draw further amounts by presenting justifications acceptable to the Fund.

Thus, the United States, with its quota of $6.7 billion, could draw nearly $1.7 billion "essentially automatically," and would be given "the overwhelming benefit of the doubt" on drawings up to $6.7 billion plus any amount of net sales of dollars by the Fund.

The drawing rights described above relate to the Fund's $28 billion of resources contributed as quotas by member countries. The Fund may also borrow from its members. In 1962, 10 major industrial countries agreed to lend to the Fund up to $6 billion (see Table 19–3). These agreements to lend are not un-

Table 19–3 Fund borrowing arrangements (millions of dollars)

LEADING COUNTRY	AMOUNT OF COMMITMENT
United States	$2,000
United Kingdom	1,000
Germany	1,000
France	550
Italy	550
Japan	250
Netherlands	200
Canada	200
Belgium	150
Sweden	100
Total	$6,000

SOURCE: International Monetary Fund, *International Financial Statistics*, June, 1963, pp. 2–3.

conditional. For one thing, any funds lent may be relent by the Fund only to one or more of the countries signatory to the agreement, not to other members of the Fund. Moreover, each loan is subject to approval by the lending countries. However, this is an important addition to the resources at the disposal of the Fund, especially for meeting short-term credit movements from and among the countries that are financially important. The United States can draw up to $4 billion from these funds in addition to its drawing rights related to its quota at the Fund.

There are also several limited arrangements for international monetary cooperation and lending, such as those among the Scandinavian countries and through the Bank for International Settlements at Basle. These will not be discussed here.

Special Drawing Rights

At the beginning of 1970, as mentioned earlier, the IMF initiated a scheme for the creation and issue of Special Drawing Rights (SDRs), sometimes referred to as "paper gold." These are unconditional rights to draw currencies of other countries and are described by the IMF as "unconditional reserve assets created by the

Fund to influence the level of world reserves; they are allocated to participating members in proportion to their Fund quotas." SDRs are stated in terms of gold, each having a gold value equal to that of the U.S. dollar before August, 1971. They are used as a means of payment among national monetary authorities and held by these agencies as international reserves. Nearly $3.5 billion of SDRs were issued at the beginning of 1970, another $3 billion at the beginning of 1971, and still another $3 billion at the beginning of 1972, for a total of $9.5 billion. The timing and magnitude of further issues will be determined by the IMF.

It seems likely that SDRs or some similar type of asset, will play an increasing role in the international-liquidity system in the future. Such a scheme provides a mechanism through which the world can deliberately regulate the size of total international reserves and their rate of growth, rather than allow them to be determined by the vagaries of gold production, nonmonetary demands for gold, and the balance-of-payments position of a major nation, such as the United States.

AN OVERALL VIEW

In summary, the principal components of the international monetary system are commercial banks; other institutions, such as brokers and dealers in foreign-exchange markets; central banks and exchange-stabilization funds; and some international monetary institutions, of which the International Monetary Fund is by far the most important. At the center of the mechanism are the commercial banks of the various countries, interconnected through foreign branches and a complex network of correspondent relationships. Most international payments are made by transferring deposit claims against banks, and the banks operate this mechanism. For each nation, the principal source of these means of paying other countries is the nation's flow of receipts from other countries. However, each nation also needs some source of international liquidity in order to be able to meet, for at least a short period, a possible excess of payments over receipts. The major responsibility for providing international liquidity has devolved on central banks, governments, and international institutions. There are two principal sources of international liquidity: international-reserve assets and facilities for borrowing gold or moneys acceptable to other countries.

Table 19–4 summarizes the international-reserve positions in mid-1971 of all countries except the U.S.S.R., mainland China, and some communist satellites. Note that the data refer to a time before the dollar crisis of August, 1971. Because of that crisis and for other reasons, policies relating to international reserves are likely to change in the future. The *international-reserve position* of a country is officially defined by the IMF as the sum of holdings of gold, SDRs and foreign exchange by the country's government and central bank plus its reserve position in the IMF. The last-named item is any unused part of its gold tranche at the Fund against which it can draw essentially automatically.

Table 19–4 brings out several points of interest. (1) In mid-1971, gold con-

Table 19–4 Official international reserve positions, June 30, 1971 (billions of dollars)

COUNTRY OR AREA	TOTAL	GOLD	SDRS	FOREIGN EXCHANGE	RESERVE POSITION IN IMF
United States	$ 13.5	$10.8	$1.2	$ 0.3	$1.4
United Kingdom	3.6	0.8	0.5	2.3	–
Canada	4.9	0.8	0.4	3.2	0.5
Germany	16.7	4.0	0.5	11.2	1.0
France	5.7	3.5	0.4	1.8	–
Italy	6.1	2.9	0.2	2.7	0.3
Netherlands	3.5	1.9	0.5	0.6	0.5
Belgium	3.2	1.6	0.4	0.7	0.5
All other countries	47.6	10.5	1.8	32.8	2.7
Total	$104.8	$36.8	$5.9	$55.6	$6.9
Percent of total	100.0	34.8	5.6	53.0	6.6

SOURCE: International Monetary Fund, *International Financial Statistics,* December, 1971, pp. 18–23.

stituted only about 35 percent of total international reserves. Its relative role as an international-reserve asset has been declining and is likely to fall even further in the future. Gold monetary reserves actually declined by nearly $3 billion between 1965 and March, 1968 as demands for hoarding and other nonmonetary purposes exceeded new gold production. Virtually no gold has been purchased for monetary purposes since March, 1968, and this policy is likely to be continued in the future. (2) The largest component of international reserves, comprising 53 percent of the total, is in the form of official holdings of foreign exchange. These consist mostly of claims against American dollars. Although it is difficult to predict the future role of this type of reserve, it seems highly likely that it will decline relatively, and perhaps also in absolute amount, in favor of some other type of reserve asset, such as SDRs. (3) Reserve positions in the IMF constituted 6.6 percent of total international reserves. This component may increase in absolute amount as IMF quotas are increased, but there seems to be no reason to expect that its relative share will rise. (4) SDRs constituted only 5.6 percent of total international reserves on the date shown. However, it is almost certain that SDRs, or some similar asset that can be created by an international institution, will grow both in absolute amount and as a share of the total. This is virtually assured by a combination of conditions: needs for larger international reserves as world production and trade increase; the unlikelihood of a significant increase in the stock of monetary gold; and the desire of many countries to rely less heavily than in the past on foreign exchange as a component of their international reserves.

To meet their needs for international liquidity, the official agencies of the various nations also have access to borrowing facilities. Among these are borrowings from the IMF in excess of gold tranche positions, borrowing under swap arrangements among the Federal Reserve and various other central banks, and less formal and less permanent borrowing arrangements among the various national central banks and governments.

INTERNATIONAL ROLES OF THE DOLLAR

Three international roles or functions of the dollar and of short-term claims denominated in dollars can be distinguished.

1. International means of payments. As we noted earlier, dollars are widely used not only in payments by Americans to foreigners and *vice versa*, but also in transactions among entities of other nations.

2. Store of value—the demand for asset purposes. Private foreigners normally hold very large amounts of short-term, dollar-denominated earning assets. There are many reasons for this: the wide array of liquid earning assets available in American markets, the high state of development of our financial institutions, the excellence of our foreign-exchange markets, and so on.

3. Component of international reserves of foreign countries and international monetary institutions. Because of foreign demands for short-term dollar claims for such purposes, the stock of American liquid liabilities to the rest of the world is normally very large. For example, in mid-1971, total short-term liabilities to foreigners exceeded $50 billion. Although such a large stock of short-term claims on dollars served useful purposes, its existence poses danger for the international-liquidity position of the United States. An unfavorable event, such as a sharp rise of interest rates abroad or loss of confidence in the exchange rate on the dollar, can lead to large outflows.

The capacity of the United States to meet its short-term liabilities is not limited to its international reserves in the form of gold, SDRs, foreign exchange, and its reserve position in the IMF. These are supplemented by various borrowing arrangements.

1. Borrowings from the IMF. Requests to borrow an amount not exceeding the United States' quota, $6.7 billion, would be given "the overwhelming benefit of the doubt," and further amounts could be borrowed on the basis of a justification.

2. Outstanding swap agreements with other central banks aggregating $11.2 billion.

3. The possibility of other borrowings from foreign central banks and governments.

4. The possibility of mobilizing private United States short-term claims against foreigners.

For a long time these monetary defenses were adequate. However, as we shall see in Chapter 27, they did not prevent the dollar crisis of August, 1971, at which time the United States government terminated the convertibility of dollar claims into gold or other reserve assets.

Selected readings

International Monetary Fund, *Annual Reports* and *International Financial Statistics*
(monthly) , Washington, D.C.
Scammell, W. M., *International Monetary Policy,* 2nd ed., London, Macmillan, 1961.
Yeager, L. B., *International Monetary Relations,* New York, Harper & Row, 1966.

CHAPTER 20

INTERNATIONAL PAYMENTS AND EXCHANGE RATES

Having presented the mechanism of international payments, we shall now analyze in some detail the various types of international flows of receipts and payments. We shall have two principal purposes. The first is to illuminate interrelationships among national economies—to show how changes in income levels, price levels, and interest rates in one country affect the economies of other countries. The second is to describe the supplies of a nation's currency and demands for a nation's currency in the exchange markets. For these purposes, concepts and statistics relating to balances of payments are invaluable.

A NATION'S BALANCE OF PAYMENTS

The balance-of-payments concept has been officially defined as follows:

> The balance of payments of a country consists of the payments made, within a stated period of time, between the residents of that country and the residents of foreign countries. It may be defined in a statistical sense as an itemized account of transactions involving receipts from foreigners on the one hand, and payments to

foreigners on the other. Since the former relate to the international income of a country, they are called "credits," and, since the latter relate to international outgo, they are called "debits."[1]

Several points concerning a nation's balance of payments deserve emphasis.

1. It is not a balance sheet showing the nation's international assets and liabilities at a point in time. Instead, it shows *for some stated period of time* the *flow* of that nation's receipts from the rest of the world and of its payments to the rest of the world.

2. Following the conventional rules of double-entry accounting that any entity must account for the use of all its receipts and must show the sources of all its payments, a nation's payments and receipts for any period must be exactly equal. Thus, the payments side accounts for all the uses of the nation's receipts from the rest of the world, and the receipts side accounts for the sources of the funds used to make total payments to the rest of the world.

3. One nation's receipts are payments for the rest of the world, and its payments are receipts for the rest of the world.

International transactions are essentially the same as domestic transactions; they are all included as purchases and sales of goods and services, purchases and sales of financial claims, and unilateral transfers. However, to facilitate description and analysis they are classified in a more detailed way in Table 20–1. We

Table 20–1 Components of the United States balance of payments

RECEIPTS (OR CREDITS)	PAYMENTS (OR DEBITS)

1. Exports of goods and services
  a. Merchandise
  b. Services
  c. Income on foreign investment
	1. Imports of goods and services
	  a. Merchandise
	  b. Services
	  c. Foreign income on investments in the United States

2. Unilateral receipts 3. Sales of long-term claims 4. Sales of short-term claims 5. Sales of gold and other reserve assets	2. Unilateral payments 3. Purchases of long-term claims 4. Purchases of short-term claims 5. Purchases of gold and other reserve assets
6. Errors and omissions	6. Errors and omissions

shall start with three items that are included in the "income and product account" of the United States. Our exports of goods and services, which we shall designate by (X), are obviously a source of receipts. They represent the part of our GNP that is supplied to the rest of the world. They include not only exports of commodities, but also many types of services, such as transportation services, banking, and other financial services, and services to foreign tourists in the United States. They also include income earned on American claims against other coun-

[1] U.S. Department of Commerce, *The Balance of Payments of the United States,* Washington, D.C., U.S. Government Printing Office, 1937, p. 1.

tries. On the other hand, our imports of goods and services, to be designed by (M) are obviously payment items. They include purchases of commodities and many types of services and also income paid to foreigners on their claims against this country. Unilateral transfers refer to gifts and grants. They are a source of receipts when the United States receives gifts and grants, and a payment item when our people or government make gifts or grants to the rest of the world. We shall deal with *net* unilateral transfers, designating them by (U). In most years since World War II, this has been a significant net payment item in our balance of payments.

As already noted, these are the only three items in our balance of payments that enter directly into our national-income and product accounts. A few further comments on them will prove helpful when we later discuss interrelationships among the various national economies on income and product account. Our exports of goods and services (X) may be viewed not only as a receipt item in our balance of payments but also as the value of foreign demands for our output and as the value of our output made available for use by the rest of the world. Our imports (M) may be viewed not only as a payment item in our balance of payments but also as the amount of our national income that is used to demand output from the rest of the world. (X − M) is usually referred to as "balance on goods and services." This has been a net-receipt item during most years since World War II, although it was a net-payment item in 1971. Unilateral transfers (U) have usually been a net-payment item; they represent the value of our exports for which we receive no compensation either in the current period or later. Net foreign investment (NFI) is equal to (X − M − U) (see Table 20–2). At an

Table 20–2 Balance of payments items in the national-income and product accounts of the United States, 1970 (millions of dollars)

Exports of goods and services (X)	$62,902
Less: Imports of goods and services (M)	59,311
Equals: Balance on goods and services	$ 3,591
Less: Net unilateral transfers (U)	3,148
Equals: Net foreign investment (NFI)	$ 443

SOURCE: *Survey of Current Business,* July, 1971, p. 32.

earlier point, we added NFI to gross private domestic investment to obtain a total that we called "gross private investment," and we indicated that it, like domestic investment, is an offset to private savings—a way that saving can be reinjected into the spending stream. *NFI* can also be viewed as that value of our output and exports during a period that is used to change the amount of our net financial claims against the rest of the world. When *NFI* is positive, it is the amount by which we increase our net financial claims against the rest of the world by means of purchasing claims against other countries or retiring claims formerly held against the United States by other countries. When *NFI* is negative, it represents the decrease of our net claims against the rest of the world required to finance the excess of $(M + U)$ over (X) during that period.

All other transactions in the balance of payments involve purchases and sales of some type of financial claims. Our sales of long-term claims to foreigners are a source of receipts. These include both equity claims and long-term debt claims. Some of these are foreign purchases of long-term claims against American entities; others are foreign purchases of long-term claims formerly held by Americans against foreign entities. On the other hand, American purchases of long-term claims from foreigners are a payment item. These include both American purchases of long-term claims against foreign entities and American purchases of long-term claims against the United States that were formerly held by foreigners. We shall use L to designate the amount of American sales of long-term claims for any period to foreigners minus purchases of long-term claims by Americans from foreigners. Thus, L is a net-payment item when, as occurs in most years, American purchases of long-term claims from foreigners exceed American sales of such claims to foreigners.

Similarly, American sales of short-term claims to foreigners are a source of receipts, because the foreigners must pay for these assets. These transactions take many forms: foreign purchases of deposits and other short-term claims against American banks and other financial institutions, foreign purchases from Americans of short-term claims against foreign entities, foreign purchases of short-term claims against American governmental units and business firms, repayment by foreigners of short-term debts to Americans, and so on. On the other hand, American purchases of short-term claims from foreigners are a payment item, because we must pay foreigners for these assets. These purchases also take many forms: American purchases from foreigners of deposits and other short-term claims against foreign banks and other foreign entities, American purchases from foreigners of short-term claims against American banks and other American entities, and so on. Thus, transactions in short-term claims are a source of net receipts in the United States balance of payments when American sales of such claims to foreigners exceed American purchases of such claims from foreigners, and a source of net payments when American purchases exceed American sales of such claims.

Gold and other international reserves are best viewed as forms of financial claims. Sales of these reserve assets by the United States to the rest of the world are a source of receipts, because buyers must pay for them. On the other hand, purchases of reserve assets by the United States are a payment item, because we must pay for them. The final item, "errors and omissions," sometimes called "unrecorded transactions," is simply an admission of errors in estimating values and an acknowledgement of the failure to identify some transactions. It is a net payment or net receipt item reflecting values in the balance of payments that cannot be identified. It is suspected of being composed largely of unrecorded transactions in short-term financial claims.

As already noted, a nation's total receipts and its total payments for any stated period must be exactly equal. Yet a nation is sometimes said to have a "surplus" or a "deficit" in its balance of payments, both implying inequalities of receipts and payments. These apparently conflicting views are easily reconciled. It would indeed be rare for a nation to have an exact balance of receipts and payments on every major class of transactions entering into its balance of payments. Instead, it usually experiences net receipts on some types of transactions which must be balanced by net payments on others. The general notion of a surplus or deficit is fairly straightforward: A nation is considered to have a surplus during a stated period if its net receipts on account of some types of transactions are balanced by net payments on other accounts in such a way as to improve its "net international-reserve position" or its "net international-liquidity position." This can be reflected in a net increase in its stock of official international-reserve assets, or a decrease of selected types of debt liabilities to foreigners, or some combination of the two. A nation is said to have a deficit when its net payments on account of some types of transactions are balanced by net receipts on other accounts in such a way as to deteriorate its "net international-reserve" or "net international-liquidity" position. This can be reflected in a net decrease in its stock of official reserve assets, or an increase of selected types of debt liabilities to foreigners, or a combination of the two. Unfortunately, however, there is no general agreement on specific definitions of these key terms. Nations use differing definitions, and the United States has employed several. The key issue is this: Which items in the balance of payments should be placed "above the line" in computing the surplus or deficit and which should be placed "below the line" and considered as means of financing the surplus or deficit?

We can illuminate some of the major issues by using data for 1970 to consider two concepts of the balance used in the United States. One concept is "the net-liquidity balance." Under this concept, all items in the balance of payments except two are placed "above the line" in computing the size of the surplus or deficit. The two exceptions, which are placed "below the line" and considered to be a means of financing the surplus of deficit, are (1) the net change during the period in U.S. official reserve assets and (2) the net change in liabilities to foreign official reserve agencies plus the net change in net liquid liabilities to private foreign entities. The latter is equal to the net change in liquid liabilities to foreign private entities minus the net change in liquid claims against them.

These principles are illustrated by the data for 1970 (see Table 20–3). Note that payments are designated by a minus sign, and the absence of any sign denotes receipts. The balance on goods and services was a surplus of $3,591 million. However, our deficits, or net payments, on all other items "above the line," these totaled $8,310 million. Thus the balance on a net liquidity basis was a deficit of $3,852 million. This deficit was balanced or financed by net sales of $2,477 million of official reserve assets, and a net increase of $1,375 million in net liquid liabilities to foreigners. The latter resulted from a decrease of $5,969 million in net liquid liabilities to private foreigners which was more than offset by an increase of $7,344 million in liabilities to foreign official reserve agencies.

Table 20–3 United States balance of payments, 1968–1970 (millions of dollars) (—) denotes payments or debit; omission of sign indicates receipt or credit.

	1968	1969	1970
Exports of goods and services (X)	$50,623	$55,600	$62,902
Imports of goods and services (M)	— 48,134	— 53,589	— 59,311
Balance on goods and services (X − M)	2,489	2,011	3,591
Net unilateral payments (U)	— 2,875	— 2,910	— 3,148
Net purchases of long-term claims (L)	— 963	— 1,980	— 3,482
Purchases of short-term nonliquid claims on foreigners (S)	231	— 602	— 548
Errors and omissions (E)	— 493	— 2,603	— 1,132
Sum of U + L + S + E	−$ 4,100	−$ 8,095	−$ 8,310
Balance on net liquidity basis (B = (X − M) − (U + L + S + E))	−$ 1,610	−$ 6,084	−$ 3,852*
Settlement of liquidity balance			
Net change in U.S. official reserve assets	— 880	— 1,187	2,477
Net change in net liquid liabilities	2,490	7,271	1,375
Balance on official reserve-transactions basis	1,641	2,702	— 9,821
Settlement of balance			
Net change in U.S. official reserve assets	— 880	— 1,187	2,477
Net change in liabilities to foreign official reserve agencies	— 761	— 1,515	7,344

* After allowance for receipts of $867 million of SDRs. Deficit before this allowance was $4,719 million.
SOURCE: Adapted from *Federal Reserve Bulletin,* September, 1971, pp. A74–A75.

Another concept of the surplus or deficit is "the official transactions balance." The principal difference between this and the net liquidity balance is that the item "change in net liquid liabilities to private foreigners," is shifted from "below the line" to "above the line." It will be noted that in 1970, the deficit on the official transactions basis was $9,821 million, or nearly $6 billion more than the deficit on the net liquidity basis. This resulted from the fact that net payments in that amount were made to reduce net liquid liabilities to private foreigners. The deficit of $9,821 million on the official transactions basis was financed in part by a reduction of $2,447 million in U.S. official reserve assets and in part by an increase of $7,344 million in liabilities to foreign official reserve agencies.

A comparison of data for 1969 with those for 1970 will dispel any notion that for each period a deficit on an official reserve transactions basis must be larger than that on a net liquidity basis. In 1969, there was a deficit of $6,084 million on the net liquidity basis, but a surplus of $2,702 million on the official reserve transactions basis. This difference of nearly $8.8 billion was primarily the result of very large net borrowings abroad by private Americans, principally by American commercial banks. In fact, it was largely because of large receipts from these private short-term borrowings that the United States was able to increase its stock of official reserve assets and to decrease its liabilities to foreign official reserve agencies. The situation was reversed in 1970 as American banks made large net payments to private foreigners to reduce their liquid liabilities.

Having surveyed the various types of economic transactions between a nation and the rest of the world, we shall now explore economic interrelationships among national economies, starting with interrelationships through exports and imports of goods and services.

EXPORTS, IMPORTS, AND INCOME LEVELS

The composition and size of any nation's exports and imports obviously depend on many conditions, not only those at home but also those in other countries with which it trades or could trade. Among these are all the conditions that determine comparative advantages in the production of various products: relative endowments of the various types of natural resources, of various types of human labor, and of capital; relative states of technology; and so on. Also highly relevant are the preference patterns of people in that nation and in other nations for the products of the different countries—the tastes and preferences that help determine demand functions. In a full-scale study of international economics, these conditions would be analyzed in detail. However, since we are interested primarily in the monetary aspects of international economic relationships, we shall assume that these other conditions are given and constant. This enables us to concentrate on two forces that are clearly relevant to the behavior of exports and imports: the level of national incomes and the price level in each country relative to price levels abroad. Each nation's demand for imports is affected by the level of its income, and both its demand for imports and its ability to export are affected by the level of its prices relative to those abroad. We shall first explore relations between income levels and levels of imports and exports.

For this purpose it will be convenient to reclassify some of the items in our earlier statements of national output and income. When we were highlighting domestic aspects, we expressed the value of a nation's output, or total expenditures for its output, as $Y = C + I + G$. It will be remembered that I included gross private domestic investment plus net foreign investment. Also, consumption, gross private domestic investment, and government purchases included an import component. Now we break down these values. C_d, I_d, and G_d will now include only domestic expenditures in these forms for *domestic* output. X represents expenditures for the nation's output by the rest of the world. Thus, in terms of the total value of a nation's output or total expenditures for its output,

$$Y = C_d + I_d + G_d + X \tag{1}$$

This formulation makes it clear that changes in foreign expenditures for X can raise or lower the demand for a nation's output.

At an earlier stage, we expressed the disposal of a nation's disposable income as $Y = C + G + S$, including in C and G an import component. Now we break this down and include imports (M) as a way of using national income. Thus,

$$Y = C_d + G_d + S + M \tag{2}$$

A nation uses some of its disposable income to buy domestic output for consumption and government use, some to buy imports, and the remainder for saving. Like saving, imports are a "leakage" from the income stream of an individual country, because they are a part of the value of its output and income that is not returned to the market as a demand for domestic output.

Other things equal, a nation's demand for imports is a positive function of its income. It will use some part of each increase of its income to buy more imports. Some of these will be in finished form, such as perfume, foreign cars, Paris hats, or machine tools. Some will be in the form of imported raw materials or components needed for production, such as iron ore, wool, petroleum, or tin. On the other hand, a nation typically decreases its expenditures for imports when its national income falls. We shall use $\Delta M/\Delta Y$ to denote "the marginal responsiveness of imports to income." The size of $\Delta M/\Delta Y$ is likely to be relatively large for countries heavily involved in foreign trade. For example, it may be 25 percent or even higher for such countries as Denmark, the United Kingdom, or Belgium. However, for more self-sufficient countries, like the United States, it is likely to be smaller.

We must also modify our statement of the multiplier. If saving is the only "leakage," the multiplier is $1/(\Delta S/\Delta Y)$. But as soon as $\Delta M/\Delta Y$ is greater than zero, the multiplier becomes

$$\frac{1}{(\Delta S/\Delta Y) + (\Delta M/\Delta Y)}$$

Thus, $\Delta M/\Delta Y$ tends to decrease the size of the multiplier. For example, if $\Delta S/\Delta Y = 0.4$ and $\Delta M/\Delta Y = 0$, the multiplier is $1/0.4 = 2.5$. But if $\Delta M/\Delta Y = 0.1$, the multiplier is $1/(0.4 + 0.1) = 2.0$. We shall use this very simple form of multiplier, although it does not take into account any "backwash" effects on demand for the nation's exports resulting from induced changes of income levels abroad. This will be accounted for in other ways.

Increase in domestic incomes

Let us first consider the case in which country A's output and income are increased by an upward shift of C_d, I_d, or G_d demands, which do not involve any shifts of export or import functions. Such increases could reflect upward shifts of the consumption function, or the investment-demand function, or the adoption of expansionary fiscal or monetary policies. Let us assume that the autonomous change is a $10 billion increase of the I_d demand. This, of course, tends to induce increases in consumer demands in the familiar multiplier fashion. Now, however, we must recognize that some fraction $(\Delta M/\Delta Y)$ of each increase of income will be used to increase imports, and is thus a leakage from the nation's income stream. The multiplier effects can be expressed as

$$\Delta Y = \Delta I_d \frac{1}{(\Delta S/\Delta Y) + (\Delta M/\Delta Y)}$$

Assuming that $\Delta I_d = \$10$ billion, $\Delta S/\Delta Y = 0.4$, and $\Delta M/\Delta Y = 0.1$, we find that

$$\Delta Y = \$10 \text{ billion } \frac{1}{0.4 + 0.1} = \$20 \text{ billion}$$

With this rise of Y, the nation's imports (ΔM) will tend to increase by an amount equal to $\Delta Y (\Delta M/\Delta Y)$. With $\Delta Y = \$20$ billion and $\Delta M/\Delta Y = 0.1$, $\Delta M = \$20$ billion $\times 0.1 = \$2$ billion. The rise of country A's domestic income levels has served to worsen its balance-of-payments position.

This example of an autonomous change in the level of one nation's income demonstrates several important points:

1. To the extent that a nation's imports are responsive to its income level, domestic multiplier effects will be smaller.

2. Changes in the level of a nation's income affect its balance-of-payments position by changing, in the same direction, its payments for imports. We shall emphasize later, when we consider exchange-rate theory, that as a nation's level of income grows higher, it is likely to supply more of its money in exchange markets to pay for imports.

3. Since one nation's imports are exports for the rest of the world, changes in the income level of one country tend to be transmitted to other countries through changes in its demand for their exports. Thus, a rise of incomes in country A, which increases its demand for the exports of others, can initiate increases of income abroad.

Although the simple multiplier analysis used above is helpful, it should not be assumed that the effects will be exactly those indicated by this analysis. One thing that the analysis ignores is "backwash" or "feedback" effects from induced changes of income levels abroad. For example, the increase of country A's demand for the exports of others tends to raise, both directly and through multiplier effects, the level of their output and income. Some parts of these increases in foreign income are likely to be used to increase demands for the exports of country A. The size of these feedback effects is important for two reasons: (1) to the extent that they occur, they offset the increase of imports by country A, reduce its net leakages on foreign-trade account, and enlarge its domestic multiplier effects; and (2) they also reduce the extent of the worsening of country A's balance of payments—some part of the increase of A's imports will be offset by the induced rise of foreign demands for its exports.

The multiplier also ignores effects on the money supplies of country A and of the rest of the world. The rise of country A's imports tends to increase its payments to the rest of the world and may even produce a deficit in its overall balance of payments. Suppose that country A makes net payments by selling gold to the rest of the world. This, as we found earlier, tends to reduce bank reserves in country A, to restrict credit, and to raise interest rates. To the extent that this occurs, it will tend to restrict demands for domestic output in A and to snub the upward multiplier effects. In the rest of the world, which receives the gold, the effects are in the opposite direction. However, it should be remembered that the monetary authorities in country A or the rest of the world, or both, may elect to offset the domestic effects of these gold flows.

Further, the multiplier ignores the behavior of interest rates. Interest rates in country A tend to be increased for two reasons: (1) because of the rise of its income level, and (2) because of any restriction of its money supply that is allowed to occur. In the rest of the world, the receipt of gold and any monetary expansion that is permitted to occur tend to lower interest rates, but any rise of income induced by the increase of country A's demand for its exports tends to raise interest rates. As already noted, the rise of interest rates in A tends to snub the rise of its income level. And a rise of interest rates in A relative to those abroad tends to attract inflows of funds to purchase its securities, or at least to decrease outflows of funds. This, of course, tends to help A's balance of payments.

Finally, the multiplier ignores effects on price levels. Up to this point, the analysis has assumed price levels to remain constant, so that changes in income were changes in real income. This may be realistic if output is still below full-employment levels even after the increases of demand. But suppose that price levels in A are increased relative to those in the rest of the world. This will tend to decrease A's exports and also to increase its imports as the people of A are induced to substitute imports for higher-priced domestic products.

In summary, autonomous increases in a country's income level do indeed have powerful international effects. To the extent that they induce increases in the country's demand for the exports of the rest of the world, they serve to spread the rise of incomes. They also worsen the country's balance-of-payments position. But the "real income effects" tell only a part of the story. Also relevant are changes in the money supplies of the various countries, changes in price levels, and changes in interest rates.

Decrease in domestic incomes

An autonomous decrease in the level of a nation's income tends to have international effects that are just the reverse of those described above: to decrease its demands for the exports of other countries, to decrease its payments to them, and to decrease the quantities of its money offered in foreign-exchange markets. Here again, the full story includes effects on money supplies, price levels, and interest rates.

Changes in demand for a nation's exports

We have now seen how changes in the level of a nation's income emanating from internal sources can spread to other countries and affect balances of payments. Let us now see how a nation's income level and balance-of-payments position can be affected by changes in foreign demands for its exports. Suppose that the initial change is a $5 billion increase in foreign demands for its exports. This has two important direct effects: (1) It directly increases total demand for the nation's output and induces upward multiplier effects, and (2) it increases the nation's receipts for exports and improves its balance-of-payments position. This may tend to increase the nation's money supply and to decrease money supplies abroad.

However, the story is not yet ended. As the nation's income rises because of both the initial increase of demand for its exports and the induced multiplier effects, its demands for imports will rise. This tends both to raise incomes abroad and to increase the supply of the nation's money in exchange markets. Thus, we find that the initial change of demand for the nation's exports, which improved its balance of payments, tends to lessen the size of its favorable balance by increasing the nation's demand for imports.

Changes in money supplies may also affect the readjustment process. Suppose that the initial increase in the country's receipts for exports is received in gold, and that this is allowed to increase bank reserves, to expand the money supply, and to lower interest rates. Suppose also that gold-losing countries contract credit and raise interest rates. The fall of interest rates in the gold-receiving country has two types of effects:

1. It serves to stimulate domestic investment and to raise further the level of the nation's income. This, in turn, stimulates further increases in its imports and payments to other countries. Thus, an expansion of the money supply in the gold-gaining country makes more powerful the forces tending to eliminate the country's initial excess of receipts over payments. This excess will most likely also be reduced due to the monetary contraction in the gold-losing countries which tends to lower their incomes and reduce their demand for imports.

2. The fall of interest rates in the gold-gaining country, together with any rise of interest rates in the gold-losing countries, tend to induce capital outflows from the gold-gaining country, or at least to inhibit inflows. This, too, tends to offset the initial excess of receipts over payments.

Of course the monetary authorities of the gold-gaining country, of the gold-losing countries, or both, may prevent changes in their balances of payments from affecting bank reserves, money supplies, and credit conditions. However, to the extent that they do prevent such changes, they reduce the power of the forces that serve to bring international receipts and payments back into equilibrium. The outcome also depends somewhat on the behavior of price levels. Suppose that prices in the gold-gaining country are increased by the initial increase of demand for its exports, the induced upward multiplier effects, and the expansion of its money supply, while prices abroad remain constant or fall. This rise of its prices relative to those abroad will tend to reduce its exports and to increase its imports, both of which serve to reduce the excess of its international receipts over its payments.

We have given but a few examples of the interrelationships of national economies through transactions on income and product account. However, these examples do indicate how changes in income levels originating in one country or group of countries can spread to others, how the income level of a country can be altered by changes in foreign demands for its output, and how all of these things affect the flow of international payments and the behavior of each nation's international reserve.

INTERNATIONAL CAPITAL FLOWS

The various national economies are interconnected not only through transactions on income and product account, but also through transactions involving the purchase and sale of long-term ownership and debt claims and short-term claims. These international capital flows are of interest for two reasons: because of their effects on balances of payments, and because of their effects on the supply of investable funds, interest rates, and income levels in the various countries. For example, suppose country A receives large inflows of funds from foreign purchases of long-term securities or short-term claims. This is obviously a receipt item in its balance of payments. It also adds to the supply of investable funds in the country and tends to lower interest rates, thereby affecting the nation's income level. On the other hand, outflows of such funds from a country are payment items in its balance of payments, which tend to decrease its supply of investable funds and to raise interest rates.

Differences in the marginal productivity of capital among countries constitute a basic, long-term force inducing international flows of capital funds. These differences in the marginal productivity of capital from country to country result from such things as differences in stocks of savings and capital goods relative to supplies of natural resources and labor, differences in technology, differences in managerial capacity, and so on. In a world characterized by perfect competition, absence of risk, and unfettered movements of funds, differences in the marginal productivity of capital would be reflected in differences in interest rates; residents in areas of high interest rates would sell financial claims in areas of low interest rates in order to command more capital; and the process would continue until the marginal productivity of capital and interest rates were equalized in all areas. There are, of course, many obstacles to international purchases and sales of financial claims. Among these are government restrictions, incomplete knowledge of opportunities, and fear that property rights will not be protected. However, very large international flows of funds on capital account do occur. Some of these are in response to basic long-term forces of the types described above and are at a fairly steady rate. However, both the directions and rates of flow are affected significantly by shorter-run factors, such as cyclical fluctuations in national economies, changes in relative levels of interest rates in different countries, and changes in expectations concerning the future behavior of exchange rates among national currencies.

Some holders of financial claims, especially those with only small portfolios, give little or no consideration to the possibility of holding financial claims against foreign entities and confine themselves to claims against entities in their own countries. This is not true of many financial institutions and of wealthier individuals who are more sophisticated financially; in making and adjusting their portfolios, they consider not only available alternatives at home but also those in at least some other countries, and they presumably seek to achieve the most favorable combination of yield, safety of principal, and liquidity. Other things equal, the proportion of assets held in the form of claims against other countries will vary directly with the height of interest rates abroad relative to those at home. Thus, when interest rates rise in some countries and not in others, funds tend to flow from areas of lower interest rates to areas with higher interest rates. Residents of countries with the higher interest rates tend to lend more at home and less abroad, while residents of countries with the lower interest rates tend to lend less at home and more abroad.

Monetary authorities recognize the responsiveness of capital flows to interest-rate differentials, and they sometimes influence the latter in order to affect their balance-of-payments positions. For example, suppose that a country wishes to reduce the deficit or increase the surplus in its balance of payments. It may adopt a restrictive monetary policy and raise interest rates in order to reduce outflows of capital funds and even to increase inflows. On the other hand, a country that has an undesired surplus in its balance of payments may seek to lower interest rates at home in order to reduce inflows of funds and even to induce outflows. At times, however, this responsiveness of international capital flows to interest-rate differentials can be embarrassing to central banks in their pursuit of domestic objectives. Suppose, for example, that one country or group of countries is restricting credit and raising interest rates in order to combat inflationary pressures at home, while another country or group of countries is following an expansionary monetary policy and lowering interest rates in an effort to raise domestic levels of output and employment. Large flows of funds to the countries that are trying to restrict credit add to their supplies of investable funds and lessen the degree of restriction. And the country trying to increase domestic supplies of credit may experience a worsening of its balance-of-payments position without achieving the desired amount of credit ease at home.

A second factor affecting investors' choices among claims on domestic and foreign entities is relative safety of principal value. Both domestic and foreign claims are subject to default risks and to the market risk that interest rates may increase in the future. Two other types of risk should be mentioned: The first of which may be called "political risks." These include such possibilities as outright confiscation or confiscatory taxation, refusal to allow payments to foreigners, emergence of a government that will not enforce private property rights, and so on. As such events come to be expected in a country, large capital outflows are often induced. The other type of risk is the "exchange risk"—the possibility of changes in exchange rates among national moneys. Changes in expectations concerning exchange-rate behavior sometimes induce very large anticipatory or speculative movements of funds. For example, suppose that for some reason there arise expectations that the exchange rate on the dollar may decline significantly, or, stated otherwise, suppose that it is expected that exchange rates on other currencies will rise significantly in terms of dollars. Foreign holders of claims on dollars may rush to sell them before the anticipated depreciation, using the proceeds to buy claims against other currencies. Americans may also rush to exchange dollars for claims against other currencies.

Relative liquidity is a third factor affecting investors' choices among domestic and foreign financial claims. The very high liquidity of short-term claims against dollars makes them a popular investment for foreigners. However, expected changes in relative liquidity can induce large-scale movements of funds. For example, threats of war abroad or other developments abroad that reduce expected liquidity of foreign claims can lead to large shifts of funds to the United States.

We shall now proceed to use much of the preceding materials to develop an analysis of exchange-rate determination. As a first step, we shall look at the nature and functions of exchange rates.

EXCHANGE RATES

Whenever things are exchanged against each other, there must, of course, be some rate or ratio of exchange between them; there must be some type of "price." By the *exchange rate* between two monetary units we mean simply the number of units of one money required to buy one unit of the other. Either monetary unit may be employed as the unit for stating the price of the other. For example, a situation in which 2 Philippine pesos exchange for 1 United States dollar could be stated either as $1 = 2 Philippine pesos or as 1 Philippine peso = ½ dollar. Also, a change in the exchange rate to $1 = 3 Philippine pesos can be expressed either as a rise in the exchange rate on the dollar relative to the peso or as a decrease in the exchange rate on the peso relative to the dollar.

Structure of exchange rates in a given market at a given time

In our later discussion, we shall find it convenient to speak of "the" exchange rate between two national moneys in a given market at a given time. In fact, however, there is not a single rate but a cluster of rates between the two moneys, though all fall within a narrow range. The differentials involved are of three main types.

1. Differences between dealer's buying and selling prices. For example, a dealer may pay only $2,400 for a £1,000 draft on a London bank at the same time that it would charge $2,404 for such a draft. It is out of this margin between selling and buying prices that exchange dealers pay their expenses and make profits.

2. Differences in maturities of the claims. At some given time, the array of rates on sterling in the New York market might be as follows:

Cable rate	$2.40⅛
Sight rate (banker's demand drafts)	2.40
Rate for 60-day banker's bills	2.39⁵⁄₁₆

Thus, at any time, the cable rate is highest, followed by the rate on sight or demand drafts and then by the rate on time bills. This is because of differences in the time that sterling is paid out abroad. If a cable order is used, the selling bank loses that amount of its sterling balance almost immediately. If the bank sells a sterling demand draft, it does not lose its sterling balance until a few days later when the draft has traveled to London and has been presented for payment. In effect, the bank has the use of the funds during the intervening period. Lowest of all is the exchange rate on time drafts or bills, because these are not payable until a future date. The rate on a sterling time draft is equal to the rate on sterling demand drafts less interest to the maturity of the time bill.

3. Differences in the degree of safety and liquidity of the claims. A claim on a well-known and highly regarded foreign bank will bring a higher price than a claim on a less highly regarded bank or on a nonbank debtor in whom confidence is not so high.

When we refer to "the" exchange rate between two moneys we shall, unless otherwise specified, mean the rate applicable to sight or demand drafts on highly regarded banks. It will be assumed that the prices of other claims cluster around this rate in their appropriate competitive positions.

Exchange arbitrage

Competition tends to establish one rate of exchange between two moneys in a given market at a given time. For example, the dollar price of sterling cables tends to be the same at all New York banks at a given moment. But may not exchange rates between two moneys be quite different in two widely separated markets, such as New York and London? This is impossible if movements between the markets are unrestricted, largely because of the possibility of arbitrage. By *arbitrage* we mean the simultaneous purchase of something in a cheap market and its sale in a dear market to profit from price differences between the markets. *Speculation,* on the other hand, is a means of deriving profit by taking advantage of the price differences between different points in time. Arbitrage and speculation should not be confused.

Exchange arbitrage is accomplished through cable orders. Let us consider first what is usually called *two-point arbitrage.* Suppose that the cable rate in New York is £1 = $2.41 at the same time that it is £1 = $2.40 in London. An arbitrageur—who may be the foreign-exchange department of a big New York bank—could make abnormally large profits out of this discrepancy. He could sell a £100,000 cable in New York for $241,000 and at the same time order his London correspondent to draw a $240,000 cable order on New York and sell it for £100,000. Thus, in a matter of minutes, the arbitrageur would make a gross profit of $1,000; he would sell in New York for $241,000 the sterling that he purchased in London for only $240,000. The effect of these transactions is to equalize exchange rates in New York and London. The sale of sterling in New York tends to lower its dollar price there, and the offer of dollars for sterling in London tends to raise the dollar price of sterling in that market. Exchange rates must be practically the same in the two markets after arbitrageurs have completed their operations. In fact, discrepancies as large as the one assumed in our example could hardly occur in a market free of restrictions, for exchange arbitrageurs are always on the alert and can make good profits from very small margins. For this reason, we can, with little inaccuracy, speak of one exchange rate between two moneys at a given time without specifying the market to which we are referring. This obviously is not possible if movements of funds between the markets are restricted.

DETERMINANTS OF EXCHANGE RATES

Since an exchange rate is a price, we should be able to use ordinary supply-and-demand analysis, arguing as usual that the exchange rate is determined by both supply and demand functions. We shall begin our discussion with the case in which official agencies do not peg exchange rates or otherwise intervene, but allow exchange rates to be determined by free-market forces. To illustrate the principles involved, we shall analyze the dollar price of the British pound sterling, or what is the same thing, the sterling price of the dollar, and shall state our analysis in terms of the supply of and demand for sterling.

The next step is to define supply and demand and to identify their components. By the supply of sterling, we mean a function or schedule showing the quantities of sterling that would be supplied in exchange markets per period of time at each of the various possible dollar prices of sterling. Its components are the payment items in the British balance of payments—amounts of sterling supplied to purchase imports of goods and services and to buy various types of financial claims from foreigners. By the demand for sterling, we mean a function or schedule showing the quantities of sterling that would be demanded in exchange markets at the various possible dollar prices of sterling. The components of these demands for sterling are the receipt items in the British balance of payments; that is, quantities of sterling demanded to pay for British exports of goods and services and to purchase various types of financial claims from the British. Let us now use simple statics to show how supply and demand functions determine exchange rates.

Supply function of sterling

The purpose of a supply schedule stating supply as a function of price is the usual purpose of isolating the effect of price (in this case, the exchange rate) on quantities supplied. Such a curve can be drawn only if we assume that all other conditions affecting supply are given and constant. Listed below are the principal factors which, for the moment, we assume to be given and constant.

1. The level of real income in Britain
2. The level of prices and costs in Britain relative to those of other countries
3. Levels of interest rates in Britain relative to those of other countries
4. Expectations as to future exchange rates on sterling

5. Tastes for British products relative to those of other countries
6. Other factors relevant to the productivity and comparative costs of British and foreign products

Later, we shall see how changes in these conditions tend to shift the supply function for sterling.

The supply function of sterling is represented by the *SS* line in Figure 20–1. It is shown as a positive function of the exchange rate on sterling; that is, the higher the exchange rate on sterling, the greater will be the quantity of sterling offered in the exchange market. The reason for this is that the higher the dollar price of sterling, the cheaper will be the sterling price of imports, the greater will be the quantity of imports demanded by Britain, and the greater will be the sterling value of imports if the price elasticity of British demands for imports, stated in terms of sterling prices, is greater than unity. This becomes clearer as we remember that increases in the dollar price of sterling are accompanied by decreases in the sterling price of the dollar. For example, a rate of £ = $1 is obviously the same as $1 = £1; £1 = $2 is equivalent to $1 = £½; and £1 = $3 is equivalent to $1 = £⅓. Suppose that the American price of some export to Britain is $1 per unit. In terms of sterling, the cost of the import to the British will be £1 if the exchange rate is £1 = $1, only £½ if the exchange rate is £1 = $2, and only £⅓ if the exchange rate is £1 = $3.

It will be helpful to remember that, other things equal, an increase in the exchange rate on a nation's currency tends to encourage its imports, and that a decrease in the exchange rate on a nation's currency tends to discourage its imports.

Demand function for sterling

The demand function for sterling, represented by the *DD* line in Figure 20–1, assumes that all other conditions except the exchange rate are given and constant. The most important of these conditions are the following.

Figure 20–1 Demand for, and supply of, sterling

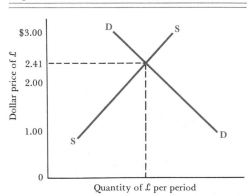

1. The level of real income in the rest of the world
2. The levels of prices and costs in Britain relative to those of other countries
3. Levels of interest rates in Britain relative to those of other countries
4. Expectations as to future exchange rates on sterling
5. Tastes for British products relative to those of other countries
6. Other factors relevant to the productivity and comparative costs of British and foreign producers

Later, we shall see how changes in these conditions can increase or decrease the demand function for sterling. The demand function for sterling is shown as a negative function of the exchange rate on sterling; that is, the higher the exchange rate on sterling, the smaller will be the quantity of sterling demanded in exchange markets. This is because higher exchange rates on sterling make British exports of goods and services more expensive in terms of other currencies. For example, suppose that the sterling price of some British good is £1. The dollar cost of the good will be $1 at an exchange rate of £1 = $1, it will be $2 at an exchange rate of £1 = $2, and $3 at an exchange rate of £1 = $3.

Thus, we find that, other things equal, a nation's exports are discouraged by a rise of the exchange rate on its currency and encouraged by a decrease of their exchange rate on its currency.

It will be remembered that we are dealing with the case in which the authorities do not attempt to peg exchange rates or intervene directly to affect their behavior, and that they allow exchange rates to be determined by market forces. In this case, the exchange rate can be in equilibrium only when the quantity of sterling demanded is exactly equal to the quantity supplied, leaving neither an excess demand nor an excess supply. Figure 20–1 shows that, with the given *DD* and *SS* curves, this can occur only at the exchange rate £1 = $2.41. At any higher rate, there would be an excess supply of sterling. The supply of sterling would be larger because British imports would be cheaper in terms of sterling, and the demand for sterling would be smaller because British exports would be more expensive to foreigners. On the other hand, there would be an excess demand for sterling at any lower exchange rate on sterling. Demands for sterling would be larger because the cost of British exports in terms of foreign currencies would be lower, and supplies of sterling would be smaller because the sterling price of imports would be higher.

SHIFTS OF SUPPLY AND DEMAND FUNCTIONS
IN EXCHANGE MARKETS

We shall now use comparative statics to show how changes in selected economic and financial conditions can shift demand and supply functions in exchange markets, thereby tending to change exchange rates. We shall pay special attention to changes in price levels, income levels, and interest rates.

Change in level of British prices and costs relative to levels abroad. Suppose, for example, that Britain experiences a domestic inflation of her price and cost levels.

As the sterling prices of British products rise, the demand curve for sterling will shift to the left and downward. British goods will now be more expensive at each level of exchange rates and British exports will be discouraged. This rise of British price levels will also shift the supply curve of sterling downward and to the right. As the prices of competing domestic products rise, the British will demand more imports at each exchange rate on the dollar.

Thus, we find that if British prices rise more than prices elsewhere, the exchange rate on sterling will tend to be lowered, both by shifting the demand function for sterling downward and to the left and by shifting the supply function of sterling downward and to the right. When a country inflates its domestic price levels significantly while prices elsewhere remain relatively constant, it usually cannot balance its receipts and payments without reducing its exchange rate to maintain its exports and discourage imports.

It should be noted that the same result may occur if British prices remain constant while prices elsewhere fall. The decline of prices elsewhere will make British exports relatively expensive to foreign buyers unless the exchange rate on the pound is reduced sufficiently. Also, British imports will be cheaper in terms of sterling unless the fall of prices abroad is offset by a fall of the sterling exchange rate and a rise of exchange rates on foreign moneys. Note that Britain may be able to prevent her domestic price level from falling with price levels abroad if she reduces sufficiently the exchange rate on sterling. A fall of British price levels relative to levels abroad would tend to raise the rate on sterling, both by increasing the demand for sterling at each exchange rate and by decreasing the supply of sterling at each exchange rate.

Changes in level of real income in Britain. A rise of real income in Britian would tend to increase British imports at each level of exchange rates and thereby to increase the supply of sterling in exchange markets. It would therefore tend to lower the sterling exchange rate if the demand schedule for sterling remained constant. On the other hand, a fall of real income in Britain would tend to decrease the British demand for imports at each exchange rate, to decrease the supply of sterling at each exchange rate, and to raise the sterling rate in exchange markets.

Changes in level of real income in the rest of world. An increase of real incomes in the rest of the world tends to raise the demand for British exports at each exchange rate, to increase the demand for sterling at each exchange rate, and to raise the rate on sterling. Note that, to the extent that the rise of foreign demands for British exports is allowed to raise the exchange rate on sterling, Britain may be enabled to escape inflationary effects on her domestic price level. On the other hand, a decline of real incomes abroad tends to decrease the demand for British exports at each exchange rate, to lower the demand for sterling at each rate, and to reduce the exchange rate on sterling. By allowing the sterling exchange rate to fall, thereby making British exports cheaper in foreign moneys, Britain may be able to reduce the extent to which the decrease of foreign demand will reduce British exports, and she may do this without reducing the sterling prices of her exports.

Changes in level of interest rates in Britain relative to levels elsewhere. Suppose that British interest rates rise relative to those elsewhere. This will at least reduce capital outflows from Britain and may induce inflows. Thus, by decreasing the supply of sterling or increasing the demand for sterling, it will tend to raise the sterling exchange rate. A fall of interest rates in Britain relative to levels elsewhere tends to have the opposite effect, that is, to reduce the demand for sterling and increase the supply of sterling for international capital flow purposes.

Changes in expectations concerning future sterling exchange rates. Changes in expectations may be very important in evoking speculative capital flows. Suppose, for example, that there arise expectations that the rate on sterling will fall sharply in the future. The demand curve for sterling may be shifted to the left and downward immediately as people postpone their purchases of sterling. The supply curve of sterling may be shifted to the right and downward as people sell sterling and buy foreign moneys. Both the decrease of the demand for sterling and the increase of its supply will cause a decrease in the exchange rate on sterling. This decline of the sterling rate will, of course, stimulate British exports and discourage British imports.

What will be the economic effects of such a decline in the sterling rate induced by a speculative capital outflow from Britain? These effects depend in part on prevailing economic conditions. The results of a decline in the sterling rate may be welcome if the British economy is depressed. The decline of the sterling rate will shift the demand schedule upward for British exports at each price level in terms of sterling and thus stimulate British export industries. Also, by making imports more expensive in terms of sterling, the decreased sterling rate will discourage British imports and enable import-competing industries to raise their prices. But suppose that the British economy is already under heavy inflationary pressure. The fall of the sterling exchange rate will intensify the pressure. The upward shift of foreign demands for British products will tend to raise their sterling prices. And the rise of the sterling prices of imports will add still further to British inflationary pressures.

On the other hand, newly created expectations of a future rise in the price of sterling can lead to an immediate decrease in the supply of sterling, an increase in the demand for sterling, and a rise of the sterling exchange rate. This will tend, of course, to discourage British exports and stimulate British imports. Such a development would hardly be welcome when Britain was in a state of unemployment.

This discussion indicates one reason why nations do not like speculative capital flows that make their exchange rates fluctuate in an erratic manner. Such fluctuations can have serious effects on their export industries, their import-competing industries, their price levels, and their entire economies.

CONCLUSIONS

The preceding section has shown how exchange rates could be determined and changed by supply and demand functions under a freely flexible exchange-rate system in which neither the central bank nor the government intervened to peg or otherwise directly influence the behavior of exchange rates. In the next chapter, we shall consider exchange-rate systems in which the central bank or government pegs rates within narrow limits. Even in this case, however, the analysis presented above is highly relevant, because it helps to explain how much gold and other international reserves the central bank and government will gain or lose in the process of stabilizing the exchange rate, what level of rates will prove to be tenable, and what processes will bring international receipts and payments into equilibrium.

Selected readings

Machlup, F., *International Trade and the National Income Multiplier,* Clifton, N.J., Kelley, 1943.

Machlup, F., "The Theory of Foreign Exchange," *Economica,* November, 1939; February, 1940. (Reprinted in American Economic Association, *Readings in the Theory of International Trade,* eds. Howard S. Ellis and Lloyd A. Metzler, Homewood, Ill., Irwin, 1950.)

Nurkse, R., *Conditions of International Monetary Equilibrium,* Essays in International Finance, No. 4, Princeton, N.J., International Finance Section of Princeton University, 1945.

CHAPTER 21

INTERNATIONAL MONETARY POLICIES

This chapter will deal with two principal topics: exchange-rate systems and methods of equating international receipts and payments. Policy choices in these fields are important, not only for the behavior of international trade and capital movements, but also for the ability of nations to promote their domestic economic objectives. Although we shall often refer to national policies in these fields, it should be remembered that in all international transactions at least two nations, and usually many more, are involved, and that the actual behavior of an individual nation's exchange rate and balance of payments depends not only on its own policies but also on those of other nations. This fact underscores the importance of the nature and degree of international cooperation.

One major policy issue is the choice of an exchange-rate system. Here there are two broad alternatives. One is to peg the exchange rate within narrow limits, achieving this through official purchases and sales of gold or other international reserves. The other is a system of floating or flexible exchange rates. However, we shall find that these are very broad categories and that the actual systems within each category can differ significantly.

A different, but closely related, policy issue is that of choosing methods of dealing with deficits and surpluses in balances of payments. Suppose that a nation has a deficit in its balance of payments; this is obviously a surplus in the balance of payments of the rest of the world. Each nation may respond in one or more of several ways (see Table 21–1). For example, a deficit country may "absorb" the

Table 21–1 Methods of dealing with a surplus or aeficit in the balance of payments

1. Absorb it by allowing international reserves to change
2. Repress it
3. Eliminate it by adjusting
   a. Exchange rates
   b. Income levels
   c. Relative price levels
   d. Relative interest-rate levels

deficit by allowing its international reserve position to shrink. How long it can do this depends on the size of its deficit and the size of its international reserve and facilities for borrowing foreign moneys. It may "repress" the deficit by imposing direct cotrols on international trade and payments. For example, it may impose controls on all exchange transactions and may ration payments so that they do not exceed receipts, or it may impose higher tariffs or quantitative restrictions on imports and prohibit or limit capital outflows. Such measures can indeed equate international payments and receipts, but they have serious consequences for world trade and capital movements and for the efficiency of the world economy.

The deficit nation, together with the surplus nations, may eliminate the deficit. One way is to reduce the exchange rate on the nation's money. Other ways are to adjust income levels, relative price levels, and relative interest-rate levels.

These methods may be used singly or in various combinations. Policy choices in this field are closely interrelated with choices concerning exchange-rate systems. For example, to the extent that a country allows its exchange rate to change as a means of eliminating surpluses and deficits, it need not rely on the other methods. But if a country adamantly pegs its exchange rate at a fixed level, it must rely on the other methods. If its command over international reserves is limited, it can absorb deficits for only a limited period. And, if it is unwilling to repress trade and payments, it must fall back on adjustments of levels of income, prices, and interest rates.

EXCHANGE-RATE SYSTEMS

Let us now look at some of the principal attributes of exchange-rate systems, starting with flexible exchange rates.

Flexible exchange rates

In the preceding chapter, we dealt with the case of freely floating exchange rates, under which no official agency buys or sells currencies to peg exchange rates or to influence behavior of exchange rates. That behavior is determined by other demand-supply conditions in exchange markets. The exchange rate on each currency will be in equilibrium at that level that will equate the nation's receipts and payments, and will change as demand and supply functions for the currency change.

It should not be assumed that because an exchange rate is flexible it will in fact fluctuate widely. There have, of course, been numerous historical cases in which exchange rates did fluctuate widely and even wildly. These variations usually occurred during wars, postwar inflations, or deep depressions, and reflected pathological monetary and fiscal conditions. In fact, in most of these cases, nations had resorted to flexible exchange rates only after monetary and financial disorders had made fixed exchange rates untenable. There is no reason to believe that flexible exchange rates would need to fluctuate rapidly or widely to equilibrate balances of payments if the monetary and fiscal policies of the various nations were directed toward promoting reasonable stability of price levels and approximately full employment.

The great advantage claimed for a policy of freely floating exchange rates is that it gives a nation the freedom to pursue domestic economic objectives. If its exchange rate is allowed to adjust in such a way as to equilibrate its balance of payments, a nation need not for this purpose resort to direct controls over international trade and capital movements. And it need not allow concern over the state of its balance of payments and international reserves to influence its monetary and fiscal policies. Such policies can be directed solely to promoting such domestic objectives as full employment, rapid economic growth, and relatively stable price levels.

Freely floating exchange rates also have disadvantages.

1. Uncertainty as to future exchange rates creates exchange risks and may impede international trade and capital movements. For example, an American who buys exports from Britain and promises to pay in sterling runs the risk that the dollar price of sterling will rise above expected levels. And a British exporter who sells for dollars runs the risk that the sterling price of dollars will fall below expected levels. Exchange risks can be even more serious for capital movements, and especially for long-term capital. For example, you may be reluctant to make a long-term loan to a Frenchman in return for his promise to repay francs because of uncertainty as to the future dollar value of the franc. For similar reasons, a Frenchman may be reluctant to promise to repay a debt in dollars. Forward-exchange markets and speculative activities in them can lessen the burden of these risks, but these facilities are sometimes expensive and inadequate. They are usually not available to bear exchange risks on long-term lending and borrowing. In comparing exchange risks under flexible and pegged exchange-rate systems, one should not assume that such risks are absent or negligible under a nominal system of pegged rates, because pegged rates may be changed, sometimes by significant amounts.

2. Changes in a nation's exchange rate that are not necessary for longer-run equilibration of its receipts and payments may cause unnecessary disturbances in

a nation's economy, and especially in its import-competing and export industries. Suppose, for example, that there is an abnormal flow of short-term capital to nation A, which raises the exchange rate on its currency significantly above its longer-term equilibrium level. This increase of its exchange rate will tend to increase the cost of A's exports in terms of foreign currencies, and thus will lower output and employment in its export industries. The rise of the exchange rate will also lower the cost of imports, thus discouraging output and employment in A's import-competing industries. Suppose that at some later time the outflow of short-term funds is abnormally large and this lowers the exchange rate on A's currency significantly below its longer-term equilibrium level. This would encourage employment and output in both its export and import-competing industries. Such domestic disturbances resulting from erratic changes in exchange rates would not be welcome in any nation, least of all in those nations heavily dependent on exports and imports.

Attitudes toward a policy of freely floating exchange rates differ widely, largely because of differences of judgment concerning the behavior patterns of rates under such a system. The optimists believe that actual rates would deviate only slightly from their longer-term equilibrium, and that through time adjustments would be relatively smooth and orderly. The pessimists disagree. A basic issue is this: Would private speculation in exchange markets be predominantly and reliably stabilizing, or would it at least on some occasions, be destabilizing? The optimists argue essentially as follows: Private speculators, or at least those persons who speculate successfully, base their decisions on a careful analyis of the basic factors that determine the longer-run equilibrium level of an exchange rate. When the market rate rises significantly above this level, the speculator will sell the currency, thereby pushing its rate back toward equilibrium. On the other hand, if the speculator buys the currency when its price falls significantly below the long-term equilibrium level, this will tend to raise the currency's price. Thus, the speculators who make money and survive are those who correctly estimate the longer-term equilibrium level of the exchange rate and operate in a stabilizing way. Financial failure will eliminate those speculators who are wrong in their estimate of the level of the longer-term equilibrium rate or who speculate in a destabilizing way.

Pessimists challenge both the conclusion that stabilizing speculation will always predominate and the conclusion that destabilizing speculators will lose money and be eliminated. To make their point, the pessimists sometimes use stock-market speculation as an analogy. They admit that much speculation in shares of stock tends to be stabilizing. However, they contend that for considerable periods of time destabilizing types of speculation may predominate and even be highly profitable. For example, suppose that at some time the price of a particular stock is already above what you consider to be its longer-run equilibrium level, but that you expect its price to rise further because of a developing "bullish" sentiment among other participants in the market. Your purchases will be destabilizing in the sense that they will tend to push the price still further above its longer-term equilibrium level, but they will be profitable if you succeed in selling before the price again falls to the level of your purchase price. Similarly, you can reap a profit by selling a stock that is already priced below its longer-run equilibrium level, thereby tending to depress the price, if you are correct in your expectation that other "bearish" sellers will depress the price still further before it rises again. Pessimists may exaggerate the dangers of destabilizing private speculation, but they properly cast doubts on the optimistic contention that such speculation will be predominantly and reliably stabilizing.

Largely because of such doubts, many advocates of flexible exchange rates favor official intervention on at least some occasions. Under such a system, the authorities do not peg exchange rates within narrow limits, but they do intervene at times to buy and sell moneys in exchange markets to influence exchange-rate behavior. The nature and degree of intervention vary widely. At one extreme, the authorities intervene only infrequently and only for the purpose of preventing "disorderly movements"; they do not attempt to influence the longer-term trends of exchange rates. In other cases, they intervene more frequently and do attempt to affect the level of exchange rates over longer periods. As the authorities try to hold fluctuations within narrower and narrower limits, the system assumes the characteristics of pegged exchange rates.

Official intervention under a policy of flexible exchange rates raises important problems. One problem is the estimation of the longer-term equilibrium level of an exchange rate. There is no assurance that official judgments will be any better than those of private speculators. Moreover, official decisions may be unduly influenced by pressures from economic groups, such as exporters and industries competing with imports. When official intervention influences the longer-term level of an exchange rate, there is the problem of determining what that level should be. There is a real danger that some nations will try to manipulate the rate to achieve an undue national advantage. For example, nation A may try to drive down the exchange rate on its money to give greater advantage to its export industries and greater protection to its import-competing industries; nation A may do this despite the fact that it already has a surplus in its balance of payments. Nations B, C, and D may retaliate. The result may be a "war of exchange rates," with disruptive effects on trade and capital movements. Such behavior is most likely to occur in depression periods when nations try to export their unemployment, but it is by no means unknown in periods of prosperity. These disadvantages of the manipulation of exchange rates highlight the need for an international understanding or agreement concerning the appropriate behavior of exchange rates, and illustrate the need for some means of promoting cooperation among national exchange authorities.

Pegged exchange rates

One of the most common exchange-rate policies has been that of pegging exchange rates within narrow limits over considerable periods of time. Almost all of the major national currencies were interlinked through fixed rates under the international gold standard that prevailed during the years preceding World War I. Most nations returned to pegged rates during the 1920s, following the breakdown of the old system during World War I, and the principle of pegged rates was embodied in the Bretton Woods Agreements that led to the establishment of the IMF. Such systems are likely to play important roles in the future even though there is increasing support for more flexibility in exchange rates. The technique of pegging exchange rates, like that of pegging the price of wheat, the price of gold, or the price of a government security, is basically simple. A monetary authority or someone else stands ready to supply at some fixed price all the nation's money that is demanded from it at that price, and to demand at some fixed price all the nation's money that is offered to it at that price. Sometimes a monetary authority itself enters the exchange market and does the pegging. In other cases, it merely provides others with a means of doing so. Let us consider that latter case first.

Private dealers in exchange will maintain virtually stable exchange rates between gold-standard moneys if the nations issuing those moneys stand ready to buy and sell gold at a fixed price and to allow gold import and export by private operators. For example, suppose that at some time the dollar is defined as 13.71 grains of pure gold. This is equivalent to setting a gold price of $35 an ounce, for an ounce contains 480 grains. Suppose that, at the same time, the British define the pound as 32.9 grains of pure gold. This is the same as setting a gold price of £14.6 an ounce. The mint parity, or par of exchange, between the dollar and the pound will be £1 = $2.40 because the gold content of the pound is 2.40 times that of the dollar; or, to state the relationships another way, the dollar price of gold is 2.40 times the sterling price of gold. As long as both countries freely buy and sell gold at these fixed prices for international purposes, the dollar-sterling rate can deviate only slightly from this mint parity, or parity of exchange. This is because exchange dealers can acquire sterling by using dollars to buy gold and then sell the gold for sterling, and they can use sterling to buy gold and then sell the gold for dollars. For example, you might, if regulations permitted it, buy in New York 10,000 ounces of gold for $350,000. Suppose that the cost of shipping the gold to London, including your necessary profit, is $3,320. The total cost of the gold delivered in London will be $353,320. You can sell the gold there for £146,000 at the official buying price. The cost of acquiring each British pound in this way is 353,320/146,000, or $2.42. The exchange rate on the pound could not rise above this level because, at this rate on sterling, dealers would stand ready to supply all that might be demanded. The pound can rise higher and the dollar can fall lower only if the United States ceases to sell gold freely at the fixed price for export, or if the British cease to buy it freely at the fixed price.

Similarly, dealers could, if permitted, buy £146,000 in exchange markets, use it to buy 10,000 ounces of gold in London, and sell the gold in New York at the official price for $350,000. Suppose that the cost and necessary profit to the dealer is $3,320. His net realization in dollars will be $346,680, and his net realization per pound will be 346,680/146,000, or $2,375. The exchange rate on the pound cannot fall below this level as long as exchange dealers can freely use sterling to buy gold at a fixed price and can freely sell the gold for dollars at a fixed price. At this rate on sterling, dealers will buy all offered to them.

Note that when private dealers were relied on to stabilize exchange rates, the maximum deviations of actual rates from their parities depended on the costs of shipping gold which could vary from case to case, depending on such things as distance, shipping, and insurance rates. In general, however, the limits, stated as a percentage of parity, were quite narrow, usually not more than about 1 percent above and 1 percent below parity. Such narrow limits tended to be carried over when monetary authorities replaced private dealers as stabilizing agents. For example, under the IMF agreements, nations endeavored to keep their exchange rates within a band of 1 percent above and 1 percent below parity. However, during recent years there has been growing support for "widening the band" to permit somewhat more flexibility in rates. We shall discuss this later.

In recent years, techniques for pegging exchange rates within narrow limits have come to differ in at least two respects from those described above. In the first place, monetary authorities rely less—usually not at all—on the activities of private-exchange dealers to set the limits and intervene in the exchange markets themselves. In the second place, the authorities do not always use gold as an intermediary. Instead, as noted in an earlier chapter, they often buy and sell foreign moneys directly, using for this purpose their holdings of foreign moneys or current borrowings of foreign moneys. For example, suppose that the British monetary authority undertakes to prevent the exchange rate on sterling from rising above $2.42 and from falling below $2.38. Whenever the exchange rate on the pound rises to $2.42 (that is, when the rate on the dollar falls to £1/$2.42), the monetary authority uses sterling to demand dollars. It may then continue to hold the dollars or it may exchange them for gold. On the other hand, when the exchange rate on the pound falls to $2.38 (the exchange rate on the dollar rises to £1/$2.38), the monetary authority sells dollars in exchange for sterling. For this purpose it needs a sufficient supply of dollars, gold, or SDRs that can be sold for dollars, of some other currency that can be sold for dollars, or an ability to borrow dollars.

If other demands for sterling and other supplies of sterling are such as to equalize the demand for, and the supply of, sterling at some rate between $2.42 and $2.38, the government authority need not intervene at all. But the supply of sterling may exceed other demands for it at the support price. For example, at the rate £1 = $2.38, the supply of sterling may greatly exceed other demands for sterling, so that the authority must sell large amounts of its gold and foreign-exchange holdings to buy an amount of sterling equal to the difference between its supply and the demand. Such a situation is depicted in Figure 21–1. If this disequilibrium continues for very long, Britain may be drained of all her holdings of gold and foreign exchange.

Equilibration of receipts and payments
with pegged exchange rates

What policy should a nation follow when it faces a disequilibrium in its balance of international payments and is balancing its receipts and payments only by drawing down its holdings of gold and foreign assets or by building up large short-term debts to foreigners? This is one of the most important policy problems in the entire field of international finance. The nation may, of course, lower its exchange rate to equalize the demand for, and supply of, its money in exchange markets. Or it may resort to direct controls over its trade and payments in order to hold its payments down to the level of its receipts. Let us suppose, however, that Britain refuses to resort to a depreciation of her exchange rate or to restrictions on the freedom of trade and payments.

The drain on Britain's international reserves at the pegged exchange rate of £1 = $2.38 can be ended only by developments that will shift the demand curve for sterling upward and to the right, shift the supply curve for sterling upward and to the left, or shift both to a sufficient extent to equalize the demand for sterling and the supply of sterling at a rate equal to or more than £1 = $2.38. Several types of developments in other countries can assist in this process:

1. A rise of price levels abroad would increase the demand for sterling at each exchange rate by increasing the demand for British exports. It would also tend to reduce the supply of sterling by discouraging British imports.

2. A rise of real incomes abroad would shift the demand curve for sterling to the right.

3. A decrease of interest rates abroad, to the extent that it lessened capital flows out of Britain and induced or increased a flow of capital to Britain, would reduce the supply of, and raise the demand for, sterling.

All these developments could help to raise the demand for sterling relative to the supply of it and to ease the drain on Britain's international reserves. How-

Figure 21–1 Disequilibrium with pegged exchange rates

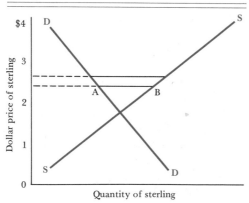

Quantity of sterling

ever, if these developments do not occur abroad, or are not sufficiently strong to close the payments gap, one or more of the following things will have to happen in Britain:

1. A fall of British price levels, which would tend to increase the demand for sterling by cheapening British exports and to decrease the supply of sterling by reducing British imports.

2. A fall of real income in Britain, which would decrease British imports and the supply of sterling.

3. A rise of interest rates, which, to the extent that it reduced the outflow of capital from Britain or increased capital inflows, would tend to reduce the supply of sterling or to raise the demand for sterling.

Adjustments of precisely these types will tend to be made "automatically" if the deficit and surplus countries subject their monetary policies to the "discipline of their balance of payments" and "follow the rules of the international gold-standard game." These "rules" originally applied to international gold movements, but they are also applicable to a system of pegged exchange rates in which the central bank buys and sells foreign moneys, thereby tending to create and to decrease bank reserves within the country. The essence of these "rules" is that the deficit country should allow its loss of gold or other international reserves to restrict its money supply, and that the surplus countries should allow their increases of gold and other international reserves to expand their money supplies.

Suppose that the deficit in the British balance of payments resulted from a decrease of its exports as other countries shifted their demand from British products to their home products. First, there are the "income effects." Both the decline of demand for its exports and the induced decrease of consumption expenditures at home serve to lower total demands for British output. In the surplus countries, the opposite occurs; demands for their output are increased both by the shift from British products to home products and by the induced rise of consumption expenditures.

Then there are the monetary effects. As the Bank of England makes net sales of gold and foreign exchange, it reduces the reserves of the joint-stock banks, thereby tending to restrict credit and to raise interest rates. It can accentuate monetary restriction by selling securities or calling loans. The monetary restriction and rise of interest rates in Britain serve both to attract funds from abroad (or at least to reduce outflows) and to lower domestic demands for output.

As central banks in the surplus countries make net purchases of gold and foreign exchange, they create reserves for their banks, thereby encouraging expansion of their money supplies and a decrease of interest rates. They can accentuate this if, as their international reserves increase, the central banks buy securities or expand their loans. The fall of interest rates in these surplus countries serves both to encourage outflows of funds to the deficit country and to increase demands for output in the surplus countries.

Such are the "automatic" processes of equilibrating international receipts and payments if both deficit and surplus countries follow these "rules of the game." Capital flows to the deficit country tend to be induced by both the rise of interest rates there and the fall of rates in the surplus countries. More fundamental is the fall of demands for output in the deficit country and the rise of demands for output in the surplus countries. Suppose first that money wage rates and prices are quickly and completely flexible and that changes in demands for output are reflected only in changes in prices. The fall of prices in the deficit country and the rise of prices in the surplus countries will serve to equate international receipts and payments by increasing exports and decreasing imports of the deficit country, and causing reverse effects in the surplus countries. Thus, if money wage rates and prices are quickly and completely flexible, international payments and receipts may be equated through adjustments of the price levels of the various countries.

What if money wage rates and prices are inflexible, at least in the downward direction? Changes in demands for output can still equate international receipts and payments, but by changing levels of real income. Increases of demands for output in the surplus countries can, by raising their real incomes, increase their demand for the exports of deficit countries. And the fall of demands for output in the deficit country can, by lowering its level of real output and income, decrease its expenditures for imports. The deficit country can become too poor to demand imports in excess of its current international receipts. In other words, it can eliminate the deficit in its balance of payments by creating a deficit in its real income or output.

It is easy to see why countries intent on promoting such domestic objectives as maximum employment and output, rapid economic growth, and price-level stability are often highly reluctant to follow "rules of the game," which require that their monetary and fiscal policies be dominated by their balance-of-payments and international-reserve positions. Countries with surpluses in their balances of payments are sometimes reluctant to expand their money supply for fear of inflationary consequences. Countries with deficits are even more reluctant to follow restrictive monetary and fiscal policies if this threatens their employment and growth objectives. They often take offsetting actions, such as central-bank purchases of securities, to prevent their loss of gold or other international reserves from restricting credit and raising interest rates.

However, if a country insists on pegging its exchange rates at a fixed level, and will not adopt restrictive fiscal or monetary policies despite a persistent deficit in its balance of payments, it is likely to be drained of its international reserves, to be forced to impose direct controls over its international trade and payments, or both.

SOME CONTROVERSIAL ISSUES

What should be the relative responsibilities of surplus and deficit countries for eliminating surpluses and deficits under an international system of fixed exchange rates? Deficit countries usually reply that the surplus countries should solve the problem by increasing their imports, by lending more, or by giving more aid. Surplus countries, on the other hand, often retort that the deficit coun-tries should tighten their belts, show some self-discipline, and cease trying to live beyond their means.

Few would contend that surplus countries should make the adjustment when they are already maintaining approximately full employment and stable or rising price levels, and when the deficits of the deficit countries are clearly attrib-utable to their own highly inflationary monetary and fiscal policies. It would be too much to ask surplus countries to eliminate their surpluses by inflating prices at a rapid rate. A more appropriate remedy in this case is for the deficit countries to reform the domestic policies that created their deficits. This may include a realistic adjustment of their exchange rates, accompanied by domestic reforms.

Consider, however, a quite different case in which the deficit countries have relatively stable price levels and their deficits were created by a sharp fall of real incomes and output in the surplus countries. The surplus of the latter countries was created by the decline of their demands for imports. The deficit countries could, of course, eliminate their deficits by adopting deflationary policies to lower their levels of real incomes and prices. However, a more attractive alterna-tive is for the surplus countries to adopt expansionary monetary and fiscal policies to raise their levels of real income and to increase their expenditures for imports.

The following rules of conduct seem appropriate under a system of fixed ex-change rates:

1. A deficit country undergoing domestic inflation should solve both prob-lems by adopting restrictive monetary or fiscal policies.

2. A surplus country with domestic output and income well below full-employment levels should solve both problems by adopting expansionary mone-tary or fiscal policies.

Unhappily, there are many situations not covered by these rules. For exam-ple, suppose some countries have large surpluses in their balances of payments along with actual or threatened inflation, while others have deficits in their bal-ances of payments despite the presence of unemployment and excess capacity at home. Should the surplus countries inflate still more to equate balances of pay-ments? Should the deficit countries create still more unemployment to eliminate their deficits? A sensible alternative, if the imbalance of international payments is large and persistent, would be to adjust exchange rates.

Adjustments of pegged rates

Although the IMF agreements envisaged virtually a worldwide system of pegged exchange rates, they also provided for adjustments of exchange-rate parities "to correct a fundamental disequilibrium." The latter term was not defined, but its general meaning was clear: Exchange-rate adjustments were not only permissible but to be encouraged as a means of dealing with imbalances in international pay-ments that could be remedied otherwise only at "excessive cost." For example, suppose a country has a large and persistent deficit in its balance of payments which it could eliminate while retaining its existing exchange rate only by placing restrictions on imports and capital exports or by resort to monetary and fiscal policies so restrictive as to prevent it from achieving full employment and its attainable rate of economic growth. Faced with such a "fundamental disequilibrium," the nation should lower its exchange rate to an equilibrium level and peg it there. On the other hand, a nation with a large and persistent surplus should raise the exchange parity on its currency.

The IMF agreements provided no guidelines to regulate the size or the frequency of the adjustments of exchange parities. Such decisions were postponed until they could be based on experience. As the years have gone by, more and more economists and some public officials have come to believe that, in practice, adjustments of parities have been too infrequent and individually too large. Too often adjustments have been made only after a large maldistribution of international reserves has occurred, trade and capital movements have been restricted, and some nations have paid too high a price in terms of output and employment. Such critics believe that if a system of pegged rates is to be retained, parities should be adjusted more promptly and in steps small enough to avoid the large speculative flows of funds that are often induced by prospective large changes in exchange rates. Several reforms have been suggested for these purposes. One is simply a change in the attitudes and practices of the IMF and its member nations; it is recommended that they adjust parities more promptly as disequilibrium appears. Another suggested reform is the widening of the band around parities. For example, the present limits of 1 percent above and 1 percent below parity might be replaced with limits of 3 percent above and 3 percent below parity. This would permit somewhat greater flexibility of actual exchange rates without changing parities.

However, this arrangement would not be adequate by itself if the existing parity seriously overvalued or undervalued a currency. For example, if the parity on a currency were considerably above the equilibrium level of its exchange rate, the actual rate would fall to the lower official support level and stay there. On the other hand, if the parity on a currency were considerably below its equilibrium exchange rate, the actual rate would rise to the upper support level and stay there. To remedy such situations, it has been suggested that a policy of widening the band be supplemented by a scheme of "sliding" or "crawling" parities. These would provide for slow and gradual adjustments of parities in response to the behavior of actual exchange rates during a preceding period. For example, parities might be altered once a month; the parity for a currency during any month would be determined by taking the average of the actual rates for the 12 months immediately preceding the month in question. Thus as the trend of actual market rates descended from the old parity, both the parity and the band limits would be adjusted downward, but at a pace slow enough to avoid large disturbances to capital flows. The same principles would apply as the trend of actual market rates on a currency increased from its old parity. If such "automatic" adjustments of parities proved to be inadequate or inappropriate, they could be supplemented or modified through discretionary changes.

EXCHANGE RESTRICTIONS AND OTHER DIRECT CONTROLS

Up to this point, our discussion of methods of equilibrating balances of international payments has assumed that there are no official restrictions on international transactions and payments. However, governments can take various types of direct action that will affect the nation's payments, receipts, exchange rates, and international reserves. In some cases, these actions are taken primarily for other reasons, and their effects in exchange markets are incidental. In others, they are taken primarily because of their effects in exchange markets.

These direct actions are of various types, of which the following are merely examples:

1. Increased tariffs on imports. By increasing the cost of imports, these may reduce the nation's imports and its demand for foreign moneys.
2. Quantitative restrictions on imports. These take various forms. A nation may put only a few types of imports under quota, or it may go as far as to prohibit all imports except those specifically licensed by the government.
3. Taxes on exports, subsidies on exports, and quotas on exports.
4. Restrictions on exchange transactions. These merit more detailed consideration.

Exchange restrictions

Exchange restrictions apply to any departure from a system of free, multilateral, international payments. They therefore include all restrictions on the types of transactions in exchange markets, the prices that may be received or paid for moneys, the use of receipts from abroad, the purposes for which international payments may be made, and so on. The first widespread use of exchange restrictions in peacetime came during the Great Depression of the 1930s. Many nations adopted them as world trade shrank, capital movements became disorderly, balance-of-payments problems multiplied, and exchange-rate stability was threatened. During World War II, all belligerent and most neutral countries instituted comprehensive systems of exchange control. In the typical case, receipts from abroad had to be surrendered at a fixed price to the central bank or an official exchange-control authority, no one could make a foreign payment without official permission, and both the types and amounts of foreign payments were strictly limited. At the end of the war, many countries were exercising strict control over all exchange transactions and were pegging exchange rates at levels that could not be supported if freedom of international payments were restored. One of the major problems since World War II has been that of lessening these restrictions, so that greater freedom of trading and lending could be restored. As of 1972 many restrictions have been removed, but some remain.

Exchange restrictions vary greatly in their comprehensiveness and their severity. In the early 1930s, their initial purpose in many cases was only to prevent abnormal capital flows out of a country—to prevent speculative flights into foreign moneys. Countries often insisted that they wished to preserve normal short- and long-term capital movements to finance international trade and investment. These restrictions had several closely related purposes: to protect the size of the country's international reserve, to enable it to use these reserves for more important purposes, and to prevent or to lessen the decline of the nation's exchange rate.

The problem of preventing "abnormal" capital movements, while maintaining "normal" capital movements, turned out to be extremely difficult. In practice, it is often virtually impossible to distinguish between normal and abnormal transactions. Furthermore, as soon as a nation refuses to allow foreign withdrawals of funds, its ability to attract new funds from abroad is greatly reduced. Finally, these restrictions can be enforced effectively only with a large organization and strict supervision of all exchange dealings, because funds can be withdrawn from a country in many ways. For example, many methods were devised to smuggle funds out of Germany. People made automobile parts and accessories out of gold and silver, painted them over, and drove the cars to Switzerland. They smuggled jewelry out of Germany and sold it abroad. German exporters underbilled their foreign buyers and made arrangements for the excess funds to be placed in accounts abroad. German importers overpaid their foreign suppliers and arranged for the extra funds to be held abroad for them.

The difficulty of regulating capital exports was but one reason why many nations came to apply exchange restrictions to virtually all types of international transactions. Perhaps more important was the feeling that these restrictions were a useful method of defending exchange rates, protecting international reserves, protecting home industries, and regulating all types of international trading and lending. A complete exchange-control system usually includes the following:

1. The government fixes the exchange rate on its money considerably above the level that would prevail in a free market.

2. Exchange dealings are centralized in the government and its authorized agencies.

3. All recipients of receipts from abroad are required to sell them to the exchange authority at the official rates.

4. No payment can be made abroad for any purpose without a permit, and in most cases an allocation of exchange, from the exchange authority.

Almost uniformly, an exchange rate pegged under a system of exchange controls overvalues the nation's money; the pegged rate is above the rate that would prevail with freedom of payments. For example, a South American country may peg its exchange rate at 1 peso = \$.20, or \$1 = 5 pesos when the market rate would be \$1 = 10 pesos if the market were free of restrictions. At the pegged rate, the supply of pesos will exceed the demand for pesos; the demand for foreign money will exceed the supply of it. Such a situation has important implications. One result of the overvaluation of the peso is that the country's exports become more expensive to foreign buyers, and this is likely to depress the nation's total export earnings. And, since the nation's capacity to pay for imports may be limited to the value of its exports, its imports are also depressed. Another result is that the demand for foreign money exceeds the available supply, and thus the exchange authority faces a rationing problem. Finally, the presence of exchange restrictions and an excess demand for foreign moneys makes the development of a black market in foreign exchange likely. Those whose demands are not fully met by allocations from the exchange authority may seek additional supplies elsewhere and be willing to pay higher prices for them.

Exchange rationing

Let us now look at some of the problems of exchange rationing, assuming that the authorities are largely successful in maintaining a single exchange rate. Faced with an excess of demands for foreign exchange over available supplies, the exchange authorities must answer questions such as: How much do we allocate to each individual, business firm, and governmental agency wanting to make payments abroad? How much do we allocate for each general type of payment, how much for payment of debts abroad, how much for payments of interest and dividends, how much for foreign investment, how much for foreign travel, and how much for each of the various types of goods and services that might be imported? Should we merely ration by type of payment, or should we also ration payments to individual countries? And, if the latter, what volume of payments should we permit to be made to each country?

Experience with exchange control and exchange rationing has varied from country to country, but there have been many common problems. One problem is maintaining fairness and honesty in rationing foreign exchange among competing individuals and business firms. When the total value of imports is limited, an allocation of foreign exchange can be extremely valuable. For example, if but little foreign exchange is allocated for auto imports, an importer might buy an American car for $2,500 and sell it in his own country for the equivalent of $15,000. If the government does not capture this excess profit with an import tax, the importer may share it with government officials. Friendships, family ties, political affiliations, and financial generosity to government employees and officials have too often played important roles in exchange rationing.

In general, countries have severely restricted exchange allocations for payments of foreign debts and transfers of interest and dividends. They have classified some types of imports as "essentials" and have given them preferential allocations while discriminating against "nonessentials." Domestic political considerations often influence these classifications. For example, imports that would compete with the output of politically powerful domestic industries are discriminated against, whereas exchange allocations for imports that are noncompetitive are more generous.

Exchange-allocation policies have also been used as an instrument for forcing bilateral trade balancing. Thus, Argentina has favored payments to Britain over payments to the United States, because the British are better customers for its exports. Germany used exchange rationing during the 1930s for political and military purposes. Payments to countries evidencing "the proper attitude" were permitted on a liberal scale, but payments to other countries were niggardly.

These examples should suggest how powerfully exchange-rationing policies can influence a nation's internal structure of production and prices, and the types and directions of its international trade.

Multiple exchange rates

We noted earlier that there can be but one exchange rate on a nation's money at any time if exchange dealings are free of restrictions. But more than one rate becomes possible as soon as restrictions are imposed; those whose demands for foreign money are not fully satisfied at the official rate may be willing to pay a higher rate. In our forgoing example, those whose demands for dollars are not fully met at the official rate of $1 = 5 pesos, may be willing to pay 10 pesos or even more for extra dollars. Also, some of those who own or can get dollars will try to avoid selling them at the official rate of 5 pesos, and will make them available in the black market at some higher price. In many cases, these black markets become well organized even though they are illegal. Let us suppose that the black-market rate becomes $1 = 10 pesos. The initial reaction of exchange-control authorities toward black markets is usually one of strong opposition; they want the entire supply of foreign money surrendered to them. After a time, however, some of them come to believe that the black-market rate provides a useful way of stimulating exports. For example, some of the nation's exporters may not be able to compete successfully if they have to sell their dollar receipts at the official rate of 5 pesos to the dollar, but they will increase their exports markedly if they can sell their dollars at the black-market price of 10 pesos. The exchange authority may therefore wink at such an "informal depreciation" of the peso in a limited number of transactions. Later, the exchange authority may formally set up a legal multiple exchange-rate system.

Some of these multiple exchange-rate systems are extremely complex. Let us use a simple system to illustrate the principles involved. Suppose that a South American country retains the "official rate" of $1 = 5 pesos and establishes two additional rates: an "export rate" of $1 = 7 pesos and a "free rate" of $1 = 10 pesos. If demands for dollars are not fully met at these prices, a higher black-market rate on dollars may appear. The exchange authorities then define the types of dollar receipts and payments to which each of the official rates applies. Multiple exchange rates are a powerful instrument.

Let us see first how multiple buying prices for dollars can be used to influence the nation's exports and dollar receipts. If the exchange authority wishes to discourage its nationals from borrowing abroad, it may force them to sell borrowed dollars at the official rate of 5 pesos, but if it wishes to encourage capital inflows, it may purchase borrowed dollars at the export rate of 7 pesos, or even at the free rate of 10 pesos. The rates paid for dollars received for exports usually depend on the type of export involved. Dollars received for some types of exports must be surrendered at the relatively low official price of 5 pesos. These are usually exports that can compete successfully at that rate and for which the foreign demand is believed to be relatively price-inelastic. The authorities may believe that the nation's dollar earnings will be greater if foreigners must pay 20 cents for each peso than they would be if fewer cents would buy a peso. Dollar receipts for certain other types of exports may be purchased at the export rate of 7 pesos. This may both raise the peso price of the exports and lower their dollar prices. Dollar receipts for certain highly favored types of exports may be purchased at the high free rate of 10 pesos.

Multiple exchange rates also affect a nation's payments and imports. If the authority wishes to encourage a certain type of payment, it supplies foreign money at a low price; if it wishes to discourage a certain type of payment, it charges a high price for the foreign money. For example, if it wishes to discourage payments of foreign debt and transfers of interest and dividends, it may sell dollars for the purpose only at the high free rate of 10 pesos. Thus, it is enabled to repay a given peso obligation with fewer dollars. To encourage certain types of "essential" imports, and to hold down their peso prices, it may sell dollars at the low official rate of 5 pesos. These may be things imported for government use, machinery or supplies to promote economic development, raw materials used in producing exports, or essentials that enter into the cost of living. But dollars to pay for other imports may be available only at the export rate of 7 pesos, or at the free rate of 10 pesos. These imports may be discriminated against because they are "nonessentials," or their peso prices may be forced up to help import-competing industries. For example, dollars to pay for steel imports may have to be bought at the free rate of 10 pesos to afford protection to the nation's budding steel industry.

Multiple selling rates have also been used to regulate the sources of imports. To encourage imports from selected countries, the authority provides foreign exchange at a low price. To discourage imports from other areas, it provides foreign exchange only at very high prices.

Brief and incomplete as it has been, this account of exchange restrictions should indicate the power and breadth of their influence. They are indeed a wide departure from the old system of free, multilateral, international payments. Their original purpose was primarily to equilibrate international receipts and payments, to protect international reserves, and to avoid or to lessen the extent of exchange-rate depreciation. But once these restrictions were highly developed and made applicable to virtually every type of international transaction, they came to be used for many other purposes as well—they were used not only to limit total imports, but also to regulate types and sources of imports and the relative prices of imports; to protect import-competing industries in varying degrees and to protect new domestic industries until they were established; to regulate the types of exports and to subsidize or penalize various types of exports; to bargain with other countries and force bilateral balancing of trade and payments; and so on. The very existence of these restrictions—and the possibility of their use to prevent or to limit repayments of foreign debt and transfers of interest and dividends—hampered international capital movements. Such restrictions not only reduce the total volume of world trade, but also misdirect it and prevent the achievement of the most efficient types of regional specialization in production. It is therefore easy to see why those who highly value the advantages to the free world of free multilateral trade and payments work toward elimination of exchange restrictions and toward reliance on other methods of equilibrating international receipts and payments.

CONCLUSIONS

We have now completed our survey of the international monetary system and of international monetary interrelationships and policies. Our survey has devoted special attention to international reserve or liquidity systems, exchange-rate systems, and methods of equilibrating international receipts and payments. Each of these fields presents many policy issues with important implications not only for international trade and capital movements but also for the behavior of output, employment, and price levels in the various countries. Moreover, policy choices in any one of these fields have significant consequences for the others.

The following list of some of the basic policy questions in the various fields will suggest both the large number of issues and their interrelatedness.

A. Issues relating to the international liquidity systems

1. How much international liquidity does the world need and at what rate should it grow to avoid restriction of trade and capital movements and both deflationary and inflationary pressures? The answer depends in part on the nature of the exchange-rate system and on the readiness of nations to eliminate deficits and surpluses in their balances of payments. A huge amount of reserves may be required if exchange rates are rigidly pegged over long periods and if nations fail to take quick and effective action to equilibrate their receipts and payments. The reserve requirement will be smaller if exchange rates are flexible or if other actions are taken quickly to equilibrate receipts and payments.

2. What should be the forms and proportions of the various components of international liquidity? What should be the roles of gold, of SDRs, of holdings of claims against foreign moneys, and of borrowing facilities?

3. Should the existing system be supplemented or replaced by an international central bank with discretionary power to create and regulate international reserves?

B. Issues relating to the exchange-rate system

1. Should exchange rates be rigidly and narrowly pegged over long periods regardless of the cost in terms of other objectives?

2. Should exchange rates be pegged, but adjusted if defense of an existing rate becomes costly? If so, what principles should guide adjustments and what techniques of adjustment should be used?

3. Should rates be allowed to float freely without official intervention?

4. Should rates be flexible, but with official intervention? If so, what should be the criteria for intervention?

C. Issues relating to methods of eliminating deficits and surpluses

1. As a means of equilibrating international receipts and payments, what should be the relative roles of direct controls over trade and payments, adjustments of exchange rates, and adjustments of incomes, price levels, and interest rates? These policy questions are obviously interrelated with those concerning the international-liquidity and exchange-rate systems.

2. What should be the relative responsibilities of surplus and deficit countries in eliminating imbalances in international payments?

D. Issues relating to national sovereignty and international economic interdependence

Among the sovereign rights claimed by each nation is the right to determine its own monetary and fiscal policies. Yet it is an incontrovertible fact that the economic policies of each country affect significantly, and in some cases powerfully, economic developments and welfare in other countries. This situation poses serious economic and political questions.

1. What basic principles should serve as a guideline to resolve these issues?

2. What types of international understandings, agreements, and institutions would best promote workable solutions?

Selected readings

Halm, G. N. (ed.), *Approaches to Greater Flexibility of Exchange Rates: The Burgenstock Papers,* Princeton, N.J., Princeton University Press, 1970.

Lary, H. B., *Problems of the United States As World Banker and Trader,* Princeton, N.J., Princeton University Press, 1963.

Scammell, W. M., *International Monetary Policy,* 2nd ed., London, Macmillan, 1961.

Yeager, L. B., *International Monetary Relations,* New York, Harper & Row, 1966.

PART SIX

AMERICAN MONETARY POLICY

CHAPTER 22

UNITED STATES MONETARY POLICIES, 1914–1929

With this chapter, we begin a lengthy discussion of monetary policy, with special emphasis on American monetary policies since the establishment of the Federal Reserve System in November, 1914.

As noted earlier, the formulation and execution of monetary policy involve at least three elements:

1. Selection of objectives—the choice of goals or purposes to be promoted.

2. Development and use of monetary institutions and instruments to promote the chosen objectives.

3. The use (at least implicitly) of some theory as to the economic effects of the various possible monetary actions.

We shall be interested in the evolution of all these elements in monetary policies. What have been the objectives or goals of our policies? How have these changed through time, and why? How have changing goals affected actions? How has the Federal Reserve developed its control instruments and how has it used them? In what ways or for what reasons has it changed its use of instruments? What types of monetary theory seem to be the bases for its policies, and how have these changed through time?

The purpose of this and subsequent chapters is not only to tell the story of past episodes; it is also to give us an opportunity to analyze policy formation and execution in specific situations, to provide a basis for understanding the present status of monetary policy, and to emphasize that monetary policy is continuously —and, at times, discontinuously—in the process of change.

BACKGROUND

When Congress passed and President Wilson signed the Federal Reserve Act in late 1913, the international gold standard was in its heyday. Gold had achieved its status as a truly international monometallic standard only in the latter part of the nineteenth century. Before 1870, few economically important countries other than Great Britain were on gold standards; most nations had adopted silver or bimetallic standards. But during the last 30 years of the nineteenth century and the first few years of the twentieth, the gold standard became widely accepted (see Table 22–1). The United States instituted its new gold standard in 1879.

Table 22–1 Dates of adopting gold standards*

Great Britain	1816	Holland	1875
Germany	1871	Uruguay	1876
Sweden		United States	1879
Norway	1873	Austria	1892
Denmark		Chile	1895
France		Japan	1897
Belgium		Russia	1898
Switzerland	1874	Dominican Republic	1901
Italy		Panama	1904
Greece		Mexico	1905

* The dates are approximate only, because some of the countries made the change from bimetallism or silver monometallism to gold in several steps.

The first years of the new gold standard were stormy ones, especially in the United States. This was primarily because they were years of deflation. The United States had followed highly inflationary monetary and fiscal policies during the Civil War; these were reflected in a doubling of the price level and in a fall of about 50 percent in the gold value of the inconvertible paper dollar. It was decided that prices would have to fall so that the dollar could again be given its old prewar gold value of 23.22 grains. When this was accomplished in 1879, the price level had already fallen more than 50 percent below its Civil War peak. But the price decline did not end at that point; it continued into the 1890s. Those who opposed falling prices joined forces with those who were infuriated by "The Crime of '73" and wanted to "do something for silver" in condemning the gold standard and in demanding more money of almost any type: more greenbacks, more silver money, and more of anything that would end the price decline and help silver. Then at the end of the century, almost abruptly, the clamor subsided, and the brief "golden age of gold standards" began. This was due in part to an upsurge in the growth of banking, but more to an upsurge in gold production, following the invention of the cyanide process of amalgamation and the new gold discoveries in the Rand district of the Transvaal and in the Klondike-Yukon area. The world's rate of gold production during the early years of the twentieth century was more than three times that in the period preceding 1896. The total money supply in the United States (coins, paper money, and checking deposits) tripled between 1896 and 1914, and wholesale prices rose more than 40 percent. Occasional complaints against the rising cost of living were lost among the praises of prosperity.

Those responsible for enacting the new Federal Reserve legislation had no intention of basically modifying the existing monetary standard. They implicitly assumed that the new system would operate within an international gold-standard framework and probably that it would follow the old rules of the international gold-standard game. What they could not know was that, before one year would pass, and even before the new Federal Reserve banks could be organized and opened for business, the old type of international gold standard would be a thing of the past. World War I was declared at the beginning of August, 1914, and carried almost all countries into inflation and off gold standards. Until 1925, only the United States and a very few other countries were on gold. During this period of more than 10 years, the old rules of the international gold-standard game were irrelevant, because there was no such standard. And the new standards that were established in the latter half of the 1920s were far different from those of the prewar period. In the meantime, the Federal Reserve had faced the task of helping to finance a major war.

THE PERIOD OF UNITED STATES NEUTRALITY, 1914 TO 1917

The war had already been declared in August before the Federal Reserve banks first opened for business in November, 1914. One of the first effects of the outbreak was to create crises in almost all financial markets, including those in the United States. Several forces combined to produce crisis conditions here: the necessity of repaying large, short-term debts to London, the unavailability of new credits from Europe, large foreign sales of securities on the New York Stock Exchange, German threats to ocean shipping and interruption of United States exports, domestic cash withdrawals from banks, and withdrawals by banks in the interior of some of their deposits with their city correspondents. At times, it was feared that a full-fledged banking panic would occur and that gold payments would have to be suspended. The worst had passed, however, when the Federal Reserve banks opened in November. By the late spring of 1915, the United States was enjoying an export boom. Demands for its products were becoming almost insatiable as neutrals turned to it for products formerly purchased in Europe and as the Allied Powers bought heavily to meet their essential civilian needs and to promote their war efforts. Between August 1, 1914 and the entry of the United States into the war in April, 1917, United States exports totaled $11,585 million, while its imports were only $5,531 million, leaving an export surplus of $6,054 million. Foreign buyers paid for these huge net purchases in three principal ways: They resold in the United States $2,000 million of their holdings of United States securities, borrowed $2,375 million, and shipped $1,100 million of gold. Since the United States gold stock had been only $1,572 million at the beginning of the war, these imports increased it by nearly 70 percent. No one had ever anticipated such gold inflows. Both the great increase in the foreign demand for United States exports and the flow of gold into bank reserves created strong inflationary pressures.

During the period between the opening of the Reserve banks in late 1914 and the entrance of the United States into the war in April, 1917, Federal Reserve officials had no opportunity either to develop meaningful objectives or to use their instruments of control effectively. It was obvious to them that they should not, in response to the gold inflow, follow expansionary policies and enhance inflationary pressures. Yet they could do nothing to offset or to sterilize the expansionary effects of gold inflows. They had almost no assets to sell and they had no power to raise member-bank reserve requirements. They had to stand by while the money supply rose from $11.6 billion in mid-1914 to $15.8 billion in mid-1917. Wholesale prices had already risen more than 50 percent when the United States entered the war.

THE WAR PERIOD, 1917 TO 1919

With this country's entrance into the war, the Federal Reserve entered a new phase. The system that had been created to "accommodate commerce and industry" now became a system to "accommodate the Treasury"; its dominant objective became that of assuring that the prosecution of the war would not be hindered by any lack of money, regardless of inflationary consequences. The government's fiscal policy was the one common to periods of major war—large deficits representing increases of expenditures far in excess of increases in tax collections. Federal expenditures rose from less than $750 million in 1916, to $18,515 million in fiscal 1919—nearly a 24-fold increase. For the three years ending June 30, 1919, federal expenditures aggregated $33,190 million, a huge sum for those days. This great rise in the government's demand for output, occurring when the economy was already operating at near-capacity levels, enhanced inflationary pressures both directly and through its stimulus to private consumption and investment demands. Despite the imposition of many new taxes and increases in old ones, total tax collections in the three years ending in June, 1919 were only $9,941 million, leaving a deficit of $23,248 million to be covered by new borrowing. (Table 22–2.)

The Treasury tried to borrow as much as it could in ways that would not involve an increase in the money supply. Employing a nationwide organization,

Table 22–2 Federal receipts and expenditures, 1916–1920 (millions of dollars)

FISCAL YEAR ENDING JUNE 30	EXPENDI- TURES	RECEIPTS	SURPLUS (+) OR DEFICIT (−)	CHANGE IN TREASURY GENERAL- FUND BALANCE	CHANGE IN GROSS FEDERAL DEBT
1916	$ 734	$ 783	+$ 48	+$ 82	+$ 34
1917	1,978	1,124	− 853	+ 897	+ 1,750
1918	12,697	3,665	− 9,032	+ 447	+ 9,480
1919	18,515	5,152	− 13,363	− 333	+ 13,029
1920	6,403	6,695	+ 291	− 894	− 1,185
Summary:					
1. Total for two fiscal years 1918–1919	$31,212	$8,817	−$22,395	+$ 114	+$22,509
2. Total for three fiscal years 1917–1919	$33,190	$9,941	−$23,248	+$1,011	+$24,259

high-pressure Liberty Loan campaigns, and various types of propaganda, it called upon the American people and business firms to "Save and buy bonds!" However, its receipts from these sales were far too small to cover its needs, so it turned to two principal types of borrowing that did require increases in the money supply.

1. Sales of Treasury securities, primarily shorter-term issues, to the commercial banks. This obviously involved an increase in the money supply, but the Treasury hoped, largely in vain, that it could later retire this money with borrowings from the public.

2. Sales of securities, largely of the longer-term varieties, to members of the public who would pay for them with money borrowed from the commercial banks. This, too, obviously involved an increase of the money supply, but the Treasury hoped that this new money would gradually be retired as banks brought pressure on their customers to save and repay their borrowings.

The Federal Reserve played a central role in this process by meeting the greatly increased demand for currency in circulation, and by supplying the banking system with sufficient reserves to enable it to buy Treasury obligations, to lend to others for the purchase of Treasury securities, and to meet essential private demands for productive purposes. In sharp contrast to its policies during World War II, it did this to only a very small extent by purchasing government securities itself. It supplied the funds largely by lending to commercial banks. To do this, it set up "preferential discount rates" on Federal Reserve loans collateraled by Treasury obligations. These were preferential in the sense that they were below the discount rates applicable to loans secured by commercial paper. They were also below, usually about $1/4$ percent below, the coupon rates on the various types of Treasury obligations to which they applied. Thus, a bank could make a small profit by borrowing from the Federal Reserve and buying government securities, and also by borrowing to lend to customers at an interest rate equal to the coupon rate on the security bought and pledged by the customer.

Three aspects of this policy are important:

1. In effect, it enabled the Treasury to determine Federal Reserve preferential discount rates, for it was the Treasury that determined the coupon rates on its obligations.
2. The preferential rates became the effective discount rates at the Federal Reserve banks. With great and growing holdings of Treasury obligations eligible for the lower preferential rates, banks would have been foolish to borrow at the higher rates applicable to commercial paper.
3. The Federal Reserve could not restrict the supply of credit for other uses while maintaining such ample credit supplies for the Treasury. Banks could secure reserves by borrowing on government securities and then lend as they saw fit.

The government's highly expansionary fiscal policy and the Federal Reserve's "accommodating" monetary policy were accompanied by inflation and monetary expansion. By mid-1919, when the government halted its deficit spending, both Federal Reserve and commercial-bank credit had expanded greatly. In March, 1917, just before the United States entered the war, total Federal Reserve credit outstanding was less than $300 million. In June, 1919, it was more than $2,500 million, of which $1,800 million represented bank borrowings. The nation's total money supply, which had been $11.6 billion in mid-1914 and $15.8 billion three years later, had risen to $21.2 billion by mid-1919. The wholesale price level was 25 percent higher than it was just before the entrance of the United States into the war and 95 percent above its level at the outbreak of the war.

Federal Reserve officials did not object to the domination of their policy by the Treasury's needs during the war itself or even during the period of continuing government deficits up to mid-1919. Like other Americans they, too, wanted to contribute as much as they could to the success of the war effort, and they recognized that the inadequate tax policy of the period necessitated borrowing from the banks and Federal Reserve support. But in the last three months of 1919, they grew restive and finally rebelled against Treasury domination. The Treasury's needs were now less urgent, because it had now established a small tax surplus. Moreover, inflation was again well under way. After some hesitation in late 1918 and early 1919, as the government's demand for output fell, the economy was again under strong inflationary pressures from rising exports and private domestic demands. Speculation in both securities and commodities was widespread, both Federal Reserve and commercial-bank credit were expanding, and prices and wages were rising rapidly. This was no speculative bubble on the surface of the economy; it was a strong inflation that pushed up not only the prices of output but also wages and other elements of the cost structure. Under these conditions, Federal Reserve officials wanted to increase discount rates. The Treasury objected. Although it no longer had to borrow new money to cover current deficits, the Treasury insisted that its refunding operations should not be hampered by increases in Federal Reserve discount rates. Moreover, it wanted to avoid any further declines in the prices of outstanding Liberty Bonds. The controversy became prolonged and bitter. Gradually, however, the Treasury acquiesced and permitted a series of discount-rate increases, the first of which occurred in November, 1919. In several cases, the Treasury's acquiescence was delayed and reluctant. By the end of May, 1920, discount rates at the various Reserve banks had been raised from their range of 4 to 4½ percent in the preceding October to a range of 6 to 7 percent.

The war and postwar inflation came to an abrupt halt in May, 1920. By then, however, price levels had risen markedly and both commercial-bank and Federal Reserve credit were greatly expanded. Wholesale prices were 140 percent above their prewar level. Total commercial-bank loans and investments had increased from $16.9 billion in mid-1914 to $36.3 billion, a rise of $19.4 billion, or 115 percent. Only 23 percent of this increase was in bank holdings of Treasury obligations; the remainder presented increased bank loans and holdings of private securities. Total Federal Reserve credit had risen to $3.4 billion, of which more than $2.5 billion was in the form of loans to banks. Thus, member banks entered the postwar depression owing the Federal Reserve banks more than $2.5 billion, and on these borrowings they were paying discount rates of 6 and 7 percent.

POSTWAR DEPRESSION, 1920 TO 1921

The end of the war and postwar inflation in the United States was signaled in May, 1920 by a worldwide break in the prices of such basic commodities as silk, tea, coffee, and most agricultural products. The ensuing depression, which ran into early 1922, was relatively short, but sharp and painful. Wholesale prices in general fell 45 percent, and the prices of farm products 50 percent. Millions lost their jobs, and thousands of business firms were injured by decreased demands for their products and by declines in the values of their high-priced inventories. Farmers were hard hit. Many who had bought high-priced land on credit or who had accumulated high-cost livestock and grain inventories either approached or were plunged into insolvency. Thus, both the solvency and the liquidity of the economy were seriously weakened. And the commercial banks, owing the Federal Reserve about $2.5 billion on which they were paying interest rates of 6 and 7 percent, were in no position to offer easier credit.

Not until April, 1921, about a year after the depression started, did the Federal Reserve take a single action to ease monetary and credit conditions. The Reserve banks did refrain from putting pressure on member banks to repay their borrowings; they wanted the liquidation to be orderly rather than abrupt and panicky. But they did not buy either government securities or acceptances to provide the banks with reserves and enable them to reduce their borrowings, and they did not reduce a discount rate until April, 1921. Such a policy now seems incomprehensible to those who accept the view that the major objectives of the

Federal Reserve should be to promote price stability, maximum employment, and the highest sustainable rate of economic growth. Why did the Federal Reserve follow the policies it did in the depression of 1920 to 1921?

The answer has many parts, but a basic point to be made is that the Federal Reserve had not yet come to believe that it had the responsibility of using its powers aggressively to promote economic stability. This concept of its function developed during the next few years. But the Federal Reserve had several reasons for wanting some liquidation of credit. One of these was to protect and improve its gold-reserve position. In considerable part, its policy was the traditional one of a central bank facing a threat to its reserve position and to its ability to maintain the redeemability of the nation's money in gold. The country's monetary gold stock had grown from $1.5 billion in 1914 to $2.9 billion in 1919. Moreover, a wartime campaign had succeeded in concentrating about three-quarters of the nation's gold in the Federal Reserve banks. A wartime embargo on gold exports prevented gold from flowing out until the embargo was lifted in the spring of 1919. Yet, by late 1919 and early 1920, the actual gold-reserve ratios of the Federal Reserve banks as a group were very close to the legal minimum. The Federal Reserve Bank of New York actually had deficient reserves on several occasions and had to pay penalties on the deficiencies. Several of the other Reserve banks would have been in even worse reserve positions if they had not borrowed from the other Reserve banks. This sharp decline in the reserve ratios of the Federal Reserve banks was brought about largely by the great rise of Federal Reserve note-and-deposit liabilities during the period of expansion and inflation, but it was aggravated by small gold outflows following the lifting of the gold embargo early in 1919.

This episode is interesting in part because it was one of the two occasions in Federal Reserve history when a shortage of gold led it to restrict credit (the only other instance was in the fall of 1931). It is significant that the Federal Reserve did not lower its discount rates in 1921 until its reserve position had improved markedly.

There were also other reasons why the Federal Reserve did not earlier remove downward pressures on credit. One reason was the belief that banks should not permanently hold large amounts of government securities. They should, instead, sell these securities and concentrate on commercial loans. Still another reason was the belief that member banks should not remain continuously in debt to their Reserve banks. Also important was the fact that the Federal Reserve had not yet learned how to use open-market operations for general monetary management purposes.

The 1920 to 1921 episode was extremely painful for the country and the Federal Reserve. Within a few years, the Federal Reserve had so changed its objectives and its methods of operations that it would not have dreamed of repeating its policies of 1920 to 1921. Armed with ample gold reserves—and even threatened by a plethora of gold—it began to emerge as an agency for economic stabilization.

THE POSTWAR WORLD

It was late 1921 or early 1922, when the Federal Reserve System was already more than seven years old, before Federal Reserve officials had an opportunity to develop anything like "normal" peacetime objectives and methods of monetary management. During their first two and a half years, Reserve officials had been powerless to prevent the flood of gold imports from feeding the inflation. From this country's entrance into the war until near the end of 1919, they had been chained to the objective of facilitating Treasury finance, regardless of inflationary consequences. Then, in 1920 and early 1921, their gold-reserve positions were so tight that they felt they had little freedom of action. Only now were they rid of the problem of financing a war, free of Treasury domination, and possessed of enough excess gold reserves and enough earning assets to enable them to regulate monetary conditions. But as the Federal Reserve officials sought to formulate peacetime objectives and to develop peacetime methods of operation, they did so under conditions that were never contemplated by the authors of the Federal Reserve Act and which made most of the prewar rules of central banking obsolete. The postwar world was far different from that of 1913.

The Federal Reserve Act anticipated that the new system would extend its credit almost exclusively on the basis of private-debt obligations. The Reserve banks would create funds primarily by lending to member banks on the basis of commercial paper, and even their open-market operations would be largely confined to acceptances. This was partly because of the theory that the supply of credit could be best adjusted to the needs of trade if based on short-term, self-liquidating loans for production and distribution purposes. But it was also partly because the supply of federal debt was so small; for some time, this debt had been less than $1 billion, and three-quarters of it was held as backing for national bank notes. All this was changed at the end of the war. The federal debt had grown to $25 billion and was widely held by all types of individuals and financial institutions. This altered the situation in many ways. In the first place, it increased the regional mobility of investable funds. These funds could now be shifted through interregional sales of government securities. In the second place, it enabled member banks to borrow on paper collateraled by Treasury obligations rather than commercial paper. In the third place, it provided the Federal Reserve with an excellent medium for open-market operations and facilitated the development and use of this powerful instrument.

Far more important, however, were the great changes in the world economy and in the relative position of the United States in that economy. The authors of the Federal Reserve Act implicitly assumed that the new system would operate within an international gold-standard framework and would in general abide by the old rules of the international gold-standard game. They had no reason to expect that the United States would become a major regulator of the world's monetary system, because the United States was in fact a minor financial center in the prewar period. She was still a net debtor to the rest of the world, she had few facilities for international lending, and her supply of knowledge and expertness in international monetary and financial matters was very limited. London was the almost undisputed monetary and financial center of the world. Britain was the world's greatest trading country and the world's greatest net creditor, and London was the world's center for international loans, both short- and long-term, and for international payments. In effect, the Bank of England managed the international gold standard. It is but little exaggeration to say that gold was on the sterling standard.

All this was changed at the end of the war. The United States emerged more powerful than ever. Both by repurchasing American securities from abroad and by foreign lending, she had become a net creditor to the rest of the world. Her industries, unscathed by the war, were more productive than ever. Her national income was probably greater than that of all Europe, and she was the principal potential source of savings for international lending. Almost alone, she remained on a gold standard. Within a few years she held more than 40 percent of all the world's monetary gold, and stood in danger of receiving more.

Europe, the old center of economic and financial power, was in economic and political distress. Her productive power was seriously reduced—partly because of physical destruction through military action, unrepaired wear and tear of productive facilities, lack of fertilizers, and malnutrition of workers. But at least as devastating were social, political, and economic disorders. Many governments were unstable, revolutionary movements were widespread, and international disputes were common. Inflation was rampant and financial disorders the rule. All countries had abandoned gold standards and only a few had managed to reestablish them before 1925. Great Britain's position was seriously undermined. In addition to her heavy loss of manpower in the war, she had lost much of her shipping, had sold large amounts of her assets abroad, and had borrowed more to help finance her war efforts and those of her allies. She had been forced to abandon the gold standard, to which she did not return until April, 1925. In the meantime, sterling exchange rates fluctuated widely. London was certainly in no position to play the role of manager of any type of international gold standard.

Thus, the inexperienced Federal Reserve officials found themselves at the head of the world's most powerful monetary system with an inescapable power to influence, not only the purchasing power of gold throughout the world, but also its distribution. By 1923, it was quite clear that, in the absence of an international gold standard, they could not follow the old rules of the game. By that time the nation's monetary gold stock had reached $3.7 billion and had increased $1 billion in the preceding 24 months. During the next two years, it rose another $500 million. Even if the Federal Reserve were merely to allow the "automatic" effects of gold imports to occur, an unwanted inflation might result. To reinforce these automatic effects by an expansion of Federal Reserve credit would compound the folly. The System, therefore, began a policy of "offsetting" or "sterilizing" the effects of gold flows except when, by coincidence, the effects of gold flows were consistent with the promotion of the System's objectives. But merely to reject the old rules of the gold-standard game—to ignore reserve ratios in determining policy—was not enough. Federal Reserve officials had to evolve new objectives and guides to take their place.

OBJECTIVES OF FEDERAL RESERVE POLICY

During the relatively short period from 1922 to 1924, Federal Reserve officials developed three main objectives or considerations that guided their policies during the remainder of the 1920s: (1) promotion of price-level stability and high and stable levels of business activity; (2) prevention of an excessive use of credit for speculative purposes, especially in the stock market; and (3) promotion of the restoration and maintenance of gold standards abroad. None of these objectives could be promoted by a Federal Reserve policy of passive accommodation; all required positive policies of regulation or control. It should be clear that no one of these objectives dominated Federal Reserve actions. When they came into conflict, as they sometimes did, Federal Reserve officials faced difficult problems of balancing and compromising.

Promotion of price and business stability

Starting in about 1922, at the end of the postwar depression, the objective of promoting price-level stability and high and stable levels of business activity became one of the most powerful determinants of Federal Reserve policy actions. Federal Reserve officials insisted that monetary policy alone could not assure the achievement of either of these objectives, because monetary policy regulated only the supply and cost of credit, and the behavior of prices and business activity was affected by many factors other than credit. Yet, Reserve officials insisted that the supply of money and credit should be so regulated that it would not be a source of disturbance to the economy, and that it would contribute as much as it could to economic stability. This supply should be neither so small as to reduce prices, lower business activity, and hamper economic growth, nor so large as to induce price inflation.

On several occasions during the 1920s, Congress considered bills that would order the Federal Reserve to stabilize the general level of prices. All of these were strongly opposed by Federal Reserve officials, who gave several reasons for their opposition.

1. Vagueness and technical defects of the proposals. They criticized the ambiguity of the term, "the general level of prices," and noted the diverse behavior of the various price indexes. Mr. Charles Hamlin, a member of the Federal Reserve Board, observed in 1928: "For example, in the period from 1925 to 1927 the Bureau of Labor wholesale indexes show a price decline of about 12 percent; but if you take the curve of the cost of living, the decline was barely 2 percent.

If you take a composite index like Mr. Snyder's, there was hardly any decline at all."[1] But Federal Reserve officials had more basic objections to the proposed legislation.

2. Not all price declines are undesirable. Although admitting that price declines are usually harmful, Reserve officials insisted that those resulting from general increases in efficiency may be beneficial. Price declines accompanied by proportional decreases in costs need not decrease the profitability of production nor lower the incentive to employ labor.

3. Price changes are but tardy indicators of more basic difficulties. Federal Reserve officials contended that changes in price levels may be poor guides to policy because they tend to appear only after basic maladjustments have been under way for some time. "Credit administration must be cognizant of what is under way or in process in the movement of business before it is registered in the price index. The price index records an accomplished fact."[2]

4. Concentration on behavior of prices. This might prevent the Federal Reserve from achieving other important objectives, such as the promotion of high and stable levels of business activity.

Although Federal Reserve officials opposed legislative mandates to stabilize price levels, they insisted that, in fact, their credit policies were designed to promote this objective as much as possible without an undue sacrifice of other objectives.

Figure 22–1 shows the extent to which the Federal Reserve related its policies to the behavior of industrial production, tightening credit when business activity was rising rapidly, and easing it when business was declining.

Restraint of security speculation

As indicated earlier, it was 1934 before the Federal Reserve acquired the power to regulate margins on loans for the purpose of purchasing and carrying securities. In the 1920s, it could curb the use of credit for security speculation only through general credit restraint or clumsy attempts at direct controls over the lending policies of member banks that were in debt to their Reserve banks. We shall see later how Federal Reserve attempts to curb stock speculation in 1928 and 1929 conflicted with other objectives, and prevented their attainment.

Restoration and maintenance of gold standards abroad

As noted earlier, and as indicated in Figure 22–2, almost all countries abandoned gold standards during World War I and few returned within the first six years after the end of the war. At the beginning of 1924, only the United States and a handful of small countries were on gold. A few others returned to gold during that year, but it was 1925 before a truly international gold standard began to re-

---

[1] *Hearings on H.R. 11806,* 1928, p. 393.
[2] Federal Reserve Board, *Annual Report,* 1923, p. 32.

Figure 22–1 Timing of Federal Reserve open-market operations and discount-rate changes compared with changes in the volume of industrial production, 1922–1935

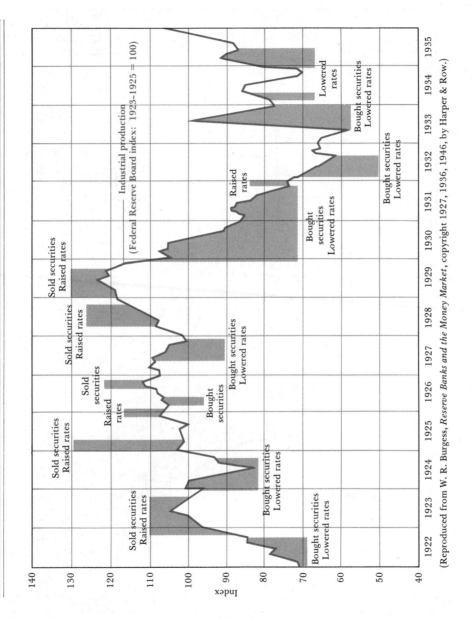

(Reproduced from W. R. Burgess, *Reserve Banks and the Money Market*, copyright 1927, 1936, 1946, by Harper & Row.)

Figure 22–2 Countries on the gold standard, 1921–1938

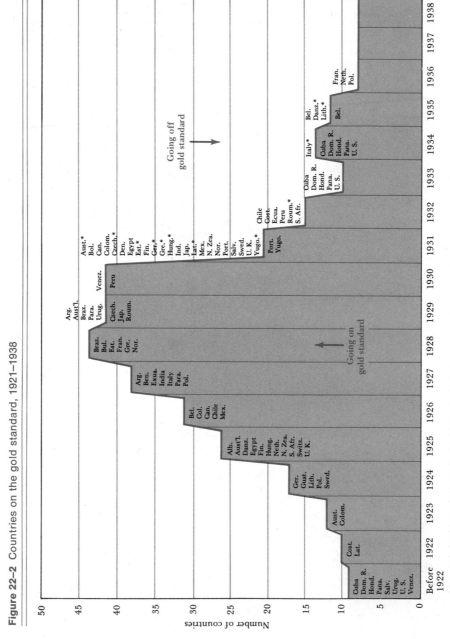

*Suspended gold standard, retained gold standard briefly, and abandoned it again.
(SOURCE: U.S. Treasury.)

appear. In the meantime, monetary and financial disorders were widespread. Great Britain and some other countries succeeded in stopping inflation in 1920; in other countries, inflation continued until after the mid-1920s. In some countries, price levels merely doubled; in some, they rose eightfold; and in some extreme cases, they rose by the billionfold. All types of domestic difficulties promoted monetary disorder: extraordinary expenditures for reconstruction and reparations payments, political instability, unbalanced budgets, easy-money policies to help the finance ministers manage their huge floating debts, and so on. The international exchange market performed erratically. Exchange rates on the various national currencies fluctuated widely, reflecting not only changes in the domestic purchasing powers of those currencies but also erratic and speculative international shifts of funds induced by such things as expectations of further inflation, domestic and international political disturbances, and uncertainties arising out of the great complex of reparations and war-debt obligations.

These countries wanted to return to gold standards. More important to them than that, they wanted to end inflation and deflation at home, to restore more stable fiscal and monetary policies, and to achieve stability of their currencies in exchange markets. Still more fundamentally, they wanted to restore their productive power and achieve social and political stability. For this purpose, many of them needed loans or grants from abroad. In this whole process of stabilization and recovery, the United States could have been most helpful. But the United States government of that day would not provide the necessary funds or even enter officially into cooperative international programs for such purposes. It might provide small grants in the early postwar period to prevent actual starvation and deal generously with its debt claims against its former allies, but it would not go further. This was partly because of United States isolationism, and partly because of the current philosophy that government should limit the scope of its activity. If United States funds were to be supplied for foreign reconstruction and stabilization purposes, they would have to come from the Federal Reserve and private sources.

It was under these conditions that the Federal Reserve System, under the leadership of Governor Benjamin Strong of the Federal Reserve Bank of New York, sought to assist both in the reestablishment of gold standards abroad and in making them function in an acceptable manner. The Federal Reserve had several reasons for desiring the reestablishment of an international gold standard. One was altruistic: Strong was deeply sympathetic with those who had suffered during the war and postwar disturbances, and wanted to see them prosper again. But he also believed that stabilization abroad was in the interest of the United States. For one thing, it was necessary to end gold flows to the United States. Time and again he warned that the only way to stop these inflows and to avoid the danger of gold inflation at home was to help put other countries back on gold standards. Moreover, foreign trade of the United States would benefit. This was partly because stabilization within foreign countries would raise their real incomes and their demands for imports, and partly because stability of exchange rates would promote trade.

Federal Reserve assistance in the restoration and maintenance of gold standards abroad was of several types. For one thing, the Federal Reserve extended stabilization credit to foreign central banks. When a nation had formulated an overall stabilization program that appeared to be appropriate, the Federal Reserve would extend a credit—a commitment to lend gold or dollars—to its central bank. The Federal Reserve acted alone in extending a $200 million line of credit to the Bank of England when Great Britain returned to gold in April, 1925. In most of the later stabilizations, it acted in cooperation with other central banks, sometimes with as many as 12 or 13 of them. These central-bank credits often served useful purposes even when they were not drawn upon. For one thing, they created confidence in the ability of the central bank to maintain gold payments, thereby discouraging speculative withdrawals from the country, and, in some cases, even inducing an inflow of funds. These credits also assisted countries in securing foreign loans. In most of the stabilizations, foreign central-bank credits to the nation's central bank were supplemented by private loans to the nation's government. These private loans might not have been made available in the absence of the central-bank credits and the implied approval of the nation's stabilization program by foreign central bankers. Federal Reserve officials and other central bankers, especially Governor Montagu Norman of the Bank of England, often performed useful services in helping countries formulate and gain acceptance of stabilization programs. (Table 22–3.)

On some occasions the Federal Reserve also made funds available to countries after they had returned to gold. It did this by making outright loans or by purchasing claims against the nation's currency in the foreign-exchange market.

Of more interest to us at this point is the extent to which the objective of promoting the restoration and maintenance of gold standards abroad influenced the general monetary policies of the Federal Reserve. In the 1920s, and especially after 1923, this objective led to easier, or at least to less restrictive, general credit

Table 22–3 Credits extended to foreign central banks by federal reserve banks*

DATE	BANK RECEIVING CREDIT	AMOUNT
1925	Bank of England	$200,000,000
1925	Banking Office of the Ministry of Finance of Czechoslovakia (approx.)	5,000,000
1925	Bank of Poland	10,000,000
1925	National Bank of Belgium	10,000,000
1927	Bank of Poland	5,250,000
1927	Bank of Italy	15,000,000
1929	Bank of Roumania	4,500,000
1929	National Bank of Hungary	2,000,000
1931	National Bank of Australia	1,083,000
1931	National Bank of Hungary	5,000,000
1931	German Reichsbank	25,000,000
1931	Bank of England	125,000,000

* For a comprehensive study of these credits, see A. Goldstein, "Federal Reserve Aid to Foreign Central Banks," *Review of Economic Studies,* February, 1935, pp. 79–98.

policies. Easier credit policies in the United States could, in two principal ways, help other countries to gain or retain gold and international reserves, and to follow more liberal or less restrictive policies at home:

1. By raising United States national money income and price levels; this would increase United States imports and payments of gold and dollars to other countries while discouraging foreign purchases in the United States.

2. By discouraging flows of capital funds to the United States, and by encouraging capital flows out of the United States; this applies to both short- and long-term funds. We shall see later that, after the restoration of gold standards, there was a great volume of short-term funds that proved to be highly sensitive to differentials between interest rates in the principal international financial centers, and especially between New York and London. When London was having difficulty in attracting and holding enough gold to maintain gold payments without an excessively restrictive monetary policy at home, Governor Strong and Governor Norman agreed that, to the extent possible without undue sacrifice of other objectives, they should try to keep interest rates in New York below those in London. This would have a double effect, they hoped. In the first place, it would shunt short-term international funds away from New York and toward London. In the second place, it would divert some part of the world's long-term borrowing away from London and toward New York. This would militate against a further concentration of gold in New York, lessen payments from Great Britain, and give the rest of the world access to a larger supply of gold and dollars.

The objective of helping other countries undoubtedly created an easier monetary policy in the United States, especially after 1923. One outstanding case was in 1924, when an aggressive easy-money policy, the first in the history of the Federal Reserve, was undertaken both to combat recession at home and to stimulate capital outflows. Another was in 1927, when the System again initiated an aggressive easy-money policy to combat recession, to stimulate foreign lending, and to repel short-term funds from New York. On still other occasions, Federal Reserve policies were probably easier or less restrictive than they would have been in the absence of this objective. Yet, Governor Strong and other Federal Reserve officials insisted that they would not sacrifice their domestic objectives to promote international cooperation. For example, Strong rejected summarily a foreign suggestion that the Federal Reserve should deliberately induce price inflation in the United States in order to expel gold, increase the international reserves of other countries, and enable them to follow more liberal monetary policies. He would not, he asserted, sacrifice his objective of promoting stable price levels at home. He also warned his colleagues abroad that the Federal Reserve would tighten credit, despite the unfortunate international effects of such a policy, if faced at home by commodity-price inflation or excessive stock-market speculation. The latter did occur in 1928 and 1929 and led to a restrictive Federal Reserve policy that injured other countries both by attracting large volumes of short-term funds to New York and by decreasing long-term lending of the United States abroad.

By 1927, the process of restoring gold standards was largely completed, although a few stragglers joined during the next two years. But the new gold standards differed in both form and functioning from those of the prewar period. For one thing, gold-coin standards had largely disappeared except in the United States. Most of the major countries adopted gold-bullion standards to economize gold. Also, gold-exchange standards became far more important than they had been before the war. A large number of the smaller countries adopted pure gold-exchange standards. Several of the larger countries also went on some type of mixed gold-exchange standard, holding a part of their international reserves in gold and a part in the form of claims against some other nation's money. For example, the Bank of France held both gold reserves and very large claims against New York and London. This great growth of gold-exchange standards and of the practice of holding international reserves in the form of claims against foreign financial centers was a major reason for the presence of a huge volume of short-term international funds highly sensitive to interest-rate differentials. Moreover, the world now had two important financial-center countries. Before the war, London was the one great monetary and financial center, and so was not likely to suffer large net withdrawals of funds. Now it had to share the position with New York.

These developments increased the vulnerability of center countries. The countries that held great volumes of claims against these centers might demand payment in gold, thereby putting the center countries under deflationary pressure and even forcing them to suspend gold payments. Also, the presence of more than one important monetary center made possible large shifts of funds that could embarrass the country losing the funds and perhaps also the country receiving them. For example, a highly restrictive policy in the United States might raise interest rates in New York and attract a large inflow of funds from London, thereby putting Britain under deflationary pressure and also defeating, at least in part, the efforts of the Federal Reserve to reduce the total supply of credit.

The new standards were more highly managed than the old ones. After years of freedom from the discipline of gold, central banks were less willing to follow the old rules of the gold-standard game and to initiate more restrictive policies when they lost gold and more expansionary policies when they gained gold. "Offsetting" and "sterilizing" actions became far more common than they had been before the war. This meant, of course, that the process of equilibrating international receipts and payments was inhibited, as was also the redistribution of gold. For example, the refusal of France to allow her money supply to increase in response to very large gold imports permitted gold inflows to continue at the expense of other countries. Also, the reluctance of countries to permit gold exports to restrict their supply of money and credit made the processes of terminating gold outflows and protecting their supply of international reserves ineffective, or at least sluggish.

The new, international gold-standard system was also characterized by disequilibrium relationships among the various national price levels as stated in terms of gold. In the prewar period, these price-level relationships were pretty well equilibrated. But many of the countries returned to gold on terms that either "undervalued" or "overvalued" their currencies in relation to those of other countries. For example, France almost certainly undervalued the franc in foreign-exchange markets when she stabilized it in 1926. She gave it a gold value equivalent to 3.92 cents, as against 19.3 cents in the prewar period. But this low exchange rate of the franc together with the price level within France made that country a cheap country in which to buy and an unattractive one in which to sell, so that her receipts exceeded her international payments on trade account. Her refusal to allow her gains of international reserves to raise her domestic price level permitted this excess of receipts to continue. On the other hand, Great Britain almost certainly returned to gold on terms that made her domestic price level in terms of gold too high. The pound sterling was given its prewar gold content, so that the exchange rate on the pound hovered around $4.8665. But the British domestic price and cost levels had not been reduced enough to make Britain an attractive market in which to buy when each pound cost about $4.8665. As a result, British export industries did not thrive. A reduction of British wage rates and other costs of production would have stimulated her export industries, but her cost structure had become inflexible downward. The functioning of the new gold standards suffered from these disequilibrium relationships among national price levels.

We shall see later that several of these aspects of the new gold standards contributed to their breakdown in the 1930s: the widespread use of gold-exchange standards, the large volume of international short-term funds highly sensitive to interest-rate differentials and to shifts of confidence in foreign currencies, disequilibrium relationships among the various national price levels, and the reluctance of countries to follow the old rules of the gold-standard game to equilibrate their balances of payments.

We have seen here that by 1922, Federal Reserve officials realized that the old rules of the gold-standard game were obsolete, and that new objectives and guides would have to be developed. Within the next two years, they had developed three principal sets of considerations that guided their policies during the next decade: promotion of price-level stability and high and stable levels of business activity, prevention of an excessive use of credit for speculation, and promotion of the restoration and maintenance of gold standards abroad.

DEVELOPMENT OF FEDERAL RESERVE INSTRUMENTS

While the Federal Reserve was developing new policy objectives and guides in the 1922 to 1924 period, it was also making remarkable progress in developing its instruments of control. The outstanding event of the period was the discovery and development of open-market operations in United States government securities. Never, before 1922, had the Federal Reserve bought or sold these securities for monetary-management purposes. The relatively small purchases and sales that had occurred were for such purposes as to provide earnings for the Reserve banks, to retire some national bank notes, and to assist the Treasury. Moreover, they were made by the individual Reserve banks without any sort of centralized co-ordination. Two very important events occurred in 1922 and 1923. In the first place, the Federal Reserve discovered how these operations might be used for monetary-management purposes. In the second place, the execution of these operations was centralized in a Federal Reserve committee. After the discovery and development of this device, the Federal Reserve had three principal instruments: discount rates, open-market operations in acceptances, and open-market operations in United States government securities.

Within a short time, the Federal Reserve was using open-market operations in government securities for both defensive and dynamic purposes. This was an excellent defensive weapon with which to offset or to sterilize the effects of gold inflows and outflows. It was also used to offset net cash inflows or outflows domestically and also large net Treasury receipts or expenditures. For dynamic purposes, it proved to be extremely useful, because the Federal Reserve could itself determine both the timing and amount of its purchases and sales. The following pattern of dynamic operations soon developed: If the Federal Reserve wished to restrict credit, it pursued this objective by first selling government securities. This reduced the volume of any excess reserves that previously existed and forced banks to borrow more heavily to repair their reserve positions. This in itself restricted credit to some degree and raised market rates of interest. The Federal Reserve would then decide whether and to what extent it would intensify restrictive pressures by raising its discount rates and its buying rate on acceptances. When it wished to initiate easier credit conditions, it would usually begin by purchasing government securities, which gave some banks excess reserves and enabled others to repay some of their borrowings at the Reserve banks. This directly eased credit somewhat and reduced market rates of interest. If the System wished to intensify the ease, it then reduced its discount rates and acceptance-buying rates.

FEDERAL RESERVE POLICIES, 1923 TO 1929

Having discussed the objectives of the Federal Reserve and its development of instruments for regulation, let us now look briefly at some of the principal episodes in Federal Reserve policy after the end of the postwar depression.

By 1923, the economy was well on its way to recovery, and prices were rising slowly. The Federal Reserve therefore initiated a mildly restrictive policy. It sold more than enough government securities to offset the $250 million net increase of the monetary gold stock, thereby forcing member banks to increase their borrowing somewhat. Market rates of interest rose slightly, and the Federal Reserve raised its discount rates—the New York rate rising from 4 to 4½ percent.

Easy money, 1924

In 1924, the Federal Reserve initiated its first peacetime aggressive easy-money policy. In the early months of the year, it moved cautiously to lessen the degree of restraint that had existed in late 1923, when member banks had owed the Federal Reserve about $800 million. In May, it began to act more vigorously. In all, it raised its holdings of government securities from $118 million to $488 million, or a net increase of $370 million. These purchases, together with continued gold inflows, enabled member banks to reduce their borrowings to less than $300 million. As market rates of interest fell, the Reserve banks lowered their discount rates. The Federal Reserve Bank of New York reduced its rate from 4½ to 4, then to 3½, and finally to 3 percent. Money-market conditions became the easiest they had been at any time since the war.

This easy-money policy was initiated for both domestic and international reasons. A recession seemed to be starting; agriculture was still depressed in many areas, industrial production showed a downward drift, and wholesale prices declined about 3 percent during the first half of the year. If the recession was not serious enough to require an aggressive easy-money policy, it at least seemed to permit such a policy to be followed without adverse effects. The other major objective of the policy was to promote United States lending abroad, and to create conditions that would hasten the restoration of gold standards and end the unwanted flow of gold to the United States. Governor Strong welcomed this opportunity to bring interest rates in New York below those in London. He had reason to think that conditions had now developed to the point that his international objectives might soon be achieved. For one thing, the Dawes Plan for the temporary settlement of the controversial reparations question had created a more favorable atmosphere for international lending. For another, it appeared that England might soon return to gold if favorable conditions could be created.

The easy-money policy probably contributed to the rapid recovery of business activity during the latter half of 1924. It certainly increased United States lending abroad. Aided by both easy-money conditions and the improvement of international conditions, United States loans to other countries in the latter half of 1924 were far above their level in previous years. The larger outflow of United States dollars, and perhaps also the diversion of international borrowing away from London, tended to raise the exchange rate on sterling. At the beginning of the year it had been $4.25; by the end of the year it was $4.70, only 3 percent below its prewar parity. Soon thereafter Britain began to make plans for her return to gold. It is also significant that the flow of gold to the United States was stopped in 1924, and was not resumed for three years. This easy-money policy may also have contributed, as some of its critics allege, to the subsequent growth of stock-market speculation.

Relative calm, 1925 to 1926

The objective of promoting the restoration and maintenance of gold standards abroad counseled a relatively easy-money policy during this period. Several countries had returned to gold standards with Britain; others soon followed. Continued large United States lending and avoidance of flows of funds to New York were desirable not only to help additional countries return to gold, but also to enable countries that had already returned to maintain their international reserves without excessively restrictive monetary policies. Nor did the objective of preventing commodity-price increases call for very restrictive policies. After recovering in late 1924 and the first few months of 1925, wholesale prices drifted slightly downward during the remainder of the decade. But stock speculation began to threaten. Recovery from the 1924 recession and rising stock-market activity evoked a more restrictive policy in early 1925. The System sold about $250 million of government securities and raised its discount rates, the New York rate increasing from 3 to 3½ percent. As speculation continued to grow, the New York Reserve bank raised its rate to 4 percent at the beginning of 1926. This rate was reduced to 3½ percent in April, 1926, as speculative activity subsided, but was restored to 4 percent in August when stock-market activity again surged upward. Speculation had already become a problem, but the worst was yet to come.

Easy money again, 1927

The Federal Reserve's second aggressive easy-money policy also had both domestic and international objectives. A recession in domestic economic activity again threatened, and wholesale prices began to fall slowly early in 1927. At least as important to the policy makers was the fact that several foreign countries were losing international reserves, or could maintain them only by adopting more restrictive monetary policies. The rise of interest rates in New York accompanying the more restrictive Federal Reserve policy in the latter part of 1926 was tending to attract funds from abroad and to restrict foreign lending by the United States. Gold inflows, which virtually had been halted since 1924, were resuming. Federal Reserve officials feared that these developments would not only injure other countries, and especially Britain, but would also renew the flow of gold to the United States and reduce the foreign demand for United States exports, especially for agricultural products. The situation was further complicated by conflicts between the Bank of France and the Bank of England. France finally succeeded in achieving a de facto stabilization of the franc in late 1926. This was accompanied by a rapid repatriation of funds that private French holders had formerly held abroad, and especially the repatriation of funds in the form of claims against London. When the Bank of France bought these claims, it acquired the power to drain very large amounts of gold from London. In the midst of a controversy with the Bank of England, it withdrew some gold and threatened to withdraw more if the Old Lady of Threadneedle Street did not conform its policies to the wishes of the Bank of France. It was to discuss these and other matters relating to international conditions that Governor Strong invited representatives of the Bank of England, the Bank of France, and the German Reichsbank to meet with him in early July, 1927.

The easy-money policy of 1927 was initiated late in July after this meeting, although it was not derived from this meeting nor from the issues discussed there. The Federal Reserve purchased about $300 million of government securities and lowered discount rates from 4 to 3½ percent. These actions were accompanied by an easing of money-market conditions. This easy-money policy probably contributed to the recovery of business activity in the latter half of 1927 and it clearly was effective for international purposes. The inflow of foreign funds was decreased, and American foreign lending maintained. The inflow of gold was reversed; within the next year about $500 million of gold flowed out of the United States. Most European central banks were able to survive the year without adopting more restrictive policies. Again, however, the easy-money policy may have encouraged stock speculation.

The stock market, 1928 to 1929

From the beginning of 1928 until after the great crash in October, 1929, the objective of preventing an undue use of credit for stock-market speculation virtually dominated Federal Reserve policy. The objective of promoting stability of prices and business activity was cited in support of the first move toward credit restriction in early 1928. But neither this objective nor that of promoting the maintenance of viable conditions abroad was responsible for the degree of restriction achieved by 1929. Between the end of 1927 and mid-1929, the Federal Reserve sold about $450 million of government securities. On the latter date, it had only $147 million left. To maintain their reserve positions during the latter part of 1928 and the first nine months of 1929, member banks had to go into debt to the Federal Reserve by about $1 billion. This was by far the largest volume of member-bank borrowings since 1921. All the Reserve banks raised their discount rates several times. Starting at 3½ percent in 1927, the New York bank rate was raised to 4 percent in February, 1928; to 4½ percent in May; to 5 percent in July; and then, a year later, to 6 percent in August, 1929. Market rates of interest, both short- and long-term, rose markedly. The rate applicable to call loans on the stock exchange was especially volatile. In late 1928, it was often above 8 percent, sometimes considerably above this level. In 1929, it ranged even higher. This rate became very important, partly because it was the rate to which short-term international funds responded.

Federal Reserve officials faced many perplexing questions as they tried to evaluate the behavior of the stock market, and to formulate their policies relative to it. One of these cannot yet be answered satisfactorily: "What would constitute a reasonable level of stock prices, assuming continued prosperity and continuing economic growth?" It has since become fashionable to laugh at those who defended as reasonable the highest levels reached in 1929. But no less silly were those who began to predict a crash as soon as stock prices began to rise above their depressed levels in 1921—levels that were below those of the prewar period (see Table 22–4). Even now we cannot be sure that the levels reached by June, 1928, would have proved unreasonable if prosperity had continued. It is important to note that, between mid-1928 and September, 1929, stock prices rose more than they had during the preceding four years. Moreover, after the crash, they quickly regained half their losses and during the first half of 1930 the average stock price was above the mid-1928 level. Only as the country slid into depression and despair did stock prices fall so low as to make those of mid-1928 look absurdly high. But these prices were absurdly low, assuming any chance of business recovery.

Table 22–4 Indexes of common stock prices (1935–1939 = 100)

PERIOD	TOTAL	INDUSTRIAL	RAILROAD	PUBLIC UTILITY
1913	71	40	240	90
1921	58	47	164	68
1924	77	63	204	92
1925	95	80	238	111
1926	106	90	265	117
June, 1927	122	103	316	135
December, 1927	141	122	336	149
June, 1928	153	134	336	173
September, 1929	238	195	446	375
January–June, 1930	175	141	364	276
June, 1932	36	30	38	64

SOURCE: Board of Governors of the Federal Reserve System, *Banking and Monetary Statistics*, 1943, pp. 479–481. These indexes are those of Standard and Poor's Corporation.

Federal Reserve officials always insisted that their chief concern was not with the level of stock prices, but with the use of credit for speculative purposes. They therefore faced the perplexing question of determining the boundary line between "reasonable" and "unreasonable" amounts for this purpose. The volume of credit used to purchase and to carry stocks certainly increased markedly during this period. Much of this credit was not borrowed through brokers. But Table 22–5 shows that loans to brokers nearly quadrupled after 1924, rising to $8.5 billion on the eve of the crash. The sources of these loans should be noted. Taken as a group, commercial banks did not increase their loans of this type. Other lenders accounted for all the increase; on the eve of the crash, they were supplying two-thirds of all these loans. These other lenders, attracted to very high call-loan rates, were of many types. They included not only individuals and financial intermediaries, but also nonfinancial corporations and foreign lenders. The flow of funds from foreign centers was very embarrassing to several central banks.

Table 22–5 Loans to brokers (millions of dollars)

DATE	TOTAL	BY NEW YORK CITY BANKS	BY OUTSIDE BANKS	BY OTHERS
December 31, 1924	$2,230	$1,150	$ 530	$ 550
December 31, 1925	3,550	1,450	1,050	1,050
December 31, 1926	3,290	1,160	830	1,300
December 31, 1927	4,430	1,550	1,050	1,830
June 30, 1928	4,900	1,080	960	2,860
December 31, 1928	6,440	1,640	915	3,885
October 4, 1929	8,525	1,095	790	6,640
December 31, 1929	4,110	1,200	460	2,450

SOURCE: Board of Governors of the Federal Reserve System, *Banking and Monetary Statistics*, 1943, p. 494.

Federal Reserve officials were perplexed as to how to limit the supply of credit for stock speculation. They did not then have the legal power to impose margin requirements—the power that has since proved effective in limiting the volume of credit used for this purpose without curtailing the supply and raising the cost of credit for other purposes. Nevertheless, the Federal Reserve Board tried, early in 1929, to achieve this result by applying "direct action" to banks that were in debt to their Federal Reserve banks. Through its own pronouncements and through the various Reserve banks, it informed members that they should not make loans on stocks for speculative purposes while borrowing at the Federal Reserve. This device failed to get a fair trial because several of the Reserve banks did not favor its use, at least not in the absence of further increases in discount rates. Nevertheless, it is highly unlikely that this type of direct action could have succeeded in curtailing loans on stocks without at the same time curtailing the supply and raising the cost of credit for other uses. It applied only to banks that were currently in debt to the Federal Reserve. These banks probably accounted for only a small part of this type of credit, and some of them would have curtailed their loans for other purposes in order to repay the Federal Reserve rather than call their highly lucrative stock-market loans. The action by the Board did not reach nonborrowing banks, and certainly not the various types of other lenders who rushed in to lend more, probably at the expense of other types of lending or spending, as call-loan rates rose.

Lacking any effective type of selective control, the Federal Reserve tried to regulate the situation through general credit restriction. It hoped that restrictive policies could kill the speculative fever and reduce the demand for speculative loans quickly, so that easier policies could then be instituted. Unfortunately, "legitimate business" and the international situation proved to be more vulnerable than the stock market.

These restrictive credit policies had almost no adverse effect on the international situation during the first half of 1928. United States foreign lending continued at a high level, and gold continued to flow out of the country. But the situation grew worse in the latter part of 1928, as credit conditions became tighter. The rate of foreign flotations in the United States market in the latter half of 1928 and the first half of 1929 was only 65 percent the rate in 1927; in the latter half of 1929 it was less than one third of the rate in 1927. Moreover, large amounts of funds flowed from abroad to New York—some to buy stock, more to take advantage of the high interest rates attainable there. These developments forced several European central banks to sell large amounts of their foreign-exchange holdings and ship gold to support their currencies. More than $260 million of gold flowed to the United States between mid-1928 and October, 1929. Many foreign central banks were impelled to raise their discount rates and to adopt generally more restrictive policies in order to protect their reserve positions.

By mid-1929, the domestic business situation had begun to deteriorate. This was, perhaps, partially due to the fact that the marginal efficiency of investment had been shifted downward by the large net accumulations of capital during the protracted investment boom. But it was at least aggravated, if not initiated, by the high cost of loanable funds, both short- and long-term.

The rest of this story is now well-known history. After several weeks of vacillation, the stock market crashed in October, 1929. With it crashed the "new era." The problems of the next decade were not to be those of excessive bullishness.

Selected readings

Brown, W. A., Jr., *The International Gold Standard Reinterpreted, 1914–1934,* New York, National Bureau of Economic Research, 1940, 2 vols.

Burgess, W. R., *Reserve Banks and the Money Market,* rev. ed., New York, Harper & Row, 1946.

Chandler, L. V., *Benjamin Strong, Central Banker,* Washington, D.C., Brookings Institution, 1958.

Goldenweiser, E. A., *American Monetary Policy,* New York, McGraw-Hill, 1951.

Nurkse, R., *International Currency Experience, Lessons of the Inter-War Period,* Geneva, League of Nations, 1944.

CHAPTER 23

MONETARY POLICY IN THE DEPRESSION, 1930–1941

At the time of the stock-market crash, and even in 1930, no one could foresee that the depression into which the world was sliding would be the most devastating in its entire history and would be a major contribution to political and economic upheavals and even to the outbreak of a second world war. This depression lasted more than a decade and came to an end only in World War II. At its depth in the United States, the depression had reduced national money income by 50 percent, and real output and income by 25 percent. One worker out of four was without a job and many others were working only part time. Business firms failed by the tens of thousands, farmers lost their farms, and families their homes. Amidst falling incomes and price levels, the monetary and financial system virtually collapsed. The gold-standard system that had been so laboriously reconstructed in the latter half of the 1920s had largely disappeared by 1932. The United States banking system, weakened earlier, collapsed in 1933. Many other financial institutions closed their doors, or at least ceased to function effectively in the saving-investment process. International lending came to a standstill. The whole complex of war debt and reparations obligations, which had been such disturbing issues in the 1920s, was largely repudiated. It is hardly surprising that under such circumstances monetary policies became unorthodox.

UNITED STATES MONETARY POLICIES, 1930 TO 1931

There was little that was novel in United States monetary policies from the time of the crash in October, 1929, until the autumn of 1931. The government did not enter the field, and Federal Reserve policies followed the general patterns of 1924 and 1927. The Federal Reserve began to relax its restrictive policy and to ease credit almost immediately after the crash. By the end of the year, it had increased its holdings of government securities by about $300 million, and had reduced its discount rates. The New York rate was first reduced from 6 to 5 and then to 4½ percent.

Policies during 1930 and the first eight months of 1931 followed the same pattern. The System gradually added another $250 million to its holdings of government securities. By August, 1931, it held about $700 million of these securities, or $550 million more than were held at the time of the crash. Largely because of these purchases and a net gold inflow of about $600 million, member banks were enabled to reduce their borrowings from about $1 billion to about $200 million while maintaining approximately constant the dollar volume of their reserves. Discount rates were reduced several times. In six steps, the New York bank lowered its rate from 4½ percent at the beginning of 1930 to 1½ percent in May, 1931. Rate reductions at the other Reserve banks were smaller.

Federal Reserve policies during this early period have been criticized as too slow and too timid. Critics point out that even as late as August, 1931, member banks still owed the Federal Reserve about $200 million and had excess reserves of only about $120 million. They believe that the Federal Reserve should have purchased a much larger volume of government securities and acceptances to enable member banks to repay all their borrowings and to accumulate several hundred millions of dollars of excess reserves. This criticism is well justified.

Starting about September, 1931, the Federal Reserve allowed credit conditions to tighten significantly, and these tighter credit conditions persisted for several months. Two major developments were responsible for this. One was an upsurge of bank failures which damaged confidence in banks and induced large withdrawals of cash from the banking system. These began in 1930. Prior to that time, cash had been flowing into the banking system, reflecting decreased needs for currency in circulation as payrolls and retail trade declined. By October, 1931, the volume of coin and currency outside the banking system was about $1 billion larger than it had been in mid-1930. Still more cash drains occurred in early 1933. The other major event leading to tighter monetary conditions in the United States in the last part of 1931 was the breakdown of the international gold standard.

THE BREAKDOWN OF GOLD STANDARDS

Four South American countries had suspended gold payments by the end of 1930. Twenty-three others, including Great Britain, abandoned gold in 1931. By the end of 1936, practically all countries had either left gold or had modified their old gold standards in fundamental respects.

What brought about this worldwide breakdown of gold standards? One basic factor was the devastating decline of real incomes and price levels, which decreased demands for exports and lowered the foreign-exchange earnings of exporting countries. Especially hard hit were countries that relied heavily on exports of raw materials, which suffered severe price dips. With great decreases in their export earnings, these nations found it difficult to reduce their international payments correspondingly and to protect their gold and other international reserves.

A second basic factor was the virtual cessation of international lending. During the latter part of the 1920s, many countries had come to rely heavily on foreign borrowings to meet their international payments and protect their international reserves. United States net lending abroad was over $700 million in 1926, over $1,000 million in 1927, and about $850 million in 1928. In 1929, largely because of tight-money conditions, these loans shrank below $300 million. Such lending practically disappeared as the Depression deepened, the prospects of repayment darkened, and some foreign debtors began to default on their outstanding obligations. During 1931 to 1932, repayments to the United States actually exceeded her new foreign lending by nearly $500 million. Many countries could not bear the strain of losing their receipts from foreign borrowings and of making net payments of interest and principal at a time when their receipts for exports were falling.

A third factor was the presence of a huge volume of short-term international debt. We have already seen that the widespread use of gold-exchange standards involved very large foreign holdings of claims against financial centers, such as London and New York. Moreover, many countries, such as Austria, had borrowed heavily abroad on short term. All of these debts were payable on demand or on short notice. And foreign creditors were likely to demand payment the moment they came to fear that the debtors could not pay or that the debtor's currency would depreciate in terms of gold. In its first manifestation, the international panic was an international banking panic.

The international panic began in May, 1931 with the failure of the Credit-Anstalt, the largest bank in Austria. This caused both foreigners and Austrians to doubt the ability of any Austrian bank to meet its obligations, and thus they withdrew large amounts of funds from the country. So great was the flood of withdrawals that it exhausted large loans from the Bank of England and the Bank for International Settlements as well as Austrian holdings of gold and foreign money; consequently, Austria was forced to terminate the convertibility of her money in gold. Many creditors found their remaining credits frozen and depreciating in terms of gold.

The panic was now on. Fearful creditors, remembering losses in Austria, began to withdraw their credits from Berlin, and frightened Germans joined the run. Within a few weeks and despite sizeable loans from the Bank of England, the Bank of France, the Bank for International Settlements, and the Federal Reserve Bank of New York, Germany suspended gold payments in July, 1931 and placed strict limitations on international payments of all kinds. Millions of dollars' worth of short-term foreign credits were frozen in Germany.

Reinforced, the panic swept on to London, from which credits were rapidly withdrawn. An increase in its discount rate by the Bank of England, which was supposed to attract and retain foreign funds, seemed rather to publicize the fact that England was in financial difficulties, and thereby hastened withdrawals. Even a $250-million joint credit from the Federal Reserve Bank of New York and the Bank of France was insufficient to stop the run or to cover withdrawals, which amounted to $975 million from July to late September. England departed from gold on September 21, 1931. The retreat from gold now became a rout. By April of 1932, gold standards had become inoperative in the following countries:[1]

Argentina	Denmark	Iraq	Rhodesia
Australia	Ecuador	Irish Free State	Russia
Austria	Egypt	Japan	Spain
Bolivia	El Salvador	Jugoslavia	Sweden
Brazil	Estonia	Latvia	Turkey
Bulgaria	Finland	Newfoundland	United Kingdom and
Canada	Germany	New Zealand	dependencies
Chile	Greece	Nicaragua	Uruguay
Colombia	Honduras	Norway	Venezuela
Costa Rica	Hungary	Paraguay	
Czechoslovakia	India	Portugal	

This dramatic breakdown of the international gold standard affected monetary and economic conditions in the United States in at least two ways. In the first place, as we shall see later, it evoked large gold withdrawals from this country. In the second place, it tended to decrease the demand for United States exports and to lower their dollar prices. Most foreign currencies depreciated in terms of gold and in terms of dollars after their countries left gold standards. As shown in Table 23–1, most foreign currencies had depreciated at least 30 percent in terms of the dollar by early 1933. As foreign buyers saw it, the dollar had become much more expensive in terms of their own currencies. They would therefore buy fewer United States products unless the dollar prices of these products fell enough to offset the rise in the price of the dollar in the foreign-exchange market. Thus, the depreciation of foreign currencies tended to depress United States export industries, including agriculture. Also, by making foreign products cheaper in terms of dollars, it tended to stimulate United States imports, which did not

[1] H. V. Hodson, *Slump and Recovery, 1929–1937*, London, Oxford. 1938, p. 92.

Table 23–1 Decline of selected foreign exchange rates, 1929–February, 1933*

MONEY	AVERAGE PRICE IN DOLLARS IN 1929	AVERAGE PRICE IN DOLLARS IN FEBRUARY, 1933	PERCENTAGE DECLINE OF MONEY IN TERMS OF DOLLARS
British pound	$4.857	$3.422	30
Canadian dollar	0.992	0.835	16
Argentine peso	0.951	0.586	38
Brazilian milreis	0.118	0.076	35
Indian rupee	0.362	0.258	29
Chilean peso	0.121	0.060	50
Danish krone	0.267	0.153	43
Norwegian krone	0.267	0.175	34
Swedish krona	0.268	0.183	32
Portuguese escudo	0.045	0.031	31
Australian pound	4.81	2.72	45

* This table deliberately omits money that was inconvertible in terms of gold and which was artificially pegged, at least in official markets, at high prices. Most of these moneys were depreciated in unofficial or black markets.

please some of those in import-competing industries. Many persons observed that this was what the world needed to bring international balances of payments into equilibrium and end the excess of United States exports over her imports. But such international objectives were not prized highly by a nation in the midst of depression. One of the major objectives of the United States policy of lowering the gold content of the dollar in 1933 and 1934 was to lower the exchange rate on the dollar, thereby tending to increase United States exports and to raise their dollar prices, and also to discourage imports and help import-competing industries.

UNITED STATES MONETARY POLICY, SEPTEMBER, 1931 TO MARCH, 1933

Let us now return to United States monetary policies during the period from Britain's suspension of her gold standard to the breakdown of the United States banking system in March, 1933.

Tighter money, September, 1931 to February, 1932

Almost as soon as Britain suspended gold payments, foreign demands for gold shifted to the United States. Gold losses were $250 million in September and $450 million in October. The restrictive effects of these gold outflows were reinforced by an upsurge of cash withdrawals from the banking system. Between August, 1931 and February, 1932, these net drains were almost $700 million. The Federal Reserve did not buy securities to offset these external and internal drains. As a result, member banks had to increase their borrowings by more than $600 million, and also suffered a $440 million net reduction in their reserves. Most of the Reserve banks raised their discount rates. The New York rate rose from 1½ to 2½ percent and then to 3½ percent. Market rates of interest rose, and credit became less available.

Why did Federal Reserve officials refuse to buy securities in the open market to offset these drains, and why did they actually raise discount rates in the face of a continuing and even accelerating decline of business and employment? Perhaps one reason was their fear that gold drains would become larger and prolonged. Another was that their gold position was precarious. The problem was not with the ratio of their gold reserves to their Federal Reserve note and deposit liabilities; this was comfortably above its legal minimum. Rather, their problem was created by a provision in the Federal Reserve Act, requiring that Federal Reserve notes be collateraled dollar for dollar, and that the only assets eligible to serve as collateral were gold and commercial paper discounted by borrowing member banks. As member-bank borrowings declined and reduced Federal Reserve holdings of commercial paper, more gold had to be used as collateral. To the extent that Federal Reserve purchases of government securities enabled member banks to reduce their borrowings, the problem was intensified. At one time the volume of "free gold" was only $500 million. This impasse was finally broken in February, 1932, when Congress passed the Glass-Steagall Act permitting the Federal Reserve banks to use government securities as collateral for Federal Reserve notes. The Federal Reserve began almost immediately thereafter to purchase government securities.

Easy money, March, 1932 to early 1933

Early in March, 1932, the Federal Reserve embarked on a program of purchasing government securities; its purchases during that year exceeded by far its purchases of any preceding year. At the end of February, it held $740 million of government securities; at the end of the year its holdings were $1,855 million, an increase of $1,115 million. These purchases permitted member banks to reduce their borrowings by about $600 million and to increase their reserve balances by $500 million. At the end of the year, member banks had more than $550 million in excess reserves. The New York bank reduced its discount rate from 3½ to 3 percent and then to 2½ percent. Most of the others left their rates unchanged at 3½ percent throughout the year. Market rates of interest declined again, but many banks were, by this time, in no position to increase the availability of credit.

Banking panic of 1933

At the end of 1932, there was some reason to hope that monetary and financial conditions in the United States had been improved and would continue to improve. The banks had over half a billion in excess reserves, gold outflows appeared to have ended, and cash withdrawals from the banking system had recently slowed down. But the solvency and liquidity of individuals, business, and financial institutions had been seriously undermined by the prolonged and serious declines of real incomes and of the prices of output and assets. Many borrowers were in no position to pay their debts promptly, if at all. Thousands of banks were therefore illiquid, if not insolvent. Any sharp jar to confidence could topple the entire structure. The storm broke in Detroit with the failure of the Union Guardian Trust Company, which was one of the largest banks in Michigan and was also closely connected with many other banks. So great was the blow to public confidence and so panicky were withdrawals from other banks that the governor of Michigan, on February 14, 1933, declared an eight-day banking holiday. The panic quickly spread to other states. By March 4, every state in the Union had declared bank holidays, and bank deposits were no longer redeemable in cash. President Roosevelt's decree of a four-day, nationwide banking holiday, beginning on March 6, merely recognized the existing situation.

The panic period was characterized by gold and currency withdrawals. The country's monetary gold stock declined about $250 million. Net cash withdrawals from the banking system were nearly $2 billion, and would, of course, have been larger if banks had not closed their doors so soon. These drains forced member banks to increase their borrowings at the Federal Reserve by $1.2 billion and to reduce member-bank reserves by more than $800 million.

From the closing of the banking system in March, 1933 until the end of the decade, the relative role of the Federal Reserve in United States monetary policy was less than it had been earlier. The government now entered the field and acted vigorously and sweepingly, if not always wisely. Moreover, as a consequence of its policies and of developments abroad, the banking system was, within a few years, so amply supplied with excess reserves as to be largely beyond control by the Federal Reserve.

THE NEW DEAL AND MONETARY POLICY

One of the first projects of President Roosevelt and his Administration after they assumed office on March 4, 1933, was that of reactivating a closed banking system. But their actions went far beyond this. Within a short time, they had suspended the gold standard, depreciated the dollar in gold, established a new and quite different type of gold standard, provided for the monetization of great amounts of silver, and established many new financial institutions.

Reopening the banks

The objective was to reopen the banks and to do so in such a way as to restore confidence in their solvency and liquidity, to prevent further cash withdrawals, to encourage cash to flow back into the system, and to enable the banks to resume their lending function. The first step was to discover the condition of the banks. All supervisory authorities quickly surveyed the banks and divided them into three classes. Those that were in good condition were permitted to reopen quickly. Those that were in hopeless condition were closed permanently. The middle group of banks that were not sound enough to open immediately but that were capable of being saved, were given help and allowed to open when their condition had been repaired. Most of this help came from the Reconstruction Finance Corporation, a government credit agency that had been established in 1932. A temporary deposit-insurance program was instituted to restore confidence in the safety of deposits.

The public responded remarkably well. By the end of March, $1.2 billion in cash had been redeposited with banks; another $700 million flowed back before the end of the summer. In the latter part of the year, the Federal Reserve provided banks with additional funds by purchasing $600 million in government securities. Largely because of these developments, member banks were able to reduce their debt to the Federal Reserve from $1.4 billion at the time of the panic to only about $100 million late in the year, and, at the same time, to add $900 million to their reserve balances. Their excess reserves rose to about $800 million. From this level, excess reserves continued to rise, largely because of the surge of gold imports that began in 1934.

Gold policies

One of President Roosevelt's first official acts was to suspend the gold standard. Gold exports were prohibited, banks and other financial institutions were forbidden to pay out gold domestically, and everyone was ordered to surrender to the Treasury all his holdings of gold and gold certificates. It was at first thought that these were merely temporary measures that would be rescinded as soon as confidence was restored. But the old gold-coin standard and the old gold dollar were gone forever.

The prolonged depression and the severe decline of price levels had generated many schools of monetary expansionists similar to those that had been extant during the long deflation that followed the Civil War. Some schools would settle for more money of any kind, others wanted more of a particular type of money. Some of the more conservative groups urged a greater expansion of Federal Reserve credit. Vocal groups in the South and West, remembering the battle cries of the late nineteenth century, demanded free coinage of silver at the old 16-to-1 ratio. Others looking at the current use of "scrip," "prosperity checks," "corn money," and "cotton money" in a number of states, demanded national issues of scrip. Some wanted large issues of greenbacks of the Civil-War type. Technocrats wanted a whole new monetary system, using the erg as the unit of account. Still others demanded an increase in the price of gold.

These influences were reflected in legislation enacted in May, 1933, which gave the President unprecedented discretionary powers to expand the money supply in many ways.[2] The President himself, or the Secretary of the Treasury acting under presidential direction, was empowered to:

1. Enter into agreements with the Federal Reserve Board and the Federal Reserve banks for the latter to buy directly from the Treasury, and to hold up to $3 billion of federal government securities in addition to those already in their portfolios.

[2] This legislation was included in Title III of the Farm Relief Act approved by the President on May 12, 1933.

2. Issue United States notes (greenbacks) in amounts not to exceed $3 billion. These were to be legal tender for all debts.
3. To fix the gold value of the dollar by proclamation, with the limitation that it should be reduced more than 50 percent.
4. Fix the silver value of the dollar and to provide for the unlimited coinage of both gold and silver at fixed ratios. The President could reestablish a bimetallic standard in this country alone, or he could enter into agreements with other countries to establish international bimetallism.
5. Accept silver at a price not to exceed 50 cents an ounce in payment of debts from foreign governments, the total accepted in this form not to exceed $200 million. Any silver acquired in this way was to be coined into silver dollars and held as backing for additional silver certificates.

The President did not use his discretionary powers to sell government securities directly to the Federal Reserve or to issue greenbacks. He did, however, take massive action with respect to gold and silver.

The dollar began to depreciate in terms of both gold and foreign currencies as soon as President Roosevelt suspended the gold standard. That is, the dollar prices of gold and foreign exchange began to rise. For example, between February and June, 1933, the British pound rose from $3.42 to $4.14, the Canadian dollar from 83.5 to 89.9 cents, and the French franc from 3.92 to 4.80 cents. It soon became evident that exchange rates might behave in a disorderly manner, and that countries might even resort to competitive devaluation, each trying to lower the exchange rate on its own currency relative to others in order to stimulate its exports and discourage imports. To deal with this and other issues, an international monetary conference was held in London in June, 1933. One proposal was that all important countries should enter into an agreement to return to some sort of gold standard. That many other countries would have agreed to this is doubtful. In fact, however, the proposal was killed when President Roosevelt refused, stating that to stabilize the dollar in gold was a far less important objective than that of raising the American price level to promote recovery and then stabilizing it. Soon thereafter he began vigorously to use his power to increase the dollar price of gold. From September 8 to October 24, the Secretary of the Treasury stood ready to buy newly mined domestic gold at a price equal to the best price available in free markets abroad. On October 24, this price was $29.80 per ounce, or 44 percent above the old mint price. Following President Roosevelt's instructions, the Reconstruction Finance Corporation began, on October 25, to buy gold at gradually increasing prices. These month-end prices were:[3]

DATE	RFC PURCHASE PRICE PER FINE OUNCE	PERCENTAGE OF OLD MINT PRICE ($20.67)
October 31, 1933	$32.12	155
November 29, 1933	33.93	164
December 30, 1933	34.06	165
January 31, 1934	34.45	167

[3] See Secretary of the Treasury, *Annual Report,* 1934, p. 205.

Thus, by the end of January, 1934, the price of newly mined domestic gold had been raised 67 percent above the old mint price; the gold value of the dollar had been reduced about 40 percent.

It is clear that the gold-buying program to raise the price of gold was undertaken as part of the general program to raise commodity prices. This was emphasized in the President's October 22 radio address just before the RFC gold-buying program was begun.[4] What is not as clear, however, is the process by which the enhanced price of gold was expected to increase the prices of other goods and services. Some critics have accused the President of accepting fully the rather naive theories held by one of his monetary advisers, Professor George F. Warren, regarding the relationship between gold and price levels. Professor Warren, pointing to alleged long-run correlations between the monetary value of gold stocks and the height of price levels, argued that an increase in the price of gold would raise domestic price levels in a short period of time and almost in proportion to the increase in the price of gold. With many qualifications, there is some tendency *in the long run* for the monetary value of gold stocks and price levels to move in a parallel manner. Even in the short run, an increase in the price of gold can be used to increase the monetary value of gold stocks and the size of bank reserves, thereby *permitting* an expansion of the money supply. But there is no assurance that the total money supply, being largely composed of bank deposits, will rise proportionally in the short run, or that an increase of the money supply, even if achieved, will increase spendings proportionally, or even that increased spendings will effect proportional changes in price levels. The extent to which the President was influenced by Professor Warren's theory is not known.

It seems likely, however, that a stronger motive for raising the dollar price of gold was the one mentioned earlier: the desire to lower the value of the dollar in terms of foreign money, thereby increasing the foreign demand for our exports, especially for farm products, and raising the prices of these goods in terms of dollars. This is indicated in the President's notes for his radio address on October 22, 1933.

> At this point it may be said that the depreciation of foreign currencies, prior to 1933, had had the effect of making the dollar more expensive in terms of those foreign currencies. Thus it took more pounds, more francs or more marks to buy a dollar than it had formerly and, since the prices of our export products are determined in terms of dollars, it took more pounds, francs and marks to buy our export products. The effect of this had been to contribute to the serious decrease in our foreign trade, not because our own prices, in terms of dollars, had risen, nor because our own products were of an inferior quality, nor because we did not have sufficient products to export. But because, in terms of foreign currencies, our products had become so much more expensive, we were not able to obtain our fair share of the world's trade. It was, therefore, necessary to take measures which would result in bringing the dollar back to the position where a fair amount of foreign currency could again buy our products; that is, to make the dollar cheaper

[4] This speech is reproduced in *The Public Papers and Addresses of Franklin D. Roosevelt,* vol. ii, pp. 420–427.

in terms of pounds, francs and marks. This was the process which commenced in March, 1933, and which had to be continued until that level was reached. It was not desirable to make this level too low, because then our own importers would find it difficult to buy foreign merchandise. But it was clear that the level had been too high, and we wanted to find the appropriate level.[5]

Table 23–2 shows the extent to which the increasing dollar price of gold was reflected in rising exchange rates on selected foreign currencies. At the end of

Table 23–2 Dollar prices of selected foreign moneys, February and September, 1933, and January, 1934

MONEY	PRICE IN FEBRUARY, 1933	PRICE IN SEPTEMBER, 1933	PRICE IN JANUARY, 1934	PERCENTAGE INCREASE, FEBRUARY, 1933 TO JANUARY, 1934
English pound	$3.422	$4.665	$5.032	47
French franc	0.032	0.058	0.065	103
Australian pound	2.722	3.713	4.088	50
Canadian dollar	0.835	0.965	0.992	19

January, 1934, with the passage of the Gold Reserve Act, the United States re-established a gold standard. The principal provisions of this act were the following:

1. The President was authorized to fix the gold value of the dollar at not less than 50 percent nor more than 60 percent of the old level. This meant that he could define the dollar as not less than 11.61 grains nor more than 13.93 grains; the price of gold could be fixed at not more than $41.34 nor less than $34.45 an ounce—the latter being the price reached by January under the gold-buying program.

On January 31, 1934, the President set the price of gold at $35 an ounce, expressly reserving the right to alter it as the country's interest might require. Not until 1945 was this discretionary power repealed.[6] The gold content of the new dollar was 13.71 grains, a reduction of 40.94 percent. The Treasury reaped a handsome profit by raising the price of gold from $20.67 to $35 an ounce. It gained $14.33 on each of its nearly 196 million ounces of holdings, or $2,805 million.

2. The act nationalized all gold, provided that all profits or losses resulting from changes in the price of gold should accrue to the Treasury, and ended the domestic redeemability of currency in gold.

3. It ended the coinage of gold for domestic use and provided that all existing gold coins should be formed into bars.

4. It provided that gold might be held, transported, imported, exported, and otherwise dealt in only in accordance with regulations prescribed by the Secretary

[5] *Ibid.*, vol. ii, p. 428.

[6] The buying price is actually ¼ percent below $35 and the selling price is ¼ percent above it.

of the Treasury with the approval of the President. In practice, these regulations permitted free purchases and sales of gold to foreign central banks and governments, but limited domestic holding and dealing to "legitimate" commercial, industrial, artistic, and scientific purposes.

5. It provided that $2 billion of the gold profits should be used to establish an exchange-stabilization fund under the Secretary of the Treasury. Thus, the Secretary was given broad powers to regulate foreign-exchange rates and even to affect domestic credit conditions through his management of the exchange-stabilization fund.

In summary, the nation had abolished the gold-coin standard, established a limited gold-bullion standard, decreased the gold content of the dollar 40.94 percent, and raised the price of gold 69.33 percent.

Silver policies

By the end of 1932, the market price of silver had fallen to only 24.6 cents an ounce, a price that far from satisfied the silver-mining interests and their spokesmen in Congress. These groups argued that a greater monetization of silver and an increase of its price would not only assist the silver-mining industry, but would also help the country to emerge from depression and deflation. They even introduced a new argument that Bryan had not used: We should raise the price of silver to help "the teeming millions in the Orient." They pointed out that as the price of silver fell, the prices of Oriental silver money declined in terms of gold money, thereby—they argued erroneously—decreasing the purchasing power of Oriental countries in the world markets. Their remedy was as simple as it was fallacious; raise the price of silver, thereby raising the prices of Oriental silver money in foreign-exchange markets, and also raising the purchasing power of the Orient in world markets.

As already noted, the legislation of May, 1933 gave the President broad discretionary powers to accept silver in payment of war debts, to purchase the metal, to establish bimetallism, and to enter into international silver agreements. He did not establish bimetallism, and only limited amounts of silver were received in payment of war debts.[7] Nevertheless, the Treasury acquired very large amounts of silver under other programs. Senator Pittman, an ardent silverite and a United States delegate to the London Economic Conference in mid-1933, persuaded a number of silver-using and silver-producing countries to agree to measures raising the price of silver. The joker in the agreement was soon revealed. In effect, the United States had agreed to purchase annually an amount of silver equal to its entire domestic production, whereas the commitments of other countries were small indeed. The President ratified the London Silver Agreement in December, 1933, ordering the Treasury to purchase the entire domestic output at 64.64 cents an ounce. This price was about 50 percent above that previously prevailing.

---

[7] For an excellent brief discussion of American silver policy, see G. Griffith Johnson, *The Treasury and Monetary Policy, 1932–1938*, Cambridge, Mass., Harvard University Press, 1939, pp. 161–200.

Still dissatisfied, the proponents of silver pushed through the Silver Purchase Act of 1934. This Act directed the Secretary of the Treasury to purchase silver at home and abroad until the monetary value of the silver stock should be equal to one-third of the value of the monetary gold stock, or until the market price of silver should rise to the level of its monetary value ($1.29 an ounce). It also provided that in order to prevent excessive profits to speculators, no more than 50 cents an ounce should be paid for silver located in the United States on May 1, 1934. The President implemented the latter provision in August by nationalizing all silver at this price. Fortunately, the law did not prescribe the speed of silver purchases by the Secretary of the Treasury. He therefore bought as slowly as political conditions permitted. Nevertheless, his purchases were very large. Table 23–3 shows that, during the period 1934 to 1942, the Treasury purchased

Table 23–3 Silver production in the United States and silver purchases by the government, 1934–1942 (ounces and dollars in millions)

| YEAR | SILVER PRODUC-TION IN THE U.S. (OUNCES) | SILVER ACQUIRED BY U.S. GOVERNMENT | | | | | | | |
		NEWLY MINED DOMESTIC SILVER (OUNCES)	(DOLLARS)	NATIONALIZED SILVER (OUNCES)	(DOLLARS)	FOREIGN SILVER (OUNCES)	(DOLLARS)	TOTAL ACQUISITIONS (OUNCES)	(DOLLARS)
1934	32.5	21.8	$ 14.1	110.6	$55.3	172.5	$ 86.5	304.9	$ 155.9
1935	45.6	38.0	27.3	2.0	1.0	494.5	318.2	535.5	346.5
1936	63.4	61.1	47.3	0.4	0.2	271.9	150.3	333.4	197.8
1937	71.3	70.6	54.6	–	–	241.5	108.7	312.1	163.3
1938	61.7	61.6	42.4	–	–	355.4	156.9	417.1	199.3
1939	63.9	60.7	40.1	–	–	282.8	120.5	343.5	160.6
1940	67.0	68.3	48.5	–	–	139.8	50.9	208.1	99.4
1941	71.1	70.5	50.1	–	–	72.6	27.1	143.1	77.2
1942	55.9	47.9	34.0	–	–	14.3	6.0	62.2	40.0
Total	532.4	500.5	$358.4	113.0	$56.5	2,045.3	$1,025.1	2,657.9	$1,440.0

SOURCE: *Treasury Bulletins.*

more than 2.6 billion ounces of silver at a total cost of more than $1.4 billion. It paid for the silver by issuing Treasury currency in the form of silver certificates. These silver acquisitions were of three types: (1) small amounts of nationalized silver purchased at 50 cents an ounce, (2) over 2 billion ounces of foreign silver purchased at an average price of 50.1 cents an ounce, and (3) about 500 million ounces of newly mined domestic silver. Newly mined domestic silver was, from the beginning, given preferential price treatment. But the initial price of 64.64 cents an ounce did not satisfy the silver groups for long. In 1939, they pushed through a law ordering the Secretary to pay 71.11 cents an ounce for all newly mined domestic silver offered to him. In 1946, they again entered the fray, raising the price to 90.5 cents an ounce. These purchases were discontinued only in 1963.

As massive United States purchases doubled the price of silver in world markets, "the teeming millions in the Orient" wished for fewer "helpful" friends. Rising exchange rates on silver currencies decreased the ability of these countries to export without drastic reductions in their domestic prices. This deflationary pressure was intensified as some of their silver money was melted and exported. In the end, most silver countries abandoned silver standards, and adopted inconvertible standards or tied their money to the dollar or the British pound. Thus, the long-run effect of United States silver policy was to reduce still further the monetary use of silver abroad.

Other relevant New Deal measures

We cannot review here all the other New Deal measures that affected the structure and functioning of the monetary and financial system. Several of them related to the Federal Reserve System. A number of amendments effected a greater centralization of authority in the System. For the first time, the System was given legal authority to regulate margin requirements on security loans and to alter member-bank reserve requirements.

Many new institutions were established to restore the flow of credit. Among the most important of these were the FDIC and many new agencies in the fields of housing and agricultural credit.

THE GOLDEN AVALANCHE

Monetary conditions in the United States prior to her entrance into World War II at the end of 1941 were largely dominated by the inflow of gold and silver resulting from the combination of United States policies and developments abroad. Largely reflecting silver purchases, Treasury currency outstanding rose about $1 billion between the end of 1932 and the end of 1941. This tended, of course, to increase directly both the public's money supply and member-bank reserves. But far greater was the increase in the monetary gold stock. At the end of 1933, the United States monetary gold stock was at $4 billion; eight years later it was at $22.7 billion; this was an increase of $18.7 billion (see Table 23–4). A small part of this increase resulted from domestic gold production and melting of gold scrap; another part ($2,805 million) resulted from the revaluation of the existing gold stock when the price of gold was increased in early 1934. But by far the largest part—more than $16 billion—came from net gold imports. Some of these gold imports reflected the excess of United States exports of goods and services over her imports, but a very considerable part represented the movement of capital funds to the United States, many of them seeking safety from political and military threats abroad.

The period was one of greatly increased gold output in all gold-producing areas. This rise began early in the Depression, even before the price of gold began to rise. With its price pegged by monetary authorities, gold was the only commodity whose production was enhanced by deflation. Declines in the prices of other things lowered the cost of producing gold. But marked increases in the price of gold while the prices of other things remained constant, or at least did not rise in proportion, enhanced gold production still more. Table 23–5 indicates that by the late 1930s the output of gold in ounces was double its level in the 1920s. And,

Table 23–4 Monetary gold stock of the United States, 1929–1941* (millions of dollars)

END OF YEAR	MONETARY VALUE OF GOLD STOCK	INCREASE DURING YEAR	VALUE OF DOMESTIC GOLD PRODUCTION	NET GOLD IMPORTS
1929	$ 3,997			
1930	4,306	$ 309	$ 43	$ 280
1931	4,173	— 133	46	145
1932	4,226	53	46	— 446
1933	4,036	— 190	47	— 174
1934	8,238	4,202	93	1,134
1935	10,125	1,887	111	1,739
1936	11,258	1,133	132	1,117
1937	12,760	1,502	144	1,586
1938	14,512	1,752	149	1,974
1939	17,644	3,132	162	3,574
1940	21,995	4,351	170	4,744
1941	22,737	742	170	982
Addendum: Dec. 31, 1933– Dec. 31, 1941		$18,701	$1,178	$16,655

* For basic data and explanations of the contents of these figures, see Board of Governors of the Federal Reserve System, *Banking and Monetary Statistics,* Washington, D.C., pp. 522–525, 536.
SOURCE: Board of Governors of the Federal Reserve System, *Banking and Monetary Statistics,* p. 542; *Federal Reserve Bulletin,* various issues.

Table 23–5 World gold production

PERIOD	PRODUC-TION (MILLIONS OF FINE OUNCES)	INDEX OF PHYSICAL GOLD PRODUCTION, AVERAGE (1923–1929 = 100)	VALUE OF GOLD PRODUCTION* (MILLIONS OF DOLLARS)	INDEX OF VALUE AVERAGE (1923–1939 = 100)
1923–1929 (annual average)	18.8	100	$ 388.6	100
1930	20.9	111	432.1	111
1931	22.3	119	460.7	119
1932	24.1	128	498.2	128
1933	25.4	135	525.1	135
1934	27.4	146	958.0	247
1935	30.0	160	1,050.0	270
1936	32.9	175	1,152.6	296
1937	35.1	187	1,229.1	316
1938	37.7	201	1,319.6	340
1939	39.5	210	1,383.7	356
1940	41.1	219	1,437.3	370
1941	36.2	193	1,265.6	326

* $20.67 an ounce, 1933 and earlier; $35 an ounce in 1934 and later.
SOURCE: Board of Governors of the Federal Reserve System, *Banking and Monetary Statistics,* p. 542; *Federal Reserve Bulletin,* various issues.

because of the increase in the price of gold, the dollar value of current gold output was more than triple its level of a decade earlier.

The supply of gold for monetary purposes was further augmented from two other sources. Large but unknown amounts came from the melting of gold scrap as both the price and the purchasing power of gold rose. Larger amounts were released from hoards in the Orient. For example, during the relatively prosperous 1920s, British India absorbed about 3½ million ounces of new gold each year. But, as her own prosperity dwindled, and as the purchasing power of gold abroad rose to unprecedented levels, she threw large amounts of the yellow metal on world markets. Her net exports for the period 1931 to 1940 amounted to 41 million ounces, worth about $1.4 billion.

OTHER ASPECTS OF MONETARY POLICY, 1934 TO 1941

As noted earlier, monetary conditions in the United States had again become relatively easy by the latter part of 1933. Member banks owed the Federal Reserve only about $100 million and held nearly $800 million of excess reserves. Then came the great inflow of funds from the Treasury's silver purchases and the golden avalanche. By mid-1934, member-bank borrowings had fallen below $50 million. From that time until well after America's entrance into World War II, they rarely amounted to as much as $10 million. Banks did not need to borrow; they were swamped by excess reserves. The latter rose from less than $800 million in late 1933, to $2.9 billion in mid-1936. In the latter part of 1940, they were above $6.6 billion. Federal Reserve discount rates were of little importance under these conditions, but, by mid-1935, they had been lowered to 1 percent at the New York and Cleveland Reserve banks, and to 1½ percent at the other Reserve banks. They were not raised again until after World War II.

By mid-1936, when the excess reserves of member banks had reached $2.9 billion, and gold was still flowing in rapidly, Federal Reserve and Treasury officials feared that they might lose control of the situation, and that inflation might occur. The country had not yet recovered fully from the Depression. About 14 percent of the labor force was still unemployed and real national output was still about 5 percent below its level in 1929. Nevertheless, real output had already risen about 37 percent above its lowest level in 1933 and was still rising, and whole-sale prices had risen 23 percent although they were still 16 percent below their levels in 1929. Federal Reserve and Treasury officials agreed that to protect against inflation in the future, they should take some of the "slack" out of the system without going so far as to restrict current credit.

They took two actions to achieve this end. For one thing, the Board of Governors for the first time used its recently acquired power to change member-bank reserve requirements. In three steps—the first on August 16, 1936, and the last on May 1, 1937—it doubled all these requirements, thereby setting them at the maximum level permitted by law. In addition, the Treasury embarked on a policy of "sterilizing" all gold imports. Between the end of 1936 and mid-1937, it sterilized about $1.3 billion of gold inflows, thereby preventing this amount from augmenting the public's money supply, commercial-bank reserves, and Federal Reserve bank reserves. It did this by selling government securities to get the funds with which to pay for the gold and then adding the gold to its own "cash holdings" without issuing gold certificates against it. In effect, it engaged in an offsetting open-market operation.

As a consequence of these Federal Reserve and Treasury actions, the excess reserves of member banks were reduced to $750 million by August, 1937. These excess reserves seem to have been widely distributed, because member-bank borrowings did not rise above $24 million. Credit conditions tightened to some degree. In 1938, business activity declined sharply but briefly, reflecting largely a shift from inventory accumulation in 1937 to inventory decumulation in 1938. Both the Federal Reserve and the Treasury thereupon reversed their policies. On April 16, 1938, the Board of Governors lowered member-bank reserve requirements (see Table 23–6). In the same month, the Treasury "desterilized" about

Table 23–6 Member-bank reserve requirements, 1936–1941

	PERCENTAGES IN EFFECT					
	1917– AUG. 15, 1936	AUG. 16, 1936	MAR. 1, 1937	MAY 1, 1937	APR. 16, 1938	NOV. 1, 1941
Demand deposits						
Central Reserve						
cities	13	19½	22¾	26	22¾	26
Reserve cities	10	15	17½	20	17½	20
Other	7	10½	12¼	14	12	14
Time deposits	3	4½	5¼	6	5	6

$1.2 billion of its idle gold holdings, adding that amount to both member-bank reserves and Federal Reserve bank reserves. These actions, together with continued gold inflows, quickly brought excess member-bank reserves above $3 billion, from which level they continued to rise.

Money-market conditions were extraordinarily easy during the rest of this period. Short-term, open-market rates were especially low. The yield on Treasury bills was usually less than ½ percent, sometimes much less. Yields on long-term securities gradually fell to less than 2 percent, far below their levels of more than 3½ percent in 1929 and 3⅓ percent in 1930.

This period witnessed a very important innovation in the objectives of Federal Reserve open-market operations in United States government securities— a change that proved to be highly significant both during World War II and in the postwar period. Prior to 1937, Federal Reserve purchases and sales of government securities were primarily for the purpose of affecting the reserve positions of member banks, thereby regulating general monetary and credit conditions. But in 1937, for the first time in its history, the Federal Reserve bought long-term government securities primarily because of the direct effects of its purchases upon their market prices. In this case, it bought long-terms to bolster their prices and sold short-terms to prevent the operation from increasing member-bank reserves. Between this time and the entrance of the United States into World War II, the Federal Reserve engaged in several operations of this nature. Sometimes it bought long-terms to bolster their prices; at other times, it sold these securities to retard increases in their prices. (Table 23–7.)

Table 23–7 Member–bank reserve positions on selected dates, 1933–1941 (averages of daily figures, in millions of dollars)

PERIOD	ACTUAL RESERVE BALANCES	REQUIRED RESERVES	EXCESS RESERVES
Last quarter, 1933	$ 2,612	$1,839	$ 773
February, 1934	2,822	1,931	891
June, 1934	3,790	2,105	1,685
June, 1935	4,979	2,541	2,438
June, 1936	5,484	2,891	2,593
July, 1936	5,861	2,954	2,907
May, 1937	6,932	6,005	927
August, 1937	6,701	5,951	750
May, 1938	7,587	5,062	2,525
June, 1939	10,085	5,839	4,246
June, 1940	13,596	6,900	6,696
December, 1940	14,049	7,403	6,646
June, 1941	13,201	7,850	5,351
December, 1941	12,812	9,422	3,390

SOURCE: Board of Governors of the Federal Reserve System, *Banking and Monetary Statistics*, Washington, D.C., 1943, pp. 371–373.

Federal Reserve officials insisted that they would not "peg" these prices at an inflexible level. They would allow the prices and yields of these securities to adjust themselves to levels consistent with the other objectives of monetary policy. The only purpose of Federal Reserve intervention, they insisted, was to prevent "disorderly" markets in these securities and to secure "orderly" adjustments of prices and yields. But it proved to be but a short step from a policy of maintaining "orderly markets" to one of pegging these security prices at inflexible levels, and this step was taken early in World War II.

FEDERAL FISCAL POLICIES

A brief look at federal fiscal policies during the 1930s will illuminate some aspects of the behavior of money during this period. After criticizing President Hoover for deficit financing and after taking initial steps to reduce government expenditures, President Roosevelt soon embarked on a policy of increased expenditures and deficit financing. Even before the beginning of the defense program in 1940, federal expenditures had risen to more than three times their level in 1929. Some of the increase represented a rise of expenditures for public works and other goods and services, some transfer payments to the public, and some grants to state and local governments. But for many reasons, of which only a few can be noted, these increased expenditures did not succeed in ending the Depression before the United States embarked on a massive armament program. (Table 23–8.)

Table 23–8 Federal expenditures and receipts, 1929–1941 (billions of dollars)

CALENDAR YEAR	PURCHASES OF GOODS AND SERVICES	OTHER EXPENDITURES	TOTAL EXPENDITURES	RECEIPTS	SURPLUS (+) OR DEFICIT (−)
1929	$ 1.3	$1.3	$ 2.6	$ 3.8	+$1.2
1930	1.4	1.4	2.8	3.0	+ 0.2
1931	1.5	2.7	4.2	2.0	− 2.2
1932	1.5	1.7	3.2	1.7	− 1.5
1933	2.0	2.0	4.0	2.7	− 1.3
1934	3.0	3.4	6.4	3.5	− 2.9
1935	2.9	3.6	6.5	4.0	− 2.5
1936	4.8	3.7	8.5	5.0	− 3.5
1937	4.6	2.6	7.2	7.0	− 0.2
1938	5.3	3.2	8.5	6.5	− 2.0
1939	5.2	3.8	9.0	6.7	− 2.3
1940	6.2	3.9	10.1	8.6	− 1.5
1941	16.9	3.6	20.5	15.4	− 5.1

SOURCE: U.S. Department of Commerce, *National Income*, Washington, D.C., 1954, pp. 170–173.

1. Small scale of federal spending. At the beginning of the Depression, in 1929, when GNP was at about $104 billion, total federal expenditures were only $2.6 billion, or 2.5 percent of GNP. Thus, even a large percentage rise of government expenditures from this level had but a small leverage effect relative to the capacity level of output.

2. Long delay in instituting the policy. The economy had been deteriorating for more than three years before any deliberately expansionary expenditures policy was adopted.

3. Increases of effective tax rates. Time and again old taxes were increased and new ones imposed. This is reflected in the rise of tax collections, while GNP remained below its level in 1929. For example, in 1937, when GNP was still 13 percent below its level in 1929, federal tax collections were up 84 percent. A considerable part of the expansionary effects of increased government expenditures was absorbed by the increase of effective tax rates, which inhibited the rise of disposable private incomes. Government deficits during this period averaged about $2.5 billion a year, or less than 2⅓ percent of the 1929 level of GNP.

As a result of these fiscal policies, the federal debt rose from $16 billion at the end of 1929 to $41.4 billion at the end of 1939 and then to $57.5 billion by the end of 1941. A major part of the rise in the money supply during the latter part of the 1930s reflected increases in bank holdings of these obligations.

THE MONEY SUPPLY

Such liberalizing actions as were taken by the Federal Reserve in the early part of the Depression did not succeed in preventing a large decrease in the money supply. Between mid-1929 and mid-1933, the money supply fell from $26.1 billion to $19.2 billion, a decline of $6.9 billion, or 26 percent. Table 23–9 shows that the

Table 23–9 The money supply and its direct determinants, 1929–1939 (billions of dollars)

	AMOUNT, JUNE 29, 1929	AMOUNT, JUNE 30, 1933	AMOUNT, DEC. 30, 1939	CHANGE, 1929–1933	CHANGE, 1933–1939
Sources					
Monetary gold	$ 4.0	$ 4.0	$17.6	–	+$13.6
Treasury currency	2.0	2.3	3.0	+$ 0.3	+ 0.7
Federal Reserve credit	1.4	2.2	2.6	+ 0.8	+ 0.4
Commercial-bank credit					
Loans	35.7	16.3	17.2	– 19.4	+ 0.9
U.S. government securities	4.9	7.5	16.3	+ 2.6	+ 8.8
Other securities	8.7	6.5	7.1	– 2.2	+ 0.6
Total sources	$56.7	$38.8	$63.8	–$17.9	+$25.0
Competing uses					
Foreign deposits	$ 0.4	–	$ 1.2	–$ 0.4	+$ 1.2
U.S. government balances	0.6	$ 1.2	3.9	+ 0.6	+ 2.7
Time deposits	19.6	10.8	15.3	– 8.8	+ 4.5
Capital accounts (net)	10.0	7.6	7.2	– 2.4	– 0.4
Total competing uses	$30.6	$19.6	$27.6	–$11.0	–$ 8.0
Money supply					
Demand deposits	22.5	14.4	29.8	– 8.1	+ 15.4
Currency outside banks	3.6	4.8	6.4	+ 1.2	+ 1.6
Total	$26.1	$19.2	$36.2	–$ 6.9	+$17.0

major reason for this was the $19 billion decrease of commercial-bank loans and security holdings.

Between June, 1933 and the end of 1939, the money supply rose from $19.2 billion to $36.2 billion. Thus, at the end of this period, the money supply was 90 percent above its level at the bottom of the Depression, and 40 percent above its level in 1929. This rise resulted largely from the rise of the monetary gold stock and increased commercial-bank holdings of federal securities. This rise of the money supply was accompanied by a less than proportional rise in expenditures for output. While the money supply rose about 90 percent, GNP in current prices increased 63 percent from $56.0 billion in 1933 to $91.1 billion in 1939.

CONCLUSIONS

Monetary conditions in the United States during the period beginning in 1934 were far easier than any the country had seen prior to that time. The banking system was flooded with excess reserves. Yet the nation did not recover fully from the Depression until about eight years later, after it had entered World War II. Should we conclude from this experience, as some have done, that monetary policy must always be ineffective in combating depression and unemployment? Only somewhat less sweeping and more tentative conclusions seem justified. One is that the effectiveness of an easy-money policy is likely to be seriously reduced if the policy is long delayed. The liberalizing policies employed in 1930 and the first eight months of 1931 were not aggressive; some member banks were still in debt to the Federal Reserve and others held only relatively small amounts of excess reserves. Few were in such condition that they felt excessively liquid and impelled to seek additional earning assets. Then came the 1931 episode and the restrictive policies accompanying it. The easy-money policy of 1932 lasted only a few months, terminated by the banking panic of early 1933. The Depression had already been under way for more than three years before an aggressive easy-money policy of some duration was followed. By this time, the economy was so depressed, the liquidity and solvency of borrowers so impaired, and excess capacity so widespread, that easy money was unlikely to bring a surge of recovery even if it slowed the decline.

Another important point suggested by this experience is that the effectiveness of monetary policy may depend greatly on the soundness of financial institutions. About 1,350 commercial banks closed their doors in 1930, another 2,300 in 1931, still another 1,450 in 1932, and 4,000 in 1933. Many other types of financial institutions were also failing. In such a situation, the public became afraid to entrust its money to these institutions, and the institutions, fearing runs, were in many cases unwilling to make investable funds available. It is to be hoped that many of the institutions and practices adopted since the 1930s have made our financial system less vulnerable. Among these are better regulation of financial institutions and practices, the FDIC, the FSLIC, insurance of mortgages, the Federal Home Loan banks, and so on. But perhaps the best insurance against a collapse of financial institutions is to prevent the serious depressions that weaken them. This may require not only prompt and aggressive monetary policies but also prompter and more aggressive fiscal policies than were employed in the 1930s.

Selected readings

Beyen, J. W., *Money in a Maelstrom,* New York, Macmillan, 1949.
Chandler, L. V., *American Monetary Policy, 1929–1941,* New York, Harper & Row, 1971.
Hawtrey, R. G., *Bretton Woods for Better or Worse,* London, Longmans, Green, 1946.

Hodson, H. V., *Slump and Recovery, 1929–1937*, Oxford, 1938.

Johnson, G. G., Jr., *The Treasury and Monetary Policy, 1932–1938*, Cambridge, Mass., Harvard University Press, 1939.

Paris, J. D., *Monetary Policies of the United States, 1932–1938*, New York, Columbia University Press, 1938.

CHAPTER 24

MONETARY POLICY, 1941-1951

With the entrance of the United States into World War II in December, 1941, the Federal Reserve again became, as it had been during World War I, a servant of the government's fiscal policy. All conflicting objectives were pushed aside; its overriding objective became that of assuring that the nation's war effort would not suffer from any lack of money. Moreover, it was to assure that the huge war effort would be financed without any rise of interest rates above the low levels prevailing in early 1942.

WARTIME FISCAL POLICIES

The federal government's fiscal policy during this period followed the usual pattern for all-out war, but on a huge scale. Its expenditures rose tremendously. Just before the beginning of the defense effort in mid-1940, government expenditures were at an annual rate of about $9 billion. By the fourth quarter of 1941, they had risen to an annual rate of more than $25 billion. By 1944, they were above $95 billion. Thus, at the peak of the war effort, federal expenditures were more than 10 times their level before the beginning of the defense program and were themselves greater than total GNP at any time during the 1930s. More than 40 percent of the nation's output was being purchased for government purposes. Between mid-1940, when the accelerated defense program began, and mid-1946, when the wartime deficits ended, federal expenditures totaled more than $383 billion. This was more than twice as much as the federal government had spent during the preceding 150 years, nearly 100 times as much as it spent during the Civil War, and 10 times as much as it spent during World War I. (Table 24–1.)

Table 24–1 Cash operating outgo, income, and deficits of the federal government, 1940–1946 (millions of dollars)

FISCAL YEAR ENDING JUNE 30	CASH OPERATING OUTGO	CASH OPERATING INCOME	CASH OPERATING DEFICIT
1941	$ 14,060	$ 9,371	$ 4,689
1942	34,585	15,291	19,294
1943	78,979	25,245	53,734
1944	94,079	47,984	46,095
1945	95,986	51,051	44,935
1946	65,683	47,784	17,899
Total	$383,372	$196,726	$186,646

SOURCE: L. V. Chandler, *Inflation in the United States, 1940–1948,* New York, Harper & Row, 1951, p. 62. Much of the material in this and the following chapter is taken from this book.

Tax collections were increased greatly, but not nearly as much as expenditures. The result was, of course, huge deficits. These averaged more than $40 billion a year during the period of active participation of the United States in the war; in one year they were nearly $54 billion. For the six years following mid-1940, federal deficits totaled nearly $187 billion. The Treasury therefore faced the necessity of borrowing huge amounts to cover these deficits. In fact, its net borrowings during this six-year period were $199 billion, of which $187 billion was required to cover its deficits and $12 billion was used to increase its money balance.

The Treasury again tried to borrow as much as it could in ways that would not involve an increase in the money supply. It used all the devices developed during World War I as well as new ones to sell securities to nonbank buyers: great bond-selling campaigns, pleas by movie stars and national heroes; 100-percent clubs; payroll-deduction plans; and so on. It did succeed in getting nonbank investors to increase their holdings of Treasury obligations by $109 billion. But this was not enough; the commercial banks increased their holdings by $68.3 billion, and the Federal Reserve banks by $21.3 billion.

WARTIME MONETARY POLICY

Federal Reserve assistance to Treasury financing during World War II differed in at least two important respects from that in World War I. In the earlier war,

Table 24–2 Federal borrowings, their use and their sources 1940–1946 (millions of dollars)

FISCAL YEAR ENDING JUNE 30	FEDERAL CASH OPERAT- ING DEFICIT	INCREASE OR DECREASE (—) OF TREASURY'S GENERAL FUND BALANCE	NET CASH BORROW- ING	NET INCREASE IN AMOUNT OF FEDERAL INTEREST-BEARING DEBT HELD			
				BY NONBANK INVESTORS	BY FEDERAL RESERVE AND COM- MERCIAL BANKS	BY COM- MERCIAL BANKS	BY FEDERAL RESERVE BANKS
1941	$ 4,689	$ 742	$ 5,431	$ 2,143	$ 3,318	$ 3,600	—$ 282
1942	19,294	358	19,652	12,869	6,761	6,300	461
1943	53,734	6,515	60,250	28,498	30,757	26,200	4,557
1944	46,095	10,662	56,757	32,913	23,899	16,200	7,699
1945	44,935	4,529	49,464	27,173	22,691	15,800	6,891
1946	17,899	— 10,450	7,439	5,431	2,191	200	1,991
Total increase for period	$186,646	$12,356	$199,003	$109,027	$89,617	$68,300	$21,317

SOURCE: L. V. Chandler, *Inflation in the United States, 1940–1948*, New York, Harper & Row, 1951, p. 72. This table was computed from various tables in *Treasury Bulletins*. It should be noted that the figures relating to debt reflect only the debt held outside the federal government itself; they do not include an increase of about $22 billion in federal debt held by government agencies and trust funds. These securities involved no borrowing outside the government itself; as the Treasury collected and spent social security taxes, it issued to the trust funds under its control, government securities indicating a future obligation to pay social security benefits.

the Federal Reserve itself bought very few Treasury obligations; it gave its assistance primarily by lending to banks. In World War II, it lent very little to banks; it created additional money primarily by purchasing Treasury obligations, most of them in the open market rather than directly from the Treasury. It did establish very low preferential-discount rates on loans collateraled by short-term Treasury obligations, but banks requested few loans. They did not need loans; they could get reserve money even more cheaply by selling short-term Treasury obligations to the Federal Reserve. Interest-rate policies also differed markedly in the two wars. Interest rates were allowed to rise during World War I. In general, each new bond issue carried interest rates somewhat above those on earlier issues. During World War II interest rates were not allowed to rise at all.

In March, 1942, the Federal Open Market Committee agreed with the Treasury that, in general, the level of interest rates and yields on government securities should not be allowed to rise during the war and pledged the full co-operation of the System to this end. This promise was fully kept. Interest rates in general were at that time low by historical standards, and short-term rates were abnormally low relative to longer-term rates. This was partly because of the low demand for investable funds during the Depression, partly because of the huge volume of excess reserves in the banking system. At the end of 1941, the latter were still above $3 billion. The pattern of yields stabilized by the Federal Reserve during the war period reflected these conditions. On 90-day maturities, this yield was $\frac{3}{8}$ percent; on 9- to 12-month maturities it was $\frac{7}{8}$ percent, on 5-year maturities, it was $1\frac{1}{2}$ percent; on 10-year maturities, it was 2 percent; and on the longest marketable Treasury issues, it was 2½ percent. The shape of this yield curve should be noted carefully, because it was to have important consequences.

The Federal Reserve's technique for preventing these various yields from rising—for preventing the prices of the securities from falling—was simple: It merely stood ready to buy without limitation all of these securities offered to it at the selected levels of prices and yields. In short, it stood ready to monetize, with high-powered reserve money, all the government securities offered to it by the banks and all other types of holders. As shown in Table 24–3, the System increased

Table 24–3 Maturities of governments held by the Reserve banks, 1941–1946 (last Wednesday of the month; in millions of dollars)

DATE	WITHIN 90 DAYS	90 DAYS TO 1 YEAR	1 YEAR TO 2 YEARS	2 YEARS TO 5 YEARS	OVER 5 YEARS	TOTAL
December, 1941	$ 96	$ 97	$247	$ 477	$1,337	$ 2,254
December, 1942	1,199	886	242	1,408	2,254	5,989
December, 1943	7,256	2,457	224	488	1,190	11,615
December, 1944	12,703	4,064	760	620	918	19,065
December, 1945	15,839	7,000	0	508	691	24,038
June, 1946	17,877	4,436	46	449	582	23,390

its holdings of Treasury obligations by $21.3 billion between the end of 1941 and June, 1946. Its purchases were concentrated in the short maturities; in fact, its holdings of the longer maturities actually declined during the latter part of the war. This was partly because of the very large Treasury issues of short maturities, partly because of the shape of the yield curve. Private investors tended to shun the short maturities with their low yields and to purchase the longer-term, higher-yield obligations. At their Federal Reserve support prices, these longer-term obligations were just as liquid as the shortest maturities. They could be riskier than the short obligations only if purchased above the support price or if the support price were lowered or withdrawn. Most investors were confident that the latter would not happen during the war, and they suspected that support would be continued into the postwar period.

This passive, open-market policy had several important consequences, not only during the war but also in the postwar period.

1. The Federal Reserve thereby abandoned control over its volume of government holdings, the volume of bank reserves, and the money supply. To prevent yields from rising, it had to buy all securities offered to it, regardless of the identity of the seller and regardless of the purpose for which the newly created money would be used. Thus, banks and nonbank investors alike could get new money from the Federal Reserve at will, the only cost being the yield sacrificed on the securities sold.

2. The cost of getting such funds was the low yield on short-term government securities, because banks and all other types of financial institutions held billions of these.

3. By holding down interest rates on government securities, the Federal Reserve also held down interest rates on loans to private borrowers and assured a highly liberal supply of credit for private uses. The reason was that all holders of government securities retained complete freedom to sell these holdings and to shift to other assets. Thus, not only banks, but all other lenders as well could get funds from the Federal Reserve to satisfy private demands, and they would do so in great volume if yields on private obligations tended to rise.

Table 24–4 shows that during the six years following 1939, the money supply rose from $36.2 billion to $102.4 billion, for an increase of 183 percent. By far the

Table 24–4 The money supply and its determinants, 1939–1945 (end-of-year figures, in billions of dollars)

	1939	1945	NET INCREASE 1939–1945
Sources			
Monetary gold stock	$17.6	$ 20.1	$ 2.5
Treasury currency	3.0	4.3	1.3
Total Federal Reserve credit	2.6	25.1	22.5
Commercial-bank credit			
U.S. government securities	16.3	90.6	74.3
Loans	17.2	26.1	8.9
Other securities	7.1	7.3	0.2
Total sources	$63.9	$173.5	$109.6
Less:			
Amounts absorbed by competing uses			
U.S. government deposits and cash holdings	$ 2.0	$ 25.9	$ 23.9
Time deposits	15.1	29.9	14.8
Other competing uses	10.6	15.3	4.7
Total competing uses	$27.7	$ 71.1	$ 43.4
Equals:			
The money supply			
Demand deposits	$29.8	$ 75.9	$ 46.1
Currency outside banks	6.4	26.5	20.1
Total money supply	$36.2	$102.4	$ 66.2

most important direct contributors to this increase were the $74.3 billion rise of commercial-bank holdings of government securities and the $22.5 billion increase of Federal Reserve holdings.

While following a passive general monetary policy, the authorities tried to prevent or limit nonessential private borrowing by using selective credit controls. For example, in the autumn of 1941, the Federal Reserve imposed for the first time a selective control over consumer credit, fixing maximum loan values and maximum periods of repayment. Banks were admonished to refuse loans for non-essential purposes. Authorities were established to pass upon the essentiality of new security issues. But these and other selective credit controls were far less effective in containing inflationary pressures, and even in limiting the expansion of credit for private purposes, than were the great variety of direct controls imposed on the economy early in the war.

THE WARTIME ROLE OF DIRECT CONTROLS

It soon became evident that the government's fiscal policy would create strong inflationary pressure as output approached capacity levels, if not before. The huge rise of government expenditures directly increased the demand for output; it also contributed greatly increased amounts to private money incomes. Increased tax collections recovered some of this money from the private sectors, but not nearly enough to prevent disposable private incomes from increasing greatly. With greater disposable incomes, consumers would, if left free to do so, increase their consumption demands. The multiplier would operate upward, perhaps raising consumer spending at a greater rate than government spending. Something of the same nature would happen to business spending. Prospects for profitable new investment were highly favorable, disposable business income was greatly increased, and credit was cheap. It became clear that something would have to be done to prevent consumers and business from spending as much as they wanted to spend and could afford to spend with their large and rising disposable money incomes. Inflationary pressures would have to be "repressed." This was not only to prevent or limit price inflation; it was also to prevent rising private demands from diverting productive resources away from the war effort.

A whole series of direct controls was established for these purposes. These controls included price ceilings on virtually every type of output, ceilings on wages, and ceilings on rents. It was illegal for anyone to charge or to pay more than these prices. Also included were many types of controls over the production, distribution, and use of output. In general, producers could buy equipment and supplies only if permitted to do so by the government, and the quantities that they could buy were limited. Thus, total business spending was held down because the quantities of things business could buy were limited and the prices business could pay were limited by ceilings. In short, business was forced to spend less than it wanted to, many businesses were unable to spend all their current disposable incomes, and the inability of business to spend limited its demand for investable funds.

Consumer spending was similarly repressed. Consumers were forbidden to pay prices above the legal ceilings and the quantities of goods available were limited. Many were rationed. Many others, such as automobiles and most other consumer durables, simply were not produced. Thus, consumer spending was repressed and households were virtually forced to save far more than they would have done in the absence of direct controls.

The repression of private spending was not, of course, complete. Consumer spending did rise, as did also the wholesale and cost-of-living price indexes. The latter did not reflect actual price increases that occurred through upgrading, quality deterioration, and black markets. Yet the repression was remarkably successful in view of the strength of the inflationary pressures.

In short, the country had not been in the war very long before it was in a state of suppressed inflation, or widespread, excess demands. The demand for output at existing prices had become far greater than the available supply. As the war progressed, these inflationary pressures grew—partly as a result of the huge accumulation of private savings. For the years 1940 to 1945, inclusive, personal saving amounted to the huge sum of $132.6 billion and corporate net saving aggregated $28.5 billion. Total capital-consumption accretions of $72.5 billion also enabled business to increase its liquidity to the extent that these funds could not be spent for replacement of plant and equipment. The private sectors used these huge savings in two principal ways: (1) to retire debt—many households and businesses were enabled to retire their debts completely or at least to reduce them markedly; (2) to acquire liquid assets—between the end of 1939 and the end of 1945, individual and business holdings of liquid assets rose from $69 billion to $227.5 billion, an increase of $158.5 billion. Not only the size of this increase but also the liquidity of the assets should be noted. Of the total increase, $59 billion was in holdings on money itself—demand deposits and currency. Another $21.4 billion was in time deposits. Still another $75 billion was in highly liquid Treasury obligations. The nonmarketable issues, such as the E bonds, were redeemable at the Treasury on demand. The marketable issues were, in effect, redeemable on demand at the Federal Reserve at their support prices. The other $3.2 billion increase of liquid assets was in shares of savings and loan associations.

CONDITIONS AT THE END OF WORLD WAR II

The country had not escaped overt inflation during the war. By the end of 1945, consumer prices were 31 percent, and wholesale prices 39 percent, above their levels of six years earlier. Repressed inflationary pressures were very strong. The private sectors had accumulated a huge volume of liquid assets. Their money balances were now 183 percent above their level in 1939, and their total holdings of liquid assets were up 230 percent. Moreover, both business firms and households had accumulated unsatisfied wants in large volume. Many business firms that had spent little or nothing for investment purposes during the Depression, and had been prevented from spending during the war, now wanted to replace, to expand, or to modernize their plants and equipment. Large numbers of families, feeling that they had lived like Spartans during the war, now wanted to go on a spending spree and to buy the cars and other things that had not been available during the war. The inflationary potential in increased private spending was large indeed.

But there was another side to the story, a side that led many persons to forecast deep depression and widespread unemployment rather than inflation for the postwar period. Many feared that the decrease of government spending following the cessation of hostilities would bring disaster. The sharp drop of federal expenditures from their level of almost $100 billion a year would directly decrease the demand for output, set off a downward multiplier effect on consumption, and leave industry with so much excess capacity that virtually no investment expenditures would be justified. Such gloomy forecasts were one, but by no means the only, reason for the early dismantling of direct controls. They were also a force for a continued easy-money policy. When the predicted depression did not develop immediately after the war, many people continued to insist that it was "just around the corner."

As the war drew to a close, the government quickly began to relax and to remove the whole complex of direct controls. Rationing of consumer goods was dropped almost immediately, and other controls over the use of raw materials and the production, distribution, and use of output were dismantled. Wage controls were abolished almost as soon as the war ended. Many goods and services were exempted from price controls immediately and other price ceilings were raised. By mid-1946, price controls were largely inoperative, and in the autumn they were abolished. Rent ceilings remained as almost the only remnant of the wartime system of direct controls.

Prices rose immediately as direct controls were relaxed and removed. During 1946 alone, wholesale prices rose more than they had during the entire 1939 to 1945 period, and the cost of living advanced two-thirds as much as it had during the preceding six years. By August, 1948, when prices reached their first postwar peak, wholesale prices had risen 120 percent, and the cost of living 76 percent, since 1939. Two-thirds of the total rise of wholesale prices and three-fifths of the increase in the cost of living had occurred since the end of the war.

MONETARY POLICY, 1946 TO 1948

Although direct controls over the economy were removed, Federal Reserve policies remained chained to their wartime objectives and methods of implementation. The System still used its powers to peg the prices and yields on Treasury obligations, and the pegged pattern of yields for some time was the same as it had been through the war. The range was from $3/8$ percent on 90-day maturities to a ceiling of $2\frac{1}{2}$ percent on 25-year Treasury bonds. In short, during a period of full employment and inflation, the Federal Reserve was pegging a general level and pattern of interest rates that had evolved during the nation's worst depression. Not until March, 1951, more than five years after the end of the war, did the Federal Reserve completely abandon this pegging pattern.

This passive open-market policy of supplying additional Federal Reserve funds to anyone presenting securities at their pegged prices was potentially far more dangerous in the postwar period than it had been during the war. The wartime system of direct controls had effectively limited private demands for credit. As limitations on the quantities that they could purchase and on the prices they could pay limited their total spending, households and business firms limited their demands for credit. But as these limitations were removed, private buyers again became free to bid against each other for larger quantities, to pay higher prices, and to demand larger loans for the purpose. Moreover, all types of financial institutions were in a position to meet almost any forseeable increase in private demands for credit, and to do so at low interest rates as long as the Federal Reserve pegged yields on government securities, because they held huge amounts of these obligations. For example, at the end of 1945, commercial banks held $90.1 billion; life insurance companies, $20.6 billion; mutual savings banks, $10.7 billion; and savings and loan associations, $2.4 billion. Households and nonfinancial business firms also had large holdings which they could sell to get money to lend to others or to finance their own spending.

Reasons for the pegging policy

Why did the Federal Reserve continue, despite inflation, to maintain easy-money conditions through its pegging policy? In part, it was because of the widespread fear of unemployment. The long depression of the 1930s had left its indelible impression and almost a depression psychosis. Almost every year brought new forecasts of a coming decline. Moreover, the nation's new determination to promote the achievement and maintenance of "maximum employment, production, and purchasing power" was embodied in the Employment Act of 1946. Treasury and Federal Reserve officials were reluctant to take any action that might jeopardize the maintenance of prosperity. The policy was also made more acceptable by the current lack of faith in the efficacy of monetary policy. There was a widespread feeling that experience in the 1930s had proved that monetary policy was ineffective in combating depression. Many now asserted that it would be equally useless as an instrument for fighting inflation—that mildly restrictive policies would not be effective and that policies restrictive enough to halt price increases would throw the country into depression.

Concern for Treasury financing and for the prices of outstanding Treasury obligations was a major reason for continuing the policy. The Secretary of the Treasury was a strong and persistent advocate of pegging, and a stubborn opponent of increases in interest rates. Several of the relevant arguments are worth noting.

1. Increased rates on the federal debt would add greatly to the already large interest burden.

2. Fluctuating prices and yields on governments would greatly complicate the Treasury's refunding operations, a serious matter with about $50 billion of the debt maturing within a year and nearly $100 billion within five years.

3. An increase of yields on government securities, which without a rise of coupon rates would mean a decline of their prices, would impose capital depreciation on financial institutions and other holders and might lead to panicky selling and loss of confidence in financial institutions. Officials recalled the drastic decline of bond prices in 1920, when the federal debt was only $26 billion, and pointed to the greater possibilities of panic now that the debt was nearly 10 times as large and represented about 60 percent of all debt in the country.

4. Disturbances in the prices and yields of government securities would be transmitted to private securities and jeopardize prosperity. It was argued that not

only low interest rates, but also stability of interest rates and bond prices promoted prosperity.

Open-market policy

Until July, 1947, nearly two years after V-J Day, the Federal Open Market Committee continued to prevent yields on government securities from rising above the pattern selected in early 1942. In 1946 and early 1947, the prices of long-term government securities rose somewhat above the pegged level. This was primarily because the extremely low level of short-term rates led investors to "play the pattern of the rates" and to shift their purchases toward the longer-term obligations. The first break from the wartime pattern came in July, 1947, when the Federal Reserve persuaded the Treasury to allow it to eliminate the ⅜ percent buying rate on Treasury bills. The next break came the following month, when the Treasury agreed to the elimination of the ⅞ percent rate on 9- to 12-month certificates of indebtedness. But this did not mean that the Federal Reserve had ceased to limit increases of the yields on these shorter-term obligations. It had merely shifted its policy to one of maintaining the rates fixed by the Treasury on new issues.

Several aspects of open-market policy during the remainder of this period deserve emphasis:

1. Not until March, 1951, did the Federal Reserve permit the prices of long-term Treasury securities to fall below par or permit their yields to rise above 2½ percent. The prices of these obligations might rise above par, but the Federal Reserve intervened to the extent necessary to prevent their prices from falling below par.

2. In the last analysis, it was the Secretary of the Treasury who set the yields on new issues, and therefore determined the rates to be maintained by the Federal Reserve. And the Secretary consented to rate increases only reluctantly, belatedly, and to a limited extent. By the end of 1948, when the first postwar inflation had reached its peak, the yield on Treasury bills had been allowed to rise only from ⅜ percent to 1.13 percent, and that on 9- to 12-month certificates from ⅞ percent to 1¼ percent. The results of these increases could hardly be considered high interest rates for a period of inflation.

3. This willingness of the Federal Reserve to buy government securities in unlimited amounts robbed its other instruments of all or almost all of their effectiveness for restrictive purposes. In effect, this policy provided the banking system and others with a means of escape from other Federal Reserve attempts to restrict them.

Other monetary policies

The Federal Reserve employed two types of selective credit controls during this period. In 1946, as stock-market activity began to rise markedly, the Board of Governors raised margin requirements on security loans to 100 percent, thereby putting the stock market on a "cash basis." This action probably inhibited the rise of stock prices and prevented a situation in which a highly speculative stock market might have enhanced inflationary expectations. It did not, of course, restrict the supply of credit for other purposes.

Regulation W, the selective control over consumer credit that had been imposed in the autumn of 1941 under the authority of an executive order of the President, was continued until November, 1947. It was then removed because Federal Reserve officials felt that they should exercise such a control only when specifically authorized by Congress to do so. They again imposed the control briefly following a temporary authorization by Congress in August, 1948. While it was in effect, Regulation W probably retarded to some degree, although it did not stop, the growth of consumer credit.

The Federal Reserve also increased discount rates three times. The first came in the spring of 1946, when the Reserve banks eliminated the ½ percent preferential rate applicable to loans collateraled by short-term Treasury obligations; this left in effect their 1 percent rate, which was raised to 1¼ percent in January, 1948, and to 1½ percent the following August. These rate advances probably exerted some influence toward firmness, but their effects were small because the banks were largely out of debt to the Federal Reserve, and were likely to remain so while they held so many short-term Treasury obligations that they could sell to the Federal Reserve at will.

From October, 1942 until February, 1948, the Board of Governors maintained member-bank reserve requirements at the highest levels permitted by law, except that requirements against demand deposits in central reserve city banks were at 20 percent rather than at the maximum level of 26 percent. The Board of Governors then raised these latter requirements to 22 percent in February, 1948, and to 24 percent in June. In August, Congress enacted legislation giving the Board temporary permission to raise these requirements above the old maximum levels. The Board thereupon raised requirements against demand deposits at all classes of member banks by 2 percentage points, and against time deposits by 1½ percentage points. In all, these 1948 increases raised required member-bank reserves by about $2.5 billion. Such a large increase of requirements would ordinarily have restricted credit markedly. In this case, the major effect was to evoke sales of an additional $2 billion of securities to the Federal Reserve. There was an accompanying slight increase of interest rates, but the effectiveness of the increases in reserve requirements was largely negated by the passive, open-market policy.

The main argument of this section is not that these other Federal Reserve actions were wholly ineffective, but that the effectiveness of these restrictive actions was largely offset by the willingness of the Federal Reserve to supply reserve funds by purchasing Treasury obligations at relatively low and relatively stable yields.

MONETARY POLICY, 1949 TO MID-1950

After the first postwar peak of prices was reached in August, 1948, there followed more than a year of mild deflation. By the end of 1949, the cost of living had fallen 5 percent and wholesale prices were down 11 percent. In fact, 1949 was a year of mild recession, with small declines of both production and employment. This was largely because net accumulations of business inventories in 1948 gave way to net decumulations of inventories in 1949. The Federal Reserve halted its vain attempts to restrict credit, and initiated an easier money policy. Early in the spring of 1949, it eliminated its regulation of consumer credit. The temporary authorization to employ this type of regulation expired in June. It also lowered member-bank reserve requirements. In several steps, beginning in May and ending in September, it lowered reserve requirements against demand deposits by 4 percent at all classes of member banks. Requirements against time deposits were reduced from 7½ to 5 percent. The Treasury lowered somewhat the yields on its new issues, and the Federal Reserve stood ready to prevent market rates from rising above these lowered levels.

Under these conditions of mild deflation, the controversy between the Federal Reserve and the Treasury died down. In such a situation, there is no necessary conflict between the objective of promoting general economic stabilization, including stability of price levels, and the objectives of holding down interest costs on the national debt, facilitating Treasury financing operations, and preventing decreases in the prices of outstanding Treasury bonds.

By early 1950, the decline in business activity and prices had stopped, and recovery was well under way. There was still some unemployment, but economic activity was at a high level. As to the future course of business activity and price levels, there was wide disagreement among economic forecasters. The outbreak of fighting in Korea late in June, 1950 ended this uncertainty and ushered in a new upsurge of inflation.

MONETARY POLICY AFTER THE OUTBREAK
OF FIGHTING IN KOREA

The outbreak of fighting in Korea, and this country's decision to intervene, inspired a surge of buying by consumers and business firms. Remembering the scarcities and price increases of World War II, consumers rushed into the markets to get ahead of the hoarders. Business firms also hastened to replenish their inventories and to make net additions to them. Only later, toward the end of 1950, did the rise of government expenditures for military purposes add its inflationary effects to the rise in private spending. Much of this latter increase was financed by sales of liquid assets, decreases in holdings of idle money balances, and expansions of credit. The velocity of money increased appreciably, redemptions of savings bonds rose, consumer credit expanded, and business loans increased markedly. Between May, 1950 and March, 1951, the cost of living rose 8 percent, and wholesale prices 19 percent. During the rest of 1951, price levels remained relatively constant, the cost of living rising slightly and wholesale prices declining a little.

With the resurgence of inflation, the controversy between the Federal Reserve and the Treasury flared anew. The Federal Reserve wanted to restrict credit to curb the rise of prices, while the Treasury insisted that it continue to hold interest rates at an inflexibly low level. This controversy had begun to develop even before the Korean outbreak. Foreseeing a possible revival of inflation, the Federal Reserve had on two occasions—one late in 1949 and the other early in 1950—requested the Treasury to postpone public announcement of rates on its future short-term issues in order to see whether a rise in rates might be in order. On both occasions, the Treasury responded by announcing immediately that the forthcoming issues would bear yields no higher than those currently being maintained in the market. And, on both occasions, the Federal Reserve obediently continued to hold market rates in line with those on the new Treasury issues. But in August, 1950, the controversy came out into the open and the Federal Reserve publicly defied the Treasury. On the same day and at almost the same hour the two issued conflicting public announcements. The Federal Open Market Committee announced the System's determination to fight the current inflation and to use all its powers to this end. At the same time, the Treasury announced a new $13 billion issue of short-term securities with yields no higher than those currently prevailing in the market. Despite this Treasury challenge, the Federal Reserve proceeded to tighten credit. To prevent the Treasury's financing from failing, the System purchased most of the new issue at the yields fixed by the Treasury. Then it sold some of its other holdings in the market on terms that raised the market yields of short-term obligations. It also raised its discount rates from $1\frac{1}{2}$ to $1\frac{3}{4}$ percent. This controversy in 1950 related only to short-term issues; the Federal Reserve continued to prevent the prices of long-term government bonds from falling below par.

In early 1951, the controversy spread to the prices and yields on long-term Treasury bonds. A major reason for the Federal Reserve's rebellion was its fear that its other attempts to contain inflation would be ineffective as long as it had to peg the prices of these securities. In January it raised member-bank reserve requirements against demand deposits by 2 percent. Acting under new congressional authorization, it reimposed selective controls on consumer credit and imposed a similar selective regulation on credit for residential construction. It also encouraged commercial banks, insurance companies, savings banks, and some other financial institutions to enter into a voluntary credit-restraint program to prevent or lessen the extension of credit for "nonessential" purposes. But Federal Reserve officials doubted that these measures alone could stop the inflation. The policy of pegging Treasury bond prices at par would have to end.

In early 1951, the conflict between the Federal Reserve and the Treasury became dramatic. In January, the Secretary of the Treasury publicly announced that, during the defense period, all the government's issues of marketable securities (for new money as well as for refunding purposes) would bear interest rates no higher than $2\frac{1}{2}$ percent. He also implied, without stating it specifically, that the Federal Reserve had agreed to this policy. Reserve officials denied that this was true. The President and the Council of Economic Advisers then entered the dispute to support the Treasury position. After a White House conference with Federal Reserve officials, the President publicly announced that the Federal Reserve had, in effect, agreed to the Treasury's announced policy. This the Federal Reserve publicly denied. Now that the controversy was common knowledge and involved the President himself, it became a hotly debated issue in Congress, in the newspapers, and in financial circles. The Board of Governors finally informed the Treasury that, as of February 19, it was no longer willing to maintain the existing situation in the government-securities market. After further negotiations, the Treasury and the Federal Reserve jointly announced on March 4, 1951, their now-famous "accord":

> The Treasury and the Federal Reserve System have reached full accord with respect to debt-management and monetary policies to be pursued in furthering their common purpose to assure the successful financing of the Government's requirements and, at the same time, to minimize monetization of the public debt.

The Treasury–Federal Reserve accord of March 4, 1951 stands as a landmark in American monetary history, because it marked the end of inflexible pegging of the prices of Treasury obligations. Nine years after it had first adopted the policy in March, 1942, the Federal Reserve had finally regained at least some freedom to refrain from purchasing all securities offered to it, to limit its creation of bank reserves, and to restrict credit when necessary to prevent inflation. To the extent that it was freed from the task of supporting Treasury operations, it could now direct them more toward promoting economic stability.

Selected readings

Brown, A. J., *The Great Inflation, 1939–1951*, London, Oxford, 1955.
Chandler, L. V., *Inflation in the United States, 1940–1948*, New York, Harper & Row, 1951.
Fforde, J. S., *The Federal Reserve System, 1945–1949*, London, Oxford, 1954.
U.S. Congress, Joint Committee on the Economic Report:
  Subcommittee on Monetary, *Credit and Fiscal Policies, Report,* 1950.
  Statements on Monetary, Credit, and Fiscal Policies, 1949.
  Subcommittee on General Credit Control and Debt Management, *Monetary Policy and Management of the Public Debt,* 1952.
  (All published by U.S. Government Printing Office, Washington, D.C.)

CHAPTER 25

MONETARY POLICY, 1951–1959

Although the Treasury–Federal Reserve accord of March, 1951 freed Federal Reserve officials from the shackles of an unflexible pegging policy and gave them greater latitude to develop new policy patterns, it did not provide them with new patterns. Reserve officials now faced the task of developing new policy objectives and guides and new patterns of policy implementation. They were not hampered by any lack of power to expand or contract the supply of money and credit. Holding more than $21 billion of gold certificates and having actual reserve ratios nearly double the required level, the Reserve banks had ample capacity to expand money and credit whenever that might be appropriate. Their holdings of more than $22 billion of government securities at a time when total member-bank reserves were about $19 billion provided them with more than adequate power to restrict. Their problem was not a lack of power; it was rather a problem of deciding how and for what purposes to use their power. We shall highlight three of their major problems: (1) interpretation and implementation of the Employment Act of 1946, (2) determining the relationships of monetary policies to the management of the national debt, and (3) reassessment of the relative roles of their policy instruments.

THE EMPLOYMENT ACT OF 1946

This Act was an outstanding landmark in the history of American economic policies because it was the first time the federal government assumed the responsibility of using its powers and those of its agencies to promote "maximum employment, production, and purchasing power." Both the Act itself and its legislative history clearly established that the nation had become more intolerant of unemployment than it had ever been before. The passing of the Act also demonstrated to Federal Reserve officials that they were expected to participate in the fight against unemployment. However, the Act neither defined its economic objectives in operational terms nor prescribed methods of implementation. These items were not incorporated in the Act—but left for later resolution—because they required decisions that could only be based on more extensive experience. For example, the Act did not define "maximum employment." That this did not mean literally a zero rate of unemployment was indicated by the defeat of a proposal to include in the Act the term "full employment." Thus, the general objective was to keep unemployment to a "feasible minimum." Some economists thought this would be about 5 percent of the labor force, but others set it at lower levels.

The Act did not specifically refer to the behavior of price levels. However, it became increasingly clear that the nation had developed less tolerance for price inflation. After 12 years of price increases that had raised the cost of living nearly 90 percent, the nation wanted a higher degree of price stability. The Act was never amended to include this objective, but federal officials inserted it by interpretation. By the mid-1950s, they included among their stated objectives that of promoting "relative stability of the price level" or "relative stability of the purchasing power of the dollar."

The Act did not specifically mention the objective of promoting real economic growth, although this may have been implied by the term "maximum employment and production." As the nation became increasingly conscious of its growth potential, this objective was given greater emphasis, and Federal Reserve officials included among their stated objectives the goal of promoting "the highest sustainable rate of economic growth."

Thus, Federal Reserve officials often stated that their stabilization responsibilities were "to promote continuously high levels of employment, the highest sustainable rate of economic growth, and relative stability of the purchasing power of the dollar." It soon became evident that these are not always fully compatible.

Both the Employment Act and its legislative history indicated that monetary and fiscal policies together were to be used to promote the objectives of the Act, but neither the Act nor its history indicated the relative roles of monetary and fiscal actions in the "policy mix." Some officials expected that prime reliance would be placed on flexible and timely adjustments of government expenditure and tax policies, with monetary policies in a largely supporting role. Others would reverse the roles. The years following the Act demonstrated that both types of policies were used, but often with a large part of the burden falling on monetary policy.

MONETARY AND DEBT-MANAGEMENT POLICIES

During the period of pegging before March, 1951, the Federal Reserve entered the government-securities market for two principal purposes: (1) to stabilize the prices of securities that were already outstanding, and (2) to assist the Treasury in selling new issues, whether these were to secure new money to cover current deficits or to pay off maturing issues. For the latter purpose, the Federal Reserve frequently purchased a part of a new issue that others were not willing to buy at the yield rates fixed by the Treasury, and it sometimes bought oustanding issues of comparable maturities to "make room in the market" for the new Treasury issue.

The immediate purpose of the Federal Reserve at the time of the accord was not to withdraw completely from the government-securities market and leave both the prices of outstanding Treasury obligations and current Treasury-financing operations completely on their own. To withdraw support completely and abruptly after such a long period of pegging would have been both impossible and undesirable. Erratic, and perhaps even panicky, declines in the prices of outstanding securities would not only injure holders and jeopardize the future marketability of new long-term issues, but might also disturb the markets for private obligations and upset economic stability. Nor could the Federal Reserve immediately withdraw all support of Treasury financing operations. To permit a new issue to fail and perhaps force the Treasury to default on a part of the national debt was unthinkable. The Federal Reserve's immediate purpose, therefore, was merely to secure somewhat greater flexibility—to permit the prices and yields of outstanding government securities to vary more widely and to induce the Treasury to put more realistic yields on its new issues and to rely less heavily on Federal Reserve support. However, its longer-run purpose was to work toward a situation in which its open-market policies would be shaped almost exclusively by economic-stabilization objectives, and its purchases and sales would again be directed exclusively toward regulating the reserve position of the banking system rather than toward directly influencing the prices of Treasury obligations, new or old.

With respect to oustanding government securities, Federal Reserve policy for some time immediately following the abandonment of pegging was to "maintain an orderly market." Federal Reserve officials insisted that this did not mean that they would limit the extent to which the prices of these securities would be permitted to decline if the price decline was consistent with the attainment of other

Federal Reserve objectives. It meant only that they would assist in keeping these adjustments "orderly" rather than "erratic" or "disorderly." The System then shifted to a policy of "preventing a disorderly market." This was not merely an exercise in semantics; it indicated a greater Federal Reserve tolerance of fluctuations in the prices of government securities, a lessened readiness to intervene to influence these prices directly, and a greater reliance on private purchasers and sellers to maintain "orderly" conditions. By the spring of 1953, the Federal Reserve had arrived at a new rule that would "normally" or "ordinarily" guide its open-market operations: It would not buy or sell longer-term Treasury obligations (those with maturities of more than a year), but would confine its operations to short maturities, preferably Treasury bills. This has come to be known popularly as "the bills-only doctrine." The Federal Reserve also decided that thereafter it would not ordinarily engage in "swap operations," buying some maturities to raise their prices or to limit their price declines and selling others.

Federal Reserve officials had several closely related reasons for wanting to stay out of the market for long-term obligations and for confining their operations to bills and other short maturities where the direct effects of their purchases and sales on the prices of the securities would be much smaller.

1. They undoubtedly feared that if they continued to operate in the long-term market, they might again be shackled by an inflexible pegging policy. A policy of pegging prices inflexibly at some point below par could be almost as shackling as pegging at par.

2. They wished to avoid possible charges that their sales of long-term securities, or even their refusal to buy them, had unfairly imposed losses on holders.

3. The reason stressed most by Federal Reserve officials was their desire to create conditions in which private buyers and sellers would themselves develop an orderly and self-reliant market. They argued that as long as private operators in this market expected Federal Reserve intervention, they would not perform the ordinary security-market functions of taking speculative positions, buying when they thought prices were too low, selling short when they thought prices were too high, and arbitraging among the various issues to establish reasonable yield relationships. It was hoped that, after the Federal Reserve's withdrawal from the long-term market, private operators would themselves develop a "broad, deep, and resilient market."

The ability of the Federal Reserve to withdraw its support from current Treasury-financing operations depended to a great extent on the attitudes and policies of the Treasury. If the latter persisted in fixing low rates on its issues, the Federal Reserve would either have to support them or risk being blamed for the failure of Treasury financing. In fact, however, the Treasury gradually adjusted its financing policies to the current monetary policies of the Federal Reserve and conscientiously tried to make the yields and other terms on its new issues such that they could be sold without Federal Reserve support. The Treasury's cooperation was sufficient to enable the Federal Reserve to adopt two more rules by the spring of 1953: Ordinarily it would not buy any part of a new issue at the time of sale, and it would not at that time buy any outstanding issue of comparable maturity.[1]

Thus, by the spring of 1953, the Federal Reserve had moved far from its policies during the period before March, 1951, and had developed four rules that would "ordinarily" or "normally" be followed:

1. It would not deal in securities with maturities in excess of a year and would confine its open-market operations to short maturities, preferably bills.
2. It would not engage in swap operations.
3. It would not buy any new Treasury issue at the time of offering.
4. At the time of a new Treasury issue, it would not buy any outstanding securities of comparable maturity.

The Federal Reserve departed from these "normal" rules only twice during the first five years after their adoption. The first deviation occurred in late 1955, when the System was following a restrictive policy and the Treasury offered a large new issue with a maturity in excess of a year. The Treasury believed the issue had been made sufficiently attractive to enable all of it to be sold to private purchasers, but it soon became apparent that some of the issue would remain unsold. The Federal Reserve thereupon violated three of its rules all at once: It bought some of the new, longer-term issue and then sold some of its holdings of other maturities to mop up the reserves created by its purchases. The second departure occurred in July, 1958 after the dispatch of American troops to Lebanon following the revolution in Iraq. The prices of long-term government securities, including prices on a recent issue, declined. Moreover, the Treasury had just announced a new issue, which was not attracting purchasers in sufficient volume. The Federal Reserve intervened to purchase some of the outstanding longer-term issue and some of the new issue. To mop up the reserves created by these purchases, it sold other maturities out of its portfolio.

These exceptions highlight two points. The fact that there were only two exceptions to the "normal" rules in over five years indicates how far the Federal Reserve had moved away from the policies it had followed before March, 1951. It also indicates how far the Treasury, in its debt-management policies, was willing to depart from its old objective of borrowing at continuously low interest rates and to move toward adjusting its policies to the economic-stabilization policies of the Federal Reserve. But these exceptions also highlight the fact that Federal Reserve policies cannot completely ignore federal debt management and that the problems of reconciling debt-management and Federal Reserve policies directed toward economic stabilization could become even more serious in the future. It is not hard to imagine situations in which restrictive Federal Reserve policies to combat inflation might be seriously hampered by an unsympathetic Secretary of the Treasury faced with the problem of selling large new issues to meet maturing obligations and to cover current deficits.

[1] This was not interpreted as preventing the Federal Reserve from taking a part of a new issue in exchange for its holdings of a maturing issue.

As we shall see later, the Federal Reserve abandoned the bills-only policy in 1961.

RELATIVE ROLES OF FEDERAL RESERVE POLICY INSTRUMENTS

One reason for the need to reconsider the relative roles of the principal Federal Reserve policy instruments was the virtual disappearance of Federal Reserve lending to member banks during the preceding 17 years. From 1934 to World War II, member banks were so swamped with excess reserves that only a very few banks had any need to borrow. After that time, most members had adjusted their reserve positions through buying and selling government securities. Many bankers, especially younger bankers, had never applied for a loan and knew little or nothing about Federal Reserve lending policies. Moreover, Federal Reserve officials were by now inexperienced in the use of this instrument and needed to reconsider the whole problem of discount policy and discount rates.

Attitudes toward revival of Federal Reserve discounting varied widely. At one extreme, a minority favored not only reviving discounting, but also raising its relative importance to the level it had enjoyed in the 1920s. At the other extreme, some people advocated the complete elimination of discounting, considering it to be a "slippage" that decreased the accuracy of Federal Reserve control over the volume of member-bank reserves. The outcome was a compromise. Member banks were permitted to borrow, but normally for only limited periods and only to meet such reserve needs as the banks could not reasonably be expected to meet from other sources.

Open-market operations in government securities emerged as the most important policy instrument. The Federal Reserve retained its power to alter member-bank reserve requirements, but it used this power only infrequently.

Let us now see how the Federal Reserve used the greater flexibility of action that it regained in March, 1951.

FEDERAL RESERVE POLICIES, MARCH, 1951 TO THE SPRING OF 1953

The rise of prices initiated by the Korean conflict ended in March, 1951, with the cost of living up 8 percent and wholesale prices up 19 percent from their levels prior to the outbreak. There followed a period of more than four years of relative price stability. In mid-1955, the consumer price index was only 3 percent above its level in March, 1951. The wholesale price index actually declined 6 percent. This reflected a fall in the prices of farm products that more than counterbalanced a rise in other wholesale prices. The period up to early 1953 was one of high production and employment. GNP rose from $329 billion in 1951 to $347 billion in 1952, and to an annual rate of $369 billion in the second quarter of 1953. Unemployment was at a minimum. Out of a total labor force of more than 66 million, unemployment averaged only 1.9 million in 1951 and 1.7 million in 1952. In the spring of 1953, it fell to the extraordinarily low level of 1.3 million.

Under these conditions, the Federal Reserve allowed interest rates to rise somewhat during the remainder of 1951 and in 1952. It took no action to reduce the volume of bank reserves, but as the demand for bank credit rose, it did not supply additional reserves by purchasing government securities. As a result, the excess reserves of member banks declined somewhat, and in 1952 member-bank borrowings were often above $1 billion, and, at times, rose to $1.5 billion. The prices of long-term government securities were about 4 percent below par by the end of 1952.

By early 1953, Federal Reserve officials began to fear a resumption of inflation. Prices had not begun to rise, but the economy was already operating at close to capacity levels, unemployment was at a minimum, demand was still rising, and Federal Reserve officials thought they detected a speculative building up of inventories. They therefore intensified their restrictive policy. For one thing, they allowed current gold exports and a reduction of Federal Reserve float to lower member-bank reserves by about $1 billion. Member-bank borrowings were kept above $1.2 billion during the first four months of the year. In January, the discount rate was raised from 1¾ to 2 percent, its highest level since 1934. Interest rates rose to their highest levels in 20 years and the prices of long-term Treasury obligations fell about 10 percent below par. Credit stringency became severe as expectations of still tighter money and even higher interest rates led lenders to withhold funds and borrowers to rush in to anticipate their future needs. In May, 1953, the Federal Reserve began to ease the situation. It now became evident that the immediate danger was not inflation, but recession.

EASY MONEY, 1953 TO 1954

The recession of 1953 to 1954 was short and relatively mild. GNP, at annual rates, declined from $369 billion in the second quarter of 1953 to $359 billion in the third quarter of 1954, a drop of 3 percent. This decline was entirely accounted for by a shift from inventory accumulation in early 1953 to inventory decumulation, and by an $11 billion decrease in federal expenditures for national security purposes. Other demands for output held up very well, and consumption expenditures actually rose about $4 billion. The latter was due, at least in part, to a $5 billion tax reduction at the beginning of 1954, and to the automatic decrease of tax collections and the automatic rise of transfer payments in response to the fall of GNP. The number of unemployed rose above its extraordinarily low level of 1.3 million in the spring of 1953, but it did not quite reach 3.5 million, or 5 percent of the labor force.

The Federal Reserve used all its major instruments to ease credit and to combat the recession. Early in May, 1953, it began to buy short-term government securities in the open market; by the end of June it had increased its holdings by nearly $1 billion. Although this action enabled banks to reduce their borrowings and to increase their excess reserves, it did not succeed immediately in lowering interest rates. This failure was, at least in part, because the financial community did not believe that the Federal Reserve had really reversed its tight-money policy and was working toward easier credit conditions. Open-market purchases had not proved to be an effective means of announcing the change of policy. It was partly for this purpose that the Board of Governors reduced member-bank reserve requirements against demand deposits at the beginning of July. Requirements against these deposits at central reserve city banks were decreased by 2 percent, and those at other member banks by 1 percent. This freed about $1.2 billion of reserves. The System then bought an additional $500 million of government securities, bringing the total increase since April to $1.5 billion.

The combined effect of these actions was to ease member-bank reserve positions markedly. By November, 1953, member-bank borrowings had fallen from their high level of about $1.2 billion in the early months of the year to about $500 million; excess reserves had risen from around $500 million to $700 million. In February, 1954, all the Reserve banks lowered their discount rates from 2 to 1¾ percent and in April reduced them to 1½ percent.

In June and July, 1954, the Board again lowered member-bank reserve requirements. This time it reduced requirements against time deposits by 1 percent and requirements against demand deposits by 2 percent in central reserve cities and 1 percent at other member banks. This freed more than $1.5 billion of reserves. Simultaneously, however, the Federal Reserve absorbed about $1 billion of these released funds by selling government securities.

By mid-1954 credit conditions were very easy. Member-bank borrowings were less than $200 million, and excess reserves were above $800 million. The money supply had risen about $3 billion during the preceding year. It rose another $6 billion during the latter half of 1954. Interest rates, which had fallen during 1953, declined still further. The yield on Treasury bills fell below ¾ percent. The prices of long-term government securities again rose above par.

This easy-money policy almost certainly helped shorten the recession, reduce its severity, and hasten recovery. It was especially helpful in stimulating residential construction. Expenditures for this purpose, which had been $11.1 billion in 1952 and $11.9 billion in 1953, rose to annual rates of $14 billion in the third quarter of 1954 and $15.9 billion in the first quarter of 1955.

Some Federal Reserve officials later wondered whether they had not eased credit too much, continued the easy-money policy too long, and provided both the public and the banking system with too much liquidity. Between the initiation of the easy-money policy in May, 1953, and the end of 1954, the public's money supply increased from $125 billion to $134 billion, a rise of 7.2 percent. Commercial banks were also put in a much more liquid condition. For one thing, they had been enabled to reduce their borrowings from $1.2 billion to $400 million and to increase their excess reserves from $500 million to $800 million. In addition to these improvements, they had increased their holdings of government securities by more than $10 billion, and many of these were short-term obligations that could be sold quickly and with little loss by the banks. This greatly enhanced liquidity of both the public and the banks contributed to the subsequent rise of spending and prices. But it does not necessarily follow that the policies of 1953 to 1954 were too easy and too prolonged. Perhaps the error was in not moving more aggressively as business recovery approached an inflationary stage.

TIGHT MONEY, 1955 TO 1957

The recession reached its trough in the second quarter of 1954, and was followed first by recovery and then by a boom that culminated in the third quarter of 1957. During this three-year period, GNP at current prices rose $86.7 billion, or 24.2 percent. Unemployment, which was about 3.4 million in mid-1954, averaged 2.6 million in 1955 and 1956 and fluctuated around this level during the first 10 months of 1957. This represented less than 4 percent of the labor force.

Table 25–1 shows that increases in all the major categories of spendings for output contributed to the rise of GNP. In view of the widespread complaints

Table 25–1 GNP and its components, 1954–1957 (at annual rates in billions of dollars)

	SECOND QUARTER, 1954		1955		1956		THIRD QUARTER, 1957
Total GNP	$358.9		$397.5		$419.2		$445.6
Personal consumption	236.5		256.9		269.4		288.3
Gross private domestic investment	47.2		63.8		68.2		66.7
Net foreign investment	— 0.4		— 0.4		1.3		3.6
Government purchases of goods and services, total	75.5		77.1		80.3		87.0
Federal	48.3		46.8	47.1		50.9	
State and local	27.3		30.3	33.1		36.1	

SOURCE: *Survey of Current Business,* July, 1958, pp. 5, 15.

against the Federal Reserve's "excessively restrictive" credit policy, it is interesting to note that expenditures for gross private domestic-investment purposes rose more than 40 percent during the three years following the third quarter of 1954, and that state and local expenditures, some of which were financed with borrowed money, rose 32 percent. Investable funds became "scarce," not because their supply was reduced, but because the demand for them increased markedly.

Prices remained stable until mid-1955 and then began to rise, slowly at first, and then more rapidly. By October, 1957, consumer prices had risen 5.6 percent and wholesale prices 6.6 percent.

The Federal Reserve began to reduce the degree of credit ease as business activity started upward in the latter part of 1954, and then permitted tighter credit conditions to develop during the period from early 1955 to November, 1957. Its policy during this period may be characterized as almost purely defensive rather than aggressive. That is, it did not attempt to reduce the money supply despite the fact that the latter had risen more than 7 percent in the year and a half preceding 1955. Instead, it merely held the money supply approximately constant, and refused to allow it to expand in response to increases in the demand for it. The 24 percent rise of GNP expenditures was financed almost entirely by an increase in the income velocity of money. And the rise of interest rates was due largely to the sharp rise in the demand for investable funds while the money supply was not permitted to rise significantly.

Let us now see more specifically what the Federal Reserve did during this period. It did not raise member-bank reserve requirements at all. Its most aggressive action was in the first part of 1955, when it sold over $1 billion of government securities, thereby forcing the banks to borrow more heavily and to draw down their excess reserves in order to support the existing money supply. Member-bank borrowings, which had averaged less than $200 million for several months after July, 1954, averaged about $800 million during this period. In the last part of the period, they were close to $1 billion. And the excess reserves of member banks fell from $800 million to about $500 million. Federal Reserve discount rates, which had been lowered to $1\frac{1}{2}$ percent in April, 1954, were raised to $1\frac{3}{4}$ percent in April, 1955, and then in six more steps to $3\frac{1}{2}$ percent. The last increase, which occurred in August, 1957, brought these rates to their highest level since 1932.

This combination of a defensive Federal Reserve policy and the investment boom, which greatly increased the demand for investable funds, raised market rates of interest to their highest levels in 25 years.

We have already seen that these increases in interest rates did not prevent investment expenditures from rising more than 40 percent, that Federal Reserve policies did not prevent total expenditures for output from rising 24 percent, and that they did not prevent the cost of living from rising 5.6 percent and wholesale prices 6.6 percent. Does this prove, as some economists have asserted, that monetary policy cannot stop inflation? We shall not at this point speculate on the probable effects of a more aggressively restrictive policy, but a few comments on the actual events and policies of the period may be enlightening. In the first place, one should not expect a rise of interest rates to prevent a rise of investment expenditures when the rise of rates is itself produced by an upward shift of the investment-demand schedule. The marginal-efficiency-of-investment schedule undoubtedly shifted sharply upward during this period, so that spenders for investment purposes were willing to spend much more at each level of interest rates or to spend the same amounts at much higher levels of interest rates. An actual rise of investment expenditures could have been prevented only by a sharp decrease in the supply of investable funds at each interest rate, and this did not occur.

In the second place, it would be unreasonable to expect that a policy of holding the money supply stable in the face of a sharp rise of investment-demand schedules would succeed in preventing a rise of either investment spending or GNP. An induced rise of interest rates and the apparent "scarcity" of money almost inevitably lead some members of the community to find ways of "economizing" on their money balances—of holding smaller balances relative to their expenditures. This is especially true if the community enters the boom period with abnormally large balances relative to its current expenditures.

In short, a purely defensive policy of holding the money supply constant should not ordinarily be expected to prevent actual increases of investment expenditures and GNP in the face of upward shifts of investment-demand schedules, because the induced rise of interest rates will lead to an economizing of money balances relative to expenditures—to a rise of expenditures relative to money balances. But, in principle at least, the Federal Reserve could have reduced the money supply enough to offset any unwanted effects of increases in the income velocity of money.

EASY MONEY, NOVEMBER, 1957 TO JULY, 1958

In November, 1957, the Federal Reserve relaxed its restrictive policy and again moved toward credit ease. For several months, the various economic indicators had presented a confusing patterns. Several indicators suggested a continuance of the boom and of price increases. GNP had increased from quarter to quarter, unemployment in October was at its lowest level in many months, and both the consumer price index and the wholesale index set a new high record almost every month. On the other hand, several indicators suggested that the boom was losing its vigor and might soon give way to recession. Industrial production had been falling for several months. The rate of growth of GNP was declining, as also was the rate of price increases. Late in the autumn, both official and private surveys revealed that business expenditures for plant and equipment, which had been at unprecedented levels in 1956 and the first three quarters of 1957, would begin to decline in the fourth quarter and would continue to fall through 1958.

The boom reached its peak in the third quarter of 1957 and gave way to recession. By the first quarter of 1958, GNP had fallen nearly $20 billion, or about 4.5 percent. This decline was slightly greater than those in the recessions of 1949 and 1953 to 1954. Unemployment, which had been 2.5 million in October, averaged above 5.1 million in the first quarter of 1958. Changes in business-inventory policies were a major contributor to the recession. In the third quarter of 1957, business was adding to its inventories at an annual rate of $2.2 billion; in the first quarter of 1958 it reduced its inventories at an annual rate of $9.5 billion. This shift accounted for $11.7 billion of the decline of GNP. But as so often happens, the shift in business-inventory policy was induced at least in part by more basic changes in the economy. For one thing, the predicted decline of business expenditures for plant and equipment began. For another, federal-procurement policies in the autumn shifted expectations. Perhaps partly to combat inflation, but more for the purpose of holding its expenditures within the total budgeted for the fiscal year and to avoid raising the debt limit, the federal government sharply reduced its new orders for military equipment, reduced its progress payments for military equipment in process of production, and suggested to many firms that they stretch out their production over a longer period. Moreover, net foreign investment fell, largely because of a decrease in the foreign demand for United States exports. Personal-consumption expenditures held up remarkably well, declining less than 1 percent. This was in large part because of the automatic decline of tax liabilities and the automatic rise of unemployment compensation and other transfer payments that bolstered disposable personal incomes. (Table 25–2.)

Table 25–2 GNP and its components, 1957–1958 (seasonally adjusted annual rates, in billions of dollars)

	THIRD QUARTER, 1957	FIRST QUARTER, 1958	CHANGE, THIRD QUARTER, 1957– FIRST QUARTER, 1958
Total GNP	$445.6	$425.8	−$19.8
Personal consumption	288.3	286.2	− 2.1
Gross private domestic investment	66.7	49.6	− 17.1
Residential construction (nonfarm)	$16.9	$17.1	+$ 0.2
Other construction	19.7	19.2	− 0.5
Producers' durable equipment	28.0	22.9	− 5.1
Net change in business inventories	2.2	− 9.5	− 11.7
Net foreign investment	$ 3.6	$ 0.5	−$ 3.1
Government purchases of goods and services	87.0	89.5	+ 2.5
Federal	$50.9	$50.9	..
State and local	36.1	38.6	+ 2.5

It was under these conditions that the Federal Reserve relaxed credit restriction and moved toward easy money. In October, 1957, its open-market policy was designed to avoid a further tightening of the market and to ease it slightly. The first decisive move came in mid-November, when discount rates were reduced from 3½ to 3 percent. Market rates of interest, and especially long-term rates, immediately fell sharply. The Open Market Committee cautiously purchased government securities to enable banks to reduce their borrowings and increase their excess reserves, as is shown in Table 25–3.

In February, March, and April, the Board of Governors lowered member-bank reserve requirements against demand deposits in several steps. The total reductions were 2 percent for central reserve city banks, 1½ for reserve city banks, and 1 for country banks. The effect was to lower required reserves by about $1.4 billion. These actions, together with those in the open market, enabled member banks to reduce their borrowings and to increase their excess reserves. By March, their excess reserves exceeded their borrowings by nearly $500 million, almost the reverse of the situation during the period of credit restriction. The Reserve banks lowered their discount rates three more times, bringing them down to 1¾ percent in mid-April.

These liberalizing Federal Reserve actions were accompanied by a sharp decline of short-term interest rates. The yield on Treasury bills, which had averaged about 3.6 percent in October, had fallen well below 1 percent by May.

Table 25–3 Member-bank borrowings and excess reserves, 1957–1958 (averages of daily figures in millions of dollars)

	BORROWINGS	EXCESS RESERVES	NET BORROWED RESERVES (MEMBER-BANK BORROWINGS MINUS EXCESS RESERVES)	NET FREE RESERVES (EXCESS RESERVES MINUS BORROWINGS)
July, 1957	$ 917	$534	$383	
August	1,005	534	471	
September	988	522	466	
October	811	467	344	
November	804	512	292	
December	710	577	133	
January, 1958	451	573		$122
February	242	567		325
March	138	633		495
April	130	623		493
May	119	666		547

SOURCE: *Federal Reserve Bulletin,* various issues.

Long-term rates proved less responsive. After dropping sharply immediately after the first reduction of discount rates in mid-November, they began to drift downward much more slowly, and by May had begun to rise. The very easy conditions prevailing in the short-term credit market were not evident in the long-term market, for several reasons. One was the extraordinarily large volume of new, long-term bond issues. State and local governments borrowed heavily, both to finance current expenditures and to retire short-term debt issued during the period of high interest rates. So did corporations. The federal government also floated several long-term issues, primarily to retire short-term debt. This became a highly controversial matter, for many believe that, in periods of recession, the Treasury should borrow only on short-term obligations and should refrain from issuing long-term securities that would compete with private long-term issues and tend to decrease the availability and increase the cost of long-term credit for private investment. These heavy borrowings in the long-term market while short-term loans were being repaid help to explain the disparity in the behavior of short-term and long-term interest rates. Some observers insisted that this was an occasion when the Federal Reserve should have abandoned the bills-only doctrine and bought long-term securities. A majority of Federal Reserve officials rejected this view.

TIGHT MONEY AGAIN, 1958 TO 1959

The recession that started in the third quarter of 1957 proved to be shorter than many economists had expected, and it reached its low point in April, 1958. The economy then began a recovery that continued until the second quarter of 1960.

GNP had risen 13 percent by the fourth quarter of 1959, and 17 percent by the second quarter of 1960. However, this proved to be the weakest recovery in the postwar period. Demands for output and actual output failed to rise as fast as the productive capacity of the economy. Unemployment, which had claimed 7.4 percent of the labor force in February, 1958, did decline to 4.9 percent by mid-1959, but thereafter climbed to some degree. During the last half of 1959 and first half of 1960, it averaged 5.5 percent. (Table 25–4.)

Table 25–4 GNP of the United States during selected periods, 1958–1960 (billions of dollars at annual rates)

	FIRST QUARTER, 1958	FOURTH QUARTER, 1959	FIRST QUARTER, 1960	SECOND QUARTER, 1960	THIRD QUARTER, 1960
Total GNP	$432.9	$488.5	$501.7	$504.8	$503.7
Personal consumption	287.4	318.8	323.9	329.9	329.8
Gross private domestic investment	53.9	73.2	79.1	73.5	70.3
Net exports of goods and services	1.7	.0	1.4	2.4	2.8
Government purchases	89.8	96.5	97.2	99.0	100.8

Thus, this "prosperity" period was characterized by a level of unemployment comparable to the levels that prevailed during the recessions of 1949 and 1954. There were widespread complaints about the slow rate of economic growth in the United States relative to growth rates abroad. The weakness of the recovery was reflected in stability of prices. The wholesale price index did not rise, and the consumer price index rose only 1.5 percent from early 1958 to the end of 1959. Nevertheless, fears of inflation were widespread. The almost uninterrupted rise of prices for nearly 20 years and the failure of prices to decline in the 1957 to 1958 recession convinced many that we were in danger of adopting inflation as a way of life.

It was largely because of fear of inflation that the Federal Reserve abandoned its easy-money policy in May, 1958 and initiated a restrictive policy that was to permit interest rates to rise to their highest levels in 30 years. By December, 1959, when rates reached their peak, yields on 3-month Treasury bills were around $4\frac{1}{2}$ percent; those on 9- to 12-month Treasury issues, about 5 percent; and those on long-term federal issues, about 4.27 percent. In broad outline, Federal Reserve policy during this period was quite similar to that during the 1955 to 1957 boom. The Federal Reserve did not attempt to reduce the money supply; it only followed a policy of "leaning against the wind," of preventing the money supply from increasing in response to the rising demand for money balances. Large gold outflows of about $2.6 billion between the end of April, 1958 and the end of 1959 tended to reduce bank reserves. A large part, but not all, of these reserve losses were offset by Federal Reserve purchases of securities. As shown in Table 25–5,

Table 25–5 Reserve positions of all member banks on selected dates, 1958–1960 (millions of dollars)

PERIOD	TOTAL RESERVES HELD	REQUIRED RESERVES	EXCESS RESERVES	MEMBER-BANK BORROWINGS AT THE FEDERAL RESERVE	NET FREE RESERVES
April, 1958	$18,394	$17,772	$623	$130	$493
May, 1958	18,194	17,543	651	119	532
August, 1958	18,580	17,946	635	252	383
November, 1958	18,540	18,034	506	486	20
March, 1959	18,429	17,968	460	601	− 140
May, 1959	18,580	18,132	448	767	− 318
September, 1959	18,593	18,183	410	903	− 493
December, 1959	18,932	18,450	482	906	− 424
January, 1960	18,878	18,334	544	905	− 361
February, 1960	18,213	17,758	455	816	− 361
March, 1960	18,027	17,611	416	635	− 219

SOURCE: *Federal Reserve Bulletin,* various issues.

total member-bank reserves remained almost unchanged during the period. However, banks were able to maintain their reserves at this level only by markedly increasing their borrowings from the Federal Reserve from about $119 million in May, 1958 to more than $900 million in the last part of 1959. The free-reserve position of banks also changed markedly. In April to May, 1958, banks had net free reserves of about $500 million. By the last part of 1959, the decline of their excess reserves and increase of their borrowings from the Federal Reserve put banks in a position of having net borrowed reserves of more than $400 million. Such, in broad outline, was the open-market policy of the Federal Reserve. As in the earlier period of restriction, the Federal Reserve did not raise member-bank reserve requirements, but it raised its discount rate four times, elevating it from 1¾ percent in the spring of 1958 to 4 percent in September, 1959.

In the summer of 1958, the Federal Reserve again departed from its "normal" rules for open-market operations, to prevent disorderly declines in the prices of long-term government securities. The market for long-term bonds had shown signs of weakness for several weeks. One reason for this was the very-large volume of long-term government and private issues during the first months of the year as long-term rates fell below what were considered "normal" levels. Another was the almost unexpected and early end of the recession, which led many people to expect higher interest rates in the near future. Still another reason was widespread speculation in a recent long-term issue. Then came the dispatch of United States troops to Lebanon, which led to a sharp decrease in private demands for long-term obligations. On July 18, 1958, the Federal Reserve announced tersely that it would "buy Treasury securities other than short-term securities." This announcement, together with very small purchases of the long-term obligations, was sufficient to restore order in the market, and the Federal Reserve quickly withdrew.

But soon thereafter the Treasury faced current financing problems. It feared that private buyers would not take all of a $13.5 billion, August 1 issue of one-year 1⅝ percent certificates of indebtedness. The Federal Reserve purchased enough of these to assure the success of the issue. At the same time, it sold enough of its other holdings to prevent an easing of the reserve position of the banks. After this episode, it returned to its "normal" rules of open-market operations.

As already indicated, the peak of interest rates was reached around the end of 1959. The Federal Reserve then began a cautious relaxation, largely because of the high level of unemployment. In the summer of 1960, as a new recession loomed, the Federal Reserve began to move more positively toward an easy-money policy. Then it was faced by an unhappy fact: Even the United States could have its freedom of action limited by considerations related to balance-of-payments and international-reserve positions.

CONCLUSIONS

The period of about nine years extending from the Treasury–Federal Reserve accord in March, 1951 until the summer of 1960, when considerations relating to the nation's balance of payments began to influence monetary policy, may be considered to be a "reconversion period" for the Federal Reserve. At the beginning of the period, the Federal Reserve had not followed a restrictive policy in more than 17 years. For more than nine years its overriding objective, which greatly limited its ability to promote other goals, had been to prevent increases of interest rates on long-term government securities. Now it had regained freedom to elevate other objectives and to develop new ways of using its policy instruments. However, conditions at that time were far different from those of the 1920s and early 1930s. One important change was the great growth of the national debt, which could not be ignored completely. Another change was symbolized by the Employment Act of 1946: The nation was now determined not only to avoid serious depressions, but also to maintain continuously "maximum employment, production, and purchasing power."

This chapter has described how the Federal Reserve used its newly regained flexibility of action. It gradually reduced the extent of its direct intervention to stabilize the prices of government securities and to assist in Treasury financing. The two recessions of 1953 to 1954 and 1957 to 1958 were countered with expansionary monetary policies. The booms and threatened inflations of 1952 to 1953, 1955 to 1957, and 1958 to 1959 invoked monetary restriction, which consisted mainly of limiting increases in the money supply in the face of rising demands.

At the end of the 1950s, the stabilization program had been successful in the sense that there had been no major depression in the 15 years following World War II. However, there had also been at least partial failures and problems that threatened to persist and perhaps to become more serious. First, there were the three recessions of 1949, 1954, and 1958. Although these were mild and short by historical standards, they were bitter disappointments to those who had hoped for continuously low unemployment and a continuously high rate of economic growth. A second disappointment was the incompatibility of price stability on the one hand, and low levels of unemployment and high rates of economic growth on the other. Many people had hoped that stability of price levels could be maintained even with unemployment rates as low as 2 or 3 percent. Now they witnessed price increases while the unemployment rate was 4 percent or even higher. This development led to widespread debates concerning the various alleged sources of inflation—demand-pull, cost-push, sellers' inflation, and so on. There also developed growing support for an "incomes policy" or "wage-price guidelines" to supplement policies regulating the behavior of aggregate demand.

Unfortunately, the difficulties that appeared in the 1950s did not end with that decade.

Selected readings

Ahearn, D. S., *Federal Reserve Policy Reappraised, 1951–1959,* New York, Columbia University Press, 1963.

Friedman, M., *Dollars and Deficits,* Englewood Cliffs, N.J., Prentice-Hall, 1968.

U.S. Congress:

Joint Economic Committee, various hearings and reports since 1952 on monetary and fiscal policies.

Senate Committee on Finance,

Investigation of the Financial Condition of the United States, 1958.

(All published by U.S. Government Printing Office, Washington, D.C.)

CHAPTER 26

MONETARY POLICY, 1960–1971

Only twice during its first 45 years was the Federal Reserve impelled to adopt more restrictive or less expansionary policies because of concern about its own reserve position, the nation's balance of payments, or the international reserve position. One of these exceptions occurred in 1920; the other, in 1931. At other times, the United States not only maintained a strong international reserve position but also tended to have a surplus in its overall balance of payments. We have already noted the huge gold inflows in 1915 to 1917 and the further inflows in the early 1920s that concentrated more than 40 percent of the world's monetary gold stock in the United States by 1924; the further inflows in the late 1920s and the first year and a half of the 1930s; the golden avalanche following 1933; and the influx of still more gold between the end of World War II and the end of 1949. On the latter date, the United States held about two-thirds of the world's gold reserves. By this time many people had accepted the hypothesis of a "chronic dollar shortage"—a chronic tendency for the United States to run a surplus in its balance of payments and to gain international reserves at the expense of the rest of the world.

By the autumn of 1960, this era had ended. The United States had a large deficit in its overall balance of payments, its net international reserve position had shrunk, and its ability to prevent a depreciation of the exchange rate on the dollar had become subject to doubt. Its position continued to deteriorate as the United States incurred deficits in its balance of payments during almost every year through 1971, thereby losing international reserves and greatly increasing its short-term liabilities to the rest of the world. This culminated in dramatic actions in August, 1971, which terminated the redeemability of the dollar in gold and other reserve assets and allowed the dollar to depreciate in terms of major foreign currencies.

Thus, since 1959, the United States has had to face new policy questions. What, if anything, should it do to eradicate or decrease the deficit in its balance of payments and to repair its international reserve position? To what extent should its general monetary and fiscal policies be made more restrictive to promote this objective? When this objective conflicts with domestic objectives relating to output and employment, which should take precedence? How and to what extent could the various objectives be made more compatible? Before we describe the nation's answers to such policy questions—a major purpose of this chapter—we will find it useful to survey briefly the behavior of the domestic economy from 1960 to 1971 and to review the various developments in the international monetary situation.

THE DOMESTIC ECONOMY

To describe the principal macroeconomic developments in the American economy since 1959, it will be useful to divide the period into two parts: that prior to mid-1965 and that following mid-1965. The first was characterized by excessive unemployment and sluggish growth; the second, by extensive and prolonged price inflation.

1960 to mid-1965

Starting at about mid-1960, the economy began to slide into a recession, which continued into the first quarter of 1961. The actual decline of GNP was less than 1 percent. However, this small decline of output, together with the continuing growth of the labor force and rising output per man-hour, produced a sharp rise of unemployment. By the fourth quarter of 1960, unemployment had reached 6.5 percent, and it remained at or above this level for over a year. Business activity began to rise again after the first quarter of 1961, but its rate of growth was far too sluggish to match the increase in total productive capacity provided by a growing labor force, continuing advances in technology, and an increasing stock of capital goods. The result, until mid-1965, was a persistence of excess capacity and excessive unemployment. In no year during this period was the unemployment rate as low as 5 percent (see Table 26–1).

During this period there was a clear conflict between the objective of de-

Table 26–1 Average unemployment rates, 1960–mid 1965 (percent of civilian labor force)

YEAR	RATE (PERCENT)
1960	5.6
1961	6.7
1962	5.6
1963	5.7
1964	5.2
1965 (first half)	5.2

SOURCE: *Federal Reserve Bulletin,* various issues.

creasing the deficit in the balance of payments and the desire to increase the rate of real economic growth and lower the unemployment rates.

The period since mid-1965

The relative stability of price levels which had prevailed since 1958, ended soon after America began to expand its involvement in the Vietnam War and in mid-1965. From that time through the end of 1971, prices rose every year. Total increases during the period were about 33 percent in consumer prices and 23 percent in wholesale prices.

In the earlier years of this period, and certainly between mid-1965 and the third quarter of 1968, this was predominantly a demand-pull inflation, which occurred as aggregate money demands for output rose faster than real output could be expanded. During the three years following mid-1965, GNP at current prices rose by $200 billion, or more than 26 percent. As multiplier analysis would suggest, a major part of the increase was contributed by increases in personal consumption expenditures. However, these increases were largely induced by sharp autonomous increases of three other types of demands for output. The largest of these was the rise of expenditures for output by the federal government, which amounted to $35.5 billion, an increase of more than 54 percent, during the three-year period. A major part of the increase was related to the Vietnam War, but other federal expenditures also rose. No significant increase of federal taxes occurred until mid-1968. Expenditures for output by state and local governments also rose sharply, increasing by $32.5 billion, or 47 percent. Thus total government expenditures for output rose nearly $68 billion, or more than 50 percent, in a period of only three years. These increases were augmented until the fourth quarter of 1966 by a sharp increase of private investment for purposes other than residential construction, this increase amounting to nearly $26 billion, or 33 percent. In view of these large and rapid increases of expenditures for output, it is no wonder that prices were pulled upward. (Table 26–2.)

The behavior pattern of demands for output altered somewhat after mid-1968. One reason why is that the federal budget ceased to be a source of further

Table 26–2 GNP and selected components at current prices: annual rates, 1965–1971 (billions of dollars, seasonally adjusted)

| PERIOD | TOTAL GNP | GOVERNMENT PURCHASES OF GOODS AND SERVICES | | | GROSS PRIVATE DOMESTIC INVESTMENT OTHER THAN RESIDENTIAL CONSTRUCTION |
		FEDERAL	STATE AND LOCAL	TOTAL	
1965–1Q	$ 662.8	$ 64.4	$ 67.0	$131.5	$ 77.9
2Q	675.7	65.5	68.9	134.4	78.3
3Q	691.1	67.6	71.3	138.9	81.5
4Q	710.0	70.1	73.2	143.3	85.8
1966–1Q	729.5	72.8	75.2	148.0	90.1
2Q	743.3	75.6	77.7	153.4	96.4
3Q	755.9	80.5	80.1	160.7	94.9
4Q	770.7	82.1	83.0	165.2	104.1
1967–1Q	774.4	87.7	86.5	174.2	92.4
2Q	784.5	90.1	88.2	178.4	87.4
3Q	800.9	91.4	89.9	181.3	92.0
4Q	815.9	93.6	92.9	186.5	94.2
1968–1Q	834.9	96.4	97.2	193.6	91.0
2Q	858.1	98.9	99.4	198.3	96.7
3Q	875.8	100.9	101.4	202.1	96.6
4Q	891.4	101.9	104.7	206.7	100.9
1969–1Q	907.6	100.9	107.5	208.5	103.0
2Q	923.7	99.8	110.1	209.9	105.4
3Q	942.6	102.5	111.6	214.1	112.8
4Q	951.7	102.1	114.2	216.3	109.8
1970–1Q	956.0	100.2	117.1	217.3	101.2
2Q	968.5	96.8	119.7	216.5	104.2
3Q	983.5	96.1	124.0	220.1	109.9
4Q	988.4	95.9	127.9	223.7	104.5
1971–1Q	1,020.8	96.7	131.5	228.2	107.4
2Q	1,040.0	96.0	133.6	229.6	112.9
3Q	1,053.4	97.6	136.2	233.8	108.1
4Q	1,072.9	100.3	140.5	240.8	115.0

increases of total expenditures for output. Legislation enacted in June, 1968 imposed a 10 percent surtax on personal and corporate income taxes and reduced some types of expenditures. Only in 1970, when excess capacity and increased unemployment were beginning to appear, did federal fiscal policy again become expansionary to a significant degree. State and local expenditures continued to increase throughout the period. Private investment for purposes other than residential construction began to rise again in the latter part of 1968 and continued upward until about mid-1969, when the rise was halted by a highly restrictive monetary policy.

We have emphasized that in the earlier years of the period, and certainly during the period preceding the third quarter of 1968, this was predominantly a "demand-pull inflation." The same might be said, although with less certainty, of the first months of 1969. However, by the early months of 1970, the situation

had clearly changed. At least partly because of more restrictive federal fiscal policies and very stringent monetary policies in 1969, the rate of increase of aggregate
demands for output had slowed down. Moreover, underutilization of labor and
plant capacity was becoming more evident. Excess capacity was appearing in
industry after industry, and the unemployment rate was rising. The latter rose to
5 percent by mid-1970, to more than 6 percent at the end of the year, and averaged
about 6 percent during the first half of 1971 (see Table 26–3). Price inflation
continued unabated despite these developments.

Table 26–3 Unemployment rates, as percent of civilian labor force (seasonally adjusted)

	1965 (PER-CENT)	1966 (PER-CENT)	1967 (PER-CENT)	1968 (PER-CENT)	1969 (PER-CENT)	1970 (PER-CENT)	1971 (PER-CENT)
January	4.8	4.0	3.7	3.6	3.3	3.9	6.0
February	5.0	3.7	3.7	3.7	3.3	4.2	5.8
March	4.7	3.8	3.7	3.7	3.4	4.4	6.0
April	4.8	3.7	3.7	3.5	3.5	4.8	6.1
May	4.6	4.0	3.9	3.6	3.5	5.0	6.2
June	4.7	4.0	3.9	3.7	3.4	4.7	5.6
July	4.5	3.9	3.9	3.7	3.6	5.0	5.8
August	4.5	3.9	3.8	3.5	3.5	5.1	6.1
September	4.4	3.8	4.1	3.6	4.0	5.5	6.0
October	4.3	3.9	4.3	3.6	3.9	5.6	
November	4.2	3.7	3.8	3.4	3.4	5.9	
December	4.1	3.8	3.7	3.3	3.4	6.2	

SOURCE: *Federal Reserve Bulletin,* various issues.

By this time in 1971, the inflationary process had become in large part a
cost-push and mark-up inflation. Hourly wage rates, including fringe benefits,
rose much more rapidly than output per man-hour, thereby increasing labor costs
per unit of output. To compensate for these increased costs, most employers tried
to increase their prices. As shown in Table 26–4, unit labor costs rose more than

Table 26–4 Indexes of compensation per man-hour, output per man-hour,
and unit labor costs in private nonfarm industries (1967 = 100)

YEAR	COMPENSATION PER MAN-HOUR	OUTPUT PER MAN-HOUR	UNIT LABOR COSTS	PRICE LEVEL OF OUTPUT OF THESE INDUSTRIES
1965	89.2	95.1	93.9	94.8
1966	94.6	98.4	96.2	96.8
1967	100.0	100.0	100.0	100.0
1968	107.3	102.9	104.3	103.6
1969	114.5	103.2	111.0	108.0
1970	122.3	103.8	117.8	113.2

SOURCE: *Economic Report of the President,* 1971, p. 236.

4 percent in 1968, and more than 6 percent in both 1969 and 1970. They continued upward in 1971. In view of the strong inflationary expectations that had developed, it is easy to see why demanded increases in money wages were so large. Workers demanded wage increases large enough to offset not only past increases in the cost of living but also expected future increases.

This situation of continued price inflation in the face of excessive unemployment and underutilization of other productive resources presented a dilemma for conventional monetary and fiscal policies. More restrictive policies to combat price inflation would almost certainly lead to increased unemployment, but more expansive policies to promote real economic growth and employment would probably stimulate price inflation and create still stronger inflationary expectations. Because of this dilemma, proposals for some sort of direct wage and price controls or for a wage-price review board received increasing public support. Finally, in August, 1971, President Nixon reluctantly imposed a 90-day freeze on wages and prices.

Later we shall discuss in some detail official policy responses during this period of inflation since mid-1965, but our next task is to survey major developments in the international monetary situation. Three relevant domestic developments during the inflationary period should be kept in mind.

1. Both by stimulating imports and by discouraging exports, the large rise of American costs and prices led to a deterioration of the country's international balance on goods and services account.

2. The size and duration of the inflation and the apparent unwillingness or inability of American authorities to take effective measures to halt it, decreased confidence that the existing exchange rate on the dollar could be maintained and set the stage for speculative outflows of capital funds.

3. The heavy reliance on monetary policies, and the attendant wide fluctuations of American interest rates, induced very large international flows of capital funds, and especially of short-term funds. For example, the highly restrictive monetary policies of 1966 and 1969, which were accompanied by increases of American interest rates to their highest levels in more than a century, led to large inflows of funds. Such flows were not welcomed by either American officials or the authorities of some of the countries losing funds. On the other hand, lower interest rates in the United States sometimes led to unwanted outflows of funds, which contributed to the deterioration of the American balance of payments.

DEVELOPMENTS IN THE INTERNATIONAL
MONETARY SITUATION

We shall now survey some of the reasons for the change in the balance-of-payments position of the United States.

In the years immediately following World War II, while war-torn and war-deprived countries were still in the process of restocking and reconstruction, demands for American exports were almost insatiable. Our net exports of goods and services were large enough to enable us to make large loans and grants of foreign aid to the rest of the world and still to increase our gold reserves.

By the end of 1949, our gold stock had reached the huge value of $24.6 billion, which was about two-thirds of the world total. However, the situation began to change about the time of the outbreak of war in Korea, and the large surplus in the United States balance of payments was gradually replaced by chronic deficits. Major contributors to this turnabout were the recovery of productive capacity in other major industrial countries, devaluation of the British pound and several other currencies in 1949, and inflation in the United States during the Korean conflict. In any case, we have had a deficit in our balance of payments during every year except two (1957 and 1968) since 1949. During every year through 1970, we had a positive balance on goods and services account. For the years 1950 to 1959, inclusive, these surpluses on account of goods and services aggregated more than $25 billion. But huge as they were, these net receipts on goods and services account were not sufficient to cover our net payments to the rest of the world in the form of unilateral transfers and net purchases of long-term and short-term claims. The result was an overall deficit in the period from 1950 to 1959 of $17.3 billion (see Table 26–5). Deficits have continued since 1959, so that the aggregate deficit for the years 1950–1970, inclusive, was more than $49 billion.

These large and prolonged deficits inevitably reduced the net international reserve position of the United States. At the end of 1949, the official international reserves of the United States exceeded $26 billion, while total short-term liabilities to foreign countries were less than $6 billion. By the end of 1959, our international reserves had declined to $21.5 billion, while our liquid liabilities to other countries had risen to $16.2 billion. And by the end of 1970, our international reserves had shrunk further to $14.5 billion, while our liquid liabilities to other countries had swelled to more than $41 billion (see Table 26–6).

The United States was not the only nation to experience large imbalances in its balance of payments during this period. Of course, the deficits in the United States balance of payments had as their counterparts surpluses in the balances of payments of other countries. However, the experiences of other countries varied widely. Some, of which Germany is an example, tended to have large and persistent surpluses, while others, of which Great Britain is an example, tended toward large and persistent deficits. This situation is hardly surprising in view of the fact that while nations were attempting to maintain fixed exchange rates they were often reluctant to direct their monetary and fiscal policies to the eradication of their deficits or surpluses. To a large extent, these deficits and surpluses reflected imbalances on account of goods and services and long-term capital movements. However, they were often exacerbated by large international movements of short-term funds.

It seems likely that by the early 1960s, the flow of short-term funds among the principal international financial centers was more mobile than it had ever been before. This was only partially due to the removal of official restrictions—free

Table 26–5 U.S. balance of payments, 1950–1970 (millions of dollars)

YEAR	BALANCE ON GOODS AND SERVICES	OVERALL BALANCE ON LIQUIDITY BASIS $(= \Delta R - \Delta D)$	CHANGE IN OFFICIAL RESERVE ASSETS (ΔR)	CHANGE IN LIQUID LIABILITIES TO REST OF WORLD (ΔD)
1950	$ 1,892	−$ 3,489	−$1,758	+$1,731
1951	3,817	− 8	+ 33	+ 41
1952	2,356	− 1,206	+ 415	+ 1,621
1953	532	− 2,184	− 1,256	+ 928
1954	1,959	− 1,541	− 480	+ 1,061
1955	2,153	− 1,242	− 182	+ 1,061
1956	4,145	− 973	+ 869	+ 1,842
1957	5,901	+ 578	+ 1,165	+ 587
1958	2,356	− 3,365	− 2,292	+ 1,073
1959	310	− 3,870	− 1,035	+ 2,835
1960	4,133	− 3,901	− 2,143	+ 1,758
1961	5,622	− 2,371	− 606	+ 1,764
1962	5,149	− 2,204	− 1,533	+ 670
1963	5,984	− 2,670	− 378	+ 2,292
1964	8,580	− 2,800	− 171	+ 2,627
1965	7,121	− 1,335	− 1,222	+ 115
1966	5,300	− 1,357	− 568	+ 789
1967	5,213	− 3,544	− 52	+ 3,492
1968	2,493	+ 171	+ 880	+ 709
1969	1,949	− 7,012	+ 1,187	+ 8,199
1970	3,672	− 4,715	− 3,344	+ 1,371
1950–1959 Total	$25,421	−$17,300		
1960–1970 Total	$55,216	−$31,738		
1950–1970 Total	$80,637	−$49,038		

SOURCE: *Economic Report of the President,* various issues; *Federal Reserve Bulletin,* various issues.

Table 26–6 The international reserve position of the United States on selected dates (millions of dollars)

END OF YEAR	OFFICIAL INTERNATIONAL RESERVES	SHORT-TERM LIABILITIES TO FOREIGN COUNTRIES		
		TO CENTRAL BANKS AND GOVERNMENTS	TO OTHER	TOTAL
1949	$26,024	$ 2,908	$ 3,052	$ 5,960
1959	21,504	9,154	7,076	16,231
1960	19,359	10,326	7,045	17,371
1970	14,487	20,066	21,803	41,869

SOURCE: *Federal Reserve Bulletin,* various issues.

flows of funds had been permitted in many earlier periods. However, among the many other developments that also contributed to this mobility were: more rapid and cheaper methods of communicating information about market conditions and opportunities, closer relationships between American bankers and businessmen and their counterparts abroad, the rise of business organizations doing business in many countries, greater sophistication of American bankers in the field of international finance, development of new techniques in international finance, and so on. This greater fluidity of capital flows has much to commend it. However, on several occasions it has proved to be highly disturbing to countries receiving inflows as well as to those suffering outflows. One of its drawbacks is that it reduces the independence of national monetary policies. For example, suppose that for domestic reasons country A wants a restrictive monetary policy and high interest rates while country B wants a more expansionary policy and lower interest rates. Massive flows of funds from B to A not only tend to weaken B's balance of payments and to strengthen A's, but also to lessen the ability of both to achieve their interest-rate objectives. Moreover, high mobility facilitates massive international movements of funds in anticipation of changes in exchange rates. For example, the United States experienced large outflows of funds on several occasions when confidence in the exchange rate on the dollar weakened, Britain suffered huge outflows before the pound was devalued in 1967, and Germany experienced massive inflows on several occasions when its currency was expected to be revalued upward. International flows of $2 billion or more within a short period were by no means uncommon.

From their first appearance, in 1950, until about 1960, deficits in the American balance of payments were welcomed as almost wholly beneficial to the rest of the world. The general reaction was, "Only good can come from a loss of gold by the United States. It is about time that the country traded some of its sterile gold for useful goods or income-yielding assets and augmented the international reserves of other countries, who need them so badly." Our deficits provided the rest of the world with tremendous amounts of liquidity. We took none of the new gold flowing from gold production and from sales by the Soviet Union, leaving this to be added to the international reserves of other countries, and our deficits provided them with large amounts of gold and claims on dollars. Large amounts of these funds remained in the possession of private foreign banks and other private foreign holders, but very large amounts flowed into the official reserves of other countries. These were made available initially in the form of claims against dollars, but central banks and governments could convert them into gold. Thus, the official gold and foreign-exchange reserves of all foreign countries rose from $20.3 billion at the end of 1949 to $37.6 billion at the end of 1959, for an increase of 85 percent.

By increasing the liquidity of the rest of the world, our continuing deficits played a major role in restoring a system of relatively free multilateral trade and payments. The shackling system of exchange controls and trade restrictions prevailing in the early postwar period has already been described. These not only

restricted and distorted international trade, but also reduced to a trickle the international flow of private capital. All this began to change, slowly at first and then
more rapidly, as more of the industrialized nations improved their balance-of-payments and international reserve positions. By 1960, most of the financially important countries had liberalized their trade policies and had removed practically all restrictions on short-term capital movements.

Attitudes toward deficits in the balance of payments of the United States
had begun to change by 1960, and they changed even more during the following
years as the deficits continued, as American international reserves shrank and her
liquid liabilities to foreigners rose, and as it became increasingly clear that the
United States would not follow monetary and fiscal policies restrictive enough to
terminate the deficits. Deficits that were earlier considered to be beneficial to the
world as a whole now came to be regarded as at best dangerous and at worst
catastrophic for the international monetary system.

Major criticisms of the balance-of-payments situation were of two related
types. The first was that if American deficits were not eradicated, or at least reduced markedly, confidence in the exchange rate on the dollar would deteriorate
and the dollar would depreciate in terms of gold. The first dramatic indication of
decreased confidence in the dollar occurred in the autumn of 1960, when large
speculative purchases in the London gold market pushed the price of gold above
$40 an ounce, more than 15 percent above the American official price of $35. This
led, in October, 1960, to the formation of the London Gold Pool by the Federal
Reserve, the Bank of England, and several other major central banks. From
that time through mid-March, 1968, the Pool supplied sufficient gold from official
reserves to prevent the gold price from rising above $35.20 an ounce. However,
there was still a lack of confidence in the United States' ability to maintain gold
value of the dollar. A number of central banks held claims against dollars only
reluctantly, fearing that these would depreciate in terms of gold and their own
currencies. However, at least the larger and more responsible central banks recognized that an attempt to convert their dollar claims into gold would probably
precipitate a monetary crisis, with dire effects on the international monetary
system.

A second criticism was that it was basically unsound to allow the world's
supplies of international reserves and liquidity to be so heavily influenced, and
even dominated, by the state of the American balance of payments. It would indeed be an unlikely coincidence if the size of the American deficit were such as to
increase the world's supply of international reserves at an optimum rate. More
specifically, a number of countries complained that excessive American deficits
were increasing international reserves too rapidly and inducing inflation abroad.
Central banks were forced to purchase the excess dollars to prevent the exchange
rate on the dollar from falling, and these purchases expanded the reserves of their
banking systems.

Although there were widespread demands that the United States eradicate
its deficits, or at least reduce them sharply, it became increasingly evident that

such actions could seriously affect the world economy if they were not accompanied by other monetary reforms. For one thing, the measures adopted by the United States to eradicate its deficits could affect other countries adversely. Use of highly restrictive monetary and fiscal policies for this purpose might precipitate a recession, or at least a slowing down of economic growth, thereby reducing the demands for exports. And few nations would welcome a depreciation of the exchange rate on the dollar, because this would make American exports more competitive and would decrease American demands for the exports of other countries. Thus, at least some critics who demanded an end to American deficits seemed opposed to the measures that would be necessary for the purpose.

However, a central question was this: "If the principal source of increases in international liquidity in the postwar period—deficits in the American balance of payments—disappears, or is sharply reduced, how can we achieve an orderly and adequate growth of the supply of international liquidity?" Increasing supplies of liquidity would clearly be needed to accommodate and promote growth of international trade and capital movements. It became increasingly evident during the 1960s that the world's monetary gold stocks would not grow fast enough to provide the necessary increases. World gold production averaged about $1.4 billion a year, and was supplemented in some years by significant gold sales by the Soviet Union. A large part of these new gold supplies was absorbed by private hoarding and in industrial and artistic uses, but until 1965 there were some additions to the world's monetary gold stocks. After that time, nonmonetary demands for gold exceeded new supplies, so that the London Gold Pool had to make net sales out of official reserves to keep the market price from rising above $35.20. Net sales were only $45 million in 1966, but they soared to nearly $3 billion during 1967 and the first 2½ months of 1968. It was under these conditions that the cooperating central banks announced in mid-March, 1968 that they had terminated the London Gold Pool, that henceforth they would sell gold only to each other and not to private buyers, that the price in these transactions would remain at $35 an ounce, and that they would not purchase any gold not already in official reserves. Most other important central banks agreed with these principles. Thus, there would be no further monetization of gold and no reliance on gold as a source of increased international liquidity.

During the 1960s, the air was filled with proposals for reforms of the international reserve and liquidity system. Two proposals that were widely discussed failed to be adopted. One proposal was to raise the official price of gold from $35 to $70, or even to $105, an ounce. The other suggestion was to establish an international central bank that would create and regulate the supply of international reserves in much the same ways that national central banks regulate supplies of reserves for their domestic-banking systems. Among the reforms that were adopted were increases in the resources of the IMF and more liberal lending policies by that institution; the establishment and enlargement of "swap facilities" among the leading central banks; and numerous other extensions of credit, some on a large scale, by central banks to each other. The reform with the greatest long-run consequences for the international monetary system was the adoption of the SDR scheme, which has already been described.

However, despite its long-run potentialities, the SDR scheme did not immediately solve the major problems of international liquidity. It did not immediately control the size of international reserves, because these were still subject to change by American deficits. And it did not effectively restore confidence in the exchange rate on the dollar, because it did not reduce the huge outstanding volume of American liquid liabilities to the rest of the world; it did not terminate, or even reduce, deficits in the American balance of payments; and its additions to the international reserves of the United States—amounting to $867 million at the beginning of 1970 and another $717 million at the beginning of 1971—were too small to restore confidence. Thus, it remained possible for further adverse developments to precipitate a dollar crisis. This happened in mid-August, 1971, when the President terminated redemption of the dollar in gold and other reserve assets, and stated his strong desire to see the dollar depreciate significantly in terms of foreign currencies.

This event was preceded by further deterioration in the nation's balance of payments, especially during 1970 and the first 7½ months of 1971. The balance on goods and services account, which had averaged a surplus of more than $5 billion annually from 1961 to 1967, declined thereafter, and in the first half of 1971 produced a deficit for the first time in many decades. Large short-term capital outflows made much greater contributions to the deterioration of the American balance of payments. During 1970 and about the first three months of 1971, these occurred primarily because interest rates in the United States were falling faster than those in the principal foreign financial centers. As already noted, a combination of a highly restrictive monetary policy and large demands for credit in 1969 raised interest rates in the United States to their highest levels in more than a century. This was accompanied by huge flows of short-term funds to the United States, the largest component being borrowings of Eurodollars by American banks. The flow reversed in early 1970 as the Federal Reserve adopted more liberal policies, and interest rates in the United States declined relative to those abroad. The United States deficit on an official-settlements basis rose to the huge total of $10.7 billion for 1970, and became even larger in 1971. We shall later describe in some detail how outflows of funds from the United States, originally in response to differentials in interest rates, developed into a flood of speculative outflows, culminating in President Nixon's action on August 15, 1971.

SPECIFIC MEASURES RELATING TO
THE BALANCE OF PAYMENTS

Although the United States has been concerned almost continuously since 1959 about the deficits in its balance of payments and the deterioration of its international liquidity position, it has not been willing to sacrifice domestic objectives relating to economic growth and employment by adopting general monetary and fiscal policies restrictive enough to bring its balance of payments into equilibrium. The nation has, however, taken a wide variety of actions directed toward improving its balance of payments without recourse to more restrictive general monetary and fiscal policies. For example, the United States persuaded several governments (notably those of Germany, France, and Italy) to prepay some of their debts to the United States, to buy military supplies in the United States, to bear a larger part of the burden of providing foreign aid, and to open their long-term capital markets to foreign flotations. The United States also took several steps to reduce American expenditures abroad. For example, it decreased the amounts of duty-free imports that tourists could bring back. It limited the freedom of military personnel to maintain their families abroad. It gave still greater preferences to American products in purchasing supplies. And it "tied" government loans and grants to the purchases of American products. By 1968, it was requiring that more than 90 percent of all government loans and grants be spent in the United States. Many of these measures are highly mercantilistic and, if long continued, will tend to lower the efficiency of the world economy.

Direct restrictions on capital movements

Many measures were adopted to discourage outflows of short-term and long-term funds. Some of these directly restricted such outflows. For example, purchases of foreign stocks and of bonds with a maturity of a year or more, except those of less developed countries and a few others, were subjected to an "interest-equalization tax," which was designed to increase by about 1 percentage point the annual cost to foreigners of obtaining funds in the American market. Under strong pressure from the government, most financial institutions and large nonfinancial corporations agreed to "voluntary-restraint" programs to curb outflows. Commercial banks agreed to limit their foreign loans to existing levels, other financial intermediaries also restricted their foreign lending, and corporations reduced their direct investment abroad. These programs became less "voluntary" when the President issued an executive order formalizing them in early 1968.

Adjustments of interest rates abroad

Other measures did not place direct restrictions on capital outflows but sought to reduce them without a general increase of interest rates in American markets. For example, several foreign countries lowered their interest-rate levels to inhibit inflows of funds. One purpose was clearly to help decrease the outflow from the United States. But recipient countries did not welcome funds that might later prove to be "hot money," and which interfered with their efforts to restrict credit.

To minimize the extent to which they would have to rely on a decrease of their general levels of interest rates to inhibit inflows, some countries adopted special methods. For example, Switzerland reached a gentleman's agreement with its banks that they would not accept new demand deposits from foreigners, that time deposits from foreigners would not receive interest, and that new foreign deposits with a maturity of less than six months would be subjected to a charge of 1 percent per annum. The banks also agreed to avoid using foreign funds to purchase Swiss securities, real estate, and mortgages. Germany imposed high reserve requirements on increases of deposit liabilities to foreigners, and for a time forbade payment of interest on foreign-owned deposits.

Operations in exchange markets

The American authorities also began to operate in foreign-exchange markets in order to influence international flows of funds and to conserve gold. Before 1961, the Federal Reserve and the Treasury did not buy and sell foreign moneys to influence the dollar exchange rate. They kept the dollar within narrow limits solely by purchasing and selling gold. In March, 1961, the Treasury broke this precedent by reactivating the Exchange Stabilization Fund, and by beginning to buy and sell convertible moneys. The account was managed by the Federal Reserve. A year later, in March, 1962, the Federal Reserve began similar operations on its own account. Operations for both the Treasury and the Federal Reserve are under this jurisdiction of the FOMC and are carried out through the Federal Reserve Bank of New York. The manager of these accounts now operates in the spot-exchange market (the market for immediate delivery of the moneys involved) and in the forward-exchange market, which deals in contracts to deliver or to receive moneys at some stipulated time in the future.

Operations in spot markets can have several purposes. One is to affect expectations concerning future rates. For example, purchases of dollars (that is, sales of foreign moneys) to limit or prevent a decline of the exchange rate on the dollar may succeed in creating expectations that the dollar will not decline. Federal Reserve sales of foreign moneys to buy excess dollars in exchange markets can also prevent the latter from being sold to foreign central banks, which might use them to demand gold. Federal Reserve operations in spot markets have been in significant volume, as have those of some other cooperating central banks and governments.

Operations in forward markets also affect expectations concerning the future course of exchange rates and are sometimes used for this purpose. However, we shall concentrate here on the use of this device to influence the direction and rate of international capital flows by affecting the relative net rates of return available in different countries.

To illustrate the principles involved, let us suppose that a German investor has funds that he is willing to lend in either Frankfurt or New York, depending on relative rates of return in the two markets. If he does lend in New York, the dollars that he intends to loan will be bought for marks in the spot market. At the same time that he purchases dollars in the spot market, he will sell them for marks in the forward market in order to repatriate his funds at the end of the loan period. His relative *net* returns will depend not only on the heights of interest rates in New York and Frankfurt but also on the relationship between the spot rate at which he buys dollars and the forward rate at which he sells dollars. For example, if the forward rate on the dollar is at a 2 percent discount relative to the spot rate, he will lose 2 percent on his exchange transactions and will find it more profitable to lend in New York only if interest rates there are at least 2 percentage points higher than in Frankfurt. On the other hand, if the forward rate on the dollar is at a 2 percent premium relative to the spot rate, he will gain 2 percent on his exchange transactions and will find it more profitable to lend in New York unless interest rates there are at least 2 percentage points below those in Frankfurt. Thus, it is possible for American markets to attract and retain funds even if American interest rates are lower than those abroad.

On several occasions since 1960, outflows of funds from the United States were encouraged by the existence of large forward discounts on the dollar. This was especially serious when the countries whose currencies were at a considerable forward premium also had interest rates above those in New York. Several foreign central banks as well as the Federal Reserve and the Treasury therefore bought dollars forward (that is, they sold the foreign currencies forward) to decrease the forward discount on the dollar. For example, in late 1960 and in 1961, the German Bundesbank, in an effort to encourage short-term investment broad and to discourage inflows, offered to purchase forward dollars from its banks at a premium. The Bank of Italy entered into similar arrangements. The United States Treasury first began to operate in the forward market in March, 1961, and the Federal Reserve entered on its own account a year later. Some of their operations have been very large. For example, at one time in 1961, the Treasury had sold forward more than 1 billion Deutsche marks, equivalent to about $250 million. At another time in 1962, forward sales of Swiss francs amounted to nearly $150 million. Similar operations also occurred in other currencies and at other times.

Operations of these types in both spot and forward-exchange markets serve useful purposes and may become permanent monetary instruments for the following reasons:

1. They can be used to influence expectations concerning the future course of exchange rates and thus to influence speculative flows of short-term funds.

2. By influencing forward premiums and discounts, they can reduce the extent to which given interest-rate differentials induce flows of funds.

3. They can, at least for a time, reduce gold losses.

Thus, they can be very helpful in dealing with speculative flows and for limited periods of time. They do not, of course, correct basic imbalances in international payments.

Changes in Regulation Q
(ceilings on interest rates on time deposits)

For five years prior to 1962, the highest rate that any commercial bank was permitted to pay on any class of savings or time deposit was 3 percent. Big banks in New York and a few other centers complained that these low ceilings prevented them from competing effectively for foreign funds, with the result that deposits were lost and outflows of funds increased. Largely, although not solely, in response to this situation, ceilings were raised in January, 1962, so that the highest rates available on time deposits were increased from 3 to 4 percent. In October of that year, Congress permitted the Federal Reserve to remove ceilings on rates paid on deposits of foreign central banks and governments. Ceilings were raised still further in the following years, partly for international and partly for domestic reasons. Thus, banks were permitted to pay higher rates, not only to foreign private holders, but also to American firms that might lend abroad.

One purpose of these actions, and especially of the earlier ones, was to make higher returns available to holders of dollar deposits without necessarily raising the rates paid by American borrowers. However, the higher rates also had important domestic repercussions, because they induced a rapid increase in domestic holdings of time and savings deposits at commercial banks.

MONETARY POLICIES, 1960 TO LATE 1965

The measures described above were directed specifically to the objectives of improving the nation's balance of payments and of stemming gold outflows, and some of them to providing more freedom to pursue expansionary domestic objectives. We now turn to an examination of other aspects of monetary policies during this period of excessive unemployment.

We have already noted that the economy began to slide into a recession in mid-1960, that the recession reached its nadir in the first quarter of 1961, and that thereafter GNP rose without interruption but at such a slow pace that excessive amounts of unemployment and excess capacity persisted. The first response of the Federal Reserve to the onset of the recession was to move toward a more liberal policy, just as it had done in the earlier postwar recessions. It purchased government securities in the open market and lowered member-bank reserve requirements, thereby enabling the banks to reduce their borrowings and increase their excess reserves. Moreover, discount rates, which had been at 4 percent, were lowered to 3½ percent in June and then to 3 percent in August, 1960. These actions, together with decreased demands for funds, brought a reduction of interest rates in the open market. For example, the yield on 90-day Treasury bills, which had averaged 3.87 percent in the first quarter and 2.99 percent in the second quarter, declined to 2.36 percent in the third quarter of 1960. But there the decline virtually stopped; these rates stayed at about the same level through the third quarter of 1961 and then increased slightly.

Monetary policy during this period of excessive unemployment is best described as only "moderately expansionary," and less expansionary than in earlier postwar recessions. For example, Federal Reserve discount rates, which had been reduced to 1½ percent in 1954 and to 1¾ percent in 1958, were not reduced below 3 percent in this period. The average annual rate of growth of the money supply was less than 3 percent. The decline of market rates of interest, and especially of short-term rates, was not as great as in earlier recessions. It appears almost certain that in this period concern about the balance of payments did, to some extent, motivate the Federal Reserve to follow less expansionary policies than it would otherwise have followed.

"Operation Nudge"

In an attempt to reconcile its international and domestic objectives, the Federal Reserve modified its open-market policy, trying to "nudge" short-term rates higher relative to long-term rates. The height of long-term interest rates in the United States relative to those abroad obviously influences the flow of long-term funds to other countries. However, during this period, Federal Reserve and Treasury officials believed that short-term rates were the more important in determining international flows of funds, whereas long-term rates were more important in determining domestic investment spending. They therefore sought to raise short-term rates relative to long-term rates. Note that they faced two separable policy problems: (1) to regulate the overall reserve positions of the banks, and thus influence the general or average level of interest rates; and (2) to influence the relative heights of short-term and long-term rates. The attempts of the Federal Reserve and the Treasury to raise short-term relative to long-term rates are usually called "Operation Nudge," although some people referred to these operations as "Operation Twist."

To illustrate the principles involved, we assume that the Federal Reserve has already determined the overall reserve position of the banks. The basic technique of the "nudge" is to increase the supply of Treasury bills and other short issues available to banks and the public relative to the supply of long-term government bonds. This is done through both Treasury debt-management operations and Federal Reserve open-market operations. For its part, the Treasury increases the supply of Treasury bills and other short maturities outstanding. It does this in several ways: by outright "swaps" of Treasury bills for outstanding longer maturities, by concentrating new issues in the short-term area, by purchasing longs rather than shorts for its own investment accounts, and so on. These operations tend, of course, to decrease the average maturity of the federal debt. To prevent this, or at least to decrease its extent, the Treasury has used an "advance-refunding" technique. That is, by issuing longer-term obligations, it has refunded issues that still have a few years to run.

In comparable ways, the Federal Reserve can increase the supply of Treasury bills and other short maturities available to the banks and the public: by selling shorts and buying longs, by purchasing longs rather than shorts to supply bank reserves, and by providing banks with reserves or excess reserves by other means that do not require it to purchase shorts. To do this, however, the Federal Reserve had to abandon its controversial "bills-only" (or "bills-usually") policy. Some steps in this direction were taken in late 1960, when the FOMC began to buy certificates, notes, and bonds with maturities up to 15 months. On February 20, 1961, it abandoned "bills-only," announcing, "The System Open-Market Account is purchasing in the open market U.S. government bonds and notes of varying maturities, some of which will exceed five years." Since that time, it has dealt in a wide range of maturities. However, its swaps and purchases of long maturities have been in only modest volume.

Its desire to avoid decreasing the supply of short maturities available to the public may also have been a minor factor in the Federal Reserve's decisions to meet a part of bank needs for reserves by allowing them to count all of their vault cash as reserves and by reducing reserve requirements against time and savings deposits from 5 to 4 percent in late 1962.

It is very difficult to assess the effects of "Operation Nudge," partly because the operation was so limited in scale. Federal Reserve swaps of shorts for longs were small, as were its net purchases of longer maturities. Moreover, the Treasury offset these operations to some extent by issuing longer-term securities. It does seem likely, however, that the overall effect was to make short-term rates slightly higher relative to long-term rates than they would otherwise have been.

The Federal Reserve and the Treasury again employed the techniques of "Operation Nudge" in the early part of 1971, when the objective was again to lower long-term rates to stimulate domestic investment and to lessen declines of short-term rates which would encourage capital outflows. The Federal Reserve supplied additional bank reserves primarily by purchasing long-term bonds, and the Treasury met its borrowing needs primarily by issuing short-term, rather than long-term, obligations. These actions probably raised short-term rates at least slightly relative to long-term rates, but they did not stem the outflow of funds.

Fiscal policies

As another means of reconciling domestic and international objectives, the government adopted a more expansionary fiscal policy. It recognized that a fiscal policy that succeeded in raising domestic income and output would tend to worsen the balance of payments by increasing imports. But, unlike an expansionary monetary policy, it would not tend to lower interest rates or to encourage capital exports. In fact, to the extent that it succeeded in increasing the demand for domestic output and in raising the expected profitability of domestic investment, it would tend to keep funds at home.

In 1962, two steps were taken to encourage private investment. One was a liberalization of depreciation rules, which permitted firms to write off their investments more quickly for tax purposes. The other was enactment of an *investment-tax credit*, which permitted business firms to deduct from their income-tax liabilities an amount equal to 7 percent of their purchases of new plant and equipment. This was, in effect, a subsidy for new investment.

In late 1962, President Kennedy proposed a sizeable reduction of personal and corporate income-tax rates, but Congress delayed the reduction until 1964. The reduction, which became effective in steps in 1964 and 1965, amounted to $15 billion at the levels of GNP prevailing in 1965. It clearly had the desired effect of increasing the rate of growth of demands for output. It would have been even more useful if it had been instituted at least two years earlier.

MONETARY POLICIES, LATE 1965 TO OCTOBER, 1966

We have already described the upsurge of expenditures for output after mid-1965: the large and rapid increases of expenditures by the federal government, the continuing increases of expenditures by state and local governments, and the rise of business expenditures for purposes other than residential construction that continued until the third quarter of 1966. These induced large increases of consumer spending. Despite these upsurges of spending, no significant federal tax increases were enacted before June, 1968.

One effect of these large and rapid increases in expenditures for output was to reduce unemployment. Despite large additions to the labor force, the unemployment rate fell from 5.5 percent in mid-1965 to 3.2 percent in October, 1966. Another effect was price inflation. Price levels had been relatively stable during the seven years preceding mid-1965. For example, since 1958 the wholesale price index had risen less than 2.5 percent and the consumer price index had risen only about 9 percent. However, between June, 1965 and October, 1966 wholesale prices rose 3.3 percent and consumer prices went up 4 percent.

Thus, in the face of highly expansionary fiscal policies, it became the task of the Federal Reserve to try to contain the inflation by restricting supplies of money and credit while demands for credit were large and rising. The federal government had to borrow large amounts to finance its mounting deficits, and state and local governments were also large net borrowers. Business firms demanded large amounts of funds in both long-term and short-term markets to finance their rising expenditures for fixed equipment and inventory and also, in mid-1966, to meet accelerated tax payments to the government. In the years immediately preceding 1965, nonfinancial corporations received an average of $20 billion a year from outside sources; this rose to $32.7 billion in 1965 and $37.6 billion in 1966. The combination of a restrictive monetary policy and rising total demands for credit in 1966 raised interest rates to their highest levels in more than 40 years.

The Federal Reserve took two important policy actions on December 6, 1965. One was to raise the maximum rates that banks might pay on time deposits (see Table 26–7). Ceiling rates on savings deposits were left unchanged but those

Table 26–7 Maximum interest rates on time deposits, 1965

	MAXIMUM RATES EFFECTIVE:	
TYPE OF DEPOSIT	NOVEMBER 4, 1964	DECEMBER 6, 1965
Savings deposits	4	4
Time deposits		
30–89 days	4	5½
90 days and more	4½	5½

on time deposits were raised to 5½ percent. The major purpose of this action was to enable banks to retain time deposits and compete effectively for funds in the face of rising interest rates on other short-term assets. Banks, and especially large banks, had outstanding large amounts of negotiable certificates of deposits (CDs) which would mature in December, and which might be withdrawn if their yields were not adjusted upward. Federal Reserve officials believed that the large rise of the ceilings would make the ceilings ineffective and leave banks free to bid effectively for funds. However, by midsummer of 1966, following sharp increases of rates on other assets, these new ceilings were again "pinching."

The Federal Reserve's other major action in December was to increase discount rates from 4 to 4½ percent. In retrospect, it appears that the increase should have been made earlier. However, President Johnson and many others criticized the increase, asserting that it was premature and would unduly inhibit the growth of employment and output. Perhaps partly because of such criticisms, the Federal Reserve followed a somewhat liberal open-market policy for several weeks. It allowed unborrowed reserves of member banks—i.e., their total reserves less amounts borrowed from the Federal Reserve—to rise by $942 million from November, 1965 to January, 1966. During the same period the money supply expanded by $2.7 billion and total savings and time deposits at commercial banks were increased by $2.5 billion. However, in the spring of 1966, the Federal Reserve began to move toward a highly restrictive policy. By restricting its purchases of government securities, it prevented any significant rise in the supply of unborrowed reserves during the five months following April (see Table 26–8). The money supply did not increase at all between April and the end of the year, although transactions demands for money balances rose with the continued increase of GNP.

In the meantime, banks—and especially large banks—were experiencing unexpectedly large increases in demands for business loans. Many bankers found to their consternation that while their outstanding loan commitments were far larger than they had thought, some of their most valued depositors unexpectedly demanded accommodation. To meet such demands, banks scrambled for funds. They raised their borrowings from the Federal Reserve above $700 million, so that their negative free reserves—the excess of their borrowings from the Federal Reserve over their excess reserves—averaged above $300 million from April through October. They attempted to attract more time deposits, but the Federal Reserve refused to raise ceiling rates even though rates on other short-term assets had become higher. As a result, few banks could attract additional time deposits and some suffered net withdrawals, especially of large-denomination CDs. The banks also sold federal and state and local government securities at large losses; they paid 6 percent or more in the market for federal funds; and some of the most sophisticated banks paid 7 percent or more for Eurodollar loans. By September, many banks were forced to use nonprice rationing to limit the increase of business loans, and interest rates were at their highest level in more than four decades. The entire structure of rates shifted upward, but short-term rates rose the most (see Table 26–9).

Table 26–8 Member-bank reserves and the money supply (reserves in millions; money supply and time deposits in billions, seasonally adjusted)

	TOTAL RESERVES	UN-BORROWED RESERVES	EXCESS RESERVES	BORROW-INGS AT THE FEDERAL RESERVE	FREE RESERVES	MONEY SUPPLY	TIME DEPOSITS AT COM-MERCIAL BANKS
November, 1965	$21,958	$21,506	$369	$452	—$ 83	$165.7	$145.5
December	22,719	22,265	452	454	— 2	167.4	147.0
January, 1966	22,750	22,348	358	402	— 44	168.4	148.0
February	22,233	21,755	371	478	— 107	168.0	148.8
March	22,160	21,609	305	551	— 246	169.3	149.5
April	22,528	21,902	358	626	— 268	170.9	151.4
May	22,487	21,765	370	722	— 352	170.2	153.0
June	22,534	21,860	322	674	— 352	171.1	153.7
July	23,090	22,324	408	766	— 358	169.6	155.3
August	22,655	21,927	338	728	— 390	169.6	156.6
September	23,240	22,474	398	766	— 368	170.5	157.1
October	23,333	22,600	302	733	— 431	169.6	156.8
November	23,251	22,640	389	611	— 222	169.2	156.8
December	23,830	23,273	392	557	— 165	170.3	158.0
January, 1967	24,075	23,686	373	389	— 16	169.6	160.5
February	23,709	23,347	358	362	— 4	170.4	163.2
March	23,405	23,296	435	199	236	172.8	165.3
April	23,362	23,228	309	134	175	172.1	167.3
May	23,284	23,183	370	101	269	174.1	169.3
June	23,518	23,395	420	123	297	176.2	172.4
July	23,907	23,820	359	87	272	177.9	174.6
August	23,791	23,702	387	89	298	179.1	177.2
September	24,200	24,110	358	90	268	179.2	178.9
October	24,608	24,482	286	126	160	180.3	180.8
November	24,740	24,607	403	133	270	181.2	182.5
December	25,256	25,018	341	238	103	181.5	183.5
January, 1968	25,840	25,603	375	237	138	182.4	183.7
February	25,610	25,249	391	361	30	182.6	185.0

Table 26–9 Selected interest rates (percent yield per annum)

	AVERAGE, 1964	AVERAGE, 1965	JUNE, 1966	JULY, 1966	AUGUST, 1966	SEPTEMBER, 1966
3-month Treasury bills	3.55	3.95	4.54	4.86	4.93	5.36
9–12-month Treasury bills	3.76	4.09	4.40	4.98	5.10	5.21
Long-term government bonds	4.15	4.21	4.63	4.75	4.80	4.79
4–6-month commercial paper	3.97	4.38	5.51	5.63	5.85	5.89
Corporate bonds Moody's Aaa	4.40	4.49	5.07	5.16	5.31	5.49

SOURCE: *Economic Report of the President,* January, 1968, pp. 272–273.

Disintermediation

As indicated in an earlier chapter, a large part of the public's saving, and especially of household saving, usually flows to financial intermediaries in exchange for such claims as shares in savings and loan associations, deposits at mutual savings banks, and claims against life insurance companies. This process was shocked severely by the sharp rise of interest rates on competing financial assets between March and September, 1966. Hardest hit were the savings and loan associations, which were accustomed to large net inflows of funds. The average monthly increase of their oustanding shares had been $881 million in 1964 and $698 million in 1965. Net inflows were far smaller in 1966, and during four months there were net outflows (see Table 26–10). The net outflows in April and July were

Table 26–10 Monthly changes in principal liabilities of selected financial intermediaries, 1964–1966 (millions of dollars)

	SAVINGS SHARES IN SAVINGS AND LOAN ASSOCIATIONS	DEPOSITS AT MUTUAL SAVINGS BANKS	TOTAL ASSETS LESS POLICY LOANS OF LIFE INSURANCE COMPANIES
Average monthly changes, 1964	+$ 881	+$354	+$655
Average monthly changes, 1965	+ 698	+ 300	+ 740
January, 1966	− 77	+ 246	+ 700
February	+ 528	+ 218	+ 556
March	+ 838	+ 379	+ 487
April	− 773	− 327	+ 572
May	+ 387	+ 116	+ 454
June	+ 1,185	+ 243	+ 473
July	− 1,508	+ 205	+ 852
August	+ 124	+ 166	+ 288
September	+ 631	+ 384	+ 330
October	− 56	+ 105	+ 750
November	+ 614	+ 148	+ 653
December	+ 1,732	+ 680	+ 585

SOURCE: Derived from data in the *Federal Reserve Bulletin,* various issues.

large. At the end of October, their total outstanding shares were $10 million below their level at the end of March. Faced with the virtual cessation of net inflows, and fearing large withdrawals, savings and loan associations found it difficult to meet their outstanding commitments to lend on mortgages and were unable to make many new commitments. This was a sharp blow to the residential construction industry, which relies so heavily on these institutions for financing.

Mutual savings banks were also affected, but less severely. Their monthly net inflows of deposits had averaged $354 million in 1964 and $300 million in 1965. These inflows fell sharply in 1966, averaging only $174 million per month during the first 10 months, a decrease of 42 percent from the 1965 level.

Life insurance companies faced a somewhat different problem. Flows of funds to them did not decrease. However, many of them had contracted to lend to their policyholders on demand, and at 5 percent, amounts up to the cash surrender values of their policies. As other interest rates rose, policyholders greatly increased their demand for such loans. The result was a shrinkage in the net flows of funds available to life insurance companies for purchasing other types of assets, primarily mortgages and corporate bonds. Net inflows of funds for such purposes had averaged $655 million per month in 1964 and $740 million in 1965. After January, 1966, these inflows fell sharply, averaging only $500 million per month during the next eight months, a decrease of 33 percent below the 1965 level.

Thus, the three types of financial intermediaries that contribute most heavily to the financing of the residential construction industry were forced to restrict their mortgage lending. This restriction, together with high interest rates, brought a sharp fall in residential construction. Measured from their levels of a year earlier, new private-housing starts had fallen 28 percent by July, 1966; in October, the decline reached 40 percent. These declines brought loud protests from the building industry, Congress, and some others.

The Federal Reserve was much concerned by these developments. It feared that nonbank financial intermediaries would be squeezed even more and would, in at least some isolated cases, suffer large withdrawals. It was also worried about the heavy impact of these developments on construction. Thus, it was faced with the problem of determining how to ameliorate the situation. One approach would have been to shift toward a less restrictive general monetary policy in order to curb the rise of interest rates, or even to lower them. And this consideration was a factor in the Board's refusal to approve increases in discount rates during July. (Seven of the Reserve banks proposed that their discount rates be raised from $4\frac{1}{2}$ to 5 or $5\frac{1}{2}$ percent but the Board disapproved all of these proposals.) But to relax general monetary policy would, of course, increase the danger of inflation. Therefore, the Federal Reserve sought "selective" measures that would enable it to slow the rate of increase of business loans by banks, reduce the flow of funds into time and savings deposits at commercial banks, and reduce the diversion of funds away from nonbank financial intermediaries. It was especially concerned with large banks, whose business loans were expanding most rapidly and who were bidding most actively for funds.

Selective measures

The Federal Reserve adopted several types of selective measures. One was to tighten ceilings on time-deposit rates. As noted earlier, the Board action in December, 1965 established ceiling rates of 4 percent on savings deposits and $5\frac{1}{2}$ percent on all types of time deposits. As competing market rates rose sharply during the summer, there were widespread requests that the ceilings be raised to enable banks to retain deposits and perhaps attract more. This the Board refused to do. In fact, in July and again in September, it actually rolled back ceilings on some types of time deposits. The maximum rate on large-denomination time deposits—those of $100,000 or more—remained at $5\frac{1}{2}$ percent; ceilings on smaller denominations were reduced to 5 percent. These actions had two principal purposes. One was to reduce the diversion of funds away from nonbank financial intermediaries. The other was to slow the expansion of business loans by limiting the ability of banks to attract funds. Total savings and time deposits grew very slowly between April and September.

Another action with selective effects was to increase reserve requirements on certain types of time deposits. For nearly four years prior to July, 1966, reserve requirements on all classes of savings and time deposits had stood at 4 percent. However, in two actions—one in July and the other in September—the Board changed the regulations. Reserve requirements on savings deposits and on the first $5 million of time deposits at each bank were left unchanged at 4 percent, but those on bank time deposits in excess of $5 million were raised to 6 percent. Thus, the change was directed at the larger banks. Although these actions tended to have some generally tightening effects, their principal purpose was to inhibit the bidding for time deposits by large banks, and thus to lessen their expansion of business loans. With required reserves at 4 percent, they could lend an amount equal to 96 percent of their time deposits; with the requirement at 6 percent, they could lend an amount equal to only 94 percent of their time deposits. It is doubtful that these mild actions were very effective.

The Federal Reserve also resorted to moral suasion. By early summer, Federal Reserve officials were stating that business loans were expanding too rapidly, that this was inflationary, and that the investment boom might prove to be "unsustainable" in the sense that it would lead to a temporary glut of fixed capital and inventory, which would lead to a later decline. Discount officers admonished banks that sought to borrow "too frequently or too much" while expanding their business loans "too rapidly." The moral-suasion effort culminated in a letter of September 1 which was sent to all member banks and to the press.[1] The letter made several points:

1. Some expansion of business loans is required, but the national interest would be better served by a slower rate of expansion.
2. Bank liquidation of municipal securities and other investments creates pressures on financial markets; "a greater share of bank adjustments should take the form of moderation in the rate of expansion of loans, and particularly business loans."
3. "Member banks will be expected to cooperate in the System's efforts to hold down the rate of business loan expansion—apart from normal seasonal needs—and to use the discount facilities of the Reserve Banks in a manner consistent with these efforts."
4. Banks cooperating by curtailing business loans rather than disposing of securities will be eligible for a longer period of discount accommodation if needed.

It is difficult to assess the effects of this letter. The expansion of business loans did begin to slow down at about this time, but not necessarily as a result of the letter. One factor that may have contributed to the slow down is that many

[1] For the text of the letter, see *Annual Report of the Board of Governors for 1966*, pp. 103–104.

banks had already begun to screen loan applications more closely. Also, demands for business loans were becoming less ebullient. However, it does seem likely that moral suasion by the Federal Reserve, including the September letter, played at least some small role in slowing the expansion of business loans.

The peak of strains in financial markets was reached in September. In October, the Federal Reserve decided to move no further toward restriction; and in December, it began to move toward a more liberal policy.

MONETARY POLICIES, LATE 1966 TO NOVEMBER, 1967

This shift in monetary policy was primarily in response to a weakening of private investment spending, because government expenditures continued to rise without abatement. However, expenditures for residential construction had fallen significantly by the fourth quarter of 1966, business spending for inventory accumulation fell sharply in the first two quarters of 1967, and business expenditures for plant and equipment also declined, but only slightly. The Federal Reserve responded to this situation with a number of liberalizing actions. In late December, it quietly withdrew its letter of September 1. In March, it lowered from 4 to 3 percent reserve requirements against savings deposits and against the first $5 million of time deposits at each bank. The effect was, of course, to decrease overall reserve requirements, but also to have most of the initial benefits accrue to the smaller member banks. In April, all the Reserve banks lowered their discount rates from 4½ to 4 percent. The FOMC bought large amounts of government securities. These actions enabled member banks to increase their unborrowed reserves by nearly $2 billion in the year following October, 1966; member-bank borrowings from the Federal Reserve fell from more than $700 million to less than $100 million, and net free reserves rose from a negative figure of about $400 million to a positive figure of more than $270 million. The money supply rose by about $10 billion, or 6 percent.

Market yields on short-term and long-term debts moved in disparate ways. Short-term yields fell during the first half of 1967 and then rose during the second half—although they did not reach their peaks of 1966. For example, yields on 90-day Treasury bills fell from 5.39 percent in October, 1966 to 3.49 percent in July, 1967, and then rose to 5.01 percent in December. The decline of market rates on competing short-term assets while ceiling rates remained unchanged permitted a large increase in time deposits at commercial banks, which amounted to more than $13 billion, or 15 percent, during the year following October, 1966. These developments also brought large inflows of funds to other financial intermediaries, and especially to savings and loans associations, which helped revive residential construction. On the other hand, yields on long-term debt declined only briefly and then rose to record levels. For example, yields on corporate bonds rated Aaa by Moody's declined from 5.44 percent in September, 1966 to 5.03 percent in February and then rose almost continuously to 6.19 percent in December. This disparate behavior of short- and long-term yields resulted from a combination of factors—expectations of continuing inflation and rising rates in the future, fear of unavailability of credit in the future, and the squeeze on liquidity in 1966. Both financial institutions and other business firms had reduced their liquidity markedly by late 1966. Financial institutions preferred short-term liquid assets to rebuild their liquidity, and other business firms issued huge amounts of long-term debt to make sure that they could command funds and to reduce their reliance on bank loans.

In retrospect, it is clear that Federal Reserve policies during this period were excessively expansionary. By October, 1967, these policies had become subject to criticism, not only by outsiders but also by a minority within the FOMC. Critics pointed to the continuing rise of government expenditures while Congress still refused to raise taxes, to the renewed increase of private investment spending, to the higher rate of increase of total spending for output, to the continuing domestic price inflation, and to the worsening of the nation's balance of payments. Such considerations alone would probably have led to the adoption of less expansionary monetary policies before the end of 1967—even in the absence of financial disturbances abroad. In fact, however, action was precipitated by events surrounding devaluation of the British pound on November 18 from a parity of $2.80 to $2.40. This was followed by large capital outflows from the United States and by sharp increases in gold hoarding. As we have already seen, this culminated in the dissolution of the London Gold Pool and the introduction of the two-tier price system for gold in mid-March, 1968.

MONETARY POLICIES, NOVEMBER, 1967 TO JUNE, 1968

From November, 1967 through June, 1968, when Congress finally voted to raise taxes and to decrease federal expenditures, Federal Reserve policies were less expansionary than they had been in the preceding period, but they were still not very restrictive. They probably would have been more restrictive if Federal Reserve officials had not feared that such actions would jeopardize enactment of the tax and expenditure legislation then being considered by Congress. However, a number of restrictive actions were taken. Discount rates were raised from 4 to $4\frac{1}{2}$ percent in November, 1967, to 5 percent in March, and to $5\frac{1}{2}$ percent in April. Reserve requirements on demand deposits in excess of $5 million at each bank were raised by $\frac{1}{2}$ percent for all classes of member banks. The Federal Reserve did continue to purchase government securities, but at a slower rate. As a result of these policies, unborrowed reserves of member banks rose only $539 million between October, 1967 and June, 1968, member-bank borrowings from the Federal Reserve rose from $126 million to $692 million, and net free reserves of member banks declined from a positive level of $160 million to a negative level of $341 million.

Both short- and long-term interest rates rose significantly. For example, between October, 1967 and June, 1968, the yield on 3-month Treasury bills rose from 4.55 to 5.54 percent and that on Aaa corporate bonds rose from 5.82 to 6.28 percent. Judged on the basis of the behavior of monetary aggregates, monetary policies in this period appear less restrictive. The money supply rose at an annual rate of 7.2 percent and time deposits at commercial banks increased at an annual rate of 8.1 percent. In addition to these increases, total expenditure for output rose at an annual rate of 10.5 percent, and the consumer price index increased at an annual rate of 4.5 percent. By this time, an increasing number of people were complaining that Federal Reserve policies were being guided too much by the behavior of interest rates and not enough by the behavior of the money supply.

MONETARY POLICIES, JUNE TO NOVEMBER, 1968

In late June, 1968, a full three years after federal expenditures began their rapid rise, Congress finally passed the Revenue and Expenditure Control Act, which provided for a 10 percent surtax on personal and corporate income taxes and a reduction of $6 billion in federal expenditures. This action was widely expected to be highly effective in restricting the rise of aggregate demands for output, in curbing price inflation, in lowering interest rates by reducing government borrowing, by lessening inflationary expectations, and by making feasible a less restrictive monetary policy. In fact, some feared an "overkill" if the restrictive fiscal actions were not accompanied by some relaxation of monetary policies. Federal Reserve officials shared these views. At a meeting on June 18, the FOMC instructed the manager of the open-market account, ". . . that if the proposed fiscal legislation is enacted, operations shall accommodate tendencies for short-term interest rates to decline in connection with such affirmative congressional action on the pending fiscal legislation so long as bank credit expansion does not exceed current projections."[2] Such a policy of "accommodation" was followed from the end of June through November, 1968. During this period, Federal Reserve holdings of government securities were increased by $2 billion, which permitted the unborrowed reserves of member banks to rise by $1.2 billion. Discount rates were lowered from 5½ to 5¼ percent in August. The money supply rose from $190 billion to $196 billion, for an increase of 3.2 percent. Interest rates declined until September and then began to rise gradually.

By December, it had become only too clear that the fiscal actions initiated in June were less effective than had been expected. Total expenditures for output were rising rapidly, price inflation continued, and the balance of payments was deteriorating. It was under these conditions that the Federal Reserve shifted to a more restrictive policy in mid-December.

MONETARY POLICIES, DECEMBER, 1968 TO FEBRUARY, 1970

The restrictive policy initiated in mid-December, 1968 became more stringent during 1969 and was not terminated until February, 1970. Monetary and fiscal policies did not attempt to decrease total expenditures for output or even to pre-

[2] *Annual Report of the Board of Governors of the Federal Reserve System,* 1968, p. 166.

vent any further increases. Instead, they tried to slow down the rate of increase of money demands for output, and hoped that the restricted rise of demands, together with the growing productive capacity of the economy, would gradually slow down the rate of price inflation with a minimum of depressing effects on employment and real economic growth. These hopes proved to be overly optimistic.

Monetary policies were highly restrictive. As we shall see later, the money supply was allowed to rise only slightly despite continuing increases in demands for money balances for transactions purposes. And monetary restrictions, together with rising demands for credit, raised market rates of interest, both short-term and long-term, to their highest levels in more than a century. For example, Table 26–11, showing monthly averages of yields, indicates that the peak levels reached

Table 26–11 Market rates of interest, November, 1968–February, 1970 (yields in percent per annum)

PERIOD	3-MONTH TREASURY BILLS	PRIME 4–6-MONTH COM-MERCIAL PAPER	FEDERAL FUNDS RATE	PRIME RATE CHARGED BY BANKS	U.S. TREASURY BONDS	AAA CORPORATE BONDS
November, 1968	5.45	5.92	5.81	6.25	5.36	6.19
December	5.94	6.17	6.02	6.50–6.75	5.65	6.45
January, 1969	6.13	6.53	6.30	7.00	5.74	6.59
February	6.12	6.62	6.64	7.00	5.86	6.66
March	6.01	6.82	6.79	7.50	6.05	6.85
April	6.11	7.04	7.41	7.50	5.84	6.89
May	6.03	7.35	8.67	7.50	5.85	6.79
June	6.43	8.23	8.90	8.50	6.06	6.98
July	6.98	8.65	8.61	8.50	6.07	7.08
August	6.97	8.33	9.19	8.50	6.02	6.97
September	7.08	8.48	9.15	8.50	6.32	7.14
October	6.99	8.56	9.00	8.50	6.27	7.33
November	7.24	8.46	8.85	8.50	6.51	7.35
December	7.81	8.84	8.97	8.50	6.81	7.72
January, 1970	7.87	8.78	8.98	8.50	6.86	7.91
February	7.13	8.55	8.98	8.50	6.44	7.93

SOURCE: *Federal Reserve Bulletin,* various issues.

during this period were 7.87 percent for 3-month Treasury bills, 8.84 percent for prime commercial paper, 9.19 percent for federal funds, 8.5 percent on bank loans to prime customers, 6.86 percent on long-term government bonds, and 7.91 percent on the highest grade corporate bonds. In view of both the large rise of interest rates and the high levels reached, it is not surprising that financial markets were at times turbulent, that large amounts of funds were diverted away from financial intermediaries and into higher yielding open-market assets, and that large amounts of funds flowed to the United States from foreign financial centers.

The Federal Reserve used all its major instruments for restrictive purposes. Discount rates were increased from 5¼ to 5½ percent in December, 1968 and to 6 percent in April. Another action in April raised reserve requirements against demand deposits at all member banks by ½ percent, thus increasing required reserves by about $650 million. Federal Reserve open-market policy was such as to prevent any significant increase in the unborrowed reserves of member banks (see Table 26–12). During most of 1969, these reserves were at or below the levels pre-

Table 26–12 Member-bank Reserves, the money supply, and time deposits at commercial banks, November, 1968–February, 1970 (Reserve data in millions of dollars, and the money supply and time deposits in billions of dollars)

PERIOD	TOTAL RESERVES	BORROWING AT THE FEDERAL RESERVE	UNBORROWED RESERVES	NET FREE RESERVES	MONEY SUPPLY (SEASONALLY ADJUSTED)	TIME DEPOSITS (SEASONALLY ADJUSTED)
November, 1968	$26,785	$ 569	$26,216	−$ 245	$196.0	$201.8
December	27,221	765	26,456	− 310	197.4	204.8
January, 1969	28,063	697	27,366	− 480	198.1	203.7
February	27,291	824	26,467	− 596	199.3	203.2
March	26,754	918	25,836	− 701	200.1	202.5
April	27,079	996	26,083	− 844	201.0	202.1
May	27,903	1,402	26,501	− 1,102	201.6	201.7
June	27,317	1,407	25,910	− 1,064	202.4	201.2
July	26,980	1,190	25,790	− 1,074	203.1	198.1
August	27,079	1,249	25,830	− 946	202.6	195.4
September	26,971	1,067	25,904	− 831	202.8	194.8
October	27,340	1,135	26,205	− 992	203.2	194.2
November	27,764	1,241	26,523	− 998	203.5	194.0
December	28,031	1,086	26,945	− 829	203.6	194.6
January, 1970	28,858	965	27,893	− 799	205.2	193.3
February	27,976	1,092	26,884	− 819	204.5	193.5

SOURCE: *Federal Reserve Bulletin*, various issues.

vailing in late 1968, and even in February, 1970 they were only 1.5 percent above their level of a year earlier. The banks were faced with a difficult dilemma: While the Federal Reserve refused to provide additional reserves through open-market purchases, customer demands for bank loans were high and rising rapidly. Banks, therefore, were anxious to obtain funds from whatever source they could find. Their borrowings from the Federal Reserve reached $1.4 billion in May, 1969 and averaged more than $1.1 billion through the rest of the year. Banks would have liked to borrow much more from the Reserve banks at the prevailing discount rate of 6 percent, but they knew the Federal Reserve would disapprove, and some considered it prudent to conserve some borrowing power for use in an emergency. Many banks would have liked to have attracted more funds by raising their rates on savings and time deposits, but the Federal Reserve refused to raise the ceilings. As yields on competing assets rose, banks in general were not only unable to attract more funds but also suffered net outflows. Withdrawals from large-denomination negotiable CDs were especially large. As shown in Table 26–12, the trend of total time and savings deposits at commercial banks were descending through 1969; by December, these deposits were 5 percent below their level of a year earlier.

Banks competed with each other in many ways for the existing supply of reserves.

1. They borrowed federal funds. Increased demands for these funds, together with decreases in the supply of excess reserves, pushed the federal-funds rate to very high levels. During the last half of 1969 this rate averaged about 9 percent, or 3 percentage points above the Federal Reserve discount rate.

2. They sold some of their holdings of securities, especially obligations of the federal government and of state and local governments, thereby accentuating rises of yields on these securities.

3. They sold some of their loans and participations in their loans. Some of these sales were outright and some were under repurchase agreement.

4. Their subsidiaries and affiliates issued commercial paper and made the proceeds available to the banks. The amount of bank-related commercial paper outstanding appears to have increased more than $3 billion during the year.

5. They borrowed huge amounts of Eurodollars, mostly through their foreign branches. Liabilities of American banks to their foreign branches rose from $8.5 billion in January, 1969 to a peak of more than $15 billion in November and averaged above $14.5 billion during the rest of the year. On many of these borrowings banks paid interest rates in excess of 10 percent.

Despite their competitive scramble for funds, banks were forced to curtail expansion of their loans to customers, including business firms. They did this to some extent by increasing interest rates. For example, the prime rate was increased in three steps to 8.5 percent. However, banks also used various types of nonprice rationing. Firms that could not meet all their needs through bank borrowing turned to other sources—to issues of commercial paper, to expensive long-term financing, to sales of liquid assets, to increases in their accounts payable, and so on. Well before the end of the year, many firms were in a highly illiquid condition.

As in 1966, the sharp rise of market yields was accompanied by financial disintermediation. This was evidenced primarily in a decreased net flow of funds to financial intermediaries, although some institutions suffered net withdrawals. The shrinkage of net inflows was especially severe during the second half of 1969. For example, during that period, outstanding shares of savings and loan associations rose only $0.6 billion, total deposits at mutual savings banks increased only $0.9 billion, and the total volume of funds available to life insurance companies for purposes other than policy loans increased only $3.4 billion. These developments tended to reduce sharply the supply of mortgage funds, thereby depressing residential construction. The Federal National Mortgage Association and the Federal Home Loan Bank Board supplied some assistance by issuing and selling in the market large amounts of claims against themselves and channeling the proceeds to the principal mortgage lenders. However, these actions were not sufficient to prevent a net reduction in total funds supplied to mortgage markets.

Thus, no matter what criteria one may use, monetary policies in 1969 were highly restrictive. We have already mentioned the rise of interest rates to their highest levels in more than a century, the tight rein kept on the unborrowed reserves of member banks, and the shrinkage of total time and savings deposits at commercial banks. The money supply rose 3.1 percent during 1969, but the annual rate of increase during the second half of the year was only 1 percent. Total bank credit rose by 3.4 percent during the year.

We noted earlier that it was hoped that these monetary policies together with fiscal policies would gradually reduce price inflation with a minimum of depressing effects on employment and real economic growth. By the early months of 1970, it was becoming increasingly clear that the plan was not working. On the one hand, price inflation continued unabated. Increases for 1969 as a whole were 6 percent for the consumer price index, 4.8 percent for the wholesale price index, and 4.7 percent for the GNP price deflator. The rate of increase did not fall as the year progressed. Wages increased much faster than productivity, thereby raising unit labor costs. On the other hand, real economic growth and employment were affected adversely. Real GNP grew less than 3 percent during 1969; and in the fourth quarter of the year, its growth was completely halted. In the first quarter of 1970, real GNP was 1 percent below its level in the third quarter of 1969. The unemployment rate, which had averaged about 3.3 percent during the first months of 1969, reached 3.9 percent in January, 1970 and 4.2 percent in February; by May, it was about 6 percent.

MONETARY POLICIES AFTER FEBRUARY, 1970

Federal Reserve officials were in a quandary as they reviewed their policies at the beginning of 1970. They knew that industrial production had been falling for five months, that growth of real GNP had halted, and that unemployment was rising; they had good reason to believe that the situation would deteriorate further in the absence of positively expansionary actions. But they also knew that there were no signs of a decrease in the rate of price inflation, that inflationary expectations were strong and widespread, that the balance of payments was already in bad condition, and that a more expansionary monetary policy could well lead to large outflows of funds. This mixed situation explains why there were different judgments in the Federal Reserve during the first weeks of 1970, with some officials favoring a continuation of restrictive policies and others advocating relaxation. It also explains why the Federal Reserve moved cautiously for several weeks after it decided, in mid-February, to adopt more expansionary policies.

Not only monetary policies but also federal fiscal policies became more stimulative in 1970. The 10 percent surcharge on income taxes was terminated in two stages, the first of several tax reductions contained in the Tax Reform Act of 1969 became effective, and federal expenditures increased sharply, mainly through larger grants-in-aid to local governments and through transfer payments to individuals. As it moved toward more liberal policies, the Federal Reserve emphasized monetary aggregates—such as the money supply and the volume of bank credit—more than it had in earlier years. However, it continued to devote attention to the behavior of interest rates.

As usual, the Federal Reserve relied primarily on open-market operations to effectuate its policies. It purchased only cautiously at first, but more aggressively after mid-1970. In December, the unborrowed reserves of member banks were 8.5 percent above their level in June and 8 percent above their level in February (see Table 26–13). Further increases came in early 1971. Net free reserves of member

Table 26–13 Member-bank reserves, the money supply, and time deposits at commercial banks, 1970–1971 (reserve data in millions of dollars, and the money supply and time deposits in billions of dollars)

PERIOD	TOTAL RESERVES	BORROWINGS AT THE FEDERAL RESERVE	UNBORROWED RESERVES	NET FREE RESERVES	MONEY SUPPLY (SEASONALLY ADJUSTED)	TIME DEPOSITS (SEASONALLY ADJUSTED)
January, 1970	$28,858	$ 965	$27,893	−$ 799	$205.2	$193.3
February	27,976	1,092	26,884	— 819	204.5	193.5
March	27,473	896	26,577	— 781	206.6	195.3
April	28,096	822	27,274	— 704	208.3	198.5
May	27,910	976	26,934	— 795	209.2	200.3
June	27,567	888	26,679	— 701	209.6	202.2
July	28,128	1,358	26,770	— 1,217	210.6	208.2
August	28,349	827	27,522	— 682	211.8	213.2
September	28,825	607	28,218	— 335	212.8	218.5
October	28,701	462	28,239	— 208	213.2	222.2
November	28,558	425	28,133	— 305	213.5	225.0
December	29,265	321	28,944	— 49	214.6	230.4
January, 1971	30,488	370	30,118	— 91	214.8	235.3
February	29,880	328	29,552	— 127	217.3	240.9
March	29,686	319	29,367	— 120	219.4	246.1
April	29,885	148	29,737	— 8	221.1	248.3
May	30,419	330	30,089	— 18	223.9	251.4
June	30,023	453	29,570	— 322	225.6	254.4
July	30,547	820	29,727	— 658	227.5	256.8

banks rose from a negative level of more than $800 million in February, 1970 to a negative level of less than $100 million in December, and then fluctuated around this level during the first five months of 1971. The downward trend of member-bank borrowings from the Federal Reserve was temporarily interrupted during the late spring and early summer of 1970 by disturbances in the commercial-paper market associated with the financial distress of the Penn Central Transportation Co. The failure of this firm to meet its maturing commercial-paper obligations, and rumors that other important firms might follow suit, led to a sharp reduction of supplies of funds to the commercial-paper market and to fears that many businesses would be unable to roll over their commercial paper. The Federal Reserve took two actions to deal with this situation. First, it invited banks to borrow from their Reserve banks the amounts that would be needed to lend to firms that could not roll over their maturing commercial paper. Second, it suspended interest ceilings on large-denomination CDs with maturities of 30 to 89 days, thereby enabling banks to bid freely for these funds. These actions were sufficient to prevent a financial crisis.

Although the Federal Reserve relied primarily on open-market purchases for easing purposes, it also took several other actions. In January, it raised ceiling rates on time and savings deposits by amounts ranging from $1/2$ to $3/4$ percent. Similar actions were taken by the FDIC for nonmember banks and by the Federal Home Loan Bank Board for savings and loan associations. The principal purposes of these actions were to bring ceiling rates more in line with yields on competing assets and to encourage flows of funds to financial intermediaries. The rise of ceilings and the subsequent decline of market yields on competing short-term assets led to a rapid reintermediation. From their February level, total time and savings deposits at commercial banks rose 4.5 percent by June, 19.1 percent by December, and 31.5 percent by June, 1971. Outstanding shares at savings and loan associations rose 2.7 percent in the first half of 1970, 8.2 percent for the year as a whole, and 20.4 percent for the 18 months ending in June, 1971. Increases of deposits at mutual savings banks were 2.5 percent for the first half of 1970, 6.8 percent for the year, and 16 percent for the 18 months ending in June, 1971. These large inflows played a major role in raising supplies of mortgage funds and in stimulating residential construction.

Federal Reserve discount rates were reduced from 6 to $5\frac{3}{4}$ percent in November, 1970, and to $5\frac{1}{2}$ percent in December; three more reductions in early 1971 brought them down to $4\frac{3}{4}$ percent in February. In November, 1970, the Federal Reserve reduced reserve requirements against time deposits at each member bank in excess of $5 million from 6 to 5 percent. However, some of the expansionary effects of this action were offset by an accompanying action that subjected bank-related commercial paper to the same reserve requirements that were applicable to time deposits.

These actions permitted the money supply to rise much faster than it did in 1969. Increases above the level in February, 1970 were 2.5 percent by June, 1970, 4.9 percent by the end of the year, and 10.3 percent by June, 1971.

Both short- and long-term interest rates declined sharply in early 1970 as soon as it became evident that the Federal Reserve planned to relax its restrictive policies. However, after this initial reaction, short- and long-term rates behaved in different ways (see Table 26–14). Short-term rates declined almost continuously until the spring of 1971. In contrast, long-term rates rose sharply for several months and by mid-1970 were even higher than they had been in 1969. There appear to have been two major reasons for this behavior. One was the continuance of strong inflationary expectations, which made some people reluctant to purchase long-term bonds. The other was a huge increase in new bond issues, which rose from $44 billion in 1969 to more than $78 billion in 1970. More than half of the

Table 26–14 Market rates of interest, 1970–1971 (yields in percent per annum)

PERIOD	3-MONTH TREASURY BILLS	PRIME 4–6-MONTH COMMERCIAL PAPER	FEDERAL FUNDS RATE	PRIME RATE CHARGED BY BANKS	U.S. TREASURY BONDS	Aaa CORPORATE BONDS
January, 1970	7.87	8.78	8.98	8.50	6.86	7.91
February	7.13	8.55	8.98	8.50	6.44	7.93
March	6.63	8.33	7.76	8.00	6.39	7.84
April	6.50	8.06	8.10	8.00	6.53	7.83
May	6.83	8.23	7.94	8.00	6.94	8.11
June	6.67	8.21	7.60	8.00	6.99	8.48
July	6.45	8.29	7.21	8.00	6.57	8.44
August	6.41	7.90	6.61	8.00	6.75	8.13
September	6.12	7.32	6.29	7.50	6.63	8.09
October	5.90	6.85	6.20	7.50	6.59	8.03
November	5.28	6.30	5.60	7.25–7.00	6.24	8.05
December	4.87	5.73	4.90	6.75	5.97	7.64
January, 1971	4.44	5.11	4.14	6.50–6.00	5.91	7.36
February	3.69	4.47	3.72	5.75	5.84	7.08
March	3.38	4.19	3.71	5.50–5.25	5.71	7.21
April	3.85	4.57	4.15	5.50–5.25	5.75	7.25
May	4.13	5.10	4.63	5.50	5.96	7.53
June	4.74	5.45	4.91	5.50	5.94	7.64
July	5.39	5.75	5.31	6.00–5.50	5.91	7.64
August	4.93	5.73	5.57	6.00	5.78	7.59

increase was accounted for by government issues, but corporate-bond issues rose from $18.3 billion to $30.3 billion. The latter mainly reflected the efforts of business firms to rebuild their liquidity positions which had deteriorated markedly during the period of monetary restriction.

After reaching their peak in mid-1970, long-term interest rates declined sharply and almost continuously until the spring of 1971.

Thus, by mid-1971, despite the continuing price inflation, both monetary and fiscal policies had been stimulative for nearly 18 months. However, unemployment continued to hover around 6 percent. These developments will be discussed further in the next chapter.

Selected readings

Heller, W. W., and M. Friedman, *Monetary vs. Fiscal Policy,* New York, Norton, 1969.

Okun, A. M., *The Political Economy of Prosperity,* Washington, D.C., Brookings Institution, 1970.

CHAPTER 27

THE DOLLAR CRISIS OF 1971

On Sunday evening, August 15, 1971, President Nixon appeared on nationwide television to announce what he described as "The most comprehensive new economic policy to be undertaken by this country in four decades." Although the accuracy of this description is debatable, there can be no doubt that the announced changes were dramatic and sweeping, that at least some of them have not only short-run but also important long-run implications, and that they represented sharp departures from the policies previously followed by his Administration. Up to that time, he had staunchly defended his "game plan" for dealing with domestic inflation and unemployment and had flatly rejected all proposals for any kind of wage-price guidelines or wage-price review board. Now he imposed a 90-day freeze on wages, prices, and rents; stated that the freeze would be followed for a temporary but indefinite period by a program providing more flexible direct controls; and proposed further tax reductions to combat unemployment. His reversal on international monetary policies was no less dramatic. Prior to this announcement, he had affirmed and reaffirmed his determination to maintain the existing exchange rate on the dollar. Now he terminated convertibility of the dollar into gold and other reserve assets, declared his determination that exchange rates on other currencies should rise in terms of the dollar, and imposed a 10 percent surcharge on all dutiable imports.

The general public reaction was highly favorable, perhaps not so much as a result of the specific nature of the actions but as a result of a feeling of relief that "at last something is being done about the economic mess." A complex mess it certainly was: unabating price inflation in the face of excessive unemployment and underutilization of plant capacities, and a deficit in the nation's balance of payments that was not only continuing but was growing to mammoth proportions. Some type of comprehensive program was clearly indicated; piecemeal actions would not suffice.

BACKGROUNDS OF THE CRISIS

Let us now concentrate on the events in 1970 and the first 7½ months of 1971 to see how the crisis developed.

Domestic developments

We have already seen that, following the highly restrictive monetary policies of 1969, both monetary and fiscal policies became more stimulative in early 1970. The federal government increased its expenditures and lowered taxes, and the Federal Reserve adopted a moderately expansionary policy. By July, 1971, the money supply had risen 11 percent above its level in February, 1970, and time deposits at commercial banks had grown nearly 33 percent. Both long- and short-term interest rates had fallen sharply, although their decline was interrupted during the weeks preceding the crisis.

These policies were accompanied by some increase in real output. For example, GNP in real terms rose about 2.4 percent between the second quarter of 1970 and the second quarter of 1971. However, the growth rate was too small to reduce unemployment. During the summer of 1971, the unemployment rate hovered around 6 percent, about the same level that had prevailed during the preceding eight months and significantly above the levels of early 1970. At the same time, price increases continued at a rate above 5 percent with little sign of abatement, and currently negotiated wage increases were far above prospective increases in productivity per man-hour.

The monetary and fiscal authorities were in a dilemma. More restrictive policies to combat price inflation would raise unemployment above its already excessive level would probably be ineffective, at least in the short run, in curbing excessive wage increases which were creating cost-push pressures. On the other hand, more expansionary policies to combat unemployment would promote inflation, strengthen inflationary expectations, and accelerate deterioration in the balance of payments. Under these circumstances, direct limitations on wages and prices might eliminate or lessen cost-push pressures, permit a larger part of any increase in aggregate demand for output to be reflected in increases in real output and employment, and combat inflationary expectations. Also, termination of convertibility of the dollar into gold and other reserve assets, and a subsequent decline of the exchange rate on the dollar, would serve to equilibrate the balance of payments and give monetary and fiscal authorities greater freedom to concentrate on their domestic objectives.

The balance of payments

As noted earlier, the nation's deficit in its balance of payments, measured on an official reserve-transactions basis, was $10.7 billion in 1970, far larger than it had been in any preceding year. This deterioration resulted in part from a shrinkage of the balance on goods and services account, but much more from huge outflows of short-term funds on private account. The latter was initially in response to widening differentials in interest rates, as rates in the United States fell much faster than those in foreign financial centers. The balance of payments deteriorated still further in 1971. By the second quarter, there was actually a deficit on goods and services account. Short-term funds continued to flow out. During the first two months, these flows were still largely in response to differentials in interest rates. However, by March, speculative movements began to develop and outflows later grew to a flood.

Basic conditions in the balances of payments of the United States and a number of other countries were highly favorable to exchange speculation. Of course, no one could be certain that exchange rates would be realigned, or if they were realigned, no one could be sure of what changes any realignment would entail. However, the situation provided speculators with opportunities for significant profits with only a very small probability of significant losses. The American balance of payments was basically so weak that there was virtually a zero probability that the exchange parity on the dollar would be increased, and a significant probability that the dollar would decline in exchange markets. On the other hand, the balances of payments of a number of other countries were so basically strong that there was virtually a zero possibility that exchange rates on their currencies would be reduced, and a significant probability that they would be increased. Two of the "strongest" currencies were those of Germany and Japan, but most of the currencies of Western Europe were considered strong in comparison to the dollar. What better odds could a speculator want?

By April, there were large speculative flows of funds out of the United States and into various other countries—especially into Germany. These flows were not welcomed by the United States. They were welcomed even less by the recipient countries, whose central banks had to purchase huge amounts of dollars in order to prevent exchange rates on their currencies from rising above their upper limits. Then there occurred an event that might have attracted little attention under other circumstances: The main German economic research institutes recommended that the mark be revalued upward or allowed to float. After a high-ranking German official commented favorably on the proposal, inflows to Germany accelerated. The German central bank had to purchase $1 billion on May 3 and 4 and another $1 billion during the first 40 minutes of trading on May 5. At that point, the German central bank announced that it would buy no more dollars. Similar actions were taken immediately by the central banks of the Netherlands, Switzerland, Belgium, and Austria.

Over the following weekend, the Swiss franc was revalued upward by 7.07 percent and the Austrian schilling by 5.05 percent. The German mark and the Dutch guilder were allowed to float. These actions did not stop or even reduce speculative flows. Confidence in the dollar was eroded further by the United States' inability to halt the deterioration in its balance of payments and by its lack of progress in reducing the rate of inflation. Many thought that the foreign currencies that had already been revalued or allowed to float would rise still more, and that other countries might take similar actions.

Both the outflow of private funds and the deficit in the balance of payments of the United States were huge during the first 7½ months of 1971. For example, the net outflow of private short-term funds during the first seven months of 1971 was at least $7 billion and may have been considerably larger. The deficit in the balance of payments for the first half of 1971, as measured on the official reserve-transactions basis, was $11,264 million, and it continued to rise thereafter. During the first seven months of 1971, official reserve assets of the United States were drawn down by $2,356 million and liquid liabilities to foreign official reserve agencies rose by $12,896 million. On August 6, a report by a congressional sub-committee asserted that the dollar had become overvalued, and that the situation should be corrected through a general realignment of exchange rates. On the same day, the Treasury reported a $1 billion loss of gold and other international reserves. Outflows of funds accelerated sharply, and over the following week $3.7 billion flowed into foreign central banks. Such were some of the principal developments preceding the President's announcement of August 15.

COMPONENTS OF THE NEW ECONOMIC POLICY

Direct controls of wages, prices, and rents

As already indicated, the freeze order had several related purposes: to arrest the wage-price spiral, to weaken inflationary expectations, to enable a large part of any rise of demands for output to be reflected in increases of real output and employment, and to make more expansionary monetary and fiscal policies feasible. It was obvious that the freeze itself could be no more than a temporary stopgap, and that over a longer period it would become unacceptable and ineffective. One reason was that the freeze included many inequitable and disequilibrium price and wage relationships. For example, some employers had raised wages but had not yet raised their prices; others were in the reverse positions. Some recently negotiated wage increases had become effective and were therefore allowable; others had been negotiated but not yet effective and were therefore not allowable;

and so on. Such maladjustments might be tolerated for 90 days, but probably not much longer. A second reason that the freeze had to be only temporary was that it relied almost solely on voluntary compliance for enforcement.

When the 90-day freeze terminated in mid-November, it was followed by Phase II—a flexible program to limit, but not prevent, increases of wages and prices. Administration of the program was entrusted to three bodies appointed by the President: (1) the Cost of Living Council, a body within the executive department; (2) a Pay Board—a tripartite board composed of five public members, five members from labor, and five from business; (3) a Price Commission composed of seven public members. The Pay Board and Price Commission were given a high degree of autonomy, and the Cost of Living Council intervened only infrequently.

President Nixon refused, as he put it, "to create a bureaucratic monster" to administer wage and price controls and insisted that compliance should depend largely on voluntary cooperation. At least partly to minimize the required number of enforcement personnel, the Phase II administrators divided industry into three categories. The first, including only a few of "the largest and most significant industries," were permitted to raise wages and prices only with prior approval by the Pay Board and the Price Commission. The second, including some other large industries, were free to raise wages and prices but were required to report these increases. The third, including by far the largest number of business firms, were free to increase wages and prices, subject only to later inspection and protest. The coverage of price controls was reduced significantly in January, 1972, when the Cost of Living Council exempted from controls some types of rentals and all retailers with annual sales of less than $100,000. Coverage of both wage and price controls was reduced further in the following months.

The control authorities faced difficult problems in formulating standards for allowable wage and price increases. The standards announced were that on the average, wages should rise no more than 5.5 percent and prices no more than 2.5 percent a year. It was believed that these wage and price standards would be mutually consistent if average productivity per man-hour rose at an annual rate of 3 percent. However, the announcement of such average goals did not really solve the problem of standards, because it left unanswered such questions as: Which wages and prices should be allowed to rise more than the average, and how much more? Which should rise less than the average, and how much less? Under what conditions, and to what extent, should an employer experiencing an increase of his wage rates be permitted to raise the prices of his products? As might be expected, such questions proved to be highly controversial.

The first months of Phase II were stormy ones. At times it appeared that the labor members of the Pay Board might resign, and that labor would refuse to cooperate. Several of the early wage increases approved by the Board were far in excess of the 5.5 percent goal, and some of the price increases were well above the 2.5 percent standard. There were also many charges of violations of wage, price, and rent ceilings—although the actual extent of such violations is not known—

and several complaints that buyers were being hurt by increases in the prices of exempted products. Despite these difficulties, however, it appeared clear in the spring of 1972 that the control system had been at least partially and temporarily effective in preventing costs and prices from rising as fast as they would have risen in the absence of the direct-control system.

At the same time, there were several reasons to believe that this system would become less effective with the passage of time, and especially as employment and output approached their full-employment levels. For example:

1. Excess unemployment and excess plant capacity persisted until at least the autumn of 1972. The partial success of the wage-price control system under these conditions provided no basis for expecting similar success as aggregate demands for output rose fast enough to pull employment and output toward their full-employment levels.

2. A large number of products were exempted from price controls, and the system relied heavily on voluntary compliance due to the scarcity of enforcement facilities. These conditions virtually assured that price rises would become increasingly numerous, that those whose prices were more tightly controlled would become increasingly restive, that increases in the cost of living would militate against holding the line on wage increases, and that maladjustments of relative prices and wages would become more widespread.

For reasons such as these, it seemed highly likely in the autumn of 1972 that within a few months the Phase II-control system initiated in November, 1971 would be changed markedly or even abandoned. What its sequel would be was not at all clear.

International aspects of the new economic plan

Termination of convertibility of the dollar into gold and other reserve assets was a severe shock to the international monetary system that had been established nearly 25 years earlier under the Bretton Woods Agreements and forced reconsideration of almost all aspects of that system.

Exchange-rate realignments. The most immediate impact of the new economic plan was on the stability of exchange rates, because the dollar was now free to float. American authorities would no longer sell reserve assets or purchase dollars to limit declines of exchange rates on the dollar, nor would they buy reserve assets or sell dollars to depress the dollar in terms of other currencies. The behavior of exchange rates was to be determined by other participants in the market, including both private transactors and official foreign institutions. However, both the President and the Secretary of the Treasury made clear their determination that exchange rates on other currencies should rise markedly in terms of the dollar. For many weeks, they made no specific recommendations, but it was rumored that they would insist on an average appreciation of other currencies in the range of 12 to 15 percent. This would mean an improvement of perhaps $13 billion in the balance of payments of the United States.

The reaction of most foreign officials to changes of such magnitude was shock and disapproval. They contended that such large increases of exchange rates on their currencies would seriously damage both their export industries and their import-competing industries and might precipitate an economic recession. Even those who conceded that some depreciation of the dollar was appropriate believed that a smaller adjustment would be adequate. However, the issue was by no means confined to the size of the average appreciation of other currencies in terms of the dollar; it also included realignments of exchange rates among other currencies. It was obvious that whatever might be the *average* appreciation of other currencies in terms of the dollar, exchange rates on some currencies should rise considerably more than the average and others should rise considerably less. But differences in the percentage changes of the various currencies in terms of the dollar would bring changes in exchange rates among those currencies. The currencies that increased by the largest percentages in terms of the dollar would appreciate in terms of the currencies that had appreciated by small percentages in terms of dollars. Thus, to protect and promote its position in international trade, each nation tended to fight for a smaller appreciation of its currency relative to the dollar and also for a smaller percentage increase than those applicable to other currencies. For example, Germany and other nations that believed the United States was asking for an excessive average appreciation of foreign currencies in terms of the dollar, nevertheless wanted the largest percentage appreciation for the Japanese yen, so that the latter would become more expensive in terms of their own currencies. France wanted the German mark to appreciate more than the French franc, and so on.

Controversies were sharpened and probably prolonged by the temporary 10 percent surtax imposed by the President on all dutiable imports. This was designed as a bargaining device, to be withdrawn when foreigners had made "adequate" concessions to American demands, which extended beyond the realignment of exchange rates. The President and the Secretary of the Treasury asserted that the United States was not responsible for the international crisis; they claimed that the crisis had resulted from the activities of speculators and from the uncooperative and harmful policies of other countries. Those countries had not taken action to eradicate the surpluses in their balances of payments, their contributions for the support of NATO forces in Europe were inadequate, and their international trade policies were generally too restrictive and particularly discriminatory against American exports. No mention was made of similar protectionist policies in the United States. Resentment against the import surcharge was enhanced by its blunderbuss nature: It applied indiscriminately to exports of countries with deficits in their balances of payments as well as to those with surpluses, to underdeveloped as well as developed countries, and to countries with liberal trade policies as well as those that were highly protectionist. Whatever may have been the merits of the import surcharge as a bargaining weapon, it presented at least three dangers: that the resentment it created would make it more difficult to arrive at acceptable realignments of exchange rates, that it would lead to an international trade war, and that it would further encourage the already-growing protectionist sentiment in the United States.

European governments responded to President Nixon's announcement on August 15 by closing their exchange markets and keeping them closed for a week. During this period, they tried to arrive at a common response to the American actions. After the attempt failed, revealing wide differences among the countries, exchange markets were reopened on an uncoordinated basis on Monday, August 23. No country changed the exchange parity of its currency. France adopted a double exchange rate, a commercial rate and a financial rate. The latter was allowed to float upward, but the former was held to its old upper limit. All the other countries allowed their currencies to float; they would no longer buy dollars and supply their own currencies in such a way as to prevent exchange rates on their currencies from rising above their old upper limits. However, they did not permit a "free float"; their official agencies intervened extensively, usually to buy dollars in order to decrease the extent of the decline of the dollar exchange rate. For about two weeks, the Japanese authorities bought dollars freely to prevent any rise of the exchange rate on the yen. However, on August 28, after buying $4.4 billion, they allowed the yen to float upward, but with continued official intervention to limit the rise.

American authorities were unhappy about the inervention by foreign agencies, and referred to the situation as "a dirty float." They wanted "a clean float," under which the behavior of exchange rates would be determined solely by demand and supply conditions without official interference. As might be expected, other countries refused to end their intervention, but they gradually allowed rates on their currencies to rise.

Although the central issue in these controversies was the realignment of exchange rates among the various national currencies, the controversy extended to the mechanics of achieving realignments. What specific actions should be taken to achieve the realignments that came to be agreed upon, whatever those might be? Debate on this issue became heated. One basic question was: In terms of what common unit should the prices of the various national currencies be stated? Several alternatives were available. One option was to state the prices of all currencies in terms of a selected national currency, such as the dollar. If this were done, parities among national currencies would be determined by their relative prices in terms of the dollar. For example, if prices were set at currency A = $2 and currency B = $0.50, the parity would be 4B = 1A. This alternative was rejected because many countries refused to accept a "dollar standard." Another alternative was to state the prices of all currencies in terms of SDRs. This was not adopted, probably because SDRs were so new and had never been used as a basic unit of account; in fact, the value of the SDR was stated in terms of gold. Not surprisingly, it was finally decided to follow the traditional practice of using gold as the common unit of measurement. Under this system, parities among currencies depend upon the relative values of the currencies in terms of gold or, what amounts to the same thing, the relative official prices of gold in terms of the various currencies. For example, if the official prices per ounce of fine gold are set at 40 units of currency A and 160 units of currency B, the parity will be 4B = 1A. Note that this method can be used to determine parities among currencies even though no gold is purchased or sold by the monetary authorities. In other words, a change in the official price of gold does not necessarily imply that the authority will purchase or sell gold at that or any other price.

An increase of the parity of another currency in terms of the dollar can be achieved by increasing the official price of gold in terms of dollars, by lowering the price of gold in terms of the foreign currency, or by employing various combinations of the two actions. This is because the parity of the other currency in terms of the dollar is equal to $\dfrac{\text{the dollar price of gold}}{\text{the price of gold in the other currency}}$.

Suppose, for example, that it is desired to increase by 10 percent the parity on another currency in terms of the dollar. This could be achieved by raising the dollar price of gold by 10 percent, while the price of gold in terms of the other currency remained unchanged. Alternatively, it could be achieved through a decrease of approximately 9 percent in the price of gold in terms of the foreign currency while the dollar price of gold remained unchanged. Or it could be achieved through various combinations, such as a 6 percent increase in the dollar price of gold together with approximately a 4 percent decrease in the price of gold in terms of the foreign currency.

It soon became apparent that the various governments were by no means indifferent concerning the methods to be used to realign exchange rates. For several weeks, the American authorities insisted that they would not even consider raising the dollar price of gold. Some other countries, notably France, insisted that they would allow exchange rates on their currencies to rise only if the United States "made a contribution" by increasing the dollar price of gold. The American authorities appeared to believe that devaluation of the dollar in terms of gold would be viewed as a sign of weakness and as an admission of policy mistakes by the United States. These authorities continued to maintain that other countries had caused the trouble, and it was their responsibility to take actions to remedy it. France, on the other hand, insisted that the crisis had been created by American mistakes, and that the United States should admit this and raise the dollar price of gold. However, there were also more substantive reasons for such differences in attitudes. For one thing, each government knew that a significant increase of the exchange rate on its currency in terms of the dollar would be deeply resented by members of both its export and its import-competing industries. If the government itself raised its exchange rate by lowering the price of gold, its responsibility for the results would be clear, and it might suffer severe political consequences. However, if the same increase in its exchange rate resulted from an increase in the dollar price of gold by the American government, the political impact on the nation's government might be softened, although the economic impact on the country would be the same.

Another consideration related to effects on the value of each nation's stock of international reserves in the form of gold, SDRs, and dollars. Consider two cases:

1. A nation decreases the price of gold in terms of its own currency while the dollar price of gold remains unchanged. As measured in terms of its own currency, the value of all types of its international reserves will decrease. However, as measured in terms of gold or dollars, the value of its international reserves will remain unchanged.

2. The nation does not change the price of gold in terms of its own currency, but the dollar price of gold is increased. As measured in terms of its own currency, the value of its gold and SDRs will remain unchanged but the value of its dollar holdings will decline. However, as measured in terms of dollars, the value of its dollar holdings will remain unchanged, but the value of its gold and SDRs will rise.

Such considerations seem much less important than the main issue—realignment of exchange rates—but they were hotly debated.

For many weeks following August 15, both American and foreign authorities tended to maintain their initial positions, and there was little progress toward a realignment of exchange parities. Gradually, however, both sides moved towards more cooperative attitudes. The American authorities became willing to agree to a small increase in the dollar price of gold as a part of a broader program and implied that they might reduce the amount of concessions required as a condition for removing the 10 percent surtax on imports. Foreign authorities gradually accepted the idea that some appreciation of their currencies in terms of the dollar was inevitable and allowed their currencies to float upward, although still with official restraints.

Finally, on December 18, representatives of the Group of Ten, including 10 leading industrial countries, arrived at an agreement. Although some aspects of the agreement did not conform to the rules of the IMF, the IMF approved it as an interim arrangement. The agreement had three principal parts:

1. Realignment of exchange parities, or, as they were called in the agreement, "central rates." Representatives of the United States agreed to request Congress to raise the price of gold from $35 to $38 an ounce, an increase of 8.57 percent. This would raise by 8.57 percent the exchange of parities on currencies of those countries that did not change the price of gold in terms of their currencies. France and Britain followed this course (see Table 27–1). Five other major countries lowered the price of gold in terms of their currencies, so that all their parities in terms of the dollar rose by more than 11 percent. Italy and Sweden raised their prices of gold, but by only about 1 percent, so that their parities in terms of the dollar rose nearly 7.5 percent. Thus, parities on currencies of other countries accounting for a major part of world trade were increased in terms of the dollar. Canada did not fix a new parity but allowed her currency to float upward.

Table 27–1 Changes in exchange rates of major currencies in relation to the dollar, January 1, 1971–December 31, 1971

CURRENCY	PERCENTAGE INCREASE
Japanese yen	16.88
Swiss franc	13.88
West German mark	13.58
Netherlands guilder	11.57
Belgian franc	11.57
French franc	8.57
United Kingdom pound	8.57
Swedish krona	7.49
Italian lira	7.48
Canadian dollar	*

* No new parity was adopted for the Canadian dollar and it continued to float.
SOURCE: *Economic Report of the President,* January, 1972, Washington, D.C., U.S. Government Printing Office, 1972, p. 143.

2. Widening of the band between official intervention limits. The old limits had been 1 percent above and 1 percent below parity; the new limits were 2.25 percent above and below.

3. Immediate removal of the 10 percent surcharge on dutiable imports by the United States. This was welcomed by foreign countries, who had feared that the United States would require many more trade concessions before removing the tax.

However, in entering into the agreement described above, the United States had not abandoned its demands that other countries accord more liberal treatment to American exports and, in some cases, limit their own exports to the United States, and it was still at least determined to use its bargaining power to force concessions. A formal increase in the price of gold to $38 an ounce required Congressional action. American negotiators warned their counterparts that in the absence of trade concessions, Congress might refuse to raise the price of gold or might attach highly protective provisions to the legislation.

Haggling over such issues continued for more than seven weeks following the December 18 agreement, and it was not until February 9, 1972 that the President formally asked Congress to raise the official price of gold from $35 to $38 an ounce. Congress complied, but the purpose of the legislation was merely to facilitate a modification of exchange parities, and there was no commitment to buy or sell gold at the new price or any other price.

Convertibility of the dollar into international reserve assets. In the agreements of December 18, the United States made no commitments concerning restoration of convertibility of the dollar in terms of gold or other international reserve assets. However, it is likely that most representatives of the participating countries expected that realignment of parities, with new and widened official intervention limits, would be followed as soon as practicable by measures to restore convertibility. They must therefore have been disappointed as it became evident that the Americans were in no hurry at all to begin considering this problem and especially when, in mid-February, the Secretary of the Treasury stated that convertibility would not be restored during 1972, but that some progress toward that objective might be made in 1973. The strong implication was that in the meantime there would be little or no official intervention by the United States to prevent the exchange rate on the dollar from falling below its lower intervention limit.

Around the time of the December agreement, the difficulties of keeping the exchange rate on the dollar within its new intervention limits tended to be underestimated. Observers were correct in stating that for the forseeable future it would be easy to prevent the exchange rate on the dollar from rising above its upper intervention limit. Foreign central banks, holding more than $45 billion of liquid claims on dollars, would be both able and more than willing to supply enough dollars for this purpose. They proved to be wrong, however, in forecasting that the problem of preventing the exchange rate on the dollar from falling below its lower intervention limit would be largely solved for some time by a huge reflow to the United States of the short-term funds that had gone abroad during 1970 and 1971. The reflow did not occur. A major reason for this was that, partly because of the Federal Reserve easy-money policy, interest rates in the United States were below those in foreign financial centers. Other reasons included the long delay in ratifying the increase in the dollar price of gold and fears that the dollar would be allowed to decline further. As the hoped-for return of short-term funds failed to materialize, the American balance of payments remained in heavy deficit.

As the United States continued to refuse to take any action to prevent the dollar from falling below its lower intervention limit, foreign monetary authorities faced a painful but familiar dilemma; they had to choose between purchasing still more unwanted dollars and allowing the exchange rate on the dollar to decline still more. Most of them reluctantly decided to buy more dollars. By the summer of 1972, the dollar holdings of foreign central banks had soared above $53 billion. These would have been even larger if Japan and several European countries had not instituted direct control on capital inflows. Among the devices used were prohibition of interest on deposits by foreigners, negative interest rates on deposit liabilities to nonresidents, special reserve requirements ranging up to 100 percent on increases of deposit liabilities to foreigners, prohibition of sales of earning assets to nonresidents, and limitations on borrowing abroad.

Thus, uncertainty continued to shroud the international monetary system. No one could forecast whether the new parities would remain unchanged, when full convertibility of the dollar into some type of international reserve would be accomplished, or precisely what steps would be taken to achieve that end. However, it was clear that three major types of problems would have to be solved: (1) elimination, or at least a marked reduction, of the deficit in the American balances of payments; (2) removal of at least a part of the huge "overhang" of short-term claims against dollars held so reluctantly by foreign monetary authorities; and (3) reform of the international liquidity system.

MONETARY AND FISCAL POLICIES

As noted earlier, one of the purposes of both the system of wage and price controls and the termination of the convertibility of the dollar was to achieve greater freedom to expand aggregate demand in order to reduce the unemployment and underutilization of capacity that still prevailed in August, 1971. Both fiscal and monetary policies were used for this purpose.

Fiscal policies

Expansionary fiscal actions included both tax reductions and expenditure increases by the federal government. Tax reductions were of several types: provision of more liberal depreciation rules for business, a 7 percent tax credit for business purchases of equipment, repeal of the 7 percent excise tax on automobiles, an increase of personal exemptions under the federal income tax from $650 to $675 for 1971 and $750 for 1972, and an increase of the minimum standard deduction on income from $1,000 to $1,300. Federal expenditures began to rise in late 1971 and were accelerated in the first half of 1972 to provide more stimulus to the economy. The overall budget deficit for the fiscal year ending June 30, 1972 was forecast to reach more than $38 billion. A major part of this reflected a shortfall of revenues because GNP was so far below its full-employment level. The full-employment deficit—that which would have resulted if the unemployment rate had averaged only 4 percent—was estimated at about $8 billion.

The President's proposed budget for the fiscal year ending June 30, 1973, which he submitted to Congress in January 1972, provided for some further stimuluation of the national economy, primarily through increasing federal expenditures by at least $10 billion. It seemed likely, however, that Congress would press for larger increases, partly to promote a larger rise of aggregate demands, but perhaps even more to expand specific government programs of nonmilitary types.

Monetary policies

As we saw in the preceding chapter, the Federal Reserve began to move toward an expansionary policy in February, 1970. By the end of the year, the whole structure of interest rates had fallen, the money supply had risen nearly 5 percent, and large amounts of funds were flowing into financial intermediaries; these funds included time deposits at commercial banks. Expansionary policies were continued throughout 1971 and at least until the autumn of 1972, though their degree of expansiveness varied from time to time. During 1971, discount rates were decreased in four steps from 5½ to 4½ percent, the lowest level since early 1968. As usual, however, the Federal Reserve relied largely on open-market operations, purchasing enough government securities to offset currency and other drains and to increase the unborrowed reserves of member banks (see Table 27–2). The latter rose nearly 8 percent during 1971, but the rate of increase was

Table 27–2 Member-bank reserve positions, 1971–1972 (millions of dollars, monthly averages of daily figures)

PERIOD	TOTAL RESERVES	UNBORROWED RESERVES	BORROWING AT THE FEDERAL RESERVE	EXCESS RESERVES	FREE RESERVES
December, 1970	$29,265	$28,944	$321	$272	—$ 49
January, 1971	30,488	30,118	370	279	— 91
February	29,880	29,552	328	201	— 127
March	29,686	29,367	319	199	— 120
April	29,885	29,737	148	140	— 8
May	30,419	30,089	330	312	— 18
June	30,023	29,570	453	131	— 322
July	30,547	29,727	820	162	— 658
August	30,455	29,651	804	198	— 606
September	30,802	30,300	501	206	— 295
October	30,860	30,500	360	207	— 153
November	30,950	30,544	406	257	— 149
December	31,308	31,200	108	156	48
January, 1972	32,865	32,845	20	173	153
February	31,922	31,889	33	124	91
March	31,921	31,822	99	233	134
April	32,565	32,456	109	136	27
May	32,812	32,693	119	104	— 15
June	32,518	32,424	94	180	86

SOURCE: *Federal Reserve Bulletin,* various issues.

lower in the first half of 1972. The money supply rose 6.2 percent during 1971 and 3.6 percent in the first half of 1972. Increases of time and savings deposits at commercial banks were 17.9 percent in 1971 and 7.8 percent in the first half of 1972. The stated objective of the Federal Reserve was to provide enough money and credit to promote and support a recovery output and employment but not so much as to rekindle inflationary pressures and expectations.

OUTPUT, EMPLOYMENT, AND PRICES

After declining slightly at the end of 1969 and in the first quarter of 1970, real GNP began to rise again, slowly at first and then somewhat faster. By mid-1972 it was about 9 percent above its level in the first quarter of 1970. However, the actual rise of output was too small to offset the rise of overall productive capacity resulting from the continuing increase of the labor force, the increasing stock of capital goods and advances in technology, so that both employment and output remained well below their full-employment levels. Neither the presence of excess capacity nor the system of wage and price controls had stopped price inflation, though the rate of price increases had declined somewhat. The price level of output as a whole had risen about 3 percent during the preceding year.

The economic outlook remained uncertain in the autumn of 1972. Both employment and output were expected to continue to rise through at least the first half of 1973, though there were differences of opinion concerning both the speed and the duration of the rise. The outlook for the behavior of prices was especially cloudy. This resulted from several types of uncertainty: uncertainty as to the speed and extent of future increases of aggregate demand for output; uncertainty as to the time when wage and price controls under Phase II would be further relaxed or removed and what their sequels would be; and uncertainties as to the extent of wage increases in 1973, when a record number of wage contracts would come up for renewal. One thing did seem certain—that we still face problems.

Selected readings

Burns, A. F., "Some Essentials of International Monetary Reform," *Federal Reserve Bulletin,* June, 1972, pp. 545–549.

Okun, A. M., *The Political Economy of Prosperity,* Washington, D.C., Brookings Institution, 1970.

Schultz, C. L., R. E. Fried, A. M. Rivlin, and N. H. Teeters, *Setting National Priorities: The 1973 Budget,* Washington, D.C., Brookings Institution, 1972.

CHAPTER 28

THE FUTURE

The preceding chapters have surveyed the American monetary and banking system—its institutional structure, principles of operation, objectives, and policies.
Its history has been characterized by both continuity and change. Elements of
continuity are so strong that one cannot understand present structures and policies without referring to events and ways of thinking that date back many
decades, even to the early nineteenth century. There have also been changes—
some gradual, some abrupt and discontinuous, some noncontroversial, but most
have been highly controversial. Viewing the situation from the vantage point of
1972, there is no reason to believe that the conflict between continuity and change
is at an end or that future changes will be any slower or less pervasive than the
changes in the past. No one can forsee all of the changes that might occur, but
enough tensions and conflicts are already apparent to insure that the future will
be far from static. We shall mention only a few of the major issues that are already
apparent or are likely to develop.

THE INTERNATIONAL SETTING

In suspending the convertibility of the dollar into gold and other reserve assets on August 15, 1971, President Nixon effectively suspended the operation of the international monetary system that had evolved under the Bretton Woods Agreement. He thereby forced a reconsideration of virtually all aspects of that system. However, neither this action nor the many actions that followed it in the next few months provided enduring resolutions of basic issues or established a new system that can be expected to be permanent.

In establishing new parities, though with a wider band between official intervention limits, the monetary authorities of most countries again revealed their strong preference for a system of pegged-exchange rates rather than flexible or floating rates. However, this decision leaves many questions: Under what conditions will parties be realigned? Will they be changed only rarely and in large steps, or more frequently and in smaller steps? What specific methods will be used to change parities? Such questions will have to be answered as the pattern of realigned parities proves to be inappropriate and produces large deficits for some countries and large surpluses for others. At least some of the realigned parities were probably inappropriate even under the conditions existing at the time of their adoption. Other parities will become inappropriate with the passage of time if, as seems almost certain, most nations continue to refuse to allow their monetary and fiscal policies to be dominated by their balance-of-payments positions rather than by their domestic objectives. The issue of the "optimum flexibility of exchange rates" is still very much with us.

Also unresolved are many issues relating to the international reserve and liquidity system. Gold will almost certainly have a declining role in this system. The greatest likelihood is that little or no more gold will be purchased for monetary purposes. However, even if some gold is purchased for monetary purposes its role in the monetary system is still likely to decline. One reason for this is that little gold is likely to be offered to the monetary authorities in the absence of a very large increase in official prices for gold or large gold discoveries or a sharp decline of nonmonetary demands for gold. Also, countries are unlikely to adopt any system in which the size and rate of growth of international reserves would be dominated by the vagaries of gold mining and nonmonetary demands for gold.

The international roles of the dollar are also uncertain. The dollar will probably remain the major medium of international payments. Private foreigners will also probably hold large amounts of dollar-denominated claims as investment assets. However, in making such forecasts, one should remember that once the British pound was *the* great medium of international payments and London was the supreme international financial center. The dollar will almost certainly have a smaller role as a component of official international reserves than it did in the years preceding the crisis of 1971. Even if foreign monetary authorities forget and forgive the depreciation of the dollar in terms of gold, SDRs, and major national currencies, they will oppose any system in which the size of international reserves is dominated by the state of the balance of payments of the United States.

Almost by default, a greater role will be played by SDRs or some other type of reserve asset that can be created and managed by the IMF or some other international institution. As the role of this type of asset is expanded, the SDR scheme will undoubtedly be modified. In the past, the amounts of issues were planned several years in advance, and lump sums were issued at the beginning of each year. This procedure is likely to be replaced by a more flexible system, in which decisions regarding the amounts of issues are made more frequently.

A natural line of evolution would be toward an international central bank exercising continuous management of the supply of international reserves and liquidity. Such a bank would face policy problems similar to those that confront national central banks.

MONETARY OBJECTIVES

The Employment Act of 1946 is a major landmark in the history of American economic policy. Even as late as the early 1930s, few people would have believed that in less than two decades the federal government would accept responsibility for promoting "maximum employment, production, and purchasing power." As of 1972, we have achieved one major objective of the Employment Act; we have not had a major depression in the 27 years that have elapsed since World War II. Yet the performance of the economy has failed to meet fully the rising aspirations of the American people. Very large amounts of potential output and employment have been lost during six minor economic recessions and some other periods of sluggish economic growth. Also, the economy has proved to be prone to price inflation. Much of the inflation has been associated with the aftermath of World War II, the Korean conflict, and the intervention in the Vietnam War, but the rate of price increases has been uncomfortably high in some other periods. The nation still faces the problem of reconciling its objectives of price stability, continuously high levels of employment, and economic growth.

Problems of implementation still remain. It was expected that the objectives of the Employment Act would be promoted primarily through the use of monetary and fiscal policies to regulate the behavior of aggregate demands for output, but the relative roles of monetary and fiscal policies were not specified. The record of fiscal policies for stabilization purposes has been spotty. The "automatic fiscal stabilizers" have been helpful on many occasions—although they have sometimes inhibited economic recovery, as in the early 1960s—and discretionary tax and expenditure policies have at times contributed to stability. In general, however, fiscal policies have disappointed those who expected them to be adjusted flexibly and quickly. There are many reasons for this: sluggish congressional procedures and an unwillingness to delegate authority to the President, a continued lack of conviction on the part of some congressional leaders that economic stabilization should be a dominant consideration in fiscal policies, partisan politics, and so on. Fiscal policies have not yet made their maximum contribution to economic stabilization. This has shifted a major part of the burden to monetary policy. On some occasions, as in 1966, monetary policy alone bore the burden of combatting inflation while fiscal policies were excessively expansionary. The results were the highest interest rates in more than 40 years, heavy impacts on the construction industry and on nonbank financial intermediaries, and unwanted increases of interest rates in foreign financial centers.

Monetary policies since World War II have been superior to those in earlier periods. The Federal Reserve has shown more wisdom in selecting its objectives and more sophistication in the use of the instruments at its command. However, it is still far from exercising a precise control of the behavior of aggregate demands for output. This is partly because of the associated problems of inadequate economic forecasting and of lags in the effects of monetary policy. We know that the effects of a policy action do not appear immediately; instead, they appear only after a lag and are spread through time. However, we have inadequate knowledge of the length and variability of the lags involved. Milton Friedman and some other economists are so impressed by these difficulties that they would abandon discretionary anticyclical monetary policies and would increase the money supply at a steady rate regardless of current economic conditions and the nature of economic forecasts. Others believe that anticyclical policies, with all their shortcomings, will yield more favorable results than would the Friedman formula. This is obviously an area in which we need more understanding, and greater understanding will lead to modifications of monetary and fiscal policies.

Although we can not yet precisely control the behavior of aggregate demands for output, there is a growing feeling that even if control of aggregate demand were completely precise, it could not alone reconcile our various economic objectives to an optimum degree. We need other measures to achieve more favorable "trade-offs" between price stability on the one hand and continuously low levels of unemployment and high rates of economic growth on the other. We have already mentioned a number of such proposals, including measures to increase the geographic and occupational mobility of labor, "incomes policies," wage-price guidelines, wage-price review boards, and more formal systems for direct controls of individual wages and prices. We do not know which, if any, of these measures will become permanent features of national economic policy. One thing is clear, however: none of them can be a substitute for appropriate control of aggregate demand.

THE FINANCIAL STRUCTURE

The financial system has changed markedly in recent decades, and there is no reason to believe that change is at an end. We can expect further changes in the structure of the commercial-banking system, in the range of functions performed by commercial banks, and in the allocation of functions among commercial banks and other types of financial institutions.

Commercial banking

We noted earlier that during recent decades there has been a rapid trend away from independent unit banks and toward multiple-office banking. This has occurred in two principal ways. One way is through branch banking, in which a single banking corporation establishes branch offices either *de novo* or by absorbing previously existing banks. Another way of replacing the unit bank is through group banking, in which a holding company acquires control of two or more banks, which may or may not operate branches. Market pressures for larger multiple-office banking systems continue unabated. States that formerly prohibited both branch and group banking are now permitting one or both, and states that formerly permitted them but limited their scope are now relaxing the restrictions. There is even some support for new federal laws to permit national banks to branch across state lines. It is clear that if the government does not impose restraints on the banking system, in a few decades the system will be composed of far fewer banks, each operating a large number of offices spread over a wide geographic area.

Public policies relating to banking structures face difficult issues. We want banking units large enough to reap the major economies of scale. At the same time, we want to preserve and even to promote competition in markets for banking services. Officials are still searching for optimum solutions, but they are hampered by inadequate knowledge of the extent of further economies of scale as banking units become larger and larger and also lack information regarding the precise relationship between banking structure and the degree of competition.

The scope of functions performed by commercial banks has also changed and is likely to change even more in the future. In the 1930s, following the widespread failures of banks, public policies tended to restrict the scope of banking functions, the professed purpose being to promote the safety of banks and to protect bank depositors. Also, most bankers were hardly in a mood to be venturesome. However, bankers have become much more venturesome and innovative in recent years and public policy has become somewhat more permissive. In many cases, a bank has itself expanded the range of its functions. In the late 1960s and early 1970s, this occurred to an increasing extent through one-bank holding companies, an arrangement that provided for a holding company to own and control one commercial bank and one or more subsidiary corporations. Among the services performed by such subsidiaries are provision of computer services; selling or underwriting various types of insurance; factoring; rental and leasing of equipment; serving functions similar to those of savings and loan associations; forming and managing real-estate investment trusts to make short-term construction loans, provide long-term mortgage credit, and develop real estate; operation of travel agencies; provision of investment and management advisory services;

and operation and sale of mutual funds. Where a one-bank holding company is used for these purposes, the commercial-banking corporation does not itself expand the scope of its functions. However, when the various corporate veils are pushed aside, one finds that a wide range of functions have been brought under common ownership and control. The conventional line between commercial banking and other types of financial institutions has been breeched.

Other financial institutions

The distinction between commercial banks and other financial institutions is also becoming blurred as other institutions—primarily savings and loan associations, mutual savings banks, and credit unions—assume functions formerly provided exclusively or primarily by commercial banks. It is by no means certain that commercial banks will continue to be the only type of financial intermediary providing demand deposits that serve as a means of payments. Many of the other financial intermediaries already provide means of payments to their customers, mostly to households. To date, they have done this primarily by providing checks or other orders on their own demand deposits at commercial banks, not by permitting transfers of financial claims against themselves. However, a few states have allowed credit unions and savings banks to accept demand deposits and to permit these to be transferred to third parties as a means of payment. In late 1971, a presidential commission recommended that all these thrift institutions be allowed to provide checking accounts and credit cards to nonbusiness entities. It also recommended that: federal charters be provided for mutual savings banks so that they could be established in all 50 states, instead of only 18 states as at present; that all the thrift institutions be permitted to make unsecured loans to consumers; and thrift institutions be allowed to provide trust services, to sell insurance, and to operate and sell mutual funds.

Although it is too early to forecast precisely the course of future developments, there does seem to be a strong trend away from highly specialized institutions and toward institutions performing a wider range of functions. Such changes highlight important issues of public policy. Some of these relate to the structure of the authorities that regulate the various types of financial institutions. At the present time, regulatory authority is widely scattered; it is divided between state and federal authorities, and at each governmental level it is divided among several agencies. This arrangement has several disadvantages. Each agency tends to become an advocate for the types of institutions under its jurisdiction and to promote their interests relative to those of others. Also, nonuniformities of regulations favor the growth of some and inhibit the growth of others, even though the inhibited institutions may be more efficient. As the various types of institutions come to be increasingly similar and more directly competitive, the entire regulatory structure should be reconsidered.

Other issues relate to the substance of regulatory policies. As always, the objective of maintaining the safety and soundness of institutions will have to be balanced against the objective of enhancing their usefulness to the community.

Also, regulations applicable to the various types of financial institutions should be such as to make survival and growth dependent on relative efficiency in the performance of financial functions, not on unjustifiably discriminatory regulations. We have already noted some of the discriminatory regulations that have significantly affected the structure of the commercial-banking system. For example, in the years before 1914, the growth of national banks was seriously inhibited by higher reserve requirements; higher capital requirements; and inability to lend on real estate, to establish trust departments, and to accept bills of exchange. State-chartered banks and trust companies were given a large competitive advantage. Since 1914, members of the Federal Reserve System have been subject to higher reserve requirements, higher capital requirements, and some other regulations more restrictive than those on nonmember banks. Discriminatory regulations also affect the relative competitive positions of commercial banks and other financial institutions. For example, the ability of commercial banks to compete with other types of financial intermediaries for time and savings deposits is inhibited by higher reserve requirements and sometimes by lower ceiling rates. Taxes on commercial banks are generally higher than those on mutual forms of intermediaries. On the other hand, there seems to be no good economic reason why the thrift institutions should be excluded from consumer loans or various other types of earning assets that may be acquired freely by commercial banks.

In the interest of securing an efficient financial system, the general principle should be: Similar functions are subject to similar regulations, regardless of what type of institution performs them.

THE FEDERAL RESERVE

The Federal Reserve has changed markedly since its inception in 1914 and will undoubtedly continue to change in the future. Starting with only limited objectives, it developed into an agency for continuous monetary management, and since 1946 it has used its powers to promote the purposes of the Employment Act. Although classified as an independent central bank, it is, and must be, responsive to changing national policies and aspirations. As a creature of Congress, it must comply with congressional mandates, and it often responds to changing public demands even in the absence of a mandate.

The location of the power to control monetary policy is also likely to change still more. Since many other countries have nationalized their central banks and asserted government power to control monetary policies, there is no assurance that something similar will not happen to the Federal Reserve. Further shifts may occur in the location of powers within the System. When the Federal Reserve was created, most of the power was decentralized among the 12 Reserve banks; now it is largely centralized in the Board of Governors and the FOMC, although some vestiges of power remain with the directors and officers of the Reserve banks. It is by no means impossible that at some time in the future the officers and directors of the Reserve banks will lose their remaining power, that the shares of stock in the Federal Reserve held by member banks will be retired, and that the latter will lose their power to elect directors of the Reserve banks.

The concept of membership and nonmembership in the Federal Reserve may change significantly, and the distinction may even be abolished. As noted earlier, the Board of Governors has repeatedly recommended to Congress that all banks accepting demand deposits be subject to the same reserve requirements and be given access to Federal Reserve discount facilities. The same principles might apply to nonbank financial intermediaries as they accept demand deposits and need access to Federal Reserve facilities for check clearing and collection. Also, there is no good economic reason why other regulations applicable to member banks should be more restrictive or different from those applicable to nonmembers performing similar functions. If such changes occur, the significance of membership would largely disappear. However, history suggests that such changes will meet strong opposition.

There are also likely to be changes in the Federal Reserve's role in regulating the structure and practices of banks. Much of the time and energy of Federal Reserve personnel are now devoted to supervising and examining banks and to passing upon proposals for establishing *de novo* branches, bank absorptions, and acquisition of banks by holding companies. These functions are now shared in a somewhat unsatisfactory way by the Federal Reserve, the Comptroller of the Currency, the FDIC, and the Department of Justice. There have already been many proposals that all of these functions be concentrated in one agency, which might be one of the established agencies or a new one. The responsible agency might well be given jurisdiction over not only commercial banks but also other types of financial intermediaries serving similar functions.

MONETARY AND FISCAL THEORIES

We noted earlier that all policy actions must be based on theory, implicit or explicit, and that policies are unlikely to be better than the theory on which they are based. Both monetary and fiscal theories have been improved markedly in recent decades, and improvements in economic understanding have contributed to improvements in monetary and fiscal policies. Economists rightly contend that policies would be better if policymakers were guided by the best theory available. However, economists must admit that they still have much to learn, especially about quantitative relationships, such as the strength of the effects of a given monetary or fiscal action, lengths of lags, and the distribution of effects through time. Econometric studies have cast considerable light on these subjects, but many of the findings are inconclusive and some are contradictory. Much more remains to be done.

CONCLUSIONS

This chapter has not attempted to catalog all of the existing unresolved issues in this field, still less to forecast all those that may develop in the future. However, incomplete as it is, it should have succeeded in making one major point: there is no reason to believe that processes of change in our monetary and financial structures, practices, objectives, and policies are nearing an end. A wise commentator once observed, "To some problems there are no solutions, only outcomes." He might have added, "And the outcomes are unlikely to be permanent."

Selected readings

Report of the President's Commission on Financial Structure and Regulation, Washington, D.C., U.S. Government Printing Office, 1971.

INDEX

Page references in italics are to tables and page references in bold face are to illustrations.

Acceptances, 223–224
Accounting, double-entry, 117–119
Accounting systems, 7–8
American Stock Exchange, 58
Assets, 10
  in accounting, 117–118
  commercial banking, 162–165, 168–173
  customer loans, 174–175
  and debts, 47
  diversification, 72–73
  insurance of, 79
  and investments, 49
  liquidity of, 48, 60, 71, *82*
  open-market, 173–174
Austria, bank failure, 499–500

Balance of payments, 403–404
  British, 443–445, 445–448
  capital flow, 439–441
  definition, 428–429

  and dollar crisis, 586–587
  international, 5
  net liquidity balance, 432
  official transactions balance, 433
  surplus and deficit, *450*
  United States, *429, 430, 433, 557,* 561–565
Balance sheet, 117
  combined, 168
Bank of America, 116
Bank of England, 457, 492
  during Crash, 499
  and gold standard, 480
Bank of France, 488, 492
Bank for International Settlements, 418
Bank of Massachusetts, 89
Bank of New York, 89
Bank of North America, 89
Bank note, 37, 38
Bank Note Reporter, 97
BankAmericard, 170

Banking, commercial-loan theory, 222
crises, 102, 103–104, 108–109
debt purchasing, 54
evolution, 36–41
fractional reserve, 39–40
group, 111–112
international, 407–426
Banking Act of 1933, 191
Banking Act of 1935, 110, 130, 223, 238
Banks, 82–83
absorptions, 109–110
central, in international transactions, 417–419
reciprocal currency, 418, *419*
charters, 90, 92, 93–94, 110
collapse (1933), 32
commercial. *See* Commercial banks
correspondents, 408–410
de novo branches, 109–110
early development, 88–93
failure, 32, 108–109
federal, 26
and Federal Reserve, 80. *See also* Federal Reserve banks
free-banking laws, 94
government regulations, 41–42
investment, 56
laws, 94, 97–101
loans, 99
mutual savings, 76
new, 110–111
panic of 1933, 502–503
and politics, 92, 94
power over money supply, 39–41
private, 26–27
promissory notes, 26–27
reopened, 503–504
reserves, *231, 232*
of commercial banks, 138–141
increase in, 178–179
in national banking system, 99, 103–104
savings, 571
state, 90, 92, 93–98, 100–101, 110
abuses, 94–98
expansion and contraction, *96*
in Federal Reserve system, 189–190
number, *100*
Banks for Cooperatives, 77
Barter, 17, 333
pure, 5–7
unit of, 7–8
Baumol, W. J., 309 *n.*
Benton, Sen. Thomas, 92
Biddle, Nicholas, 93
Bills of Exchange, 38
Bimetallic standard, 21, 29–31
Board of Governors, 251, 264, 265
and member bank requirements, 238, 239–240, 241, 242

Brokerage houses, 70–71. *See also* Stockbrokers
Building and loan associations. *See* Savings and loan associations

Cambridge equation, 327
Capital, defined, 118
formation, 48–49
international flow, 439–441
and investment, 49
movements, 562
and productivity, 48–49
restrictions, 562
stock, 48
Capital accounts, 117, 118
Capitalist societies, economic motivations, 15, 16
Capitalization, 64
Central reserve city banks, 102–103
Certificates of deposit (CDs), 59, 161, 162
Checking deposits, 13, 26–27, 42, 121–124
Circulating medium. *See* Exchange
Circulating promissory notes, 25, 26
Claims, debt. *See* Debt claims
equity, 49–50
insured, 79–80
Coinage, 36
by U.S. Treasury, 42
Coinage Act of 1791, 29–30
Coins, 13
disadvantages, 37
silver, 25
token, 25. *See also* Full-bodied money
Collectivistic society, 16
Commercial banks, 42, 75–76, 82, 603–604
assets, 116–117, *125*, 162–165, 168–173
open-market, 173–174
balance sheet, 119–121
branch banks, 106
chain banks, 106
change in assets, *127*
checking deposits, 121–124
claims against, 124–128
composition, 116–117
control of, 137–138
customer loans, 174–175
debts, 114
definition, 114–115
deposits, 128–132
in Federal Reserve System, 188–190
holdings, 275, *277*
interbank payments, 132–133
liabilities, 160–165
liquidity, 163, 165–168, 222, 223
loans, 115
loans to, 165–168
note issue, 115
number of banks, 105, *106, 107*
objectives, 136–138

Commercial banks (*Continued*)
  reserves, 138–141, 178–179
  size, *116*
  unit banks, 106
Commercial-paper houses, 57
Common denominator of value. *See* Unit of
  value
Common measure of value. *See* Unit of value
Compensation, per man-hour, *554*
Competition, imperfect, 318
Comptroller of the Currency, 87, 98–99, 105,
  110, 198, 199
Consumer finance companies, 77
Consumption, and debt, 46–48
  efficiency, 47, 48
  personal, 352–353
  and saving, 348–353
Contracts, 6–7, 9
Correspondent relationships, 133–135. *See
  also* International transactions
Cost of Living Council, 588
Council of Economic Advisers, 322
Counterfeiting, 25, 97
Country banks, 102–103
Credit, 333
  book, 47
  cards, 170
  defined, 45
  extensions, 45
  instant, 170–171
  money, 20–21, 24–27, 42
  parole, 47
  stock of, 52–54
  systems, 27
  and transfer of resources, 45
Credit unions, 76–77
Credit-Anstalt (Austria), 499
Currency, 233. *See also* Dollar; Gold; Silver
  certificates
Current yield, 63

Dawes Plan, 491
Debt claims, defined, 50
  and institutions, 50
Debt money, 20–21. *See also* Credit
Debts, bank deposits, 44
  and consumption, 46–48
  corporate, 53
  defined, 45
  economic functions of, 45–46
  international, and stock-market crash, 499
  and investment, 48–50
  and monetary institutions, 44
  net, 52
  new, 52
  outstanding, 52–54, 67
  and production, 51
  stock of, 52–54

  and transfer of resources, 45
  United States, 52–54
Default, risk of, 61
Deferred payment, 9
Deficit units, 51–52
Deflation, and bank failure, 109
  1930s, 3–4
Demand, derived, 308
  and investment, 353–358
  for labor and output, 311
  for output, 311–313
  shifts, **312**
  and supply, 305–309
Deposits, 38
  in checking accounts, 121–123
  derivative, defined, 122
  expansion and contraction, 141–158
  interbank, 132–133
  primary, defined, 122
  public's demand for, 128, 129, *130*
  time, 161–162
Depression, exchange restrictions, 419–420
  1929, 105, 109, 220, 221, 264, 276, 493–496
  1930s, 3–4
  post–World War I, 477–478. *See also* U.S.
    Government, monetary policies
Derivative functions, 7
Dewey, Davis R., 93 *n*.
Discounting, 64–67
Disequilibrium conditions, 18, *456*
Diversification, 70–71, 72–73
Dollar, amount of interest, 63
  background of crises, 585–587
  and breakdown of gold standard, 500, 501
  during Civil War, 31
  content, 30, 31
  convertibility, 594–596
  depreciation, 505
  exchange rates, *594*, 595
  floating, 589–594
  vs. foreign currencies, 32
  and gold standard, 593–594
  gold value reduced, 32
  inconvertibility, 31
  international position, 4, 426
  as monetary unit, 29–30
  multiple buying prices, 464–465
  and new economic policy, 587–596
  prices, *507*
Drafts, 44

Economic dynamics, 309–311
Economic Dynamics (Baumol), 309 *n*.
Economic systems, effect on monetary policy,
  17–19
Economy, deficit units, 51–52. *See also* United
  States
Employment, 597–598
  full, 18

Employment Act of 1946, 534–535, 601
Enterprisers, 16–17
Equilibrium conditions, 17, 456–458
Eurodollar deposits, 166–167
European economy, post–World War II, 480
    response to Phase II, 589–596
Exchange, 8–9
    arbitrage, 442–443
    markets, 445–448, 562–564
    rates, 441–443, 505, *594*
        charges, 190
        during Depression, 461
        determinants, 443–445
        of dollar, *594,* 595
        flexible, 450–453
        IMF agreements, 460
        multiple, 464–466
        pegged, 453–461; British, 455–456
        political considerations, 463–464
        realignment, 589–594
    rationing, 463–464
    restrictions, 461–463, 464–465
    value, 17, 18
Exchange Stabilization Fund, 563
Expenditures, *286*
    domestic investment, 286–287
    exports, 288–289
    personal consumption, 285
    purchases, 289
    rate, 326–329
Exports, domestic, 288–289
    and breakdown of gold standard, 500
    capital, 462
    international, 434–439
    United States, 288–289

Farming economy, 16–17
Federal Advisory Council, 194
Federal Deposit Insurance Corporation, 76,
        87, 109, 191, 198, 199, 582
    purpose, 104–105
Federal funds market, 59–60, 166
Federal Home Loan Bank, 80, 267, 582
Federal Housing Administration, 79
Federal Intermediate Credit Banks, 80
Federal Land Banks, 77
Federal Open Market Committee, 193–194,
        225, 242, 250–251, 521, 528, 563, 574
Federal Reserve Act, 102, 103, 183, 186, 219–
        220, 222, 229, 251, 472, 502
Federal Reserve banks, 490
    advances, 219–223
    assets, 209, 211–212
    capital accounts, 209
    claims against, 59–60
    control, 191–193, 194–195
    debt, 504, 512
    deposits, 210–211
    discounts, 219–223

establishment, 183
excess reserves, 512, 513
international reserve assets, 212–214
liabilities, 209
maturities held, 522
notes, 210–211
ownership, 190–191
size, *188*
stock, 190–191
and the Treasury, 191. *See also* Federal Re-
    serve System, member banks
Federal Reserve Bulletin, 230
Federal Reserve System, 31–32, 42, 44, 80, 82,
        101, 103, 134, 138–139, 303
    acceptances, 224–225
    advisory capacity, 203
    balance sheets, 209–210
    banking supervision, 198–199
    Board of Governors, 192–193, 248, 267
    business stability, 481–482
    vs. other central banks, 183–184
    center countries, 488
    check clearing, 199–201
    commercial banks in, 116
    consumer credit controls, 266
    coordination, 252
    credit to Bank of England, 486
    credit to foreign banks, 486–489
    currency, 233
    as depository, 203
    and deposits, 128–131
    and Depression of 1929, 493–496
    discount-rate changes, *483*
    discount rates, 247–250, 491, 529, 569
    distribution, *187*
    easy-money policy, 487, 490–491, 492–493,
        538–541, 543–545
    expansionary policies, 254
    float, 227–229
    foreign deposits, 234–235
    foreign-exchange holdings, 219
    future role, 605–606
    gold holdings, 214–218
    and gold standard, 482–489
    government securities, 522, 535–537
    holdings, 274–275, 278
    instruments, 489–490
    and interest rate, 255–256, 267–268
    legal-reserve requirements, 267–268
    liabilities, 229, 571
    liberal periods, 258
    long-term securities, 513–514
    member banks, borrowing, 247–250, 501–
        502, *545*
        loans to, 221–223
        requirements, 188–190, 237–242, *513*
        reserves, 230–233, 257–260, *514,* 540, *545,*
        547, 570, 578, 579, 581, 597
    membership, *189*

Federal Reserve System (*Continued*)
  monetary control, 262, 269
  monetary management, 207–208
  monetary policies, 526–529
  and money supply, 256–257
  moral suasion, 250–251, 263–264, 573–574
  nonprice methods, 247
  notes, 25, 26, 42
  offsetting, 480–481, 488
  open-market account, 256
  open-market operations, 242–247, *483*, 490,
    513, 515, 522–524
  Operation Nudge, 566–567
  paper money, 44
  pegging policy, 527–528
  policies, during World War I, 474–477
    post–World War I depression, 477–478
    1923–1929, 490–496
    1931–1932, 501–502
    1946–1948, 528–529
    1951–1953, 538
    1953–1954, 539–541
    1955–1957, 541–543
    1957–1958, 543–545
    1958–1959, 545–548
  policy actions, 255–260
  policy instruments, 538
  preferential discount rates, 475, 476, 477
  preventive measures, 512–513
  price stability, 481–482
  promotion of economic stability, 481–482
  proposed changes, 195–198
  purchases government securities, 502, 504
  purpose, 104, 184–186
  raises time-deposit rates, 568–569
  rates paid, 16
  real-estate controls, 266
  Regulation W, 266
  Regulation X, 266
  responsibilities, 220–221
  restrictions, 492, 495
  restrictive periods, 253–254, 258
  SDR certificates, 218–219
  security loans, 264–266
  selective control, 528–529, 572–574
  and speculation, 482
  sterilizing, 480–481, 488
  stock in, 168
  and stock market, 493–496
  structure, 186–190, 195
  tight money, 541–543
  and Treasury, 202–205, 221, 233, 261–262,
    530–532
  U.S. government obligations, 224–227
  wartime assistance to Treasury, 520–522
Federal Savings and Loan Insurance Corporation (FSLIC), 76
Fiat money. *See* Circulating promissory notes

Financial intermediary, 81
  defined, 69
  diversification, 71–72
  economic bases, 70–71
  government intervention, 79–81
  insolvency, 78
  liabilities, *571*
  management problems, 78
  and risk, 72–73
  sponsorship, 77
  types, *75–77*
  and withdrawal of funds, 73–75
Financial markets, 54–60
Fire and Casualty insurance companies, 77
First Bank of the United States, 89–90
Fisher, Irving, 326, 339, 340, 383
Fisherine type of equation, 326
Foreign exchange, 219, 410–412
  exchange arbitrage, 411
  forward markets, 411
  spot markets, 411
France, undervalued franc, 489
Free banking, 94, 98
Friedman, Milton, 256, 337
Full-bodied money, 21–23

*General Theory of Employment, Interest and
  Money* (Keynes), 325
German Reichsbank, 492
Glass, Carter, 185
Glass-Steagall Act, 502
Gold, 415, 495
  and balance of payments, 438
  bullion, 36
  certificates, 23, 212, 214–218
  in dollars, 30
  and Federal Reserve, 480–481
  as financial claim, 431
  flow, 492
  international reserves, 35, 424–425
  limited, 32–34
  new role, 600
  paper, 35
  shortage, 478
  policies, 213
  prices, *22*, 510, 512, 592, 593
  production rise, 473
  stock, 217, 273–274, 278, 556
    pre–World War I, 474
    United States monetary, *511*
    world, 560
  system limited, 34–35
  United States stops buying, 34
  world production, *511*
Gold-bullion standard, 32–34
Gold-coin standard, 31–32
Gold Reserve Act of 1934, 214

Gold standard, 21–22
  adoptions, 472
  breakdown, 499–501
  in colonial America, 30
  international, 479–480, 482–489
  managed, 32
  in nineteenth century America, 30
  participating countries, *484*
  suspended by Roosevelt, 504–508
Gold Standard Act of 1900, 184
Goldsmiths, 37, 38
Government National Mortgage Association,
      77
Governments, backing, 23–24, 25
  credit money, 41–42
  debt management, 398–401
  definition of money price, 21, 22
  disposable income, 389–391
  expenditures, *387, 395*
  financing Civil War, 31
  fiscal policies, 394–398
  gold redemption, 29
  influence on banking, 41–42
  issuance of credit money, 24–27
  loans, 79
  monetary and fiscal policies, 402–404
  overexpansion of money supply, 29
  purchases, 386–387
  redemption problems, 29
  saving, 390–391
  tax-collection function, 397–398
  tax receipts, 388–389
  transfer payments, 387–388, 397. *See also*
      Monetary authority; United States Gov-
      ernment
Great Britain, gold standard, 489
  incomes policy, 322
  leaves gold standard, 499, 500
  London as world financial center, 480
  pegged exchange rates, 455–456
  post–World War I, 480
Greenbacks, 26, 31
Gross National Product (GNP), 282–291
  and components, *541, 544, 553*
  as expenditures for output, 285, *286*
  as group income shares, *290*
  as national income, 289–291
  1929–1971, *284*
  during selected periods, *546*
Group of Ten, 593–594

Hamilton, Alexander, 88
Hamilton, Walton, 15
Hamlin, Charles, 481–482
Hodson, H. V., 500
Holding companies, 112

Imports, 434–439
  duties, 594

  essential, 463
  and multiple exchange rates, 465
  surtax, 590
Income, debt and, 46, 48
  disposable, business, 294
  flow, 45–46, 48, 51–52, 298
  government, 291–294
  and international transactions, 446–447
  and investment, 383–385
  levels, 446–447
  national, 51–54
  personal, 296
  private, 297–298, 301, 391
  surplus units, 51–52. *See also* Gross Na-
      tional Products
Income statement, 117
Inflation, 4, 601
  periods: World War I, 476, 477
    World War II, 525
    1950, 530–532
    1970–1971, 323
Information media, financial, 55–56
Institutions, and debt, 50
Interbank relations, 132–135
Interest rates, 63–68, 334–335, 341, 379, 438,
      570, 583
  Federal Reserve, 523
  market rates, *577, 583*
  on time deposits, *568*
  World War II, 521. *See also* Regulation Q
International Bank for Reconstruction and
      Development (World Bank), 77, 419
International correspondents, 134, 135. *See
      also* International transactions
International Monetary Fund (IMF), 35,
      214, 215, 218, 418, 419–424, 560, 593,
      601
  drawing rights, 422–424
  fund-borrowing arrangements, *423*
  membership, 421
  policies, 422
  quotas, *421*
  sales of currencies, 420–423
  special drawing rights, 423–424
International monetary situation, 555–561
International monetary systems, and gold
      standard, 35
International transactions and banks, 408–411
  capital flow, 439–441
  central banks, 417, 419
  exchange rates, 441–443
  exchange risk, 440
  flow, 413–414
  foreign-exchange markets, 410–412
  free markets, 412–413
  functions of money, 408
  imports and exports, 434–439
  and income levels, 434–439
  liquidity, 414–416, 418

International transactions and banks *(Continued)*
  management, 416, 417–419
  multilateral, 412–413
  payments, 403–404, 410
  political risks, 440
  reserves, 415–416, 424–426
  role of dollar, 426. *See also* International Monetary Fund
Investment, and capital formation, 49
  and debt, 48–50
  defined, 49
  and demand, 353–358, *365, 371*
  disinvestment, 287
  domestic, 286–288
  and income, 383–385
  marginal efficiency, 355–358
  marginal responsiveness, 358–360
  negative, 287
  private, 49
  return, 356
Investment banks. *See* Banks
Investment companies, 77
Investment-tax credit, 567
IOUs, 37

Jackson, Andrew, 91, 92, 93
Jefferson, Thomas, 88
Johnson, G. Griffith, 508 *n.*

Kennedy, Pres. John F., proposed tax reduction, 567
Keynes, John Maynard, 313, 325, 341, 343, 348, 356–357
  liquidity trap, 402

Labor, marginal value product, 317–318
Legal tender, 12
Legislation, on coinage, 29–30
  to create bimetallic system, 30
  establishment of a monometallic standard, 31
  stabilization of the dollar, 31
Liabilities, in accounting, 117, 118
Liberty Loan campaign, 475, 477
Life insurance companies, 77, 571–572
Liquidity, 14, 165–168
  of assets, 71
  defined, 60
  and financial intermediaries, 78
  sources, 80
Loans, 170–171
  to brokers, *494*
  commercial, 169–170
  customer, 174–179
  government, 79
  international, 499
    during Crash of 1929, 500

National Banking Act, 99
National banking system, 103
London Economic Conference (1933), 508
London Gold Pool, 559, 560, 575
London Silver Agreement, 508

Market facilities, 81
  customer-loan, 174–178
  financial, 54–60
  open, 173–179
Marshall, Alfred, 327
Marshallian K, 327
Master Charge, 170
Means of payment. *See* Exchange
Medium of exchange. *See* Exchange
Member banks. *See* Federal Reserve banks
Metal standards, market value, 25. *See also* Gold; Silver certificates
Metals, evolution as currency, 36
Mill, John Stuart, 17–18
Mint ratio of dollar, 30
Monetarists, 337–338
Monetary authority, 28–29
Monetary institutions, issuance of money, 44
  soundness of, 517. *See also* International Monetary Fund
Monetary management, 35
  controls, 263
  negative, 263
  positive, 263
  selective, 263, 268. *See also* Federal Reserve System; United States Treasury
Monetary policies, 18–19
  1965–1966, 568–569
  post–World War II, 602
Monetary standards, 28–35
Monetary systems, changes in, 35
  consolidated balance sheet, 271–273
  gold stock, 273–274
  international, 600–601
  SDR certificates, 273–274
Monetary theory, 302–305
  classical model, 313–316
  departures from classical model, 317–320
  post–World War II, 321–323
Monetary unit. *See* unit of value
Money, availability, 334
  classification, *21*
  creation of, 18
  debt, 271
  defined, 11–15
  demand, 329–332, 332–335
  examples, 11–12
  expenditures, 326
  flows, 281–282
  holding balances, 330–332
  income velocity, *328*
  liquidity-trap hypothesis, 341–343
  markets, 57

Money, availability (*Continued*)
 ratio to GNP, *328*
 reciprocal currency, 418, *419*
 as reserve, 415–416
 stock, 326
 supply, 210, 270–278, 329, 376–379, 382–385
  behavior, 276–278
  capital accounts, 275–276
  currency, 274
  decrease in, 516
  determinants, *277, 516, 523*
  factors, *276*
  Federal Reserve holdings, 274–275
  gold stock, 273–274
  and interest rates, 382–385
  nonmonetary liabilities, 275–276, 278
  post-Depression, 516
  SDR certificates, 273–274
  supply and demand, 36
 velocity, 326
Money and Banking (White), 97 *n.*
"Moneyness," 13
Monopoly questions, 105
Morris plan banks, *188*
Mortgage companies, 77
Mortgages, home, 79
Multiplier, the, 360–362, 365, 366, 436–437
Mutual Savings Banks. *See* Banks
Mutual savings and loan associations, 76

National bank notes, 101–102
National Banking Act, 98, 100, 101
National Banking System, 93, 98–104
 shortcomings, 101–104
National-income accounting, 282
Near-moneys, 13–15
Net worth defined, 118
New Deal, 503–510
New York as monetary center, 488
New York Stock Exchange, 58
Nixon, Richard M., and dollar crisis, 584
 creates control boards, 588
 new economic policy, 587
Norman, Gov. Montagu, 417, 486, 487

Open Market Committee, 544
Open market operations, announcement effects, 245
 defensive, 246, 247
 dynamic, 247
 patterns, 245–246
 purchases and sales, 243, 244–245
 repurchase agreements, 243
Open-market policy. *See* Federal Reserve System
Operation Nudge, 566–567
Orders to pay, 44

Output, 597–598
 demand functions for, **311**
 and income, 51
 increased demand for, 311–313
 prices, 318–320. *See also* Demand
Overbanking, 108, 110
Ownership, shares, 51–52. *See also* Shareholders

Paper money, 13, 24, 42, 43, 92
 destructibility of, 25. *See also* Representative full-bodied money
Pay Board, 588
Payments, and multiple-exchange rates, 465
 system, 333
Phase II. *See* United States government, monetary policies
Pittman, Sen. Key, 508
Portfolios, 72
 regulation of, 79
Price Commission, 588
Price and Price Policies (Hamilton), 15
Prices, 597–598
 control, 587–589
 defined, 7
 expectations, 334
 inflation, 312–313. *See also* Inflation
 levels, 379–382
 of output, 318–320
 post–World War II, 321–323
 stabilization, gold, *22*
 support programs, 79
 and supply and demand, 305–309
 wage-price guidelines, 322–323
Primary functions, defined, 7
Principal, safety of, 60–61
Principles of Political Economy (Mill), 17
Private pension funds, 77
Production and debt, 51
Profit and loss statements, 117
A Program for Monetary Stability (Friedman), 256 *n.*
Purchasing power, 8
 generalized, 9–10
 gold, 23

Raguet, Condy, 97 *n.*
Reconstruction Finance Corporation, 503–504, 505–506
Rediscount facilities, 80
Regulation Q changes, 564–565
Regulation W, 529
Rent control, 587–589
Representative full-bodied money, 20–21, 23–24
Representative token money, 25
Reserve city banks, 102–103
Resources and capital stock, 48–49

Revenue and Expenditure Control Act, 576
Roosa, Robert, 235
Roosevelt, Pres. Franklin D., during banking panic, 503
  gold policies, 504–508
  reopens banks, 503–504
  silver policies, 508–510
  and value of dollar, 505–509

Safety of principal, 60–61
Savings, bonds, 161, 162
  business, 351–352
  certificates, 161, 162
  and consumption, 348–353
  and debt claims, 50
  defined, 46
  and income, 48
  and investment, 48, 49, 50
  passbook, 161
  personal, 352–353, 525
  supply shift, *375*
Savings and loan associations, 76
Say's Law, 314
Second Bank of the United States, 91–93
The Second Bank of the United States (Dewey), 93 *n.*
Secondary reserves, 82
Securities, brokers, 70–71
  dealers, 57
  defined, 57
  direct, 81
  exchanges, 58–59
  indirect, 69
  liquidity, 58
  loans on, 170–171
  marketability, 57–58
  markets, 57
  over-the-counter market, 59–60
  primary distribution, 56–57
  risks, 60–61
  secondary markets, 57–60
Seigniorage, 24
Shareholders, 49–50
Short runs, 18
Silver certificates, 25, 31
  in dollars, 30
  limited buying, 31
  policies in the United States, 508–510
  prices, 25
  production, *509*
  standard, 21
    in colonial America, 30
Special Drawing Rights (SDRs), 35, 212
  certificates, 218, 273–274
Specialization of capital, 5
  in United States, 15–16
Speculation, 412, 442, 492
Spending during World War II, 524–525

Spot-exchange market, 563
Stabilization, of dollar, 31
  in terms of commodity, 29
Standard of value. *See* Unit of value
State banks. *See* Banks
Statics, 306, 309–311
  comparative, 306, 371–379
  simple, 370–371
Sterling, and British economy, 444–448
  exchange rate, 455
  supply function, 443–445
Stockbrokers, 57, 58–59
  loans to, *494*
Stock market crash, 1929, 493–496
Stock savings and loan associations, 76
Stocks, prices, *494*
  trading, 53–54
  underwriting, 56. *See also* Securities
Store of value, money as, 9–11
Strong, Gov. Benjamin, 417, 485, 487, 491, 492
Supply, and demand, 305–309
  classical theory, 313–317
Surplus, defined, 118
Surplus units, 51–52
Surtax, 590

Tax Reform Act of 1969, 580–581
Time deposits, 125
Token coins, 25
Trade, 5
  in United States, 15–16

Unemployment, 4–5, 323
  rate, *552, 554,* 568
Union Guardian Trust Company, Detroit, 503
Unit of account. *See* Unit of value
Unit of value, in barter, 6–7
  money as, 7–8
United States, Civil War economy, 472
  commercial bank holdings, 275, 277
  early bank system, 184–186
  economy, 51, 52. *See also* United States Government, monetary policies
  financial institutions, future role, 602–605
  international reserve position, *557, 561–565*
  isolationism, 485
  liabilities, 426
  loans abroad, 491
  presidential monetary powers, 504–505
United States Constitution and banking, 90
United States Department of Justice, 105
United States Government, adoption of gold standard, 472–473
  balance of payments, *429, 430, 433, 557*
  bank tax, 100
  borrowing, *521*

United States Government (*Continued*)
breakdown of gold standard, 500, 501
cash operating outgo, income and deficits, *520*
debt, 52–54
  management policies, 535–538
direct controls, 524–525
direct issues, 56
disposable income, 291–294
dissaving, 293–294
easy money, 539–541, 543–545
exchange-rate policies, 213
expenditures, 515
federal bonds, 99, 101
and Federal Reserve, 205, 473. *See also* Federal Reserve System
financial institutions, 79–81
fiscal policies, 1930s, 514–517
  World War II, 519–520
  1960s, 567
  1971, 596
gold policies, 33–34, 213. *See also* Gold stock, *217, 511*
and International Monetary Fund, 423
investment, 299–300
monetary policies, pre–World War I, 473–474
  World War I, 474–477
  post–World War I, 474–478, 479–481
  1931–1932, 501–502
  1932–1933, 502
  1934–1941, 512–514
  World War II, 111, 520–524
  1946–1948, 514–529
  1948–1950, 529–530
  Korean War, 530–532
  1951–1959, 533–549
  1960–1971, 550–583
  Phase II, 588–589
money supply, 12–13, 15–17, 42–43. *See also* Money
open market, 528
pegging, 527–528
purchases, 289
saving, 293–294, 299–300
securities, 171–172
short-term claims, 431

silver policies, 508–510
special drawing rights, 213–214
tight money, 541–543, 545–548
wartime controls, 524–525, 526
wartime monetary policy, 520–524
United States notes, 26
United States Treasury, 42, 98
accord with Federal Reserve, 532
bills, 171, 513
bonds, 171, 531
currency, 42, 43, 274, 278
debt, 220
and Federal Reserve, 202–205, 221, 224–227, 233, 530–532, 536, 537
foreign exchange, 219
and gold, 31, 32–34
gold purchases, 214–219
liberalizing action, 262
monetary operations, 271
notes, 171
Operation Nudge, 566–567
paper money, 44
and pegging policy, 527–528
restrictive actions, 261–262
sales of securities, 475–476
during World War II, 474–477
silver purchases, 508–510
special drawing rights certificates, 218
sterilizes gold imports, 512–513
wartime borrowing, 520

Veterans Administration, 79

Wage control, 587–589
Wages, 317–319
  1971 freeze, 323
  rates, post–World War II, 321–323
Warren, George F., 506
Wilson, Woodrow, 472
Wingfield, B. Magruder, 189 *n.*
Wire transfers, 201–202
World Bank. *See* International Bank for Reconstruction and Development

Yield, defined, 61–62
  to maturity, 63
  nominal, 63